TOO BLACK TO FAIL

THE OBAMA PORTRAITS AND THE POLITICS OF POST-REPRESENTATION

MARC JAMES LÉGER

Ottawa

www.redquillbooks.com
ISBN: 978-1-926958-36-1

Library and Archives Canada Cataloguing in Publication

Too black to fail : the Obama portraits and the politics of postrepresentation / Marc James Léger.

Léger, Marc James, 1968- author.

Includes bibliographical references.

Canadiana 20220207135 | ISBN 9781926958361 (softcover)
1. Obama, Barack, 1961- —Portraits. 2. Obama, Michelle, 1964- —Portraits. 3. Presidents—United States—Portraits. 4. Art—Political Aspects—United States—History—21st century. 5. Art and society--United States—History—21st century. 6. Identity politics—United States—History—21st century. 7. United States—Politics and government—2009-2017.

Classification: LCC E908.3 .L44 2022 | DDC 973.932092/2—dc23

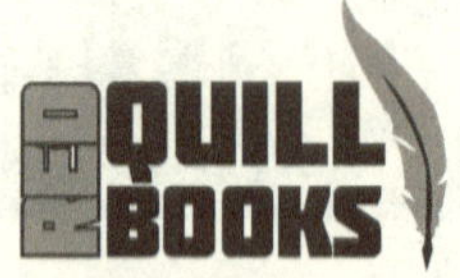

RQB is a radical publishing house.

Part of the proceeds from the sale of this book will support student scholarships

TABLE OF CONTENTS

PREFACE

In 2016, disappointment regarding the failures of the Obama administration seemed to pale in comparison with the Trump fiasco. One would not have known this given the Democratic Party's obsession with overblown allegations of Russian meddling in the election. As Thomas Frank deftly stated in his book, *Listen, Liberal*, American progressives had lost their way and the party of the people was in obvious disarray. Although none of this came as much of a surprise to the left, there was reason to worry, not only because a madman was now in the saddle, but because the liberal centre was in complete denial about its role in his victory.

Donald Trump managed to win the election with deceptions about bringing back good paying jobs and xenophobic promises of patriotic glory. It was easy enough to see that he knew how to raise the ire of liberal elites, who played into his game all too well. And they wanted to, I argue, because they prefer to blame Trump than to fight for socialist equality. In this context, writing a book about Trump seemed less important to me than an examination of the contradictions of today's "progressive neoliberalism." As a crystallization of this tendency, the Obama portraits looked to me to be an appropriate subject. As part of my analysis, it would be necessary to address the race and class debate as well as the way that American politics is locked in a bipartisan framework. Socialism appears here as a third term and as the only alternative to the two-party system. Moving the goalposts of politics further towards left field not only means organizing the working class, but also disengaging culture and subjectivity from the postmodern intellectual frameworks that have informed academic writing and activist new social movements. Going against this status quo, *Too Black to Fail* has hopefully contributed something to the reanimation of radical thought among a new generation of leftists. After the culture wars of the 1980s and 90s, and after the resurgence of emancipatory universalism in the first decade of the twenty-first century, I consider how the hasty return to identity politics after Occupy Wall Street has mostly served the agenda of the 10 and 1 percent.

A first draft of this book was completed in September 2019 and the manuscript was updated through to February 2022. All of the issues that are addressed in these pages were in evidence before the 2020 Democratic Party primaries began. Neither did Obama's role in the nomination of Joe Biden as party leader nor did the Black Lives Matter protests change anything much to my initial insights and arguments. After Bernie Sanders ended his 2020 campaign, all of the woke elements that no one had heard a word from beforehand came out to back Biden against the incumbent Trump, who was now demanding reparations from China for a naturally occurring virus that he did very little to prevent from spreading. Trump eventually attempted a fascist coup d'état to take back what he told people was a stolen election. Like his Democratic predecessor, Biden decided to look forward and allow the guilty, which included officials in the White House, Congress, the Senate, the Pentagon, the CIA, the National Guard and the Capitol police, to mostly go unpunished, calling for unity and asserting the need for a strong Republican opposition. If *Too Black to Fail* was not published ahead of the 2020 U.S. presidential election, as I had planned, it nevertheless addresses identity and class debates that continue to divide the left and that demand a stronger principle and policy orientation.

Among the more particular issues that I address, developments unfolded over the course of 2020-21 in relation to the George Washington High School murals and the 1619 Project. Regarding the murals, the dauntless efforts of the George Washington High School Alumni Association led to the school being placed on the National Park Service's survey of historic American buildings, which is one step away from inclusion in the Service's national registry. This would give the building and the artworks contained within it federal landmark status. As well, efforts the rename the George Washington High School on the view that its namesake was a slaveholder were successfully thwarted by the Association. It has been a pleasure and a privilege for me to play a role in helping to save the Arnautoff murals from destruction and I wish to acknowledge here the friendly exchanges of Lope Yap, Jr., Robert Cherny, Gray Brechin and Todd Cronan. With regard to the 1619 Project and related subjects, I have enjoyed communications with Tom Mackaman and David Walsh at the invaluable *World Socialist Web Site*. Thanks to the *WSWS* for giving me the opportunity to help inform workers about misguided efforts to destroy the murals by Sam Kerson that were made for the Vermont Law School – a case that will hopefully be resolved in favour of the artist and the public interest.

Racialist attacks by institutions against outstanding progressive art is a small indication that the radical project is on the defensive. In the United Kingdom, the Department of Education has sought to outlaw anti-capitalism as an "extreme political stance" that is equivalent to anti-Semitism and terrorism. Similar policies are now being drafted by Republican lawmakers in the United States and elsewhere. This new McCarthyism is accompanied by seemingly progressive forms of conservatism and censoriousness that are now known as cancel culture. Some of this is related to identity issues and diversity mandates as well as intersectional models of research and activism. Since I started working on this book, not only have I been cancelled by some former comrades and colleagues, but I have also received some words of appreciation from others who are afraid to write as I do for fear of reprisal. In my case, working as an independent scholar has allowed me a measure of autonomy that I fear intellectuals and artists are not being granted by ostensibly radical allies and colleagues. For these reasons, I am particularly grateful to George Rigakos and Red Quill Books for publishing a title that others have disingenuously sought to contrive as controversial rather than critical.

Besides a delay in publication, I experienced for the first time in my scholarly life difficulties with image requests. The demand of a copyright owner to review a scholar's work as a condition for copyright permission qualifies as unacceptable terms and conditions. It is a sad sign of the times that well-established and remarkably wealthy contemporary artists whose works are held in public collections seek to control the discussion of their work in scholarly publications. Where permission was not made possible without such conditional terms, or where fair use guidelines could not be resorted to in the interest of scholarly inquiry, images of some of the works discussed in this book have not been included. On the other hand, I am grateful to those artists and gallerists who shared their brilliant work with me and my readers. Special thanks go to Theodore Harris for kindly entertaining my request to use on the cover of this book images of the Obama portraits incorporated into one of his "mousetrap" works, which were inspired by a collage work by Romare Bearden. As incitements to speech, or "mouth-traps," as I understand these works, I hope that I have not disappointed anyone.

I wish to thank Rosika Desnoyers for her helpful comments on draft versions of this book and other writings. It is always nice to have a longtime friend you can talk with about the latest insanity. Thanks to Andrew Hartman for kindly agreeing to read the book for an endorsement. Lastly, thanks to comrade Cayley for not only suffering my requests to wait to talk to me until I'm finished writing another sentence, but for hearing out my jibber jabber about this, that and the other.

INTRODUCTION

The left once dismissed the market as exploitative. It now honors the market as rational and humane. The left once disdained mass culture as exploitative; it now celebrates it as rebellious. The left once honored independent intellectuals as rebellious; it now sneers at them as elitist. The left once rejected pluralism as superficial; now it worships it as profound.

– Russell Jacoby, *The End of Utopia*

In the United States of Republican president Donald Trump, the presidency of Barack Obama seemed like a golden age of civility and cosmopolitanism. While no one expected that a standing president could single-handedly take the country on a drastically different course, and Obama's vaunted bipartisanship was never a promising formula for much in the way of radical change, there was a sense that with Trump something was lost and that in some ways the Obama presidency was, or might have been, the last chance for a break with decades of conservative government. Trump's campaign slogan, Make America Great Again – a phrase derived from one of Ronald Reagan's speeches – thus appeared and functioned as the kind of divisive sabotage that Obama had been careful to avoid. Not only did it promise to bring back the jobs that had long ago been automated, offshored and outsourced, but it cast the previous administration as 'not great.' The black intellectual Ta-Nehisi Coates considered the election of the reality show billionaire as the judgement of a racist country that had been holding its breath for eight years and whose incredulity towards the possibility of 'Good Negro Government' had only increased during that time.

According to Coates, as for many who make race relations definitional of American politics, Trump's supporters were anxious to deliver government power back to the people to whom it rightfully belonged.[1] Obama himself advanced this idea in his 2020 memoir, stating that Americans had been "spooked by a black man in the White House" and voted for Trump as "an elixir for racial anxiety."[2] Among liberal progressives, the narrative of white revanchism was the best explanation for this dreadful turn in the wheel of fortune. For the American working class, however, the wheel had been spinning since at least the 1970s, and the Obama administration turned out to be consistent with what came before. The extent to which the 2016 election was a protest vote against decades of class restoration rather than the singular expression of white racism is elucidated by the 2016 exit polls, which indicated that almost half of Americans were primarily concerned with economic insecurity, while identity issues and immigration registered at less than one percent. We also know that support for the Republicans, regardless of who it is that voted for Trump, stayed at the same level from 2008 through to 2016, but that the extra support the Democrats enjoyed declined by 8 million over two elections to eventually reach the same low level as the Republicans. Miraculously, for many Democratic Party partisans, none of this decline in voter support had anything to do with Obama or with the New Democrats' Third Way policies. Conveniently, the shift in voter behaviour was explained as a reaction to Obama's identity, as exemplified by the 'birthers' who had refused to acknowledge Obama's citizenship, even after he produced his official documents.[3] According to this line of interpretation, the same sort of identitarian animus was directed against Hillary Clinton in her 2016 bid for the presidency. The more long-term view suggests that over two decades, the George W. Bush era had blended into the Obama years and the Trump madhouse. As the political science scholar Adolph Reed Jr. has put it with regard to the bipartisan consensus, Obama was the warm-up act to Trump. With more Wall Street support than any other candidate in 2008, the only thing that set Obama apart from the rest of the Democratic Party establishment, Reed says, was the pigment of his epidermis.[4]

In contrast to 2016, the results of the 2020 exit polls show not only the influence of the Black Lives Matter protests but also the influence of virtue signalling by the corporate media and the centrist establishment. Fuelled by right-wing extremism, Democratic partisanship had succeeded in redirecting questions of political economy around race and identity. Without a mass political movement on the left, substantive social change around issues like economic inequality, climate change, militarism, unemployment, homelessness and the lack of affordable health care, remains disconnected from the question of policing and incarceration. This shift away from class solidarity and the critique of political economy has led to forms of anti-racism that are compatible with contemporary capitalism, including black authenticity, racial uplift, theories of white privilege, woke posturing and biological determinism. All of these are cultural politics that have no clear political orientation. The official portraits of president Barack and first lady Michelle Obama are emblematic of this situation.

In 2016, portraits of the Obamas were commissioned to grace the walls of the National Portrait Gallery. In 2018, after the unveiling of the paintings, the director of the NPG raved that attendance at the museum had skyrocketed, proof as it were of the fact that America is not a country of anti-immigrant xenophobes, racists, sexists and homophobes. This boost in attendance was undoubtedly due to the acquisition of the Obama paintings, which, the moment they were first exhibited, increased the number of visitors to the museum by 300 percent. Even before Trump won the 2016 election, largely due to wall-to-wall news coverage of his antics, Americans had found a new Oedipal figure – better than Vladimir Putin. In no time at all the two were lumped together as Trump was said to be in the pocket of the Russian oligarch. After the Mueller investigation into Trump collusion with the Russians ended up empty-handed, Democratic Party conspiracy theorists were still out with their bloodhounds, backed up in the endeavour by Hillary Clinton's ravings in *What Happened* that the Russians, with the help of Julian Assange, were out to get her and undermine American democracy. Clinton wrote: "Despite Trump's attempts to cover for Putin, cybersecurity experts and U.S. intelligence officials were confident that the Russians were behind the hack [of her emails]."[5] As though Americans had forgotten what a farce the Mueller investigation turned out to be, Clinton and House Speaker Nancy Pelosi later blamed the January 6 storming of the Capitol building on collusion with the Russians. Although home-grown terrorist organizations and right-wing militias are well-known to American intelligence agencies, the corporate media once again propagated the idea that racist white workers rather than general social crisis and ruling-class machinations were to blame for the Republican-backed riot. Average workers, it turned out, comprised only ten percent of the January 6 mob.

In November 2020, the next elected president, Joe Biden, appointed the most diverse cabinet on record, with the ostensible goal of appeasing the progressive wing of the party.[6] Rather than progressive policy on economic inequality, unemployment, the coronavirus pandemic, police reform, immigration reform, foreign policy, health care or education, the cabinet included Avril Haines as CIA deputy director (the woman responsible for Obama's drone assassination programme), Kamala Harris as Vice President (a South-Asian and African-American specialist in the prosecution of the poor), Alejandro Mayorkas as head of the Department of Homeland Security (the Latino deputy secretary of Homeland Security who helped Obama become known as the Deporter in Chief), Linda Thomas-Greenfield as ambassador to the U.N. (an African-American expert in colonial exploitation), Janet Yellen as treasury secretary (the woman who helped Bush and Obama with the bank bailouts) and Neera Tanden as senior advisor (the Indian-American chief executive of the Center for American Progress and defender of U.S. imperialism in Libya, Syria and Iraq). All seven of Biden's initial communications team, almost all of them drawn from the Obama administration, were white and minority women. Needless to say, Biden's white male nominations were no more progressive. Despite the commitment of these and several other minority nominees to social reaction, the argument that such millionaire representation on the Biden cabinet 'matters' was heard even among nominally left figures.[7]

The Obama portraits are part of the quandary we are in today where identity politics mix with global capitalism and the postmodern renunciation of left universality. In the further reaches of academic post-structuralism, problems of political economy are given an ideological fix as 'social justice' issues rather than matters of class struggle. One is increasingly obliged to demonstrate the relevance of class politics to identity politics. The irony of the development of academic anti-Marxism is that culturalist post-politics are now denounced by conservatives along with the socialist agenda. The 'grievance studies affair' that was orchestrated by Helen Pluckrose, James Lindsay and Peter Boghossian sought to demonstrate that identity-obsessed academics are willing to publish articles recommending that humans be trained like dogs as an effective means to combat rape culture, or that white students should be placed in chains as a way to teach them about their unacknowledged white privilege. While the hoax did more to underscore the neoliberalization of education than to advance social theory, it did reveal the extent to which postmodern notions of identity and difference maintain only a thin veneer of progressivism.[8]

The myopia of identity politics, which crowns people like Obama and Clinton with an ideological halo, has given an advantage to rightists like Trump. To the left of this struggle between neoliberal centrism and anti-democratic authoritarianism is a fragmented and marginalized radicalism. As postmodern theory separated issues of identity and difference from universalism, macro-politics and political economy, contemporary "woke" identitarianism has gradually and unwittingly revived ideas that were historically associated with conservative reaction, including anti-universalism, race reductionism, cross-class alliance for the sake of nationalism and notions of organic totality. This mixes with philosophical nihilism and reduces politics to the logic of empowerment. The reassertion of identity-oriented activism after the macro-political thrust of anti-globalization, the movements of the squares and Occupy Wall Street has something of what John Roberts refers to as the reasoning of unreason.[9] While Roberts is concerned to account for the reappearance of the populist and fascist right, much of what he describes also characterizes identitarian endeavours. The rejection of an unconditional universalism accompanies the abstraction of capitalist social relations in a politics of agency, as he puts it, that is bereft of transformative change. Although capitalism polices radical anti-Enlightenment particularism so as to stabilize the conditions for accumulation and an inclusive and expansionist free market liberalism, it nevertheless accepts particularisms that attack the cause of unconditional rights for all. Particularism is accepted as a justification for capitalist exploitation and consumer democracy, but not as part of the extension of universal secular egalitarianism beyond capitalism. Consequently, where the solution to capitalist exploitation is not the universalism of liberalism, it is the narrow, communitarian and regressive universalization of capital as the "universalization of human finitude."[10] Along these lines, Trump's politics were part of the tradition of counter-revolution. Bypassing codes of civility, his pro-American particularism opposed almost anything that was not ostensibly "white, male and Christian," from environmentalism and immigration to public safety and the right to protest.

An early analysis of the Trump phenomenon is a broadside by Mikkel Bolt Rasmussen titled *Trump's Counter-Revolution*. Rasmussen describes the purpose of his book as, first, an analysis of Trump as a "late-capitalist fascism that solves the economic crisis by returning to an imagined idea of a national community through protectionism and nationalist measures," and second, a critique of the "opposition between Trump and democracy," which, he says, was "a staple of liberal discourse since Trump's election."[11] Rasmussen defines Trump as a symptom of the problems of capitalist crisis, a notion that echoes the slogan of the San Francisco-based Party for Socialism and Liberation: Trump is the Symptom, Capitalism is the Disease, Socialism is the Cure.

According to Rasmussen, Trump's election was a vague and uninformed protest against the neoliberal policies of deregulation, privatization and cuts to social programmes. Like Brexit in the U.K., Trump's nationalist policies were said to appeal to the discontent of the working class by promising protectionist solutions and public investment. The Trump presidency was also said to be a reaction to the rise of global protest movements and an effort to redirect discontent, defining Americans as the master race and Trump as its strong leader. Not unlike fascist predecessors, Trump used mainstream and mass media platforms to whip up resentment, employing against his opponents the kind of pop cultural and blatantly discriminatory attacks that pre-empt criticism.[12] Rasmussen argues that Trump's "postmodern fascism" promised to restore the white male petty bourgeoisie and the American nation to its former greatness. According to Trump's rhetoric, the decline of the U.S. was due, in part, to the influx of immigrants and refugees from Mexico, who could only be deterred by building a wall between the two countries.

Rasmussen is correct that the Trump counter-revolution was a reactionary measure against alter-global forces of resistance. As an aphorism attributed to Walter Benjamin has it, the rise of every fascism bears witness to a failed revolution.[13] There is, however, a class element to the critique of an ostensibly outraged and white petty bourgeoisie. There has indeed been a rise to cultural hegemony of a global petty bourgeoisie, but this now dominant post-ideological and post-class disposition is characteristic not only of those who voted for Trump, but also of a significant proportion of mainstream liberals as well as the progressive left. The petty bourgeoisie, which is comprised of small business workers, no-collar office workers, service workers, students and creatives, and which is culturally expansive as a cross-class phenomenon, includes those people who supported Hillary Clinton and Joe Biden as the lesser of two evils. Moreover, it is identitarian liberals who invented the 'brocialist' meme to slander the Bernie Sanders campaign in 2016 and 2020. They were reinforced in their assault on the left by the postmodernist dismantling of the vestiges of Marxism. Trump's apotheosis, one might say, was the result of a widespread social counter-revolution that coincides with the abandonment of class politics and the rise of neoliberal knowledge and culture industries. As a movement by and for the ruling class, abetted by the neoliberal centre, the far right is a symptom of the crisis of neoliberal hegemony and a movement directed against the working majority.

Identity is an unavoidable fact of life and is related to the modalities of identification and disidentification. These modalities are operative in racism as well as anti-racism, both of which can be put to the service of capitalism. Who are the Obama supporters who are de facto anti-racist and consider his presidency to have been a milestone of social progress? In the introduction to their edited text, *Hopeless: Barack Obama and the Politics of Illusion*, Jeffrey St. Clair and Joshua Frank argue that Obama was the embodiment of the new multiculturalism.[14] His vaguely liberal ideology, defined as post-racial and post-partisan, was responsible for illegal wars, drone strikes, the bailout of corrupt bankers, the failure to close Guantánamo Bay, the maintenance of a recessionary economy, the outsourcing of manufacturing, ten-to-twenty percent unemployment, increased wealth inequality, the protection of torturers, extensive government surveillance and the extra-judicial killing of U.S. citizens. What, these authors ask, did Obama's followers think of American politics throughout his two campaigns?

> What was running through their minds when the mists finally parted to reveal that Obama was implementing cunning tracings of Bush-era policies on everything from the indefinite detention of uncharged prisoners in the war on terror to raids on medical marijuana distributors in states where medical pot has been legalized?[15]

Like Rasmussen, St. Clair and Frank suggest that after Obama, the American right wanted their country back, not from corporate capitalism, but from immigrants, blacks, public employees, teachers, scientists and homosexuals. The ignorance of this conspiratorial right, however, appears more contemptible than the heedlessness of the neoliberal "moderates," whose failures simply do not register.

Rasmussen argues that race issues and racial privilege have been essential to American politics since the founding of the nation. Politicians like Trump are looking to racism and protectionism as new means to enforce neoliberal capitalism. In this context, whites are said to have unfair advantages in a colourblind and white supremacist society, as noticed in racial disparities in infant mortality, policing, incarceration, education, housing, wealth and employment. In order to challenge politicians like Trump, he says, the critique of capitalism is only a half measure, since "only an end to whiteness as a socio-political category can create the conditions of possibility for an American democracy."[16] According to this view, a colourblind movement like Occupy Wall Street was "corrected" by Black Lives Matter, which demanded not only police reform, but compensation for structural violence and exclusion. He writes:

> If Occupy was the youth in New York and California, and Black Lives Matter was the black population, then Trump's supporters are the white and blue-collar workers outside of the metropolis, who reject the last 30 years of economic restructuring and demand the restitution of the previous (white) welfare of a previous era.[17]

Rasmussen chides leftist commentators like Mike Davis, Nancy Fraser and Naomi Klein for criticizing the Democratic Party for its dependence on global finance capital and therefore ignoring how a return to working-class politics, as represented by Sanders, focuses on fighting neoliberalism at the expense of the history of racial disadvantage. Such social democracy, he argues, ignores how nostalgia for Franklin D. Roosevelt's New Deal and Lyndon B. Johnson's Great Society were alliances between the white working class and capitalism at the expense of black workers.[18] He writes: "It was white work and white welfare within the framework of state-sponsored capitalism, and that, of course, is no kind of ideal today."[19]

Rasmussen is among many on the contemporary progressive left who have made race issues central to anti-capitalist politics. Wielding increasingly trendy but relatively unexamined terms like 'structural racism' and 'racial capitalism,' the radical left is in the process of neoliberalizing itself in the name of anti-racism. This book argues instead that intersectional calls for 'race and class' analysis on the left risk weakening radical materialism in favour of the liberal pluralist ideology that has shaped the discourse of anti-racism since the postwar period. According to Paul Frymer, from the 1930s to the 1980s, the U.S. federal government's methods of promoting civil rights within trade unions was ultimately to the detriment of both the Civil Rights movement and the labour movement.[20] As Touré Reed argues,

> Democratic presidential administrations – from Kennedy to Obama – have unquestioningly failed to address the structural sources of racial disparities. However, far from reducing race to class, liberal social policy since the Cold War has tended to abstract racial disparities from the political-economic forces that generate them.[21]

In Reed's estimation, postwar liberalism has been race reductionist rather than class reductionist. This makes even historical study subject to distortion. For example, the New Deal excluded agricultural workers and domestic servants, which left out the majority of blacks and maintained the Southern way of life. These restrictions, no less racially motivated than other forms of Jim Crow discrimination, are sometimes attributed to the gains that had been secured through the allotment of land to the families of black WWI soldiers. The view that New Dealers colluded with Southern racists, however, ignores the fact that three out of every four domestic and agricultural workers who were excluded from Social Security were white, and other mostly white work sectors were also excluded. Blacks who worked in other areas were covered and millions benefited from various other aspects of the New Deal, whose programmes were disproportionately beneficial to blacks when compared to the rest of American society. Similar efforts to discount the bourgeois revolutions and the Civil War have affected contemporary historiography. Although the conceit of academic intersectionality is that it is non-reductionist, the fact remains that it is by a large a product of postmodern academia with little to offer the radical left. According to Barbara Fields, the function of slavery was not the production of white supremacy, but rather the production of cotton or sugan cane. Or as Ellen Meiksins Wood has argued, the link between primitive accumulation and capitalism that is presumed by the notion of racial capitalism obscures the fact that historical forms of imperialism did not necessarily develop capitalist relations and imperatives. Contemporary forms of academic and activist anti-racism that take identity for granted detach race issues from their conditions of socio-economic production. And the reasons for this have everything to do with contemporary conditions of socio-economic production.

Despite the emphasis that left politics gives to political economy, a non-reductionist and non-determinist materialism must also address questions of ideology. While Rasmussen calls for an anti-racist leftist internationalism, the situation in the U.S. found Trump's white authoritarian capitalism opposed to Obama's post-black capitalism, Clinton's post-feminist capitalism and Sanders' multicultural populism. Trump is not only the product of four decades of neoliberal policy, but also of the ideology of the progressive liberal centre, including its academic identity politics and post-political new social movements. In response to Max Horkheimer's statement that "whoever is not prepared to talk about capitalism should also remain silent about fascism," we should add to this the challenge that whoever is not prepared to talk critically about identity politics should also remain silent about capitalism.[22] Rasmussen is correct to say that identity issues are issues of class struggle. However, one needs to think this through in dialectical terms and not simply as a politics of anti-oppression that is to be synthesized with anti-exploitation. We could begin, then, by proposing three interrelated axioms: 1) the particularity of identity has nothing to do with the universality of culture and politics, 2) identity is one of the means through which culture and politics are deployed, 3) identity politics is central to the culture and politics of the neoliberal era.

There are countless perspectives on the relation between identity and class. The Marxist thesis of this book is that *whereas racial and sexual differences are not inevitably conflictual, labour and capital are inherently antagonistic.* Philosophically speaking, antagonism is inherent to the division between subject and object, which takes an infinitely multiple number of social forms. It is easy enough to appreciate that this gap is not a justification for oppression. However, not every form of oppression is directly determined by capitalist social relations. Racial and other forms of discrimination and domination pre-exist capitalism and are not exclusive to Western culture. Capitalism, however, structures social relations in ways that are specific to its world historical transformations. It is the ways in which global neoliberal capitalism structures ideology around identity, culture and lifestyle that is pertinent to us today, even if attention to these issues does not bring us very much closer to the kind of society-wide system change we require if we are to tackle the most daunting political challenges of our times, from imperialist wars and climate change to world poverty and global divisions of labour exploitation.

Postmodern and post-structural theories have taught cultural theorists to believe that societal norms must be challenged, that ideologies naturalize unacknowledged interests, and that transformation is preferable to the stability of political, ethical and aesthetic standards. Such paradigms can be used indiscriminately against nationalistic chauvinism as well as democratic socialism. If the left is to dissolve Trump-like symptoms and leave behind the era of neoliberal globalization, it must rid itself of the myth of an inoperative class politics. The working class has been made into the convenient foil of a post-political end-of-history ideology that has reduced class struggle and socialist politics to the totalitarian tragedies of the twentieth century. The liberal class has chattered ad nauseam about its Trump symptom because Trump is the result of its project to eradicate the left. Trump's strategy advisor Stephen Bannon once remarked, "the longer [the Democrats] talk about identity politics, [we] got 'em. I want them to talk about racism every day. If the left is focused on race and identity, and we go with economic nationalism, we can crush the Democrats."[23] The liberal middle class ignores to everyone's disadvantage the concerns of the working majority. Has the identitarian left done the same?

Kim Sajet, the director of the National Portrait Gallery, suggested that the portraits of the Obamas that were made by Kehinde Wiley and Amy Sherald in 2018 are like icons that are drawing in secular pilgrims to reflect on the past, but also, as they take a selfie and buy merchandise in the museum store, dream about a potential future in which presidential power is defined by the racial identity of the sitters.[24] What do these latter-day pilgrims think when they look at the paintings? An answer might be ventured by considering the 2020 primaries. The popularity of Bernie Sanders caused the Trump Republicans to make anti-socialism the focus of their 2020 campaign. Trump sought to sideline Sanders so that he could then campaign against a right-wing Democratic nominee. In September 2019, Pelosi announced an impeachment inquiry against Trump's investigations into Biden's son's ties to a Ukrainian gas oligarch. This game of establishment infighting deflected attention from the political struggle within the Democratic Party, which colluded with Trump's immigration policies, increased military budget and corporate tax cuts. In his State of the Union address in January 2019, Trump declared that "America will never be a socialist country," this being only a few degrees of separation from Hillary Clinton's position on why the U.S. should not be a socialist country and Elizabeth Warren's assurances to Wall Street that she is capitalist to the bone. At a National Republican Congressional Committee dinner, Trump warned in McCarthyite fashion that socialism is threatening to destroy America, a perspective seconded by the creation of an anti-socialism caucus in the House of Representatives, no doubt prompted by the twenty-fold increase in strike activity in 2017 from preceding years. In March 2019, former president Obama responded to the Bernie 2020 campaign with a speech in Berlin where he denounced leftist criticism of the Democratic Party. Working behind the scenes with Pelosi, Obama helped to prevent the drive towards the left within the party and successfully promoted Biden, his former Vice President, as an identity politics candidate – a tough sell for a blooper-prone grifter with a dismal track record on race and gender issues.

After Sanders won the popular vote in the first three primaries, his campaign was poised to win either a majority or a plurality of delegates at the Democratic National Convention. With only one week remaining until

Super Tuesday, the Democratic establishment scrambled to block his path. In the South Carolina primary, African-American Congressman James Clyburn, a member of the Congressional Black Caucus, encouraged a Biden vote. Leaders in the Caucus directed poor and working-class blacks to oppose Sanders by emphasizing Biden's association with Obama and his promise to elect a black Vice President or Supreme Court judge. Following the South Carolina primary, Obama called nominee Pete Buttigieg to have him drop out of the race. Senate Majority Leader Harry Reid called Amy Klobuchar to do the same. These candidates' supporters were now encouraged by Obama to vote for Biden, who in comparison with Sanders had next to no grassroots support, could not raise donations beyond the billionaire class, was incoherent in debates and aggressive towards citizens at town hall meetings. Without any ground game and with no path to victory, Warren, who had campaigned against Sanders and other nominees on gender politics, decided to remain in the race. Buttigieg and Klobuchar dropped out of the race to give their supporters to Biden and Warren stayed in the race to prevent her supporters from going over to Sanders.

With Obama's support, a bellicose establishment crony scored large majorities with African-American voters, especially in Alabama. In contrast, Sanders did well among Latino voters. Sanders won only 23 percent of the votes among educated women. As for his popularity with young people, these voters turned out in smaller numbers in 2020 than in 2016. Despite the Sanders campaign going to great lengths to emphasize solidarity across identity groups, the neoliberal Biden, who has a history of discriminatory policies, did best among African Americans who consider race issues to be more important than economic inequality. According to Keeanga-Yamahtta Taylor, Biden's success on Super Tuesday "reflects the fact that we haven't fully interrogated Barack Obama's tenure."[25] If one was to pursue the sort of reasoning that accounts for the Trump presidency as the fault of a racist white working class, then by the same logic, the results of Super Tuesday would oblige us to consider that African Americans are politically self-destructive, easily manipulated and anti-Semitic. That is precisely the kind of reasoning that this book rejects by suggesting instead that the lesson of the 2016 and 2020 elections is the problematic nature of a politics that privileges identity and demographics over universalist policies and class solidarity against neoliberal ideology.[26] According to Dan Kovalik, the fact that the left-liberal obsession with racial and gender equality has practically eclipsed democratic concerns and led Americans to "lionize a mass murderer like Obama who destroyed tens of thousands of [mostly black and brown] lives" is "downright pathological."[27]

On April 8, 2020, in the midst of the emerging coronavirus pandemic, and with trillions of dollars being funnelled into the U.S. economy to prop up the business elite, the Obama Democrats came through with their choice for the leadership: a corporate lackey who promised investors that nothing will change. Regardless, something did change after even Sanders and Warren came around to endorse Biden. If in 2016 the Trump victory could wrongly be attributed to the racism of the white working class, the Biden nomination was the outcome of a concerted effort on the part of the establishment to prevent even the slightest concession to the interests of working people. Possibly for the first time since 2008, Obama no longer appeared too black to fail but quite simply the neoliberal operative that he always was. This was evident as the CARES Act bailed out the wealthy while working people were being forced back into unsafe workplaces or onto the unemployment rolls. By the end of April, support for Trump was increasing among black and Latino voters. In May, Biden told Charlamagne tha God, host of *The Breakfast Club* radio show: "If you have a problem figuring out whether you're for me or Trump, then you ain't black."[28] Tellingly, concern for the fact that Biden is an elderly white male was greater among affluent suburban whites than among African Americans and Hispanics.

By August 2020, after failing to properly handle the pandemic – including a recommendation to inject disinfectant as a preventive measure – and after having deployed federal police to quell Black Lives Matter protests in the aftermath of the police murder of George Floyd, Trump increased his support among black and Latino voters. Although almost 90 percent of black voters are Democratic Party supporters, the GOP's well-packaged pseudo-populism maintained its appeal with minority voters beyond the attention given by liberals to white racial grievance. In other words, when minority voters support Trump, the explanation provided by the media is that this is due to the fact that they are less affluent and less educated, and not due to the fact that the Democratic Party is increasingly associated with the interests of the billionaire class, which causes many voters to either ignore elections or switch brands. Working-class voters who opt for Trump are defined as dupes since the GOP is even less a party for working people than the Democrats.[29] The assumption here is that political ideology is homologous to economic interests. Yet this elementary definition of politics fails to account for the policies of even the most principled Democratic Party politicians.[30]

If the nomination of Biden to lead the Democratic Party was a referendum of sorts on the Obama legacy, then the choice of Kamala Harris as Vice Presidential nominee sealed the deal. The 2020 Democratic National Convention celebrated this victory by including veterans of the 1996 *Republican* National Convention, including Colin Powell, John Kasich and Cindy McCain. After

Biden won the presidency, Obama did a series of interviews to promote the first volume of his new memoir. This was accompanied by uses of contemporary art to rejuvenate his image, including a 2020 portrait of Obama by Jordan Casteels that was presented in the context of an interview in *The Atlantic* and an interview with the television show *60 Minutes* filmed in the Smithsonian's National Portrait Gallery, with Obama seated in front of the official portrait of Abraham Lincoln. Striking a thoughtful attitude, Obama defended his two terms by contrasting them with the brutality of Donald Trump and Genghis Khan.[31] In his posing as a wizened leader, Obama talks about progress and goodwill, all the while setting the lowest bar for himself and his accomplices. Despite his presidency, Obama presented himself as a man of the people who is not only concerned with the world economy but with the spiritual needs of the least of these.

The journalist Krystal Ball has argued that the definition of privilege is the luxury to care more about the demographics that help you win elections than about substantive class issues. "To the extent that there is a fascist movement in America," she says, "you might consider the way it has been fuelled by all who join hands in bipartisan unity to screw over the working class and shower largesse on the wealthy and the well-connected."[32] Ball's critique of moral preening and virtue signalling on the Democratic Party "left" sums up the mystique that has bedevilled the flocks of tourists that have gone to see the Obama portraits.

Too Black to Fail takes a dual political and cultural approach to uncover the Obama portraits, and by implication, the race and class issue in the U.S. The first chapter of this book provides a detailed description of the Obama portraits, the statements made by the artists to the media and the statements made by the Obamas. It then examines the references in the Barack Obama portrait to other works in the history of U.S. presidential portraiture. This is followed by contextual references to George W. Bush's hobbyist art and the kitsch painting by Andy Thomas that was hung by Trump in the White House. The semiotics of political portraiture is addressed, as is the way in which contemporary art is being developed in relation to the kind of symbolic representation that has very little to do with aesthetics or politics and more with the rhetoric of empowerment. The chapter advances the concept of 'post-representation' in relation to autonomist theories of neoliberal governance.

The next chapter considers the legacy of the Obama administration. It begins with the question of race and the fetish of the first black presidency as a form of ideological jouissance that allowed people to overlook Obama's policy choices, which in many cases were more regressive than those of his Republican predecessor. Obama's early career is addressed, as is his attitude towards the black agenda. Divided in two sections, 'too big to fail' and 'too big to jail,' the Obama administration's successes and failures are assessed in terms of domestic and foreign policy, leaning heavily on the failure side of the equation with respect to harmful decisions made in the areas of economic policy, tax cuts, social security, campaign financing, manufacturing, employment, labour policy, health care, education, ecology, immigration, policing, criminal justice, civil liberties, militarism and human rights. Obama's choices are shown to have adversely affected black and minority constituencies especially, a problem that was not improved by the office of Attorney General Eric Holder, despite his expansion of the Civil Rights Division. Obama's two terms in office are shown to have increased social inequality and made the world a more dangerous place. The chapter concludes with an examination of the idea of the 'extreme centre' and the 'death of the liberal class' as discussed by Tariq Ali and Chris Hedges. A notion of 'neoliberal reverse colourblindness' is then put forward, which argues that anti-racism and celebritization were the only stratagems available to Obama to gloss over the failures of his administration.

The third chapter develops the idea of 'woke aesthetics' as the overall conceptual framework for the kinds of art practices that were chosen as befitting this creative departure in presidential portraiture. A brief mention of some of the main tenets of postmodern theory and contemporary art activism is supplemented with Nancy Fraser's theory of 'progressive neoliberalism,' according to which identity groups aspire to social recognition within the ideology of corporate capitalism. Woke aesthetics is defined as a belated 'postmodernism of reaction' combined with identitarianism. A brief description of Sherald's art practice is followed by a lengthy analysis of the work of Wiley. His influences and education are considered, as is his method of streetcasting, which brings into play notions of homosexuality as outlaw desire. Wiley's work with corporations and his effort to develop his practice into branding and cross-platforming is presented in relation to various models of critical theory, from the writings of W.E.B. Du Bois to Frantz Fanon, Herbert Marcuse, Nina Power and Mark Fisher. The chapter concludes with a comparison of the work of the two Obama portraitists with Zanny Begg and Elise McLeod's *City of Ladies*, a work with similar motifs but far more progressive politics and aesthetics.

The fourth chapter on 'racialism and its discontents' develops the issue of how it is that anti-racism and anti-universalist race exceptionalism justifies the kind of nefarious neoliberalism that defines the policies of Barack Obama and the art of Kehinde Wiley and Amy Sherald. The chapter develops the critique of racialism from the perspective of emancipatory universality and class analysis. It is divided into sections that classify different types of politicized knowledge. A section on 'activists' describes the work of Black Lives Matter as well as the academic field of Critical Race Theory. Both are subject to critiques by Adolph Reed, Cedric Johnson, Paul Street, Tom Carter and Keeanga-Yamahtta Taylor.

A section on 'the scapegoat' looks at the ways in which the white working class has been blamed for the rise of Trump and the far right, a postulate that ignores the reality of voting patterns in 2008, 2012, 2016 and 2020. The section on 'devil's advocates' focuses on Touré Neblett and John McWhorter's respective theories of post-blackness and the final section on so-called 'cultural Marxism' addresses the work of Karen and Barbara Fields in relation to the decolonial movement in education and alt-right critiques by people like Jordan Peterson of postmodern social engineering. A section on race 'managers' critiques the writings of Eric Michael Dyson, Ta-Nehisi Coates and Michelle Alexander as representative of mainstream neoliberal racialism. This contrasts markedly with a section on 'the intellectuals,' which explores the ideas of non-racialist social critics like Cornel West, Walter Benn Michaels, David Harvey, Adolph Reed and Ellen Meiksins Wood. These critics combat racialism in favour of different types of left universalism. Their work contrasts with race 'brokers' like Chris Chen, Asad Haider, Nikhil Pal Singh, Joshua Clover and David Roediger, who combine race and class issues in ways that weaken both class critique and the universalist foundations of emancipatory politics.

The fifth chapter on 'black capitalism and embedded history' is divided into two interrelated sections that examine the ways in which claims to historical significance are made when controversies arise around political symbols and political statements. The case of NFL quarterback Colin Kaepernick raises the problem of political correctness in situations where multi-million-dollar sponsors like Nike are engaged in wokewashing. The question of black capitalism is addressed in relation to celebrity branding and promotional crossovers into diversified investments. The notion that sports events and celebrity musicians are "making history" is promoted by corporate sponsors and the media in such a way that identity and market choice work to substitute a seemingly class-neutral democratic politics, if not a recuperated black radical agenda, for progressive politics more generally. The marketing of Obama as a cool candidate is shown to have merged with the consumer politics of hip hop and sports celebrity. The chapter then examines the controversies surrounding the attempt by racialists to destroy the New Deal WPA murals on the life of George Washington in the George Washington High School in San Francisco. As a flashpoint of national debates around historical memory and distinctions between revolutionary and neoliberal worldviews, the case of the Victor Arnautoff murals reveals the extent to which woke capitalism has eroded, or failed to erode, radical political consciousness. The *New York Times*' 1619 Project, with its race-based attempt to reframe revolutionary history, is also addressed in these terms. The two cases are developed in relation to the question of fascist ideology as the political unconscious of postmodern historicism. As racialism takes root in academia and mass culture, a do-it-yourself micro-fascism instrumentalizes allyship in favour of post-representational art and politics.

The conclusion to this study proposes a revised version of the museum label that accompanies the painting of Barack Obama in the National Portrait Gallery. Black populism and the limits of the black Marxist concept of 'racial capitalism' are discussed in relation to the rise of right-wing authoritarianism since postmodernism. A politics of emancipatory universalism is put forward as an antidote to the kind of neoliberal identitarianism that justifies injustice in the name of justice.

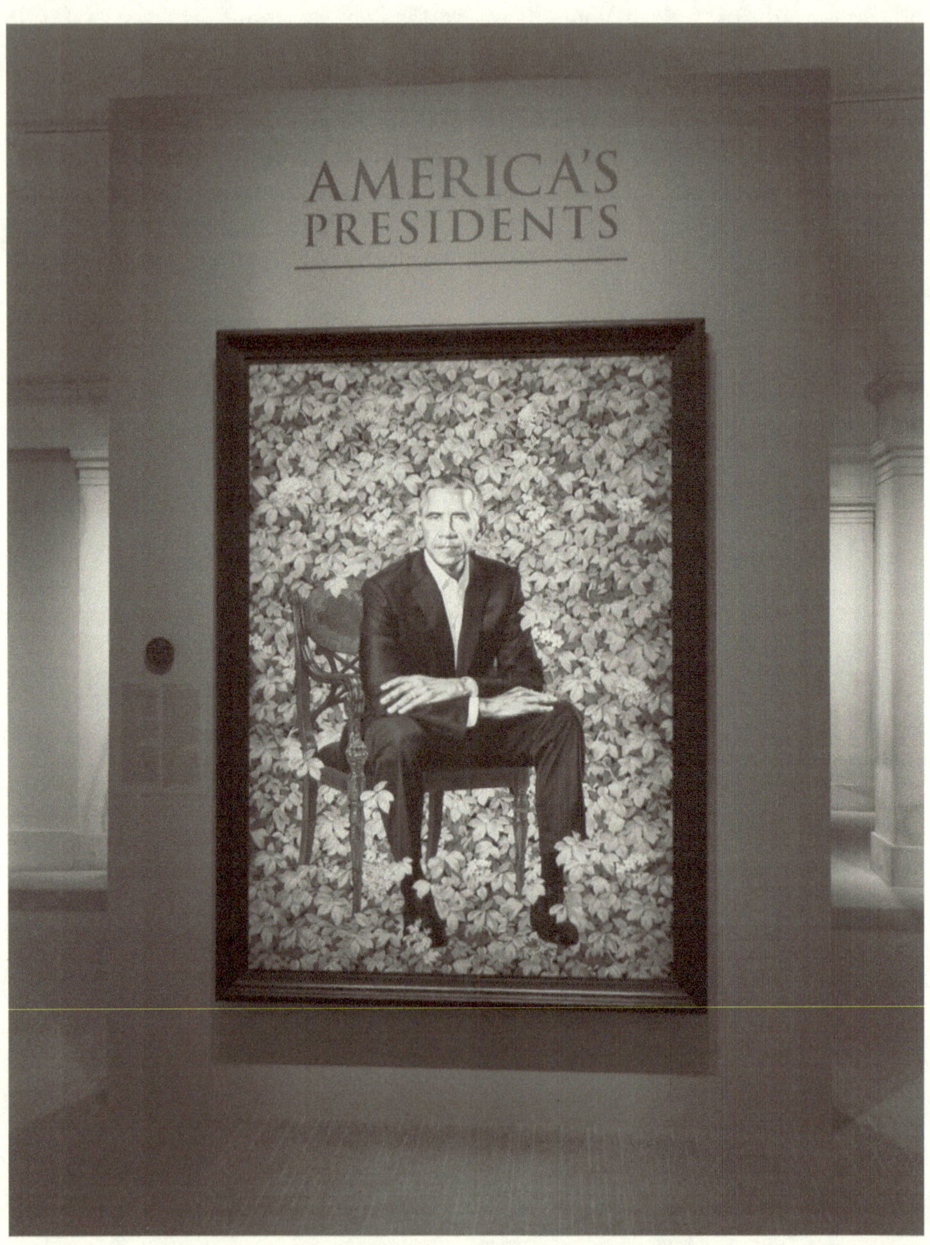

Kehinde Wiley's portrait of former president Barack Obama in the exhibition ***America's Presidents*** at the National Portrait Gallery, Washington, D.C. Detail of photo by Mark Gulezian. Courtesy of the National Portrait Gallery, Smithsonian Institution.

CH. 1: A TRAP FOR THE GAZE

My wallpaper and I are fighting a duel to the death. One of us has to go.

– Oscar Wilde

The obscene virtual dimension is inscribed into an ideological text in the guise of the fantasmatic background that sustains the emptiness of the Master-Signifier.

– Slavoj Žižek, *The Parallax View*

Barack Obama is the first black President of the United States and therefore the first black president to be featured in the Smithsonian's National Portrait Gallery. The portrait of Barack Obama was painted by Kehinde Wiley and the portrait of Michelle Obama was painted by Amy Sherald. These are the first black artists to be featured in the National Portrait Gallery collection of presidential portraits.[1] On the advice of White House curator William Allman, White House interior designer Michael Smith and Harlem Studio Museum director Thelma Golden, the Obamas chose Wiley and Sherald, who met with the POTUS and FLOTUS to discuss their respective views on portraiture and the aesthetic strategies they would use for these works. The overall commission process was curated by Taína Caragol, Dorothy Moss and the NPG, which raised $500,000 in private funds from benefactors. These two official portraits have been added to the permanent collection of the National Portrait Gallery. While the image of Barack Obama is shown in the exhibition of presidential portraits, the painting of Michelle Obama was first presented in the recent acquisitions section. The unveiling of the works on February 12, 2018, attracted celebrities as well as politicians, including Tom Hanks, Steven Spielberg, Joe Biden, Eric Holder and David Axelrod. The unveiling was reported to be a significant event since the artists chosen by the Obamas make work that one can readily associate with contemporary art rather than the more sedate realm of conventional portraiture. By all accounts, the portraits are the most successful in the recent history of this practice. They generated a considerable amount of online activity, including commentary on a viral photograph by Ben Himes that shows a two-year old girl named Parker Curry staring at the larger-than-life portrait of Michelle Obama. People lined up for hours to take photographs of the paintings and sales at the museum shop increased by 200 percent in the first year after these acquisitions. In 2018, two million people visited the museum, doubling the average attendance numbers.

An Effect of Grace

Before this commission, Kehinde Wiley was already known to Barack Obama, who in 2015 had presented him with the U.S. State Department Medal of Arts Award for cultural diplomacy through the visual arts. After being accepted for the assignment, Wiley worked with Obama for six hours, took thousands of photographs and leafed with him through art history books for something that Obama would like him to emulate. Obama asked him to do something unprecedented. Wiley had to explain what he would do differently, not only with regard to other presidential portraits, but also in relation to his typical working method of drawing on imagery from the Western art canon that he subverts by replacing whites with contemporary black sitters.

Wiley's large, almost life-size painting depicts Obama in a photo-realistic manner that is offset with the artist's characteristically bright colours. Obama is shown seated midway in a wooden antique chair – a possible reference to African furniture and sculpture. He leans forward with his arms crossed and his hands resting on his knees. He looks directly at the viewer while his head is slightly turned to his left. His feet are similarly turned inward, which imparts a sense of awkwardness as well as athletic poise. Although he has an air of seriousness, he also looks inquisitive. He is dressed in a dark semi-casual Friday suit with an open collar white shirt and no tie. His watch, a vanitas motif, is half-exposed. Like everything else in the painting, the watch seems to refer to the balance of opposites. It is possibly an allegory of half measures. These elements are standard enough and the painting would have gone unremarked if it was not for the fact that both the chair and the figure are lodged in a background of green leaves that cover parts of the chair as well as Obama's left arm, his ankles and his feet. The foliage includes a smattering of flowers that refer to his life trajectory, with blue lilies from Kenya, where his father is from, Arabian jasmine from Hawaii, where he grew up and studied, and chrysanthemums, which are the official flower of Chicago and refers to the city where he met Michelle Obama and launched his political career.

Part of the framing of this work is the wall label, which reads:

> Barack Obama, born 1961. Forty-fourth president, 2009-2017. Barack Obama made history in 2009 by becoming the first African American president. The former Illinois state senator's election signaled a feeling of hope for the future as the U.S. was undergoing its worst financial crisis since the Great Depression. While working to improve the economy, Obama enacted the Affordable Care Act, extending health benefits to millions of previously uninsured Americans. Overseas, he oversaw the drawdown of American troops in the Middle East – a force reduction that was controversially replaced with an expansion of drone and aviation strikes. Though his mission to kill al-Qaeda founder Osama bin Laden was successful, his pledge to close Guantanamo prison went unrealized.[2]

At the unveiling ceremony, Wiley described the painting thus:

> This is our humanity. This is our ability to say: 'I matter. I was here.' The ability to be the first African-American painter to paint the first African-American president of the United States is absolutely overwhelming. (...) In a very symbolic way what I'm doing is charting a path on earth through those plants that weave their way. There's a fight going on between [Obama] in the foreground and the plants that are trying to announce themselves underneath his feet. Who gets to be the star of the show? The story of the man who inhabits that story? (...) But there are also botanicals that are going on there that nod towards his personal story. It's the story of the man who inhabits that story. It's all chance-driven.[3]

Wiley ended his statement with what looked to be a Hands Up, Don't Shoot gesture that was too subtle to be definite. The idea that the work is made by a black artist who works with the Western canon to challenge the 'white gaze' led only a few reporters to suggest that the work is also designed to challenge the 'heterosexual gaze.' Wiley's reference to the plants in that regard is a mainstay of his art. However, the artist did something additional and rather extraordinary that made the Twittersphere freak for a short while: he painted an oversized spermatozoid shape inside a vein on Obama's left temple. In addition, although no one has remarked on this fact, he painted the folds in the president's crotch to look as though he has a vagina rather than the usual male anatomical bona fides. The fact that Obama has his arms crossed, with his wedding ring prominently showing, indicates that he is barring his sex, one would assume, first and foremost, from the artist's gaze.

These unusual elements, which are not mentioned in the catalogue that was published to accompany a traveling exhibition of the portraits, adds innuendo to two kinds of statement that Wiley has made.[4] The first type addresses issues of racial identification. As he said to the BBC: "The reality of Barack Obama being the president of the United States – quite possibly the most powerful nation in the world – means that the image of power is completely new for an entire generation of not only black American kids, but every population group in this nation."[5] The second type refers to issues of sexuality. In a statement made to National Public Radio, Wiley said: "What we're positing here is a new vision of the possible, one which is inclusive, one that says yes to people who happen to look like me and one that will increasingly catch fire as we go on to inspire young people to imagine new possibilities."[6] The reference to people who "look like me" refers to Wiley's blackness, but it also refers to the way that he desiringly looks at men when he scouts for models for his paintings. Wiley was clear to credit Obama with the agreement to go ahead with the work: "The painting stands out as a game changer, really. And I think that's in keeping with the type of bold leadership and authentic voice that this President gave to this nation."[7]

Obama himself seems to have seconded Wiley on this issue. In an Instagram post after the unveiling, he thanked the artist, stating that "generations of Americans – and young people from all around the world – will visit the National Portrait Gallery and see this country through a new [inclusive and optimistic] lens."[8] At the unveiling Obama credited Wiley for changing the way people think of privilege and power. He mentioned that he had asked Wiley to "bring it down just a notch" and not make him look like Napoleon.[9]

It is anyone's guess if Obama is playing an inside game with the artist or if he and the American public were placed in the role of innocents, oblivious to the subtext of the artist's work. One of Wiley's most well-known paintings, *Napoleon Leading the Army Over the Alps*, is a large-scale work from 2005 that is based on Jacques-Louis David's 1801 classic, *Napoleon Crossing the Alps*. Wiley's version depicts an unnamed black model who is shown wearing Timberland boots, camouflage pants and red designer brand Starter Sportswear tennis wristbands, a possible allusion to fist-fucking. The family name indicated on the rock below says Williams instead of Napoleon, which some have read as an allusion to the association of black names with the names of former slave owners, and which, along with the rearing horse's harness, alludes to sexual bondage. Wiley's *Napoleon* also has a pattern of spermatozoa on its wallpaper background, along with sperm shapes that are carved into the cartouches of the ornate gilded frame. The artist's portrait is carved into the cartouche that crowns the frame.

The sperm symbol that is used in the Obama portrait has several possible allusions, from political power, defined exclusively in terms of male virility, to the artist's signature and brand concept, and possibly also, as a representation of the 'whiteness' that is encoded in Obama's bloodstream. If Nelson Shanks's portrait of Bill Clinton was rejected by the former president because it depicted the shadow of Monica Lewinsky's dress, Wiley's send-up to the scandal of sex and power is "out loud and hidden all at once."[10] This reiterates Michel Foucault's notion of sex as a secret that is spoken about ad infinitum, which is more or less consistent with Freudian psychoanalysis.[11] As Oscar Wilde once stated, much about sex has little to do with sex and more to do with power. On the pithiest level, we could say that when gay sexuality no longer causes a scandal, one must look for new ways to *épater l'hétérosexuel*, which risks making the artist into his own joke, more a matter of self-loathing than social critique. There are nevertheless important reasons why such work is less an embarrassment to the White House than it is fully consonant with the politics of post-representation.

The better of the two paintings is without question Amy Sherald's portrait of Michelle Obama, which was Sherald's most interesting work up to that point. It shows the First Lady seated with a large, sleeveless Milly brand gown that reaches both edges of the bottom of the painting, creating a tall, pyramidal shape. She has one arm resting over her opposite knee and the other fashionably supporting her chin. Like her husband, her head is turned away slightly but her eyes look assuredly and intelligently at the viewer. As is typical of Sherald's paintings, the skin colour of her black subject is painted in a grisaille that the artist uses as a device with which to emphasize her sitters' interiority and personality, the ordinariness of blackness and the artifice of painting. The grey skin tone as well as Obama's black hair matches some of the patterning on the mostly white dress. At the same time, sky-blue nail polish matches the monochromatic background, creating a surface tension between the figure and the background.

The wall label at the National Portrait Gallery reads:

> Michelle LaVaughn Robinson Obama, born 1964. Michelle Obama remembers growing up on the South Side of Chicago and thinking "being smart is cooler than being anything in the world." After earning degrees from Princeton University and Harvard Law School, she joined Sidley Austin LLP, where she met Barack Obama in 1989. Guided by the desire to improve her community, she left the firm in the mid-1990s to begin a career in public service. She directed community and external affairs for the University of Chicago Medical Center prior to moving to Washington in 2009. During her husband's two presidential campaigns, Mrs. Obama delivered poignant speeches that centered on her family's commitment to serving others and highlighted the importance of her role as a parent. As a first lady, she focused on women's rights, LGBTQ rights, children's health, and military families.[12]

As a conversation piece, the focus of the painting is the dress, so much so that one could argue that Michelle Obama chose two artists for this portrait

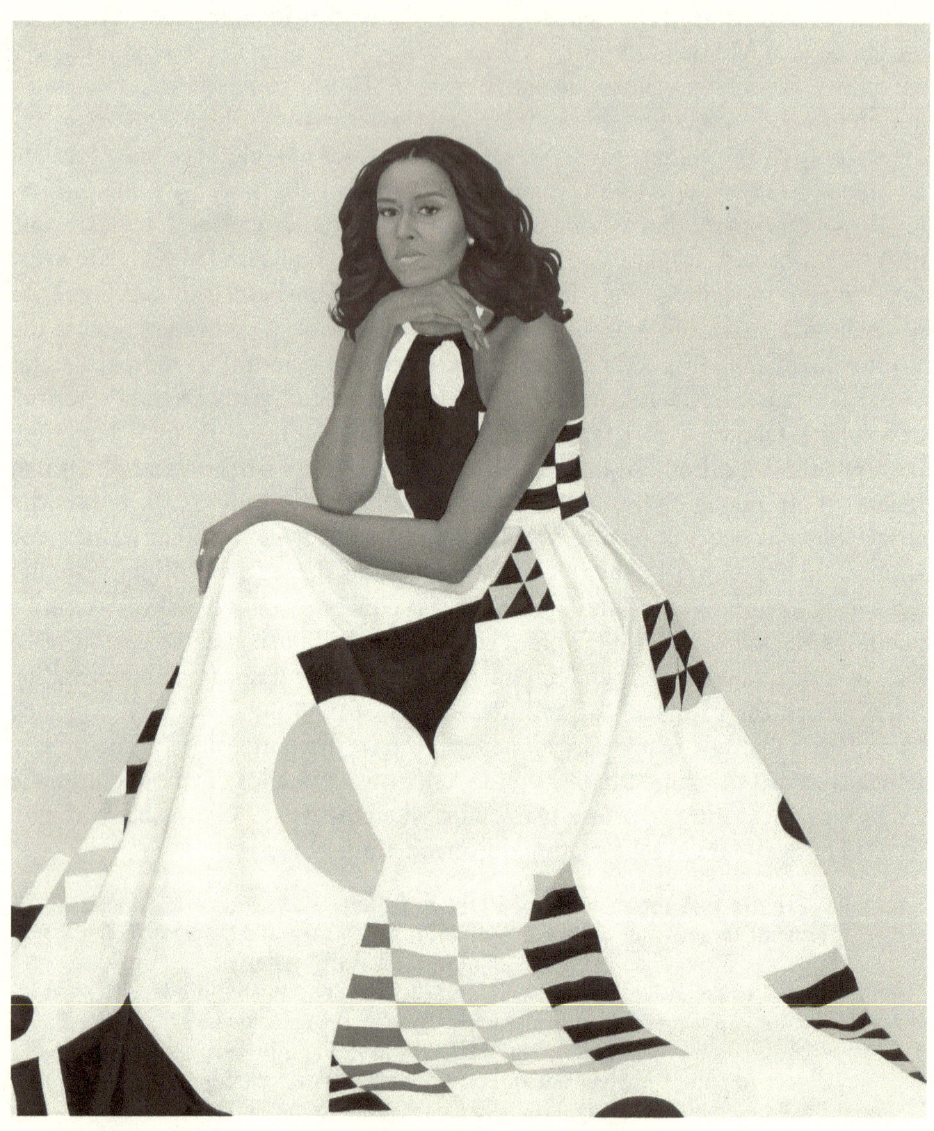

Amy Sherald, ***Michelle LaVaughn Robinson Obama***, oil on linen canvas, 183.2 x 152.7 cm (6 x 5'), 2018. Courtesy of the National Portrait Gallery, Smithsonian Institution.

commission. Milly is the designer label of Michelle Smith, one of Obama's favourite designers. Milly is the label that she wore on her first day in the White House and on other special occasions. On first blush, the pattern looks like a Piet Mondrian design or something along the lines of post-Cubist art. Smith refers to it as a "clean, minimal geometric print" that is "forward thinking" and "without a reference to anything past or nostalgic."[13] This automatic association with European modernism prepares the way for a surprise twist insofar as the patterning is also said to have been inspired by Gee's Bend quilts, which date from the mid-nineteenth and early twentieth century, and which were made by a small rural community of African-American quilters descended from plantation slaves. Just as Gee's Bend quilts were made from remnants and rough materials, including feed bags, the designer dress is made of cotton poplin, a material sometimes used for work clothes. Known for her no-nonsense attitude, and in this regard for her preference for reasonably-priced American labels like J.Crew, ASOS and The Gap, Obama chose the affordable $400 dress so that she can be remembered for her approachability and, all things being equal, concern for the poor. It was chosen from the Milly Spring/Summer 2017 ready-to-wear collection, which is inspired by animus towards Trump and by the desire for equality in human rights, race and sexuality. According to Michelle Smith, the simple lacing and ties indicate the "feeling of being held back" and that "we're not quite there yet."[14] As Kate Betts argues, Michelle Obama's style choices exemplify her belief that she is helping to liberate a new generation of women.[15]

Sherald came into the orbit of the Obama White House after winning the 2016 Outwin Boochever Portrait Competition, a prestigious prize that includes a commission for the NPG and an accompanying exhibition that tours the country. As Sherald prepared the exhibition, she commented: "Having the White House up the street during the Obama administration was a constant reminder that this country we live in would not be as great as it is without people that look like me."[16] The question of political representation is complicated by the history of liberal democracy, but the notion that popular sovereignty can be reduced to racial similarity presumes that identity is coterminous with political democracy. Sherald's grisaille technique and the Milly dress make for a small but significant difference from the notion that seeing is believing. She insists that her work can be read universally as a message about our common humanity, with Michelle Obama being described as exemplary and uniquely authentic. In her media statements, Sherald made relatively uncomplicated associations between her desire to paint ordinary people who are black like her and the desire to see black politicians in places of power. As she puts it, "[s]omething big happened in history, something happened that wasn't supposed to happen and I think they should be represented in that way."[17]

Given the history of slavery and the disenfranchisement of black Americans, the momentousness of the first black presidency is without question. Michelle Obama chose to acknowledge this but with modesty concerning the fact that she and her husband were the first people to fill that role. She did this by comparing the two NPG portraits to cooking a thanksgiving dinner for strangers, stating that the best meal you can serve others is the one you love to make for yourself.[18] She also noted at the unveiling that no one in her family had ever had their portrait painted, adding:

> I am thinking about all of the young people, particularly girls and girls of color, who in years ahead will come to this place, and they will look up and they will see an image of someone who looks like them hanging on the wall of this great American institution. I know what kind of impact that will have on those girls, because I was one of those girls.[19]

This statement no doubt incentivized the popularity of the photograph of Parker Curry staring at the large painting and reportedly saying that she thought it was a painting of a queen. Obama later met with the toddler and her family, dancing with her to Taylor Swift and tweeting: "Parker, I'm so glad I had the chance to meet you today (and for the dance party)!" The portraits and the emphasis on future generations sums up the notion of the Obama legacy as one in which, as Deana Haggag argues, culture was used to change the world.[20] Ever since Jacqueline Kennedy made the White House a platform for style politics, presidential administrations have either used or avoided culture as a means to make political statements.[21] The Obamas are known to have added important artworks to the White House collection while at the same time demonstrating their interest in American popular culture. Their choice of Wiley and Sherald as portrait painters was an act of cultural brinkmanship, balancing artistic interest, which is unusual for this type of commission, with accessibility, defined in terms of visual legibility as well as the fact of the Obama election victory as a benchmark in civil rights.

Can't Knock the Hustle

Most of what was written in the mainstream media before, during and after the unveiling of the portraits emphasized the fact that the Obamas are to be remembered for being the first African Americans in the White House and for being culturally sophisticated, as evidenced by their decision to support contemporary artists rather than conservative portrait painters. It was recognized that the Obamas added important modern and contemporary artworks to the White House collection – works by Edward Hopper, Mark Rothko, Joseph

Albers, Robert Rauschenberg, Alma Thomas, Susan Rothenberg and Sam Francis – and also supported the talent of African-American pop artists, as noticed in Barack Obama's end-of-year playlists. The Obamas were chic, progressive and self-assured, with enough confidence in their cultural tastes to award the National Portrait Gallery commissions to two African-American painters working in a postmodern style. This emphasis on aesthetics caused something of a rupture in the tradition of American presidential portraiture, drawing attention away from Obama as a political figure and emphasizing instead what appears to be the Obamas' cultural capital. As Christopher Knight aptly stated:

> Out across the land, a culture war is raging. It's the sauce of the unprecedented public response to this Smithsonian commission, which far surpasses the unveiling of any presidential portrait before it. In the White House, the Obamas were the first of their kind. At the Smithsonian, the artists are the first of their kind.[22]

Satisfied with their turkey dinner, almost none of the mainstream journalists took this unprecedented occasion to discuss either aesthetic or political issues with anything but the usual mendacity, much of it spoon-fed by official sources. What was discussed, almost exclusively and in large part due to the choice of artists, was the question of identity.

On the other side of mainstream adulation, the Internet spawned a good deal of inflammatory clickbait, as Knight calls it. Much of this was due to the revelation that Wiley had painted a sperm shape in the vein of Obama's forehead, which led to a frenzy of meme activity, from the serious to the silly. Some bloggers noted that the leaves in the background were repeated in several places, as though Wiley had cheated. Others noted that the leaves have what looks like the number 666 encoded in the pattern. Some noticed that Obama's right hand seems to have a sixth finger. Different parodies of the work had him sitting on a toilet, disappearing into the background foliage or wearing a Guantánamo Bay boiler suit. Instead of prison, the green leaves rather conjure an Ivy League setting, which calls to mind Thomas Frank's critique of the technocratic class as an invading army of "well-graduated" professionals.[23] Wiley's green leafy background also invites comparisons with Michelle Obama's healthy-eating proselytism in her book *American Grown: How the White House Kitchen Garden Inspires Families, Schools, and Communities*, adding another layer of hip innuendo with Obama appearing as Michelle's recommended meal. In response, Wiley insisted that nothing about his painting could detract from Obama's "insane energy," even if he and the president thought of the portrait as a "jagged little pill we tossed into the world" in order to see what would happen.[24] Wiley later downplayed the notion that he had intentionally generated all of the

Internet hype and stated that the negative reactions to the painting had more to do with the culture wars and the usual political antagonisms than anything having to do with the work itself.[25] Sherald was more fortunate, receiving only vague criticism for her portrait's lack of verisimilitude.

In terms of art criticism, the media response had little to say that is specific to art theory, mostly due to the fact that the magic realism aspects of postmodern portraiture are hardly radical statements, except for the fact that the paintings are made by African-American artists, which in today's diversity-obsessed art world received more than passing attention. On the art side, to the extent that this distinction is allowed, only Vinson Cunningham proffered a modicum of conceptual terminology, wondering if the portraits were an "exercise in canon-making or sneaky deconstruction."[26] Overall, race politics took precedent as the measure of serious criticism, with Peter Schjeldahl declaring imperiously that in such work, race is a condition for resetting the course of Western art.[27] Steven Nelson anchored Wiley's and Sherald's work in a tradition of representation that goes back to W.E.B. Du Bois's *American Negro* exhibition at the 1900 exhibition in Paris, which showed some 500 photographs and 200 books written by African Americans, as well as Booker T. Washington's publication that same year of *A New Negro for a New Century*, which includes 600 photographs of African Americans.[28] Chiquita Pascal took a related, but slightly more ingenuous tack by arguing against the expectation that people of colour, black women especially, should feel obliged to support other black artists. Sherald's thoughtful painting of Michelle Obama, she argued, deserves consideration as work that asks people to think twice about the visual clues of blackness. Vigilance about having one's artwork recognized implies being prepared to criticize the work on an aesthetic level, not because the aesthetic is more important than the political, but indirectly because of the importance of politics.[29]

This line of identity-specific analysis, whatever one thinks of it, is not accessible to everyone in the same way. This is perhaps why few people, other than Internet pranksters, bothered to criticize the work. In the first year of media reporting on the portraits, the art critic Ben Davis made the only politically incisive assessment. Acknowledging that it is rare for the unveiling of presidential portraits to be on the order of art news, he accounted for this by noting the similarity between the "art-world power players" and "liberal big wigs" who attended the unveiling. The choice of Kehinde Wiley made complete sense since he is "one of the most pop-culture-friendly of art-market stars," known not only for his paintings but for collaborating with corporations like FIFA and the TV show *Empire*.[30] The difficulties of Obama's two terms, from extra-judicial killings to the crackdown on whistleblowers, NSA surveillance and deportations, which Davis claims were happily forgotten in the age of Trump, gave the liberal establishment and the public "an opportunity … to comfort itself with the ennobled imagery of its own heroes."[31] However, after Trump, even the ratings of George W. Bush improved. "Somewhere, deep down, on the level of subtext and unintended meanings," Davis wrote, "this strange, strange political portrait ends up being about how the man must be abstracted from the nitty-gritty of his legacy to become the symbol that his followers desire him to be."[32] More relevance can be given to the strange, however, than most commentators were able to muster. In order to make the case for this, one must look not only to the images collected by Du Bois and Washington, but to the association of Obama with figures as disparate as Abraham Lincoln, Theodore Roosevelt, John F. Kennedy and George W. Bush.

The Brass Menagerie

Wiley's portrait of Obama is displayed in the National Portrait Gallery Hall of Presidents and was first presented as part of an exhibition titled *America's Presidents*. Both the White House and the NPG have a complete set of portraits of America's presidents, from George Washington to Barack Obama and ongoing. At the end of a presidential administration, official portraits are made of the President and the First Lady, as well as the vice president, cabinet secretaries and senior officials. The White House also issues official photographs of the president and senior officials. Portraits of the First Lady began to be painted when Edith (Theodore) Roosevelt oversaw the restoration of the White House. These began to be commissioned officially in the 1960s, after Jacqueline Kennedy founded the White House Historical Association. In 1994, George W. Bush instituted the practice of commissioning a second set of portraits of the President and the First Lady for the NPG, which recommends artists for the task. Until the twentieth century, Congress raised the funds required for official portraits, a practice that is now supported by private donations that are raised by the White House and the NPG for their respective collections.

Art historians outside of the United States have little or no reason to be aware of any of the works in either the White House or the NPG collection, excepting perhaps the portrait of Theodore Roosevelt painted by John Singer Sargent, or the portrait of John F. Kennedy made by Elaine de Kooning. Beyond these two, the interest of presidential paintings is for the likenesses conveyed by portraits, many of them made before the advent of photography, and for the minimum of historical and political symbolism that can be registered through pose, clothing, setting and select objects. Until the twentieth century, these works tended towards sombre colours of ochre, black and brown, with highlights around the face and hands. The solitary male figures are invariably seated or standing, their arms folded, holding a document or some other notable item, or relaxed to the side. Similarly, their eyes either return the gaze of the viewer or look off to the side. Not much seems to change in this unremarkable tradition. Even in this staid bailiwick, however, Wiley has proven to be knowingly obstreperous. His one-upmanship has not only served his brand image but also jockeys for prepotency in this to date exclusive gentlemen's club.

Presidential portraits are typically approached as symbolic and political documents. The different versions of Gilbert Stuart's 1796 portrait of George Washington commemorate the end of the Revolutionary War in 1783. The inspiration for the work tells us more about Alexis de Tocqueville than about neo-classicism. Stuart depicts Washington as a 'man of the people' rather than a monarch. Tucked under Washington's writing desk, on the floor, are books with the titles *American Revolution* and *Constitution and Laws of the United States*. There is not much to relate to the Obama portrait until George Peter Alexander Healy's 1869 painting of Abraham Lincoln, the sixteenth U.S. President. The portrait-length picture of the seated leader of the Civil War is without doubt the obvious reference for Wiley's composition. A Wiley fan might even appreciate the floral designs that decorate the edges of the red rug at his feet and the red upholstery of his chair. Like the Obama picture, this one also has a series of counterbalances, with a three-quarter profile making Lincoln's shaded right eye completely black. His chin rests pensively in his right hand, whose extended index finger points not only to the heavens above but also to his eye, a possible reminder that slavery was the blind spot of the Revolutionary era. His right arm braces the arm of the chair, just as Washington held the sword of justice. This portrait of Lincoln is derived from Healy's 1869 painting *The Peacemakers*, which shows Lincoln seated in the company of generals Ulysses S. Grant, William Tecumseh Sherman and Admiral David Dixon Porter. This meeting from the last days of the Civil War shows the four figures interacting, yet also talking past one another. The rainbow outside the window behind Lincoln is reminiscent of the rainbow in the top right corner of Stuart's portrait of Washington. From the years of John F. Kennedy to George W. Bush, *The Peacemakers* was displayed in the White House Treaty Room. There is also a copy of the work in the Pentagon. It appears as a background image in George H.W. Bush's official portrait, painted by Herbert Abrams in 1994. It was moved to the George W. Bush Presidential Library in 2002 and moved again by Obama to the President's Dining Room in the White House. As it happens, Obama chose Lincoln's birthday, February 12, for the unveiling of the NPG portraits, bringing a close to his two terms in office, which began in Springfield, Illinois – Lincoln's hometown.

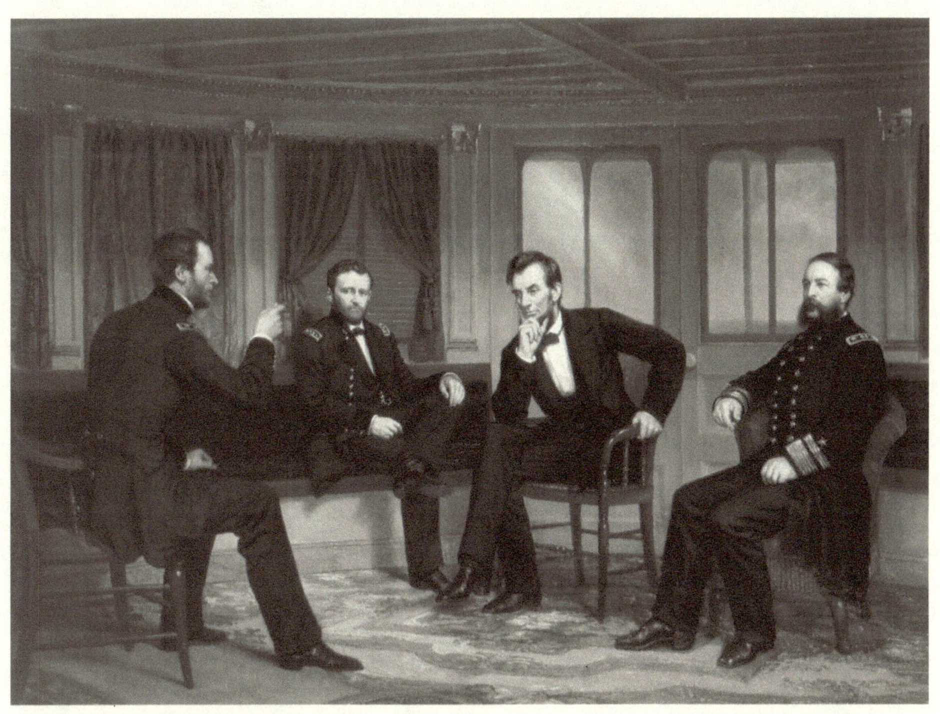

George Peter Alexander Healy, ***The Peacemakers***, 1868. Oil on canvas, 119.7 cm x 159.1 cm. Courtesy of The White House Historical Association.

All of these references amount to more than enough political content to serve the commission's purpose. However, Wiley's portrait also sends up Nelson Shanks's 2006 NPG portrait of *William Jefferson Blythe III*, which has a shadow in the work that the artist says is a reference to the Monica Lewinsky affair. Clinton's missing wedding ring adds to the caper. Any other painter of the genre might wonder how it is that Shanks manages to sell his dull paintings for anywhere between $500,000 and $900,000. Other considerations include the fact that the Clintons' 2001 and 2004 White House portraits were painted by Simmie Lee Knox, who has made paintings of politicians like Thurgood Marshall and Eric Holder, as well as celebrities like Hank Aaron, Bill Cosby and Oprah Winfrey. Knox's paintings of the Clintons are the first White House portraits commissioned to an African-American artist. His painting of Hillary Clinton shows her right hand casually leading the eye to her 1996 book, *It Takes a Village: And Other Lessons Children Teach Us*, which discusses how it is that society can enable children's success. If bling is the thing, on might prefer Ginny Stanford's 2006 painting of Hillary Clinton, a realistic portrait in profile with flanking gold leaf panels designed in a *fin de siècle* art nouveau idiom.

One could blame the Reagans for all this baroque kitsch entering the stream of presidential culture. In that respect, George W. Bush was not to be left behind. While his 2008 NPG portrait shows him casually dressed and mugging for the camera from his retreat at Camp David in Maryland, the more intriguing work is John Howard Sanden's White House portrait, which shows Bush Jr. standing in front of W.H.D Koerner's *A Charge to Keep*, a 1916 painting that is thought to be about cowboy missionaries, known as circuit riders, who spread Methodism across the Alleghenies. A Methodist since the 1970s, Bush used the title of the painting for his autobiography. Although the meaning and attribution of the work have been contested, it bears a striking similarity to another painting by Koerner, which was used as an illustration for a 1916 story in the *Saturday Evening Post* about a horse thief escaping a lynch mob in Nebraska, with the caption: Had His Start Been Fifteen Minutes Longer He Would Not Have Been Caught. Bush instructed that his White House portrait should be slightly smaller than the White House painting of Bush Sr. Without the CIA credentials and wherewithal of his father, the younger president made use of cowboy imagery to give legitimacy to his war against Iraq and protection of the homestead. Obama was not known to wear a cowboy hat, but he also kept the charge, spreading the gospel of Manifest Destiny to Pakistan, Syria, Libya and Yemen.

Dogs Playing Poker

In *Mythologies*, the French semiologist Roland Barthes has a short entry on "Photography and Electoral Appeal." He argues that images of political candidates presuppose the power to convert, and that, because of this, the photograph seeks to establish a link between the candidate and the voter. This link is rhetorically modulated by the candidate's way of dressing, posture and manner, condensing the social totality into an "anti-intellectual weapon."[33] He gives as an example the political portraits of the populist Pierre Poujade, a French petty-bourgeois politician and supporter of the Nazi collaborator Philippe Pétain. Poujade was anti-intellectual, anti-parliamentary, xenophobic, anti-Semitic and a supporter of the Algerian War. He encouraged people to divest from official politics and not pay taxes. In terms of electoral democracy, the essence of Poujadism was to communicate to voters: "Look at me. I am like you."

The function of the image of the politician is to convey something irrational that transforms the candidate, his programme, family and background, as well as attitudes and style of life, into ideological bait. The lure is the potential for the image to be interpreted as a likeness of the voter. The voter who takes the bait thus votes for themselves. This explains why so many people have lined up to take selfies with Obama's portrait. The typical attitudes struck by candidates,

Barthes writes, vary from respectable or sanctimonious, to genteel and searching. Both the Obamas have their heads turned slightly away from the viewer, but their eyes look confidently forward. Their portraits have the features of a candidate who combines thoughtful reflection and wilful action:

> the slightly narrowed eyes allow a sharp look to filter through, which seems to find its strength in a beautiful inner dream without however ceasing to alight on real obstacles, as if the ideal candidate had in this case magnificently to unite social idealism with bourgeois empiricism. This last type is quite simply that of the "good-looking chap," whose obvious credentials are his health and virility. Some candidates, incidentally, beautifully manage to win on both counts, appearing for instance as a handsome hero (in uniform) on one side of the handout, and as a mature and virile citizen on the other, displaying his little family.[34]

Political imagery has a petty-bourgeois function, which the sociologist Pierre Bourdieu attributed to family photography.[35] It effects, according to Barthes, a blackmail of moral values, uniting in one indexical sign family, race and nation, as well as honour, heroism and the future. If one is to accept the official and mainstream line about the Obama portraits, their poses would carry forward what Barthes says about the combination of a realistic outlook with an inspiring nod towards an undefined "other domain" and place of "higher humanity":

> the candidate reaches the Olympus of elevated feelings, where all political contradictions are solved: peace and war in Algeria, social progress and employers' profits, so-called "free" religious schools and subsidies from the sugar-beet lobby, the Right and the Left (an opposition always "superseded"!): all these coexist peacefully in this thoughtful gaze, nobly fixed on the hidden interests of Order.[36]

On most of these counts, the Obama paintings are business as usual, which is why more has been made about the way that race issues and aesthetic interest signal a departure.

After Obama, Donald Trump would also seem to have destabilized the political order once and for all. Neither successful as a businessman or virtuous as a politician, Trump came to power by behaving more like a scary clown than as someone concerned with humanity and the social order. He made this plain enough when he announced in 2019 his Trump Made America Great Again complex for the wealthy Manhattan neighbourhood of Hudson Yards. The complex is expected to include a Presidential Library with a strip club, massage parlour and mini-golf course. Trump tweeted that he hopes to include in the centre editioned copies of Maurizio Cattelan's *America* (2016), a golden toilet that the artist originally made to criticize U.S. imperialism.

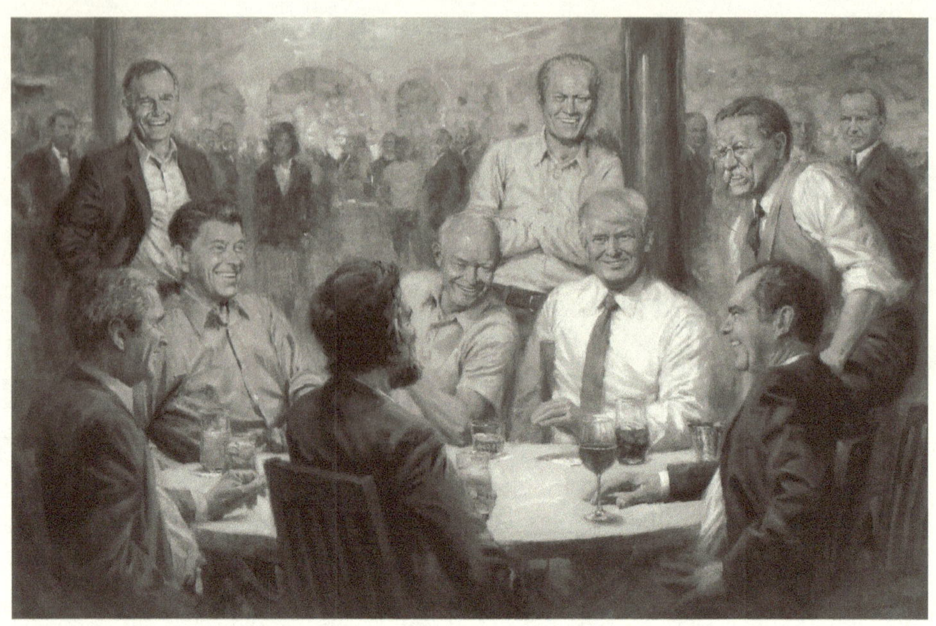

Andy Thomas, ***The Republican Club***, c.2017. Courtesy of and © Andy Thomas.

In October 2018, Trump displayed in the White House a print of an Andy Thomas painting called *The Republican Club*. Based loosely on the classic kitsch paintings by Cassius Marcellus Coolidge of dogs playing poker, and otherwise influenced by the illustration art of Fredric Remington, Charles Russell and Howard Pyle, Thomas made separate paintings of Democrats and Republicans sitting around a political convention table – an imaginary space of presidential and partisan kinship that spans historical eras. In the Republican version, which Trump hung outside the Oval Office in his personal dining room, Trump is depicted drinking Diet Coke and sharing laughs with George Bush Sr. and Jr., Gerald Ford, Dwight Eisenhower, Warren Harding, Calvin Coolidge, Teddy Roosevelt, Richard Nixon, Ronald Reagan and Abraham Lincoln. The Democrat version includes Barack Obama, Franklin Roosevelt, Andrew Jackson, Woodrow Wilson, Lyndon Johnson, Harry Truman and Bill Clinton. In both paintings, the same woman is seen in the background walking towards the table. She represents the first, yet unknown Democratic or Republican woman president. Trump's redecoration of the Oval Office and White House have been said to be like the Thomas painting: bizarre, gaudy, tacky and tasteless. Trump mentioned to Thomas that he did not like most portraits of himself. One presumes then that Trump likes this kitsch likeness, which is also sold as a 550-piece jigsaw puzzle.[37] Trump's display of *The Republican Club* in the White House confirms Clement Greenberg's rationale in "Avant-Garde and Kitsch":

> the main trouble with avant-garde art and literature, from the point of view of the fascists and Stalinists, is not that they are too critical, but that they are too "innocent," that it is too difficult to inject effective propaganda into them, that kitsch is more pliable to this end. Kitsch keeps a dictator in closer contact with the "soul" of the people. Should the official culture be one superior to the general mass-level, there would be a danger of isolation.[38]

As film critic J. Hoberman puts it, Trump is not the amusing, Hollywood production code Reagan type, but is rather a product of the polluted ecosystem of talk radio, reality TV and social media.[39] His supporters are less likely to have watched *Lassie* than *Jackass*.

Today's neoliberal politicians are neither interested in getting close to the people, as Greenberg suggests, nor in getting people to see themselves in their politics, as Barthes proposes. That would be the stance adopted by people like Bernie Sanders or Jeremy Corbyn, who, to put things in marketing terms, have a product orientation. Greenberg argued that kitsch welcomes and cultivates insensitivity, that its fake sensations and spurious formulas demand nothing from its audience except their money. Politicians since Jimmy Carter are not selling themselves since even they do not believe that their policies will be beneficial to the masses. And with Trump, politics is now a *Celebrity Apprentice* experience whose ultimate purpose is to make people untrusting of government institutions. This is more or less the argument that was put forward by the Sots artist Alexander Melamid, who stated that Trump is the "perfect avatar" of the culture created by radical students, the counterculture and narcissistic artists like himself who are associated with the avant garde.[40] However glib, Melamid's argument resonates with Angela Nagle's thesis that the counterculture's anti-establishment values have today morphed from the fringe and the mainstream into the viral cynicism of alt-right transgression.[41]

The most boiled-down expressions of cynical reason in American painting are without doubt the paintings made by George W. Bush, which were revealed to the public through an email hack in 2013. Bush's tightly cropped portraits have the tonal range and flat quality of paint by numbers, but without its formulaic detailing. His portraits include paintings of himself, his father, Tony Blair and Vladimir Putin. He does not attempt to editorialize with these works or add any symbolic content. At the level of surface, they are potentially as interesting to contemporary art viewers as the paintings of Reginald Gray or Kurt Kauper, but without any sense that the artist is more than an amateur enthusiast. When Bush thought to add some thematic complexity to his art by making 98 portraits of U.S. veterans, which are presented in his 2017 book *Portraits of Courage*, he did not produce a series that is different from anything a socially engaged artist might have made, except for the fact that Bush is responsible for sending as many as four million American soldiers to war and causing hundreds of thousands of deaths in Iraq. According to a review in *The Guardian*, "it's precisely this dramatic irony that gives *Portraits of Courage* its numinous and haunting quality."[42]

Equally numinous are Bush's painting of a Guantánamo Bay prisoner in an orange boiler suit being attacked by a police dog, portraits of Saddam Hussein and Osama bin Laden with clown faces, and a painting of the Abu Ghraib prisoner who was made to wear a bag over his head, his arms outstretched like a crucified martyr tied to electric wires. The overruling of Hamdan v. Rumsfeld by the U.S. Supreme Court implies that Bush's sanction of the torture of Iraqi detainees in 2003, which includes abuse, rape and murder, is actionable as a Geneva Conventions war crime. Michelle Obama told the NBC *Today* show on October 11, 2018, that she and Bush have the same function:

> He is my partner in crime at every major thing where all the formers gather. So we're all together all the time, and I love him to death. He's a wonderful man. He's a funny man. [...] Party doesn't separate us. Color, gender – those kinds of things don't separate us. It's the messages we send. If we're the adults and the leaders in the room and we're not showing that level of decency, we cannot expect our children to do the same.[43]

Obama said this when she launched her memoir, *Becoming*. Becoming what, one might wonder. Becoming responsible for the deaths of one million Iraqis, flouting the Constitution, expanding domestic spying and giving tax cuts to the wealthy? In these terms, Barack Obama also admitted his guilt by association during the 2016 election, when he stated that the two parties are on the same team. The minimum of difference between *The Democratic Club* and *The Republican Club*, between the party of the centre-right and the party of the far right, is increasingly reducible to their stance on diversity, a difference that is bridged in Andy Thomas' works by the approach of the same corporate woke candidate. *Guardian* critic Joshua David Stein is trite in saying that Bush's paintings are ironic and for further suggesting that Bush's portraits of veterans force the viewer to consider how naiveté functions in both art and government policy. According to Melamid, Andy Warhol argued that making money is art. George W. Bush, whose net worth is a modest $39 million, and who rakes in $150,000 for speaking engagements, can be construed in this Pop art sense as a neoliberal version of the political leader as artistic demiurge.[44]

Although the Obama portraits are more artistically challenging than previous presidential portraits, from the perspective of contemporary art they are a derivative form of second-generation postmodernism, with all that this implies with regard to work that is made after the recuperation by the culture industry of such developments as the deconstruction of the opposition between high and low culture, simulation and the representational sublime, irony and the semiotic mediation of reality, the death of the author, the reduction of epistemology to the ontology of matter, as well as the performativity of gender, race and sexuality. They are atypical, however, insofar as they are not defined by the standards of what Bourdieu referred to as cultural capital.

In *The Rules of Art*, Bourdieu argues that the social space encompasses the field of power.[45] The field of power has as one of its subfields the field of cultural production, which includes large-scale mass production as well as small-scale production. Small-scale production involves works by consecrated or canonical artists that display a high degree of cultural capital and a low degree of economic capital. This includes works by the bohemian avant gardes that have a somewhat lower degree of cultural capital. Works with a low degree of cultural-symbolic capital and a higher degree of economic capital correspond to large-scale production like Hollywood films or journalism. On the whole, Bourdieu ignores the field that has a paucity of cultural capital but a high degree of symbolic capital as well as a high degree of economic capital, which would include painters like Bush. Bourdieu's *On the State*, a publication based on his lectures at the Collège de France between 1989 and 1992, describes the state as a regulator of the symbolic "meta-capital" that organizes social fields such as law, education, culture and the professions. This symbolic capital is in the process of being disorganized insofar as the neoliberal state renounces its mandate as the disinterested representative of the public interest.[46]

The shift towards creative industries, which now encompasses the corporatization of universities and museums, emphasizes the next-to-zero autonomy side of Bourdieu's model and represents the accelerated reduction of cultural autonomy to neoliberal heteronomy.[47] This phenomenon is reinforced by the emphasis given to the concept of power in contemporary discourse theory. The logic of empowerment is widely promoted by identity politics. A painter like Wiley makes the kind of art that is more concerned with the field of power than the field of culture. Since the Obama commission, Sherald's work has been gradually pushed in this direction as well and she now receives massive amounts of likes on Facebook and Instagram. This kind of success is the price that Sherald is paying, or rather, is going to be paid, for making the kind of work that has only a modicum of autonomy. Although this kind of work is not without technical skill and visual interest, it does raise the question about whether or how portrait painting can participate in the non- and anti-commercial aims of ambitious art.

The Obama presidency was an occasion in which every American, especially blacks and minorities, could find inspiration. However, as Adolph Reed argues, "while most Americans probably considered the [Obama] victory an important, positive statement, few among the most politically sophisticated could suggest its likely impact beyond the symbolic."[48] This symbolic transcendence of historical obstacles to equality of opportunity are easily separated, he adds, from the social programmes that one might associate with racial justice, conceived in terms of black mass politics, providing instead anti-racist platitudes and an institutional expression of socially-minded neoliberalism. Similarly, the Obama portraits are inscribed in the field of political power defined by state authority and in the symbolic space of an emergent politics of post-representation. Whether one looks at the two paintings' text, context or subtext makes little difference to the issues involved. In other words, the works by Wiley and Sherald do not challenge but confirm the ideological values they were made to commemorate.

The Science of Imaginary Solutions

For a creative class weaned on the cultural politics of representation and cultural politics of difference, the assertion that the Obama portraits participate in a culture and politics of post-representation may come across as somewhat antipodal. What does the concept of post-representation offer in terms of political possibilities and what does it imply in terms of ideological foreclosure? The first and most direct expression of post-representation is political anti-representation, also referred to as post-politics and sometimes associated with Italian workerism.[49] Michael Hardt and Antonio Negri's theory of the multitude, for instance, advocates a leaderless, grassroots and horizontalist politics of new social movements that look beyond the representative politics of parliamentary parties and elections, unions and the mainstream press.[50] Rather than alienating one's political power through the constituted power of delegates and state institutions, the notion of constituent power anticipates a subject 'in itself' and that agitates 'for itself' through direct action. Well-known groups and movements that engage in post-representational politics include Indymedia, Anonymous, WikiLeaks and Occupy Wall Street. Versions of constituent power have also been proposed in relation to formal politics with for instance the digital democracy strategy of governance proposed by the Five Star Movement in Italy and the civil disturbances orchestrated by the Gilets Jaunes in France.

After leftist activists had assessed the limited impact of the anti-globalization anti-summit protests of the late 1990s and 2000s, Occupy Wall Street activists drew on the tactic of urban occupations that had been experimented with by the Spanish *indignados* and the movements of the Arab Spring. Simon Tormey describes OWS as one example of anti-representational politics. This "event-movement," he says, can be thought of as becoming-*something* – a non-affiliated, non-programmatic, rhizomatic set of tactics that are designed to bring attention to wealth inequality and that are coordinated to protect commons through the sharing of knowledge on social media.[51] Tormey cites Hardt and Negri's notion that traditional political representation affects a "disjunctive synthesis" that separates political representatives from the masses.[52] The 'post-politics' that emerged in the late 1960s and 70s marked the decline of representational politics and the emergence of 'post-representative' affinity groups, protest movements and direct action tactics like squats and carnivals. New social movements have since then organized against war, nuclear weapons, environmental degradation as well as around identity politics and anti-discrimination. Recent expressions of post-representational politics include the People's Action Network, EuroMayDay, Reclaim the Streets, the World Social Forum, Occupy Wall Street, Idle No More, Black Lives Matter, MeToo, Women's March, March for Our Lives and Extinction Rebellion.

Post-representational movements consider that representative democracy is constrained by corporate control and by institutions like the United Nations, NATO, the World Bank, the IMF, the G7 and the G20, none of which are democratically accountable and in many cases dictate state policy, expropriate public wealth, prevent regulation, promote free trade, privatize social services and dismantle labour laws as well as international treaties.[53] These institutions by and large impose the kind of neoliberal policies that have replaced the state protection of full employment and social welfare with a new form of political-economic organization that has deregulated and liberalized government policies in favour of the requirements of capital accumulation. As advocated by Bill Clinton and Tony Blair, the 'Washington Consensus' declared that the social democratic guarantee of occupational safety, health care, civil rights, environmental protections and world peace would be replaced by policies that "liberate" corporate power and re-establish market freedoms.[54]

In their theory of the multitude, Hard and Negri argue that the conditions for democracy on a global scale are made possible by the biopolitical organization of life and labour in a digitally networked global economy.[55] Biopolitical production organizes the shared basis of ideas, images, affects and relationships. It also organizes the private property and state security regimes of what they call "empire," which refers to the supra-national level of globalization.[56] As a Foucauldian concept, the notion of biopower accepts the premise that power organizes the forms of resistance to exploitation and precarity. Autonomists also make use of Marxist theory to elaborate the forms of post-Fordist production that are no longer limited to industrial blue-collar labour and are instead dispersed throughout the service sector and various forms of so-called immaterial labour, a fabric of production and immanent process of cooperation that defends global citizenship against the tendency of empire to regulate flows for the sake of accumulation.

Autonomist theory is not Marxist insofar as it is anti-dialectical and relies on reified and countercultural oppositions like open/closed, constituent/constituted and rhizomatic/arboresque. It accepts the tendencies that are at work in neoliberal governance and proposes, not unlike Karl Marx, that any communist alternative will emerge as a result of the contradictions of the new modes of production. Traditional forms of leftist insurgency cannot work against empire because like the multitude empire is distributed and polycentric. Hardt and Negri nevertheless believe that a constituent network can undermine the network of the war machine. However, in order to act as a network, the multitude must abandon the notion that they are unified as a people or as the working class. In terms of identity politics, Hardt and Negri's notion of difference is a world in which race and gender no longer matter, and more specifically, where identity is sufficiently deterritorialized as to no longer be thought of in terms of autonomy or separatism.[57] Their use of Deleuzian concepts like becoming and desiring production is compatible with similar philosophical notions like Giorgio Agamben's idea of whatever singularity.[58] The ontological reality of the multitude is neither based in the interchangeability of individuals nor on collective unity, but is instead a singularity that develops through cooperation and hybridization.

In practical terms, Hardt and Negri's post-representational politics comes down to a positivist logic of swarms, nomadism and migrations, of Internet memes, media invasions, myths and conspiracies that break with the expected. This is the opposite of a political programme or even a list of demands. Against the notion of sovereignty, whether political or aesthetic, biopolitical production transforms the conceptual and material possibilities for any kind of identity or centralization of value and power in a hierarchy of elements. The multitude is a "body without organs," referring to the notion of organs that refuse the unity of the political body or the distinction between inside and outside, private and public. Since sovereignty is on the side of capital, the multitude is against the enclosure of the commons that has been accelerated by the cybernetic revolution. The multitude is neither liberal nor socialist, they argue, nor is it anarchist or vanguard. However, it is sometimes assumed to be opposed to the neoliberal governance that leads to economic crises and the destabilization of traditional values and ways of life. Political resistance, according to this line of thought, automatically gives rise to authoritarian forms of power that limit popular sovereignty in favour of the freedoms of the market and the interests of the wealthy. Neoliberal governance, they argue, even advances through the traditional custodial powers of the welfare state, from the War on Poverty to the War on Drugs and War on Terror, incentivizing autonomy through the entrepreneurialization of the self as human capital in a society of risk and debt. Job retraining, lifelong learning and identity crises of various sorts are consequences of the rhizomatic networks, capital flows and media viruses that are a fact of life for the multitude in the life-work continuum of empire.

Although they do not like to acknowledge the fact, Hardt and Negri's autonomist analysis of biopolitical production does not escape the Marxist theory of base and superstructure. The totality of capital does not preclude post-representational forms of politics, which Hardt and Negri associate with the most advanced stage of the capitalist relations and mode of production. The fact that today's creative and knowledge industries are based on the surplus produced by an increasingly proletarianized global population is not the focus of their work. What matters to them is the potential for social transformation brought about by "the rule of everyone by everyone."[59] Nor is the upward redistribution of wealth, or what David Harvey describes as accumulation by dispossession, something with which their work is directly concerned.[60]

We could say that the post-representational era of the multitude is divided between those who experience the world in the Foucauldian terms of disciplinary societies (factories, barracks, prisons, slums) and those who experience the world in terms of Deleuzian control societies (offices, schools, museums, parks). The culture of the petty-bourgeois intermediary classes is now a global culture. It would be foolish to think that social cooperation and political non-participation by themselves can solve the crises of capitalism. We could argue that global capitalism with a multicultural face and a Guy Fawkes mask corresponds perfectly to the disjunctive synthesis of the new forms of non-sovereignty that are instituted by the politics of post-representation. We do not find behind the Guy Fawkes mask the real person who may someday be able to enjoy the commons. What we find is the person who enjoys wearing a Guy Fawkes mask. By the same token, multicultural diversity in the age of global markets is also a mask. The problem is this: neither the diversity agenda nor the multitude aims for a universal emancipation beyond capitalism. Both are inscribed within and adjusted to global capitalism. On the one hand, as Slavoj Žižek argues, the obsession with minorities loses sight of the proletarian position, which is increasingly automated, offshored or reduced to the category of redundant surplus labour. On the other hand, the deterritorializing flows of the network society create a new kind of totalitarianism where unfreedom and oppression are experienced by individuals as their opposite.[61] This in part explains the growing hegemony of right-wing politics, where today's oligarchies manufacture and manipulate popular resentment as means to reinforce and militarize the system of capital circulation. From pizzagaters to anti-vaxxers, the multitude is getting uglier by the day.

The outcome of this first approach to post-representation conditions a second. Laura Bazzicalupo argues that the contemporary dissolution of political representation leads to a restless search for new ways of doing politics, a reflexive post-representational condition that is premised on the crisis of liberal democracy and actually existing socialism. The disjunctive synthesis, as Hardt and Negri define it, between government and the governed has become the *dispositif*, she argues, of the neoliberal state. Bazzicalupo writes: "It is this sovereignty that today is not completely accomplishing its synthetic-ordinative function, placed side by side with and/or substitute[d] by … the 'cognitive format' of neoliberal governmentality."[62] For this author, the subject of democracy refers to a Foucauldian mechanism of representation that is premised not only on a present absence – the empty place of power as a condition for a politics that is based on the exclusion of a constitutive outside, which opens a path to vindication – but also, the gap between the people and themselves.[63] As Žižek argues, power is not most effective when it addresses people as normal subjects but rather when it addresses them as divided subjects. The inconsistent aspect of a power structure can be the basis of its subversion, but it can also function in terms of an obscene power that indicates to people that it is not to be taken seriously.[64] For post-representational politics, according to Bazzicalupo, institutions are to be modified according to a deconstructive emphasis on the occupation of power as the immanence of life and against notions of transcendence, sovereign power or separation. As opposed to the management of appearances, being-together in common appeals to actuality, vitality, productive desire, self-organization and self-generation – "the 'movement' [as] a multitude of living singularities."[65]

Bazzicalupo cautions that anti-representational revolt can be easily absorbed by capitalism. Neoliberal government and the post-Fordist "spirit of capitalism," she writes, produces libertarian subjectivity, affirming reality and extending capitalist rationality through processes of subjectification.[66] For such theoretical immanentism, sovereign power is not so much top-down or contradictory than it is biopolitical, diffuse and productive. The neoliberal state imagines itself to be a kind of post-representational power, with individuals and groups defined as vectors of power. Governance is pragmatic and flexible rather than exclusionary or oppressive, replacing sovereignty with empiricism, management and consensus. Citizens are encouraged to empower themselves directly "without the discredited mediation of democratically and procedurally legitimated representative forms."[67] The real-time surface simulation of 'the people,' either through the mainstream media or through social media, effects a populism of "hegemonic immanentist hyperrealism."[68] Political relations no longer signify or represent anything that is semantically meaningful in terms of universality and equality, she argues, but they can be reduced to the image of a powerless leader who nevertheless participates in the political process. This is the flipside to the micro-practices of resistance that do not seek to occupy state power but leave it in place as the condition against which the contingencies of hegemonic contestation can be articulated.[69]

The implication of these two definitions is that post-representational politics could be explained in terms of a semantic after-the-fact representation of the experiences and defeats of the left in the twentieth and early twenty-first centuries. Against the workerist view that the so-called old left is inoperative, Alain Badiou understands the experiences of the international workers' movement as constituent features of an invariant communist hypothesis.[70] These include: the betrayal of the revolution by Stalinism, leadership cults, forced collectivism, cronyism in government, violent purges of bureaucrats and dissidents, the reduction of revolution to the needs of modernization and economic competition, the policy of non-interference with imperialist powers, the conflation of the function of the vanguard party with the institutions of state power, and lastly, the failure to dissolve the need for the party into the democratic control of social reproduction. In other words, any radical critique of the politics of post-representation should not only consider the failure to reach a communist stage of human development, but also the development of left strategies that aim beyond the current situation and create opportunities that are not pre-determined by unmediated data sets, semantic units, and so on. In Badiou's terms, such politics would be exceptions to the immanence of things rather than their ratification, as is the case with post-politics.

Postmodern critiques of dialectical approaches to the contradictions of capitalism are, from the perspective of Marxism, situational. Insofar as socialist regimes have failed to bring about the end of capitalism, post-representational politics on the radical ultra-left and the neoliberal right have sought to develop anti-organizational systems that avoid permanent, hierarchical and delegated forms of authority. The reduction of politics to biopolitical production, however, should not be considered a more solid basis for emancipation than the orthodox appeal to historical necessity. The horizontalist and identitarian left's fixation on the failures of communist modernism is related to blockages in the contemporary conjuncture. Is the way out, as Žižek might suggest, to accept the hopelessness of our predicament?[71] How can we reinvent the left project?[72] The prospect of a new beginning, as Žižek says elsewhere, is what separates class struggle from the one-dimensionality of a consciousness that is inscribed in positivist materialisms like Foucauldian biopower.[73] Post-structuralist models of post-representation are therefore inadequate to a comprehensive critical theory. Regardless, they are necessary to understand if one is to offer a radical explanation and critique of contemporary ideology.

We Tortured Some Folks

Today's post-representational practices conform to biocapitalism as a simultaneous claim to and disavowal of political representation. One wonders, in this regard, if contemporary culture can do anything to advance the cause of emancipation. In *Wretched of the Screen*, media artist and theorist Hito Steyerl dismisses the notion that contemporary art can be critically distinguished from the "bling, boom and bust" of post-Fordist speculation. In the midst of neoliberal austerity, she argues, the hype around contemporary art is not so different from the affective dimensions of deregulation and the upward redistribution of wealth.[74] How does this work? Steyerl suggests that the technological conditions of visual culture in a digital age moves representation away from the function of verisimilitude towards algorithmic probabilities and modification through applications. With regard to electoral politics, she writes:

> The representational paradigm assumes that you vote for someone who will represent you. Thus the interests of the population will be proportionally represented. But current democracies work rather like smartphone photography by algorithmically clearing noise and boosting some data over other. It is a system in which the unforeseen has a hard time happening because it is not yet in the database. It is about what to define as noise – something Jacques Rancière has defined as the crucial act in separating political subjects from domestic slaves, women and workers. Now this act is hardwired into technology, but instead of the traditional division of people and rabble, the results are post-representative militias, brands, customer loyalty schemes, open source insurgents and tumblrs.[75]

We could with this make some sense of an Obama promotional campaign in which the would-be president posed for *GQ*-style images taken by the controversial photographer Terry Richardson, who was known in the early 2000s for bringing a 1970s soft porn aesthetic into fashion photography, and who has since then been criticized for harassing his female models. The images appeared in *Vibe* magazine in September 2007. One of the photographs shows Obama shaking hands with Richardson and the two of them grinning while gesturing some thumbs up. Although they are posed against a white background, they look as though they are having a great time at a late evening gathering, the kind of party imagery that one associates with lifestyle magazines.

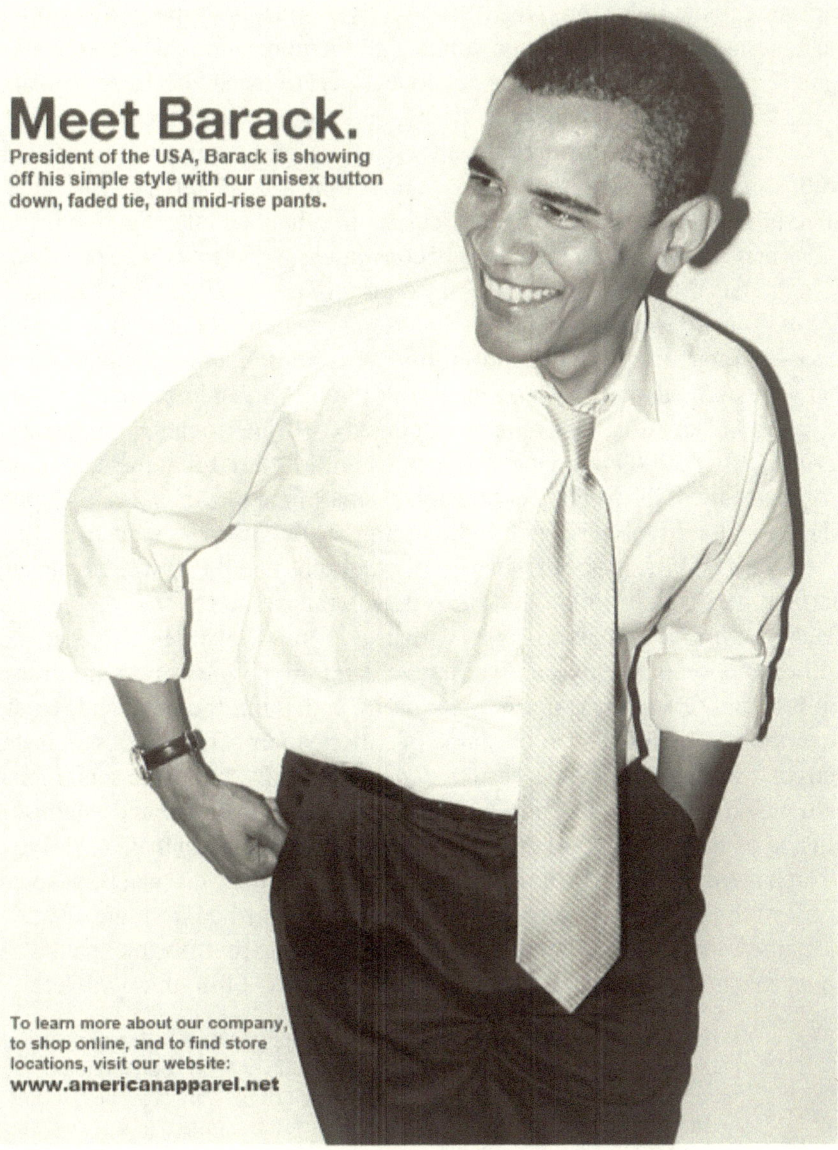

Anonymous Obama American Apparel meme based on a Terry Richardson photo shoot for *Vibe* magazine, 2007. Source: Internet.

The stylistic similarities between Richardson's photographs of Obama and American Apparel advertisements led to one of the images being anonymously appropriated and remade into an American Apparel meme. Notwithstanding the fact that American Apparel owner Dov Charney also has a record of sexually harassing his female employees, the affectively positive aspect is its similarity to the advertisements that depicted young staff members modelling company clothes against a white background. The negative aspect of these images is their similarity to the thumbs ups that American Army soldiers and CIA officers gestured in the selfies they took with tortured detainees at the Abu Ghraib prison in Iraq. Photographs of the abuse came to public attention in April 2004. The Supreme Court ruled in 2006 that these and similar cases of 'enhanced interrogation techniques' in Afghanistan and Guantánamo Bay constituted war crimes. The case brought to light the fact that the Office of Legal Counsel issued in 2002 what became known as the 'Torture Memos,' which included government documents that advocated the use of torture to coerce and intimidate foreign detainees, a set of practices that were applied after the 2003 invasion of Iraq. Almost immediately after taking office on January 20, 2008, Obama rescinded OLC interrogation guidelines for the period 2001 to 2009, redacted the memos and declared that the state would not prosecute any of the military contractors, Department of Defense or CIA personnel who had been involved in either the writing of the memos or the use of torture.

This confluence of the fashion photographs and the torture memos updates Barthes' 1950s description of a *Paris Match* magazine cover showing a saluting black youth in a French uniform, which the semiologist defined as an example of the function of myth as an instrumental signifier. One important difference is the fact that Obama was not a low-ranking cadet, but the president. He hails us nevertheless, in this case in the name of American imperialism. As an instance of depoliticized speech, myth does not deny complexity, but gives social relations a natural and eternal appearance, passing from history to nature and establishing the illusion of clarity. The kind of neoliberal post-representation that is involved in the Obama meme is what Barthes defined as a meta-language that can be adapted to the needs of the occasion, an expediency that he distinguished from the operationality of meta-politics, or "myth on the left."[76] Against the multiform expansiveness of bourgeois myth, Barthes defines the "imperfection" of myth on the left:

> the Left always defines itself in relation to the oppressed, whether proletarian or colonized. Now the speech of the oppressed can only be poor, monotonous, immediate: his destitution is the very yardstick of his language: he has only one, always the same, that of his actions; metalanguage is a luxury, he cannot yet have access to it. The speech of the oppressed is real, like that of the woodcutter; it is a transitive type of speech: it is quasi-unable to lie; lying is a richness, a lie presupposes property, truths and forms to spare.[77]

If truth and lies were superseded by postmodernism's floating signifiers, what is it that we are dealing with here? Alan Kirby argues that the death of postmodernism, much like its birth at the moment of the destruction of the Pruitt-Igoe housing project in 1972, was marked by the fall of the Twin Towers in 2001. What replaced it is what he refers to as pseudo-modernism, defined as a new concern with the real that combines ignorance and conformity with fanaticism and global markets. He writes:

> pseudo-modernism lashes fantastically sophisticated technology to the pursuit of medieval barbarism – as in the uploading of videos of beheadings on the Internet, or the use of mobile phones to film torture in prisons. Beyond this, the destiny of everyone else is to suffer the anxiety of getting hit in the cross-fire. But this fatalistic anxiety extends far beyond geopolitics, into every aspect of contemporary life; from a general fear of social breakdown and identity loss, to the effects of a new personal ineptitude and helplessness, which yield TV programmes about how to clean your house, bring up your children or remain solvent.[78]

For Steyerl, a Kafkaesque glossiness characterizes the new mediascape where monological spam images do not reflect anything but themselves as shiny surfaces. The referent of the image, she says, is cryptic and unstable. The machinic, algorithmic processing of media spam treats politics like advertisements generated by bot armies that jump-cut between glamour, sectarianism, porn and government corruption – an Internet State Apparatus that governs an infrastructure of code and polices metadata.[79] It is not enough, as Kirby suggests, to simply say that all of us are this authorless, interactive code-based intertextual spam. The effort to fight back against image spam with reality-based representation, Steyerl argues, leads to exhaustion and back into systems, transforming artists and activists into data providers. Networked social activists are thus pressured to represent and be represented within a context of biopolitical surveillance. Against neoliberalism's authoritarian techniques of "algorithmic consensual governance," activists are pressured to develop skills in disappearance and subterfuge, doing messy and confusing things. The problem is that the pattern of "hiding in plain sight" is definitional of the post-representational strategies of both the governed and those who govern. It is as though, as Günter Grass once said, neoliberalism has realized the anarchist dream of abolishing the state.[80]

CH.2: FROM OBAMARAMA TO THE DRONE PRESIDENCY

Riot shields / Voodoo economics / It's life, it's life / It's just business / Cattle prods and the IMF / I trust I can rely on your vote

– Radiohead, 'Electioneering'

I learned we earned, got no concern / Instead we burned so where the hell is our return? / Plain and simp the system's a pimp / But I refuse to be a ho / Who stole the soul?

– Public Enemy, 'Who Stole the Soul?'

If the principal achievement of the Obama presidency was the victory over racial discrimination, is it not legitimate to ask whether his administration did anything to mitigate racial disparities in critical areas like poverty, education, housing, employment, immigration and criminal justice reform? If the question of racial disparity cannot be separated from the broader question of social inequality, how did Obama manage to convince the electorate that he was the candidate of change? As Paul Street comments, the American state and the Democratic Party that Obama governed has a disappointing history of civil rights betrayal.[1] Obama turned out to be no different in that regard from his predecessors and so his accomplishment could be limited to meeting the demands of a restrictive institutional framework. Obama's ethno-cultural identity nevertheless made it easier for him to pose as an agent of progress, all the while accommodating the domestic and imperial hierarchies of the establishment. Had Obama turned out to be more progressive on race and class issues, he would have been less suited to the centrist requirements of the Democratic Party. That, in a nutshell, is the enigma of the Obama presidency.

African Americans have many disadvantages when compared with the rest of their fellow citizens. African Americans constitute approximately 13 percent of the population, close to 40 million people. Blacks have the lowest median income of all ethnic groups and make just over half of the median household income of white Americans. Blacks collectively possess less than one percent of the nation's wealth. The black middle class is sliding into poverty faster than its white counterpart. More than 25 percent of African Americans live below the poverty level. This is due to the fact that wages, adjusted to the cost of living, have not improved significantly over the last 50 years. Black unemployment is twice the national average, even for blacks with college degrees. Half of African-American children live below the poverty level. Black teen pregnancies are twice the rate as that for whites. Suspension from school is three times more likely for black children. Residential segregation and unequal access to quality education in redlined neighbourhoods contributes to black poverty. In states with the highest poverty rates, voter abstention and voter obstruction make the difference between the two main political parties largely irrelevant. Ballot restrictions prevent third parties from emerging.

The economic difficulties that African Americans face are compounded by incarceration rates. Women lead 70 percent of black households. One reason for this is the fact that close to one million black American men are in prison. Although the U.S. has only two percent of the world's population, it has 25 percent of the world's prison population. Incarceration rates increased from roughly 300,000 to two million in the period 1970 to 2000, an average that is ten times greater than most other industrialized nations. In 2000, ten percent of black males aged 20 to 40 were in prison, which is ten times the likelihood for whites. In 2010, more than 30 percent of black male high school dropouts were in prison. Black men comprise 41 percent of the prison population and 49 percent of murder victims. Almost all black homicides, close to 94 percent, are perpetrated by other blacks, while 85 percent of white homicides are by other whites. Although the rate of violent crimes decreased in the 1990s, the incarceration rate increased, with many sentences attributed to drug trafficking and drug possession. High incarceration rates, which in part have been exacerbated by the replacement of rehabilitation with retribution, result in more crime and contribute to cycles of poverty, debt, unemployment and homelessness, making overall life chances more difficult and adding to racial prejudice, discrimination, drop-out rates, gang violence, despair and suicides. In a social system in which a white person with a criminal record has a better chance of being hired for a job than a black person without one, and in which prison becomes a means to acquire health care, food and shelter, only massive socio-economic and political change can redeem the slogan 'Yes, we can.'[2]

The increase of social inequality since the end of the postwar boom means that poor blacks are economically worse off than they were in the period before the Civil Rights era, which questions the extent to which affirmative action, black nationalism, identity politics and recent forms of intersectional anti-racism have done anything to challenge the predominant social relations. The social prospects for African Americans cannot be separated from the overall growth of social inequality in the U.S., where the top one percent doubled its assets in the period 1980 to 2014. On a global level, eight individuals – most of them American – own as much wealth as the bottom half of the entire global population.[3] Jeff Bezos, Bill Gates and Mark Zuckerberg possess more wealth than the poorest half of the U.S. population. The top five percent of earners in the U.S. have 67 percent of the total social wealth and live on average 20 years longer than the poorest Americans. Seventy percent of Americans have less than $1000 in savings. Economic inequality is reflected within identity groups, where for instance the black middle class, or those with household earnings of more than $75,000, is the fastest growing group. The black middle class represents about ten percent of blacks overall, and consists of professors, doctors, lawyers, engineers, managers and executives. Within the middle class, discrimination is mitigated and black professionals have achieved overall parity with whites. There are today some 35,000 African-American millionaires, up from 25 in 1960. Since approximately half of black households have between nothing and $6000, the African American population is the most unequal of all other ethnic groups.[4] Wealth inequality among blacks is structurally similar to wealth inequality among all other ethnic groups. Class inequality defines the terms of racial equality. In other words, and according to the discourse of racial disparity, social equality will be achieved when blacks as a group have proportionally the same percentage of millionaires and billionaires as whites.

The struggle against racism and class struggle are not different versions of the same struggle. The task before us is therefore the ruthless elucidation of this difference. Racism has been defined by Obama and many other commentators as America's 'original sin.' The function of this concept is by and large to bypass leftist class politics and to substitute history with religion. Slavery is not simply the original sin of the U.S. but is part of world history. Framing politics in terms of histories of oppression is one of the ploys that is fundamental to the ideology of *progressive neoliberalism*, which is defined by Nancy Fraser as a hegemonic bloc comprised of high-end financial sectors like Wall Street, Silicon Valley, Hollywood, as well as mainstream liberal progressives.[5] Progressive neoliberals have two rival groups, she argues. The first of these is a *progressive populism* that is comprised of the remnants of organized labour and the marginalized minority constituencies that now form the basis of new social movements. Through their forward-thinking attitudes towards diversity and cosmopolitanism, the New Democrats by and large succeeded in uniting this majority of the marginalized with the interests of corporate capitalism. The second rival is a *reactionary neoliberalism* that has the same policies of upward redistribution as does progressive neoliberalism, but mixes this with rhetorical claims to represent working Americans while at the same time defending an exclusionary ethno-national, anti-immigrant and pro-Christian social order. In terms of the 'great awakening' that is represented by BLM and MeToo, Slavoj Žižek suggests that today's politicization of difference is not a radical or subversive phenomenon but is simply the majority position.[6] This epochal change is not unimportant simply because it is mainstream. There are breakthroughs that can be achieved in terms of social equality. However, there is a tendency, on the one hand, for these gains to be restricted to the wealthy, and on the other, for them to be restricted to liberal capitalist ideology, which then allows them to be appropriated by conservative forces. The great awakening has become a conformist awokening in which the logic of victimhood is combined with or confined to the ideology of personal freedom. What Žižek does not mention in his analysis is the fact that the logic of victimhood is accompanied by a reactionary politics of victimization that also combines with the status quo. Demands for equality become justifications for chauvinism and abuses of power. On this count, Adolph Reed and Merlin Chowkwanyun warn against the discourse of racial disparity, which, they argue, rejects universality and class politics. It is, as such, compatible with the class politics of the establishment.[7] The discourse of racial disparity that has animated progressive neoliberalism is a moralizing and formalist ideology of race that is used by the liberal class to displace a dynamic historical materialist perspective.

As a belated representative of the bipartisan corporate policy framework of black capitalism, Obama contributed to the dismantling of left politics. His presidency is the supreme instance to date of the 'black faces in high places' ideology advanced in the Richard Nixon and Jimmy Carter era to neutralize the remnants of communist internationalism and Black Power nationalism. After Ronald Reagan, the New Democratic politics of Bill Clinton laid the groundwork for the Obama administration. The globalization policies advocated by corporate lobbyists and think tanks like the Heritage Foundation and the CATO Institute, who called on government to abandon the gold standard and protectionism, deregulate markets, de-unionize labour, offshore factory production, dismantle welfare, facilitate mergers, lower taxes and deflate the money supply, were further advanced by free trade policies and financial deregulation. So were the privatization whims of the military, health care industry and pharmaceuticals, food safety and energy sectors satisfied. The War on Drugs that fuelled the privatization and militarization of security services were a domestic policy equivalent to post-Cold War interventions in Serbia, Afghanistan, Iraq, Libya and Syria. In 2008, poor whites voted for John McCain and wealthy whites voted for Obama. Since Obama seemed more hip than Hillary, Americans vindicated four decades of black capitalism and neoliberal policy without even knowing it. As Matt Taibbi reported about Obama in 2007: "You can't run against him on issues because you can't even find him on the ideological spectrum."[8]

Dark Horse

The black feminist cultural theorist Hortense Spillers has argued that race is not destiny. One would not know this, however, when one examines assessments of the political career of the first African-American president. So much of the Obama presidency is defined in terms of race that to make a distinction between Obama's politics and his identity appears racist. Race, according to Spillers, is a fiction. Its illusory quality allows someone to move from black to post-black and back again. Race has no inherent meaning, even as it reifies personality.[9] Reification would seem to be an occupational hazard if you are President of the United States. Obama's political cunning, which has been noted by almost everyone, is his ability to maintain a certain distance from race as much as partisan politicking. It is appropriate then that one of the first Obama memes was the 'Hope' poster image that was created by Shepard Fairey, a street artist whose tag or brand name is Obey. The function of a Master Signifier is to occupy the place of ritual obedience. This opens a perspective on the significance of Obama as the first black president. The facts of slavery, segregation and black capitalism are exactly what made Obama, in the midst of illegal wars and on the heels of the 2008 banking crisis, the best possible candidate. The desire for Obama was the desire to not only redeem a traumatic history but at the same time to pretend that he, more than any other politician, could abolish the place he occupied. One could thus celebrate Obama's election in terms of the Lacanian notion of surplus enjoyment – a symptom that sticks out and betrays the repressed totality of everything that people know. After his election victory, as his supporters called on people to party like it's 1999, this repressed content was soon in evidence. Those who clung to the Obama fetish were the ones who maintained the fiction of Obama's racial identity, since you cannot have enjoyment and meaning at the same time. The rest were in the process of losing their pensions, their jobs, their homes or their loved ones.

Barack Obama was born in Honolulu in 1961. He was raised in Hawaii and then in Indonesia by a black Kenyan farmer and a white activist organizer from Kansas. Obama's mother and maternal grandfather supported his intellectual development and taught him the lessons of the Civil Rights movement, instilling in him an appreciation for black leaders like Frederick Douglass, Thurgood Marshall, Lena Horne, Harry Belafonte, Richard Wright, James Baldwin and Malcolm X. His parents inculcated a universalist outlook through which to understand the African-American struggle as a quest for justice and equality. Obama was educated at a leading private school, then at Columbia University and Harvard University, where he became editor and later the first black president of the Harvard Law Review. Despite his biracial identity, Obama embraced his blackness as a feature of his cosmopolitanism, combining individualism with communitarianism, patriotism and the Christian faith. In terms of black politics, his blend of universalism and particularity played itself out in varying ways, some of them linked to history and others to politics. As a beneficiary of radical freedom struggles, from the founding fathers to Abraham Lincoln and Martin Luther King, Obama thought of himself as a black *president* and not a *black* president.[10] Although he argued against the notion that racism is a thing of the past, Obama considered that all Americans share the same history and social challenges. He believed that the task of a political leader is to serve all Americans equally and he denied race-specific means to redress racial inequality. This approach found favour among whites, who responded positively to his fusion of universalism with mainstream values and middle-class interests. The contradictions of this stance could be noticed in his foreign policy rhetoric, for which he criticized American imperialism and isolationism while at the same time defending the unique role of the U.S. as the defender of capitalist democracy on the global stage.

With regard to black politics, Obama called for moral accountability and personal responsibility, rejecting the attitude that whites are to blame for the social problems that afflict American blacks, or that blacks are ontologically the victims of whites. Because he criticized blacks for stereotypical vices, many have associated Obama with a tradition of black scolds, from Booker T. Washington to Sidney Poitier, Louis Farrakhan and Bill Cosby. His refusal to use the bully pulpit to advocate for the black cause gained him the enmity of those more closely associated with the Civil Rights tradition. He argued against them that angry accusations of racism could no longer be wielded for the sake of political advantage, calling for unity across the colour line. In his 2006 memoir, *The Audacity of Hope*, Obama writes:

> Rightly or wrongly, white guilt has largely exhausted itself in America; even if the most fair-minded of whites, those who would genuinely like to see racial inequality ended and poverty relieved, tend to push back against suggestions of racial victimization – or race specific claims based on the history of race discrimination in this country.[11]

Obama's only notable connection to black nationalism was his relationship to Jeremiah Wright of the Trinity United Church, a pastor who combined black liberation theology with identitarian pride and empowerment. Unlike Wright, however, who reviled America's racism and class inequality, Obama played both sides of stereotypes, optimizing advantage so as to escape ghettoization and therefore tending towards the notion of post-racial consensus.

Although Obama's memoir rejects the notion that America is a post-racial society, his conciliatory and compromising attitude in politics was extended to identity issues. Obama privileged those in power, showing more concern for American hegemony than for anything that could be politically disadvantageous. His most outward statement of identification with black politics was his comments before and after the acquittal of George Zimmerman to the effect that Trayvon Martin, who was killed by Zimmerman, could have been his son or even himself as a teenager. In contrast to the politics of Black Lives Matter, his statement nevertheless underscored the notion that people should be judged on the basis of their character and not their race. The question of racial violence, however, is not simply avoided by reference to moral character. As Richard Hofstadter has remarked, violence in the U.S. is more pronounced among citizens than against the establishment elite and is often encouraged by elites against radical and minority groups.[12] Obama's equanimity on social inequality did not favour social reform so much as liberal capitalism as the definition and the limit of universality. Both black politics and left politics could thus be defused through liberal ideology as a philosophical standard and as moral justification for the virulence of neoliberal policies.

Obama's background as a Chicago politician coincides with his relationship with Michelle Obama. Michelle Robinson's perspective on race was informed by having grown up on the South Side of Chicago, a black middle-class enclave. Chicago was a segregated city before the 1950s. Blockbusting and white flight facilitated the settlement of black neighbourhoods in the era after and during the black northern migration. As black businesses and families prospered, black life was experienced as the norm rather than the exception, eventually transforming South Side Chicago into a black political stronghold. It is only as a university student at Princeton University, and while working on her thesis on "Princeton-Educated Blacks and The Black Community" that Michelle Obama says she experienced discrimination and became aware of her blackness. She and Barack met while working for the same law firm and married in 1992. The two shared similar attitudes towards identity issues. Michelle Obama's 'pride-gate' statement that Obama's election was the first time that she felt proud of her country was later echoed by her relief that his two terms were finally over, revealing her mistrust of the same people and process that made his election possible. As FLOTUS she avoided politics and emphasized motherhood instead, much as Barbara Bush had done before her.

From 1992 to 2004, Barack Obama taught constitutional law at the University of Chicago Law School. He cut his political teeth while working for two years as a community organizer on the South Side of Chicago and through work with a law firm specializing in civil rights litigation. His method was oriented towards building consensus between black South Siders, established political authorities and financial foundations. He was elected Senator of Illinois in 1996, 1998 and 2002, and then U.S. Senator in 2004. As a state politician, Obama relied on his Ivy League credentials and received corporate support for his bipartisan agenda. He opposed the Iraq War on pragmatic rather than moral grounds and criticized the inadequate government response to Hurricane Katrina. In 2005 he satisfied the interests of corporations and defied labour organizations by voting in favour of the Class Action Fairness Act, a law that denies citizen access to courts in legal challenges to the corporate control of labour rights, consumer rights and civil rights. This decision led many to question his credentials as a progressive. Writing for the *Village Voice* in 1996, Adolph Reed made what has now become a widely repeated assessment that is worthy of Nostradamus:

> In Chicago … we've gotten a foretaste of the new breed of foundation-hatched black communitarian voices; one of them, a smooth Harvard lawyer with impeccable do-good credentials and vacuous-to-repressive neoliberal politics, has won a state senate seat on a base mainly in the liberal foundation and development worlds. His fundamentally bootstrap line was softened by a patina of the rhetoric of authentic community, talk about meetings in kitchens, small-scale solutions to social problems, and the predictable elevation of process over program – the point where identity politics converge with old-fashioned middle-class reform in favoring form over substance. I suspect that his ilk is the wave of the future in U.S. black politics here, as in Haiti and wherever the International Monetary Fund has sway.[13]

As Obama shifted from state to federal politics, so did his support network. According to Ken Silverstein, Obama was perceived as a player who could adapt to the culture of Washington D.C. lobbyists, corporate donors, campaign consultants, pollsters and media strategists. The influence of these forces that are hostile to reform, Silverstein says, results in representative democracy getting taken off the table.[14]

Obama announced his candidacy for the presidential nomination in 2007. His March 2008 speech in Philadelphia, "A More Perfect Union," was his only speech that treated race as a special topic, making the connection between progress in race relations and other social issues like health, education, employment, climate change and militarism. He reassured white voters with his colourblind optimism and mobilized a multicultural coalition of small donors through both social media and grassroots organizations. Despite the inclusivity of his campaign, he also relied on vested interests. His top 20 contributors were Wall Street firms, including Goldman Sachs, Lehman Brothers, JP Morgan Chase, Citigroup, Morgan Stanley, Credit Suisse and Citadel Investment Group, who contributed close to $3 million to his campaign. Law firms donated more than $11 million and many of his campaign aides were registered lobbyists. Overall, Obama raised $750 million for his 2008 campaign, more than twice the amount raised by John McCain. If in his speeches Obama said that he wished to bring the U.S. closer to perfection, his method would be public relations, spending more than $50 million on media and marketing. His slogan 'Yes, we can' had more in common with the 1980s neoconservative slogan 'because I can' insofar as his campaign also promised to maintain Bush policies on big oil, energy and utility companies, the nuclear industry, the finance industry, agribusiness and the wars in the Middle East. Despite the warning signs, African Americans and Hispanics overwhelmingly voted for Obama, giving him approximately 90 percent of the black vote for both of his terms. In his 2008 acceptance speech he associated his victory with the legacy of Lincoln and King, raising the expectation that America would be leaving behind not only the problems of the Clinton and Bush administrations, but the troubled history of racism.

Too Big to Fail

When Obama was sworn into office, nearly forty million Americans lived below the poverty level, roughly 15 percent of the population, with most job growth in the low-wage sector. Nearly 16 million children lived in poverty and more than 1.6 million counted among the 3.5 million homeless. While high-wage earners in the top one percent were making an average of $1.3 million annually, the majority of Americans were earning $33,000 or less, living paycheck to paycheck. After the banking crisis, nearly 4 million Americans lost their homes, adding thousands of families to the count of homeless Americans. Unemployment was at its worst since it began to be measured in 1948, with close to 14 million unemployed and 9 million working part-time. As many as 40 million Americans received SNAP food stamps and close to 6 million lived on them entirely. Close to 50 million Americans were food insecure. Obama had promised a new economic agenda to create jobs, build infrastructure, alleviate poverty and reform the economy, health care, education and housing. How then would he balance the free market ideology of Wall Street financiers with the needs of Main Street? Clearly, community organizing would not be an effective method in Washington. While his cabinet appointments did not give blacks any preferential treatment, with fewer African Americans assigned to posts than both of his predecessors, it was nevertheless consistent with the Clinton and Bush administrations on both domestic and foreign policy, leading to a view of Obama as a Blairite pragmatist and compromiser. How one is to assess Obama's acquiescence to the financial oligarchy and the military-industrial complex is less important than its acknowledgement. Because his presidency was a sign of progress, Obama could more easily gain public support for a ruling-class agenda. Opposing reformist measures at every turn, he replaced the politics of social justice with technocratic and post-representational governance.

Defending the free market over everything else, Obama helped to neoliberalize social policy. This gets missed when former radicals like Angela Davis argue that Obama represents the defeat of the white male agenda as well as the defeat of the kind of 'colourblind' leftism that reduces social issues to political economy. At the level of political strategy, the notion of the Obama presidency as a civil rights achievement is not unrelated to public policy. Even on rights issues, Obama was not the progressive he seemed to be. Regarding abortion rights, he argued that the Freedom of Choice Act was not high on his agenda, calling on women to reduce the number of unwanted pregnancies and encouraging adoption. According to Sharon Smith, one third of American women will have an abortion in their lifetime and this rate increases as the economy worsens.[15] On the other hand, Obama supported LGBTQ rights, ending the Don't Ask Don't Tell policies of the military and repealing the Defense of Marriage Act as unconstitutional, thereby legalizing same-sex marriage and partner benefits. In 2010 he introduced the National HIV/AIDS Strategy and he also worked on HIV/AIDS prevention among sex workers. In 2014 he passed an executive order against employment and housing discrimination. He nominated a Latina judge, Sonia Sotomayor, to the Supreme Court, as well as Elena Keegan, who had served as a clerk for Thurgood Marshall, the first black Supreme Court Justice.

These few successes in social policy, including benefits to federal employees, were counterbalanced by his broader policy framework. Although it is not Obama's fault that 10 percent of the U.S. population owns 95 percent of wealth, he can be accused of contributing to this imbalance. During his time in office, the assets of the wealthiest 400 Americans increased from $1.57 to $2.4 trillion. Wages declined, debt increased and the cost of living increased, making conditions worse for minority groups especially. Based on Federal Reserve data, the People's Policy Project determined that whereas 65 percent of African Americans and Latinos own 0 percent of the total wealth of their respective groups, the wealthiest 10 percent of each group owns 75 percent of the total wealth, which is similar in numbers to whites. During Obama's two terms, the top 1 percent of African Americans increased their share of their ethnic group's wealth from 19.4 to 40.5 percent. The top 10 percent of African Americans increased their wealth in this period by an average of $285,000 and the bottom 40-90 percent lost an average of $100,000 to $350,000. As editor of the *Black Agenda Report*, the late Glen Ford argued that Obama's bipartisan austerity regime saved the banks at the expense of entitlement programmes, and this, despite the fact that in 2008 the Democrats controlled Congress. The Democratic Party's focus on deficit reduction, which is the same as GOP policy with the small difference of number amounts, attacks social welfare programmes like Social Security and Medicare first and foremost.[16] According to Dave Lindorff, these welfare programmes, the legacy of Roosevelt's New Deal and Johnson's Great Society, are not the cause of government debt and have operated on a surplus since 1981, with a surplus of $2.6 trillion in 2011. Medicare and Social Security Trust Funds were rather raided during the period 2000-2010 for the sake of the War on Terror and subsequently construed as a burden on taxpayers. Cuts to retirement benefits were then leveraged for the sake of economic stimulus and tax cuts for the wealthy.[17] Obama's Deficit Commission was eventually defamed by the AFL-CIO as a front for attacking Social Security.

The promotion of identity politics by the Democratic Party has a class character that the majority of Americans have lost the ability to perceive. The premium on identity in contemporary culture is not simply incidental to the financialization of everyday life, which Obama did much to facilitate. Obama's economic policy offered supply-side solutions to economic problems and mimicked his predecessors by criticizing overregulation, including the protective framework of the Glass-Steagall Act that had previously separated insurance companies, commercial banks and investment banks. Faced with the greatest economic crisis since the 1970s, Obama opted for corporate welfare, the suppression of wages and austerity measures that shift the economic burden onto the vulnerable. Among his first acts in office was the appointment of Clinton and Bush neoliberals as well as laissez-faire deregulators like Larry Summers, Timothy Geithner and Ben Bernanke. These people had contributed to the deregulation of derivatives trading and the creation of exotic debt instruments, thereby misleading investors and subverting banking reform. Among some of the other players in this Wall Street gang were AIG, Goldman Sachs, Lehman Brothers and Citigroup operatives like Robert Hormats, Jacob Lew, Michael Forman, Robert Rubin, Lewis Alexander, Hank Paulson and Gary Gensler.

After the 2008 economic crisis, which was entirely the fault of the Wall Street finance industry, Obama taxed the public to the tune of $24 trillion to bail out the banks and their CEO managers. Moreover, he did almost nothing to regulate Wall Street and punish the guilty, who had caused millions of Americans to lose their homes, their jobs and their pensions, leading Cornel West to refer to Obama as the "black mascot of Wall Street oligarchs and the black puppet of corporate plutocrats," a "Rockefeller Republican in blackface."[18] Obama used quantitative easing at the Federal Reserve to increase the stock values of corporations and the wealthy one percent. His post-race politics helped to smooth over the fact that poor blacks with low educational levels had been targeted for subprime loans, creating an artificial demand for assets that could be bundled and resold to hedge fund managers. In the process, rating agencies had been paid off to ignore the housing bubble for the sake of increased demand. Companies like AIG and Goldman Sachs manufactured the crisis by selling risky financial and insurance products worth trillions of dollars. AIG, which had insured the bad investments of Goldman Sachs, was considered 'too big to fail' and therefore deserving to be rescued. So was Goldman Sachs, which went on to make record profits in 2008. JP Morgan Chase made $11 billion in profits in 2009, boosted in part by the transfer of food stamp income onto debit cards. By 2019, Wall Street CEOs were taking in $27 billion in bonuses. The bailout therefore did not serve the homeowners who had lost their investments, but the perpetrators who had caused the crisis in the first place, transforming politicians into the employees of corporate donors.[19] Most of the foreclosures of 2009-2010 were associated with segregation, with for instance 71 percent of the failed 2005-2008 Wells Fargo loans in Baltimore located in black neighbourhoods. Obama did enact the Dodd-Frank Wall Street Reform and Consumer Protection Act, which brought reforms to financial regulatory agencies and the banking industry, but these measures, after the draft bill was whittled down by lobbyists, did not end too big to fail but in fact increased Wall Street control of government. Trillion-dollar banks like Bank of America, JP Morgan Chase, Citigroup, Wells Fargo, Goldman Sachs and Morgan Stanley are now beyond government regulation.[20] By the end of Obama's two terms, the banks controlled 50 percent of wealth assets.

With the country reeling from corruption vertigo, Obama instituted the 2010 American Recovery and Reinvestment Act, a $700 billion stimulus bill designed to salvage jobs and contribute to economic growth. A seemingly intelligent and compassionate decision, with spending on research, infrastructure and social needs, it was followed by Citizens United, a law that gave the same moneyed interests that crashed the economy a greater say in campaign financing. By 2011, with the economy headed once again into recession, Obama chose to avoid another stimulus and instead shifted his policy towards deficit reduction. With the eventual goal of handing Social Security over to Wall Street money managers, he reduced contributions by $120 billion. He facilitated the offshoring of wealth into foreign currencies and investments, none of which would help economic recovery. Obama then began to preach the gospel of austerity and small government, cutting public assistance and ramping up the war economy. With economic growth at a lowly 2 percent and unemployment above 8 percent, Obama ran deficits and increased government debt from $10.7 to $16 trillion. Maintaining Bush's tax cuts for the middle and upper-middle class, median wages fell and manufacturing was offshored, replaced mostly with service sector jobs that increased the number of part-time and temporary jobs from 10.7 to 15.8 percent.

At the end of Obama's first term, 14 million Americans were unemployed, with countless more underemployed or who had stopped looking for work. Here too, black workers were adversely affected, with long-term unemployment at 10 percent. In 2009 Obama did sign the Lilly Leadbetter Fair Pay Act for pay equity but one can also imagine that equity in Target and Family Dollar jobs is no equity at all. In terms of labour policy, Obama oversaw the $80 billion TARP-funded GM-Chrysler and Ford bailout by ruining the American auto industry, closing as many as 14 factories, cutting production and eliminating 35,000 jobs while at the same time driving the remaining manufacturing towards Southern states that have lax labour policies for mostly non-union workers. Detroit was hit hard, with auto worker wages reduced by half for new hires and pensions slashed. Obama's "rescue" cost taxpayers anywhere between $10 to $25 billion to save jobs and secure the support of the United Auto Workers.[21] Obama was later invited to Flint, Michigan, to witness first-hand the problem of contaminated water. This water was once the basis of the fortunes of GM but was now no longer fit for manufacturing purposes, let alone human consumption. Failing to declare the Flint crisis a federal disaster, largely to protect the wrongdoing of Wall Street investors, Obama reassured the people in this economically devastated city that by using filters the water is drinkable.[22] Although more than a dozen people died from Legionnaire's disease water poisoning in 2014-15, and countless children suffered from lead poisoning, the city and health officials who were responsible for the outbreak through a privatization money-making scheme were dismissed of charges of manslaughter by state Democrats. Since fewer than 12 percent of American workers are unionized, and with only the Democratic Party as their advocate, Obama never felt any pressure to support organized labour.

In labour policy, as in most other trouble spots, Obama blamed workers for their problems. He was more attuned to the privatization agenda that characterizes his signature legislative achievement, the Affordable Care Act, better known as Obamacare. Despite plaudits as a feat of the impossible, Obamacare was consistent with the treatment of health care as a commodity and was managed according to market principles, with cost reduction rather than service as its primary purpose.[23] It is estimated that in the U.S., one doctor commits suicide every day due to overwork and depression. Some of the stress is caused by the inability to properly provide care for patients. As many as 45,000 people die every year for lack of health insurance and the uninsured have a 40 percent above average risk of dying. Health care costs are one of the three main contributors to poverty rates, along with unemployment and taxes. In 2009, in the midst of the recession, the four largest private health insurers made more than $12 billion in profits. Obama supported universal single-payer health care as a candidate, but he dropped the idea of a public option when he became president, choosing instead to shift the burden of costs for health care from corporate employers to workers and diverting billions of dollars into the coffers of the insurance industry. Although the ACA did increase the number of people covered by health insurance by approximately 20 million, including many African Americans, the non-partisan Congressional Budget Office found that it nevertheless left 30 million Americans uninsured. The rising cost of living adds to the number of people who are uninsured. Just as costs for health insurance increased under Obamacare, so did the confusion about insurance options, benefiting the oligopolistic insurance-pharmaceutical complex, which in 2008 contributed a record amount to political candidates, with three times more to Obama than to McCain.[24]

Rather than concern for public health, Obama showed more interest in private wealth. Extending Medicare to all would have reduced administrative costs from 20 percent – about $500 billion annually, or 1.5 percent of GDP – to 4 percent, allowing hospitals to better serve those with special needs, especially the disabled and the elderly who are responsible for a larger proportion of health care costs. In comparison with other countries, U.S. health care costs amount to 17 percent of the GDP, which is on average twice the typical amount. Obama's Deficit Reduction Committee was staffed by enemies of Social Security and Medicare, who sought to raise the age of Medicare eligibility. What Obama should have considered instead was a reduction of the age of eligibility to guarantee better coverage.[25] According to Vicente Navarro, Obama should not have linked the need to reduce the cost of health care with deficit reduction. By focusing on the extension of insurance coverage, Obamacare ignored the fact that more than 150 million Americans are underinsured and are not aware of the fact until they are stuck with heath care bills. Under Obamacare, insurance premiums, deductibles and co-payments absorbed more disposable income and health care costs increased.[26]

By the end of Obama's two terms, as home values declined, life expectancy had fallen, largely due to social distress, suicides and drug overdoses. A few weeks before the 2016 election, Obama announced that health premiums would increase by an average of 25 percent, giving people less reason to vote for Hillary Clinton. Not that many voters would have known this, but Obamacare was based on Bill Clinton's endorsement of the Dutch and Swiss models of universal coverage through the private insurance system, which replaces social insurance with the for-profit insurance market, now a feature of the World Bank and International Monetary Fund agenda. One of its creators is the economist Alain Enthoven, a former Pentagon strategist who influenced Margaret Thatcher's neoconservative policy to transition the National Health Service towards a pro-market and multi-tier model that encourages preferential coverage. Like other aspects of the neoliberal attack on public institutions, this model of 'managed competition' favours the cost-benefit analysis of managers to the detriment of the knowledge of health care professionals, who are being transformed into hospital employees and losing control over their conditions of work. Had Obama chosen to implement single-payer health care, which is desired by the majority of Americans, he would not only have saved $400 billion annually, but would have bolstered the support of his constituents.

Obama's post-partisan privatization schemes also extended to education. In the first month of his presidency, he demonstrated his commitment to education by visiting an elementary charter school, underscoring the market-driven business model that would ostensibly curb underachievement among middle school students. The Washington D.C. school in question gives out $100 monthly amounts for good behaviour. Students in this school are being taught corruption and greed as the basis of citizenship. The D.C. chancellor, Michelle Rhee, has used test scores to fire principals and teachers, undermining unions in the interest of a new type of efficient school business and student customer, who now buys access to the job training that will allow them to invest in themselves as human capital. As noticed by a speech Obama gave to the United Federation of Teachers in 2008, the goal of the means-tested business model for education is for the sake of such marketable skills expediency as the creation of engineers who can build better automobiles than the Japanese and South Koreans – in other words, narrow and competitive private instrumentality rather than democratic responsibility and criticality.[27] Those who do not perform well in this system are prepared for either the precarious work life of Walmart and Amazon jobs, or for prisons, which in some cases are better funded than schools. Approximately one million students dropped out of school during each year of Obama's tenure. Almost half of black students drop out of high school, about twice the rate as their white classmates. The majority of these will have been students in underfunded schools. A 2017 study by the HOPE lab in Wisconsin revealed that close to one million students pursuing a community college education were homeless.

The fact that neoliberal ideology is part of a ruling-class agenda is evident in the field of education. Politicians like Obama who claim that they are preparing

American students to compete in the global economy ignore the fact that per capita, teachers in countries like South Korea are paid twice the amount that is paid to their American counterparts, who receive pay that is far below the international average. Students in America's elite private schools perform worse than the average public school student in Finland, where 90 percent of teachers are unionized.[28] The U.S. has an 86 percent literacy rate, a number that seems high, but which by global standards stands at 125th position, with countries like Russia, Azerbijan, Poland, Cuba and Armenia ensuring 100 percent literacy for its citizens. From 2008 to 2013, the U.S. government's Department of Education received $120 billion in post-secondary student loan interest, with an annual average of $51 billion, which is equivalent to the annual profits of the four largest American banks. The total amount of student debt in the U.S. is over $1.6 trillion, larger than the credit card debt and short only of the mortgage debt. Pursuing the path of neoliberal privatization through vouchers, charter schools, economic incentives and de-unionization, Obama legitimized the closure of public schools as well as attacks on teachers by free-marketeers and union busters like his Secretary of Education, Arne Duncan, who as the CEO of Chicago Public Schools had been known for the militarization and corporatization of schools, increasing student expulsion, instituting surveillance, closing schools and either firing dedicated staff or replacing them with cheaper new hires.[29] Obama withheld federal funding for education so as to implement Duncan's charter school policies.[30] Hundreds of thousands of teachers were laid off by reforms designed to promote private charters. Duncan considered Hurricane Katrina the best thing to have happened to New Orleans since the disaster led to the charterization of 57 percent of its schools. Although non-unionized teachers do not outperform unionized teachers, the best public schools lost mostly unionized teachers.[31] Other Democrats, like Robert Ford and Al Sharpton, promoted charter schools while receiving kickbacks from right-wing non-profits. Obama also altered Bush's race-neutral guidelines for school admission by encouraging racial preferences, an affirmative action policy that seems progressive but that dovetails with the growth of inequality.

It is not for no reason that Bush's No Child Left Behind and Obama's Race to the Top educational policies resulted, from 2017 to 2019, in the largest increase in teacher strikes in decades, with strike activity in California, Pennsylvania, Illinois, Indiana, Ohio, Oklahoma, Colorado, Oregon, Arizona, Alaska, North and South Carolina, Tennessee, Mississippi, Louisiana, Maine, Nevada, North Dakota, Arkansas, Delaware, Georgia and New Mexico. And they are not alone. Neoliberalization is causing the same forms of teacher resistance in Argentina, Brazil, Costa Rica, Columbia, Algeria, Ivory Coast, Kenya, Mali, South Africa, New Zealand, Mexico, Poland, the U.K., Iran and India. So have health care workers, transportation, civil service, retail, utility, manufacturing, high-tech and gig economy workers gone on strike in large numbers. Teachers are one of the last strongholds of public sector unions, with more than one million members in the American Federation of Teachers and more than three million members in the National Education Association. Teachers are the largest group of unionized workers and a target on the neoliberal hit list. The charterization of schools is not surprisingly supported by billionaires like Bill Gates and the Walton family, philanthrocapitalists whose free-market ideology promotes a multi-tier system and the transformation of education from a public good into a market for investment.[32] Despite the increase in union activity, one should not underestimate the role of unions in demobilizing the class struggle through concessionary contracts and threats of job cuts, leading in some instances to the development of rank-and-file insurgencies and wildcat strikes.[33] In 2018, 450,000 American workers went on strike, the highest count since the mid-1980s and a significant resurgence since the lowest levels from after the 2008 bailout, an indication of how poverty, inequality and austerity are effective tools of labour exploitation and the suppression of socialism. During the COVID-19 pandemic, back-to-school herd immunity policies were vigorously opposed by teachers, parents and students alike.

On the environment and ecology front, Obama cannot be said to have been a responsible steward. Despite the pre-election enthusiasm of Greenpeace, he supported the nuclear power industry as a solution to climate change, diverting billions in federal funding to dangerous technologies that are defended on the premise that they are cleaner than coal. Obama also promoted oil drilling on America's coastlines, even after the BP oil spill in the Gulf of Mexico. His Minerals Management Service allowed fossil fuel giants to practically manage safety issues by themselves. After the 2010 BP spill, 8 million additional acres of the Gulf were opened for drilling. Obama's Secretary of the Interior, Ken Salazar, did next to nothing to protect wildlife and endangered species, treating land management as the purview of business contractors and allowing mining, drilling, pollution, clearcutting and mountaintop removal. Obama's Secretary of the Interior, Tom Vilsak, advocated for agribusiness, which is eroding arable land, gobbling up small farms and spreading taxpayer subsidized Frankencrops over one third of U.S. cropland.[34] In relation to biotechnology, Obama avoided mandatory labels for GMOs and approved the genetic engineering of foods against the advice of scientists. Government appointees included former employees of corporations like Monsanto, Dow, Syngenta and Dupont, who spend hundreds of millions lobbying government. After industry complained about the fact that Michelle Obama had planted an organic garden, the White House ceased to mention the word organic in its publicity.[35] Although Obama proposed a cap-and-trade bill on greenhouse gases in 2009, his bill was perceived to be an exercise in greenwashing. After the 2010 mid-term elections, the administration rebranded climate change to more upbeat talk of "clean energy" and international climate financing to developing countries for sustainability and adaptation, offset by government giveaways to energy-dependent states and the fossil fuel, coal and nuclear industries as components of a supply-focused 'all-of-the-above' energy policy. Eager to develop hydraulic fracturing, offshore drilling and shale gas production, the Obama administration increased fossil fuel dependency while at the same time issuing feel-good energy efficiency standards in automobile manufacturing and building construction – consumer-level adjustments that overlook lax standards for power plants and refineries.

By 2011, despite Supreme Court mandates for the Environmental Protection Agency to regulate emissions, and in light of conservative deficit reduction obstructionism, the Obama administration was making next to no effort to combat global warming, save to distinguish itself from climate change deniers.[36] The U.S. had reduced its carbon emissions by around 15 percent, enough to remain lax on targets. Expensive non-hydro renewables like solar, wind and geothermal account for only 5 percent of the U.S. energy supply, compared to 40 percent in some European countries. Despite their 100 percent potential, renewables are mitigated by the concern for energy security and energy independence through increased dependence on fossil fuels and fossil fuel exports. Clean energy is otherwise encouraged as a matter of international competition in energy technology. Given the lack of a coherent strategy to address the climate crisis, Obama's policy objective was to keep energy prices down and prepare for health and climate change externalities.[37] When he left office, his delay of the Keystone XL notwithstanding, the U.S. was producing more oil than Saudi Arabia and more oil and gas than Russia.[38] Meanwhile, Greenland is green, corn is not growing on arable land, hurricanes ravage the Eastern seaboard and fires rage across the Southwest.

On the question of immigration, Obama earned a reputation as 'deporter-in-chief,' ousting as many as 2.7 million undocumented workers – more than any previous president. Rather than reforming immigration policy, Obama expanded the ineffective and cruel internment methods of Immigration and Customs Enforcement and Customs and Border Protection as a matter of national security. After September 11, Bush linked immigration policies to War on Terror security issues, creating law enforcement programmes that jumped from $23 million to $690 million for the period 2004 to 2011, affecting Latino and Muslim immigrants in particular. These policies were extended by Obama's 'smart enforcement' practices, which were enacted despite the fact that immigrants are less likely to commit crimes than American citizens. The number of deportations caused by the criminalization of immigrant status eventually became so suspect that in 2014 Obama responded to criticism by calling on the Department of Homeland Security to review its deportation practices.[39] Insofar as immigration law is connected to the Department of Labor, the practice of deportation falsely associates immigrant labour with unemployment and low wages. Although polls indicate that little more than 10 percent of workers are concerned about immigrant workers, 85 percent of Americans, especially the 50 million American Latinos, favour a path to citizenship for immigrant workers. The fact that immigrants contribute more to the American economy than they receive is hardly something to be celebrated since their contribution is due to a greater degree of labour exploitation. This international problem cannot be solved by trade wars, protectionism and racist bigotry.

As immigration is also under the jurisdiction of the Department of Justice, immigration raids add to the social costs of incarceration. In 2006, the U.S. spent close to $2 billion on the justice system. During Obama's two terms in office, one out of five black men have been in prison. More than 20,000 people are in solitary confinement, many of them suffering from mental illness. Although Obama opposed the War on Drugs, he defended the use of force by police and suppressed protests by trying to build bridges with law enforcement rather than by working to change the system. From the years 2009 to 2016, some 10,000 people were killed by police. Obama's Department of Justice ignored police abuse and racial profiling. Instead, he armed police departments with military-grade equipment, tripling the Pentagon's 1033 programme amounts from $34 million in 2008 to $91 million in 2010 and $787 million in 2014, the year that weaponized police showed up in Ferguson, a city in which the impoverished black population was under lockdown by a municipality that is funded through police fines.

Considered by Ford as the "biggest domestic war hawk in the history of the United States," Obama contributed to the criminalization of not only immigrants but citizens as well.[40] Obama's neoliberal policies of austerity were accompanied by securitization and the curtailment of civil liberties. He extended NSA spying and surveillance despite its illegality, spending more than $100 billion in tax dollars to intercept citizen communications with the most intrusive surveillance apparatus the world has ever seen. Obama then used more than $150 million in U.S. taxpayer money to help the UK's GCHQ do the same.

Government surveillance is justified as a matter of national security. Yet securitization did not prevent 340 mass shootings in the U.S. in 2017 alone. Even if none of these have anything to do with foreign terrorists, they are occurring at the same time that the U.S. has been involved in wars in the Middle East since 2001.[41] More than previous presidents, Obama was an instrument of intelligence agencies like the CIA, the NSA, the FBI and the State Department.[42] He invoked State Secrets Privilege to shield government wrongdoing and also extended the Patriot Act and similar emergency measures that were installed by George W. Bush, Colin Powell, Dick Cheney, John Brennan, Donald Rumsfeld and Condoleezza Rice. In terms of civil liberties, domestic policy overlaps with foreign policy. To avoid criticism, Obama shut down truth-tellers like Chelsea Manning, Edward Snowden and Julian Assange, prosecuting more whistleblowers than all previous administrations combined. He also blocked books and photographs by CIA and FBI agents that reported on torture by American soldiers. Obama partnered with police and the CIA to monitor Muslims, denying basic rights with respect to freedom of speech, freedom of assembly, association, religion, conscience and privacy.[43] U.S. intelligence is comprised of more than 1000 government organizations and close to 2000 private companies that operate from some 10,000 locations, intercepting the emails and phone conversations of citizens and the customers of compliant telecommunications companies. Illegal FBI wiretaps extend to email surveillance on foreign governments and human rights activists. Trump, for his part, advised Americans to get used to it. People like Snowden, who warn people of what is happening, are threatened with death as traitors.

Too Big to Jail

In 2009, according to the National Coalition for the Homeless, 67,000 U.S. veterans were homeless and 1.5 million were at risk of homelessness due to poverty and dismal living conditions.[44] That same year, Obama received the Nobel Peace Prize, awarded to him for his efforts in international diplomacy, especially for reaching out to the Muslim world. In 2010 he visited the home of Mahatma Gandhi, the leader of the Indian independence movement and advocate of nonviolent civil disobedience. He then went on to be the first president to be at war for every day of his eight years in the White House, ignoring anti-war activists and in 2016 dropping 26,000 bombs on Muslim countries. As the first black commander of the American military behemoth, Obama pursued the so-called War on Terror in Iraq, Afghanistan, Pakistan, Syria, Libya, Yemen and Somalia. He oversaw Special Operations in more than 138 countries, an increase by 130 percent since Bush and which led to the worst refugee crisis since WWII. Obama was without question dedicated to the expansion of the military-intelligence apparatus, extending the Patriot Act and the War on Terror that since 9/11 has killed as many as two million people, including 225,000 Americans, and cost taxpayers as much as $4 trillion dollars through deficit spending – all the better for the likes of Republican John Boehner or Democrat

Harry Reid to propose cuts to Social Security, Medicare and Medicaid. Under the rules of the Authorization to Use Military Force, Obama used drone strikes in Libya, Pakistan, Yemen, Afghanistan and Somalia, where any male of military age, whether civilian or not, could be targeted as an enemy combatant. Obama used drone strikes to kill as many as 9000 people with next to no challenge from Congress. According to U.N. Charter, drone strikes are considered illegal if the host country does not allow them, which means that Obama's drones were illegal everywhere except in Afghanistan, where the U.S. controlled a compliant puppet regime.[45]

Department of Defense spending increased during Obama's administration from $600 billion to $700 billion, which represents 34 percent of the world total for military spending and more than the next 9 countries combined. The American military destruction of Iraq and Afghanistan cost Americans $1 trillion, an average of $300 million per day, with trillions of dollars as well as thousands of human deaths unaccounted for. Obama also increased spending on nuclear weapons, across a span of three decades, for nuclear submarines, bombers, ballistic missiles, warheads and components. His war cabinet included Hillary Clinton, Robert Gates, Susan Rice and Joe Biden – Democrats with the same capitalist-imperialist worldview as Republicans like George W. Bush and John McCain. The continuation of Bush policies meant that Obama would not hold anyone accountable for war crimes. In the struggle for hearts and minds, Obama also encouraged militarism in higher education, contributing to a culture of organized violence. Student protesters and critical thinking were criminalized in the name of a market ethos that links research with military and intelligence objectives, subverting the public mission of the university.[46] As Trump took the reins from Obama, NATO war games were the largest since the Cold War. Trump's Jade Helm operations extended military training from designated sites to civilian spaces. What Matt Taibbi refers to as the two main devices of the fascist playbook, 'the big lie' and 'the scapegoat,' are now used routinely by Western powers, from Iraq's fabled WMDs to Sarin gas attacks in Syria and false claims of Russian threats to Ukraine, as means to create consent around criminal policies.[47]

American military operations in the Middle East are not only due to oil interests, but also to U.S. policy on the Israel-Palestine conflict. Ever since the 1960s, when Israel succeeded in destroying Arab secular nationalism, the country has been considered a strategic ally of the U.S. Since Israel signed a peace treaty with Egypt in 1979 and with Jordan in 1994, the country has been able to launch assaults on the neighbouring countries of Lebanon, Gaza and the West Bank without U.S. censure, leading to the war against Iraq and now threatening war against Iran.[48] Although Israel expanded settlements on Palestinian lands during his tenure, Obama claimed that Israel is defending itself. In 2008, the Israel Defense Forces killed some 300 people in Gaza and injured 800. Obama's advisor, David Axelrod, defended the incursions as acts of retaliation.

Obama applied a similar logic of just war in Afghanistan, where U.S. and NATO forces created a civil war between Pashtun nationalists, who are stronger today than in 2001, and the compliant and corrupt regimes of Hamid Karzai and Ashraf Ghani. Like his predecessor, Obama ignored the advice of Stanley McChrystal and David Petraeus, who denounced the conflict as both punitive and unwinnable, and opted instead for a counter-insurgency troop surge in the hope of pacifying the press and his Republican rivals.[49] The victory that can be said to come from bombing innocent civilians in peasant villages is the break-up of the traditional tribal system in favour of a national army that can be remote-controlled from Washington. Since the American intervention, the opium trade in Afghanistan, which was once a negligible feature of its economy, now represents the lion's share of exports, tripling in production after the U.S. invasion and nearing close to 90 percent of all global production in 2013. Obama's misguided policy of spending billions to bomb select opium farms did not prevent drug use in Afghanistan from doubling along with the doubling of unemployment.[50] The opioid epidemic has led to the worst drug crisis in American history. While Afghanistan is one of the poorest countries in the world, the U.S. in 2010 was dedicating $2 billion per week and 100,000 U.S. troops to bombing yet another country back to the Middle Ages.[51] Obama replaced the troops that were eventually withdrawn from Afghanistan with a 40 percent increase in bombings. He then sent the extra troops to neighbouring Pakistan, engaging in the so-called 'Af-Pak' situation with more enthusiasm than Bush. He pursued the Pashtun tribes that straddle both sides of the border with drones strikes, extending U.S. operations into Pakistani Kashmir. Although drone activity produces no American casualties – other than PTSD among drone operators and several suicides among Special Operation Command officers – 90 percent of the Pakistanis killed in drone strikes were "collateral" civilian deaths. In order to secure compliance from the Pakistani regime, the U.S. has killed some 16,000 Pakistani soldiers and militants, and displaced more than 3.5 million people, fuelling Islamist extremism.

The conflict in the Middle East was of course initiated with Bush's war in Iraq, which has killed more than one million Iraqi civilians and which is in violation of international law. Pursuing a policy that is euphemistically referred to as 'liberal imperialism,' Obama transformed the Iraq war into a 'black op,' or covert paramilitary operation that nevertheless involved as many as 50,000 troops in 2009. Despite his opposition to the war, Obama maintained a permanent military occupation of Iraq. The U.S. now controls Iraqi oil production and government policy. After the rise of the Islamic State of Iraq and the Levant (ISIS), which was armed in part through wilful neglect of state military arsenals, the U.S. could hardly leave Iraq. On the other hand, the U.S. has guaranteed nothing but the plunder and ruin of the country as it descended into extremism and systemic corruption. Obama expanded this theatre of operations by imposing sanctions on Iran. Even though the Americans have wished to overthrow the Iranian regime since the 1979 Revolution, they have sold weapons to Iraq as well as Iran to weaken both, later invading Iraq to divide and conquer every Muslim tendency, Kurdish, Shia and Sunni (Baathist). The U.S. has failed to stoke ethnic and civil conflict in Iran. It threatened the country against the development of nuclear weapons capacity by unleashing the Stuxnet computer virus in nuclear facilities and assassinating several nuclear scientists. Obama then boasted of the Iran nuclear deal as a milestone in diplomacy.[52] Iran agreed to the nuclear deal in the hope of improving relations with the West. Threats of military intervention resurfaced with Trump, however, whose trade sanctions caused the cost of living in Iran to triple.

Obama supported the war for regime change in Syria, authorizing special operations to train and arm anti-Bashar al-Assad rebels, many of whom were affiliated with al-Qaeda and al-Nusra jihadists. This was followed by the Russians, Iranians and Turks entering the conflict, with the U.S. vacillating on its commitments to both the Turks and the Kurds.[53] The role of the U.S. was less obvious in Syria than in Libya, an illegal war pursued without the approval of the United Nations Security Council and in defiance of Congress and the War Powers Act. Having decided that it was time for Muammar Gaddafi to be replaced, Obama shifted from enforcing a no-fly zone to attacking the country with 14,000 bombing sorties in the name of human rights, a decision overseen by Hillary Clinton, Susan Rice and Samantha Powers, and with the assistance of France's Nicolas Sarkozy and the U.K.'s David Cameron. The butchering of Gaddafi's body, which was put on public display in a Benghazi meat locker, was proclaimed a victory for the Libyan people. Due to the timing, many assumed that the Libyan intervention was part of the Arab Spring. The conflict was rather created by mercenaries and fuelled by lies that were fabricated against Gaddafi, who had offered amnesty to rebel forces. After insurgents slaughtered people in Tripoli, Obama and his allies warned that Benghazi would suffer the same fate and that Gaddafi was planning a genocide. This did come about, but only after the 2011 NATO bombing and the deposition of the Revolutionary Leader of the Libyan Arab Republic. Here as elsewhere, imperialist powers were mostly concerned to control economic resources, wary of China's economic takeover of the African continent and Gaddafi's refusal to allow Western military bases in Libya in preference for African unity through a common African currency, resource nationalism and control of Libyan oil reserves. Under Gaddafi, who had the support of the majority of the population, Libya had managed some of the most significant social welfare achievements in Africa in terms of education, health care, housing, life expectancy, gender freedom and the elimination of homelessness. The NATO intervention destroyed these gains and extended conflict to Mali, where imperialist powers stoked and weaponized ethnic conflicts. By 2017, African refugees were being sold for hundreds of dollars in Libyan slave markets.[54]

The scenario in Libya was the opposite of the more confusing conflict involving the Boko Haram in 2012, which was on the one hand targeted by the State Department as a terrorist organization and on the other hand funded through financial support to the Nigerian government. What the two cases have in common is the use of terrorism as a pretext for military takeover.[55] The illegality of Obama's actions in Libya were redoubled by the NATO murder of civilians and journalists, as well as the protection of outlaw rebels, who funnelled weapons to jihadists operating in Syria and elsewhere. Among Obama's war crimes, the Libyan intervention was carried out under the smokescreen of a 'military humanism' that justifies the destruction and control of any anti-imperialist nation that is perceived to be a threat to international security.[56] The reality is more perverse. It is not only that non-compliant state regimes are an obstacle to empire, but that manufactured conflicts are leveraged to advance the interests of the military industry, which makes short shrift of international law. The Arab Spring not only provided a pretext for the Libyan operation, however, but contributed to real worry in the establishment about democratization. The Americans were not happy about the removal of Hosni Mubarak and turned a blind eye when the regime of Abdel Fattah el-Sisi began to execute his Muslim Brotherhood opponents, now designated terrorists. Qatar and the United Arab Emirates participated in the bombing of Libya and also aided Saudi Arabia in its bombing and incursion into Bahrain. Obama sold the Saudis $100 billion in weapons and supported its destruction and control of Yemen, where the civil war has killed 100,000 civilians and brought 10 million to the brink of starvation, a situation that is considered the world's worst humanitarian crisis.[57] The bipartisan foreign policy preference for radical Islamist states authorized Obama to veto the U.N. Security Council and block actions against war crimes by the International Criminal Court.

In Ukraine, Obama ignored the civil war aspects of the Maidan uprising as fascist and anti-Russian forces took over the government. He denounced the Russian occupation of the Crimea in favour of Ukrainian territorial integrity but ignored the referendum in Crimea in which 97 percent of the population preferred accession to the Russian Federation to a full-out conflict with the capital, which is now constitutionally anti-communist. The U.S. not only mobilized support for Ukraine to isolate Russia, but in doing so stoked a civil conflict with the Russian majority in Donetsk and Luhansk, encircling Russia with NATO troops in Eastern Europe.[58] In addition to contradictory trade relations, anti-Russia and anti-China hysteria continued with Obama along lines established during the Cold War. With regard to China, Obama proclaimed a diplomatic 'Pivot to Asia,' seeking not only to redress America's trade imbalance, but to use military challenges in the South China Sea to advance its strategic interests. The pivot gave Trump the prerogative to threaten a starving North Korea with fire and fury "the likes of which the world has never seen before."[59]

American foreign policy regarding Latin America did not improve after Hugo Chávez gifted Obama a copy of Eduardo Galeano's *Open Veins of Latin America*, a critique of U.S. imperialism. A less bloody regime change operation than the one perpetrated on Libya was orchestrated in Honduras, where Manuel Zelaya was apprehended in a night raid and expulsed to Costa Rica. Although Obama denounced the coup, the U.S. was involved through the National Endowment for Democracy, the School of the Americas and assistance by the U.S. Agency for International Development to right-wing elements that funded and trained anti-government groups. These include the coup leaders and torturers that are supported by the Western Hemispheric Institute for Security Cooperation. Zelaya was denounced by the Clinton State Department, which said nothing about the coup regime's more than 1000 human rights violations, including assassinations.[60] Not unlike Gaddafi, Zelaya was not deposed for what he was doing wrong, but for what he was doing right, which included the kinds of liberal reforms demanded by trade unions, Indigenous groups and social activists, including minimum wage hikes and public control of the communications sector. Since the coup, the poverty rate in Honduras has increased by 70 percent and the country now has one of the highest murder rates in the world.

In Columbia, arguably the most right-wing country in Latin America, Obama garnered access to military bases, raising the ire of other countries in the region, least of all Venezuela, where the Trump administration assisted the self-appointed leader, Juan Guaidó, in his failed takeover attempts. Obama continued the U.S. policy of military support for the regime in Columbia, where since the late 1980s the government has displaced 4 million civilians and killed 2700 union leaders.[61] A note of optimism was struck in 2014 when Obama agreed with Cuban leader Raúl Castro to restore diplomatic relations after decades of embargo. The one-sidedness of the agreement is obvious enough when one considers Obama's failure to hold to his election promise to close the Guantánamo Bay detention and torture centre by 2010. The Bush administration had released the majority of prisoners before Obama's tenure. Afterwards, as many as 55 detainees were held indefinitely without charges, many of them resorting to hunger strikes to bring attention to their plight as 'forever prisoners' in this legal black hole.[62] Obama avoided transferring the remaining prisoners to civilian courts and granting fair and speedy trials, thereby extending the practice of indefinite detention. He did release the 'torture memos' that documented how the Department of Justice's Office of Legal Counsel had in 2002 and 2005 redefined torture so that it could be implemented by CIA operatives. He also released some of the photographs of prison torture in Iraq and Afghanistan.[63]

The function of the Guantánamo Bay dungeon was by and large supplanted by Obama's use of drone killings, which, along with assassination, torture, extraordinary rendition and indefinite detention are some of the most incriminating aspects of his presidency. Obama failed to prosecute and rather shielded the Bush administration officials and lawyers who had worked to legalize torture – people like CIA director John Brennan. He even gave some of them positions in his administration, allowing the CIA to oversee and censor the reports. He absolved torture on the basis that those who implemented the crime were acting on orders.[64] Obama is thus partly responsible for Trump's nomination of Gina Haspel, a Bush-era black site administrator, as the CIA's deputy director.[65] Changes to the National Defense Authorization Act of 1961, which abolished *habeas corpus* and basic constitutional guarantees of due process, made possible the indefinite military detention of U.S. citizens and non-citizens. By extending the War on Terror, Obama continued with practices of indefinite detention and extrajudicial assassinations by the military-intelligence apparatus. Although he banned the use of torture, extraordinary rendition allows prisoners to be sent to other countries where it can take place, despite the fact that this practice violates the U.N. Convention Against Torture. According to Steve Hendricks, under the doctrine of universal jurisdiction, any signatory of the Convention can and is obliged to prosecute a political leader, after they leave office, if any instance of the crime has gone unpunished. Bill Clinton, who signed the Convention on behalf of the U.S., ordered several cases of extraordinary rendition, as did George W. Bush. By refusing to investigate Bush's crimes, Obama simultaneously absolved himself as well as Clinton.[66] Where his own actions have been in question, as with drone strikes and assassinations, he invoked state secrets against investigations.[67]

Obama made extensive use of aerial drone strikes, which are run from out of dozens of secret facilities, with little to no oversight or even understanding by the House of Representatives. Under the guidance of the CIA and the Joint Special Operations Command, Obama authorized 'kill lists' of targets selected for assassination, preferring this method rather than ground troops to remove suspected enemies. Obama authorized some 563 drone strikes, compared with Bush's 57 strikes, killing between 400 and 800 civilians, most of these in Pakistan, Somalia and Yemen. He also supervised the targeted killing of approximately 3000 people in Iraq, Libya, Afghanistan, Pakistan, Yemen and Somalia. In addition to the creation of a global assassination network, Obama executed three American citizens without trial and due process. A former constitutional law professor, Obama flouted basic democratic procedures in a manner that is fitting of the philosophy of the Nazi jurist Carl Schmitt. He used the AUMF to kill al-Qaeda propagandist and U.S. citizen Anwar al-Awlaki by drone strike in Yemen on September 30, 2011. Al-Awlaki's 16-year-old son was later "accidentally" killed by a separate drone strike. Trump later went on to kill one of al-Awlaki's daughters.[68] Obama's barbarism was also displayed with the assassination of Osama bin Laden, which has been promoted as one of his greatest achievements as commander in chief. Bin Laden was killed with impunity in Pakistan by Special Forces that more typically exercise discretionary 'kill or capture' orders for enemy combatants. The reason that bin Laden was killed on sight was to avoid the investigation of CIA ties to al-Qaeda that date back to the 1980s and that give reason to 9/11 conspiracy theories. The unceremonious tossing of bin Laden's corpse into the sea is of a piece with the lawlessness that led to the murder of Saddam Hussein and Muammar Gaddafi.

Most of Obama's crimes were committed with the authorization of the Department of Justice headed by Attorney General Eric Holder, the first African American to occupy the post of top law enforcement officer. For those who criticize Obama's post-racial equanimity, Holder is considered by many to be more cognizant of black identity and civil rights, calling on whites to take more responsibility for the problems of racism. His Civil Rights Division had the largest budget to work with and was celebrated by the NAACP for its defence of the Voting Rights Act as well as fair housing, fair lending, education, desegregation and same-sex marriage. Holder was also praised for his work against employment discrimination and mandatory minimum sentencing.[69] He otherwise reinforced Obama's obedience to corporate, military and financial interests, including the unauthorized launching of wars of aggression, unlimited executive power to assassinate U.S. citizens without due process, drone killings, indefinite detention, failure to prosecute torture, invocation of government secrecy, the militarization of police and protection of police crimes, warrantless NSA surveillance, crackdown on whistleblowers and protesters under anti-terrorism laws (including protests in Ferguson), the deportation of millions of immigrants, ecological negligence in the Gulf of Mexico, Wall Street money laundering and the bankrupting of Detroit.[70] The sum total of these contraventions and semi-legal justifications of presidential power amount to the extirpation of democratic rights. Defying the Constitution and the Fifth Amendment, Holder introduced a distinction between judicial process and due process, giving Obama license to kill citizens and persecute Assange, Manning and Snowden under the Espionage Act. Holder was therefore the law behind most of Obama's too big to fail and too big to jail disasters, making both of them right-wing operatives who conspired against the American people and who should be prosecuted as war criminals. Obama passed the baton of state criminality to Trump, who immediately declared that the War on Poverty was over as he lowered taxes for the top 2 percent of earners, resulting in more upward redistribution of wealth and $5.1 trillion in lost tax revenue.

That Creed Reaffirmed

As a career politician, Obama's calling card was black respectability and bipartisan centrism. It would be ironic that Obama said so little about race if it were not for what this reveals about the neoliberal version of colourblindness. If neoliberalism and globalization imply that equality is to be measured by the fact that powerful people who are identified with groups that are structurally disadvantaged are beyond ethics, morality and the law, then the ideology of universality could indeed be considered bunk, if only that assessment did not fully justify the rise of the authoritarian right. In such a race to the bottom, why should anyone be less fascist than anyone else? In this regard, one might also think that it is easy enough to distinguish between ideologies that are genuinely left, right and centre. But things are not so obvious. According to the World Values Survey and European Values Survey for the years 2008 to 2014, liberal centrists are more hostile to democratic institutions than are those who are considered to be on the extreme left and extreme right. Consequently, the average citizen in Western democracies is increasingly disposed to accept authoritarian politicians as pragmatists who can get things done.[71]

Getting things done was without doubt the gist of Biden's 2020 No Malarkey campaign slogan and speeches. For the 2020 presidential race, Obama avoided having anything to do with his former vice president until it was clear that Biden was the only way to stop Sanders. Although Sanders kept his promise and began campaigning for Biden as early as March, the now entrepreneurial Obama avoided being further associated with Biden until 20 days before the November 4 election. By that time Trump had only a 13 percent chance of winning. When interviewed about his vision for 2021 and beyond, Obama shamed voters for the failures of his administration, suggesting that if progressives (had) wanted progressive legislation, they would have to "get out there" and work harder.[72]

The nihilism that is at the core of today's liberalism is nothing new. According to Chris Hedges, the classical liberal belief in the use of critical reason for the sake of human progress has been in retreat since the period after WWI, when corporate capitalism began to propagate a narcissistic mass culture and a free market bonanza for imperialist globalization. Since the Cold War, the liberal class has preferred to fight against organized labour and leftist ideas than to reform corporate state regimes. As the quest for profits polluted the ecosphere and gave way to militarism, liberal capitalism staked its hopes on science and technology.[73] One can speculate whether or not corporate power has effectively bought out and decimated the liberal class, including its moral and political leaders, intellectuals and artists.

For Tariq Ali, the death of the liberal class is more specific to the fallout of 1989. With the disappearance of the Soviet Union as an ideological challenge to unfettered capitalism, social democracy in Western Europe has been set on a course where centre-left parties align with the centre-right.[74] Neglecting leftist politics and the needs of workers, the Americanization of politics, as he calls it, makes parties redundant due to their servitude to the mechanisms of austerity – financial deregulation, cuts to public spending, tax cuts for the rich, the sale and privatization of public services, unemployment and the casualization of labour, free trade, foreign direct investment – and impunity – the economic and ecological instability that is regulated though militarism, immigration policy and policing. Like Bill Clinton, Tony Blair and François Hollande, Obama was a product of the liberal-conservative coalition that catered to the wealthy by attacking public welfare. If the only significance of Obama's blackness was his ability to encourage African-American and liberal voters to identify with vested interests, then we need to be more aware of the role that identity plays in contemporary class conflicts. Obama was the intelligence community's preferred candidate after Bush insofar as his ethnicity could be used against a populist thrust from the right or the left. The baiting of Obama as both a Nazi and a communist extremist, as a Muslim terrorist and divider-in-chief, largely served to obscure his role as an extreme centrist. In the end, however, the first black *president* did not fare as well as the first *black* president, even if he did little more for the black agenda than use some folksy language on occasion and swagger on his way to and from the podium.

The neoliberal consensus enforces the kind of reverse colourblindness that admits a person's qualities on the basis of progressive anti-racism and anti-sexism but ignores their politics. Anti-racism won Obama the support and the affection of the black middle class and the glitterati, including millionaire celebrities like Ellen DeGeneres, Jerry Seinfeld, Leonardo DiCaprio, Tom Hanks, Oprah, Jay-Z (Sean Carter) and Michael Jordan. It is celebrity groupies rather than world leaders who were represented in Obama's White House farewell video. The last concert at the White House, presented by Black Entertainment

Television, included Mavis Staples, Bob Dylan, Tony Bennett, Blind Boys of Alabama, Common, Yolanda Adams, De La Soul, Usher, Jill Scott, Bell Biv DeVoe, Chance the Rapper, Frank Ocean, Swiss Beatz, Busta Rhymes, Ludacris and Lin-Manuel Miranda. The Obamas' farewell event included Jay-Z, Oprah Winfrey, Samuel L. Jackson, Stevie Wonder and Usher on the private guest list. Actor Jesse Williams celebrated Obama's combination of smarts and cool. If smart means being able to get away with murder and cool means being indifferent to the plight of others, then Williams knows what he is talking about. It might be unfair to expect everyone to understand how it is that neoliberal policy in government and discourse theory in intellectual circles allows the politics of anti-oppression to combine with predatory capitalism and the destruction of legal rights. Regardless, the Trump victory was a small if confused indication that many Americans understood that the Obama administration did little to curb oppression. Black businesses did not benefit from Obama's economic stimulus. Unemployment among blacks grew to twice the rate for whites. Obama did nothing to mitigate incarceration, including sentences for illegal drug possession. Median black household income dropped by more than 10 percent during his tenure, double the amount for whites. Black poverty increased by 25 percent, black students were expelled at higher rates than previously, and blacks were twice as likely to be uninsured as whites. Blacks who are 25 percent less likely to own their own home, and who were sold discriminatory subprime loans, caught hell as Obama bailed out predator banksters.

As Tariq Ali argued in 2010, after Bush left the White House, there was no fundamental change other than the mood music.[75] Perhaps it is just as well if the only thing of some value that one can attribute to the Obama presidency is the soundtrack.[76] Beyond that, the post-representational logic of his administration was an instance of what happens when culture and politics are reduced to the quest for power. How is it that the radical tradition has been supplanted by the pursuit of individual wealth and status, or that corruption, scandal and the will to power has replaced a demand for justice that requires both commitment and disinterestedness?[77] The suggestion that the protests and riots against police violence that erupted in Ferguson in 2014 were indirect indictments of the Obama administration is more retrospective wishful thinking than it is evidenced by BLM critiques of Obama.[78] While protesters did criticize his policy of militarizing police forces, the role given to his Department of Justice had more to do with managing conflict through the criminalization of dissent than police reform.

After Obama, Trump was not an exception to the logic of post-representation but rather its most right-wing exemplar. When Trump emitted one of his improprieties, for instance, by stating his preference for immigrants from Norway rather than Haiti, El Salvador, Nigeria and Afghanistan, referring to the latter as “shithole countries,” the Internet glowed like a million points of light. Among his countless improprieties, Trump declared in May 2020 that he would break with tradition by not unveiling at the end of his term the official White House portrait of his predecessor. Obama’s aides suggested that he could care less so long as Trump is in office.[79] As Jodi Dean argues, Trump not only displayed his enjoyment of power and inequality, he allowed others to interpassively enjoy through him, giving people permission to express racism, sexism and hatred. If liberals also enjoyed their outrage, using Trump as a prop for their jouissance and disgust with the working class, Trump additionally allowed them to remain within their complacent scripts, directing both parties of the ruling class against socialist alternatives.[80] When during the 2020 race Trump threatened that he would not respect the results of the November election and was colluding with rightists organizing voter suppression and intimidation campaigns at voting stations, Biden, Obama and the Democratic establishment were practically silent on the matter.[81] The Democratic Party put up more resistance to shady information about Russian sources spending $1000 on Facebook ads during the 2016 election than to Trump’s direct links to the extrajudicial murder of Michael Reinoehl and a neo-fascist plot to kidnap and execute Gretchen Whitmer, the Democratic governor of Michigan.[82] On January 6, as Trump watched his followers attack the Capitol building to stop the election count, Obama was incommunicado. Beyond the neoliberal endgame, only strong working-class and anti-imperialist subjectivizations have a chance to bring about a change to the system of global capitalism.[83] Until then, and as identity politics continues to trump socialism, things are likely to continue getting very bad indeed.

CH.3: WOKE AESTHETICS

Woke: 1) To wake up in past tense. i.e. "I woke up today." 2) The act of being very pretentious about how much you care about a social issue. i.e. "While you are obsessing with the Kardashians, there are millions of homeless in the world. Stay woke."

– Urban Dictionary

If you see 'em in the streets give 'em Kanye's best / Why? They mad they ain't famous (God damn) / They mad they're still nameless (Talk that talk, man) / Her man in the store can't seem to get Kanye fresh / But we still hood famous (God damn) / Yeah we still hood Famous

– Kanye West, 'Famous'

The French philosopher Michel Foucault famously introduced *The Order of Things* with a discussion of Diego Velásquez's Baroque painting, *Las Meninas*.[1] The large canvas depicts the artist's studio in the royal palace of King Philip IV of Spain. It is ironic that Foucault mentions this work as a prelude to a book that announces the death of the subject since *Las Meninas* is a work that heralds the advent of liberal humanism. The contrivances of the painting, which bridges the world of the Renaissance and the modern era, are dedications to humanist virtue, where the vanity that is a feature of the work as a royal commission is tempered by courtly manners and studied modesty. This virtuoso display of classical mimesis captures the paradoxes of the age: the puritanical naturalism of genre pictures, the disenchantment brought about by the scientific worldview, competition through imperial art collections, and the epistemological totalizations that subtend absolutism. Foucault writes about the work as a "system of feints" in which subject and object, sovereign and vassal, oscillate like the thresholds of "two incompatible visibilities."[2] Humanist artists like Velásquez tried to surpass themselves for the glory of their patrons. Like the *trompe l'oeil* ceilings of the Carraccis, or the beggars hired by Carravaggio to model as saints and Greek gods, the entire undertaking is played as though a game. If all the world's a stage, as Shakespeare wrote, then reality has been conquered by illusion.

Exit liberal humanism. Enter postmodernism. After the world of the Renaissance artist was displaced by the conditions of independent studio production and market exchange, only the avant gardes could raise the level of culture to the status it occupied in the pre-modern world, leading in the early twentieth century to the kinds of modernist experimentation that suited the institutions of high culture, or in the case of radical experiments, that sought to transform everyday life. With the advent of postwar consumer culture and the détente of the Cold War, artistic transgressions that still made some claim to Enlightenment critique, which precludes fascist experiments, were by and large contained by the order of global capitalism.[3] With the abandonment of utopian thinking, the pessimist *philosophes* of French theory heralded the return of the Baroque. Jean-François Lyotard defined the new sublime as an effect of the post-industrial techno-scientific revolution. Whereas academic painters wanted to ennoble themselves and their professions, the democratic access to historical-political signs now belonged to the anonymous mass citizen, a "virtual prince" whose way of thinking has more in common with photography than painting.[4] This new reality does not reinstate make-believe, however, since the acceleration of obsolescence in the consumer universe accepts the infinite as immanent. Walter Benjamin's writings from the 1930s had already assessed the loss of the aura of the work of art through mass culture's rationalization of social experience. With the postmodern it was not only the aura that had withered, but also the surrounding reality. In the writings of Jean Baudrillard, the counterfeit strategies of the Baroque era had been replaced by simulation as the "dominant scheme in the current code-governed phase."[5] Paul Virilio offered the technical guide to Foucault's archaeology of the subject, assessing the human as a matter of machine logic. Nano-technological miniaturization, biotechnology and media prostheses would replace ideological superstructures as well as Althusserian infrastructures with the intra-organic intrusion into the living, ushering in a post-evolutionary and meta-designed post-body, grafted into tele-action.[6] Even if the art world understandably went crazy for the Bruce Mau-designed Zone books on the history of the human body, or Peter Greenaway's chiliastic decentrings of 'man,' Virilio's post-humanist subject was more a lab rat than the measure of anything significant. This line of thinking led to affect theory, animal studies and assemblage theory, a largely apolitical second wave of behaviourism.

Around this time, Cultural Studies scholar Dick Hebdige argued that much of the postmodernists' scaremongering was the morbid work of marginalized and overeducated cultural critics who were bored with their university jobs. Like Benjamin before him, Hebdige thought that it was better to give people something to do than to prophesize the end of everything. The style politics of subcultures could offer some kind of redemptive alternative to the "sorrow in the zeitgeist."[7] The call was gladly taken up by critics like Kobena Mercer, who looked into black hairstyles as a means to fight against Eurocentric definitions of beauty.[8] While the boom in Cultural Studies was more a facet of the culture industry than its point of self-knowledge, it nevertheless emphasized forms of resistance that exist within popular culture, a realm that critical theory had marginalized. However, if style rather than literariness could encourage cultural democracy, it could also, as Meaghan Morris argued, lead to utter banality, pre-emptively prohibiting reflection on one's complicity with capitalism, commodification and conditions of exploitation. The other side of *Crocodile Dundee* was not only the reality of Indigenous life, but also a deadly foreign policy that is live on television and in the routines of everyday life.[9]

Beneath the agential hubris of consumer politics and the vaunting of new subjectivities was the political economy of the Thatcher and Reagan revolutions that had delegitimized universality, citizenship, civil liberties, work safety, environmental and consumer protections, social security, education, housing and health care services. The oil crisis and recession of the 1970s opened the centralized state to supply-side economics, monetarism and free trade. All of this was backed up with regressive notions of individual initiative and rewards for those who work for them. Even if you found yourself at the bottom of the neo-Darwinist hierarchy, you were promised that the benefits would trickle down. Multinational think tanks wrote government policy and the mainstream media supported them by celebrating cigar-smoking entrepreneurs and attacking the down and out with television crime serials. Incredulity towards the meta-narrative of progress was expressed in the celebration of the status quo, referred to by Hal Foster as a 'postmodernism of reaction.'[10] In mass culture this could be anything from the spectacle of Michael Jackson's post-racial transformation to Madonna's blonde ambition to challenge the patriarchy by becoming filthy rich. Repeating tired clichés proved to be more lucrative with audiences than challenging them, if not oneself, with difficult art, film and music, now denounced as elitist. In contemporary art, the reactionaries took a page from Ronald Reagan: they attacked the modernist avant gardes as well as their countercultural successors and affirmed consumer populism as a strategy to outflank radical critique and create a market-friendly version of elitism. Artists returned to traditional materials, like oil painting and bronze sculpture, and went to work for Sotheby's or Saatchi rather than the people. Neo-Expressionism celebrated narcissistic flatulence and abject art offered a neurotic version of the same.

While these artists, according to Foster, hid their political affiliations, they had nothing to worry about since postmodernism had taught them recipes for success by keeping things playful, anarchic, performative, dispersed, rhizomatic, ironic, indeterminate and immanent. Fredric Jameson, along with other Marxist scholars like David Harvey and Edward Soja, came into conflict with postmodernists and feminists on account of the supposed failure of Marxist cultural analysis to give credence to questions of subjectivity and difference, which, since at least Ernesto Laclau and Chantal Mouffe's theory of radical democracy, had become *de rigueur*.[11] The conflict between 'primary' class contradictions and the 'secondary' contradictions of nation, religion, race, gender and sexuality had been short-circuited ever since Foucault reputedly dethroned the critique of political economy. The great code turned out to be Marx's *Capital* and not the Christian Bible, as Northrop Frye had thought. Postmodernists pandered a culturalized appropriation of Gramsci according to which hegemony no longer referred to capitalist exploitation but to the multiple ways in which people embody power. The politics of subjectivity made it seem that it was more important to be weirdly marginal than for people to have a decent-paying job with health benefits. Since the Seattle protests against globalization, however, the pluralist focus on difference was prorogued by the realization that progressive forces are losing the class war something fierce. The 2000s thus witnessed the re-radicalization of culture, with a politicized socially engaged art becoming what Gregory Sholette has referred to as "the unconfirmed major contender for an avant-garde redux."[12] One of the important sites for social practice art was Occupy Wall Street, which was supported by and gave rise to a number of activist artist collectives, including Strike Debt, Rolling Jubilee, Sandy Relief, Occupy the Pipeline, Occupy Homes, Occupy Museums, Gulf Labor, Natural History Museum, Flood Wall Street, Art Against Police & Displacement, Direct Action Front for Palestine, Idle No More, Decolonize This Place, MTL+, People's Climate March, Black Lives Matter and Hands Up Don't Shoot. According to Yates McKee, it is not only that many artists were involved in OWS, but that Occupy created a new situation in which contemporary art was replaced with movement-based cultural production.[13] In only a few years, the identitarian thrust of BLM and MeToo would eclipse OWS's attention to political economy, with Decolonize This Place leading socially engaged art's intersectional turn.

In the speech that he gave in Zuccotti Park, Slavoj Žižek famously said to the assembled OWS activists: "Do not fall in love with yourselves. We have a nice time here. But remember, carnivals come cheap."[14] While this statement may seem far removed from the work of Kehinde Wiley and Amy Sherald, a Lacanian connection can be made through Gina Dent's introduction to Michele Wallace's DIA project on Black Popular Culture. Dent associates blackness with the joy of collective experience, but also with Jacques Lacan's notion of jouissance. Blackness, she says, is a mythic construct, and so black people's love of blackness, in particular through cultural objects, must be recognized as a fantasy, leading from innocent romance and market conditions to a cultural politics of representation that acknowledges when it is that popular culture has supplanted oppositional practices.[15] She mentions, in this regard, Cornel West's distinction between conservative behaviourists – those who translate the personal directly into symbolic and structural oppressions – and liberal structuralists – those who assume that structural oppressions determine personal relationships. Both approaches, West says, contribute to nihilism and the occlusion of radical cultural critique.[16] The desire to see people who 'look like me' immortalized in postmodern pop art may well be a carnivalesque conceit, but these cultural artefacts also contain, to put things in the words of Mikhail Bakhtin, heteroglossic accents that indirectly register the history of class struggles.[17]

The reception of the Obama portraits involved a great deal of mediated jouissance. People fell in love with Sherald's and Wiley's paintings without much thought given to what seeing oneself represented by the Obamas had to do with postmodern culture or political economy. Their paintings invite comparison with the work of other contemporary black artists, such as Robert Colescott, Faith Ringgold, Renée Cox, Barkley Hendricks, Henry Taylor, Sanford Biggers, Kerry James Marshall, Jordan Casteel, Devan Shimoya, Jennifer Packer, Tschabalala Self, Njideka Akunyili-Crosby, Wangechi Mutu, Derrick Adams, Lynette Yiadom-Boakye, Jeff Sonhouse, Ebony Patterson, Mario Moore, Iona Rozeal Borwn, Toyin Ojih Odutola, Awol Erizku, Rotimi Fani-Kayode and Mickalene Thomas. The marketable cachet of postmodern painting draws its relevance, on the one hand, from technical skill and pictorial style, and on the other, from the field of power, as argued previously. Wiley, for instance, enjoyed his Peter the Great moment when his *Rumors of War* (2019) equestrian bronze was installed in Times Square. Celebrating queer black masculinity, the statue of a young man with dreadlocks and a hoodie was later to be moved to Richmond, Virginia, where it was to be added to the city's display of ten Confederate generals. The president of the Virginia Museum of Fine Arts board of trustees considered the acquisition the most important that the museum had ever made. By June 2020, after BLM protests erupted anew, anti-racism activists were busy tearing down Confederate monuments along with statues of Christopher Columbus, George Washington, Thomas Jefferson, Andrew Jackson, Abraham Lincoln and Theodore Roosevelt. Wiley's work was installed outside the museum a few months before Richmond's monumental equestrian statue of Robert E. Lee came down.[18]

If for decades progressive artists like Judith Baca have been calling for work that deals with public issues rather than 'cannon in the park' and 'hero on a horse' types of display, what cultural politics are served by this new sort of identitarian propaganda?[19] The status hierarchies of the art world are doubly discriminatory for black artists; first, in terms of the distributional inequality between the majority of artists and the few who achieve art world consecration in terms of dealer, gallery, critic and museum attention; and secondly, in the racial and gender inequality represented by the world's art collections.[20] However, as Cedric Johnson would have it, racial progress in today's progressive neoliberal institutions is pursued through a "low-frequency war against the working class" and the vindication of "racial and gender justice for those who are the most integrated and ideologically committed to neoliberalism."[21] For example, the institutional success of the feminist and anti-racist Nigerian émigré writer Chimamanda Ngozi Adichie is not unrelated to her support of politicians like Clinton and Obama. Her demure performance of elite privilege replays 80s yuppie ambition for the woke set, who gobble up her rudimentary righteousness with apathetic enthusiasm.

The leftist alternative to progressive neoliberalism has not to date organized as a socialist left, but rather as a pragmatic populism that is represented by politicians like Bernie Sanders, Alexandria Ocasio-Cortez and the Squad of activist politicians like Ilhan Omar and Cori Bush. Since the re-emergence of the far right, which stokes culture wars as a smokescreen with which to muddle the socio-economic foundations of class conflict, left populists tend to argue for social solidarity against what they misconstrue as the class 'reductionism' and 'essentialism' of the labour left.[22] In some ways, progressive left populism has also constituted a post-representational post-politics that shares with progressive neoliberalism an aspirational culture of recognition and social justice. The more entrepreneurial artists who are willing to ride the dragon of neoliberalism can be said to have preserved aspects of the postmodernism of reaction. An example of this can be found in Micaela Giovannotti and Joyce B. Korotkin's notion of a "neo-postmodern" Baroque. These curators of the exhibition *Neo-Baroque!* express the restorationist character of their project with the assertion that passion and beauty are back with a vengeance. Replaying the 1980s critique of minimalism and conceptualism, which echoed the way that neoconservatives criticized government regulation and taxation, they celebrate the reappearance in the twenty-first century of symbolic representation, surface splendour and abyssal ornamentation, that is, over and against intellect and ideology.[23] In the case of Wiley and Sherald, this second generation replay of the 1980s in the 2000s combines with a belated identity politics to produce *woke aesthetics*. Woke aesthetics separates social justice issues from radical left tendencies and hitches its wagon to "progressive" neoliberal ideology.

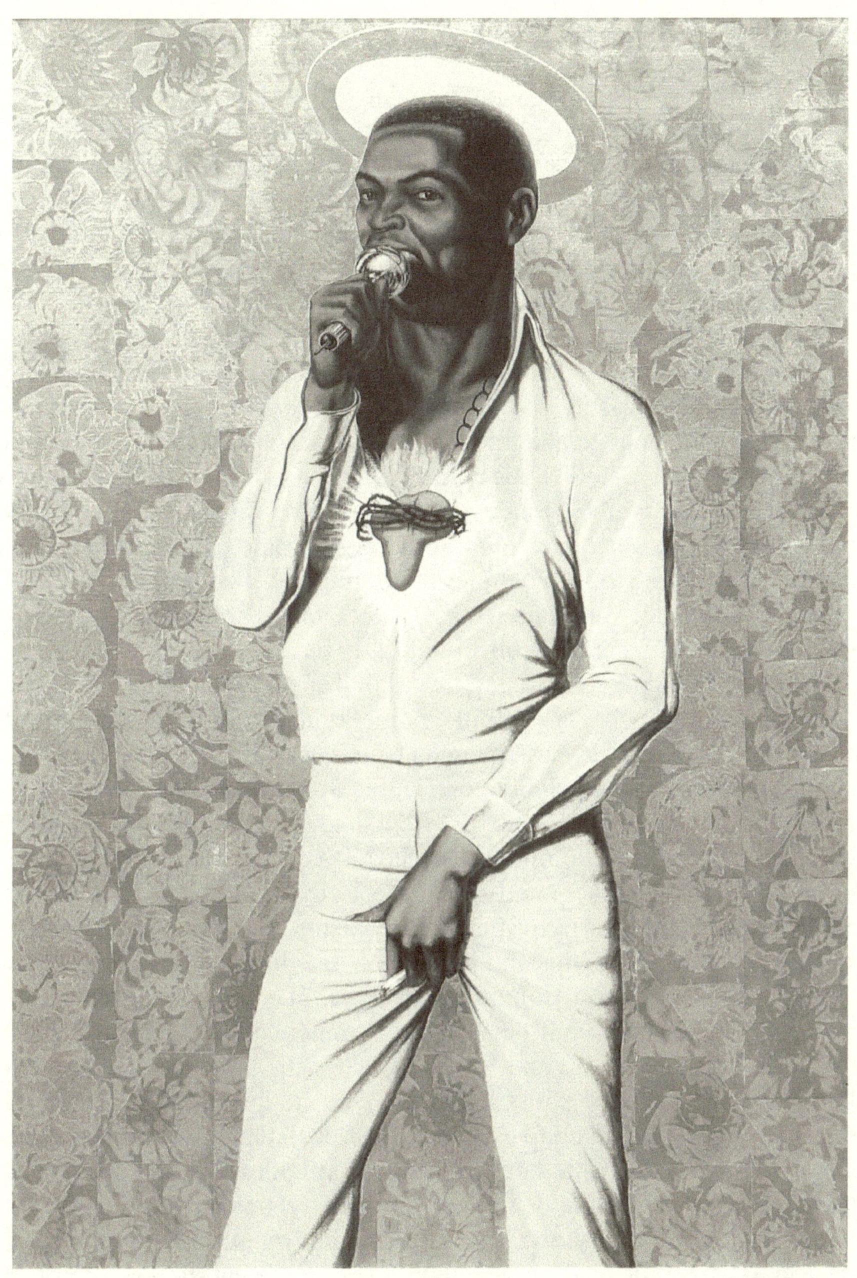

Barkley L. Hendricks, ***Fela: Amen, Amen, Amen, Amen...*** (detail), 2002. Oil and variegated leaf on linen canvas, hand-carved (by artist) and burned wooden frame, altarpiece armature, 27 pairs of high heels, 169.55 x 118.75 cm (152.4 x 101.6 cm unframed), with 152.4 cm altarpiece. © Estate of Barkley L. Hendricks. Courtesy of the artist's estate and Jack Shainman Gallery, New York.

The Artsy Vanguard

In April 2008 the website Artsy profiled Amy Sherald as part of its list of the 50 most influential artists in contemporary art. Sherald acknowledges in the interview that although it is sometimes difficult to know when an artist has become a household name, for her it is undoubtedly when she was commissioned to paint the portrait of Michelle Obama, at which point she went from working under-the-radar to instant celebrity. She was soon afterwards represented by the prestigious gallery of Hauser & Wirth.[24] Artsy's art market editor, Anna Louie Sussman, reported that after the NPG unveiling, Sherald's Chicago gallerist, Monique Meloche, received countless inquiries from celebrities and collectors around the world. Christie's New York also received calls from prospective buyers, who were happy to add their names to a waiting list that Christie's head of contemporary art, Sara Friedlander, says is comprised of people who think of the Obamas as royalty.[25] Since, on average, Sherald can paint as many as ten paintings in one year, she could not in her lifetime paint all of the people who after the White House commission would now like a portrait from her. As a condition of sale for some works, collectors are promising to eventually donate the portrait to a public collection. Early buyers paid anywhere between $8,000 and $12,000 per item, rising to $35,000 and $50,000 after Sherald won the 2016 Outwin Boochever Portrait Competition. A year before she won this National Portrait Gallery award, Sherald had been shortlisted for the presidential commission, a fact that no doubt contributed to her taking the prize from the other 2500 competitors. She is the first woman to win this Portrait Competition, an award that includes a commission for the NPG and an accompanying touring exhibition. She has subsequently won the 2018 David C. Driskell Prize, a $25,000 award from the High Museum in Atlanta, and that same year the St. Louis Contemporary Art Museum hosted a solo exhibition of her work.

Sherald was born in Columbus, Georgia, in a middle-class household. Her father was a dentist and her mother a homemaker. Her family was not particularly interested in art and Sherald was for the most part self-motivated in her decision to take the path of an artist. She graduated from Clark Atlanta University in 1997, going on to earn an MFA from Atlanta's Maryland Institute College of Art in 2004. She later moved to Baltimore. Sherald's formula for most of her paintings is the depiction of a solitary, unnamed and anonymous African-American figure shown frontally, usually from the knees up. The scale is close to life-size, but small enough, until her more recent success, to fit into an SUV for transportation. Her figures are set against a flat, colourful background, which tends to be monochromatic with a sometimes slightly organic texture. She cites Barkley Hendricks and Kerry James Marshall as her main influences.

She also credits Bo Bartlett's images of white Southern life, styled in a belated American Realism, a term that she uses to describe her own work. A Bartlett self-portrait shows him as a black man, just being himself, which was a eureka moment for Sherald as she had never before seen a painted portrait of a black individual.[26] Since 2019, she has experimented with double portraits and one can anticipate further transformations to her original portrait format.

Sherald says that her choice of models is based on a personal sense of what makes the individual captivating. She chooses people that she may or may not know and as she goes about her everyday activities. She chooses the clothes they wear, photographs them and coordinates the colour compositions into a pleasant whole. *Miss Everything (Unsuppressed Deliverance)*, the work that won her the Outwin Boochever prize, and which was made for a wealthy patron, shows a figure wearing a vintage blue dress with white polka dots and a hat that belongs to one of her aunts.[27] An inquisitive-seeming young woman with a debutante's white gloves holds an oversize teacup, possibly an enormous latte, or, as Sherald says, an oversize object like something from *Alice in Wonderland.* Her sister, who is a writer, sometimes helps Sherald compose the titles of her works, which add a touch of surrealism: *Well Prepared and Maladjusted*; *A clear unspoken granted magic*; *High Yella Masterpiece: We Ain't No Cotton Pickin' Negroes*; *They Call Me Redbone But I'd Rather Be Strawberry Shortcake*; *What's precious inside of him does not care to be known by the mind in ways that diminish its presence (All American)*; *What's different about Alice is that she has the most incisive way of telling the truth.*

While Sherald's work is very different from Wiley's, they share a logic that we could associate with the question of social justice as it is expressed in relation to recognition and distribution. The first relates to the representation of black experience and the other to the question of making a living while doing so. With regard to recognition, Sherald says that her paintings are designed to correct the lack of representation of black Americans in the art historical canon. She says:

> I was inspired to paint things that I didn't see within the art historical narrative. I'm not sure what came first, exactly. I was always drawn to the figure. It came naturally to paint people that looked like me, but then I also recognized that the art history books that I looked up weren't actually relevant. The images weren't there. I understand the importance of being represented at a cultural level and being able to see reflections of yourself, and society, in culture. I basically paint people who I want to see exist in the world, but then I want to create a narrative that's extricated from a dominant historical narrative.[28]

Sherald credits one of her MFA art teachers, Arturo Lindsay, for encouraging her to paint people who look like her. From that moment on she painted only black subjects. For her, black is not an identity, but is rather the experience of living somewhere between the categories of black and white. Blackness is rather a matter of familiarity and resemblance. The question of what it means to be American is a secondary concern. In order to avoid her work being limited to issues of race, Sherald decided to paint her models' skin tones in shades of grey. The colour choice first occurred as an accident, with grey as a layer of underpainting for brown skin. She decided to keep it grey for the new possibilities of interpretation that it allowed. The grey tone associates painting with black and white photography, which often has a family function and shows people how they would like to be seen.[29] The grey colour allows her to approach race as a construct and an artifice, however, without any suggestion that grey is a neutral colour beyond racial difference, as was the case for instance in Ursula Le Guin's 1971 novel, *The Lathe of Heaven*. Sherald views the art historical canon as a construct that her works have the ability to challenge. Her claim is that seeing people who look like you in art institutions is empowering. However, these are not the Rosie the Riveter type of images of an artist like Tim Okamura, whose multiculturalist concoctions have been featured in pop culture and in celebrity collections. In contrast, Sherald's subjects exude a calm self-possession, despite being dressed up in conspicuous buppie clothes.

Dawoud Bey associates the ordinariness of Sherald's subjects with the history of slavery and racism in the American South. Her portraits allegorize the South's imposed behavioural codes of "deferential obsequiousness" by isolating the figure from the surrounding social space.[30] The challenge is the ability to be oneself in a world filled with antagonism. Recognition therefore factors into the ability to make a living. Sherald waited tables until she was 38 and only afterwards managed to paint full time, which she says allows her to keep up with the bills. Since 2015 she has worked seven days a week to fill commissions. She defines success as staying true to who you are while at the same time taking risks and making the kind of work that she says makes her uncomfortable in terms of career stability.[31]

Just how risky is it to make commercial art and then accept a commission from the White House? Sherald's attitudes towards recognition and distribution come together in her painting of Michelle Obama. Even in this rare instance, she considers the work to be a "micro-narrative" of who the sitter is personally. Given the fact that there are roughly, on Sherald's count, only ten black women portrait painters working today, the work is diplomatic but also sends a subversive manifesto-like message, she argues, vis-à-vis the art canon. What is the nature of this challenge? Her portraits, she says, are about performing respectability politics for the gaze.[32] Sherald says:

> The gaze is really important. My subjects are no longer under the gaze of other people, they're there to meet your gaze. So if you look at a lot of European paintings, if there is a black figure in it they're usually adoring the white woman in the painting or they're there as a prop. And so the people I paint are there for a specific reason, and that's to meet your gaze. And to interact with you.[33]

Sherald's works has little to do with race politics and is rather attuned to human and spiritual qualities that are more comparable to Rembrandt than to Hendricks. In a community that is plagued by poverty and incarceration, this is a softer self-image than black Americans are accustomed to seeing. Sherald says she painted Michelle Obama in a way in which viewers can see themselves, making no distinction between fame and anonymity. She speaks about Obama in a chummy way and describes her as an inspiration to women and minorities: "I feel like she really represents what I paint, which are American people. They are black people doing stuff. You know what I mean? And black people become first ladies. For me it was natural to have her as a subject."[34] After "hanging out" in the White House Oval Office, she says, she now sees herself as an ambassador for Michelle Obama, signing autographs and posing for selfies so as to convey the personability and warmth of the former First Lady.[35]

Michelle Obama cannot be faulted for all of Barack Obama's policy choices, but she is married to him. What does Sherald's flattery say in contrast to Emory Douglas' 2013 portrait of the former president, titled *Kill Bill-NOBEL FRAUD*? The former Minister of Culture of the Black Panther Party depicts Obama with devil horns, signing his weekly 'terror Tuesday' kill list and branded with a broken Nobel Prize medal that bears the inscription Nobel Fraud. In contrast to another kind of painter, Mark Bradford, whose abstract works sell for millions of dollars, Sherald considers her commercial art in modest terms. "I knew I was going to be successful," she says. "I thought, I'll get a gallery. I'll sell a few hundred thousand dollars a year worth of art, and that'll be my life. (…) Now I see I can have anything I want."[36] Sherald's understudy is the young African-American poet Amanda Gorman. After reciting her work for Joe Biden's inauguration ceremony, Gorman went on to become BFF with Michelle Obama, Hillary Clinton and Oprah Winfrey, promoting luxury brands while at the same time inspiring black girls to buy into the system.

Viewing Habits

Sherald responded to the wave of BLM protests that erupted after the police murder of George Floyd by painting a portrait of Breonna Taylor for the September 2020 cover of *Vanity Fair*. Taylor was killed in her Louisville apartment on March 13 after two officers forced their entry on a drug-related warrant. She is one of the nearly 1000 Americans who are killed by police every year. Protests against her murder and that of other blacks occurred for months in Louisville as well as Atlanta, Philadelphia, New York, Chicago, Seattle, Portland and Los Angeles. The demands to end police violence and racism were met with further policing and denunciations by Donald Trump of the protests as the work of antifa "terrorists," anarchists and anti-American socialists. While Trump went so far as to encourage right-wing paramilitary vigilantism, Biden did little more than demand respect for the law.

The Attorney General of Kentucky, Daniel Cameron, denounced the protests as "mob justice" and also dismissed the outrage that was expressed by "celebrities and influencers."[37] Despite his anti-democratic authoritarianism, Cameron was correct to note the influence of celebrities on BLM activism. In early June, Alicia Keys, Jada Pinkett Smith, Queen Latifah, Tracee Ellis Ross, Solange, Selena Gomez and Janelle Monáe called for justice for Breonna Taylor.[38] They were later joined by Tessa Thompson, Beyoncé, Rihanna, Oprah and Cardi B. That some of the celebrity support for the protests might have something conspicuous about it came to the fore when NBA MVP Steph Curry was reported wearing custom BLM golf shoes in honour of Taylor. The shoes, which will help support Black Lives Matter, have her name printed on the left toe and her face on the right toe. The words 'Say Her Name' are printed on the shoe, as is the hashtag #blacklivesmatter.[39]

The grafting of identity politics onto neoliberal capitalism is not only the preserve of celebrities, however, but is now official Democratic Party strategy. For this, the Democrats increasingly rely on celebrity support to channel outrage about social inequality back into establishment channels. As identity-driven movement politics like BLM take precedent over a comprehensive left politics that tackles single-payer health care, ecology, demilitarization, immigration reform, a living wage and police reform, the fashionable postmodern micro-politics that appeal to middle-class suburbanites leave the interests of the vast majority of the working class out of the bipartisan setup. The focus on demographics rather than political vision and ideological programme leads to situations where the likes of Katy Perry, Lena Dunham and LeBron James do their best to get out the Democratic vote but not if the candidate is someone like Bernie Sanders. Appealing to demographic constituencies does not win majorities, let alone build them. Those who argue that identity politics actually plays a negligible role in the Democrats' campaigns ignore how the role that it does play is used to promote policies that do not address people's basic concerns.

Once identity has become your brand, it seemingly no longer matters what your politics are or what you are willing to do to gain power. That is one lesson that has not been learned since the Obama presidency. No wonder then that Sherald made an election season plug for what Mark Lilla refers to as the pseudo-politics of "identity liberalism."[40] Painting an elegant portrait of Taylor, with the headline *Breonna Taylor: A Beautiful Life*, Sherald is seemingly doing something to return beauty and dignity to a black woman whose life was not valued by the people hired to serve as her protectors. As Sherald told an interviewer: "I wanted this image to stand as a piece of inspiration to keep fighting for justice for her. When I look at the dress, it reminds me of Lady Justice."[41] The work has all of the usual Sherald trademarks: grey skin tone, a 3/4 body length, a monochromatic background and a few characteristic items, including a gold cross necklace and the wedding ring that Taylor's boyfriend planned to propose to her with. The dress was specially designed by the Atlanta-based designer Jasmine Elder, whom Sherald learned about on a digital platform that showcases black businesses. Its colour is that of Taylor's birthstone.

Since Sherald has joined the ranks of artists whose ambitions are shaped by the class interests of her wealthy patrons, one can hardly see this cover image, regardless of how lovely it is, as a work with any kind of radical political significance. It is rather a work that reinterprets Taylor's death in the terms of black capitalism. The painting was commissioned by *Vanity Fair* to grace a special issue that was guest edited by Ta-Nehisi Coates, the black intellectual favourite of the neoliberal centre. To make matters more bizarre, Sherald posed for the magazine in front of the painting and wearing what looks like nothing but a long-sleeve shirt, as though she had just woken up from her boyfriend's apartment and had nothing else to put on. Legacy Russell, a curator at the Studio Museum in Harlem, correctly questioned the aestheticization of #BreonnaTaylor for commercial purposes.[42] While Russell argues against artwork that makes black trauma into something decorative and that thereby attempts to confer dignity, she does not make the accompanying demand for the politicization of culture. The assumption nevertheless is that the hashtag politics of BLM are what is important, more so than the colour of the dress, which, Sherald says, was her main preoccupation: "I thought, What would I want if I were 26. Breonna, what colour do you want this to be? Please tell me what colour you want this dress to be."[43]

There are no taboo subjects in art but the more important question, as the writer Philip Roth put it, is the proper presentation of a problem. Knowing what your goal is will have a great deal to do with how you define the issues.

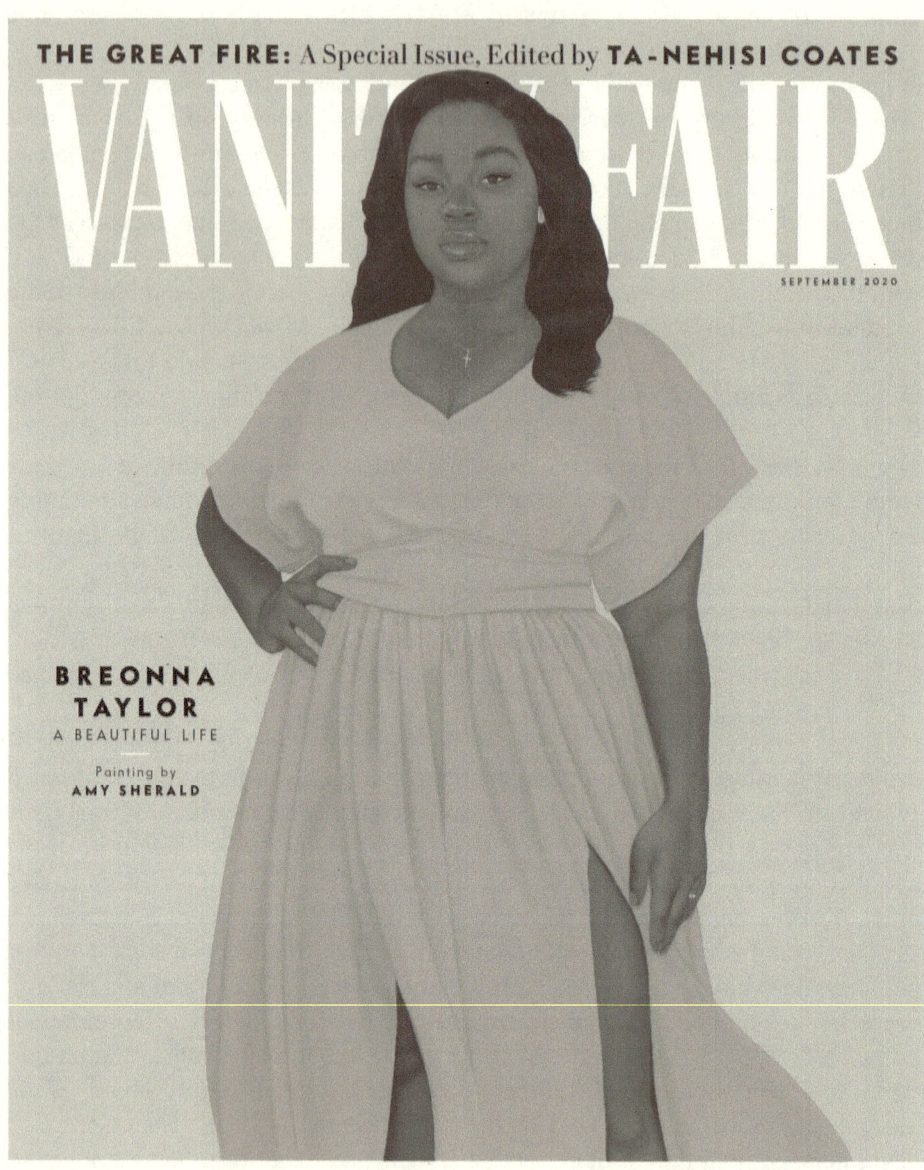

Portrait of Breonna Taylor by Amy Sherald for the cover of the September 2020 issue of *Vanity Fair*. Collection of the author.

Sherald's portrait of Taylor does have something of what the Marxist literary critic Terry Eagleton defines as fine art's mission to provide a "secular version of divine grace."[44] However, insofar as 'woke aesthetics' responds primarily to the post-representational thrust of contemporary anti-racism, it is not too much of a mischaracterization to think of the portrait, to quote Adolph Reed and Merlin Chowkwanyun, as a "self-righteous and lazy-minded expression of the identitarian discourse that has increasingly captured the left imagination in the United States since the 1990s."[45] As a demand for justice for Breonna Taylor and other victims of police murder, Sherald's cover portrait is an unintentional distillation of everything that is wrong with establishment activism.

An article by Reed and Walter Benn Michaels, titled "The Trouble with Disparity," argues against the idea that the problem that defines police violence is racism and that the solution to it is anti-racism.[46] Government and corporate support for this perspective is an indication of just how deceptively transparent this ideological illusion has become. The focus on racial disparities, black poverty and racist policing, they argue, will not eliminate inequalities. The reason for this is that racism is not the main cause of inequality, as evidenced by white poverty and the police murder of more whites than blacks. Racial inequality is driven by wealth inequality. Because that is the case, the ascension of a minority of black celebrities and professionals into the class of millionaires and billionaires – the elimination of the racial wealth gap – will do nothing to end inequality. The strategy of the neoliberal establishment to scuttle any effort at wealth redistribution supports anti-racism as ideological cover for an agenda that serves the wealthy ten percent of society at the expense of the rest.

According to people like Beyoncé, Oprah and Sherald, the main thing that blacks can do in these circumstances is limited to individual solutions, like dressing up for a potential role in the hierarchy. The notion that 'race matters,' Michaels and Reed further argue, is now a kind of folk wisdom that makes movements like BLM part of the neoliberal agenda. As class politics is now almost automatically rejected as 'reductionist,' the so-called woke left has given up on struggle and solidarity for the sake of a lottery system that transforms spiritual truths into symbols that blackmail people into submission.

Kehinde Wiley, Genius

What Amy Sherald wants has as much if not more to do with the desire for economic and social stability than it does with what Griselda Pollock has discussed in terms of "psycho-symbolic investment in the canon."[47] Sherald's work is too artistically timid to be presumed to want to have an impact on the direction of contemporary art. Kehinde Wiley, in contrast, is somewhat more ambitious. Pollock describes canon-obsession as having less to do with the desire to correct the canon through inclusion, and more to do with the production of new knowledges by insisting that sex, and in this case, race, is everywhere, making visible the ways that the canon's construction in terms of Western masculinity is premised on the marginalization of difference and is therefore a function of "its own traumatized sexual formation."[48] In this, feminist theory dispenses with one knight in shining armour and invents another: the Other that can help the invisible norm confront its unconscious inner traumas. No wonder then that Wiley is celebrated as the Napoleon of painting, the most sought-after American artist, whose work is in more than forty museum collections and who reportedly holds the world in the palm of his hand.[49]

Media personality and journalist Touré (Neblett) describes Wiley as the most successful African-American artist since Basquiat. He writes: "An art world superstar who's full of brilliance and ego, and who's willing to strip and be a nude model for his fellow artists, Kehinde Wiley is … one of the dominant painters of his generation on an artistic level and on a business level. (…) Kehinde Wiley is a genius. Flat out."[50] The reason Wiley is a genius is not because his art is particularly ingenious, but because he makes blacks look like winners and conquerors. The automobile industry recognized this aspect of Wiley's work well before the black intelligentsia. In 2004, only two years after Wiley graduated from the MFA programme at Yale University, the luxury Infiniti division of Nissan hailed him as part of their 'Infiniti in Black' marketing campaign, which celebrates emerging artists. Wiley is shown with empty stretchers and cans of paint. Against a black background the ad copy reads: "A portrait in black by Kehinde Wiley. We are the canvas. Genius. Original. Breathtaking. A style our own, never before seen, groundbreaking." This is juxtaposed with an image and description of the car: "A study in black by the Infinity G35 Coupe. With an available 298-hp, 6-speed manual transmission, sport-tuned suspension, 19-inch forged aluminum-alloy wheels and visionary design, it's more than a work in progress, it's a movement."

Kehinde Wiley was born in 1977 in Los Angeles. The youngest of six children and twin to his brother Taiwo, Wiley was raised by his mother, Freddie-May Degrate Wiley, a linguist and specialist in Ebonics – a field that studies black American language in relation to Standard American English. His father had met his mother while an architecture student at UCLA and returned to Nigeria before Wiley was born. Wiley's mother ran a flea market and sold potted plants. The Wiley kids would help her by scavenging the surrounding neighbourhood for furniture to re-sell, an activity that Wiley says gave him an appreciation for the ersatz of fake furniture and the junk aesthetic. He credits both his mother's erudite appreciation of linguistics as well thrifting as influences on his own sensibility: "Hyper-decorative stuff! So many flowers on couches! It was kitsch; it was faux-rococo meets the black American street. No matter how informed I am around different aesthetics, [those images] left something in my DNA."[51] Code switching came in handy as Wiley learned to navigate both the tough L.A. neighbourhoods and the wealthy white communities into which he and his brother were sent to study art.[52] Enrolled in art classes at California State University, he learned to draw and paint. He visited local museums where he says he was impressed by paintings of the landed gentry by Reynolds, Gainsborough and Constable.[53] He also encountered the murals of Chicano artist Glugio Nicandro (Gronk) and was impressed by Kerry James Marshall's paintings of black figures on view at the Los Angeles County Museum of Art.[54] His teen years were also marked by an art trip to St. Petersburg and admission to the Los Angeles County High School for the Arts, where he learned the skills necessary for figurative and magic realism.

Wiley pursued a BFA at the San Francisco School of Fine Arts (San Francisco Art Institute), graduating in 1999. Painting teachers Jeremy Morgan and Sam Tchakalian gave him an appreciation of technique and a sense of the usefulness of abstraction for decorative backgrounds. What the SFAI also imparted to Wiley was a greater appreciation of critical theory in relation to ethnicity. He read the writings of W.E.B. Du Bois, Kwame Anthony Appiah, Chinua Achebe, Wole Soyinka and Cornel West. He was particularly influenced by Thelma Golden's exhibition, *Black Male: Representations of Masculinity in Contemporary American Art*, which showcased 70 works by 29 artists from the 1970s to the 90s. More postmodernist than ethno-nationalist, Wiley consciously sought to produce something different from artist Betye Saar's representations of racial stereotypes. He thought instead to combine homoerotic perversion and the bombastic grand style of hip hop into a "definitive black statement" that he believed would not be reductive but could confront issues of identity in terms of a negotiated, anti-essentialist and open-ended semiotic of blackness.[55] More exactly, he aimed to make the kind of work that would appeal to upper-middle-class African-American collectors.[56]

During his MFA at Yale University, Wiley refined his approach to blackness through the writings of Henry Louis Gates and Richard Dyer. He welcomed post-structuralist theory and the deconstruction of whiteness as the ostensible universal norm of aesthetic ideology. His notion of ethnicity was enhanced by studies of the black diaspora and an appreciation of the Nigerian trickster figure Eshu Elegba, the god of confusion whose cunning unifies and differentiates opposites. For Frederick Douglass, Eshu is a common trope in slave narratives and exemplifies how a slave becomes a man by overturning expectations. All of this came together for Wiley as he worked as a teacher's assistant for the painter

Kurt Kauper, a figurative painter who manipulates the rhetoric of painting and technique as a vehicle for homoerotic topics. Wiley extended this insight with the suggestion by the curators of a Kerry James Marshall show at LACMA that his exhibitions increase the number of people of colour who visit the museum.[57] Among his stated influences, Wiley includes Vanessa Beecroft, Glenn Ligon, Su-en Wong, Lisa Yuskavage, John Currin, Gerhard Richter and Andreas Gursky.

During a year-long artist residency at the Studio Museum in Harlem, Wiley developed his approach to "streetcasting" models for his portraits. Aside from a few early works and participation in the group shows *Ironic/Iconic* (2001-2002) and *Black Romantic* (2002), Wiley came to prominence, quickly enough, after the art dealer Jeffrey Deitch signed him on for a solo exhibition at Deitch Projects. Wiley's 2003 solo exhibition *Faux Real* presented work in the signature style that he would continue to perfect through to 2017. This format is comprised of life-size paintings of young black men in hip hop attire and with poses modelled on canonical works of art. For this exhibition the models take on religious poses, some of them of female saints, angels or prophets, and are set off from decorative backgrounds that contain countless tiny gold-coloured spermatozoa. This was followed by another solo exhibition, *Passing/Posing*, also in 2003 and at Deitch's SoHo gallery. In this series of 18 paintings with arched frames and one ceiling painting, Wiley depicts young black men in the poses of Renaissance, Baroque, Rococo and Romantic paintings. The floral backgrounds of these works were painted by a team of assistants. Art critics like Holland Cotter, Mia Fireman and Holly Myers wrote approving reviews and Arnold Lehman invited Wiley to present his exhibition at the Brooklyn Museum, which acquired five of the works, including *Go* (2003), a ceiling painting that shows breakdancers in brand-name boots and sneakers ascending into the blue yonder. The opening event included the black gay opera singer and drag queen Shequida, who was dressed in a Venetian gown and was accompanied by a black classically trained string quartet performing hip hop hits in a period style. During the exhibition, hip hop music played from a video monitor at the entrance and photographs of the models were shown alongside their art history references.

By 2005, Wiley began to take the Russian formalist notion of 'struggle over the sign' as far as he could within his chosen format.[58] His *Rumors of War* series, shown at Deitch Projects and made as an oblique response to the first Gulf War, depicts black males in baggy jeans and puffer jackets in the poses of equestrian studies by Rubens, Titian, Velásquez, LeBrun and Géricault. A uniformed military band playing hip hop opened the exhibition and the gallery space was redesigned as a swank gentlemen's club with red carpeting, leather furniture, a mounted bison head and black bouncers. These triumphalist specimens were inverted in the *Down* series, also shown at Deitch Projects. In this instance, seven billboard-sized paintings show youths in the repose of fallen soldiers, martyred saints, the dead and the dying, whose transcendent monumentality is contrasted with the vulnerability and pathos of gay life on the 'down low.' While *Rumors of War* explored sexual manhood in the terms of machismo and conquest, *Down* delves into the metaphysics of saintly rapture that is part of a gay undercurrent in the classical tradition, from Michelangelo and Caravaggio to F. Holland Day and Pier Paolo Pasolini. Victoria Emily Jones suggests that these images of fallen saints addresses the victimization of black youth in the era of mass incarceration, alongside the conflation of whiteness with holiness in Western art.[59] This is hardly a necessary reading, however, as death could also function as a metaphor for the sexual prey who are the pendants to the conquerors in the previous series. One can only speculate that by adding his *Rumors of War* equestrian statue to the line of Confederate soldiers in Richmond, Wiley was intending to add gay black subtext rather than woke anti-racism to this display of civic sculptures.

Wiley went global with his 2006-2014 *World Stage* series, which extends his work to nine countries, including China (2006) – where he opened a second studio aside from his New York studio – Nigeria and Senegal (2008), Brazil (2008-9), India, Sri Lanka (2010), Israel (2011), France (2012), Jamaica (2013) and Haiti (2014). He also visited Tunisia, Morocco, Gabon, Congo and Cameroon. In each instance, Wiley streetcasted young men in the drag of American hip hop and worked with local artists, producing a set of 8-10 paintings along with an accompanying catalogue and video. In each instance, local variations allow for a more specific focus on Western representations of that part of the world, alongside indigenous cultural forms. He also branched out with his 2012 series, *An Economy of Grace*, which is his first set of works to depict women, in this instance in the poses of aristocracy and heroines. The dresses worn by the women were made in collaboration with Riccardo Tisci, the creative director at Givenchy, who designed gowns, hairstyles and makeup inspired by the Louvre collection. After the unveiling of the Obama portrait, conservative commentators made much of the fact that Wiley had described his painting of a black Judith with the head of a white female Holofernes as "a play on the 'kill whitey' thing."[60] No one remarked on the lesbian subtext of the work. The matter was not cleared up by the additional over-the-top statement that Wiley made in the NPR documentary on *An Economy of Grace* to the effect that "women have always been decorative" and that they have "never been actors or possessed real agency."[61]

At this point in the first decade of his career, Wiley had been working with more than one studio to produce series of works much in the same way that fashion houses come out with seasonal lines of clothing. Among these were collaborations with artisans who extended his work to other media. The 2013-14 *Memling* series is comprised of eight small altarpieces modelled on Hans Memling paintings in International Gothic retables of gold leaf. Bronze and marble busts were inspired by the neo-classical sculptures of Jean-Antoine Houdon as well as the legacy of slavery and phrenology. *Cameroon Study* (2010), for example, represents a black man with a striped shirt, backpack straps and a New Balance shoe on his head. Reminiscent of the stained-glass panels of Gilbert and George as well as the homoerotic confections of Pierre et Gilles, Wiley has also had tapestries and stained-glass works produced that remix his black saints with the hip hop iconography of BMW Motorsport t-shirts and Black Panther patches.

Ghetto Life

In terms of progressive neoliberalism, the question of recognition in Wiley's case is complicated by the fact that his sense of social justice is less concerned with realism than it is with the manipulation of structures of misrecognition. Having said this, Wiley is like Sherald to the extent that he values the experience of seeing the work of black artists and black subjects represented in art museums. His practice is committed to the inscription of black subjects into the Western tradition of portraiture. As he puts it: "What I choose to do is to take people who happen to look like me – black and brown people all over the world, increasingly – and to allow them to occupy that field of power."[62] The premise of his strategy is a piece of desiderata that he found on the street while he was in residence at the Studio Museum on 125th street in Harlem. The document is an FBI mugshot of a black man in his teens or early twenties. It shows his information and reads: CONFIDENTIAL: FOR LAW ENFORCEMENT USE ONLY. This chance document, not unlike Kurt Schwitters' merz fragment, has become the basis of several works, including *Conspicuous Fraud Series #1* (Eminence) (2001), *Smile* (2001), *Mugshot Profile in Blue* (2002) and *Mugshot Study* (2006).

Working with this fragment as a kind of template for his work more generally combines several layers of possible meaning. On the one hand, the objective depersonalization that is produced by official documentation and police photography is part of a system of control that "feminizes" subaltern subjects like the poor, the criminal and the working class as objects of knowledge. As John Tagg has noted, however, citing Gareth Stedman Jones, one should not overestimate the ability of disciplinary regimes to mould humans in their own image.[63] The question of power in portrait painting is nevertheless accepted by Wiley and is the reason he was drawn to the police document. As he puts it:

> It was a mug shot of an African American man in his twenties that appeared sympathetic, attractive, and it had all of his information on it – his name, his address, his social security number, and his infractions – and it made me begin to think about portraiture in a radically different way: I began thinking about this mug shot itself as portraiture in a very perverse sense, a type of marking, a recording of one's place in the world in time. And I began to start thinking about a lot of the portraiture that I had enjoyed from the eighteenth century and noticed the difference between the two: how one is positioned in a way that is totally outside their control, shut down and relegated to those in power, whereas those in the other were positioning themselves in states of steady grace and self-possession.[64]

Just as Wiley is not satisfied to reproduce the white subjects of Western art, he is also not interested in inhabiting the subject position of what is likely a straight and white New York policeman. However, he wishes to acknowledge and maintain the position of power that is structured by the mugshot image. The painting *Mugshot Study* (2006) eliminates the data of its source and focuses on the figure as a sex object. Eugenie Tsai, curator of the 2015 Kehinde Wiley retrospective at the Brooklyn Museum, compares the painting to Warhol's *Most Wanted Men*, a mural of criminal mugshots made for the New York State Pavilion at the 1964 World's Fair and an homage to gay sex as outlaw desire.[65] An entry by Touré in the retrospective catalogue emphasizes how the mediated stereotypes of the criminality of black youth shapes American culture, from police budgets to political candidates. According to Touré, Wiley sees a "wanted man" and rescues the boy's image from "the plantation of criminal expectations and fearful permutations," a repatriation that he argues liberates the boy's vulnerability, "wounded and still growing," and renders it available to Wiley. Touré writes:

> Maybe if others had seen this boy as innocent, as a boy of potential, as someone who deserved the benefit of the doubt, as someone who wasn't a problem – maybe if he'd lived a life filled with people seeing him in the generous way that Kehinde did, then maybe he wouldn't now be on this wanted poster.[66]

If Touré is no doubt correct about the notion that beliefs inform perception, it is less certain that there is anything revolutionary about sexual attraction, let alone the pederasty that Touré alludes to by referring to the figure as a boy. While Touré does not shy away from the question of visual pleasure, he is assuming that Wiley's perception lifts all taboos at once.

Wiley does not eliminate the question of prohibition with regard to so-called outlaw desire but rather resituates it within his own set of concerns. This is perhaps most obvious in the way that he goes about finding models for his paintings, which typically involves hanging out on the street with one or two assistants and looking for prospective sitters. Wiley searches for black male models aged on average between 18 and 25 years, most of them from inner-city neighbourhoods like Harlem and Brooklyn. What he looks for is the kind of macho posturing and "alpha male energy" that connotes power. Given the fact that his subjects are for the most part poor and disenfranchised, he is particularly interested in the imposture of bluster and ghetto pride, which he associates with the global marketing of blackness. These young men are 'passing,' much like animals and insects that learn to imitate their environments as a means of survival, and Wiley is the *flâneur*, who as Benjamin said about the nineteenth-century dandy, goes botanizing on the streets.[67] They are conceived and depicted as anonymous social types rather than as individuals with a unique identity. According to Brian Keith Jackson, Wiley's interactions with his models have sexual undercurrents but they do not discuss sexuality. Wiley prefers to not conflate aesthetics and sexuality and looks for ways to increase ambiguity and leave room for exploration.[68] As Wiley himself states: "My work is political and religious but it's also decidedly homoerotic. When I'm approaching these guys, there's a presupposed engagement. I don't ask people what their sexualities are, but there's a sense in which male beauty is being negotiated in each of these works."[69]

Once he has approached someone, Wiley shows them art history books from which they might choose a pose for a painting. He takes Polaroids and invites them to his studio for on average three-hour sessions where he takes photographs from which he will make a painted portrait. They choose their own clothes and work with Wiley on the selection of a pose, which can be male or gender-bending female, all of which allows for the expression of some individuality.[70] He avoids documentary realism and emphasizes the erotic aspect by artificially enhancing his models' physical attributes. He makes a drawing based on a selected photograph, which can be manipulated by computer to alter the colours and composition. In some cases, boys have been made into girls and vice versa. The models sign release forms and are compensated for their time. The artist says he enjoys the momentary state of confusion he has caused in their lives but also their spontaneous understanding of the glamour involved. A model once made his way to his studio despite having been shot in the leg the previous evening.[71] They are invited to the exhibition openings, where they can watch people gazing admiringly at their larger-than-life hyperreal portrait, and where, according to Wiley, rich old white men can mingle with the young black boys who are "moving up in the art world."[72]

There is little sense criticizing Wiley's work in terms of formalist art theory, as proposed for instance by art critic Micah Malone. Malone argues that Wiley's use of confused light sources and loose execution of the figure "appropriates the flatness and the expediency of Pop art."[73] One thinks of Mel Ramos in particular. This would hardly be an insult to the artist, who readily concedes that his works are "bombastic, syrupy, and garish."[74] To not paint himself into a corner, Wiley provides critics and journalists with different cues, saying that his works are "anti-portrait" paintings, that they are more concerned with the viewer's experience, and also that each of his works is a kind of self-portrait. These combined statements indicate that there is nothing to see: these are anti-portrait self-portraits that are about the viewer. What is more certain is that they are simultaneously autobiographical and ethnographic, sociological and glamorous, heroic and pathetic. One can question Wiley's assertion that his work acknowledges and empowers his black subjects, whom he says become important contributors to American history. "I think that it's always important not to shut the work down with any sense of high-art audience versus black-people-in-the-street audience," he claims.[75] We could say, then, that Wiley's overturning of expectations is intended to be carnivalesque by momentarily suspending power relations and thereby bringing beauty and vulnerability into visibility, pushing masculinity to the margins and blackness closer to the centre.

The question of power is further heightened by Wiley's use of decorative floral patterns in the backgrounds of his works. While his background patterns have been compared to the batik fabric backgrounds of the black and white photographs of Seydou Keita and Malik Sidibé, they more precisely originated with the austere pastel selections of the Martha Stewart Home Collection and have flat, all-over floral patterns that isolate the figure from the rest of the world. Elements like plant tendrils disturb and encroach on the figure. This play of figure and ground has less to do with Cézanne, Braque and Matisse, and is more patently illusionistic in its dramaturgy. "At times, the ground is fighting," he says. "It's taking over the figure. It's jockeying for position. (…) There is a type of hostility there."[76] The result is an oscillation in which the figure becomes background information and the floral ground emerges as part of the surface, a strategy that Wiley associates with Robert Smithson's notion of site/non-site. The difference of course is that Smithson was not interested in prudish subterfuge. In Wiley's case these strategies are pursued to enhance the sense of erotic tension, with flowers as conventional symbols of sexuality. As if the tiny spermatozoa in Wiley's backgrounds were not enough, he also includes pubic hairs as synecdoches of his presence, a practice exemplified by Jackson Pollock's drip paintings. He refers to old master paintings as "the ultimate cum shot."[77] Wiley, however, is not all about materials, in comparison, say, with the abstractionist Anthony Viti, who paints with his body and uses all of his body fluids on his large canvases. Wiley's decorative spermatozoa are at once the insignia of gay male propaganda and the trademark of a personal brand.

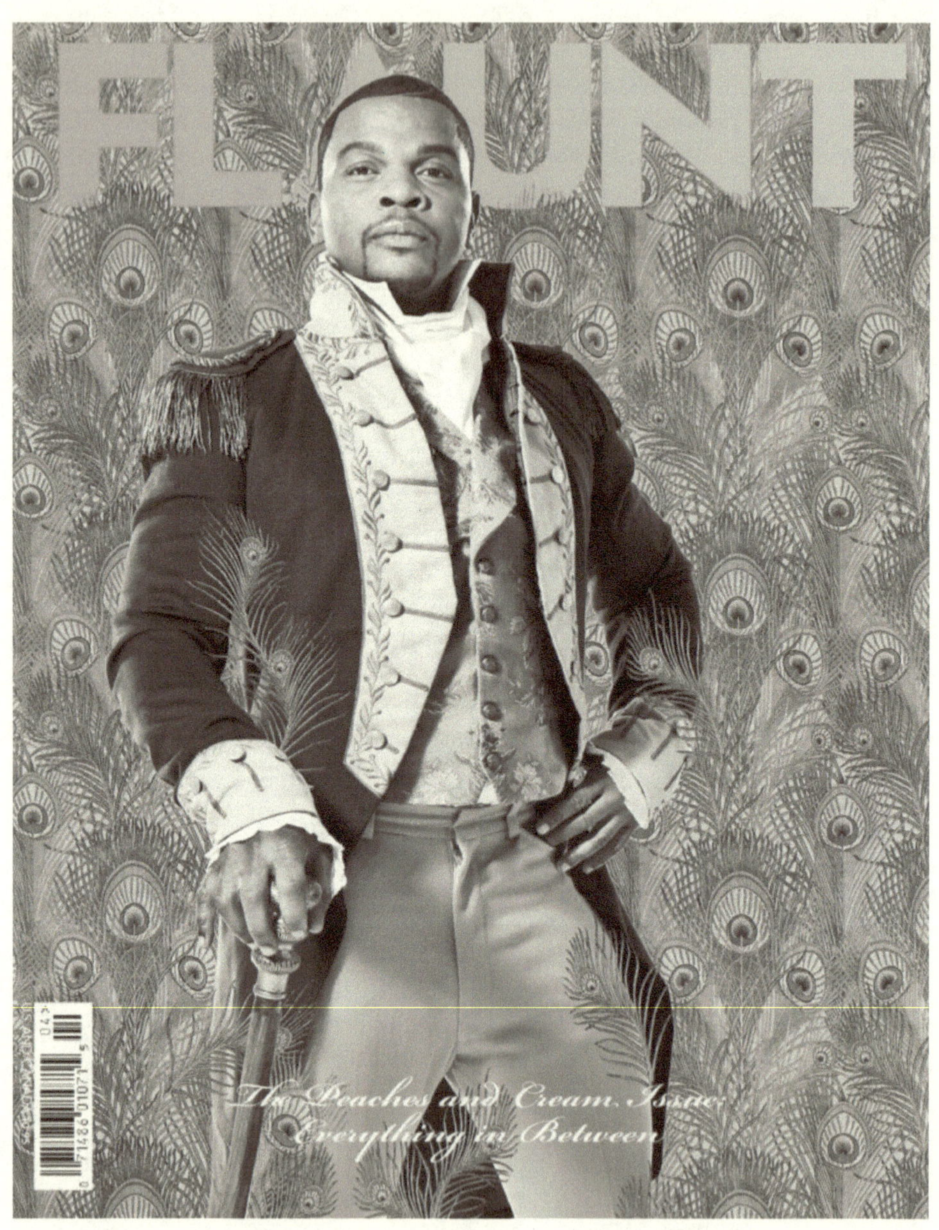

Kehinde Wiley self-portrait made for the cover of *Flaunt* magazine #114 (2011). Collection of the author.

How does all of this come together – the streetcasting gaze as outlaw desire on the down low and a figure/ground relationship that molests the ghetto pride of Wiley's subjects? The painting *Willem Van Heythuysen* (2006), for instance, is based on a 1625 Frans Hals portrait of a Calvinist bourgeois from Haarlem. It shows a black man from Harlem, New York, who wears all-white Sean Jean Sportswear and props himself with a seventeenth-century hilted broadsword. The work is only slightly different from Wiley's self-portrait on a 2011 cover of the lifestyle magazine *Flaunt*. In this case Wiley is supported by nothing less than a peacock feather background and a brass-knobbed cane. He embraces macho posturing with gusto, owning up to the fact that what he depicts is a "body language of domination" that celebrates ego "in a chest-beating way," using theatricality in the same manner as his European sources: "all I'm simply doing is using the language of the dominant culture and oftentimes being criticized for it."[78] On this score he seems less a trickster than an uncomplicated status seeker, who argues that playing the art game obliges him to go to parties and meet the right people, an activity that he compares to statecraft. The game, he says, "is knowing truly what your core interests are; knowing truly what turns you on aesthetically and personally and knowing how that interfaces with the reality of the marketplace."[79]

And Wiley plays the market very well indeed. For his *World Stage: China* series, he combined aspects of Socialist Realist poster art from the Chinese Cultural Revolution with the Qing dynasty decorative art that is typical of Chinese vase patterns – an irony given the role of Jiang Qing, Mao's wife, in the cultural policies of the era. Maoist 'model behaviour' posters are a genre of idealized young hero and martyr propaganda. Most famous is Pan Dongzi. In the widely reproduced poster *The Sparkling Star Is Handed Down Ten Thousand Generations* (1975), the model youth grins at the viewer. A rifle is strapped to his back, his arms sway and he his supported at the waist by red lilies. A 1974 film depicts him as a teenager joining the Red Army and serving as a doctor in the Second Sino-Japanese War, a reference to the intellectuals who served as 'barefoot doctors' and who helped peasant communities with ad hoc medical assistance and farm work. Wiley's send-up to the genre of propaganda posters shows figures who are comparatively unapproachable. The figure in *Support the Rural Population and Serve 500 Million Peasants* (2007) has his nose turned up at the viewer and holds his first aid carrying bag like a purse. He wears the kind of hair piece that would typically serve as a foundation for a wig, for instance, if he was drag queen, or the kind of nylon stocking that could serve as thug fashion. He is not a model type in the communist sense but rather as a haughty homie. Since he is said to have served as many peasants as McDonald's employees have flipped hamburgers, he is most likely a fashion model or porn star. Wiley

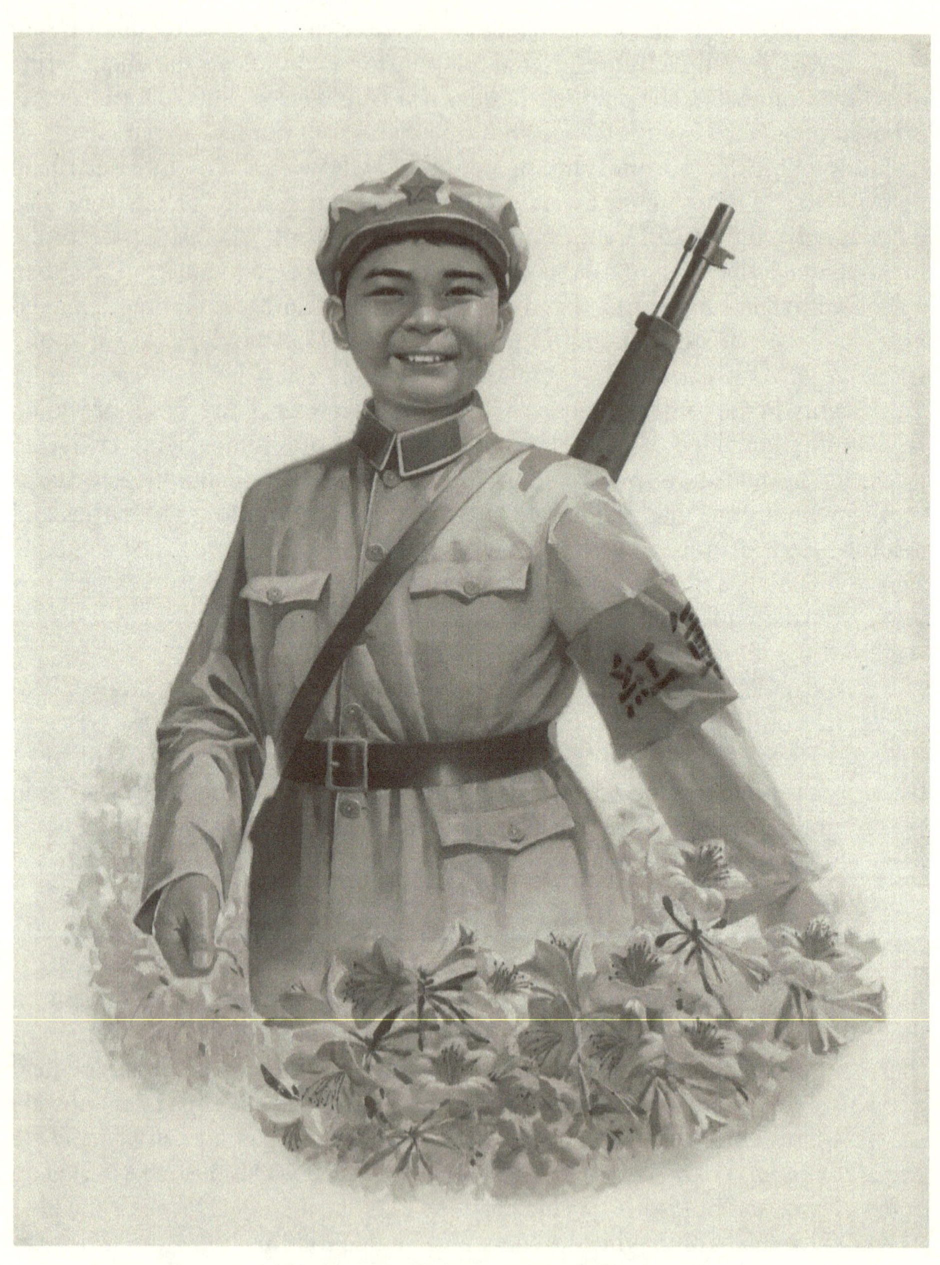

Ge Wanming, ***The Sparkling Red Star Is Handed Down Ten Thousand Generations***, 1975. Landsberger collection. Courtesy of the International Institute of Social History.

plays with ambiguity in the background as well, which has an invented pattern that is without an exact historical source. Another work in the China series, *Cheick I* (2007), shows a figure with a San Diego Padres baseball cap that has no known precedent in the Cooperstown Collection.

The play with ambiguity goes all the way down and has been associated by critics as a feature of post-blackness. For the 2001 Studio Museum exhibition *Freestyle*, the curator Thelma Golden and the artist Glenn Ligon originated the concept of post-black as a distinctly African-American take on the fluid postmodern subject, who can slide effortlessly between traditional high art and popular culture. The point of post-black, which Wiley embraces as a kind of schizophrenia, is that this new black subjectivity can improvise among historical registers, whether 60s and 70s black nationalist activism or 80s and 90s global multiculturalism. That the new black is more decidedly postmodern than revolutionary is accepted as progress beyond black trauma and marginality towards what Derek Conrad Murray identifies as the symbolic capital of marketing potential. Murray writes:

> In terms of playing on the increased financial wealth of African Americans in the last decades of the twentieth century and anticipating the enormous riches and diversity of the global hip-hop phenomenon, both *Freestyle* and Wiley's art were totally in sync, and this cohesion may have been one reason Wiley's art was deemed an immediate success.[80]

Wiley would likely accept Rebecca Walker's argument that his work can be considered in terms of post-identity as well as post-gender.[81] He says: "We're arriving at a culture where we can take it for granted what sexuality is. So it can exist out loud and hidden all at once."[82] With regard to the Lacanian notion of the gaze, it is less the case for Wiley that there is no big Other than that there is always a resistance to some form of the gaze: "I didn't want [my work] to be about being the 'gay' painter. (…) It's the equivalent of not wanting to be merely a 'black artist.' I didn't want either of those factors to dilute or distract from the conversation."[83] On an artistic level, Wiley embraces playful subterfuge rather than the exclusivity of singular meanings. One question that emerges is how can one build a politics by queering recognition? This problem shifts the balance within progressive neoliberalism from justice issues towards the question of power and therefore more towards questions of distribution than the recognition of identity.

Brandstorming

Wiley's signature style works to disrupt the codes of the Western art canon by including black subjects in the poses of Rubens, van Dyck or Ingres, conferring upon them the allure of status, prestige and privilege. In the process, Wiley interferes with social codes around black masculinity. In terms of the cultural repertoire of signs that is available to contemporary viewers, the privileges associated with white, European masculinity are not changed but dispersed.[84] Wiley compares his strategy to both cross-dressing and carjacking, where the Western tradition is "emptied out" and consumed.[85] What is more surprising than Wiley's bombast is the consensus among commentators that the artist has successfully confronted if not defeated European and American portraiture by bringing issues of race, masculinity and power into art historical discourse. The business of art criticism is not without its own kinds of subterfuge. While David Greenberg writes in *Art in America* that Wiley disrupts the hierarchies of traditional painting, the *New York Times* critic Holland Cotter declares that Wiley has made history by dethroning the old masters and putting his subjects in command.[86] Wiley is hardly the first and only artist involved in this sort of endeavour, whether we are talking about Robert Colescott's painting *George Washington Carver Crossing the Delaware: Page from an American History Textbook* (1975), the perverse Indigenous reversals of Kent Monkman or the Adult Swim television series *Black Jesus*. Connie H. Choi argues that Wiley is avoiding the double blackmail of both negative and positive stereotypes, a reasonable assessment that mitigates claims to radicality with a keener appreciation of Wiley's marketing of African-American culture.[87] We could here again credit Benjamin's reflections on Baudelaire, where the ambiguity of social relationships in commodity culture allegorizes 'dialectics at a standstill,' or the commodity as dream image and fetish.[88]

Like a latter-day Warhol, Wiley has no qualms about outsourcing the meticulous work involved in the realization of his paintings. Comparing his studio to the traditional European atelier, he hires assistants to paint the wallpaper backgrounds and the rough work for the figures. He also commissions artisans to build his ornate frames. His first studio was in New York City, followed by studios in Beijing and Dakar, with plans for others still in Columbia, Rio de Janeiro and Mumbai. At each of these sites, he employs as many as four to ten studio assistants, at low cost, as well as a local manager who coordinates the shipping of orders in time for their assembly at a designated museum exhibition. Wiley also works with assistants in the digital manipulation of photographs and with local tailors and designers in the preparation of costuming. Preferring to compare himself to a financier or a tech entrepreneur than the stereotype of the romantic "Brexit artist," as he calls it, who wants to "make autonomous art great again," he vaunts his outsourcing of creativity to low-paid assistants as a critique of the mystique of the solitary artist starving in a garret.[89]

Wiley does not reserve his strategies for anonymous everyday showboats, pimped up on a grand scale. He has also served the narcissism of rich and famous black celebrities. His paintings made an early appearance on television in the apartment of Lucious on the Fox television drama *Empire*. In 2005, he was commissioned by the TV network VH1 to paint portraits of its annual Hip Hop Honorees, including Big (The Notorious B.I.G.), LL Cool J., Big Daddy Kane, Grandmaster Flash, The Furious Five and Ice-T in the pose of Ingres' Napoleon. He has painted Kanye West and made a painting of the singer Santigold for the cover of her 2012 album *Master of My Make-Believe*. In 2008 he painted Michael Jackson in a monumental equestrian portrait as King Philip II of Spain. In 2010 the Cincinnati Art Museum commissioned a portrait of Grace Jones, with Alexander McQueen selected as the dress designer.[90] In addition to celebrity portraits, his work has been purchased by high-profile individuals, including A-list collectors Don and Mera Rubell, cyclist Lance Armstrong, musician Elton John, tennis player Venus Williams and actor Neil Patrick Harris. Playing up the question of complicity, Wiley opines: "Let's face it, I make really high-priced luxury goods for wealthy consumers."[91] According to one of his dealers, Sean Kelly, his works sell for $100,000 to $500,000, making Wiley one of the wealthiest artists of his generation.[92] Pre-empting the criticism of leftist academics, Wiley states:

> I consider art to be fun. You know, enough already with the high seriousness. You can do paintings and have fun and be respected and appeal to the general public without making your art difficult. (…) Really smart art types are sort of embarrassed by all this. It's just too much beauty, too much emotion, too many uneducated black people in the room. And they think, 'Why am I [not] special anymore?' And I'm sorry but that has to be done away with. It's possible to have rigorous work that is also joyful and celebratory.[93]

Wiley's thinking is less ideologically confused than it is Ivy League camp. He believes that with his high-priced luxury goods he is able to respond to the exclusive tastes of the elite and their "absolute celebration of decadence and empire," which he glibly justifies as part of the tradition of easel painting.[94]

Wiley not only obliges celebrities but corporations as well. On the occasion of the 2010 FIFA World Cup in South Africa, the sports company Puma commissioned him to paint portraits of three of soccer's most decorated players: Samuel Eto'o of Cameroon, John Mensah of Ghana and Emmanuel Eboué of the Ivory Coast.[95] Puma at that time was both seeking to incorporate art into its brand identity and was interested in moving deeper into the African market. The paintings were shown in a Puma-sponsored exhibition in Cape Town, *Legends of Unity*. Puma also created clothing and footwear with Wiley-patterned graphics that were worn by players during the World Cup. Puma's marketing for its One Unity Project emphasized unity over and above the diversity of the hundreds of languages spoken on the continent as well as the history of civil wars and famines. Nothwithstanding Puma's effort to create a positive brand image by sponsoring a UN project for biodiversity, the FIFA association was riddled with difficulties as its officials were found to have accepted as much as $10 million in bribe money from South Africa. This specific issue is marginal in comparison with the broader impact of the role played by the FIFA World Cup in globalization processes, which, not unlike the International Olympic Committee, transfers billions in tax revenue from the host country into untaxed and unregulated corporate profits. In concert with transnational corporations like Coca-Cola, McDonald's, Visa and Adidas, FIFA impoverishes communities in exchange for spectacle and surplus capital.[96]

Wiley takes the typical Cultural Studies approach to brands like Puma, Adidas and Nike, saying that people are both victims who submit themselves to the corporate conquest of market space as well as agents fashioning their subjectivity according to the aesthetic features of the brand.[97] He says the same about himself: "My style and design align perfectly with the Puma brand in the sense that I think what we are both trying to achieve is a sense of joy in all we do."[98] The two sides come together in the narrative that Wiley builds around brands and the story of 15-year old Michael Eugene Thomas, who was killed in 1989 by a classmate who wanted his $100 Michael Jordan sneakers. "The brands that people wear are a serious business," he says:

> I remember growing up as a kid in South Central Los Angeles, back in the 1980s, when people were being killed for Jordan sneakers. Branding says a lot about luxury, and about exclusion, and about the choices that manufacturers make, but I think that what society does with it after it's produced is something else. And the African American community has always been expert at taking things and repurposing them toward their own ends.[99]

Accepting the logic of branding, Wiley extends it to other subjects, none too small: "Africa today has a very poor brand – people think of starvation, war, and disease. But in 2010 the World Cup was in Africa for the first time. And it was an important time to see Africa as a place of celebration."[100] He has also shown his paintings as posters for the Metropolitan Opera House and on NYC yellow taxicabs through the Art Production Fund for public art. "My engagement with popular culture, with corporations, with branding, with museum space, with

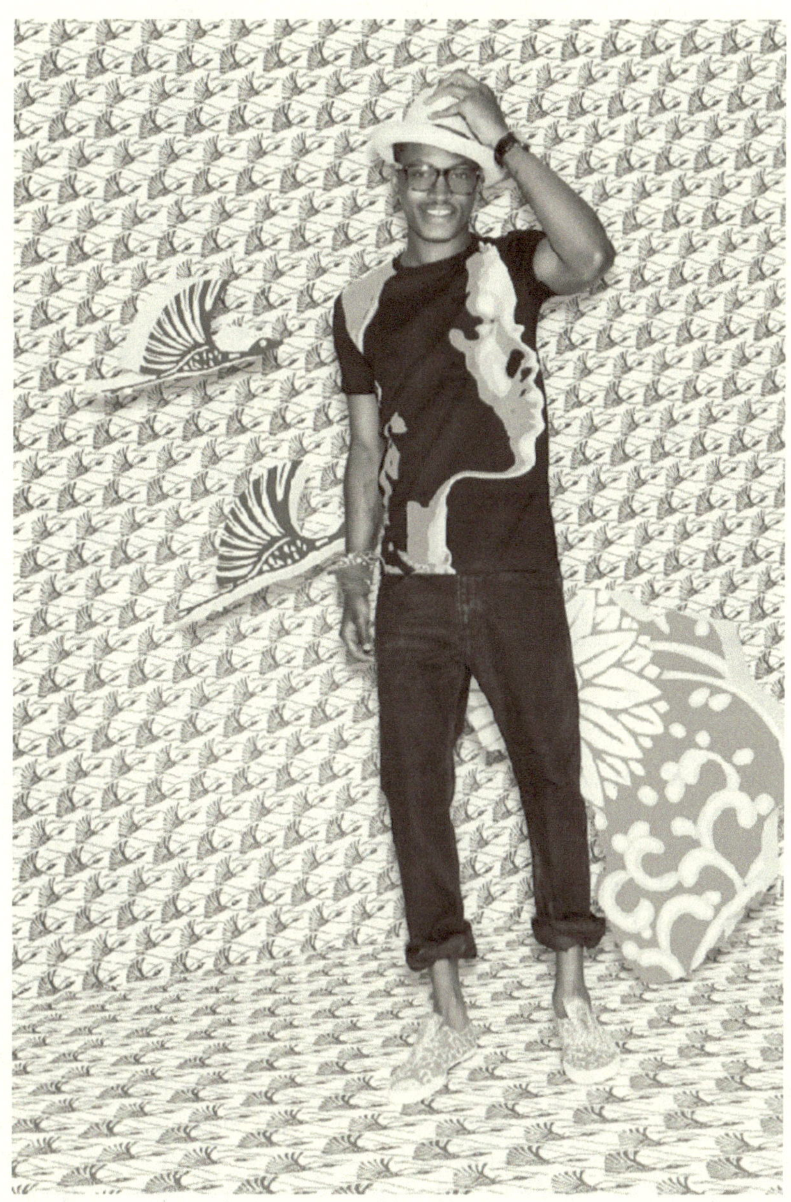

Puma Africa Lifestyle Collection. Kehinde Wiley designs for the Puma Global Football campaign and Puma's One Unity Project for the 2010 FIFA World Cup in South Africa. The campaign envisions community in Africa through soccer. Clothing, footwear and accessories pay homage to African soccer champions. Proceeds from sales go towards programmes that support biodiversity in Africa, in partnership with the United Nations Environment Program's Year of Biodiversity 2010. Courtesy of Puma and Berk Communications.

community organizations, with non-profit institutions can all exist at once," he says, without compromising his artistic integrity.[101] Regarding Obama, Wiley says that he appreciates how having had a black man in charge after the debacles in Iraq and Afghanistan created a new, international respect for the U.S. The people he meets abroad, he says, have a sense that with Obama, America "redeemed its brand."[102]

As the 'House of Wiley' becomes a global brand, the artist has been given exposure in magazines like the *New York Times*, *Style Magazine*, *Vogue* and *House and Garden*. Wiley has not only courted this attention, but has been rewarded for making business values the focus of his art. His *World Stage* series is the most obvious instance of this, prompted as it was by a 2001 Goldman Sachs report on global economic development. The report's predictions of economic development in BRIC countries (Brazil, Russia, India and China) led Wiley to plan satellite studios around the world, allowing him to tap into the global diaspora of hip hop fashions and sports brands. One of his works from the 2008 Brazil World Stage became an official art print for the 2014 FIFA World Cup.

The Brooklyn Museum, which exhibited his work in 2004 and purchased several paintings, including his *Napoleon Leading the Army over the Alps*, which was on view in the museum's main lobby, organized a Wiley retrospective in 2015 titled *A New Republic*. From February to May, the exhibition drew 150,000 visitors. The curator, Eugenie Tsai, boasted that Wiley is reshaping the canon by embracing gender difference and sexual orientation, making visible the social construction of culture.[103] The exhibition was supported by the Henry Luce Foundation, the National Endowment for the Arts and Grey Goose Vodka. Grey Goose is a subsidiary of Bacardi, the largest alcohol company in the world. Bacardi was established in Cuba in 1830 and had close ties to the country's political elite until the Che Guevara faction came to power in October 1960. Since then the Bacardi estate has built connections to U.S. political elites and the CIA. It has funded Cuban exile organizations and terrorist attacks in Cuba, assisted the U.S. in its embargo against Cuba and backed mercenaries in Nicaragua, El Salvador and Angola. Bacardi advertises its brand of Havana rum as Cuba Libre. Wiley partnered with the Grey Goose brand again in 2014 to help launch its LeMelon product, a flavour once associated with the French aristocracy. Grey Goose commissioned from him portraits honouring 'the kings of culture' in film (director Spike Lee), music (rapper, DJ and music producer Kasseem Dean, a.k.a. Swizz Beatz) and sports (NBA basketball all-star and Olympic medallist Carmelo Anthony). The works were to be auctioned in 2014 at Art Basel Miami. This series is part of a process of cross-promotion that began with the *World Stage* series and has become a modus operandi as Wiley has diversified into a multinational brand. Other series along these lines include the maritime paintings made for the exhibition *In Search of the Miraculous* (2017-18) and the "trickster" series of portraits of black artists Derrick Adams, Sanford Biggers, Nick Cave, Rashid Johnson, Glenn Ligon, Kerry James Marshall, Wangechi Mutu, Yinka Shonibare, Mickalene Thomas, Hank Willis Thomas, Carrie Mae Weems and Lynette Yiadom-Boakye. Wiley argues that cross-platforming synergy is the way the entire world works today, and not only the art world, where there is still a great deal of snobbery, he says, about 'the rules of the game,' which he thinks is not all for the worse insofar as the language of art cannot be done away with entirely.[104]

Wiley's version of woke aesthetics counters the weakening of symbolic efficiency with regard to the function of art in class society and at the same time repurposes it at will, not unlike those who welcomed the burning of the Notre Dame cathedral in 2019 as an occasion to give it a makeover. He does not resist the decay of aesthetic and cultural languages but assists this process. As Ben Davis argued in 2013, Wiley is not producing a critical image of black identity, he is "an art director selling a formula, a style, that can be translated into a lot of different mediums."[105] As if to prove Davis' point, Wiley signed on with Brillstein Entertainment Partners in 2018. The Hollywood talent agency will assist Wiley with deals for representation in film and television, licensing his paintings for the big screen and elsewhere. They will also help to identify directing opportunities for the artist, along with collaborations with screenwriters and creators, a cross-platforming that has been pursued by the artists Julian Schnabel, Steve McQueen, Sam Taylor Wood and Rashid Johnson. As Hollywood moves in on the corporatized business of contemporary art, museums become a wokewashing engine for the billionaire class.[106] In 2018 Wiley made the *Time* magazine 100 List. Praised by LL Cool J as a "creative genius," he was showcased alongside Oprah Winfrey, Rihanna, Ryan Coogler, Chadwick Boseman, Roseanne Barr, Ronan Farrow, Elon Musk, Jeff Bezos, Nancy Pelosi, Donald Trump, Prince Harry, Emmanuel Macron, Crown Prince Mohammed Bin Salman, Xi Jinping and Kim Jong Un.[107] A few years previously, confusing false modesty with charitable self-flattery, he stated that he is not interested in "overthrowing systems" or "grand sweeping political narratives," but is simply pointing to the beauty of people from underserved communities who look like him.[108]

Wiley does not simply broker local colour. He also celebrates the capitalist and imperialist power relations that bridge the epochs. In a 2015 article in *Modern Painters*, Chloe Wyma offered in two pages more criticism of Wiley's work than most of what could be read about him almost everywhere else. Wiley's Brooklyn Museum retrospective, she argued, is safer than subversive. Feeding the art crowd's taste for nobrow pastiche, the artist queers nineteenth-century pompier perversity with a "steamy display of inverted exoticism and epicene genderfuckery."[109] Acknowledging that Wiley does not seek to be activist, she extended this insight to make the point that his historicist remix of European grandees does not challenge today's race politics. His work rather participates in the mainstream pop celebration of the black "royalism" of people like Beyoncé and Jay-Z, a language of status that legitimizes conspicuous wealth and cannibalizes the imagination. Wiley's commercialism makes his statement that he is standing on the shoulders of those who survived slavery and colonialism, and nevertheless went on to create jazz, blues and hip hop, anodyne if not repulsive.[110] In comparison, the work of artists like Dread Scott, Jackie Sumell, Rick Lowe and Charles Gaines articulate unequal power relations but with a sense of struggle rather than complicity.

Jenni Sorkin argues that Wiley's work risks reducing the seriousness of issues affecting African and African-American men to the surface bling of "ghetto-fabulous fashions."[111] Very few have questioned the way that Wiley asserts the kind of authority that establishes itself through genealogies that officiate the exercise of absolute power, from wealthy Renaissance princes to the Baroque Church, the First French Empire and the Third Reich. The latter replaced French revolutionary democracy with Nazi claims to Greek-descended Aryan perfection, a new race of masters. To question Wiley's work on his own stated terms is undoubtedly too much to ask from art that operates in a world in which signifiers of wealth and power are used routinely in fashion and the mass media. One would be missing the broke Baroque bombast if not for the fact that there is very little irony in Wiley's art and next to no povera. If the anti-art of Fluxus artists flushed the canon of Western bourgeois art down the drain, creating in the process a new set of practices and concepts, artists like Wiley dispense also with the radical anti-art of the twentieth century. Save for postmodern trends in academic theory, the artist works with conservative materials and reactionary values.

Given his penchant for showbusiness, one can only receive with scepticism Wiley's 2018 series of portraits of residents of Ferguson, Missouri, the city that gave rise to the Black Lives Matter movement. One should be no less suspicious of this appropriation than the Mongrel Coalition's critique of Kenneth Goldsmith's conceptual poetry reading of Michael Brown's autopsy report, attacked as an instance of "colonial aesthetics."[112] Wiley visited the West Florissant convenience store where Mike Brown was alleged to have been stealing before he was killed by police. The series is presented in the exhibition *Kehinde Wiley: Saint Louis* (2018), which interprets eight works of art that are in the St. Louis Museum collection. Concerned with the paraphernalia of clothing and jewellery, Wiley adds to this the notion that portrait painting, much like photography, is traditionally associated with the effort to fight death.[113] This is perhaps not so far off from the Wiley who disassociates from blackness but who is interested in "bling bling" and people who ornament their bodies with Gucci and Versace, baggy jeans and hoodies. In 2019, he presented at the Galerie Templon in Paris a series of works that depict third gender Mahu sitters from Tahiti. Blending LGBTQ issues with the political correctness of MeToo, Wiley claimed to be correcting with these images the "problematic" and "exploitative" aspects of the work of Paul Gauguin, which he defines as part of a colonial history of "complicated gazing."[114] One presumes that these recent series are another way that Wiley can improve and expand his brand image. "I'm not particularly interested in providing answers to questions of morality," he said in his early career; "I'm more interested in creating situations."[115] The Situationists created situations. Wiley indulges the society of the spectacle.

How challenging is Wiley's work in a culture that has been plundering the canon for decades if not centuries? One can think of thousands of examples of canon busting, from Édouard Manet's *Déjeuner sur l'herbe* to the image of Mariah Carey in *Harper's Bazaar* as a Fragonardian nymphette. In the latter case the fact that the artist was designer Jean-Paul Goude seems hardly worth mentioning. Even the man upstairs has been called upon to fist-bump the latest moderns, with Michelangelo's *Creation of Adam* used to sell everything from Coca-Cola, Nutella and Lay's Potato Chips to Purell Hand Sanitizer. In 2004, the magazine *Sports Illustrated* repopulated the Sistine Chapel with the all-time greats of American sports, including black and female athletes. In 2006, the FIFA World Cup commissioned the repainting of the central train station in Cologne as an Adidas fresco, a Baroque *trompe l'oeil* depiction of ten soccer world champions. It was viewed by eight million travellers as well as millions of television sports fans.

Although it may not be manifestly evident, one of the important predecessors of Wiley's work is Jeff Koons. In the 1980s and 90s the Costacos Brothers produced posters that featured professional athletes in pop cultural poses, presenting people like Michael Jordan, Magic Johnson and Wayne Gretzky in flashy riffs on movie posters, transforming athletes into cowboys, soldiers, cyborgs and superheroes. Among the more well-known images was a poster of basketball champion Moses Malone as the biblical Moses. Peter Moore, who was the creative director at Nike in the early 80s, used some of these images as Nike advertisements. Inspired by Baudrillard's theory about the precession of simulacra, Koons purchased the copyright to the Moses Malone poster and re-presented it as his own work in a 1985 exhibition titled *Equilibrium*. In 2018, separate instances of this appropriated image sold for $146,000 and $185,000.

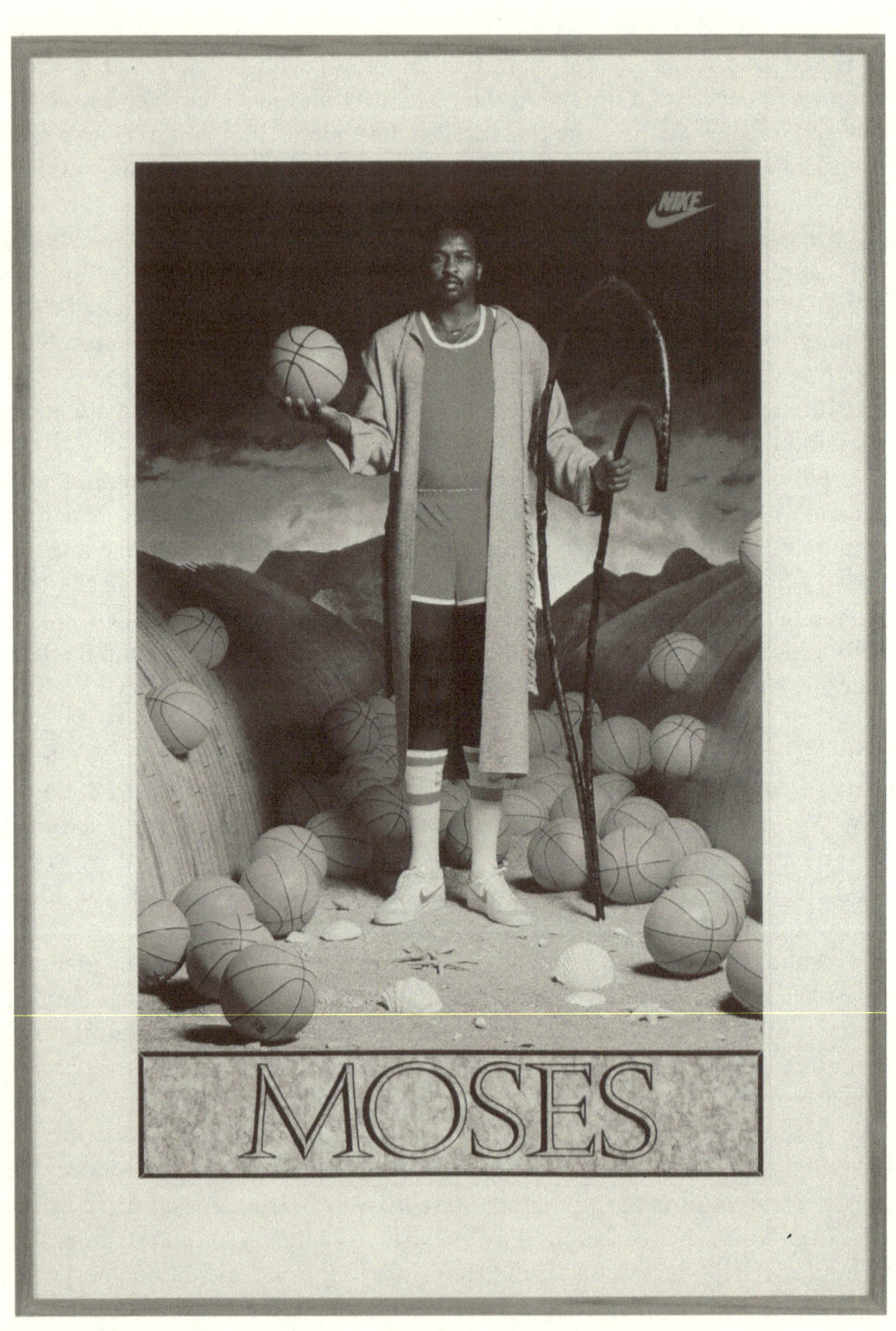

Jeff Koons, ***Moses***, 1985. Framed Nike poster, 115.6 x 80 cm. © Jeff Koons.

The interest of the image for Koons was the use of athletic prowess to escape inner-city poverty. According to Koons:

> The Nike ads were my great deceivers. The show was about equilibrium, and the ads defined personal and social equilibrium. There is also the deception of people acting as if they have accomplished their goals and they haven't: 'Come on! Go for it! I have achieved equilibrium!' Equilibrium is unattainable; it can be sustained only for a moment. And here are these people in the role of saying, 'Come on! I've done it! I'm a star! I'm Moses! It's about artists using art for social mobility. Moses is a symbol of the middle-class artist of our time who does the same act of deception, a front man: 'I've done it! I'm a star!' (...) What was paralleling this message was that white middle-class kids have been using art the same way that other ethnic groups have been using basketball – for social mobility.[116]

Wiley is not a 1980s Neo-Geo artist, but he is like Jeff Koons, Julian Schnabel and Damien Hirst in the sense that he produces work with the art market and wealthy collectors in mind. According to Chris Wiley, new levels of economic inequality have led to the penchant for speculation and a kind of vacuous abstract art that he refers to as zombie formalism. In the early 2000s, the art market came roaring back from its previous apogee in the 80s and capital once again flooded the galleries and artist studios. Art speculation combined with tax evasion, money laundering and price fixing at auction houses, where art flippers inflated the value of artworks to boost reputations. This form of unregulated fraud is seemingly a win-win for buyers and artists alike.[117] As zombie aesthetics becomes woke, diversity in whatever idiom is increasingly added to the mix, as seen for instance in the effort by millionaires to inflate the importance of the work of Jean-Michel Basquiat by driving up auction prices. As art critic Robert Hobbs argues, the way that Wiley was championed as an "immediate success" relates to the increased financial wealth of African Americans in the last several decades and the spread of the global hip hop phenomenon.[118]

As far as postmodernism goes, Wiley is a less interesting artist than Koons. Koons used advertising and marketing strategies in ways that were not only experimental but reflexive. Even in interviews Koons is a consummate pitchman. Wiley's brand strategy is comparatively prosaic, a Norman Rockwell for the age of diversity preening. How does this work as branding? Žižek comments on the symbolic efficiency of the anti-marketing aspects of works of art, where the superego injunction is: "You should be ready to pay an exorbitant price for this commodity precisely because it is much more than a mere commodity."[119] The utilitarian consideration is that Gauguin, who painted 'third people' a century earlier, exploited Tahitians for the sake of the white European gaze, but Wiley is providing a seemingly redemptive re-canonization of the same marginal subjects. This provides a deceptive cover for not only the injunction to enjoy, but to enjoy artwork that provides no particular satisfaction, like charity from the Bill and Melinda Gates Foundation. Gauguin was a genuinely talented painter and was hardly a typical European. Wiley's luxury-brand paintings are rather consistent with global capitalism and consumer design. Like much postmodern theory, they promise more than they deliver. Images of poor and minority subjects can easily be made available to consumers, but the exorbitant price of a Wiley painting adds to the illusion that Gauguin and all of the other dead, white European males are at last being displaced by women, gays and blacks. Žižek mentions a Starbucks fair-trade coffee campaign with the tag: "It's not what you're buying, it's what you're buying into." What are the intellectual and ideological premises of such wokewashed culture?

Sex, Race, Gender and Bentham

Wiley is indifferent to class analysis and radical politics. He offers no criticism of the culture industry, the art market and the neoliberalization of institutions that now trade on identity politics as if the pluralist critique of modernist formalism was the new thing. It never occurs to most people in the art world – artists, curators, instructors and critics alike – that some of the now commonplace concepts that one might find in a book like Victor Burgin's *The End of Art Theory: Criticism and Postmodernity* are themselves due for a rethink.[120] Through postmodernism, theories of aesthetic autonomy were assailed from a number of vantage points: art's political, economic and social aspects; the critique of subjective judgement; the relation of language to representation and the cross-pollination of techniques in the age of mass media. One reason why the obituary on latter-day formalists like Clement Greenberg and Michael Fried has the features of an eternal return, even in the context of today's post-Fordist creative industries, is due to the ideological screen that it now provides for the petty bourgeoisie in the creative and knowledge industries.

Postmodernists may not be as Nietzschean as they sometimes pretend. Žižek reverses Nietzsche's axiom that if God is dead then everything is permitted. On the contrary, he argues, it is due to the belief that God (or any big Other) exists that everything is permitted. The same goes for modernist aesthetics as the negative theology of contemporary art and politics.[121] Wiley's status in the art world is similar to Obama's position as the first black president. Criticism of Wiley's and Obama's deference to aesthetic and political ideology can be misconstrued as a way to deny them agency, which brings into play questions of race and power. Brian Keith Jackson states this plainly enough:

> Can the persistence of less flattering responses mean that the dominant culture continues to view the black male, even in the age of Obama, as nevertheless taboo, to be glossed over, no matter how acclaimed or highly regarded, much as even a black titan of industry, when taken out of context, becomes just another black male body on the street, to look past or scan with apprehension?[122]

When in 2013 Oprah Winfrey claimed that she was a victim of racism because she was denied the chance to buy a $38,000 handbag in a Zurich boutique, the government of Switzerland issued a formal apology through the tourism office. The question of double standards for even the rich and powerful was also in evidence during Obama's 2009 negotiation of conciliatory talks between Henry Louis Gates and policeman James Crowley, who arrested the Harvard professor after he had broken into his own home because he had lost his house keys. After criticizing the Cambridge Massachusetts police for acting stupidly, Obama was obliged to apologize, inviting both men to the White House for drinks. Obviously, not every black man who is wrongly profiled by police would be invited to the White House for resolutions.[123] Obama, however, made it seem as though it was Gates and not the police force who had to be appeased. It is as if due respect for a successful black intellectual could lift all black boats simultaneously. The point is not that none should receive any privileges so long as everyone does not, which cedes too much ground to conservatives, who are content to see to it that none do. The question, rather, is the way that inegalitarian and reductive reasoning has both overdetermined and underdetermined aspects, in this case: 1) the chances of a black artist being consecrated by the field of culture, 2) the basis on which any artist can be consecrated, and 3) what that person or collective does as an artist, regardless of their concern for recognition. The logic of 'too black to fail' reduces the last to the first point and ignores the second. The reason why Wiley is too black to fail as a second-generation postmodern portrait painter has everything to do with race and sexuality and little to do with culture, as evidenced by the fact that Wiley's approach to the traditions of the Western canon is more opportunistic than critical.

A similar set of issues was raised around the work of Robert Mapplethorpe, an artist who, as it turned out, was 'too gay to fail.' Mapplethorpe was initially viewed by art critics as a commercial artist, selling the rights to his slick photographs for commodity purposes and feeding the alt-celebrity mill with pristine black and white portraits of everyone from Louise Bourgeois to Arnold Schwarzenegger. After his death from AIDS-related causes, a retrospective of his work was shown in Washington D.C.'s Corcoran Gallery of Art. It was then that Mapplethorpe's homoerotic and sadomasochistic images came under attack by Republican politicians, leading to a court case with charges for pandering obscenity and depicting minors in a state of nudity pressed against the director of Cincinnati's Contemporary Art Center. Expert witnesses defended Mapplethorpe's work on mostly formalist grounds rather than on the basis of moral or community values – though some effort was made to address Mapplethorpe's participation in a minority lifestyle.[124] Anthropologist Carole S. Vance argued that these and similar works were attacked because they gave visibility to minority sexual subcultures.[125] The art critic Douglas Crimp had in the early 1980s considered Mapplethorpe's work to represent an outdated form of modernist appropriation. Later, in the midst of the AIDS crisis and attacks on the National Endowment for the Arts that equated homoeroticism with obscenity, Crimp altered his assessment to argue that postmodern strategies of appropriation had "shifted from a grounding in art world discourse to a grounding in movement politics," which included the work of ACT UP, Gran Fury and other artists fighting a culture that sought to make gays and lesbians invisible.[126] Crimp also addressed the way in which Mapplethorpe's nudes "depict desire as openly homosexual" and therefore contribute to gay world-making as the "prerogative of a self-defining gay subculture."[127] For Crimp, Mapplethorpe's 'postmodernism of reaction' could be more transformative than the 'postmodernism of critique' of someone like Sherrie Levine due to Mapplethorpe's rejection of the universalizing function of the museum and the presumption of an undifferentiated public. On this basis, however, Essex Hemphill criticized Mapplethorpe's objectification of black males as a reiteration of the racist stereotypes of colonial fantasy.[128] Kobena Mercer similarly argued that Mapplethorpe's images could serve racist readings as easily as they serve the artist's reputation. The extension of intertextual pleasures from gay male and interracial pornography into high art, he argued, lent Mapplethorpe's work a self-reflexivity that is most effective in the context of urban, commercial and gay male subculture. Against readings that reduce the meaning of the work to an essentialist understanding of the identity of its maker, Mercer championed works that acknowledge the diversity of the relations in which identities and artistic traditions are socially produced, which undermines assumptions that artists can directly represent the groups they are associated with.[129] Black individuals are not reducible to blacks as a group; not all blacks are the same. Similarly, the politics of reception implies that no individual or group has a monopoly on the meaning of a work.[130]

The categories of sexual difference, racial difference and gender difference have a supplementary qualification at the level of alienation. In terms of psychoanalysis, the difference between subjects is fundamental to subjectivity as such. The inability to come to terms with an inherent antagonism is resolved through the fantasy construct of the fetish. The contradictions of the Obama portraits and the Obama administration were so charged with the burden of minority representation as to be resolved essentially through compensatory idealizations. To the extent that art and politics matter as social categories, difference politics founders on its abandonment of universality. While postmodernists were at one time convinced that they had rid theory of the concept of universality as a preserve of bourgeois humanist ideology, and later as a field that hegemonizes the interests of an invisible and putatively white European masculinity and heteronormativity, the social condition for this process of cultural deconstruction is less a democratic plurality of difference and more the reality of global capitalism. Where neoliberal regimes do increasingly less at the level of socio-economic welfare, they fight the conservative right with gains for minorities within an increasingly unequal equal-opportunity exploitation. As an adjunct to such capitalist realism – to use Mark Fisher's phrase for a neoliberal capitalism that sees itself as little more than the least worse of political options – woke aesthetics conjecture that it is unfair to expect minority groups to fight against capitalism while also fighting against discrimination.[131] The question, however, is whether, by refusing to fight capitalism, the politics of anti-racism, anti-sexism, anti-homophobia and anti-xenophobia can be adequately addressed, least of all as economic inequality and political instability fuel rightist reaction. A more complicated level of analysis brings us to consider that not only is racism a feature of capitalist ideology, so is anti-racism. Today's woke wars operate as an integral part of progressive neoliberalism and as a war against the authoritarian right and the radical left. The hegemonic tactic of the intermediary petty-bourgeois class is the manipulation of identity issues in such a way as to ignore the workings of capitalism for the sake of diversity.

Observing the rules of anti-racism leads critics to overlook Wiley's cultural politics. His work is equal parts academia and pop culture, with race, gender and sexuality operating as subterfuge for black capitalist careerism. The factor that makes Wiley's work different from predecessors who represented black males as objects of erotic desire – artists like Rotimi Fani Kayode and Lyle Ashton Harris, or artists like Andy Warhol and Alexander McQueen, who operate as crossover brands – is the shift from the postmodern deconstruction of norms to the culpabilization of privilege. With the Cubists and Surrealists, the defamiliarization enabled by artefacts from colonized cultures was both a means to destabilize bourgeois ideology and to change life through artistic experimentation. Well before contemporary art scholars began writing books on the racism and sexism of Paul Gauguin, the work of Carl Van Vechten, patron of the Harlem Renaissance and literary executor of the author Gertrude Stein, divided the black literary community. His 1926 novel *Nigger Heaven* also contributed to transforming Harlem into a site of white tourism. Van Vechten's colourful wallpaper backgrounds were used to adorn portraits of celebrities like

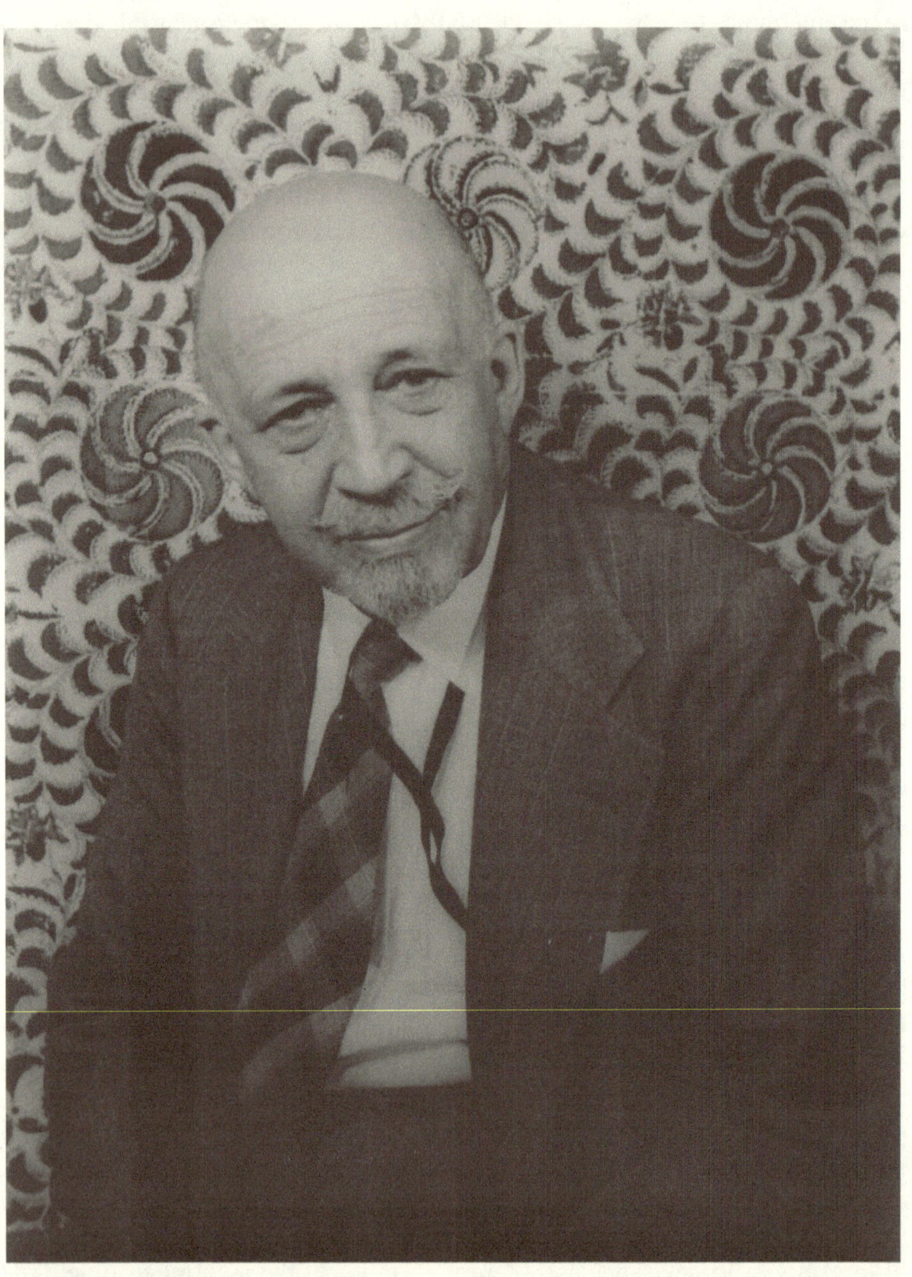

Carl Van Vechten, Photograph of W.E.B. Du Bois, 1946. Beinecke Rare Book and Manuscript Library, Yale University. © Van Vechten Trust.

W.E.B. Du Bois and Eartha Kitt, but also relatively anonymous acquaintances like Alan Meadows and Geffrey Holder, whose bare black chests and floral props recommend them as objects of sexual gratification. Van Vechten was preceded in this style of portraiture by Cecil Beaton, the socialite documentarian who photographed popular individuals like Gary Cooper, Marilyn Monroe, Truman Capote and Queen Elizabeth II. As if to extend his dominion, Beaton famously created a *Vogue* photoshoot using Jackson Pollock's drip paintings as a backdrop for models in couture dresses. To paraphrase the August 1949 issue of *Life* magazine, Beaton encouraged *Vogue* readers to think of him, and not Pollock, as the greatest living artist.

One wonders how Wiley views himself as an artist. He stated early on that painting was a place for him to disappear and imagine different possibilities for his life.[132] These possibilities would seem to have as much if not more to do with identity than with aesthetics. Although critics argue that queerness and blackness are as essential to Wiley as they were to James Baldwin, Bayard Rustin or Langston Hughes, Wiley seeks to displace the normative gaze through which the black body and gay desire are constructed. His method for doing this is the hollowing out of traditions, creating racial and gender confusion as part of a politics of queer destabilization: "Many people see my early work simply as portraits of black and brown people. Really, it's an investigation of how we see people and how they have been perceived over time."[133] Although he identifies as a gay man, Wiley says that his own experience as someone who has occasionally drifted is not black and white.[134] One reason for playing a game of ambivalence is contextual, based on the experiences of exclusion that black queer people have faced. Another is strategic, refusing the disciplinary regimes of identification. Choi argues that Wiley forces his viewers to recognize their complicity in regimes of objectification.[135] Along these lines, one might see oneself as part of a pattern, if only the lines separating race, gender and sexuality were not as oblique as a Wiley (self-)portrait.

The utopian aspects of the postmodern fantasy of a genderless and post-racial universe are based in a disavowed critique of capitalist exploitation. At an earlier moment in black cultural politics, it was still possible to imagine an escape from capitalist disciplinary regimes. For example, in *Space Is the Place*, an afro-futurist science fiction film made in 1972, jazz musician Sun Ra and his Arkestra decide to settle African Americans on a new planet, using music as the means of transportation. Sun Ra travels back in time to a Chicago strip club to confront a pimp overlord called the Overseer, a man who embodies the evil in the black community and who is a tool of the white power structure. Sun Ra and the Overlord agree to a game of cards to settle the fate of the black race. In the present, he meets with young African Americans in Oakland and opens an "outer space employment agency" to find recruits for the exodus. He is at odds with the Black Panther Party regarding the correct vision of the future for the black race. He also organizes radio interviews, a record album and a concert. Jimmy Fey, a white representative of the entertainment industry, means well but is a puppet of capitalism. Although Ra is suspected by his public of having invented the outer space gimmick to boost his record sales, NASA scientists kidnap him to extort his secrets. He is saved by students who bring him to the concert where he plays his free jazz. As NASA scientists open fire on the crowd, Sun Ra waves his hand and they reappear on his spaceship. The spaceship launches into the cosmos and Earth is destroyed.

Space Is the Place is one part black nationalism and another the cultural contradictions of capitalism as exemplified by the music industry. In contrast, Wiley's post-black and post-gender ethos could not be thought of as a form of queer afro-futurism since he considers the culture wars to be over and rather that platform capitalism allows today's artists to jump from planet to planet with a minimum of friction.[136] Similar second-generation postmodernists, like Awol Erizku and Leonce Raphael Agbodjelou, use canonical references and subterfuge to flatter their audiences with art that is mostly indifferent to cultural capital, save the question of formal composition and attractive models. Wiley has more in common with an artist like Michael Jackson than Sun Ra. When the Jackson 5 became the marketing focus of Motown records, the label licensed branded music instruments, album covers, posters, colouring books, a board game, a cartoon series and a magazine called *Right On!* The album *Destiny* was released in 1978, followed by *Triumph* in 1980. Between the two albums, Jackson released a solo album, *Off the Wall*, leading to a split from his brothers. It was followed by *Thriller* in 1982, the best-selling album of all time, winning eight Grammy Awards. By 1997, the King of Pop was selling as many as 20 million albums per year and raking in $165 million per world tour. In 1996, *Forbes* magazine placed Jackson's annual income at $35 million. Jackson died in 2009. By 2017 his estate was earning $287 million annually.

Black specificity and difference can be part of a strategy of integration into the higher echelons of capitalism. Even if the artist is deemed a sell-out by critics and other artists, their work is nevertheless accepted on the basis of black visibility. If the work is found to have integrity, even as pop culture, it may become a challenge to audiences and institutions. In these terms, Wiley has developed a double strategy: integration into the official art game through classicized references to the social margins, or Picasso in drag. Hobbs refers to Wiley's practice as a form of "conceptual realism," defining portraiture in terms of power relationships that are coercive and not simply mimetic. He identifies two aspects of this approach: 1) performing old master authority and streetwise alpha male swagger, and 2) underscoring representation as capture and performance for the controlling gaze of the other.

It is worth mentioning Hobbs's essay in detail since it is the only serious theoretical analysis of Wiley's work to date. The main problem with the essay, at the outset, is that is seeks to mobilize all of the resources of critical cultural theory without much concern for whether or not these are suited to the subject. From the two sides of power – mastery and capture – Wiley's work is said to be analogous to Foucault's theory of subjectivity and aesthetic self-fashioning within disciplinary discursive regimes.[137] The question of power in portraiture allows Wiley to rethink how painting can subsume issues of identity and history under the norms of aesthetic representation. Just as young black men can be both empowered or disempowered by their identification with hip hop, high art can become an insidious realm of capture.[138] When asked to sum up his practice in one word, Wiley says "panoptic," referring to Foucault's study of surveillance through prison architecture.[139] His streetcasting is an exploration of the automation of power in the way that people comport themselves positively and productively, based on cultural conventions. The techniques of power and of observation are thereby folded by the artist into questions of representation, ethnicity, sexuality and history.

Among his inspirations, Wiley mentions Jennie Livingston's *Paris Is Burning* (1990), a documentary film about black drag performers who battle one another by taking on female poses from fashion magazines, a practice known as voguing. According to Wiley, "[t]hose positionings were about how grand you are. It was about creating this shell, about creating this mask of power, even though you may have been one of the poorest people in the neighborhood or one of the most powerless people in the neighborhood."[140] The film and the artist are said by Hobbs to have also been influenced by Judith Butler's writings in *Gender Trouble* and *Bodies that Matter*.[141] Performing in hip hop or voguing renders the coercive norms that serve as the basis for any intelligible cultural style. Gay voguers can act straight, revealing heterosexuality as artifice rather than an invisible and therefore naturalized ontology. Wiley argues that he is performing portraiture and painting as a set of naturalized codes, playing the game of art and the art market straight.[142] With regard to Wiley's *The Dead Christ in the Tomb* (2007), a work based on a Mannerist painting by Hans Holbein, Mercer argues that the conditions to such subversion have to do with survival:

> Setting black male figures loose from prevailing codes that fix their image as a problem in need of solution, Wiley joins company with performative traditions in black diaspora self-fashioning in which the power to play with surface appearances was a matter of life and death whenever masking ensured survival in a hostile world.[143]

Not unlike the work of Kara Walker, Wiley introduces queerness into the field of vision, revealing the sexual subtext of capture, Mercer says, with black humanity imprisoned by its own beauty. Wiley would no doubt agree, as he defines the powerlessness of his models in the *Down* series as a codification of eroticism. No doubt this is what Wiley intends when he says that he knows how to appeal to wealthy patrons, as though the appreciation of unequal power relations can only come from the position of those with the disinterested luxury to be able to use it or to dispense with it at will. On this score, the reference to Foucault fails since for the postmodern philosopher power is diffuse rather than economic. Further, the economic reference and art market gambit make Wiley's critique of the male gaze and of heteronormativity suspect. Efforts to redefine economic power in terms of anti-normative prejudice turn into another strategy of status seeking.[144]

In keeping with the postmodern toolkit, Hobbs's argument makes a strawman out of the subject of humanism. He writes: "Beginning in the late nineteenth century and continuing today, humanism has been unveiled as an extraordinary masquerade, and so has its hold on portraiture and this genre's ability to construct individuals as unquestioned representations of power."[145] Humanism, from the Renaissance through to the twentieth century, is reduced by Hobbs to little more than a charade, first critiqued by Karl Marx and Sigmund Freud, and now decentred by the theories that have declared the death of the author.[146] Wiley's works are in these terms like plastic flowers laid at the grave of the Cartesian subject. The problem is that postmodernists like Wiley and Hobbs have accepted the contemporary doxa on the death of the subject without philosophical scrutiny and as justification for neoliberalism.[147] Contrary to popular academic opinion, it is discourse theory and not the Cartesian subject that is displaced by the study of Marx and Freud. Moreover, humanism – from Rabelais to Gore Vidal – has had a subversive edge vis-à-vis institutionalized forms of authority and against the fatalism of theories that do as much to make people accept existing power relations as to challenge them. The irony of Wiley's and Hobbs's Foucauldian critique of the autonomous artist is that theirs is in fact the kind of humanism that continues to legitimize the function of art in class society. This is why Wiley experiments with post-blackness and post-gender but not post-capitalism. As neoliberalism progressively reduces aesthetics and politics to the auction lot and fashionable hashtags, the class function of both high art and mass culture are marketed as 'freestyle' challenges to the status quo. To give Foucault his due, it is in this sense that Wiley's work is panoptic: cultural progress and political radicalism are disciplined by neoliberal institutions and made into the instruments of corporatized creative industries.

The Souls of One-Dimensional Folk

Wiley argues that one should be both critical and complicit, like the Nigerian trickster god Eshu, embracing contradiction and polyphony. He recognizes though that being an art canon jokester can cause problems, since even tricksters get caught in their own games:

> The games I'm playing have much more to do with using the language of power and the vocabulary of power to construct new sentences. It's about pointing to empire and control and domination and misogyny and all those social ills in the work, but it's not necessarily taking a position. Oftentimes it's actually embodying it.[148]

Wanting to see black bodies represented in the same vocabulary of power as the classical tradition is defined by Wiley as an uncanny "double consciousness."[149]

The phrase double consciousness is derived from William Edward Burghardt Du Bois's turn of the century sociology of the black race in the era of Jim Crow segregation. Although *The Souls of Black Folk* is conditioned by the thinking of its time and by biological definitions of race, Du Bois nevertheless understood race as a social construct with the potential for emancipation. He questioned whether blacks in the U.S. should strive to be Negroes, Americans or both. Whichever, black consciousness implies an anti-imperialist awareness of discrimination and of the "colour line" that distinguishes blacks and whites worldwide. The following is Du Bois's well-known definition of double consciousness:

> After the Egyptian and Indian, the Greek and Roman, the Teuton and Mongolian, the Negro is a sort of seventh son, born with a veil, and gifted with second-sight in this American world – a world which yields him no true self-consciousness, but only lets him see himself through the revelation of the other world. It is a particular sensation, this double-consciousness, this sense of always looking at one's self through the eyes of others, of measuring one's soul by the tape of a world that looks on in amused contempt and pity. One ever feels his two-ness, – an American, a Negro; two souls, two thoughts, two unreconciled strivings; two warring ideals in one dark body, whose dogged strength alone keeps it from being torn asunder.[150]

Black consciousness is a double consciousness based in the awareness of how one is perceived by white society. This gift of second sight, according to Du Bois, is what allows the "talented tenth" of elite African Americans to participate in high society and uplift the rest of the black population. This aristocracy of race is conceived as a vanguard of black professionals who are hostile to the white power structure.

Although Du Bois's elitist notion of spiritual striving is universalist in the idealist sense, it grounds consciousness in the experience of the racism that condemns blacks to poverty and lack of opportunity. Disalienation would allow blacks to live life as both Negroes and Americans, and therefore to thrive while giving attention to the problems that afflict blacks as a social group. The element of self-questioning, Du Bois insisted, is not directed against other races and in no way concedes to Booker T. Washington's strategy to compromise on political rights in order to achieve incremental gains. Disalienation adheres to the ideals of American civilization and the Declaration of Independence. Against the attitude of revolt and revenge, and of reverse racism, Du Bois rejected the attitude of conciliation that avoids conflict and along with it the responsibility for social progress.

Hobbs mentions that the revolutionary black thinker, Frantz Fanon, considered Du Bois's double consciousness to be problematic insofar as a divided ego that is at war with itself succumbs to the censoriousness of the dominant white ideology – a phenomenon described by the title of his 1967 book, *Black Skin, White Masks*. The identification of the Negro as incompatible with mainstream culture and the consequent self-hatred leads to two solutions: 1) asking others to ignore race; 2) asking others to acknowledge race and find value in what has wrongly been marked as inferior. For Fanon, both solutions are neurotic:

> In order to terminate this neurotic situation, in which I am compelled to choose an unhealthy, conflictual solution, fed on fantasies, hostile, inhuman in short, I have only one solution: to rise above the absurd drama that others have staged round me, to reject the two terms that are equally unacceptable, and, through one human being, to reach out for the universal.[151]

Hobbs remarks that Fanon's solution is to transcend colourblind universality as well as the condition of blackness defined by white culture. Fanon's solution is not a rejection of universality, however, but rather a break with race metaphysics. Fanon rejected the abstract universality and black nationalism of his compatriot Aimé Césaire. What Hobbs is less attuned to, therefore, is the dialectics of emancipation in Fanon's approach to universality. On this score, the postmodern thinkers who focus primarily on language as the basis for cultural criticism differ fundamentally from both Du Bois and Fanon. The code switching, polyphony and semiotic play that can be put on and removed at will are not simply the assets of a reflexive, dialogical and diasporic pluralism in the age of communications media, but as Brian Holmes argues, they are features of a flexible personality that has emerged alongside the paradigm of global production regimes and consumer ideology. In the world of fictitious capital, it is not simply marketing that produces profits, but market segmentation, deepening the paradigms of informational and managerial control.[152] Similarly, Paul Gilroy argues that this paradoxical loss of certainty around race accompanies not only corporate multiculturalism but also authoritarian forms of ultra-nationalism.[153] The reason for this is due to the fact that the abstract universality of pluralism is used by contemporary capitalism to bypass class politics.

There are issues left unanswered in Du Bois's question as to whether slavery and race prejudice are sufficient causes to explain the black condition.[154] One response that he gives is that it is too soon to know since racism remains a social ill despite decades of desegregation and integration. The prospect is nevertheless that racial equality will eventually allow for a fair and due consideration of black individual worth and cultural achievements. Since contributions to human civilization can come from anywhere in the world, Du Bois argued, a race ideal of strong manhood and strong womanhood in America and Africa can uplift all blacks through the highest aims.[155] The best of the race are those who make intelligence, sympathy and knowledge the foundation of their breadwinning. A second answer given by Du Bois is that racism is not a sufficient cause to explain inequality since humanity is also characterized by criminal tendencies. For instance, slavery also existed in non-white societies. This negative prospect contradicts Du Bois's belief in ideals and non-selfish strivings. In this case, racism as well as anti-racism preserve the category of prejudice and scepticism concerning the possibility of universal equality. The best that one could hope for are practical arrangements and material satisfactions. Du Bois concedes to this insofar as he believes that crime and laziness are part of the unfortunate legacy of slavery, which he notices in the reduction of education to the goal of making money and the transfer of technical skills.[156]

Although Du Bois acknowledged the problems delineated by Marxism as crucial to his ideal of civilization, *The Souls of Black Folk* defines socialism as a "cheap and dangerous" "worship of the mass" that harms higher individualism, culture and intellect. "Was there ever," he asks, "a nation on God's fair earth civilized from the bottom upward? Never; it is, ever was and ever will be from the top downward that culture filters."[157] "I sit with Shakespeare and he winces not. Across the colour-line I move arm in arm with Balzac and Dumas, where smiling men and welcoming women glide in gilded halls. (…) So, wed to Truth, I dwell above the Veil."[158] Du Bois rejects limiting success to the canon, such that no others could rise, as well as tearing down the canon, only so that others can be valorized instead.

Racism in America did not change on account of the individual striving of the talented tenth but rather due to the industrial proletarianization of Southern blacks, when black labour was valorized for its contribution to surplus through a more rational form of exploitation, which had been impeded by Jim Crow racism. Proletarianization coincided with the acceptance of black culture as part of the broader American society. Even if the exceptionalism of talented individuals served the rule of race relations, the question remains whether the rule could change without the exceptions, or, whether the rule produced its exceptions. While a discursive historicist opts for one or the other, a dialectical materialist is attentive to the contradictions that structure the problem itself. As Du Bois was more than wise to argue, "[w]e will not quarrel as to just what the university of the Negro should teach or how it should teach it," adding further that education is not merely a matter for schools.[159]

Wiley's work, we could say, is an ironic inversion or double unconscious of Du Bois's first two answers, one that calls for vigilance and the other that recognizes human failings. Having cynically accepted capitalist realism and the inevitability of race distinctions, Wiley proceeds without hesitation to hollow out the Western canon and to pander ghetto bling for the sake of destabilization. Doing so, he systematically ignores the way that capitalism conditions both as well as their interaction.

Du Bois's acknowledgement of socialism as a way to alter the capitalist conditions that limit the benefits that might come from an enlightened elite are belatedly addressed by Nina Power's study of contemporary gender politics in *One-Dimensional Woman*.[160] Power wonders why it is that contemporary feminism has satisfied itself with expensive handbags, vibrators, careers and romantic love. How did feminism become a consumer accessory, she wonders. Even if television and movies are not to be believed, how did the propaganda of being a youthful bad girl come to replace politics? Power believes that Herbert Marcuse's 1964 study, *One-Dimensional Man*, offers a paradigm for the critique of contemporary feminism's acceptance of the ideology of permissive freedom and technological domination. The satisfaction of needs and constant self-promotion does not bring autonomy but integrates gender struggles into systems of control. Reclaiming the body, occupying "male" positions of power and reverse-chauvinist attitudes, she argues, have become obstacles to equality by eroding the internationalist forms of collective organization that are based on the valorization of social labour. The struggle for representation, for example in terms of the kinds of 'top jobs' performed by war hawks like Condoleezza Rice and Hillary Clinton, or neoliberals like Theresa May and Nancy Pelosi, is an ideological trap. Race and gender are in these circumstances "decoys of democracy" that reveal "the corruptibility of identity politics."[161] Beyond the flexibilization, feminization and self-objectification of labour, for which "you are your breasts," Power addresses the problem of anti-essentialism. If desire has no humanist basis, and if women are not more sensible than men, what lies beyond destructive nihilism and cynical pragmatism?

Criticizing the industrialized pornification of sex and society, or porn duty in porn capitalism, that is, despite the fact that porn is one of the few industries in which women are paid more than men, and despite the fact that porn caters to every sexual proclivity, Power defines the social relation in the sex business as the imperative to enjoy. Against pornography's mostly individualized forms of consumption, she suggests that the politicization of sex in revolutionary communes and collectives can deregulate sex beyond bourgeois domesticity. Power's neo-Reichian body without organs does not assume that sex is inherently liberatory and therefore that a community can be founded upon it. On the contrary, a collective sexuality that is 'not one' ostensibly desublimates the secrecy of sex as defined by Foucault, questioning the naturalness of heterosexuality.

One wonders why it is that on this point Power avoids Marcuse's insights on repressive desublimation. Is it not the case that denaturalizing heterosexuality has the unintended effect of naturalizing heterosexuality? And is the violence of denaturalization not a way in which enjoyment is derived, as explained in Freud's allegory of parricide in *Totemism and Taboo*?[162] The ideal of an egalitarian and non-pathological social relation is surreptitiously absconded in Power's suggested alternative and the problem of antagonism is ideologically fixed in a prohibition against domesticity. The point of socialist feminism is not to destroy families, but to bring equality to the relations between men and women – in other words, to destroy the *bourgeois* family insofar as it is premised on patriarchal oppression. Friedrich Engels' critique of the bourgeois family sought primarily to liberate sexual relations from patriarchal domination, economic necessity and class restrictions. Marx and Engels rejected inequality in sexual relations, they did not denounce heterosexual couplings and households as 'bourgeois,' which is an attitude best left to the neo-aristocratic pretentiousness of bourgeois romantics and countercultural bohemians. Power's notion of emancipated sex in cybernetic communism, which is based on Shulamith Firestone's *The Dialectic of Sex*, finds its consumerist application in Tinder and Bumble. The prehistory of this supposedly new phase of civilization is described more than adequately in Siegfried Kracauer's *The Salaried Masses*, wherein metropolitan types "get loose" as means to fit in and climb the company ladder, a "productive revolutionizing of negativity" within capitalist relations of production.[163] The only alternative to so-called normative sex, which is a non-starter from a psychoanalytic point of view, is not more kinds of sex or sex with more kinds of people, or even sex on the barricades, but emancipation from sex as such. Although there is no escape from sexuality and sexual difference, the attempt to do so can take the form of pleasure in renunciation, or in sex beyond the pleasure principle, which has little to do with sex and still less to do with love and human needs. A genuine materialism would avoid conflating issues of class, gender and sexuality into experimental lifestyles.

The background to Wiley's work is not simply a sexualized floral imagery, but, as Wiley well understands, a global cultural-industrial complex that he prefers to engage rather than critique. Du Bois's black leadership and Power's collectivist femunism exclude a third possibility: the way that an unaccountable social antagonism, or alienation, structures all of social life. On this issue, Marcuse's *One-Dimensional Man* challenges Du Bois's double consciousness as well as Power's politicization of identity while at the same time preserving what is emancipatory in both projects. Marcuse defends autonomy, dissent and negation against the stabilization of capitalism through technological integration and conformity. While his warnings against the total administration of culture may appear quaint from various perspectives – postmodern, neoliberal, communist – it addresses the ways in which identity politics, social constructionism and new materialisms tend to limit social change to one-dimensional immanentism and positivism. The main characteristic of one-dimensionality is the belief in the prospect of a total assimilation of subjectivity to objectivity and external structures. As political opposition loses its criticality vis-à-vis the broader system of post-industrial society, resistance to capitalism appears to be impossible. Any talented tenth, in these circumstances, even if they were to oppose racism and bolster multicultural excellence, would advance capitalism and state power. For Marcuse, pluralism in social, political and economic matters is compatible with the contradictory reduction of human needs and social interests to the preservation of establishment interests. Pluralism mobilizes the needs of capitalist productivity, transforming capitalist democracy into a more efficient system of domination, perpetuating exploitation, poverty, policing and militarism.[164]

One of the keystones of Marcuse's work is the notion that consumerism redirects real needs towards a "euphoria of unhappiness" in repressive needs like relaxation, fun and socialized affect.[165] Livingston's *Paris Is Burning*, for instance, openly celebrates the stylization of suffering that is on display in the voguing clubs of the 1980s. Far from transcending sexual difference, the desublimation of gender in the gay and transgender ball scene is not in contradiction with the social reality of mainstream society – as represented by the nominal allusion to *Vogue* magazine – but accommodates itself to its ideals, much as Warhol's factory transformed people into superstar affirmations of the reconciliation of aesthetics with business culture.[166] This is not to say that the *promesse de bonheur* of the aesthetic does not also preserve the memory of suffering and thereby advance a critique of social reality. However, as Marcuse sees it, art's power of negation is only operative when it refutes the established order.

For Marcuse, art is always alienation, whether as affirmation or negation. Art's alienation from everyday reality, as either museum art or pop culture, is neutralized and subsumed within the prevailing social relations. Art does not escape subsumption by accommodating itself to everyday democratic forms. The estrangement of black culture is not remedied by marketing expensive paintings, sneakers or resin casts. In these cases, easy access turns art into a cog of the culture machine, entertaining without challenging the objectives of industrial society.[167] The desublimation of artistic alienation in the reality principle of commercial society, including the administration of libido and the life instincts, conditions "institutionalized desublimation" and "contributes to the making of the authoritarian personality."[168] Sexual freedom and human agency are managed as instruments of labour and market value. Socialization through sexuality de-eroticizes life and integrates sex into work and leisure. Woke aesthetics reduce questions of art and politics to questions of identity. They make it impossible to understand how Kehinde Wiley's late postmodern art acts as an apologia for the status quo, mobilizing libido in ways that are gratifying to managed individuals and lead to political compliance – a satisfaction that organizes submission rather than protest.[169]

The Man Who Sold the World

Wiley's rapid ascension in the world of art dealers and art museums, corporate capitalism and neoliberal government is an unintended judgement on the extent to which his work actually challenges the art historical canon. Hobbs describes Wiley's performative subversions of the masculine and European gaze of art history as an instance of the "serious-parodic stage" of the Situationist method of détournement, which implies, according to Guy Debord and Gil Wolman, that the work of appropriation is not meant to arouse indignation or laughter with regard to the original, but that the most distant elements – the Western tradition, humanism, autonomy, whiteness, masculinity, heteronormativity – would be the ones that contribute most to the overall impression.[170] At the serious-parodic stage, the artwork takes the détourned materials seriously.[171] Contrary to what Hobbs suggests, Wiley is not indifferent to the power of the art that he copies. His work should therefore not be approached as "conceptual realism," but rather as a "capitalist realist" grammar of power. This is obvious enough when we compare Wiley's work to some of its appropriations.

Consider for instance Dan Funderburgh's incorporation of the Guinness beer company logo into a Wileyesque wallpaper. The background design was created for the Guinness Africa #madeofblack campaign, which depicts the creative talent of African artists like Phyno, a Nigerian rapper, songwriter and record producer who raps in his native Igbo. The 2014 Guinness campaign is part of the company's 'Made of More' platform, which promotes a new generation of Africans who represent the "new spirit" of Africa. The "artistic heritage of humanity" is here used for basic commercial purposes. An appropriation like this one can be more readily referred to as plagiarism or emulation. As far as détournement is concerned, the work draws its meaning from the new context: an advertisement that cross-promotes the creative industries to sell beer.[172]

While for Hobbs, Wiley's work overtly mines power relations at the level of identities more than class relations, what does this have to do, if anything, with the Situationist rejection of the institutionalization of high art, and consequently, of the "civil war" they were engaged in as radical leftists?[173] What do the Situationists have to do with a progressive neoliberalism that is defined by its relation to state power? Can the Situationist project be so easily converted from a Marxist overcoming of alienation to a black capitalist realism? On the basis of a defeated class consciousness, progress is here defined as the fragmentation of symbolic regimes based on the destabilization of race, gender and sexual norms. The question then is how and whether Wiley takes art and class power seriously. Answers to these questions are thwarted by Wiley's confused statements to the effect that autonomy is eroding thanks to the connectedness of cross-platform synergy, on the one hand, and on the other, the flimsy notion that hip hop is a language of survival in a hostile world.

As a weapon of the class war, the serious-parodic stage of détournement clashes with social, cultural and legal conventions. As Debord and Wolman argue, "[t]he cheapness of its products is the heavy artillery that breaks through all the Chinese walls of understanding. It is a real means of proletarian artistic education, the first step towards a *literary communism*."[174] Cheapness is not to be conflated with ignorance or brutality – the kind of cheapness that is exemplified by alt-right trolls and wealthy politicians like Trump. An example of the latter would be the Smells Like Democracy political ad campaign by the right-wing Israeli politician Ayelet Shaked, which shows her promoting a perfume called Fascism to ironize accurate accusations levelled against her and the My Israel Zionist movement. Situationist cheapness implies egalitarianism and communism. Wiley's work cannot be said to be serious-parodic in the Situationist sense. The avant-garde tendency in détournement implies the loss of importance of the détourned elements, which, in this case would involve art history *and* hip hop, straight-white-male desire *and* queer performativity, professionalized canon *and* cross-platforming brand – all of which are subject to the "decomposition" of culture in public spheres of production.[175] Beyond that, there is barely even a hint in Wiley's work of the happy few who belong to a sign-conscious counterpublic, as

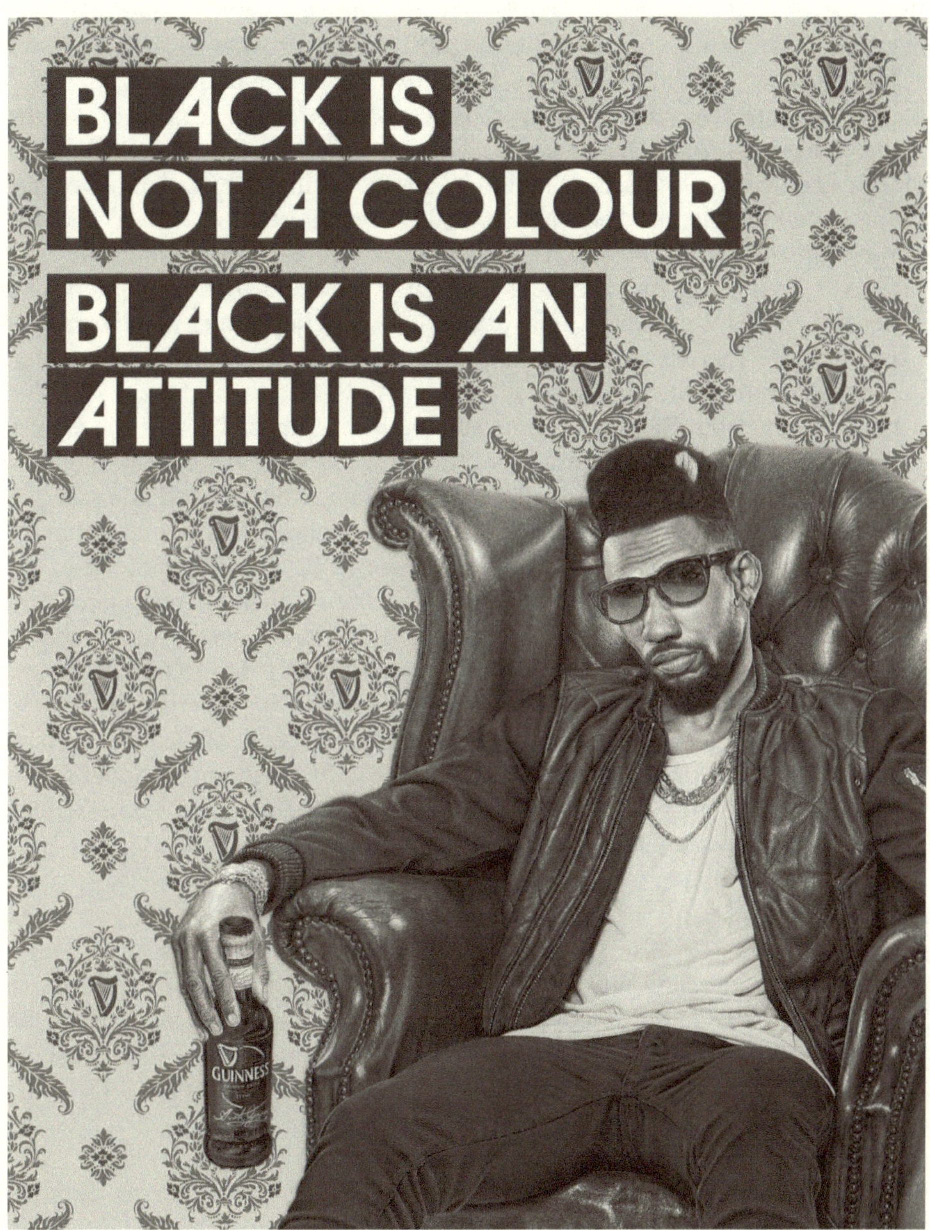

Guinness advertisement for the Guinness Africa campaign featuring the Nigerian rapper Phyno, 2014. Portrait by Steve Caldwell and background pattern by designer Dan Funderburgh. Project conceived by the AMVBBDO agency network in London with BBDO offices in Africa. Courtesy of Dan Funderburgh and The Association of Illustrators.

described by cultural critics like Mieke Bal, Norman Bryson and Michael Warner.[176] The situation that Wiley exploits is rather what McKenzie Wark refers to as the protracted spectacle of a disintegrating capitalism.[177]

A far cry from double consciousness, détournement's negation of the negation has some of the features of a Lacanian withering of symbolic efficiency. Hobbs is correct to suggest that Lacan's notion of the gaze has no empirical properties and that there is inevitably something unrepresentable and unknowable that disrupts the symbolic ordering of Wiley's figure-ground relationships.[178] However, beyond the metaphysical claptrap of the Baudrillardian sublime and Deleuzian folds, the privileged point of exclusion in Wiley's work is anti-capitalist class struggle. There is no further political activism in his post-representational second-generation postmodernism. Hobbs's mobilization of the apparatus of critical theory, from Bakhtin to Gramsci, Du Bois, Fanon, Lacan and Debord, is more promotional than appropriate. Rather, class struggle, even at the level of the sign, has been traded for dollar signs. Class has disappeared into race and sexuality; subjectivity has been made fit for exchange. Wiley's youthful black male models, even as a self-image, are allegories of the capitalization of the self.[179] The desire to see oneself reflected and refracted by the symbolic regimes of power underwrites the divided subject at the stage of its own self-consumption. What better way to describe this neoliberal condition than Maurizio Lazzarato's notion of "indebted man"?[180] In 2022, Wiley partnered with American Express to create designs for their $700 annual fee platinum credit card, adding his creeping botanicals to the company's gladiator logo. By simultaneously donating $1 million to the Harlem Studio Museum's residency programme, the artist helped to wokewash the company's philanthrocapitalist tendrils.[181]

In the Court of Charles V

The logic of post-representation is not found only in the realm of progressive neoliberalism but is also part of the logic of the alterglobal left. A counterpoint to capitalized museum art is the 2017 video project *City of Ladies* by the Australian artist Zanny Begg and the film director Elise McLeod, artists who are involved in socially engaged and anti-capitalist art practices.[181] The work is made in collaboration with several young activist women living in Paris who discuss their lives and political thoughts while also interacting with the feminist intellectuals Sam Bourcier, Hélène Cixous, Fatima-Ezzahra Benomar, Silvia Federici and Sharone Omankoy. Shown in twenty-minute samples, *City of Ladies* recombines video fragments from a database of clips into 300,000 possible narratives that invite multiples readings of feminism.

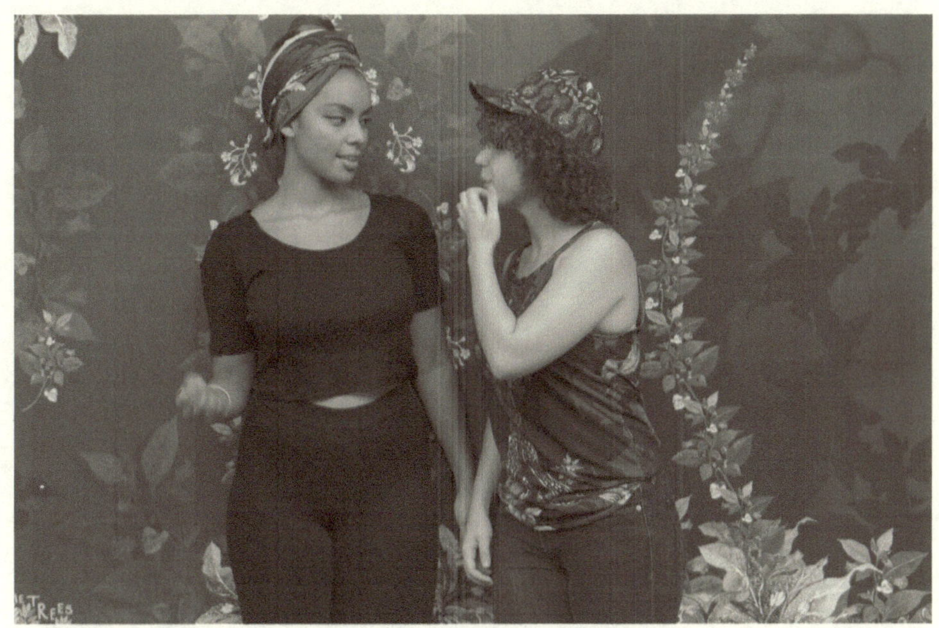

Zanny Begg and Elise McLeod, ***City of Ladies***, durational video, 2017. Courtesy of Zanny Begg.

Although most of the scenes for *City of Ladies* are filmed in everyday locations and with the young women wearing their regular clothes, these scenes are interspersed with musically enhanced interludes where they are shown in front of a plum and pink wallpaper as well as a sky-blue and cerulean wallpaper that is illustrated with repeated motifs: leaves, flowers, gendered representations of women's sexual organs, a dog named Saucy Bitch, medieval women conversing, human skulls, an activist with a blowhorn, a woman who like Daphne (in a mythological allegory of chastity) turns into a tree, the Virgin Mary, handcuffs and heart-shaped vessels. The clothing they wear in these scenes is made from fabrics with the same illustrated patterns. Rather than being sexually abducted by background motifs, as in Wiley's images, and rather than being done up in staid middle-class fashions, as in Sherald's portraits, they are enveloped in symbols that speak to their awakening social and political consciousness.

The film opens on a Paris evening in front of the allegorical statue of Marianne in Place de la République. Marianne is surrounded by three statues that personify liberty, equality and fraternity, modern values that re-inscribe the medieval virtues of faith, hope and charity. Among the subjects mentioned in the video, the girls discuss the possibility of organizing young people in proletarian neighbourhoods against the government's proposed labour reform law and use of totalitarian measures to "defend" democracy. They carry the video's wallpaper

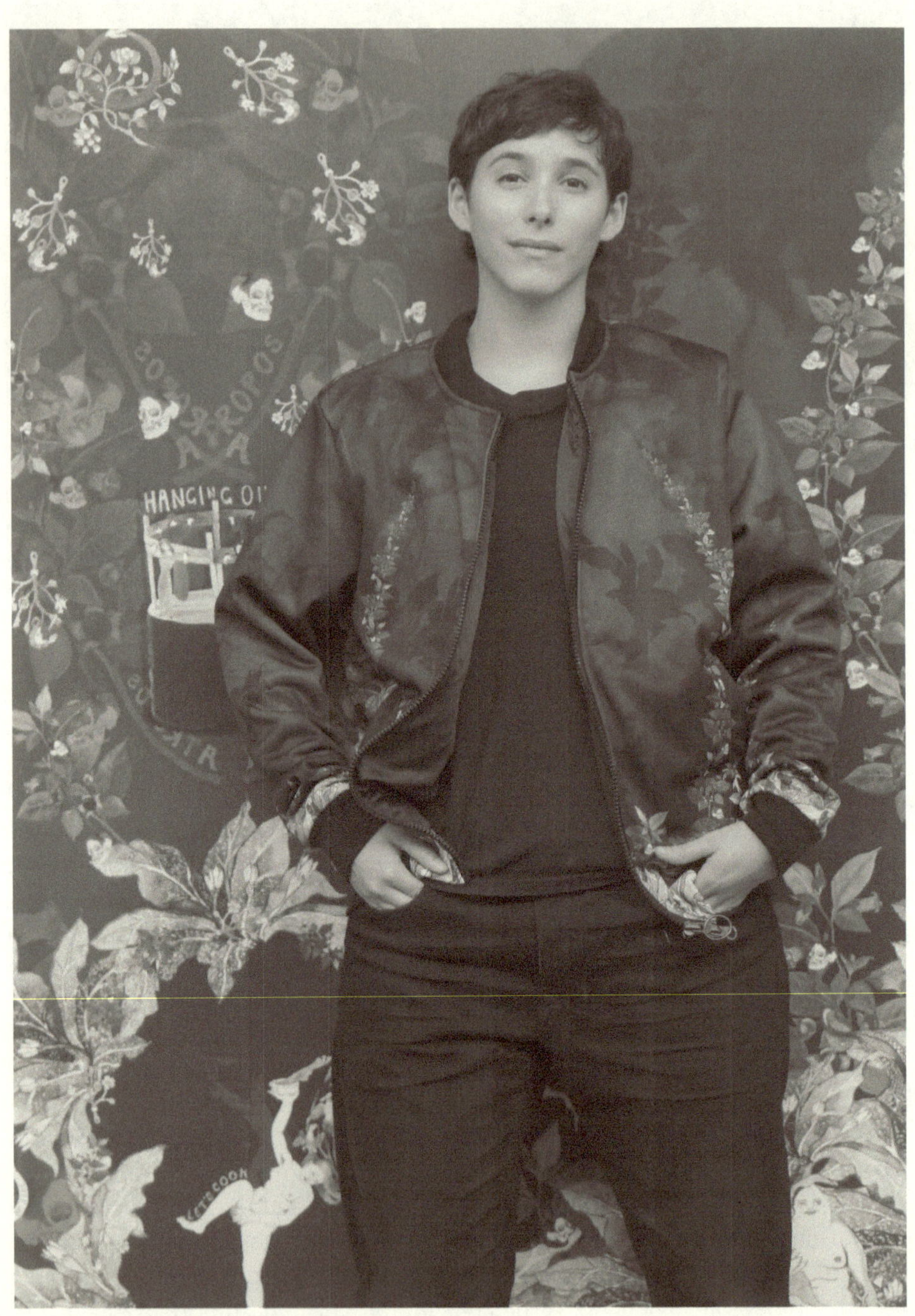

Zanny Begg and Elise McLeod, ***City of Ladies***, durational video, 2017. Courtesy of Zanny Begg.

designs and fabric patterns on protest banners. Their activism is included in street demonstrations where the banners of the General Confederation of Labour are also seen. Emergency powers have become a new normal, they say. The ravings of George Bush Jr. are heard all the way from Paris. They then sit in a casting room where one of them will be chosen for the role of Joan of Arc. The French heroine is mentioned to have appeared in the work of Shakespeare, George Bernard Shaw, Bertolt Brecht, as a Barbie doll, in the music of Patti Smith and in a film by Lars von Trier. She has more recently been made into a symbol of the right-wing National Front party.

The scene shifts to one of the girls vacuuming alongside an older co-worker. A synthetic carpet has Oriental patterns woven into it. One does not know from what country they were borrowed. Inside a posh interior, a reproduction of a May 68 poster by Atelier Populaire shows an image of a woman throwing a paving stone and a caption that says "beauty is in the streets." The young cleaner starts dancing and mentally drifts into her wallpaper universe. When she returns she looks at a copy of Friedrich Nietzsche's *The Antichrist*, then switches to Christine de Pizan's 1405 text, *The Book of the City of Ladies*. She tries on the clothes and perfume of the owner of the house, a corporate type. The businesswoman comes home to find the girl reading on the couch. Our young cleaner then rides her bicycle to meet up with her friends. On the street she sees a truck with a sign on the back that says "*louez-moi*" (rent me), which in French also means "praise me." She tells her friends that when she was at the bobo lady's house she started fantasizing about making a film. It seems she has stolen the Pizan book but we then discover that the bourgeois lady has guilt feelings, as her friend says, and lent her the book. Guilt, she argues, is not a reliable political motivation. They read from the book, which describes how women have endured centuries of assault and how they will build a walled city. "Sounds like Fortress Europe," one of them says. Another says that it is a metaphor for utopia. Pizan was considered by Simone de Beauvoir to be the first woman to use writing to defend the interests of women. She wrote ballads for court patrons and composed more than 300 works. As an advocate for the role of women in social life, she fought the sexist and misogynist ideas of her male contemporaries, in particular the view of women as evil seductresses, and offered practical advice to women. As a public intellectual who opposed scandalmongering, especially by courtly love narratives like Jean de Meun's *Roman de la Rose*, Pizan advocated that women be considered human beings while at the same time valorizing feminine qualities, which she argued are not exclusive to women. Nor are masculine qualities exclusive to men. The three women then make off, singing a song about witches and wise women.

The first of the intellectuals to be interviewed in the video is Silvia Federici. The famed socialist feminist talks about women's second-class status as lower-paid workers. Three young women listen to her discuss the history of unpaid labour.[182] Her discussion is interspersed with clips of the young cleaner stating facts, emitted like slogans, about women's work conditions: "women are paid like shit when in fact they care for you, clean your houses and raise your children." All of this takes place in the first fifteen minutes of fragments. Any one of the issues they discuss could easily be understood by the viewer. For instance, nurses in the U.S. are forced to work overtime on 16-hour shifts, with growing nurse-to-patient ratios. Reports from the American Nurses Association indicate that one in four nurses is assaulted at work on any given day. Similar reports from the Bureau of Labor Statistics show that 13 percent of nurses' days away from work are due to violence in the workplace, with health care and social service workers subject to 75 percent of reported workplace violence. However sociological and social realist, if not also postmodern and activist, the work lacks nothing in terms of styling and thoughtful construction. The only issue left unanswered, because it is not asked, is just what it is, beyond protest, that will make it such that the wages of working-class women are not so meagre in comparison with bourgeois ladies like Christine Lagarde and Marine Le Pen, whose role within the power structure is to warn that the global economy, if not the Republic, is in a state of emergency that demands more austerity measures and more scapegoating of immigrants. Beyond that, the abolition of wage labour is treated like an impractical fantasy. Nor is the commodification of ever more facets of life the solution to our problems.

CH.4: RACIALISM AND ITS DISCONTENTS

What makes itself felt in a human community as a desire for freedom may be their revolt against some existing injustice, and so may prove favorable to a further development of civilization; it may remain compatible with civilization. But it may also spring from the remains of their original personality, which is still untamed by civilization and may thus become the basis in them of hostility to civilization. The urge for freedom, therefore, is directed against particular forms and demands of civilization or against civilization altogether.

– Sigmund Freud, *Civilization and Its Discontents*

Why are there forty million poor people in America? And when you begin to ask that question, you are raising a question about the economic system, about a broader distribution of wealth.

– Martin Luther King, Jr., *Where Do We Go from Here?*

The struggle against racism reinscribes and reinforces notions of racial difference. One of the reasons why white supremacists emphasize racial hierarchy, rather than racial difference, is because, contrary to the view that white supremacy is an ideology of the white working class, racism since the turn of the previous century belongs to fascist ideology, which is a politics of domination that opposes both bourgeois universality and revolutionary socialism. Fascism is a counter-revolutionary ideology that appeals to violence against internal and external threats. Its purpose is to stabilize an inegalitarian class system. The target of fascism is not only the racial enemy but the danger that international class solidarity poses to capitalism. Various forms of fascism have today re-emerged along with the rise of virulent forms of neoliberal identity politics. Both are substitutes for the emancipatory universality of socialism. The postmodern idea that identity groups have an uncomfortable relation to class politics is more a matter of ideology than actuality. As Adolph Reed puts it: "the notion that the fault line in left-of-center politics now is between people who take a class perspective and those who take an identity-based perspective miscasts the actual tension. The identity position is itself a class position. It's just a position of a different class from the working class."[1] Those who are indifferent to this problem tend to be race-first culturalists, who can also be referred to as racialists. They may also be ethnic nationalists and in some cases intersectionalists.[2] The struggle for social equality necessitates the struggle not only against racism, but also against racialism, which requires an understanding of the political limits of anti-racism. Further problems within socialism are not only problems of social organization but problems of alienation that can be ascribed to the psychopathologies of everyday life.[3]

Taking a page from Georg Lukács' *Theory of the Novel*, in which the Hungarian critic opposed any enthusiasm for nationalist chauvinism in the context of the First World War, we could say that since the postmodern critique of meta-narratives has abated, we are similarly at the beginning of what may eventually develop as a conscious rejection of racialism.[4] We also have reason to repudiate the technocratic positivism that prevails and must develop concepts through which phenomena can be grasped. The following proposes several social typologies in relation to the race and class debate: the activist, the scapegoat, the devil's advocate, the manager, the intellectual and the broker. A section on so-called cultural Marxism is added as a chaser to these delineations. The goal here is not, as Lukács puts it, to pigeonhole concrete variations into conceptual straightjackets, but rather to provide a framework for making sense of our times and to facilitate progressive mediations of both cultural relativism and absolutism.

The Activists

In 2013, the Black Lives Matter movement emerged as an activist campaign that mobilized through the social media hashtag #BlackLivesMatter to protest racial profiling, police brutality and racial inequality in the criminal justice system. After the acquittal of George Zimmerman and the police murders of Michael Brown and Eric Garner, BLM leveraged the protests in Ferguson, New York City and elsewhere to then become involved in the 2016 Democratic Party presidential nomination campaigns. In August 2015, for example, BLM activists confronted Hillary Clinton, compelling her to acknowledge the problem of racism as a problem of ontology, in effect asking her and Bill Clinton to confess their racism rather than their policies. They offered no criticism of Obama and made no mention of the capitalist system, allowing Clinton to retort reassuringly, as Obama would have, that protest movements are a healthy sign of citizen democracy and necessary to keep governments accountable. Around the same time, BLM activists interrupted a Bernie Sanders rally, denouncing his economic populism for its avoidance of race issues and problems in the criminal justice system. Criticism is a double-edged sword. Attacking someone automatically makes them appear guilty, which is why we must often be reminded to not blame the victim and to also allow for due process in serious cases and the presumption of innocence. However, when the victim of criticism is the U.S. government and the political establishment, such considerations seem lopsided. Criticism requires that critics account for themselves. For BLM activists, hundreds of black deaths caused every year by police against an impoverished minority group whose bequest is a history of slavery and segregation is evidence enough of who the victim is in American politics. This explains why people were angered by counter-hashtags like AllLivesMatter and PoliceLivesMatter. What the reaction obscured, nevertheless, is the question of programme and leadership in BLM activism.

The Black Lives Matter (Global Network Foundation) was co-founded by Alicia Garza, who is also the director of Special Projects for the National Domestic Workers Alliance advocacy group and now operates the Black Futures think tank. One of the board members of the NDWA is Alta Starr, a black freedom movement advocate who served as a funder at the Ford Foundation. Garza has also served on the board of The Open Society, a foundation that is backed by the billionaire George Soros, who also fundraised for Hillary Clinton and whose Open Society support for BLM has been linked to the group's critiques of Sanders, a claim that is denied by the activists. BLM was also co-founded by human rights activist Opal Tometi, who is Executive Director of the Black Alliance for Just Immigration. Another co-founder of BLM is Patrisse Cullors, who is also a board member of the Ella Baker Center for Human Rights, which was founded by Obama supporter and CNN contributor Van Jones, who defined Donald Trump's election as a "whitelash" against Obama. The Ella Baker Center also receives funding from The Open Society. Although Cullors wants to train black leaders to enter government and demands reparations for blacks, she does not criticize corporate oligarchy, and for good reason since she is now the co-owner with Janaya Khan, the co-founder of BLM Toronto, of four million-dollar homes. After Cullors left BLM in 2020 due to criticism of lucrative deals with Warner Bros, YouTube and book publishers, she co-started the Crenshaw Dairy Mart art gallery in Inglewood, California, a neighbourhood in which black and Latino communities are threatened by gentrification schemes.

Very little is accomplished in the U.S. without the support of philanthropy, and so one can understand that activists would look for the financial assistance of foundations that support progressive causes. However, the need for financial support from corporate agencies does not mitigate their influence. The link to the Ford Foundation illuminates some of the problems of the BLM movement. The Foundation has pledged to channel $100 million into the BLM GNF organization, which would allow it to lobby government as a part of the Black-Led Movement Fund, which is overseen by the Borealis Foundation that is integrated with the Democratic Party. As the third largest endowment in the U.S., the Ford Foundation has ties to Wall Street, military-intelligence agencies and the corporate media. Its board consists of corporate CEOs and Wall Street lawyers. The outlook of BLM is therefore consistent with the shift in the Democratic Party over the last several decades from labour and civil rights struggles to the kind of identity politics that support the profit system and the privileges of the black middle class. BLM has mostly contributed to awareness of the need for police reform. Its 10-Point Manifesto makes many valuable suggestions to reduce incarceration: the elimination of broken windows policing of minor crimes; standardized reporting, independent oversight, as well as community accountability for police misconduct, also subject to police union regulation; better training and body cameras for de-militarized and community-appropriate police. These reforms, however beneficial, cannot be implemented without a progressive political effort that would also seek to eliminate poverty. The fact of the matter is that police violence is an index of economic equality. In the Southwest it disproportionately affects Hispanic men; in major cities it disproportionately affects black men; in Southern rural areas it affects white and black men; and in non-Southern rural areas it disproportionately affects white men.[5] In 2020, the year of the George Floyd protests, police killed 475 white people, 241 black people and 169 Hispanics. Police violence disproportionately affects men to women by a ratio of 2000 to1. The U.S., which has 4.5 percent of the world population, accounts for 14 percent of police killings, which is equivalent to the 2020-21 COVID-19 death rate. There is something wrong in this supremely capitalist state and it is not simply racism.

A key element of the racialist narrative is the endemic nature of white supremacy, a view that was reaffirmed by the Trump presidency. Aaron Morrison, the national leader of the Black Lives Matter Global Network stated on the occasion:

> Civic engagement is one way to engage in democracy, and our lives don't revolve around election cycles. We are obliged to earn the trust of future generations – to defend economic, social and political power for all people. (...) We are committed to practicing for one another in this struggle – but we do not and will not negotiate with racists, fascists and anyone who demands we compromise our existence.[6]

Like most other statements issued by BLM, it does not attribute Trump's victory to neoliberalism, global capitalism or bipartisanship, but rather focuses on racism, sexism and the resentment of whites about the ascendancy of black wealth and black political power. "In the months leading up to this election," the statement says, "we have demanded support from white people in dismantling white supremacy… We feel more than disappointed or angry – we feel betrayed."

Morrison does not address the fact that Americans voted twice for Obama, who did plenty to betray black Americans. Obama's policies, like the practice of "humane" warfare to extend the War on Terror, are surprisingly absent from Ibram X. Kendi's *How to Be an Antiracist*. Despite Kendi's emphasis on policy as the solution to racial disparities, he celebrates the fact that between 2003 and 2017, the percentage of black Americans who define racism as the primary cause of racial disparities increased from 40 percent to 60 percent.[7] According to Reed, many race-first advocates, including politicians like the late John Lewis and James Clyburn, favoured Clinton over Sanders despite the fact that a 2017 survey found that at 73 percent favourability, Sanders was more popular with African Americans than any other demographic group, including young voters.[8] In "Splendors and Miseries of the Antiracist 'Left'," Reed criticizes the best of the black activist class that has emerged since the 1960s and that is now in the throes of social media activism and intersectional identitarianism, including the youth activism around Occupy Wall Street and the Democratic Socialists of America.[9]

Reed's main point of contention is the reduction of black politics since the 1940s to equal opportunity capitalism. This has allowed the black Professional-Managerial Class to set a post-representational agenda that overestimates activist mobilization and neglects the need to build an organizational base. Reed argues that BLM is not inherently radical and has more to do with academic life and self-promoting group essentialism. It also advances a flawed, monocausal and static understanding of the racism it presumes to be fighting. How it is that one should understand racial disparities is not the same issue as how one goes about fighting against racism and related notions like institutional racism. Race, Reed writes, "should be seen as one of a class of ideologies of hierarchy based on ascriptive differentiation that is based on what people purportedly are rather than what they do."[10] Race hierarchies mediate regimes of preference and coercion that have developed over the last three centuries into differences of ascriptive status within American capitalism, including notions of heredity, criminality and feeble-mindedness. The contradiction of progressive anti-racism, he says, is its fantasy of a non-essential racial essentialism. Reed rejects the standard postmodernist logic of social constructionism. He also rejects BLM's ontologization of racism as a basis for radical politics. Identity politics is less a politics of its own and is rather an appurtenance of bourgeois ideology. The consequence is that the rise of a black millionaire club will not benefit the majority of blacks since it does nothing to challenge market forces. The convenient mixture in BLM politics of liberalism, social democracy, black nationalism and neoliberalism is more suited to product branding and communitarian rhetoric, he argues, than effective social struggle.

The promotion of black unity through the social media celebrity of astroturf spokespeople is not anti-capitalist. It rather stages symbolic connections to the militant struggles of the past and conflates contemporary conditions with the era of Jim Crow. The corruption of grassroots activism by the corporate-funded "non-profit industrial complex" is defined by the leftist social critic Paul Street as yet another "graveyard of social movements."[11] The denunciation of white hetero-patriarchy by identity careerists, Street says, attaches identity to commodity branding rather than social justice. Government and corporations are more than happy to support such groups.

Black Lives Matter emerged in the context of the so-called hashtag revolutions of new social movements, which, in the case of black politics in the U.S., allowed for distinctions to be made between the new wave of activists and the Civil Rights organizations that have in various ways become extensions of establishment political parties. As Keeanga-Yamahtta Taylor argues, the "new guard" of BLM activists define themselves as a part of a movement that is decentralized, leaderless and that approaches organizing in terms of an intersectional emphasis on multiple issues that acknowledge different forms of oppression.[12] The diversity of approaches to the Black Lives Matter cause recommends the phrase Movement for Black Lives (M4BL) as a preferable umbrella term, which has included The Black Youth Project 100, the Dream Defenders, Assata's Daughters, Leaders of a Beautiful Struggle and more than 150 other organizations, community groups and black student unions.

The fact that BLM has come under the influence of not-for-profit foundations with ties to the State Department leads to the strategic concern that whenever such groups reach a high level of popular support, they begin to function in ways that are similar to the Civil Rights organizations that they distinguish themselves from. This is doubly ironic since neither sector is similar to the Civil Rights movement of the 1960s. Although the mass multiracial protests that erupted in every state after the police murder of George Floyd were related to dire social conditions and exacerbated by the COVID-19 pandemic, the demand to defund the police was quickly reduced to racialist thinking by government representatives, who symbolically 'took a knee' against racist policing, and by corporations, which funnelled hundreds of millions of dollars into anti-racism initiatives. As the CARES Act and similar fiscal measures were in the process of bailing out the billionaire class, and as unemployment had reached Depression era levels, the political disorientation of BLM, according to Cedric Johnson, reflected the "liberal character" of social justice organizations.[13] For instance, the scholar who coined the term intersectionality, Kimberlé Crenshaw, made the revanchist argument that the resurgence of BLM activism in June 2020 was evidence of the failed universalism of the Sanders 2020 campaign.[14] You would be hard pressed to find very many people who approve of police murder, whether or not the latter are racially motivated, which is why the number of people supporting BLM protests is overwhelming. Some 20 million Americans took to the streets in 2020 to protest police murders, the majority of them white. However, as Ralph Nader argues, when in 2018 the Reverend William Barber and Liz Theoharis started a country-wide Poor People's Campaign, they received almost no press coverage and poor people did not come out to support the effort at coordinated action.[15]

Since a race politics that is class conscious creates the threat of a grassroots insurgency, establishment elites have been keen to channel anti-racist energies. By the end of 2020, BLM and related groups received some $5 billion from corporate America for anti-racism initiatives. An article in the *Washington Post* describes how after the George Floyd protests, corporate America would "no longer stay silent and promised to take an active role in confronting systemic racism."[16] The McDonald's Family Restaurant conglomerate declared that George Floyd was "one of us." JP Morgan Chase CEO Jamie Morgan took a knee. Fortune 500 corporations like Apple, Facebook, Pfizer, Proctor & Gamble and Bank of America promised they would fight back against racial injustice. Some 50 companies pledged $49.5 billion to address racial inequality, to be disbursed over a period of ten years. This represents less than one percent of the c.$525 billion in earned income that the top 50 companies make every year. However, the authors say, the money that will be doled out is mostly in the form of loans and investments that will benefit these same companies. In some cases, assistance is earmarked under special provisions that help banks avoid legal challenges and that encourage gentrification. While grants worth $4.2 billion had been made by the end of 2020, only $70 million had been disbursed to criminal justice groups. The larger portion went to groups that are focused on poverty, education, health, culture, civil rights and community investment like money transfers to black banks. By 2022, 37 companies had disbursed $1.7 billion of the pledged $49.5 billion. Most of this was oriented towards the promotion of upwardly mobile blacks through homeownership, entrepreneurial business loans in mostly the tech sector, and education, especially through grants to historically black colleges and universities. Education is seen by corporations to be less controversial than criminal justice reform, which comes under the purview of the public sector, and which is therefore more difficult for financiers to manipulate. Even when criminal justice is involved, charity prefers soft topics like cash bail and voter registration for formerly incarcerated individuals. Investment in education results in its own sorts of problems, however, as financiers seek to direct and control research infrastructures that reinforce business interests. HBCUs, these authors suggest, are engines of mobility for the black middle class. The band-aid solutions that have been prized from corporate America by BLM and the M4BL are part of the usual philanthrocapitalism that does nothing to reduce the wealth gap. These solutions do not represent structural changes to the neoliberal status quo and ongoing trends in the upward redistribution of wealth. By rejecting a public option for health care, refusing to raise taxes on the wealthy, avoiding immigration reform and the defence of civil liberties, foreign policy and military reform, criminal justice reform and election reform, the bipartisan Biden administration has made good on its promise that nothing will fundamentally change. Likewise, woke neoliberal capitalism is still neoliberal capitalism. As even charitable donors acknowledge, the post-George Floyd protest donations will not fundamentally alter the lives of black people or anyone else in the U.S.[17]

When leftists critique the ideology of the BLM movement, this, for some commentators, is proof enough that the left has a 'class reductionism' problem.[18] There are several problems with this term, least of all the fact that it is a Marxist term of disapprobation that is now used by racialists and intersectionalists against Marxists. The misuse of this term is related to the development of Critical Race Theory (CRT) and similar forms of post-structuralist identitarianism. An article written by Tom Carter on the subject helps to elaborate the problems of reductionism.[19] The teaching of CRT was attacked in ten states in the U.S. in 2021 as part of a broader assault on democracy and radicalism. Although critical of CRT, the Marxist left has no sympathy for these moves by Republicans and defends political rights. One could also view the attack on CRT as a feature of bipartisan collusion, which keeps people on both sides of the Dems/GOP divide fighting over identity politics of the left-wing and right-wing sorts, thereby leaving the socialist perspective out of politics altogether. When socialism is denounced by the far right, it is usually with reference to liberal progressives and the activist left. The radical left can nevertheless critique CRT without feeling that it is ceding ground to the conservative right. In fact, the left that is organized around the Democratic Party and the DSA – or the NDP in Canada – would benefit from more radicalism both within and outside the institutionalized sphere of state politics. The mistake that is made by state progressives like Alexandria Ocasio-Cortez is the assumption that CRT is left-wing. Not surprisingly, she mentions the term CRT at the same time that she denounces those people who critique it from the left as being "privileged" and acting in "bad faith."[20] The right, on the other hand, denounces CRT advocates for stoking national disunity.

Carter defines CRT as a field of scholarship that developed in the 1980s and 90s. More accurately, it was 'postcolonial' theory that was in vogue at that time and not CRT, which has emerged since then as a framework that more strategically manipulates the critique of whiteness. In his estimation, CRT is based on postmodern theory, racial sectarianism, subjective idealism and alignment with the Democratic Party. As the New Democrats shifted from the welfarism of the New Deal and Great Society programmes to neoliberalism plus social justice issues, defined in terms of race, gender and sexuality, the political locus of "radicalism" has shifted from left-wing parties, organizations and unions to university settings, the communications technology sector and Hollywood. Some of the themes addressed by CRT include cultural appropriation, white privilege, white supremacy, white fragility, patriarchy, toxic masculinity, safe spaces, microaggressions, rape culture, trigger warnings and standpoint epistemology.

As opposed to the Enlightenment-derived materialism of Marxism, postmodern relativism reduces scientific understanding to the status of discourses, narratives and subjective standpoint. Postmodernists argue that what we know is not as important as mining and deconstructing the conditions of possibility for knowledge, often reduced to questions of power and representation. Power rather than shared truths adjudicates how one decides, for instance, between the claims of religious groups and the claims of scientists. According to Carter, the CRT notion of "speaking your truth" and "personal storytelling" allows individuals to construct their own reality. This is consistent with the value that postmodernism attributes to *petites histoires* rather than meta-narratives that are universalist in implication, like the notion of human rights, the Marxist dialectic and Freud's discovery of the unconscious. This approach also marks the shift from the labour politics of production relations to the consumer politics of countercultures, subcultures and target audiences, a shift that coincides with post-Fordism, de-industrialization, globalization and neoliberalization. The radical subjectivism that is thereby privileged can also 'scale up' and lead for example to such counter-intuitive trends like the anti-racist critique of mathematics on the view that math has a Eurocentric bias. As Carter observes, this is the opposite of Marxist materialism, which draws on Enlightenment notions of objectivity, progress, secularism and universalism. Since CRT operates as a 'hermeneutic of suspicion' rather than a form of empiricism, it finds evidence of racism, Eurocentrism and white supremacy in nearly every aspect of society. It thus tends to operate according to the 'false consciousness' definition of ideology, using contradictory evidence to confirm the initial postulate. Since the mainstream of society is deemed to be inherently and structurally racist, only those with the proper identity can undertake the work of deconstruction. This is what is meant by the kind of 'standpoint epistemology' that is advocated by Richard Delgado and Jean Stefancic, who limit the rights of criticism to those with the "presumed competence to speak about race and racism."[21] Taken to the extreme, standpoint epistemology suggests that a patient could speak with as much competence as a doctor, or a child as a parent and teacher, etc.

One of the most problematic aspects of CRT is its reliance on the concept of race. The arbitrary categorization of people into white and black performs a double blackmail. A person is first designated as white. Then they are criticized for being white and told they have to change themselves to satisfy the arbitrary requirements of CRT experts. If one is given to neurotic virtue signalling, this may not feel like an imposition. If one's career or employment depends on it, these impositions cannot but constitute new methods of managerial control. Along these lines, women should gladly submit to the violent demands of involuntary celibates. Nothing about CRT is decidedly anti-capitalist. In this regard it betrays the Civil Rights leadership of people like Martin Luther King and A. Philip Randolph, who struggled so that all people could be treated equally and with dignity. By emphasizing social division rather than difference, CRT is at odds with the universalist and emancipatory thrust of black politics up to the 1960s. In addition, since CRT makes no distinctions between the black working class and the black bourgeoisie, it works against the possibility of multiracial class solidarity. CRT is therefore conservative on at least two counts. Whereas the work of identifying specific inequalities is a valid exercise, one cannot from this infer that all aspects of society and epistemology should be altered in order to address the problems of a minority group. Moreover, the social constructionist methodology that CRT rests upon is 'totalitarian' in its epistemological presuppositions and as such mitigates social change. That is why CRT is not an emancipatory politics but rather a racially redistributive or racially kaleidoscopic politics. That this redistribution of assets benefits primarily the black middle and upper classes makes it such that wealth inequality within racially designated groups increases. One might think that CRT is a form of anarchist "chaosophy" if it was not for the fact that it seeks to increase the amount of institutional power awarded to privileged class segments of specific racial groups.[22] This then reinforces hierarchy in the workplace. What people who benefit from diversity mandates seek to do with the power gained is not as important as gaining access to positions of power. In this regard, it is not a politics so much as a nihilistic anti-politics. However, given the fact that we exist in a capitalist world, the chances that the use of 'black ways of knowing' will be progressive is completely left to chance, which is a standard postmodern trope.

Another pernicious aspect of CRT is the fact that it is oriented towards racial separatism. With its sources in black nationalism and its anti-Eurocentrism attitude, CRT breaks with the internationalist and Marxist foundations of the black power movement and gives black nationalism a neoliberal orientation. The fact that organizations like the Academy of Motion Picture Arts and Sciences has imposed various kinds of diversity quota fulfilments gives credence to a Democratic Party agenda that is not about redistributing wealth to the majority of poor Americans, let alone the disproportionately poor African American population. It is rather designed to quell social unrest through symbolic and cultural substitutes for radical social reform.[23] Although the term 'cultural Marxism' can mean many things, those who advocate for such capitalist culturalization of politics cannot in fact be thought of as Marxists, whether as 'cultural' or 'political' Marxists. The problems of poverty, public education, housing or policing are fundamentally problems of American capitalism. These issues are approached differently in different places, but they are nevertheless the same fundamental problems when seen from the perspective of political economy and social solidarity. However, CRT explains all of these as race problems. By doing so, it puts into effect a form of race reductionism that obscures the workings of capitalism. As Carter and others mention, the Marxist critique of CRT is not meant to discount the existence of racism in society or to avoid seeking solutions to those problems. However, the brutal reality of racism does not by itself determine the best means to fight against it. Many liberals, neoliberals and conservatives are against racism. The trouble with woke racialism is that it translates social critique into middle-class identity politics.

As soon as class critiques of CRT are put forward, its advocates accuse those who disagree of denial and demand intersectional reform. As in Lizzie Borden's feminist film *Born in Flames* (1983), the charge against the left is that problems of racism and sexism would – or rather, will – continue to exist under even a social democratic government. This is an interesting yet unexamined point. Marxists argue that whereas racial and sexual divisions are not inherently conflictual, there is no possibility of class harmony under the domination of the bourgeois state. Why then would an identitarian reject a socialist government? The only possible answer to this is because they are committed to the culture war first and forever. One might also think that they do not in fact want racial or gender harmony. One thinks for example of the poet Eileen Myles's macho endorsement of Hillary Clinton as a feminist crusader. Despite social inequalities in various socialist state experiments, anti-oppression issues regarding race, gender and sexuality have not been ignored by the radical left. This misconception that operates more like an in-group rumour is a phenomenon of postwar petty-bourgeois ideology that has only gained more traction with postmodern theory and neoliberal governance. One of the most ridiculed proponents of CRT is the consultant Robin DiAngelo, who rejects the centrality of class analysis as a method that she says maintains white solidarity and protects white privilege and racism.[24] Her three-hour workshops in white self-flagellation cost universities as much as $20,000. Using spurious if not harmful forms of psychology, she and similar CRT gurus reorient ego psychology against socially widespread guilt structures. Rather than organize politics around collective action and solidarity, the corporate CRT gurus who make each individual responsible for social structures have created a petty-bourgeois reform phenomenon suited to the new Gilded Age of billionaire wealth.

As trends in leftist activist circles combine with CRT, strange hybrids and political compromises result. For instance, Carter mentions that whiteness is defined by some advocates of CRT, like Cheryl Harris, as a form of "property" that is possessed by all white people, regardless of their social status.[25] Unlike Bourdieu's sociology, this anthropological focus on guilt structures shifts the focus from a critique of the dominant capitalist system to the view that whites are the dominant class. However, the U.S. is a capitalist society and not a white supremacist society akin to the patriarchal regime in Margaret Atwood's *The Handmaid's Tale*. That such accusations come after two terms by a black president and in a world with capitalist regimes of every conceivable nationality merely underscores the race particularism that reflects the myopia of American exceptionalism. The black and brown advocacy of the racialist PMC rarely extends beyond American borders. Racial disparities, even when conceived in terms of international differences, are not by themselves political arguments. By rejecting the centrality of class or by remaking class domination into classism, CRT avoids the charge of ideological collusion with the bourgeois class. Carter writes in response: "For Marxists, yes, we plead guilty to being 'class reductionists.' Class for us is not just another form of subjective prejudice."[26] Carter explains his statement by saying that Marx was not satisfied to note the unequal distribution of wealth, which had been the case for thousands of years after human societies had produced enough surplus for there to develop social inequality between the poor and the wealthy, who guarded their bounty with the use of military force, this being the basis for the Marxist critique of the bourgeois state.

Marx's focus on the commodity and on wage labour as a contradictory social relation begins with the actuality of capitalist society in the mid-nineteenth century. Noting that capitalism's laws of development have become a global phenomenon, Marx devised a strategy of revolutionary transformation. Marxists need not plead guilty on the count of class reductionism, however. For the bourgeois class, workers are a particular class that will always exist because capitalist social relations must always exist. For the bourgeoisie, this working-class part of the social space does nothing, and should not be allowed to do anything, to transform the totality of global capitalism. Marx made this issue perfectly clear in his letter to Joseph Weydemeyer from March 5, 1852. He wrote:

> And now as to myself, no credit is due to me for discovering the existence of classes in modern society or the struggle between them. Long before me bourgeois historians had described the historical development of this class struggle and bourgeois economists, the economic anatomy of classes. What I did that was new was to prove: (1) that the *existence of classes* is only bound up with the *particular, historical phases in the development of production*; (2) that the class struggle necessarily leads to the *dictatorship of the proletariat*; (3) that this dictatorship itself only constitutes the transition to the *abolition of all classes* and to a *classless society*.[27]

Consider also this quote from Friedrich Engels' 1877 *Anti-Dühring*, where he too discusses the notion of the withering of the state in the transition from socialism to communism:

> *The proletariat seizes state power and turns the means of production into state property to begin with.* But thereby it abolishes itself as the proletariat, abolishes all class distinctions and class antagonisms, and abolishes also the state as state. Society thus far, operating amid class antagonisms, needed the state, that is, an organization of the particular exploiting class, for the maintenance of its external conditions of production, and, therefore, especially, for the purpose of forcibly keeping the exploited class in the conditions of oppression determined by the given mode of production (slavery, serfdom or bondage, wage-labor).[28]

In dialectical Hegelian terms, what this means is that the parts that constitute the different classes do not add up to the whole of the social totality, yet their relation is to one another and to the whole. This is true for class analysis as it is also true for the Marxist approach to identity issues. That is why Marxists are often misunderstood by postmodernists. For Marxists, the working class, conceived as the proletariat, is the universal class. While it is mostly only the working class that has an interest in ridding the world of capitalist social relations, only the working class has the power to do so. The plight of the working class therefore stands in for the claims that are made for all: equality, freedom, solidarity. To make good on these claims is the specific task of socialism.

Is there a limit to what woke postmodernists will say against the Marxist left? The limit is informed by today's ideology. Since many postmodern discourse theorists, social constructionists and left populists have claims to be the actually existing left, they have to characterize the Marxists who disagree with them as bourgeois or right-wing – just as critics like Reed are denounced by some for having bought into the white power structure. Although many of them claim that they do not believe in modernist macro-politics, they opportunistically resort to its terms when the need arises. This in fact is the sad irony of the concept of class reductionism when it is wielded by postmodern identitarians. Nevertheless, what one finds in such accusations is the way that identity politics has influenced their thinking. Just as whiteness studies considers whites to be guilty and inherently flawed, the postmodern left goes on the attack against the Marxist left as if it were an identity group. The problem with the bourgeoisie is that it is cis-normative. The problem with the far right is that it is racist and xenophobic. And the avenues that constitute the 'intersection' are a series of one-way streets. Whites, men and straights are not allowed to enjoy with the same license as blacks, women and queers. At best, they can do so by eating their own. Since the bogeyman version of class reductionism is not Marxist at all, the accusation shifts to individualized ad hominem attacks and futurist social media blasts. One is accused of white supremacy or one is censored according to procedural issues like 'tone' and other mysteries that Jo Freeman defined 40 years ago already as problems of organizational structurelessness.[29] A further problem is that with the advent of social media, mob-like behaviour is now affecting society at large, grade schools, business and government. While one might think that this new puritanism has something to do with social critique, the individualized nature of the attacks and the refusal to debate matters with reasoned arguments betrays the reactionary ideologies that befuddle the myriad forms of contemporary identity politics.

For Taylor, inequality among black Americans and the rise of an affluent black middle and upper class means that African Americans draw different conclusions about critical issues like police violence.[30] Any change to institutional racism, she argues, cannot occur without the transformation of capitalist social relations. The rise of a new "black left," as she puts it, requires a reciprocal understanding of common interests and of how it is that racism is used to divide workers and promote ruling-class ideas. Taylor is now among the black PMC, having earned as much as $700,000 in 2021 from the world of corporate fellowships like the MacArthur Foundation and the Guggenheim Memorial Foundation. In the last few decades, such conservative and liberal foundations that are worth more than $100,000 billion in assets have increasingly sought to buy influence in elections and national debates. In 2020, Taylor added her criticisms to those among anti-Marxists who called for the cancellation of a talk by Reed to Philadelphia and New York City chapters of the DSA, making the distinction between class politics and race politics on the left an ongoing dilemma. The activism around the M4BL is part of a social movement critique of the myths of the post-racial society and conservative attacks on state intervention. Emphasizing a class politics that places race issues at the centre of debates, Taylor champions a new black left rather than simply, the socialist left. As she sees it, black unity cannot be achieved until black and minority workers win the solidarity of white workers. White workers must come over to the cause of anti-racism against the plutocracy. Radical black leftism in this case makes a strong case for racialist logics since the universalist reforms that are advocated by people like Sanders and Reed are considered to be the old arguments of the right wing of the socialist movement. The rise of phenomena like CRT makes the prospect of a working-class movement that will advance the priority of black radicalism against 'structural racism' highly unlikely. This explains the expediency of the unfortunate concept of the white working class.

The Scapegoat

The Trump presidency has led to a great deal of speculation about those who voted for him, causing some to posit the sexism and white supremacy of the working class. As David Roediger argues in his review of Joan C. Williams' 2017 book, *White Working Class: Overcoming Class Cluelessness in America*, the stereotype of the 'white working class' was used in 2016 to explain Trump's victory and Clinton's defeat, leading to confusion about the difference between class interests and racial composition.[31] Gurminder Bhambra suggests that the post-election focus on the grievances of white workers in the rust belt is disingenuous for several reasons, including the fact that Trump was overwhelmingly supported by self-employed and middle-class whites. For the election narrative to shift from class and education levels to race issues, Trump did not need to flip the majority of white working-class voters but only a small number of former Obama supporters. The emphasis on the working class by media elites and academics to explain Trump, Bhambra argues, supports a pernicious stereotype about white identity and supposed anxieties about the loss of racial privilege. The only way to counter this, she adds, is to acknowledge the reality and history of the multiracial working class.[32] Similarly, Barbara and Karen Fields argue that the connection between labour and civil rights struggles that people used to take for granted in the 1960s has practically vanished today, so much so that when someone in the media mentions the 'working class' or 'working-class voters,' the liberal anti-racist framework that they operate with presumes that these terms imply white people, which pre-empts class struggle. The effort to blame white workers for racism then leads people to consider race rather than class to be fundamental. To know this does not make the task of the left any easier since American ideology, they argue, is an economic relation that is embedded in the ideology of race relations.[33] As far as the rust belt vote is concerned, Richard Seymour contends that there is no reason to choose between race and class issues in the 2016 election: "racist nationalism is the mythical mode through which Trump tried to address the very real economic distress of a minority of American voters."[34] It remains to be seen, however, and according to what Kwame Anthony Appiah refers to as a "cognitive division of labour," how it is that race matters to such voters, who may be motivated in differential ways with regard to identity issues.[35] The emphasis on 'whiteness' is a means to ignore class differences among whites. Ultimately, Seymour argues, the American working class does not vote because it is not represented. The notion that the white working class is accountable for Trump's victory is, according to him, a "scapegoating" that is inaccurate, incoherent, nebulous and serves as useful cover for authoritarian politics.

Given Trump's scapegoating of immigrants along with almost anyone he perceives to be the enemy of the day – including acolytes like Stephen Bannon, Mike Pence and Mitch McConnell – and given also the various kinds of social inequality that exist, it may seem perverse to consider the white working class to be the scapegoat of American politics. Regardless, this group is more structurally necessary as a scapegoat than are the various threats manufactured by the State Department. The disparagement of the white working class by liberal and educated elites is necessary to pit workers against one another rather than against establishment interests. Its most readymade references are Southern white workers in the Reconstruction era and blue-collar "hard hats" in the Nixon and Reagan years. Despite the relative veracity of charges of working-class conservatism, in both cases the structural dynamics of class society do not simply apportion blame, but more importantly, they explain it. This is not to excuse efforts to maintain white racial privilege where they occur. One could, nevertheless, argue along with Barbara Ehrenreich that liberal elite contempt for the white working class conveniently ignores such socially produced problems like declining lifespans that are due to mounting suicide rates, drug addiction and diseases of despair caused by economic stress.[36] Add to this media stereotypes along the lines of *Honey Boo Boo* and *Duck Dynasty* and you have cause for desperate people to seek vicarious forms of triumphalism through racial identification, populist resentment of elites and the conservative acceptance of societal decline.

In the case of the 2016 election, the notion of working-class reaction does not hold up to scrutiny. Rather than an increase in Trump and Republican support, what actually occurred was a decrease in voter turnout and decrease of support for the Democrats under the leadership of Hillary Clinton, who campaigned on the basis of a continuation of Reagan-Clinton-Bush-Obama policies. In addition to this, one third of the counties in the industrial states of

Wisconsin, Minnesota, Michigan, Pennsylvania, Indiana, Illinois, Ohio and Iowa that voted twice for Obama opted for Trump as a protest vote. White working-class exodus in this grouping numbers in the hundreds of thousands only and should not be over-estimated, as youth in the Midwest, for instance, voted for Green Party leader Jill Stein. In 2008, the Democrats had 69 million votes to the Republicans' 60 million votes. In 2012 and 2016 the GOP vote stayed the same while the Democratic Party vote declined to 66 million in 2012 and then to a nearly equivalent 61 million in 2016. Although Trump had only 60 million to Clinton's 60.5 million votes, he won the Electoral College. In 2016, some 100 million voters abstained or voted for a third party. Working-class Trump voters were not exclusively white, as support for Clinton fell in cities like Detroit, Cleveland, Philadelphia and Milwaukee. Many of the people who had experienced plant closures, layoffs and wage cuts throughout the previous two elections, and who happen to be white, had voted for Sanders in the Democratic Party primaries. No one in BLM, the Democratic Party or the corporate media, let alone Sanders himself, attributes the swing vote for Trump to the fact that the Democratic National Committee sabotaged these voters' preferred candidate, who had led a New Deal campaign against the party establishment and supported activist initiatives to confront corporate power.

Those who smear the working class also like to boast that Hillary Clinton received overwhelming support from middle and upper-class educated women voters. Although 37 percent of women voted for Obama, only 30 percent of eligible women voters, around 35 million, voted for Clinton. All ethnic groups increased their vote for Trump from 2012 Republican support: whites by an average of one percent; blacks by seven percent; Latinos by eight percent; and Asian Americans by 11 percent. As mentioned previously, approximately 52 percent of the people who were interviewed in 2016 exit polls cited economic issues as their main voting concern. Race and gender issues registered at less than one percent. About two thirds of respondents said that their personal economic situation had worsened in the past four years and half of these respondents voted for Trump as a candidate who promised to bring economic change. Trump's takeover of traditional DP supporters was highest among families with earnings under $30,000, ten percent of whom switched, with a six percent win from households earning up to $50,000 and a two percent win from those making $100-200,000. Clinton, on the other hand, won affluent voters over from the Republicans, gaining nine percent of households earning $100-200,000, 11 percent of those making more than $250,000 and a whopping 60 percent of those making between $2 and $3.5 million.

What the numbers from 2016 show is that blacks were proportionately more likely than whites to switch to Trump and that millionaires and the upper-middle class were far more likely than the working class to vote for Clinton, who lost ten percent of union households.[37] This is not to suggest that the wealthy did not vote for Trump, whose supporters were wealthier than supporters of previous Republican candidates, but it is to suggest that the two-party system is increasingly geared to favour the plutocracy. One should also consider that in 2016 there were 10.7 million more eligible voters than the previous election and that two thirds of this group consists of ethnic and racial minorities. Whereas Clinton focused on celebrity support in metropolitan counties, giving priority to the same social forces as Obama – Wall Street, the Pentagon, Silicon Valley and Hollywood – and with promises of tax credits for entrepreneurs rather than a progressive plan for health and employment, Trump tapped into popular discontent by campaigning against elite corruption, free trade agreements and the bugaboo of immigrant terrorists.[38] In the 2020 election, this pattern was largely the same except for the fact that fewer white male workers voted for Trump, who otherwise increased his percentage of support among all minority groups. The main difference was that exit polls showed a greater propensity, especially among Democrats, to consider race issues among the most pressing social problems.

The political philosopher Michael Bray takes a Žižekian approach to the subject of Trump voters and suggests that racialist liberals have created the imaginary figure of a pathologically racist white working class, a 'subject supposed to believe' whose revanchist resentment is the result of social and economic changes.[39] Bray argues that this phantom throwback has destroyed the idea of the post-racial society that was promulgated by Obama. Ironically, and as a feature of capitalist ideology, the post-race society was already, tacitly, premised on a vague notion of the white working class. The main problem, and we can say this is the case for both post-race advocates as well as racialists, is that the working class is presumed to be white. Another problem is the fact that racialists alienate people of all ethnic backgrounds, not only whites.

While Bray is correct to suggest that there is little to be gained by presuming that the working class is white and racist, there is even less to be gained for the left by calling on neoliberal racialists to own up to their own racism. Even if Bray criticizes post-blackness for defending the status quo, he is less aware of how it is that the critique of the capitalist reproduction of racial inequalities on a global scale can itself be premised on intellectual presuppositions that are now part of a post-representational status quo. Progressive neoliberalism, as Fraser argues, has emerged as a solution to both leftist populism and rightist authoritarianism. In the field of biocapitalist governmentality, the real subsumption of labour gradually encompasses questions of identity as part of the raw material of both capitalist production and its self-overcoming. The function of a politician like Obama is to mediate race relations for the sake of electoral victories, and it is this identitarian strategy that Trump disturbed, confirmed and rejected through his discriminatory devil-may-care invective. Railing against Trump's chauvinism does not bother his followers but it can make people blind to the politics of the extreme centre that created Trump in the first place.

The rhetoric of post-race cannot be challenged by insisting on the notion that behind the neutral neoliberal veneer lies a hegemonic whiteness. Rather, the veneer of whiteness is itself a product of the postmodern obsession with identity. Working-class atavism is therefore less a matter of racialist projection onto a 'subject supposed to believe,' as Bray suggests, than it is a matter of postmodern academia having been displaced as the 'subject supposed to know,' which has left the social field open to anti-welfare and anti-socialist reinscription. This displacement is in part due to postmodernists' rejection of critical social theory in favour of anti-dialectical immanentism and an eclectic, pseudo-left materialism.

Postmodernism's end-of-ideology relativism and social constructionist moralism have proven to be a boondoggle for radical left movements and a bounty for neoliberals. This is the lesson of the lurch of postmodern artists and intellectuals to the political right of centre. It is not only that white workers are pathologized as racist, sexist, homophobic and xenophobic, but that workers everywhere have been compelled to make victim politics and activist protest the core of their praxis, armed with little more than memes and Twitter hashtags to vent their myriad frustrations and indignation.[40] And the reason why hashtag activism feels more diverse, more multiracial and more feminist is because the working class continues to be ideologically stereotyped as consisting exclusively of blue-collar straight white males. To paraphrase Henry Kissinger on the American attitude towards Vladimir Putin: the demonization of the white working class is not a politics but an alibi for not having one. Even this interpretation may be too generous. Bray is correct that racialism and identity politics have mistakenly addressed the problems of neoliberal globalization through the critique of people deemed normative and privileged. Bray and others are incorrect, however, to think that the mere acknowledgement of the diversity of the working class is the solution to this problem.

Bray argues that the reordering of capitalist social relations according to global flows, supply chains, offshoring, warehousing, automation, privatized service work as well as regimes of debt, risk, policing and redundancy, make traditional working-class antagonisms incoherent except for their electoral expression.[41] Demands that are made to the state therefore become immediately biocapitalist. The extent to which such demands against neoliberal governance can be made coherent as class politics, for instance through candidates like Corbyn and Sanders, depends in part on the ability of the left to perceive the extent to which critical race theory, privilege theory and intersectionality have almost nothing to do with working-class politics. It is not for nothing that strategizing around identity politics by the Sanders 2020 campaign did little to alter the popular prejudice against socialism, even if most voters agreed with all of his major policy initiatives, such as free college education, universal health care and a Green New Deal. To appreciate this dilemma, one has to further consider how the politics of post-representation inform today's diversity mandates.

The Devil's Advocates

The question of race politics after Obama demands something more than the technocratic management of opportunity structures for a small number of successful people. Yet this is exactly what is propagandized as racial justice by the discourse of post-race and post-blackness. The concept of post-blackness cannot be presumed to be an unqualified benefit to black interests. Historically speaking, and as argued by Ian F. Haney-López, the notion of colourblindness was part of the legal definition of 'separate but equal' that justified Jim Crow segregation and oppression.[42] As a lawyer for the NAACP, Thurgood Marshall argued against distinctions based on race insofar as 'separate but equal' had been deployed to enforce racial inequality. Instead of emphasizing racial difference, the government dismantled Jim Crow laws. While racial neutrality did not eliminate segregation, Civil Rights lawyers gradually abandoned the notion of colourblindness in favour of race-conscious means to achieve equality. As this process developed, opponents of social equality adopted colourblindness in such a way that they could dismantle segregation while avoiding integration. In 1971, the Supreme Court ruled that the manipulation of race towards remedial ends was unconstitutional. Colourblindness was eventually used as an argument against affirmative action policies. The mass imprisonment of black Americans is today seen to be the result of colourblind policies that stand in the way of structural reform.

With the Obama presidency, colourblindness was replaced with the notion of post-racialism, which argues against the elevation of racial tensions above issues that are more important or more easily resolved. Obama argued in *The Audacity of Hope* that universal programmes, as opposed to race-specific programmes, are not only good policy but good politics, with the view that white guilt has been exhausted and that race-specific claims no longer appeal to fair-minded whites.[43] Post-race thinking emphasizes the arbitrariness of race so as to separate race from the problems that are attributed and attributable to racism. Although race is acknowledged as a social construct and a historical fact with contemporary relevance, post-race posits a break from histories of discrimination and defines contemporary racism as a vestige of the past – a mostly individual prejudice that has otherwise been defeated on a societal level.[44]

In the context of growing inequality within ascriptively black and ethnic racial groupings, the neoliberalization of race politics transforms the dynamics and functions of colourblindness as it had developed during the Civil Rights and Black Power era. As postmodern difference politics, the reduction of culture and politics to the 'matterism' of race metaphysics makes whatever blackness into a premise of black life and black success within capitalism. At best, racialism can be used to advance claims for social justice. At worst, racialism converts identity into a victim status that can be capitalized exclusively – a monopoly on history and representation that serves capitalist class interests. This capitalization of race is the unacknowledged premise of Touré Neblett's theory of post-race in *Who's Afraid of Post-Blackness?: What It Means to Be Black Now*, a book that "capitalizes" the word Black in reference to a grouping that Neblett says is "unknown" because it has been severed by slavery from its rootedness in the past.[45] Touré, as he is better known, seeks to dislodge stereotypes and limitations concerning what it means to be black, the double binds that keep people from experiencing the unlimited possibilities of blackness. The book is about what blacks, as blacks, are allowed and not allowed to be. From the start, the book's post-race metaphysics has several contradictory premises: capitalist universality, dualism and tautological reasoning.[46]

Touré begins *Who's Afraid of Post-Blackness?* with the post-structuralist paradox that because there is such a thing as the fact of blackness, there is no authentic or legitimate blackness against which one could judge whether or not something or someone is authentically black. At the outset, the hermeneutic that he sets up is politically limited, which is why Touré can casually assert that the possibilities for blackness are infinite and that it is the maximization of human potential that maximizes blackness. Signifiers in black music, for example, could derive from black male working-class hip hop styles, from middle-class and avant-garde references, or from the upper-class signifiers used by people like Jay-Z and 50 Cent. The diversity of signifiers, from heteronormative to gay and lesbian, pluralizes and broadens collective identity and mitigates policing by "identity cops." Touré cites Kehinde Wiley in this regard, who suggests that in order for blacks to do good for their community, they should first do good for themselves and push themselves beyond their limits and safe place, Wiley says, "because the white boys have always been given that free run to be individuals."[47] Global capitalism is hardly race-specific, however, and pushing oneself beyond the pleasure principle has little to do with identity. Such suggestions make Touré more of an 'identity cop' than he either admits or realizes.[48]

The point that Touré makes is that nothing should stand in the way of black success, least of all "authenticity violations" that might come from such places as the black ghetto or, an important distinction, the black left.[49] He writes: "Post-Black means we are like Obama: rooted in but not restricted by Blackness."[50] In these terms, Obama did not kowtow to Wall Street and the Pentagon. Obama is simply one of them in the same way that a neoliberal war hawk like Condoleeza Rice can be black. Do not feel ashamed of the quest for power, Touré says: "You know you're smart and you belong at Milton or Brown or Harvard or *Rolling Stone* or Goldman Sachs or whatever it is you've reached, and anything anyone else says to the contrary is a comment on them, not on you."[51] It is less the case that Touré's notion of blackness is opportunistic, suggesting that there should be no limits to the amount of power and money that blacks allow themselves, than it is that his politics are opportunistic insofar as he defends inequality and makes this the basis of his theory of post-blackness. This is another instance of neoliberal reverse colourblindness in which race is used to justify dubious politics.

Touré complicates his analysis by drawing on Lacanian psychoanalysis. The notion that blacks are captured by the trauma of victimization and abjection is, according to Derek Conrad Murray, a "dogmatic transference" that has been passed down from generation to generation. Fear of the white gaze has caused blacks to avoid anything that would shame the black community, replacing it with what Cornel West refers to as the "black normative gaze."[52] For Touré, not fearing the white gaze, or what is also known as "stereotype threat," means, for example, not being afraid to eat fried chicken or watermelon at the Ritz. Not fearing the black gaze would be something more along the lines of physicist Neil deGrasse Tyson's ravings about how much of a foodie he is, something that his mainstream interviewers like to discuss as much as his capitalist views on science. For Touré there should be no shame, whether you are black or white, about eating at the Ritz Carlton. What remains tacit in his example is that if you are black there is therefore no shame about eating at the Ritz Carlton and the added *outrance* of ordering watermelon is negated by the scandal represented by class inequality. Shame has shifted from race inequality to shamelessness about class inequality. Touré's invocation of West, who has often said that he would prefer to be in a crack house than in the White House, is used to deflect questions of politics and moral philosophy rather than elucidate them. Instead of the notion of racism as America's original sin, Touré prefers a guilt-free version of the American Creed.

Another aspect of Touré's post-racial politics is the neoliberal injunction that one should enjoy, which is part of the late capitalist emphasis on consumption rather than production. For most people, lifestyle hedonism subtends a culture of marketing and advertising that encourages living on credit. Touré's politics conforms to the social function of the executant petty bourgeoisie, the class of people who are the mediators of symbolic goods and who respond to the needs of the economy by not only stimulating consumer demand but by imposing new tastes and lifestyles. Within this logic, one can exploit one's race and gender capital for the sake of marketing new symbols and enhancing commercial profits. The needs that are specific to identity groups thereby take ideological precedent over the social relations through which such needs are defined. Touré's go-get-it provocation and anarchic individualism promotes a belated modernist adventurism. His focus on the (black) body is not incidental to the restoration of bourgeois materialism in intellectual and cultural life. This is what makes his plea for equal opportunity as well as individual and collective emancipation questionable. When such goals are separated from any acknowledgement of the difficulties of social life, and their causes, post-blackness turns social theory into an entrepreneur's guide to the power of positive thinking. To what ends? In Touré's words: to nevermind the insurrectionary sixties and instead to live the American Dream and "build more Baracks."[53] Touré is oblivious to why it is that for most people the American Dream is a lost reference.

Post-blackness is an inadequate substitute for emancipatory universality. How then can one bring an end to racism when social inequality remains a reality? Racialism responds to this dilemma by making race-specific demands, insisting on the terms of abuse, as it were, which leads to charges of reverse discrimination and the perception of anti-racist hysteria. Social constructionists take the neurotic route, deconstructing society and accepting provisional inequalities, such as the admission of racial privilege, as part of the social engineering of racial justice.[54] In both instances, historical traumas are used as pretexts for the failure if not the unwillingness to resolve contemporary problems. The question of Enlightenment universality is therefore key to today's neoteny, which is why wishing universality away cannot be the solution.

American race politics since the 1960s have been shaped by both anti-systemic tendencies as well as liberal and capitalist tendencies. Today's discussion on post-blackness keeps race politics within the fold of the ideological mainstream. New social movements, however, transform demands into the kinds of difference politics that reject universal or essentialist foundations while at the same time making specific and plural claims to emancipation. The conundrum of anti-systemic new social movements is that their neglect of the state has allowed identity and difference politics to merge with the post-ideological aspects of neoliberal governance and also with the reactionary anti-Enlightenment tradition. To the extent that anti-racism, feminism and queer politics have obfuscated class politics, they are part of the problem and not part of the solution.[55] Moreover, the success of anti-systemic new social movements coincides with U.S. hegemony on the world stage, from Hiroshima and Hanoi to Baghdad and Benghazi.[56] The concept of post-race therefore contains the historical experiences that have led to today's situation but in a mystified form. An unreconstructed bigot, from the point of view of post-blackness, finds its corollary in the failure to reconstruct those parts of the world that have been laid to waste by war, exploitation, famine and ecological damage. One could also list the many sites that decades of neoliberal neglect have led to ruin, like the Pittsburgh bridge that collapsed on January 28, 2022, only a few hours before Joe Biden visited the city to promote his infrastructure bill. The money allotted by the Biden administration to the state of Pennsylvania by the puny $1 trillion bill will not be enough to cover the cost of the inspection of its collapsing bridges. Like the May 2021 Midland, Michigan dam collapse, the June 2021 Florida condo collapse in Surfside, and the September 2021 train derailment in Joplin, Montana, the disintegration of American infrastructure corresponds directly to the rise of the post-representational politics that legitimize social inequality.

Another figure in this grouping of post-race advocates of neoliberal capitalism is the somewhat more sophisticated John McWhorter. An academic linguist and popular commentator on race issues, McWhorter has staked out a position on black liberalism and conservatism that is ideologically opposed to all of the other groups in this chapter. It is fair to say that although a liberal universalist, McWhorter is also a racialist insofar as he statedly writes "as a black person" and in defence of black American interests. His 2021 book, *Woke Racism*, is probably the most coherent critique of social justice anti-racism to have emerged on the conservative right.[57] McWhorter is not only opposed to a particular strain of the postmodern left, which he defines as "third wave anti-racism," but also to the more mainstream strands of black leadership, including the race politics of people like Jesse Jackson, Ta-Nehisi Coates and Nikole Hannah-Jones. His book is written as a how-to guide for people who have been confronted with anti-racist cancellation, which he does not define in sociological or historical materialist terms but in the more mystifying terms of religion. The attempt to transform the country with race-first consciousness is not an ideology, McWhorter argues, but a religion. His contention is that this new religion is harmful to black people, in part, because it demands that blacks think of themselves as victims who are dumber, weaker and more self-indulgent than others and therefore less deserving of equality.

Woke Racism describes several cases where competent professionals have been pilloried by the "woke mob" and fired from their jobs for statements or actions that in some cases cannot even be considered racist. Since the advent of CRT and BLM, the number of such cases has increased to the point where administrations bow to what is perceived as public pressure without any real concern for social justice or policy principles. That structural and institutional racism is now considered by anti-racism activists to be more relevant than personal prejudice makes those who are caught in the crosshairs of the accusers guilty in advance since whiteness by itself makes whites eternally culpable. The situation created by the anti-racist teachings of people like Ibram Kendi and Robin DiAngelo, McWhorter argues, replaces reason with sophistry, knowledge with experience, and truth with narrative, subjecting innocent people to the double-binds of Inquisitorial blackmail. Advancing a mostly performative form of indignation, the religious Elect, as he calls them, have gained influence in universities and the culture at large. McWhorter's political argument against the Elect is that most of the gains that could be achieved for black civil rights were achieved in the 1960s. This latest wave of anti-racism is rather a continuation of the flawed strategies of the Black Power movement and the counterculture, whose fringe behaviour is not shared by most people and whose key weapon is the charge of racism and white supremacy, which underscores the Elect's pessimistic belief that the "racial reckoning" they call for is a permanent struggle that can never be settled. The consequent performance of grievance, as well as the pleasure taken in masochistic self-flagellation, prevents society from focusing on the practical solutions that could lead to progressive social change.

There is much that McWhorter says that most progressive and fair-minded people would agree with. However, his definition of woke activism as a religion rather than a class politics works to dissemble the conservative politics that he advances. Although one might agree that the Elect do not actually care about the welfare of black people, or of whites, one should not be convinced that McWhorter does either. Just as identity issues obscure the workings of capitalism, McWhorter's intellectually lucid and often accurate critiques of third wave anti-racism serve a more dubious agenda. For instance, he is right to suggest that the essence of Elect identity is to not be white and that this agonism both reinscribes outmoded race theories and skews the ideology of post-race. Under the Elect, he says, "blackness becomes what you are not, as opposed to what you are (and only whites can define what you are not)."[58] A white anti-racist cultural critic like A.O. Scott can say the reverse: "racism is what makes us white."[59] This strategy not only invalidates individuality, it also undermines social solidarity. The question for us is this one: Does McWhorter refuse to be one of those black people who are obsessed with racial inequality, or does McWhorter refuse to be one of those people who are obsessed with social inequality? Further, is it racial identity or class status that mediates this distinction? While there is a compulsion in American society for blacks to "be black," and McWhorter does not avoid this issue, it is not of the same sort as the capitalist compulsion to competition, which affects everyone but is less obvious. If the Elect make "being oppressed" the essence of being black, McWhorter opts for a universalism that is compensatory rather than emancipatory.

The capitalist universalism that animates McWhorter's thought lacks any sense of social equality except as equal opportunity exploitation. His three solutions to America's race problem are ending the War on Drugs, teaching phonics so that poor kids have better test scores and getting past the idea that everyone should go to college. The last of these three defines McWhorter's politics best since to "value working-class jobs," as he proposes, does not for him imply higher wages and the typical programme of social democratic demands like universal health care and free college.[60] McWhorter suggests that the kinds of New Deal and Great Society reforms that were implemented in the past are utopian and impractical in today's diverse and politically polarized situation. In other words, the kind of political agenda that was advanced by Sanders in 2016 and 2020 "lacks sophistication" and "is the game of performers, not those who actually get things done for real people."[61] While McWhorter suggests that his brand of conservatism is simply practical, one cannot ignore the fact that from 2003 to 2008 he worked as a senior fellow at the corporate-funded Manhattan Institute. Formerly the International Center for Policy Research, the Manhattan Institute was founded by libertarian and free-market ideologues who have advanced the cause of personal responsibility and small government. What this implies is the entire battery of anti-democratic and anti-working-class politics: entrepreneurialism, anti-welfare policies, Reaganomics, bank deregulation, the pharmaceutical industry, gentrification schemes, charter schools, the security state apparatus, regime-change wars, anti-communism, social Darwinism, broken-windows policing, fossil fuel energy and climate change denial, tax cuts for the wealthy, etc. Some of the people associated with the Manhattan Institute and other affiliated think tanks include Antony Fisher, Bill Casey, Henry Kissinger, William F. Buckley, Daniel Patrick Moynihan, Charles Murray and Rudolph Giuliani. One could mention also that McWhorter makes regular appearances alongside the black conservative scholar Glenn Loury on *The Glenn Show* at Bloggingheads.tv. An associate of the neoconservative American Enterprise Institute and Heritage Foundation, Loury advocates the same capitalist politics of individual responsibility, entrepreneurialism, socio-economic mobility, patriotism and limited government.

In terms of post-race ideas, McWhorter's views of Obama are perhaps the most indicative. In *Woke Racism*, he compares Obama to George Washington, a historical and revolutionary figure who is anachronistically reduced by today's anti-racists to the mere fact that he owned slaves. McWhorter places Obama in a similar conundrum by suggesting that his delay on the subject of gay marriage should not be used to paint him as homophobic, as though this delay was the worst of his crimes.[62] The point of Obama's evolution on the subject is somewhat irrelevant since this legislation is considered one of the few Obama administration achievements. George Washington, in comparison, is known for more than freeing his slaves. As a prolific contributor to mainstream media, McWhorter's commentaries cover the entire Obama era. In 2008, he endorsed Obama for his native intelligence but also because having a black man in the White House would put an end to the anti-racist obsession with racism. "What I'm interested in," he said in 2008, "[and] what the Manhattan Institute is interested in is solutions. … We're talking about how we have to wait until the playing field is perfectly level. I don't think that helps anybody."[63] McWhorter perceived Obama as the perfect candidate to take the discussion away from racism as the source of poor black people's problems. With Obama, according to McWhorter, racism was no longer the main problem for blacks. "Post-racialism is a good direction to move in because if there's some separation between Blacks and Whites," McWhorter stated in 2009, "it's as if some unpleasantness is going on, like one has to have his foot on the other's neck. Are there racists? Yes. But not enough to keep a Black family out of the White House."[64] Obama could achieve this post-racial challenge while at the same time staying true to some racialist expectations, like black cultural identification, a black partner, black cadence and a black gait.[65] In addition, as the poster boy of post-racialism, Obama did not have to demonstrate the woke obsession with not being white. What McWhorter never said in his articles is that Obama would do better than most other candidates, like John McCain or Mitt Romney, to move the discussion away from class politics. Obama instead represented the kind of respectability politics that refuses to treat black people as powerless victims, McWhorter argued, by giving Americans the illusion that the system can be upended. As he wrote in 2015: "Waiting for an America with well-paying, semi-skilled jobs a short commute from black communities, with no racist sentiments and an exquisitely guilty nation with understanding of society's past abuses against black people is like waiting for a winter without snow."[66] As with the Elect that McWhorter today criticizes, there was nothing that Obama could say or do, McWhorter argued, that would please those who would criticize him for failing to be the saviour of black America and other minority groups.[67]

McWhorter's conservatively pessimistic view of American politics demands very little from elected officials except fealty to the plutocracy. This largesse is extended to Trump supporters. The Trump debacle is not due to anything the Obama Democrats and the bipartisan consensus could be accused of since many Trump voters previously voted for Obama. McWhorter prefers to think that social media like Twitter and Facebook are what changed the nature of politics by amplifying the invective of anti-racists.[68] What also got Trump elected, according to him, is the small change he promised, which is enough for McWhorter to correctly dismiss the exaggerated claims of racism among the electorate.[69] The long and the short of it, for McWhorter, is that political conservatives are correct and progressives are wrong. The common cause shared by neoliberal and postmodern anti-racists is a quandary that post-racialists like McWhorter and Neblett do very little to explain.

The Managers

The anti-Marxist thrust of racialist identity politics transforms meta-politics into questions of ontology and dubious antagonism. Identity becomes a key contradiction within the political economy, with fascism, nationalism and culture wars as three of the most common problems. Neoliberalism has domesticated diversity by making its goals consonant with global capitalism, giving rise to several generations of race managers. Such people are called upon by the dominant class to represent expert opinion on identity issues and conflicts. Race 'managers' are those who accept the conflicts of labour and capital as serious but intractable. Marxism has always cautioned against the problem of economic reductionism. However, race reductionism is more nefarious insofar as it is a form of archi-politics, which defines the political space as closed, organic and homogeneous. As a form of ultra-politics, race reductionism can go even further and depoliticize conflicts by falsely radicalizing difference into an absolute conflict between Us and Them, which limits social life to a zero-sum calculus of power relations. At best, identity managers define politics as democratic struggle within the actually existing social parameters, a para-political form of social regulation that prevents identity struggles from erupting into open conflict.[70] By itself, identity politics cannot transform capitalist social relations and has only limited relevance to the critique of political economy. For instance, equal pay for equal work is a limited benefit in an economy where class inequality is as extreme as it is today.

As the managers of identity become resentful that their politics have no progressive outlet and desperately seek to hold on to or extend their class power, they stoke woke wars that project their own ideological confusion onto those they consider the enemy identity group. Like the U.S. government, they can create or attack perceived enemies in order to produce and control followers. People who justifiably reject the assault on rights, reason and dignity by race managers are made into examples that confirm the flawed premises of the ideological attack. Since rightists typically attack people or groups by separating them piecemeal from their protective communities and eco-systems, their 'Schmittean' conflicts are waged without justification. Since their politics cannot stand up to critical scrutiny, the trials by public opinion that they stage are often supported by vested interests and used by identity managers to bypass norms of jurisprudence. This, in essence, is the problem with privilege theory, which is inherently conservative as a form of 'means tested' social justice advocacy. The rituals surrounding privilege theory, as many have remarked, are anti-modern forms of pseudo-religious expiation and propitiation. However, these sham rituals belie a class politics that is far less mysterious. The problem is that the terror and horror that is on display, as is the case with kangaroo courts and guerrilla theatre, nourish people's churlish impulses and weaken the prospect of valid outcomes to real problems. This is the reason why race managers are often celebrated more for their aesthetic, cultural and oratorial skills than achievements.

Against political regression, Reed argues that class is the only category around which mass organizations can bring into effect progressive social transformation.[71] With regard to identity politics, he writes: "The interest-group model depends on a form of elite brokerage, centred on a relation between governing elites and entities or individuals recognized as representatives of designated groups."[72] In our case, the term race manager is used to describe the form of leadership that purports to represent the interests of ascribed identity groups. Whereas Reed uses the term 'race broker' to imply what is understood here as 'race manager,' the term broker is used separately to describe individuals, groups and organizations who do not represent elite and neoliberal forms of authority, but who instead opt for a negotiated, or intersectional, definition of class and identity politics. Whereas race managers typically defend the status quo, sometimes to the point of defending reactionary agendas, race brokers tend to identify as progressive and leftist. The group 'intellectuals' is used to distinguish those who maintain the perspective of emancipatory universality from the race brokers who have adopted postmodern notions of anti-universalism and who advance a cultural politics of difference. The problem with identity brokers is that their activity deradicalizes the left and allows progressive politics to more easily combine with liberal pluralism. This tendency both causes and increases in proportion to the strength of the far right.

The limit of identity politics is that it cannot function as a meta-politics. If it was nevertheless attempted, what might a racialist meta-politics look like? Johnny Bernard Hill, a professor of religion and Dean of the Shaw University Divinity School in North Carolina, wrote in 2009 that the Obama election victory was an expression of the American Dream come true and a decisive moment for the black freedom struggle in the U.S. For Hill, Obama's election was "nothing short of a political and cultural revolution."[73] The intelligibility of the Obama presidency derived from the black freedom struggle, Hill argues, without which his leadership would have been impossible. His presidency was the outcome of the struggles of the Southern Christian Leadership Conference, the Student Nonviolent Coordinating Committee, the National Association for the Advancement of Colored People, the Congress of Racial Equality, and all those who have struggled for black civil rights, inclusive of the Poor People's Campaign that linked the struggle for racial inclusivity with democratic socialism. However, Hill argues that there had to be more to Obama's presidency than his racial identity and the shadow of America's racist past. In the era of Hurricane Katrina and black socio-economic disparity, the promise of Obama as the first black president would become a "dangerous orientation" if it did not in some way heed the colour line as well as the problems of incarceration, schooling, housing, joblessness and health care.[74]

As Du Bois noted a century ago, black leaders tend to be conservative and avoid being perceived as agitators.[75] Obama was no exception to this longstanding tradition. Given the constraints of the office, and regardless of his conciliatory attitude towards whites, Obama would inevitably be faced with criticism on all political fronts – left, right and centre. In addition to this, he would also face criticism on the basis of his identity, as being too black or not black enough, and too white or not white enough. To what extend then could Obama serve the economic and racial justice aspects that are part of the Civil Rights legacy? On this issue, Hill argues that Obama's rejection of "tribal" loyalties to the black "race" was not a matter of post-racial assimilation, but a feature of the black particularity that is a result of racism. The question of whether he was too black or not black enough, Hill argues, was irrelevant in comparison with his commitments and achievements. On the other hand, to the extent that Obama would address the social justice issues confronting most blacks, he would offend conservatives by taking on responsibility for societal problems that are not only the burden of blacks. Hill has a critique of poverty and racism, but a weak sense that there might be an alternative to capitalism. Writing in the first year of Obama's first term as President, it was possible for Hill to think that Obama's platform of job creation and corporate responsibility was an indication, in and of itself, of a sensibility that is similar to Karl Marx's conception of communism and Martin Luther King's vision of the "beloved community."[76]

It is obvious enough that Hill was optimistic about Obama, as were many progressives, up until the day he appointed his cabinet members. From that moment it became obvious that the irrelevance of Obama's blackness, when defined in terms of policy, could be acknowledged easily enough, and especially with hindsight. However, for race managers, the question of Obama's blackness gained more rather than less relevance over time. Exemplary of this strand of the black intelligentsia are Ta-Nehisi Coates and Michael Eric Dyson.

Ta-Nehisi Coates's 2017 title, *We Were Eight Years in Power*, consists of essays published in the magazine *The Atlantic* from the period 2009 to 2016.[77] Comparing Trump' election in 2016 to the era of Reconstruction, Coates argues that what white racist Americans fear more than bad Negro government is good Negro government. Coates is cognizant of how and why Hill and others in the black freedom movement would hold Obama to account and why they would be disappointed: "Presumably, all those black people who voted for Obama supported him because they thought he would advance policies that advanced them. It was hard to see how truth-telling would have improved that prospect."[78] His defence of Obama is therefore not premised on an evaluation of his commitments and achievements that is conceived independently of his identity. Coates sees Obama as the first *black* president, rather than how Obama sees himself: the first black *president*. The reason that Obama was too black to fail, according to Coates, was due to the reality of white supremacy as the hegemonic condition of political articulation and possibility. Contrary to white people's fears, according to Coates, Obama was a "measured architect" who established a framework for health care, prevented economic collapse and ended state-sanctioned torture. Although he neglected to prosecute Wall Street bankers and continued the wars in the Middle East, he, his family and their two dogs were model citizens. According to Coates, Obama was "a walking advertisement for the ease with which black people could fully integrate into the unthreatening mainstream of American culture, politics, and myth."[79] A Brooks Brothers image of black respectability, Obama avoided revolutionary political rhetoric, steered clear of corruption and scandal, and thereby denied his opponents grounds for their racist imaginings.

Believing in the inevitability of prejudice, Coates acknowledges the conservative aspects of Obama's mode of respectability politics but justifies them as an unfortunate result of slavery. In the same way, according to Žižek, that the Soviet invasion of Czechoslovakia in 1968 was a saving grace for a regime that was in economic crisis, or similar to David Graeber's argument that neoliberal capitalism would rather spend more money policing protesters than provide social welfare, Coates would rather view the Trump presidency as the predictable result of "eight years of Obama baiting" than a judgement on Obama's administration.[80] He argues that white America would rather "burn down the country if the country can't dream itself white."[81] His approach is therefore consistent with 'differential racism,' which does not define racism in terms of biological definitions of race, but posits the equality of culturally distinct groups while simultaneously providing political justification for racist anti-racism as a necessary aspect of the management of race relations.[82] To put it differently, Coates is prepared to use and abuse the history of racism for the sake of the racialist agenda and the social advancement of the class of race managers. His is a racialist equivalent of high-level corruption in right-wing trade unions that promote nationalism and the interests of capitalist employers and shareholders.

There is no reason to doubt Coates's view that Trump's white supremacy is matched by a certain level of popular incredulity towards it. How can one account for this scepticism? It is not white supremacy alone that accounts for Trump's election, but also the failings of the Democratic Party. One should therefore consider what Obama and Trump have in common. Both politicians engaged in a protracted conflict against the working poor and the political left. It is somewhat irrelevant that Obama is sophisticated and polite, while Trump is vulgar and offensive. Mark Zuckerberg and Bill Gates are similarly decent seeming, while Jeff Bezos and Elon Musk are overtly asinine. A president's congeniality is important, but it is not enough by itself to solve political problems. If it were, one could reduce politics to notions of good and evil. Such dualism and metaphysics might explain why Obama continues to enjoy a semi cult status: where for some people his 'blackness' could be found wanting in terms of political initiative, his 'whiteness' could be invoked instead, and vice versa. Too black to fail and too white to succeed in terms of social justice policy? Or, too black to succeed and too white to fail? Obama's whiteness is comparable to Margaret Thatcher's masculinity and Bill Clinton's blackness as a measure of the impossibility of reducing the plurality of any polity to the figure of the leader, that is, except for the fascist leader.

Begging the question, then, of what constitutes good government, Coates considers that the Civil Rights generation of leaders and the choreography of marches and speeches has given way with Obama and people like him to an in-between condition of reasonableness along with black particularity – no longer black, but not white either, not avoiding race, but not limited to it. Success for black Americans in politics and other areas of life comes from efforts to avoid being pigeonholed according to racially ascribed behaviours and attitudes. In a critique of the prophetic tradition championed by Cornel West, Coates says that Obama was not among the "performance prophets who live from the roar of the crowd."[83] Obama rather emerged through the tradition of black conservatives, with hard work and economic self-reliance privileged over expostulation. This conservative streak appeals to white and black Americans alike. Against stereotypes of pathology, from absentee fathers to gangsta rap and police records, the gospel of personal responsibility works in favour of the ruling class and against the grassroots strategies that are imposed on the working poor. Although Obama insisted that change comes from grassroots mobilization and not from the office of the President, he gave no support to those movements when the opportunity presented itself. If Obama was to transcend the colour line, as opposed to the class line, it would be by embodying the mythology of the middle-class vision of an all-American way of life. Good government, then, for Coates, is "bourgeois ordinariness" plus "extraordinary Americanness."[84] Black particularity supplements American exceptionalism.

How odd, then, that Hill should think of Obama, a politician who approvingly cited Ronald Reagan, as having a socialist sensibility. If Obama could be interpreted as "the most agile interpreter and navigator of the colour line," according to Coates, his presidential speeches acknowledged the existence of the middle class only.[85] What people like Hill misperceive, according to Coates, is the way in which Obama is indeed revolutionary, but a revolutionary conservative, a New Democrat who advances quietly and who, in Coates's terms, does not try to convince voters that class issues are more pressing than race issues. Coates believes that it is Obama's appreciation of Malcolm X's philosophy of self-assertion and collective self-creation that led hip hop record executives to help Obama rise to the presidency. Yet, just as MLK, X and blacks everywhere were thwarted, Coates argues, Obama was obstructed in his political agenda. When it comes to those things that Obama was not obstructed from doing, like his drone attacks, Coates supports them as "the perfect weapons of democracy."[86]

After the Obama administration, the problems associated with government could now be attributed to a black man also. For Coates, the prospect of someone like Obama using federal power may or may not have made the risks of compromise worthwhile. Even if Obama could have secured economic advantages for poor blacks, he argues, this would not address the injury of racism and white privilege. As part of this racialist narrative, Coates believes that progressives, from Bill Clinton to Bernie Sanders, have mistakenly focused on the economic worries of the majority at the expense of race-specific policies. He opposes that argument to the view that Democrats have abandoned social justice in favour of the neoliberal policies and identity politics that cause resentment among "rednecks." For Coates, then, it is racism that explains why working-class and middle-class whites would prefer to vote against their own interests than go along with Hillary Clinton's timid acknowledgements of systemic racism.[87]

Are voters tired of poverty or tired of politically correct identity politics? Or both? Is there nostalgia among Sanders supporters for the pre-identity liberalism of FDR and LBJ? Coates rejects the distinction since for him "all politics are identity politics."[88] For intellectuals like Coates, class politics and socialist internationalism are inexistent. Although race problems exist, race-specific policies are not a solution to the conflict between labour and capital, nor do they clarify questions of political orientation. Trump's electoral success leads not only to the false assertion that white supremacy is endemic to American institutions, but to a correct understanding that Trump, like his demagogic equivalents in Europe and elsewhere, turned to authoritarianism to save the global neoliberal project that reached its critical limits decades ago. The failure to confront the rise of authoritarianism is a failure of class unity against the extreme centre. For racialists like Coates, it is slavery and white supremacy that are the "necessary condition" and "existing background" of Trump's election, an approach that makes the neoliberal uses of both racism and anti-racism all the more difficult to elucidate.[89]

Although lionized by the mainstream press, which earned him a National Book Award and a $650,000 McArthur genius grant for his 2015 book, *Between the World and Me*, Coates raised the ire of progressive social critics for separating the black struggle from "colourblind" New Deal programmes. His rising tide theory of the black middle class is of a piece with Reaganomics. Combating disadvantages for blacks works best through universalist initiatives that gain broad public support. Whereas socialism seeks the destruction of capitalism, black politics cannot be based on the destruction of whites. Because white supremacy exits in the highest echelons of American institutions, according to West, Obama became "head of a white supremacist empire."[90] For West, the universality that is lost with race fundamentalism is not defined only in terms of social policy, but also in terms of moral credibility and spiritual integrity. Becoming obsessed with power inevitably leads to problems: apolitical pessimism; the disavowal of black struggle against capitalism and imperialism; inequality on a global scale; the fetishization of white supremacy as timeless and unchanging; the reduction of politics to either an individual or a tribal perception of whites; the presumption of black homogeneity; the disavowal of class society and the simplification of black history.[91] As with Touré, the usefulness of a writer like Coates to the political establishment is his separation of the black agenda from the struggles of the past and the reduction of protest politics to abstractions that are disconnected from collective organization. Coates denies this when he states: "In substituting a broad class struggle for an anti-racist struggle, progressives hope to assemble a coalition by changing the subject."[92]

Coates's race-first bourgeois politics go so far as to consider the 2016 Sanders campaign a "white agenda" that would reinforce "white supremacy."[93] Cedric Johnson denounced Coates for red-baiting the Sanders campaign on the grounds that Sanders did not advocate for reparations.[94] Like West, Johnson criticizes Coates for diminishing the involvement of blacks in socialism and social democracy, ignoring how the neoliberal assault on left politics, abetted by union bureaucracies, has destroyed people's livelihoods and created unprecedented levels of inequality. According to Johnson, Coates's perception that social democracy and left universalism would make blacks worse off, based on the shibboleth that the New Deal's Social Security Act denied benefits to sharecroppers and domestic servants, ignores two important issues: first, the limitations of those policies were not due to institutional racism on the part of the Democrats but due to the balance of class forces in the 1930s; secondly, other policies like the Works Progress Administration did benefit blacks and demonstrated the potential of public sector intervention.[95] Johnson also criticizes the way that the focus on reparations benefits the bourgeois class interests of black nationalists. Coates's "anti-racist liberalism" duplicates the Cold War focus on institutional racism and its presumption of the difference between white and black poverty. By keeping the focus on racism, Coates ignores the problems of automation, deindustrialization, unemployment, flexibilization and the neoconservative ideology promoted by the likes of Barry Goldwater, George Wallace, Richard Nixon, Bill Clinton and Donald Trump. For Johnson, Coates is among those black intellectual gadflies who play on white and black guilt, replacing the politics of solidarity with social media therapeutics.

Redistributive politics, whether understood in terms of reparations or in terms of a living wage, are not inherently anti-capitalist. Questions of emancipation are not settled with the limitation of politics to political economy. Further, the reduction of politics to the history of slavery and racism do more than maintain a race metaphysics that trades on anti-Enlightenment rhetoric. This allows racialists to come in all shapes and sizes. Coates's black populism finds its counterpart in sociologist Michael Eric Dyson's black elitism. Dyson's 2016 book, *The Black Presidency*, relates Obama's tenure to questions of representation and the "symbol systems" of American politics, which he argues makes the questions of race different to us today than they were to past generations.[96] In some respects, Dyson is less committed to race than Coates. Dyson views race as a problem in itself but not strictly for itself. Bringing race back home, Dyson defines the Obama presidency as a symbol of America to the world, a symbol to all American citizens and a symbol in particular to all black Americans.

According to Dyson, Obama's black body is a matter beyond partisan politics and instantiates America's democratic ideals as "the ultimate symbol of American life."[97] Obama's blackness cannot be post-racial insofar as it is marked by difference and brings an end to two centuries of white political monopoly. With this singular achievement assured, Obama could easily ignore the more universal aspects of race politics, for instance, by ignoring the Congressional Black Caucus and leaders like Jesse Jackson and Al Sharpton, who in turn avoided criticizing him. Radical blacks, in response, rejected the idea that Obama had taken up the "burden of representation" and refused to be bamboozled by what would be little more than another "symbolic presidency."[98] Dyson seems rather impressed with symbols, applauding Eric Holder's legacy as a "symbolic representation of black power."[99] The question of how it is that race matters is complicated by the fact that the construct of race is a fiction that can nevertheless generate material effects. What is at stake, Dyson argues, is a culture's self-image. The trouble with racism, according to him, is that it reduces what a human being can be to the image projected by a dominant white society. The problem then with Dyson's politics of racial recognition and redistribution is that is promotes racial equality as a solution to problems that may have nothing to do with race and that cannot be alleviated by anti-racism.

The problem for racial justice, as Dyson sees it, is that politics devolves into power relations rather than critical concepts and radical policies. Among the concepts that would need to be addressed if one was to proceed with a critical evaluation of Dyson's writing are the constructs of whiteness and blackness. Deconstructing whiteness as the norm of what it means to be human neither attributes nor contributes to anyone, either blacks or whites, anything that might be more desirable than what already exists. Deniability and historical amnesia are not the direct obverse of truth and memory. What racists deny others is not only memory or the particularity that is associated with historical traumas. Racism denies people's universality. Because it denies their universality it denies the damages inflicted by past traumas and the use of critical memory to work through those traumas. In this sense the singular critique of whiteness exacerbates the problems of racism. The false pretence that an abstract particular can occupy the place of power is not corrected by the reification of whiteness as the universal norm. It is not the critique of colourblind neutrality, understood as the reverse deconstruction of the obsession with race, that resolves the pathology of obsession.

Although it is self-evident that it is African Americans and not white Americans who have been marked as different, this does not make African Americans inferior to white Americans. It could, however, make African Americans a privileged category of what it means to be American. The terms of race politics and of post-blackness are less fraught by how blackness appears or is made invisible, than they are by how blackness is expected to function and therefore appear within the regimes of global capitalism. How often do bank advertisements show black workers who are too poor to take out a mortgage? Missouri representative Cori Bush, "the good Bush," made headlines in August 2021 by pushing the Biden administration to extend the pandemic eviction moratorium. She did this by sleeping on the steps of the Capitol building along with activist representatives of the more than six million Americans threatened with eviction. Can one imagine someone as respectable as Michelle Obama doing the same?

As one of many signifiers associated with trauma, the symbolic representation of blackness is made to circulate in ways that detract from its potential contribution to political and cultural progress. This explains the anxious aspects of post-blackness as a desire to escape the association with histories of oppression. In the context of post- and anti-Enlightenment nihilism, however, it is the prejudicial aspects of identity that are inflated, which is one of the reasons why privilege theory has less political validity than intersectionality, why intersectionality has less political value than radical democracy and why the latter is less radical than socialism. Post-blackness does not represent black disappearance, as Dyson argues, but is rather the integration of black history, black life and black futures into the networked circuits of capitalist exchange.[100] What difference does it make if Americans desire Obama to be non-black, half-black or totally black, since, as Dyson correctly states, such "symbolic value" "hardly put[s] a dent in the forces that pulverize black life."[101] The post-representational politics that black radicals rightly object to are imposed with a vengeance by the "democratic materialism" that makes the body, language and affect the focus of culturalized politics. Biological reduction guarantees the uses of prejudice for the sake of political manipulation. It makes race the common denominator of human association and transforms identity into a periaptic bias. Race fundamentalism thus pre-empts criticism of the Obama administration in favour of the mere fact of having a black man in charge.

Dyson defends Obama with the suggestion, against rightists, that his blackness is American to the core. He follows this with the assertion that Obama is as American as Louis Armstrong, Toni Morrison and Condoleezza Rice. This is not criticism of colourblind universalism; it is a defence of American exceptionalism. The idea that Obama is not a *black* leader but a *leader* who is black ignores the fact that Obama was not a good leader, which is not to suggest that most other Democratic presidents have done much better in the last several decades. Dyson's belief that the black torch was passed on from the prophetic tradition of MLK to the realpolitik of Obama occludes what it is that Obama took from Bush and passed on to Trump. Although Dyson chides Obama at length for not adequately representing black interests and not associating the problems of blacks with white accountability, he rarely considers how Obama defended capital interests above everything else. The "fearful racial symmetry" that Dyson associates with Obama's meritocratic stance ignores the asymmetry of its strategic significance, which is the rejection of the anti-imperialist and anti-capitalist left. Obama was not only the scold of black America, he was the scold of anyone who doubted the merits of the affluent technocracy. His reservation of the bully pulpit for the bad behaviour of underperforming blacks who self-sabotage their own path to success is rather a disavowed judgement on the U.S. itself and its role as the enforcer of global capitalism. Obama does not simply let white Americans off the hook for what hampers black progress, he lets the U.S. and its allies off the hook for what stymies human progress. One could go so far as to say that was his ultimate purpose: to renew the faith that not only had America not lost its way with neoliberalism and the wars in the Middle East, but that global capitalism represents the triumph of the American Creed.

The trouble then with Dyson and other race-centric critics is that by keeping the focus on race they distort the ways in which class issues are both distinct from and intersect with race issues. In terms of morality, black reconciliation with the status quo would seem to redeem past injustices, with survival rather than radicalization the measure of progress. If this was indeed the case, Americans would need psychiatrists more than they would need decent jobs, affordable housing and a healthy environment. Even at that, they would likely discover that their therapy is not adequately covered by Obamacare. The views of Coates and Dyson on the black presidency do not indicate that race issues are becoming a more prominent and therefore more conscious aspect of political life, but rather that they are becoming more deeply ideological. Insofar as leftist meta-politics are replaced by race metaphysics and capitalist evangelism, it is certain that racial tensions cannot be resolved – they can only be motivated, mobilized and propagandized, whether as a race war or as a war against racism. Just as capitalism in the nineteenth century no longer needed slavery, American authoritarianism no longer needs Confederate flags on its state buildings. Instead, it brings "democracy" to the Middle East, Latin America and Asia. And it fights against anyone it can blame for its declining fortunes, preferably a superpower that will justify a bloated military and security budget.

Much of this does not escape Dyson, least of all the notion that the U.S. gives an artificial importance to race and identity issues, and that because of this, the Obama presidency had a redemptive, therapeutic effect in relation to the history of race relations. In this regard, the measure of radicalism, black or white, might be how soon people broke off from Obama.[102] After he left office, Obama's defenders could more safely address his failings. And after Trump arrived in the White House, the same working people who elected Obama could be more safely denounced as racists, all the while ignoring how it is that the combination of identity politics with neoliberalism caused Clinton to lose the presidency.[103] As a commentator on NPR, CNN and MSNBC, Dyson promotes a mix of sectarian black nationalism and black neoliberalism, arguing that "Obama was at his best when he was at his blackest."[104] Like Touré, Dyson is satisfied with tautologies. If one might think that Obama was at his worst when he authorized his most destructive policies, then his record on questions of military and police violence might be thought of as Obama at his whitest.

Dyson's racialist perspective associates police violence with racism, an argument that overlooks the colour of the black and brown people who are brutalized by the multiracial U.S. military.

A less doctrinaire member of the black bourgeoisie than Dyson is Michelle Alexander, author of *The New Jim Crow: Mass Incarceration in the Age of Colorblindness*. Alexander opens *The New Jim Crow* with the accusatory provocation that racism in the U.S., as evidenced by black incarceration rates, is the same today as it was one century ago.[105] The colourblindness of the justice system, she argues, allows the status of criminality to be conflated with blackness. The mass incarceration of blacks and their subsequent marginalization through employment and housing discrimination, loss of welfare benefits like food stamps, denial of voting rights and education, is equivalent, she argues, to a new racial caste system. As many as three out of four black men in the U.S. can expect to serve time in prison. Drug-related charges in particular have increased prison sentences exponentially. The War on Drugs takes up a disproportionate amount of the $200 billion annual costs of the justice system. Of the roughly 2.5 million Americans who are in prison, approximately 40 percent are African Americans. Most sentences are due to drug convictions that disproportionately target black neighbourhoods where the CIA have used drug networks to fund its foreign campaigns. Alexander criticizes Obama's post-race colourblindness but not his class-blindness. She does not mention that the CIA's Nicaragua connection was to the Contra rebels, whose goal was to disrupt the Sandinista liberation government. The point is that Alexander prefers to define a politics and class issue as a caste issue, from which she advances a mostly moralistic critique of the Obama administration's failure to support black communities and his indifference towards the school-to-prison pipeline. She fails, however, to notice the similarity between her criticism of gangsta culture, which she says is a consequence of criminalization, and the advocacy by politicians like Obama of personal moral responsibility as a solution to incarceration rates. Embracing a now criminalized blackness, she worries, causes people to accept the stigma of criminality as a form of resistance. Black Entertainment Television's pandering of blaxploitation, she argues, is not unlike minstrel shows that were designed for white audiences, but that allow black audiences to enjoy vicariously through black celebrities who earn money and achieve fame. As the War on Drugs expanded, hip hop flourished alongside it.

Many of the problems in Alexander's discussion have less to do with criminal justice and more to do with social and cultural theory. She rejects colourblindness in favour of care and compassion for black people. The implication of her analysis is that "seeing" race implies either a white or a black gaze. Sartrean and Lacanian notions of paranoia would seem to have as much to say about the justice system as about racism. If only Lady Justice could remove her blindfold. Contrary to the evangelism of moral uplift, humans do not have higher or deeper selves, though they may strive for achievement or struggle for better conditions. Alexander strikes a correct note when she argues that in the 1970s and 80s white elites chose to exploit the vulnerability and resentment of working-class whites for political and economic gain. Tough on crime policies accompanied attacks on welfare. This system, she argues, is based on racial indifference rather than anti-black hostility since it is not concerned with the simultaneous increase of white incarceration. Whatever its contribution to culture, resentment is not a politics. The issue then is not colourblindness but the capitalist system. Nor is the logic of care and compassion able to solve the problems that are created by relations of exploitation. On this score, Alexander's solutions to end mass incarceration are essentially pragmatic: release prisoners; close prisons and let go the close to one million prison employees; curtail drug enforcement in ghetto communities; end racial profiling; legalize soft drugs and the social provision of drug treatment; eliminate mandatory sentencing; encourage re-entry programmes.

Alexander's analysis and solutions rest on a critique of universality. She criticizes the trickle-down theory of racial justice through measures like affirmative action, which, she says, divide and conquer the black community by stacking the cadres of civil rights organizations with Ivy League lawyers. Referencing MLK's programme to restructure the economy on the basis of human rights like access to food, shelter, health care, education and security, she criticizes Obama's post-black meritocracy because it ignores black poverty and incarceration. She is correct to argue that critiques of white privilege contribute to working-class resentment and that the corporate emphasis on diversity bribes blacks into the power structure at the same time that it guilts whites out of it. This sounds correct, but it runs into problems when it conservatively defines the power structure in terms of racial inequality rather than social inequality. It is less the case that racial justice cannot afford to wait for whites to give up their privileges, than that justice cannot be served by denying anyone rights and privileges. Reducing social relations to moral problems like selfishness and jealousy rationalizes suffering as a matter of policy.

What kind of society needs to create a prison population? Racial inequality in the U.S. has historical causes, but it is not a caste system because it is not based on heredity and because race discrimination has been made illegal by the elimination of Jim Crow laws. Racial prejudice and everyday forms of psychopathology are not the cause of the exponential growth of incarceration, prison labour and the for-profit prison-industrial complex. A more convincing argument for incarceration rates is the bipartisan class war against the poor.

Any challenge to the prison system in the U.S. cannot move forward without a challenge to the profit system.

In contrast to Alexander's moral exhortation, Reed addresses the criminal justice debate in relation to the political economy of race relations and the social function of anti-racism as part of the progressive wing of neoliberalism.[106] With regard to police crime, blacks are twice as likely to be killed by police as the rest of the population, and whites are killed at between 75 and 80 percent of their share of the population, which is not to say that there are not more whites killed by police overall. The emphasis on racial disparity ignores the fact that 95 percent of police homicides occur in neighbourhoods where the median household income is an annual average of $52,907 and in states that are predominantly white. People who are disproportionately in danger includes Hispanics, Native Americans and poor whites.

Excessive policing is a means to manage social inequality. The emphasis on black vulnerability by groups like BLM, Reed argues, is part of an effort to contain and suppress the "marginal and sub-employed working-class populations that are produced by revanchist capitalism."[107] Although the Black Panthers were correct, he says, to demand minority policing in black neighbourhoods, the effect of police violence on blacks has declined by approximately 70 percent since the 1960s. What has not improved since then is the leftist challenge to the upward redistribution of wealth. Transhistorical abstractions like white supremacy function as alternatives to explanations of the causes of inequality, invoking forms of individual pathology like prejudice and intolerance. The problem with managerial racialism, then, is that it relies on a concept – racism – that has no standard of evaluation. Unlike the critique of capitalism, the critique of racism has no strategic political content other than pointless injunctions to expiation, atonement and moral rehabilitation. At best, the charge of racism is innocuous; at worst, it is a pointless form of moral blackmail. The goal of racialism is not ideological purity, but the purgation of ideology as such. Today's politically correct anti-racism has practically nothing to do with race and much more to do with the post-representational politics that today govern social life and culture.

The Intellectuals

Cornel West never minced words in his criticism of Barack Obama. Equally important, he and Tavis Smiley set out in 2011 on an 18-city Poverty Tour to address the living conditions of the destitute in the U.S. and to meet with grassroots organizations dedicated to the fight against despair – Indigenous groups, immigrants and undocumented farmers, housing rights activists, seniors and elder care workers, tent cities and homeless veterans, school and free lunch recipients, soup kitchens, prisoner rehabilitation centres and Habitat for Humanity projects for the handicapped. Along the way, several stops were made to honour the legacy of Martin Luther King Jr. and the Civil Rights movement. The Poverty Tour no doubt had as part of its mission the indictment of the failure of the political class to tackle social inequality. West expressed his disappointment with Obama, arguing that he had deceived the electorate: "he posed as a progressive and turned out to be counterfeit. We ended up with a Wall Street presidency, a drone presidency, a national security presidency."[108] Given the clemency shown by Obama to the perpetrators of Wall Street fraud as well as war and torture in the Middle East, his black expression and reformist posturing became instruments of deception wielded in the interest of an empire in decline. West's dismay at the "low quality leadership" of confidence men like Obama and Holder was measured in terms of soul capital: "it's like you're looking for John Coltrane and you get Kenny G in brown skin."[109] Against this, West advocated a restoration of the "prophetic fire" of previous African-American leaders like Frederick Douglass, W.E.B. Du Bois, MLK, Ella Baker, Malcolm X and Ida B. Wells. What these people had in common was integrity in the face oppression, honesty in the face of deceit, decency in the face of insult and virtue over brute force.[110] West worries that too many today are willing to sell themselves for venality and popularity instead of moral consistency and constancy in the interest of truth and social justice, which he defines in terms of Christian love.

In an interview with Chris Hedges, one of countless given by one of the busiest public intellectuals, West denounced Obama at the same time as the rest of the black elite. The black prophetic tradition has been supplanted by the elitism and upward striving of a minority of Americans who have opted in favour of corporatization and oppression rather than education and justice. The satisfaction with Obama, he argued, was due to the hunger for a symbolic victory characterized by the narcissistic esteem for people from one's tribal milieu.[111] To make matters worse, the black leadership has been bankrupted by the establishment's spin on diversity: "this obsession with diversity that you're getting in the Supreme Court in relation to affirmative action, was a dilution and a domestication of the issue. (…) One of the ways of making sure you sanitize talk about racism is to talk about diversity."[112]

The focus of the black managerial elite on diversity in high places and success markers that are unrelated to the fate of the working majority has been the subject of the work of the literary theorist and Reed collaborator Walter Benn Michaels. Michaels has noted the ways in which diversity functions as a contemporary ideology. Although there is no scientific basis to the concept of race, the notion of racial difference is accepted as a means to confront racism. This has led to policies that promote racial diversity, for instance in university admissions, as well as through the celebration of racial difference and other kinds of identity. The emphasis on diversity, according to Michaels, has led to the marginalization of class issues in American life. As he puts it: "the idea is not just that racism is a bad thing (which of course it is) but that race itself is a good thing. And what makes it a good thing is that it is not class. We love race – we love identity – because we don't love class."[113] Because class difference cannot be celebrated, people prefer to ignore class inequality. Capitalism would rather assist the victims of racism – or some of them – than the victims of exploitation. Unfortunately, as diversity has become the ideology of the American intellectual left, questions of social inequality are tackled through the framework of identity politics, thereby undermining leftism by transforming class conflict into a matter of discrimination: the poor are "different" and in that sense they are equal to the wealthy. Whereas anti-racism prevents someone from arguing that white is better than black, few would dispute the notion that being wealthy is preferable to being poor. Since economic redistribution is treated as un-American, what the liberal class prefers is to think of conservatives like Bush and Trump as racists rather than capitalists.[114] Americans prefer the struggle against racism to the struggle against economic inequality.

One of the subjects that Michaels has addressed is the interest that business takes in diversity, with research, task forces, hiring tests, performance ratings and grievance procedures dedicated to equal opportunity, eliminating bias and improving equity. Corporate America and trade unions have fortified this consensus by institutionalizing diversity training, which is now a multi-billion-dollar industry. There are diversity products, newsletters, rankings and policies. All Fortune 500 companies have diversity training requirements. In 2014, Google is said to have spent $114 million on diversity initiatives, even if blacks were only 3.3 percent of its workforce.[115] As with advertising, diversity training is not known to yield any tangible results.[116] What the business literature critiques of diversity training ignore, however, is the successful ideological role that diversity plays in deradicalizing the left and strengthening global capitalism. As social conditions worsen, administrators in countless fields are increasingly held to account for lack of diversity, leading to moral panics and hasty remedies. The Émile-Cohl art school in Lyon, for example, digitally darkened the faces of some of the students in its advertisements to "add diversity" to the school's website. Similarly, a l'Oréal-owned beauty company in South Korea, Stylenanda, was shamed for digitally painting an advertisement model to look darker. Although criticism focused on the company's failure to hire a black model instead, the implication in such cases is that capitalism must exploit more fairly.

An instance of the propagandization of diversity policies is the 2017 Academy Awards speech by Frances McDormand, who advocated for 'diversity riders' in Hollywood films, which has since then been consolidated through diversity quotas for Oscar nominations. Her menacing speech exemplified the ways in which nihilism is re-emerging alongside right-wing populism. Its purpose is to keep mass discontent oriented towards the interests of the ruling class. The invocation of aggression as a medium for social change, as represented by her character in Martin McDonagh's *Three Billboards Outside Ebbing, Missouri* (2017), is a standard tactic of the right-wing news media, who berate progressives with the kind of misdirection that pretends to be channelling the unconscious hive mind, and this, as opposed to the wish list of corporate think tanks.[117] The pandering of stupefaction by actors like McDormand does nothing to improve the working conditions of a monitored Amazon employee on starvation wages, but it does divert attention and effort away from coordinated labour organization, which would do more to mitigate the problems of racism and sexism. Her follow-up lead role in the Chloé Zhao film *Nomadland* (2020) made destitution seem like a choice rather than a quandary. And to cap off her rightist performance as a wolf howling at the moon when she received her *Nomadland* Oscar for best actress, McDormand indirectly compared Denzel Washington's lead role in Joel Coen's *The Tragedy of Macbeth* (2021), in which she fittingly plays Lady Macbeth, as a Machiavellian inspiration for those who have the courage, like Obama, to fail with rage.[118]

Anti-racism is not wrong simply because it is supported by corporations. What this support demonstrates nevertheless is the fact that anti-racism is not automatically a struggle against capitalist exploitation. This alone is enough to explain why it is that anti-racism has become part of today's official ideology. As Michaels argues, the substitution of moral imperatives for politics obscures class issues through cultural categories. In contrast to the view that the Obama presidency was a victory for anti-racism, we are now in a situation, Michaels says, where diversity candidates will not make much of a difference to intractable problems of inequality. To explain why questions of identity are not the same as class issues, Michaels argues that workers who are on strike are not fighting to have their otherness respected. Matters of personal identity, like who you sleep with or the colour of your skin, should not have any political significance if your cause is economic equality. This does not imply the inverse: social and economic justice does entail the mitigation of problems like racism, sexism and homophobia. Obama's presidency may have produced a racist reaction, but it did not necessarily create more racism than already existed. It did, however, produce more social inequality and more social inequality can lead to more racism. The point is therefore not to dismiss questions of identity and discrimination, but to question the way that the focus on diversity contributes to the neoliberal agenda.[119] Race and class issues are in this way disconnected from one another. The way that diversity connects race and class is to redistribute wealth within identity groups. An equal number of black millionaires and billionaires is how advocates of diversity measure equality. The result is that racialists are today doing more for the privileged middle and upper classes than for the working poor.[120] In an acerbic comment on this ideology, and as a comment also on the tendency of anti-racists to project their values onto the past, Zine Magubane suggests that racialists would have considered slavery acceptable if a proportionately equal number of slave owners had been black, Latino, and so on.[121] Although intended as a joke, this statement is not so far from the imaginings of postmodernists whose ostensible dislike of Western bourgeois culture has caused them to advance a Romanticized and sometimes reactionary defence of so-called heterotopias like pirate ships, theme parks, sanatoria, witch covens or space colonies.

Michaels makes a valuable contribution to understanding the ways in which race and class do not simply intersect but are mutually and asymmetrically co-implicated. This makes class struggle more confusing insofar as progressive leftists, who are committed to anti-racism, anti-sexism and anti-homophobia, do not consider themselves to be neoliberal. The paradox is that it is not only progressive leftists who are against discrimination, but that competitive economies, as Michaels puts it, "cannot afford to discriminate."[122] However, Michaels refuses to concede politics to economic justifications of diversity, which is something that can be noticed in the work of Gary Becker, an economist and sociologist who argued that firms that discriminate add to the costs of productivity and reduce competitiveness as well as profitability. Maximizing utility and human capital, for instance, by hiring low-wage minorities, is similar to the enthusiasm of neoclassical economists for illegal immigration because it contributes to the decimation of welfare policies. Michaels objects to this anti-disparitarian notion of market-based justice because it contributes to class inequality and limits what can be achieved in terms of a left programme of social justice. His thesis is that the majority of working people are poor because of capitalist exploitation, not because of discrimination. The 50 percent of poor whites who own as little as 2 percent of total white wealth are not poor because of discrimination. Just as nineteenth-century imperialism relied on racism to justify inequality, the neoliberal legitimation of free markets champions the kind of exploitation that is managed by human resources departments that are well-trained in diversity policy.

The concern for equal opportunity is not the same as the goal of eliminating inequality. The focus on disparities between racial groups, where, incidentally, Asian Americans tend to be twice as likely as whites to number in the top 5 percent of households, leads to efforts to have less racial disparity among unequal status groups. In contrast to racial redistribution and reparations, ending class inequality through redistribution measures would eliminate the top and the bottom quintiles, a far more radical prospect than equal representation in an economic hierarchy.[123]

The politics of diversity now has the features of puritanical evangelism, demanding that people feel guilty and sacrifice for others in ways that abjure progressive thinking and promote an uncomplicated if at times virulent moralism. This is less innocent than it appears since its social function is to attack the class consciousness of a weakened left. Diversity is now also commercial, venal and fun – a surplus of narcissistic clamour and a politically safe way to engage in red-baiting. Unlike socialism, diversity is suitable to the needs of capitalism at the same time that it appears to be a progressive force of democratization. One paradox of the emphasis on diversity is that whereas the proportion of blacks who perceive discrimination has decreased from 95 percent to 65 percent in the period from 1950 to the 2000s, the proportion of whites who think of themselves as victims of discrimination has increased from 10 percent to 50 percent.[124] The reason for this is the way in which a victim politics that emphasizes discrimination has changed the way that people understand inequality, often by identifying another identity group as the cause of their disadvantage. Poor whites are now either racist or are the victims of anti-racism policies. Educational institutions increasingly promote theories of intersectionality that transform class politics into questions of discrimination, a shift that Michaels says reflects the class interests of the middle and upper-middle class. Ivy League schools that admit only a small number of applicants show more interest in affirmative action policies that support racial and gender diversity than admissions for poor students. These schools account for only a small percentage of college students and so their impact on access to education is more negligible than access to the ranks of the power elite. If race and class issues are sometimes referred to as an 'and/or' debate, anti-racists are hard-pressed to criticize women and blacks who make their way out of poverty and into professional and high-income tax brackets. However, intersectional 'andorism' does nothing to alter the growth of low-income jobs. Free higher education would do more in terms of democratic access to better-paying jobs than affirmative action does presently in the case of the top-ranked schools. It would not necessarily improve working conditions in lower-paying jobs and so the critical point about 'andorism' is that radical politics are weighted more heavily towards class issues since anti-racism cannot eliminate inequality. In contrast, the struggle against class exploitation weakens the effects of discrimination. When the left neglects the struggle for class equality, Michaels argues, it makes itself into "the good conscience of the right."[125]

Since the postwar period, the liberal critique of institutional racism has been part of an effort by the U.S. power elite to reorient black politics in the direction of establishment ideological objectives. Foremost in this discussion is Adolph L. Reed, Jr. Reed's approach emphasizes the fact that the Civil Rights movement was not a movement against racism but a movement for full citizenship that was based for the most part on the old left and the labour movement. In other words, it was animated by universalist and socialist ideals. Reed's approach to race and class raises many issues concerning today's anti-racism. The following six points summarize his varied arguments.

First, Reed rejects anti-racism on the basis of its *language and taxonomy*, which *reinforce the problem of race essentialism* and the treatment of race and class as distinct phenomena. While both sides of the race and class debate tend to ontologize the category of race, anti-racism focuses on the term race and is interested in knowing what constitutes racism. One consequence of this approach is that it reinforces the notion of racism as a timeless abstraction, with 'black liberation' also defined in vague or idealist terms. Racial injustice is consequently attributed to individual pathology, intolerance and prejudice rather than social and historical processes. By the same token, the charge of racism makes anti-racists feel good when they assign guilt to others. The obsession with whiteness, blackness and post-blackness are symptoms of this inflation of language over politics.[126] Reed thus defines race reductionism as a demand for recognition based on moral priority rather than politics:

> The contention that racism singularly defines black reality is therefore not an empirical claim, even though many advancing it seem earnestly convinced that it is. It is a lament that racism persists as a force impeding black Americans' aspirations, that no matter how successful or financially secure individual black people may be, they remain similarly subject to victimization by it.[127]

"No one in American politics with any aspirations to respectability openly embraces racism," Reed writes, "not even Donald Trump. In fact, everyone, even Trump, insists that he or she opposes it."[128] Insofar as leftist anti-racists acknowledge the ways in which capitalist relations have produced racial inequality, a further difficulty derives from an uncomplicated, ahistorical and generic understanding of capitalism. Whereas labour is without question organized on the basis of privately appropriated value and has a materially demonstrable foundation, race, Reed argues, "has no such essential foundation."[129] This brings him to reject definitions of race that are premised on essential differences, even if such differences, usually attributed to recognizable phenotypical and biological descent, are in actuality means to naturalize and legitimize ascriptive status differentiations. Racism and anti-racism are therefore ideologies that are the product of specific historical processes.[130] As the race and class debate is often reified into race-first versus class-first arguments, the treatment of racism as a normative, autonomous and predictable monolith works to mystify liberal ideology as well as social constructionist theories that emphasize difference rather than capitalist social relations.

Second, and as a result of the first point, the rhetoric of anti-racism *reduces knowledge of politics* by substituting righteous indignation, moral bombast and attitudinal dismissal for knowledge, debate and argumentation about the mechanisms and patterns of inequality that may have nothing to do with bigoted motivations. One obvious problem of race ignorance is the notion that all black people are equally oppressed and, related to this, the notion that white people invariably contribute to an all-encompassing white supremacist oppression. Social and historical problems are thereby mystified and blacks are magically absolved of the problems of capitalism and imperialism. The politics of transhistorical race essentialism makes tribal perceptions of whites useful to neoliberal notions of individual freedom. Its effects are black pessimism and fatalism about neo-colonial imperialism.

Third, anti-racism is a *flawed strategy* with regard to its own stated goal of combatting racial injustice and reduces politics to grievances. Addressing racial grievances, for example through reparations, replaces wealth redistribution across all of society. Reparations appeals to race-first thinking by racializing the notion of economic justice. The problem with reparations is that, as a designer programme, it is less solidaristic and undermines a more universal approach to poverty. A 2018 poll noted that monetary reparations are supported by 26 percent of Americans. It does not follow, Reed argues, that because black economic disparity can easily be explained with reference to the history of slavery and segregation that the solutions to such disparity should be racialized.[131] Although introduced in the late 1950s and early 1960s, and consolidated in 1969 by the Committee for Reparations for Descendants of U.S. Slaves, the issue of reparations only coalesced in 1987 with the development by the National Coalition of Blacks for Reparations of what would become bill HR40, the Commission to Study Reparation Proposals for African Americans Act that was introduced by John Conyers in 1989. Claiming reparations that had not been honoured since as far back as the era of Reconstruction, HR40 conforms to the anti-left and anti-universalist politics of black elites who do not distinguish among blacks of different classes and who otherwise make claims for advancement within multinational capitalism. The cause of reparations is therefore a consequence of the disappearance of a black working-class politics. Whereas reparations are presented as redemptive, universal social programmes are where the real struggle lies because they demand more from people than self-interest. The capitalist character of reparations was demonstrated by the use of the issue during the

2020 presidential race, with Democrat Sheila Jackson Lee presenting the bill for the first time to the full committee of the U.S. House Judiciary Committee. It was supported by Democratic Party nominees Tulsi Gabbard, Eric Salwell, Tim Ryan, Elizabeth Warren and Cory Booker. The review panel included Ta-Nehisi Coates and football player Burgess Owens, whose presentation denounced socialism and Marxism. Since Sanders had already stated that he preferred infrastructure projects and a jobs programme to reparations, the June 2019 commission appeared at a crucial moment in the DP nomination race in which both Trump and the leading Democratic candidate, Joe Biden, were denouncing socialism. The case for a national apology and economic reparations also has several built-in problems: there are no living survivors of slavery; it is not decided who would pay for reparations and who would be paid; reparations would likely rely on outdated racist concepts to determine recipients; lastly, according to the logic of reparations, there is no reason that reparations would not be made to Indigenous groups, immigrant groups and to the working class, or to foreign nations that have been devastated by American imperialism. Because the black vote is complicated by a variety of interests and ideological leanings, causes like reparations and movements like BLM create the impression that people are more committed to anti-racism than to socialist democracy. Rather than building power through a labour movement that is oriented towards socialism, what a race-first politics achieves, at best, is resistance to capitalist depredation. At worst, it accuses white workers of being racist and weakens solidarity.

Fourth, anti-racism has the opposite effect of its ostensible objective and instead *attacks the left*. Whereas official racism is proscribed by law, poverty is not. Racialists are convinced of the duality of race and class issues and separate racial justice and racial democracy from social democracy. Anti-racism is a class politics. As Reed puts it: “the race line is itself a class line, one that is entirely consistent with the neoliberal redefinition of inequality and democracy.”[132] He argues further that those who prefer an intersectional approach tend to give priority to fighting racism as the precondition for any other politics. This, he says, is the politics of the Democratic Party, which has systematically avoided economic justice since the Carter administration. Under pressure by the Republican offensive, the black political class, like the left more generally, has focused defensively on electoral victories at the expense of protecting and enhancing social programmes. The left abandoned its radical commitments in favour of a liberal reorientation that decimated labour power. One finds the same reduced ambitions in other areas, such as the feminist concern with access to government and corporate power, or the anti-war movement’s acquiescence to military intervention for the sake of democracy. The anti-racism movement has settled for the elimination of racial disparity at the expense of economic equality.

Emphasizing pragmatism, it opts for incremental changes that suppress dissent and ignores the similarities between the two main parties.

Fifth, race-first advocates have *no political constituency*. By attacking the left, racialists have demobilized black politics and created a black professional and managerial middle class that focuses on affirmative action, inclusion, diversity and the celebration of identity. The celebration of race is absurd since race is an ascriptive status that is embedded in the dynamics of capitalism. Racialists make race relations a career path in what is now a race relations and diversity management industry that consists of human resources departments, personnel agencies and consultants, all of which are concordant with the entrepreneurial and market orientation of public policy. Its calling card is the projection of positive stereotypes of black success and exemplary individuals as part of a narrative of racial triumph, as evidenced by controversies over representation in the culture industries. In addition to a $65 million book deal with Penguin for their memoirs, the Obamas have signed deals with Netflix and Spotify to promote diversity in the entertainment industry. This celebration of success and wealth has more in common with Wall Street than the black "community" that is invoked independently of any consideration of the broader American political economy. It is no different from the post-Katrina mobilization of the "black community" for the sake of privatization and the destruction of low-income housing and public schools.[133] The first film produced by the Obamas' production company, Higher Ground, is an Academy Award-winning documentary about a glass company that seeks to exploit its American workers to the same degree as its Chinese workforce. By ignoring the role of the UAW in its support of the New Democrat agenda, the film undermines socialist politics and naturalizes the global integration of the capitalist economy.

One symptom of the lack of a constituency for anti-racist politics is the replacement of a comprehensive policy orientation with a victim politics that shifts from one single-issue campaign to another, nourished by so-called grassroots and social media clicktivism. This dilettantism on the left, Reed argues, is the result of decades of defeat and marginalization. Vulnerable to enthusiasm and seeking bipartisan mainstream acceptance, left strategy is reduced to the opportunistic tactics of bearing witness, demonstrating solidarity, sending messages to those in power and standing with the oppressed.[134] The faddish blather and expressive display of black bromides function like competing brands in what Reed calls the "nonstop idiotic bread and circuses" of social media and an academy bereft of any particular strain of scholarship.[135]

Following the class politics of the black PMC, the sixth and last point addresses the actual purpose and political orientation of racialism, which is the *collusion with right-wing tendencies* of various sorts. As a product of Cold War anti-communism, anti-racism is typically anti-Marxist and makes use of the right-wing tactic of masquerading as liberal and reasonable, if not righteously angry, in order to combat radical politics. Professional anti-racists like Dyson, Coates, Tim Wise, Michelle Boyd, DeRay McKesson, Marissa Johnson, John Legend, Maulana Karenga and Molefi Kete Asante are defenders of neoliberal capitalism. Like the professional black political class of administrators, functionaries, contractors and investors, they perceive the free market as the best means to distribute wealth. Moreover, NGO-type community activists as well as academic postcolonialists often do not recognize the class tensions within race politics. Reed writes:

> In our current political moment, in which even flamboyantly race-conscious black people embrace career opportunities and ideological rationales attendant to the destruction of public education, privatization of public goods and services, and the dynamic of rent-intensifying real estate development commonly described as gentrification or neighborhood upgrading and revitalization, formulations that presume an idealized 'black community' or 'black masses' as a collective political subject obscure real processes through which the larger revanchist regime gains legitimacy among black officials and citizens as its imperatives take on the character of pragmatic common sense.[136]

In short, race-first activists, racialists and professional anti-racists contribute to the class politics of the black PMC that appeals to white liberals and bipartisan neoliberals. Their alignment with black nationalism is due to their emphasis on the centrality of racism and on a racial interpretive frame of reference for every manifestation of racial injustice. This frame of reference can encompass all social phenomena. Reed goes so far as to suggest that one should not bother making distinctions between different kinds of race-first anti-racists since all of them, even black power nationalists like Marcus Garvey, Elijah Muhammad, Floyd McKissick and Roy Innis, have proven, on the view that white people are inherently racist, willing to make alliances with right-wing forces.[137] The result of this collusion at the level of the social base is that anti-racists become the "shock troops of neoliberalism," legitimating the careers of politicians like Barack Obama, Kamala Harris and Deval Patrick.[138]

Reed decries the Obama administration as the triumph of race over ideology.[139] The Obama brand replaced politics with a desire for the vindication of black rights. By campaigning on vague notions of hope and change, Obama could avoid and delay anything related to economic justice. Obama, Reed argues, could easily present himself as the embodiment of an undefined progressivism because that is what the demoralized American left has allowed itself to become. He lived up to people's aspirations because they have none. To go beyond the neoliberal framework of the Democratic Party is to reject the stereotype that the working class is made up of white and conservative Archie Bunker types, a myth that caters to culture warriors at the expense of the socialist and democratic agenda. The logic of anti-racism makes it such, Reed argues, that voting for Obama is not proof that someone is not racist but voting for Trump is proof that they are.[140] The Trump presidency has encouraged anti-racists in and around the Democratic Party and the Democratic Socialists of America to think that the mobilization of identity politics and racialist outrage justifies the critique of class essentialism. Reed questions this as both dubious and anti-socialist.[141] The tug of war between race-first and class-first politics is asymmetric. It is all the more ideologically suspect that so few are pulling from the class side of this issue. When identity-baiting fails and the working class is proven to not be, *e ipso facto*, racist, sexist, homophobic and xenophobic, neoliberals and rightists turn more directly to red-baiting. Identity-baiting is therefore a means to forestall the more determining class conflict without, at the same time, doing anything to overcome class contradictions.

Reed's critique of politically undifferentiated appeals to black constituencies and black unity is echoed by the late Ellen Meiksins Wood's uses of political economy to criticize not only American politics, but capitalist democracy more generally.[142] A left critic of identity politics, Wood contended that we can better understand capitalist globalization by thinking of it in terms of a very broad historical sweep that dates as far back as Imperial Rome. Against the postmodern view that Western universality is inherently oppressive, Wood argued instead that the democratic thrust of identity, particularity and difference are what allow egalitarianism to coexist with empire and domination.[143] Egalitarian doctrine justifies domination through the duality of abstract political equality (pluralism and civic equality) and pragmatic or economic inequality (class inequality). In Roman Christianity, Pauline and Augustinian universality became more congenial for power than tribalism, allowing for the religious legitimation of the social hierarchy of temporal powers, including slavery, as providential. The fallen nature of humanity and the incommensurability between the city of God and the earthly city implied that there can be no justice on earth. Moral fallibility, as described by Dante and Machiavelli, made social equality a horizon of possibility, but not a plausible reality. As religion was gradually replaced by the civic religion of liberal democracy, domination was no longer obtained through direct coercion but through economic pressure. The new imperialism of global capital uses military power in order to liberate the movement of capital. People do not pledge obedience to capitalism but rather to their territorial states, which legitimize the political rights of citizens at the same time as the economic rule of global capital. Although the competitive quest for profit commodifies identity and difference, it does this through the reduction of everyone to the formal equality of abstract labour power. It is globalization, and not the colour line, that is the impersonal, natural and divine law that justifies markets and technological progress. Anti-racism participates in this globalization process.

The debate between Reed and Wood that took place at a symposium that was then published in 2002 in the journal *Political Power and Social Theory*, and later as a stand-alone monograph, relates the race and class debate to some of the more philosophical problems of Marxist analysis. In "Class, Race, and Capitalism," Wood makes several programmatic assertions that emphasize the structural difference between race and class. Rejecting the notion that race is an epiphenomenon of the material base and asserting that it is therefore distinct from class, Wood argues, first, that it is class rather than race that defines capitalist social relations, and secondly, that capitalism can exists without racism but not without class exploitation.[144] The Marxist critique of labour exploitation as the basis of the formal freedom that guarantees not only political but also property rights, makes the abolition of wage labour and the destruction of the bourgeois state the goal of revolutionary communist struggle. Whereas race hierarchies, defined by Wood as "extra-economic" mechanisms of social hierarchization, have been essential to U.S. capitalism, these and similar forms of 'civic status' hierarchies pre-date capitalism. In contrast to ancient forms of slavery and feudal social relations, capitalism is based on economic exploitation. While civic status hierarchies as well as coercive force can and have been used to reproduce class relations, slave capitalism needed to invent scientific racism to justify civic hierarchies after the advent of liberal political philosophy and the ideology of bourgeois paternalism. The latter, Wood says, justified the subordination of women, children and servants. However, neither civic status hierarchies nor coercion are constitutive of capitalism.

If capitalism is based on market imperatives that reduce all workers to interchangeable units of labour and value, regardless of personal qualities, it may also privilege certain kinds of workers for certain kinds of work and may transform particularities into marketable differences. However, that does not alter the economic imperatives that reproduce class relations in every part of the world. In contrast to the claims of racialists, Wood argues that race hierarchies and racism do not serve capitalism by reproducing race and class relations, despite the disproportionate number of blacks among the working class, but by obscuring class relations and deflecting attention away from capitalist exploitation.[145] Capitalism is indifferent to identity and is uniquely flexible in its uses of social differences in the interest of exploitation, which includes the use of gender and race conflict as means to divide the working class. Wood does not suggest that we should avoid struggles against race and gender oppression. She rather insists on their inclusion in the socialist movement. However, she does argue that capitalism can work to alter the balance of power in terms of civic hierarchies – more women and blacks in positions of authority, for example – without altering capitalist class relations. Capitalism therefore has an interest in identity politics and nationalism as means to perpetuate itself. It can do this because identity issues are not constitutive of capitalism. In this way, gender, race and sexual politics abstract identity from class politics rather than make for more concrete analyses of social relations.

In an article on race, gender and democracy, Wood cites a statement made by Issac Deutscher to American students in the 1960s: "You are effervescently active on the margin of social life, and the workers are passive right at the core of it. That is the tragedy of our society. If you do not deal with this contrast, you will be defeated."[146] The opposite, she says, is when extra-economic goals based on gender and racial equality take on an increasingly passive centrality. A paradox of the admission of more women, blacks and minorities to the ranks of the working poor is the fact that exploitation can then be attributed to causes other than capitalism. Neoliberal politicians today acknowledge the pain and suffering of identity groups in ways that are defined outside the narrow determinations of class. Although socialism cannot guarantee the elimination of gender and race oppression, it can, Wood argues, eliminate the economic needs that are served by such oppression, and it can reintegrate economic values into the political life of producers.[147] Against Reed's many points to the contrary, Marxist analysis is not naively idealist, nor can historicism solve decisive political issues. Reed's disagreement with Wood is rather a question of how one goes about doing materialist analysis. If Wood had not given priority to class analysis, her materialism would have been shorn of ideology critique and socialist politics. People who become socialist are not making a leap of faith, they are taking sides in the class struggle. The leap, insofar as it does exist, has to do with the idealist break with metaphysics.

The new imperialism does not need to justify its existence against socialism. It is enough for nation states to exist for globalization to be effective and for conflicts to be justified in terms of economic security in the service of capital markets. This much Obama understood in his bipartisan commitment to the economic sphere. Pseudo-leftists who obsess over the conservatism of the white working class ignore how postmodern post-politics and citizen activism are a justification of rather than a challenge to the system of exploitation. Such egalitarianism turns against itself insofar as it is unthreatening to capitalism.[148] In contrast to the arguments of social movement theorists, the matter is not, for Wood, a question of direct versus representative democracy. The immanentism of ideology within the mode of production simply redoubles the division between economics and politics. This is why the desire to see oneself represented in the power structure and in the person of a black president not only makes little difference to the power of capital but rather strengthens it. If the state is a necessary evil for the reign of the free market, government representatives may as well be diverse, contributing to the belief that the political class has been disabused of Enlightenment universality and its socialist counterpart. The new imperialism of the post-Cold War era, with its NATO campaigns and Patriot Act emergency measures, further ensure that no local or regional forces are allowed to interfere with state-corporate directives, either as foreign regimes or as oppositional protest movements. NGOs, development agencies and advocacy groups proliferate alongside the military contractors and the lobbying firms.

The Brokers

When truth and reason are confronted with a powerful and entrenched ideology, a dissenting knowledge is often made to serve the dominant view. The invaluable challenge represented by the work of social critics like David Harvey, Nancy Fraser, Cornel West, Cedric Johnson, Walter Benn Michaels, Adolph Reed, Fredric Jameson, Barbara Foley, David Walsh, Barbara and Karen Fields, Gregory Meyerson, Jodi Dean, Mark Fisher, Vivek Chibber, Ellen Meiksins Wood, Slavoj Žižek, Alain Badiou, and a few other kindred spirits, confronts not only a far larger number of identity and difference-oriented activists, but a middle-class academia that is saturated with intellectual tendencies that draw on post-structuralism, deconstruction and discourse theory, which for the most part define politics independently of Marxism. There are also post-Marxist and New Left tendencies that counter Marxist 'orthodoxy' with more fashionable approaches that focus on the new modes of post-Fordist production, new technologies and ostensibly new knowledges, like actor-network theory, theories of spheres or flows, theories that replace production with financialization, etc. In such instances, class issues, labour politics and leftism are distended into the kinds of materialist frameworks that dispense with the concept of totality. These approaches reinforce identity politics that are more concerned with questions of oppression than capitalist exploitation. The worse the global political, economic and ecological situation becomes, the more that academia goes to work reasserting its stance on the end of ideology. As a contingent of this revised leftism, race brokers represent a petty-bourgeois reaction to the more rigorous and principled stances developed by the aforementioned intellectuals. By and large, their work founders due to their 'decentred' materialism and their attacks on radicalism for the sake of countercultural cabbage.

One version of the new academic leftism is Chris Chen's theory of "abolitionist anti-racism," an approach that is premised on the misconception that revolutionary theory does not already include race analysis.[149] This would be one of countless strands that miss the point of Marxist analysis and have a weak conception of dialectical and historical materialism. Chen correctly notes that decolonization and Civil Rights discredited white supremacy – not that Marxism, Leninism, Trotskyism, the Popular Front, Maoism and Castroism had not done so as well – giving way to postcolonial regimes that have resorted to racialized violence for the sake of economic development. Many consider the post-apartheid capitalism of South Africa to have led to worse conditions than the pre-apartheid era. While Chen makes valuable criticisms of demands for racial equality within capitalism as well as the chauvinist-nationalist and patriotic affirmations of racialized groups, his discussion is similar to theories of 'racial capitalism' that claim to challenge the Eurocentric and Enlightenment biases of radical movements, which are accused of being race neutral and outdated insofar as they do not address the changing aspects of social conflict, from black poverty to the racially uneven consequences of the security state. According to Chen, the Marxist focus on the formal freedom of wage labour cannot adequately address the struggle against racism and so contributes to the reproduction of 'race' through differentialized economic relations and the prison system. The limit of class analysis, as well as the cultural politics of race, he argues, is the understanding of race as an 'ascriptive process' that imposes forms of racist subordination that have less to do with racist attitudes than institutional processes. When anti-racists discuss race issues as matters of identity, Chen says, status differences and the commodification of prejudices are reproduced. He also accuses socialists of reducing race to identity politics, thereby subordinating race to class and stigmatizing identity. Socialists, therefore, and presumably, view the economy as a neutral field of analysis and thereby privilege meritocratic norms.

Chen argues that an emancipatory politics would abolish identity as an ascriptive process. He notes that race and gender discrimination have weakened the American labour movement at the same time as organized labour has dwindled, leading identity groups to compete for small gains. Notwithstanding his avoidance of the contribution of labour struggles and the socialist movement to ending various forms of discrimination, his argument can be interpreted to say that it is not only identity groups that compete against one another, but that the competition between labour and capital has led to the commodification of identity as a symbolic reserve of social values. For Chen, slavery was incorporated into capitalism, making use of racial violence as part of a primitive accumulation that parallels the proletarianization of white labour. This phenomenon, he says, is active today in the production of the now redundant labour of one billion slum dwellers, which threatens labour power in the global North. Whereas Chen agrees with Frank Wilderson that this inequality is evidence of Marxism's inability to understand white supremacy as an aspect of the economic base, he confuses issues by conflating the labour movement with Marxism, suggesting falsely that the goal of communism is the integration of people into the ranks of the proletariat – or what he refers to as the capacity of surplus populations to labour -- as if labour could overtake the corporate state by putting ever more people to work.[150]

When Marx described proletarianization, he was describing the social process set in motion by capitalism, industrialization and urbanization, a process that is in effect today to an even greater degree than in Marx's time. However, Marx's nascent theories of communism did not call for more labour discipline, but for the organization of workers as the only social class who had a material interest in the overthrow of capitalism. Consequently, Marx did not distinguish between workers from different countries. On the contrary, he understood how national divisions were a threat to the workers' movement, as evidenced by his writings on the conflict between Irish and British workers and his comments on the American Civil War. The First World War further confirmed Marx's arguments, as it mobilized 70 million soldiers, most of them working class, to kill their working-class brothers and sisters in other countries. The Great War caused more than 16 million deaths and led to an influenza epidemic that killed some 50 to 100 million people. A further point that supports Marxist analysis, as argued by Wood, is that modern slavery is characterized by capitalist relations in the sense that slavery in antiquity was understood as a difference of status and not substance. Capitalists invented scientific racism to justify the uses of slavery for economic gain. This occurred in different phases but largely as the product of elite and middle-class institutions, and not as a feature of the workers' movement. In the case of anti-slavery, the motivations of abolitionists were too varied to allow for any direct comment on the emergence of socialism.

Nothing of what Chen says suggests that the universalism of revolutionary theory cannot address problems of oppression. Chen does not explain the economic value of slaves, except as a means to keep white workers subservient. He does not explain why the Civil War was fought and why desegregation was gradually achieved. This allows him to ignore three related issues: 1) the disadvantages of slavery and segregation insofar as the U.S. empire sought to justify its imperialism on the basis of universal democracy; 2) the gradual reduction of the sphere of politics in relation to economic power; 3) how the production of surplus populations is not only a means to repress labour struggles but is itself a result of the proletarianization of agricultural workers and automation. The desire of today's left-wing racialist thinkers to renovate the history of radicalism for the sake of academic novelty or multicultural social capital tends to ignore rather than explain why, at different times and in different ways, capitalism has racialized labour. It also ignores why capitalist academia may wish to 'racialize' history and socialism. What bothers postmodernists is the way that Enlightenment ideals disturb the capitalization of race and identity in ways that have only been revealed in the course of time. It is not simply that we did not know how racist Enlightenment thinkers were but that they did not know just how deeply and desperately capitalist we would become.

Racialist politics abandon the universalist and emancipatory dimension in favour of a race-oriented ontology that is subsequently historicized. By denouncing both capitalism and socialism as part of the same Enlightenment rationality, racialism understands socialism as capitalism understands it. Within Marxism, in contrast, the class subject does not have a privileged ontology except for its place in the division of labour. To argue that human subjects are not reducible to political economy, class status and labour politics does not perform the same intellectual task as the critique of political economy. Contra Chen's argument, only Marxism explains why capitalism is not inherently concerned with identity or race, except as an aspect of political liberalism's philosophy of rights. This is why the critique of "class essentialism" is a misnomer.[151] On this issue, Wood asserted the centrality and not the exclusivity of class. "If you look at the history of the United States," she wrote, "no movement has been as consistent in its struggle for racial emancipation, the emancipation of women, and so on, as the socialist movement."[152] Wood argued further that the left does not take account of diversity in the interest of working-class unity, but in the interest of human emancipation. And for this to be possible, struggles against oppression must, of necessity, be anti-capitalist.

Nor is Marxism a theory of wealth redistribution. As any socialist knows, Marx cut his teeth in the workers' movement by splitting off from the Young Hegelians and then from the Proudhonist camp. Marx not only revolutionized Hegel, he also revolutionized bourgeois materialism. Class analysis should not be misused to undermine class analysis, with capitalism surreptitiously valorized as the vanishing mediator of class, gender, race, sexuality and international relations. To argue that race is at the centre of the formal freedom that defines the capital-labour relation is simply wrong. This transforms race into a privileged commodity, as if race rather than labour power is what drives global capitalism. On the contrary, global capital makes labour productive as the privileged commodity of the global economy. Through real subsumption, capital circulation makes labour increasingly 'immaterial,' inflating the symbolic significance of race. Chen mocks Wood's Marxist view that the working class is the only subject that can end capitalism because this for him merely affirms worker self-management. Even if this was true it would hardly diminish the need to confront the problems of capitalism. The enormity of the challenge to implement socially redistributive programmes in the neoliberal era should not be used to undermine its necessity and obvious benefits.

Today's race and class debate has the characteristics of postmodern theory.[153] Most conspicuous in this regard is Asad Haider's *Mistaken Identity: Race and Class in the Age of Trump*, a call to arms whose approach to 'neither-norism' as well as 'bothandism' is as optimistic as it is confused.[154] There is much to appreciate in Haider's book, least of all his advocacy of a project of universal revolutionary emancipation and his critique of ideologies of identity that support economic elites. Among his several interconnecting arguments, Haider proposes the use of the phrase 'identity politics' by the Combahee River Collective in the late 1970s as a model for radical politics. With an emphasis on the members' lived experiences as black lesbian workers, the CRC's "Black Feminist Statement" criticized revolutionary socialism as well as the women's liberation movement on the grounds that they had not been adequately feminist and anti-racist. For Haider, what makes the Statement significant is that it performs a double operation with regard to identity: on the one hand, it identifies the situatedness of knowledge, but on the other, it does not limit the politics of identity to the members' own specific concerns. Rather, it calls for solidarity and coalition building on the basis of interrelated realities.[155] In this sense, although Haider's book seems to be a critique of identity politics, it is also a misguided critique of so-called class reductionism. The best indication of this is the fact that his starting point is the CRC and not the workers' movement, whose long history includes a vast archive of analyses and debates on questions having to do with gender, race, sexuality, religion and nationality.

With the exception of China, the internationalist left has been in retreat since the 1920s and 30s. In the postwar period, the leftist resurgence of the 1960s was already a diversified politics of civil rights, student politics, the women's movement, anti-war and ecology protest movements, as well as countercultural forms of antagonism. Most of the revolutionary struggles taking place were anti-colonial movements for national independence, all of which had to negotiate conflicting pressures with regard to revolutionary theory. However, such world-shaking projects are anathema to Haider as forms of state politics, against which he prefers the CRC collective as a model form of revolutionary grassroots politics. With this narrow framework for radicalism, Haider's critique of identity is summarized through two anecdotal episodes, which inadvertently demonstrate not only how weak the American left has become but also how microscopic is Haider's sense of revolutionary emancipation. These episodes are the failure of Occupy Wall Street to address race issues and the failure of race separatists during the 2014 student strike at the University of California at Santa Cruz to make common cause with the occupation. Against these kinds of mutual self-limitation, Haider does not revisit the history of revolutionary movements in general, but more specifically the history of revolutionary anti-racist movements, including the Black Panther Party and the Congress of Afrikan People. More recently, the "abracadabra," as he calls it, of intersectionality and privilege theory are for him grievance politics that do more to emphasize victim status and exceptionalism than the organization of mass political action. There would be no good reason to disagree with him on the latter point.

Against the ideology of victim politics, communist struggles against white supremacy have understood that race issues are essential to the workers' movement. Haider presumes that the fight against 'white skin privilege' within the CPUSA's Provisional Organizing Committee implies that class is not more fundamental than race. When people make class reductionist arguments, he says, they play into the hands of identitarian liberals.[156] This argument, however, distorts revolutionary theory. One may as well argue that one should avoid class struggle so as to not contribute further to the strengthening of capitalist democracy. One sticking point is the difference between reduction and reductionism. Failure to prevent white chauvinism in the beleaguered communist movement in the U.S. allowed racialist ideology to take up the struggle, leading to limited gains through the Civil Rights movement and the Black Power nationalism that eventually gave way to a black capitalism that advocated racial progress at the expense of class solidarity and in the context of deindustrialization. Politics was thereby reduced to the performance of black identity, which was easily disarmed in the 1980s by tough on crime policies, conservative populism, unemployment and economic recession.

The question of cultural representation is all the more acute in Haider's analysis as he turns to Stuart Hall and the Centre for Contemporary Cultural Studies approach to understanding how race became an obstacle to the development of class politics in the U.K. Insofar as racism and capitalism were approached as separate problems, with the Democratic Party and the Labour Party focused on GDP growth and trade liberalization, the right rearticulated race and class issues in favour of patriotic nationalism and individual entrepreneurialism, thereby securing the neoliberal agenda against "big government." Against Hall's analysis of authoritarian populism in his 1979 essay, "The Great Moving Right Show," Ralph Miliband's 1985 essay, "The New Revisionism in Britain," defended the primacy of the working class as the only group that can challenge the new consensus. Miliband further criticized the fragmentation of the left into new social movements. Like Hall, Haider cautions that any effort to organize workers without acknowledging how people's exploitation is lived through categories of race, gender and sexuality will inevitably fail to create the kinds of popular alliances that are required to defeat the right. In one of the most telling passages of his book, Haider mentions the solidarity that was created during the 1984-85 Miners' Strike. He writes:

> Such unexpected lines of alliance have recently been dramatized in the film *Pride* (2014), which shows the fundraising efforts of Lesbians and Gays Support Miners (a gesture of solidarity returned by the participation of Welsh miner groups at the 1985 London Pride march) and the National Union of Mineworkers' decisive support for a successful Labour Party resolution in favor of LGBT rights.[157]

The miners received support from women's groups as well. As Haider mentions, the brokering of solidarity among affinity groups did not prevent neoliberal capitalism from defeating the labour movement as well as the combined yet fragmented new social movements. Not only did Hall not anticipate this in the 1970s, he did not address the problem in the Kilburn Manifesto that he collaborated on in 2015, a reformist list of popular social demands. The culture wars and postmodern politics of the 1980s have no doubt changed mass culture and like most other society-wide phenomena have been manipulated in various ways by the ruling class. For Haider, this nevertheless confirms the fact that culture is ideology, and therefore, as Paul Gilroy has it, race is an alternative to class as a form of consciousness.[158] The bitter truth is that few postmodernists are willing to acknowledge the fact that identity politics are in part a consequence of the failures of the left. Alliances must therefore be built beyond the purview of the nation state and beyond theories that reduce politics to identitarian parochialism.

In the run-up to the 2020 presidential race, Haider's book instigated a great deal of discussion and was widely reviewed in leftist and activist journals. Among the more controversial responses was an article by Melissa Nascheck published in *Jacobin*.[159] Nascheck argues that although Haider seeks to overcome the problems posed by identity politics, his work leads in the same direction on account of his emphasis on the need to build alliances among new social movements. Rather than focus on how the ideology of racial unity supports black elites, Haider, according to Nascheck, should instead emphasize how it is that black radical politics was betrayed by postwar liberalism. In other words, there is no need to adopt a culturalist logic of race consciousness in order to understand how government policies have failed to address the problems of immiseration. In contrast to black nationalists, people like A. Philip Randolph and Bayard Rustin called for universalist social welfare policies and interracial coalitions of the working class. Comparatively, Haider's book is short on left strategy and tall on the aesthetics of militancy, as evidenced by his focus on a collective that was never associated with mass political organizations and that did not give rise to any notable achievements. Instead, the CRC was focused on its own oppression: "We believe that the most profound and potentially most radical politics comes directly out of our own identity, as opposed to working to end somebody else's oppression."[160]

Against the diverse political orientations of new social movements, Nascheck argues that socialism requires ideological cohesion, and moreover, against Haider's claims to the contrary, only socialist movements have successfully challenged capitalist class alliances. Giving a different meaning to the concept reductionism, she charges Haider with the reduction of class politics to an identity politics that emphasizes lived experience as the basis of consciousness. The real question is how can we radically change our shared experience of life under capitalism? Whereas Haider wishes to approach identity in ostensibly more 'materialist' and 'concrete' terms, Nascheck is correct to argue that he does the opposite by abstracting capitalism and anti-capitalism. Haider's 'bothandism' ignores the balance of class power, she says, and is in fact the strategy of the enemies of the left who either "worm their way into our coalition and play up identity to reshape working-class demands until they're neutralized," or are simply satisfied to become part of the liberal establishment.[161]

In an article on the Verso blog, Nikhil Pal Singh and Joshua Clover address the critique of Haider's 'bothandism' in relation to the work of Adolph Reed, who some people worry influenced Nascheck's article.[162] A few words regarding criticism of Reed allows us to return to Haider from a different perspective. Singh and Clover summarize Reed's polemic as class reductionist, which they say misconstrues Marxism and treats race as an epiphenomenon of capitalist class relations. Capitalism not only acts on race, they argue, but through race. Reed, they say, falsely treats race and class as distinct social phenomena and accuses anti-racism of undermining leftist solidarity. Their counterpoint is that Reed's critique ignores precarity and non-economic forms of coercion, two points that do not in fact stand up to scrutiny. Nevertheless, their objection is that Reed's work is outmoded insofar as he is not interested in academic postmodernism, micro-politics, post-politics and the anti-representational politics that motivate anti-oppression intellectuals. If race is the modality in which class is lived, as Hall argued, does this imply the obverse? Whereas Reed and Nascheck answer this question by addressing the issue across the long twentieth century, intellectuals like Singh, Clover and Haider operate according to a more compressed temporality.

After the rise of the anti-globalization movement, the postmodern politics of representation was admonished by the return to questions of class analysis, political economy and universality, with the post-workerist schizo-anarchism of Hardt and Negri vying for prominence with the Žižek and Badiou-led communist hypothesis. Despite the relative popularity of the latter, a neoliberalized academia is more politically compatible with the multiplicity of horizontalist social movements. Among these tendencies, dialectical materialism not only gets short shrift but is systematically falsified. Consequently, capital gets confused with class, class gets confused with society, society gets confused with reality, reality gets confused with consciousness, consciousness gets confused with pseudo-Marxism, pseudo-Marxism gets confused with Marxism and Marxism gets confused with capitalism. People may not agree with Reed's socialist politics but those who discovered his work after the fallout of the Trump presidency were introduced to a refreshing and incisive critique of the racialist racketeering that today passes for critical theory.

In response to criticism from David I. Backer and Nikhil Pal Singh, Reed has more than adequately addressed the issue of race vis-à-vis relations of production.[163] Whereas his critics consider that Reed is proposing 'eitherorism' by reducing race to a contingent, cultural construct, and therefore subordinate to class, Reed's response is that such an argument is simply inadequate class analysis. A stronger argument, he says, is not 'bothandism,' but rather an integrated concept of social relations. Race is not a function of class relations; race is the result of a process of classification that sorts groups into hierarchies of ascriptive social status and civic worth that are ideologized in terms of essential characteristics that work to stabilize a capitalist division of labour that is based on an uneven distribution of wealth and power. Race-first ideologies abstract class relations through a 'bothandist' racial capitalism, which, he argues, has become a problematic orientation on the American left. Defeatism on the left encourages culturalist and identitarian politics with "leftoid" features at the expense of radical organization.

In a more detailed critique of the internal contradictions of the Democratic Socialists of America, Reed addresses debates as to whether the organization should advance non-white, female and gender-nonconforming candidates or candidates who support universal policies. He writes:

> Those tensions resolve down to two basic alternatives: a strategy focused centrally on agitating for social-democratic programs – such as Medicare for All, free public higher education, public investment in physical and social infrastructure – intended to appeal broadly to working people of all races, genders, and sexual orientations and one that rejects that focus in favor of efforts to mobilize around issues purported to reflect the concerns of groups

marginalized on the basis of race, immigration status, sexual orientation, gender or other categories of ascribed identity.[164]

The notion that a socialist agenda cannot proceed until the problems of racism, sexism, homophobia and xenophobia are eliminated tends towards a 'do both' andorism that enables the neoliberal enemies of the left. Reed criticizes Haider's championing of the Combahee River Collective as dilettantish because it places more emphasis on will than the question of what is to be done. Likewise, 'bothandist' race and gender reductionism is vulnerable to democratic anti-left tendencies and reinforces essentialist notions of ontology, as though embodiment is the basis of a materialist politics. It also promotes the idea that the working class is white and that blacks are beyond class politics. Reed insists that race and class issues are not interchangeable and electability should not replace policy for the sake of campaign victories. Instead, socialists should forge an agenda that appeals to working people across race, gender and sexual orientation.

Haider's critique of identity politics would seem to concur with socialist politics and this may very well be adequate for setting a political agenda within activist circles. Nascheck and Reed, however, have little enthusiasm for the postmodern fine print in Haider's book. Haider's method and philosophy has a great deal in common with Ernesto Laclau and Chantal Mouffe's theory radical democracy as well as Foucauldian discourse theory. His version of intersectionality is premised on something like a deterritorialization of identity and political economy for the sake of an "insurgent universality" that looks beyond the state. In a closing section of his book, he mentions how people who protested Trump's Muslim ban in 2017 made common cause with immigrants despite the fact that many of the demonstrators were not themselves directly impacted. Against what he says is the political rationalism of Enlightenment rights discourse, one does not need to refer to someone's identity or personal interests in order to understand their opposition to American imperialism and global capitalism.[165] In a lecture that was posted online, Haider compares this kind of solidarity to Leo Bersani's discussion of sodomy as an ethics of ego self-shattering.[166] The problem with the analogy is not only that it makes "vanilla sex" seem to be equivalent to homeland security and "gay sex" equivalent to a nomadic war machine. For the sake of his very limited understanding of the problem of class reductionism, this sort of woke leftism overlooks how such a "queer" theory of affinity not only abandons what he calls the "sad passions" of belonging and attachment to one's narrowness in favour of the joy of organizing, it also affects a repressive desublimation of politics that underscores the post-Fordist flexibilization of subjectivity. Such identitarian extortion, as advanced by Judith Butler's critique of rights discourse and Wendy Brown's critique of "left melancholia," is not Marxist theory but rather neoliberal injunction.[167] Giving way on one's desire as part of an ethics of solidarity does not advance anti-capitalist struggle so much as it blackmails the left into the intersectionality swamp. Efforts at social justice should be progressive, not means tested. Human sacrifices, sexual or otherwise, will not solve our problems.

One of the bogeymen of social constructionist discourse theory is liberal individualism. Insofar as liberal political philosophy defines the subject as an agent whose political status guarantees their protection from subjection, citizenship is defined by today's anti-humanists in the terms of either a victim or victimizer. Haider distinguishes a "defensive" and "passive" juridical universalism from an "active" insurgent universalism, or what Henri Lefebvre in a different historical era referred to as revolutionary romanticism.[168] Haider does not consider that the immigrants who are looking for a better life in the U.S. are very likely motivated by what Brown refers to dismissively as the sort of "bourgeois masculinism" that seeks educational and vocational opportunities, upward mobility, protection against arbitrary violence and reward in proportion to effort.[169] Consequently, the meaning of struggle for postmodernists like Haider becomes less a matter of what one is fighting for and against than it is simply a matter of blind will.

What accounts for the contemporary compulsion towards identity, even in its anti-essentialist variants? Identity is defined by capitalist relations as more gratuitous than class because class is conditioned by work relations, which in one way or another involves coercion for the sake of survival. Identity is associated with private life, sex, culture, college and the mass media. Given the added value of underpaid Third World labour in the consumer societies of the developed North/West, class is also produced outside of the bubbles of First World Elysiums. The added value of BIPOC and LGBTQ+ for postmodernist progressives, as was the case with the CRC, is that those ascriptive traits seem to operate beyond and independently of the concerns of class. It is not that class is not lived in so many mysterious and fetishized ways, but rather that all of the concrete manifestations of hair, skin and bone 'melt into air,' as it were, as aspects of what Badiou refers to as the infinite multiplicity of ontology. No matter how mundane or thrilling, these manifestations are not in and of themselves the basis of a left politics. More nefariously, the ideological function of the obsession with anti-racism and anti-sexism is to encounter racism and sexism at a safe distance, in art, on social media and in academic essays. That is why contemporary 'woketivism' is more the concern of the PMC than the working class. The radical movement could benefit from less reliance on the postmodern strawman of a naive 50s conformism. *Father Knows Best* and *Leave It to Beaver* were already, reflexively, artefacts of Cold War propaganda. So was the corporate representation of Occupy Wall Street as a white-dominated movement with white-dominated demands – no thanks to the movement itself, whose ludicrous bro-baiting was nothing if not transference with Wall Street, now immortalized in a bronze statue of a "fearless girl."

Radical politics needs a better understanding of the alienation of socialist politics in the neoliberal era. One mainstay of leftist theory is the notion that the working class is not to be conflated with the proletariat. Marxism rejects everything that capitalism proposes as basic reality and perceives instead contradictions and abstractions. Today's anarchistic subjectivity opposes the universal in its statist forms of economic laissez-faire and juridical neo-liberalism. Yet the abstract changes into its opposite and it is humanity that becomes illusory, alienated from itself and the possibility of radical social transformation. The proletariat signifies those who bear the brunt of this alienation and who because of that have no use for the moralism that is heaped upon them. In ways that could not be anticipated by Marx and Engels, the proletariat must also abolish postmodern identity politics, in part, because they have little use for its anti-humanism. The fact that humanity does not make history as it pleases but under already existing circumstances was never meant as an apology for the status quo or for experimental forms of oppression. Postmodernism's acquiescence to the status of living dead is pure sophistry. The bourgeoisie has been exalting and crushing the individuality of workers for two centuries already. The individuality it fears is the consciousness that the working class has gained through struggle and the lucidity of socialism regarding the social praxis that can bring an end to *capitalist* alienation.[170] As William Whyte's research in *The Organization Man* revealed in the 1950s, it was CEOs at Ford and General Electric who decided that it would be best if individuals were brought into the corporatist fold. Today, joy in organization has devolved into the performance of neurotic relationality and hysterical indignation. The latter are not the result of the left's fruitless melancholia and attachment to the past, as Brown suggests. They are academic postmodernism's answer to the need for change. Or as Reed refers to contemporary social theory: Cultural Studies prattle about cultural appropriation and Orwellian chatter about privilege and whiteness.[171]

One last figure in this group of race and class brokers is the labour historian David Roediger. Roediger is well-reputed for his contribution to the study of the ways in which racism within the American labour movement has stymied anti-capitalist politics. Although he writes from the perspective of Marxism and has a commendable record of organizational involvement on the left, his work has been overtaken by social developments that make it difficult for him to accept the radical critiques of anti-racism that have been put forward in recent years. His 2017 text, *Class, Race, and Marxism*, is a sustained polemic that distinguishes his project from those who affirm the universalist character of Marxism.[172] To make his allegiance to the woke set plain enough, Roediger refers to contemporary Marxism as "class-splaining." The fact that he would concoct such a term, which echoes the ostensibly feminist notion of 'man-splaining,' is less a measure of his historical knowledge than it is an indication of where he is writing from and who he writes for. It is less a provocative challenge to the left than an admission of compromise.

Racism is a means to resolve the conflict between labour and capital. In Nazi fascism, the Jew is the figure who is blamed for pulling the strings of international capitalism. The function of the spectre of the Jew in anti-Semitism is to fantasmatically resolve, through displacement, the problems of class struggle. In progressive neoliberalism, the Jew, or any other figure of identity, is given a unique ability to transcend the problems of the labour-capital relation. Although it is certainly better that identity groups are affirmed rather than persecuted – and most of what Roediger says about racial equality is to be supported – both racism and anti-racism, from a Marxist perspective, avoid the critique of political economy and leave the inherent problems of capitalism intact.

Insofar as race and class cannot be separated, Roediger privileges historical materialism at the expense of dialectics, which would require that race relations be understood not only in terms of history but also in terms of Marxist theory. One cannot simply take on every development in structuralism, post-structuralism, discourse theory and post-Fordism without some attention to their impact on the left. The best of the "class-splainers" have managed to remain relevant over the last several decades despite the efforts of countless academics working in the humanities to bury Marxism and replace it with postmodernism. Oblivious to the immense constituency of non- and anti-Marxist scholars and students, Roediger laments the fact that "so many well-positioned" writers are placing an emphasis on class at the expense of race and gender. He dismisses them as people who imagine themselves "lonely figures sacrificing to tell the truth."[173] Given that not very many scholars are so well-placed as to be public intellectuals, one could only wish that there were more rigorous class-splainers and fewer petty-bourgeois careerists.

To prove the point that there are not that many people today who defend Marxist universality against its academic liquidation, those few that Roediger calls out for criticism are indeed well-known. *Class, Race, and Marxism* begins with a discussion David Harvey's *Seventeen Contradictions and the End of Capitalism*, a book that not only covers a vast range of issues in political economy and globalization but also makes the correct claim that identity-based struggles should not be thought to transcend the struggle against capitalism.[174] It is not possible to describe Roediger's critiques of Harvey without reproducing

Roediger's biased description. One gets a sense of this with his characterization of Harvey's "iron distinction" and "formalist" separation between anti-racism and anti-capitalism.[175] Not only is this assumption false, but one can intuit that the term that he is alluding to is 'iron curtain.'[176] Another figure who appears in this discussion is Walter Benn Michaels, whose critique of neoliberal diversity, Roediger says, has the character of a conspiracy theory. Defending the contribution of anti-racism to class struggle, Roediger objects to the idea that demands for racial justice are calls for equal distribution within an unequal society. The extent to which the demand for racial equality challenges neoliberal governance is debatable, however, especially when it ignores the globality of capitalism or when the white worker is made into a scapegoat who is seemingly unable to understand racial justice. Paul Street, Adolph Reed and Cedric Johnson are also taken to task, in particular, for their attack on Coates's criticism of Sanders' rejection of reparations.

It is telling that Roediger considers that radical left scholars are not concerned with race issues or that they believe that class analysis thrives best when there is not too much emphasis on race or so-called racial capitalism.[177] His retort is that the "most dynamic" work takes place at the intersection of class and other forms of difference.[178] Wood's work is addressed somewhat indirectly in the title of Roediger's first chapter, "The Retreat from Race and Class," which simplistically reverses some of the arguments presented in Wood's 1986 book, *The Retreat from Class: A New 'True' Socialism*.[179] Although Wood would likely have accused Roediger of identifying with radical democracy or other forms of post-Marxism, his work remains within a social democratic optic, even if at times it is equal parts white liberal guilt and sixties counterculture. Today's Marxist left, according to Roediger, either departs or fails to depart from Eugene Debs's turn of the century statement to the effect that "class struggle is colorless."[180] In Roediger's estimation, Reed wins the Eugene Debs prize since he considers the exposure of racism to be as significant as an appendix – innocuous but harmful when it flares up.[181] Reed's "misguided" class analysis, according to Roediger, targets race relations technocrats who operate with an imprecise and faulty theory of institutional racism to justify attacks on welfare. Reed and others like him are therefore said to be on the retreat from race struggles and obstructing ongoing efforts to understand the dynamics of racism.

Roediger presumes that more attention to race will undermine capitalism. What he offers is a racial analysis of class rather than a class analysis of race. Were he not only against white supremacy but also progressive neoliberalism, he might be less inclined to perceive a retreat from race and a Marxist defensiveness than a welcome renewal of leftist energies. Instead, a negligible figure like F.T.C. Manning, who was a participant at the *Seventeen Contradictions* symposium, is given the last word in relation to Harvey, whose "easy," "well-trodden" and "obvious" Marxism is said by this thinker to ignore the "materiality" of race and ethnicity.[182] Harvey argues that race is not inherent to the logic of capital and that anti-racists encounter problems with capitalists only when they become revolutionary. Manning responds to this by saying that the same is true about workers: workers only encounter problems with capitalists when they turn revolutionary. That assertion is false. Although workers become a problem to capitalists especially when they become revolutionary, workers are, even in the best of circumstances, antagonistic to the capitalist class. The same cannot be said about racialists. Manning suggests that capitalism has been as effective in coping with workers' demands as the demands of multiculturalism and gay rights. To Manning's argument that there are gender and race relations at play in all social formations, the Marxist response is that even though that is true, they are not descriptive of the specificity of capitalism. Concepts like racial capitalism or patriarchal capitalism are internal to capitalism and tend towards the reform of capitalism to advance group interests. Racial differences are not the basis of capitalist exploitation. Since sexuality and gender difference do not operate in the same way as racial difference, a related question is the tendency towards identity politics and micro-politics as transversal social movement issues that do not propose systematic alternatives to capitalism but rather seek to vary its institutional rules.[183]

At the *Seventeen Contradictions* symposium, Harvey mentioned Obama as a case in point where anti-racism fits comfortably with pro-capitalism. In his own assessment, Roediger cannot bring himself to say anything more critical of Obama than the notion that he represented the inadequacies of African-American "liberal" leadership: "The election of Barack Obama posed the issue of Black and particularly Black *liberal* roles in running an oppressive system with new force."[184] Black capitalist leadership is elsewhere given the flattering term "rulers of color."[185] Such waffling around political correctness finds Roediger coming across as disarmingly coy in his admonishments about "tone" and the need for class-splainers to avoid aggression and instead accept differing viewpoints without vilification. Here is another instance of Mark Fisher's theory of the "vampire castle," in which Roediger would fit nicely as a concern troll.[186] Fisher decried the atmosphere of humility that is demanded by today's self-styled "left," wherein the suppression of class consciousness by the academic petty bourgeoisie leads to a demoralizing atmosphere. While attacking the vampire castle can make it seem as though one is attacking the struggle against racism and heterosexism, the vampire castle is, Fisher says, an "inversion-projection-disavowal mechanism" that was created when people allowed their identities to be defined by liberal class relations. Its key features include: 1) the individualization and privatization of critique, 2) gaslighting and efforts to make critique seem difficult, 3) the propagation of guilt about privilege, even for people in subordinate classes, 4) essentialization of the enemy, despite pretences to belief in the fluidity of identity, and 5) the expression of liberal incredulity towards the predations of capitalism.[187] Against this, the reassertion of the centrality of class prevents class struggle from being organized in the interest of bloodsuckers that build solidarity with bourgeois power.

Based on Roediger's newest book, it is now easier to identify a few of the fault lines of his classic work, *The Wages of Whiteness*.[188] This study of the white working class in antebellum America takes as one of its starting points W.E.B. Du Bois's claim in *Black Reconstruction in America* (1935) that workers in the post-Civil War period accepted the conditions imposed on them by Southern elites because their whiteness provided them with small privileges in addition to the "psychological wage" they received when distinguishing themselves from blacks. Although this attention to psychology is only a fraction of Roediger's work, it is an important starting point for his research and is a theme that he develops in a several instances. How, when and why American workers defined themselves as white implies, according to Roediger, that class is not more fundamental than race to workers' sense of identity and therefore to their politics and practices. From this starting point he then suggests that racism must be examined in class terms. This leads him to focus on the working class rather than the dominant bourgeois class and its invention of ideologies of racism. Drawing on the work of Noel Ignatiev, Roediger accepts the view that the problem is not the racism of the capitalist employer, which is deemed "natural" since the bourgeoisie has an interest in maintaining its class rule, but is rather the problem of the worker, whose racism is deemed "artificial" because alien to their interests. This is a problematic starting point. Esme Choonara and Yuri Prasad note that Roediger ignores the main point of Du Bois's concept of the "psychological wage," which is the fact that it issued from the ruling class as a way to divide workers. This they say is confirmed by the historian Jack M. Bloom, who argues that the effort to imbue white Southern workers with a sense of racial superiority was a response by the planter and merchant-landlord class to their fear of losing political control – a strategy that was routed by the Populist movement in the late nineteenth century.[189] Similarly, Reed contends that racial segregation was not only a product of the dominant class, but a product of the state.[190] What Roediger accepts as a "hard-won insight" is patently inadequate as Marxist analysis since what defines capitalists, as a class, is neither the denial of the humanity of foreign ethnic groups or the humanity of workers, but the social conditions that compel them to exploit labour and accumulate surplus.[191]

Roediger's research question blames the working class for upholding racism at the same time that it makes the attenuation of racism the sole responsibility of this group since it is seemingly in their interest alone to do so. In terms of base and superstructure, the economic interests of white workers are held against them. Roediger's displacement of class struggle onto race differences allows him to avoid class issues. He addresses this complaint with a Marxist twist to the familiar Cultural Studies ploy that white workers are not dupes and that they make constrained choices in circumstances not of their choosing. The issue, though, is that in a system based on inequality it is somewhat irrelevant if you are a dupe or not and it is highly relevant that competition among workers is also competition among capitalists. Moreover, as far as the period 1800-1860 is concerned, to expect a mass of workers to display socialist class consciousness rather than liberal ideology is somewhat anachronistic since for most people there was no other social system available to consciousness except what workers may have known about revolutionary history. Although the First International emerged in 1864, it was not until 1870 that an American committee was established. It was comprised mostly of foreign-born members and never had an English-language press organ. The fact that the American section of the International never involved more than four thousand of the nearly two million American workers provides a general impression of the extent of labour radicalism at that time. For the most part, and in tenuous as well as contradictory ways, the emergence of labour politics tended to coincide with abolitionism.

Giving agency to only the white working class fails as Marxist historical materialism. And this is where psychoanalysis becomes useful. In the new era of republicanism, the privileges that free white workers could derive from the comparison between themselves and slaves had an irrational aspect that derived from their fears of dependency and their adaptation to a new, industrial era of work discipline. Roediger explains whiteness as a psychological complex that is constructed by *projecting* onto blacks, Native Americans and other immigrant groups like the Irish a self-denial of the pre-industrial pleasures of leisure and self-directed activity. In non-Hegelian, non-Marxist and only quasi-Freudian terms, Roediger argues that whiteness was constructed through otherness. While he argues more recently that this sort of post-structuralist logic is too relativistic, he believes that it can nevertheless be salvaged through reference to the formalist linguistics of Mikhail Bakhtin and vague allusions to the work of Raymond Williams. Drawing on the research of George Rawick in *From Sundown to Sunup: The Making of the Black Community* (1972), Roediger develops a Reichian notion of the repression involved in the Protestant work ethic, which attacks merry-making and postpones gratification for the sake of productivity. As both the bourgeoisie and the white working class internalized self-sacrifice and labour discipline, Roediger argues, blacks were cast as the former selves of whites in quasi-pornographic fantasies about leisure, sexuality, the celebration of life and aesthetic inclination.[192] "Whiteness took shape against the corresponding counter-images," he writes, "shunting anxieties and desires regarding relationships to nature and to sexuality onto Blacks."[193] For workers especially, anxieties about slave-like wage labour was projected onto both free blacks and black slaves, thereby giving psychic justification to attacks on black civil rights, physical attacks by white mobs and stereotyping in minstrel shows.

Roediger's and Rawick's accounts of white working-class racism may themselves be a matter of projection. Why it is that white workers would not project their imagined selves onto the middle class or onto independent workers who own their own land is anyone's guess. The countercultural aspects of Wilhelm Reich's now largely discredited ideas fail to consider how capitalism is a form of disorganization that manipulates people through confused strivings. Young eighteenth-century white workers who rioted were providing themselves with a socio-psychological pretext through which they could lie to themselves about why they are not advancing in life. Their masquerading as bucks and boys, or even as minstrels, not only hid nothing but revealed nothing. Roediger suggests that brawlers who were barely disguised in their blackface were smearing themselves to have a heightened experience of polymorphous perversity, an infantile playfulness that he argues is the opposite of capitalist anal retentiveness. Neverminding the Freudian evolutionary logic according to which the anal stage is more primitive than the genital stage, and neverminding the fact that the organization of labour not only represses pleasure but can also be a source of pleasure and satisfaction, Roediger's view that blacks were more profligate or aesthetically inclined and accomplished is of a piece with other statements by him that play to white liberal ideology, as for instance his specious notion that blacks enjoy their work more fully and that this could have been welcomed by white workers as a gift rather than spurned.[194] If nineteenth-century thinkers could be forgiven for such pseudo-scientific racism, it does not sit well with contemporary theory. The point about anxiety does make sense, however, since neither black nor white workers – or most capitalists for that matter – had a secure place in a rapidly changing social order. However, if the pressure from blacks for social equality intensified social conflicts, as Rawick argues, that likely had less to do with anxiety about racial differences than it did with the inherent limits of equality within a capitalist system.[195]

Since the rise of the New Left in the 1960s, the reinscription of categories of race and identity in culturalized politics that are more liberal and libertarian than vanguard has had woeful political effects. Abandonment of the materialist theory of class struggle in favour of theories that present class as a cultural construct that is shaped by subjectivity and contingent social phenomena has weakened the universalizing strength of radical theory. What is odd is not the persistence of Marxism but of the leftist affirmation of cultural politics in the context of globalization.[196] As Roediger himself admits, minstrel shows rarely addressed the conflicts of labour and capital.[197] Although *Class, Race, and Marxism* suggests that *The Wages of Whiteness* may have been too simplistic in its mixing of Marx and Freud, and the book received much criticism on this account, it is worth pursuing his method further to understand why it is that universality is not built solely on the basis of particulars and differences.[198]

In a 2018 discussion, Roediger and Tricia Rose, a professor of Africana studies, address what the video post description defines as the "incontrovertible" fact that Trump's election victory rested on his support among white voters and that the white working class is moving towards the political right.[199] Roediger argues that white nationalism is and is not a new phenomenon. He suggests that it rests on a self/other paradigm that requires someone to look down upon. In Hegelian Marxist terms, however, the 'self' is not a particular group but is the totality, defined by Marxists as the concrete universal of capital. In contrast, the 'other' is the plurality of others, none of whom can occupy the position of the self and the sum of which does not constitute the totality. It is less the case then that one looks down on an 'other' from the vantage point of a 'self,' but rather that through another 'other' one imagines oneself as something other than an 'other.' From a Hegelian perspective, then, there is no particularity that can embody the whole and so the politics of universality is not a matter of particularization but of historical change at the level of the totality.

In his discussion with Rose, Roediger acknowledges that the Democratic Party no longer has a class politics. Since voters are not cultural dopes, he argues, the wages of whiteness must be, in part, the answer to the enigma of Trump's election since the Democrats avoid universal welfare policies that would provide preferential benefits to people of colour. Why the Democratic Party's avoidance of such policies should contribute to the wages of whiteness is not explained. After Roediger argues along the lines of James Baldwin that whiteness makes whites miserable, Rose adds the quip that what whites will receive for their unintelligent support of Trump are the "minimum wages of whiteness." The joke is revealing in the way that it loses the argument to neoliberals in its presumption that in a capitalist society all workers can potentially live middle-class lives, if only they were not so racist and if only they would consistently vote Democrat.[200] The obverse to this is the presumption that if more working-class whites were upwardly mobile, they would have less need to hold on to their whiteness, a notion that is disputed by Roediger in his specious suggestion that immigrants who seek economic advancement want to become white. He then says that white and black unity is about to be superseded by black and brown unity, another specious notion that tacitly presumes that black and brown people are of the same mind, and further, that if they were, this would unequivocally result in social progress. Roediger doubts his own discourse when he acknowledges that many of the whites who voted for Trump also voted twice for Obama. He also notes that there is growing criticism, particularly from the political right, about whiteness studies as a form of discrimination. However, based on his discussion in *Class, Race, and Marxism*, Roediger is also aware that there is much better criticism emerging from the political left.

One obvious problem with white liberal guilt is that whiteness must always be shown to be harmful and blackness must as much as possible be shown to be beneficial. Such assertions, which falsely assume the verifiability of their terms, have more to do with turning the tables of history – if not more exactly turning the tables on the Marxist theory of history – than thinking in terms of emancipation. As Cedric Johnson has it, the sort of "psychohistory" that is central to contemporary thinking on whiteness and blackness is premised on the "false equation of identity and political interests." "Racial affinity," he argues, "is not synonymous with political constituency."[201] Yet for Roediger, whiteness is a self-justifying proposition. Put in Lacanian terms, his critique of the white gaze masks his presumption that someone can occupy the gaze. The polymorphous perversity he advocates is rather a mark of his own perverse relationship to the power structure. If whiteness is more of a burden on the working class than the PMC, it is likely because, insofar as workers resist social control, the stigma of so-called whiteness is imposed on them by today's disciplinary regimes, and this, in a way that is similar to the criminality that is imposed on blacks.

Avoiding the Real of class struggle, whiteness studies fit comfortably within the various post-disciplinary fields of American studies, race studies and Cultural Studies. Even if articulated as Marxist theory, Roediger's approach to labour affects a liberal fantasy that is more concerned with a harmonious collectivity that does not exist than with the radical tradition and the working class that does. What psychoanalysis calls for in such a situation is not more projection, but a traversal of the fantasy.[202] Žižek, who oddly enough is not mentioned in Roediger's *Class, Race, and Marxism*, argues that jouissance not only makes different cultures incompatible, but divides each cultural formation from within insofar as they are unable to relate directly to their own jouissance. Social antagonism, therefore, includes the alienation of whiteness or blackness from itself. This deadlock is resolved by projecting the unstable core of a culture's jouissance onto an other that is presumed to have full access to a consistent jouissance. Roediger's notion of pre-industrial pleasures says as much if not more about the counterculture's attitudes towards working life and the working class than it does about labour history. The presumption, in any case, is that the memory of a previous epoch contains the secret of white jouissance.

The most immediate solution to political jealousies is to not impose one's mode of jouissance onto others. Doing so, according to Bourdieu, is a key feature of the petty-bourgeois habitus.[203] In the name of a socialism from which Roediger takes a certain distance, and which is presumed to possess a consistent jouissance through the figure of the working class, Roediger withdraws from class struggle in favour of race studies, an odd thing to do in the context of the decline of labour militancy and the rise of the rightist assault on the social and political gains of the organized left. Such post-Marxist anti-universalism that perceives the real democratic struggle as the fight against racial and sexual oppression, according to Wood, is only abstractly universalistic and coincides with the "new revisionism" of the "newer left" generation that replaced the working class with the ideology of popular alliances and thereby capitulated to social democracy.[204] Whiteness studies are not concerned with the abstraction of labour, which is accepted, but with racial jouissance, which Roediger grounds in a collective identity: the nineteenth-century white working class whose labour is not defined communistically as the effort to overcome poverty and meet the necessities of life but is rather defined by its rejection of the 'pre-industrial' lifestyles of black freedmen and slaves.

Roediger defines the identity of the white worker in terms of what Žižek describes as a defensive reaction to the threat of black jouissance.[205] The interests of black workers do not come into view in this instance but remain all the more mysterious as bearers of jouissance, the *objet petit a* that white workers require to maintain their sense of themselves as undivided. The paradox, according to Žižek, is that the same holds true for politically correct anti-racism, which is parasitic on what it pretends to fight and is sustained in this by surplus enjoyment. The problem of anti-racism, then, is that it is only fantasmatically attached to its object. Such fantasies, Žižek argues, do not dissolve symptoms but gloss over the fundamental, in this case, class antagonism. Fantasies provide identity and social formations with signifiers with which to fill the void of jouissance.

As the Democratic Party becomes a party for the rich that supports race, gender and sexuality issues but attacks the working class with global trade deals, deindustrialization and increased wealth inequality, racialist fantasies should be replaced with a global solidarity of struggles.[206] The populist rejection of socialist struggle in favour of a dialogue between cultures and classes indirectly serves right-wing mobilization. As if his book had not already done enough to discredit the left, Roediger ends *Class, Race, and Marxism* with an apologia for the limits and "uneasy assumptions" of the word solidarity.[207] In a universe of biocapitalist integration, the "problematization" of the Wobbly notion that an "injury to one is an injury to all" becomes an invitation to the vampire castle. How does one recognize that race projection, as Roediger puts it, is more complexly, as Fisher puts it with regard to the conditions of class struggle in a postmodern world, an inversion-projection-disavowal mechanism? Or as Lacan would say, desire is the desire of the Other. Better to take Roger Lancaster's advice that the path forward does not involve the accumulation of minorities into a majority: "The Left must now discover how to win over the publics being represented by identity brokers with an inclusive and universalist social program."[208]

The Freedom Fighters Were Here

The smallest advances made by the left are often met with swift response by the political centre and right. This problem is exacerbated by postmodern tendencies of various sorts that reinforce political nihilism. If in the early 2000s it seemed as though the PMC was divided between its creative class and activism wings, these two factions have since the dissolution of OWS made common cause around identity politics. For example, former OWS activists, some of whom have regrouped as Decolonize This Place and Strike MoMA, have made race issues central to their new, intersectional, conception of activism.[209] Despite their anti-capitalist and anti-imperialist views, the activities of Strike MoMA share some principles with the woke politics of diversity. Their politics both competes with and complements neoliberal messaging in favour of BLM, MeToo and similar identitarian efforts. Consider in this regard the Scottish police and government's campaign to tackle hate crime through public awareness advertisements in the form of letters written to transphobes, homophobes, disablists, bigots and racists. Its purpose, according to officials, is to make Scotland the most inclusive country in the world. Written from the perspective of a hate crime witness, the letter interpellates readers as courageous citizens who would rally against various kinds of wrongdoing.

The result of the Scottish government's anti-oppression ad campaign, according to government press releases, has resulted in an increase in reports of bullying and abuse of minorities. While there is nothing wrong about the ads per se, they do ignore the problems that are created when political rhetoric avoids the causes of social conflict. This is not simply a matter of delinquency and resistance to authority. For instance, and neverminding cases of outright hostility, if bus and subway announcements recommend that able-bodied riders allow the elderly and pregnant women to be given priority in seating, even conservative riders would gladly offer their seat. However, if an advertisement designed by a privilege theorist recommended that an able-bodied white person give their seat to an able-bodied BIPOC rider on account of histories of racism, they would

Dear racists,

do you threaten people because of where they're from or the colour of their skin? Do you hurl language so vile it makes people scared to leave their homes?

Well, your hate has no home here. We're making a stand and if we see or hear anything we're calling you out and calling the police.

Yours, Scotland

Hate crime. Report it to stop it.

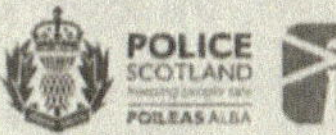

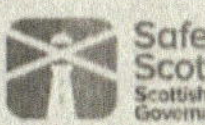

onescotland.org

Dear Racists. One Scotland, Scottish Government and Police Scotland advertising campaign against hate crime, 2018. Courtesy of the Scottish Government, OGL.

not surprisingly reject the injunction. However, such norms of decency are not what is being proposed in activist settings. For example, labour lawyer and peace activist Dan Kovalik describes the incongruities that have shaped black and white allyship within BLM activism. In some of the BLM protests of summer 2020, as many as 85 percent of protesters were white and as few as 3 percent of protesters were black. In some neighbourhoods, black residents tried to keep out white BLM protesters. Some white protesters attacked black leaders who were too conciliatory and in other cases, black leaders attacked white protesters and bystanders. The orientation towards quasi-religious expiation led some protesters in Pittsburgh to allow a minority of black leaders to use white protesters as both shields and weapons. White protesters would allow themselves to be yelled at for being white, turning protests into orgies of humiliation. Kovalik dittoes Black Panther leader Elaine Brown, who critiqued BLM for failing to create change by organizing according to a revolutionary agenda.[210] While one might think that activists are always in a position of humility vis à vis the state monopoly on violence, that perspective is more suited to sycophants than revolutionaries.

What the Scottish ads and contemporary woke activism ignore is the level of internationalist solidarity. Moreover, it calls people out rather than calling them in. It attacks bigotry rather than building a polity around shared values. Since conservatives claim to believe in bourgeois universalism, mostly at the level of economic liberalism, their only true enemy is the socialist left. Since socialist forces are not particularly powerful at the moment, no thanks to attacks against "sectarians" and "tankies," the right has focused on anti-woke culture wars against social justice activism, which the alt-right has dubbed 'cultural Marxism,' a neologism that has some validity in terms of postmodern theories but that has been transformed instead into a conspiracy theory that begins with Hegel, Marxism and the Frankfurt School, and is now said to be corrupting government and the workplace. A radical politics has an intellectual, philosophical and ideological foundation. The material force of ideology cannot be advanced solely through appeals to material needs and incentives. The rise of fascism in the twentieth century was for example fought in the name of 'spirit' and against the materialist decadence of the bourgeois class. Had such issues been considered more closely by the inventors and promoters of privilege theory and diversity training, the academic left might not have wasted as much time as it has over the last few years critiquing 'whiteness' and other straw dogs. The solution is not to give more attention to questions of pride and dignity, but to build, preserve and consolidate the radical culture of the left.

As the frightening inanities of the far right begin to display the same investment in countercultural ersatz and police stand-offs as the activist left, the question of 'what is to be done' arises anew. Short of revolutionary upheaval, the activist and new social movement left finds its identity politics reflected in the social democratic politics that have taken on board most of its concerns. The Sanders campaigns for the Democratic Party nomination, for example, adopted BLM slogans and placed minority hires in all of the top campaign positions, advertising in the early months of 2020 to minority constituencies and leaning into identity politics so as to steal some support from "minority" candidates like Elizabeth Warren, Pete Buttigieg, Kamala Harris, Amy Klobuchar and Cory Booker.[211] Whatever its merits, the problem with this campaign is that it obscured the class character of left politics and avoided making capitalism, rather than the bigotry of Trump and the greed of Wall Street, the target of the socialist left. On the first anniversary of the January 6 coup attempt, *Jacobin* editor Bhaskar Sunkara warned the populist left that too much criticism of the Democratic Party only serves the far right.[212]

The critique of Enlightenment ideals and emancipatory universality by today's postmodern social and cultural theorists is similar to Third World ideologies that sought to combine traditional religion and cultural parochialism with modernization in economic development and technology. The resulting polities upheld alternative cultural logics that championed national elites on the world stage.[213] Racialism reproduces many of the worst aspects of these experiences in postcolonial nationalism. As economic inequality increases, so does the righteous tone: Rhodes Must Fall! So also does the narcissism of small differences in a cancel culture that is inoperative at best. This matter is not settled by the work of Jean-Luc Nancy, whose notion of universalism was limited by 'necropolitical' considerations of cultural revolution and organic communion.[214] The consequent genealogies of genocide, slavery and other injustices are now part of the ideological arsenal of the ten percent of the population with six-figure annual earnings.[215] The rest play this game in accordance with the conversion strategies that would allow them to increase their diversity capital as they move precariously from educational to career settings.[216]

Among the members of this new alliance of the PMC, it is often difficult to distinguish the conformists from the activists. Such social justice warriors as have come to be designated 'cultural Marxists' rarely self-identify as such, with perhaps the brave exception of cultural theorist Sven Lütticken, who emphasizes the performativity of identity and culture in the context of alt-right uses of the term, which he defines as a "reductive culturalisation of socio-economic issues that obscures the extent to which the cultural field itself is implicated in these matters."[217] Slavoj Žižek and the economist Richard Wolff claim that they do not know where the concept comes from or what it implies. Wolff made the more obvious but nevertheless relevant comparison of Jordan Peterson's critique of 'cultural Marxists' with National Socialist campaigns against 'Cultural

Bolshevism' in 1920s Weimar Germany.[218] Žižek, on the other hand, understands the term all too well and went so far as to suggest that cultural Marxists are not Marxists.[219] In his 2019 debate with Peterson, he preferred to press him to define the term for himself. Even if Peterson is inept in his critique of Marxism – all the better to misdirect his followers – he is minimally aware of what has been occurring in academic Cultural Studies over the last few decades.

Only a cynic would avoid examining the concept of cultural Marxism for fear of providing support to the alt-right. By that measure, socialists should refrain from socialism since it can be appropriated by national socialism. One may as well fold up one's tent and call it day. Cultural Marxists are, or could be considered, those who replace the critique of political economy with the 'economy' of race or gender, or any other materially defined category, arguing, as a Marxist might, that race and gender relations transform 'socially constructed' categories into ideologies that legitimize social inequalities as natural, normal and inevitable. In other words, what Marxists refer to as secondary contradictions of nationality, religion, gender and culture are substituted for the primary contradiction, which is the struggle between labour and capital.[220] This substitution is common in postmodern understandings of materialism, which now draw on discourse theories that displace the centrality of class altogether. Žižek writes:

> Is class antagonism not also traversed by racial and sexual tensions? We should reject this solution for a precise reason: there is a formal difference between class antagonism and other antagonisms. In the case of antagonisms in relations between sexes and sexual identities, the struggle for emancipation does not aim at annihilating some of the identities but at creating the conditions for their non-antagonistic co-existence, and the same goes for the tensions between ethnic, cultural, or religious identities – their goal is to bring about their peaceful co-existence, their mutual respect and recognition. Class struggle does not function in this way: It aims at mutual recognition and respect of classes only in its Fascist or corporatist versions. Class struggle is a 'pure' antagonism: the goal of the oppressed and exploited is to abolish classes as such, not to enact their reconciliation.[221]

The accusation of class essentialism, Žižek says, misses its mark. Without dismissing ecological, feminist, anti-racist, decolonial and national struggles, class should be understood as the dynamic that overdetermines these interacting and multiple struggles. Against radical democratic and intersectional approaches, Žižek rejects the bell hooks idea that class is only one in a series of antagonisms. When class is reduced to one among other identities, he argues, class becomes another version of identity politics. The resulting 'classism' advocates (self-)

respect for workers, which Žižek says is a characteristic of both populism and fascism.

Socialist traditions of gender and race politics that extend the analysis of the mode of production and the labour market to include the family, for example, or questions of uneven development among nations, set the stage for today's more abstract forms of social theory. The two levels of contradiction need not be hierarchized for the interplay between class issues and gender issues, or class, gender, race and sexuality issues, to be analysed in the terms of historical and dialectical materialism.[222] In an exemplary statement in the history of materialist feminism, Simone de Beauvoir argued in *The Second Sex* that "one is not born, but rather becomes, a woman."[223] De Beavoir insisted that gender is constructed and that woman is the Other of man. She thereby rejected femininity as a ploy that allowed for forms of male domination like the imposition of housework or sexual promiscuity. Feminist demands included the right to education, economic independence, contraception and abortion. De Beavoir, however, shared some of the assumptions of her existentialist philosopher partner, Jean-Paul Sartre. The idea that each person is the source of their own consciousness and is condemned to be free endorsed the kind of phenomenological reduction that encouraged an idiomorphic pessimism that was compatible with bourgeois Romanticism. De Beauvoir was followed by Monique Wittig, who rejected the category "woman" as the imposition of gender ideology.[224] One might think that she was post-gender before the notion arose. From postwar existentialism to structuralism and post-structuralism, the critique of political economy was replaced with non-dialectical versions of eclectic materialism that reduced political liberalism to a much narrower form of existential nihilism. Through identity politics, the proletariat was made to represent any oppressed group and so took on a moral rather than political valence. As a prisoner of rather than a threat to Cold War cybernetics, this existential left gradually convinced itself to accept the Foucauldian trap of power-resistance, only to later clamour for Deleuzian becomings.[225]

Deborah Kelsh insists on the class character of the shift towards identity politics in the postwar period.[226] The new petty-bourgeois class provided the ruling class with two services: first, it erased or minimized knowledge concerning the priority of the production process as a contradictory production of surplus value, and second, it produced new knowledges that deny their own production in relation to the first. In other words, in order to secure promotions, salaries and material comforts, the PMC advanced identity politics that discredit classical Marxism and ideology critique in favour of theories like deconstruction or radical democracy that disabled apprehension of the social totality and instead proffered abstract notions like undecidability or the blurring of boundaries. One was encouraged, she argues, to focus on one's partiality and reject revolutionary politics.

The postmodern deconstruction of terms, concepts and classifications, especially concepts like reason, objectivity, truth, humanity, civilization and progress that are associated with Enlightenment modernity, makes the destabilization, relativization or modification of any concept in common use appear to be a challenge to the status quo. Those who defend established ideas and disciplinary fields are branded conservative. Those who produce what Thomas Kuhn referred to as 'weird science' are championed as innovative if not radical. The fact that a somewhat bloated knowledge industry produces a surfeit of theory that aims to be different but that oftentimes is less advanced and less innovative than the standards of the discipline is grist for the diploma and publishing mill, or in the case of Peterson, the media circus.[227] According to David Graeber, genuinely innovative research has declined in the last several decades despite the exponentially larger amount of research that is carried out and published.[228] Unlike postmodern pragmatism, critical theory distinguishes between those practices and techniques that serve human needs and those that reify social relations. Marx's critique of political economy, for instance, relates the activity of the individual worker to the productive activity of society, demonstrating how human beings are transformed into appendages of machines and into alienated producers and consumers.[229] While pragmatism looks for ways to create jobs, critical praxis seeks to free humanity from unnecessary toil. One symptom of today's so-called cultural Marxism is the return to the kinds of positivism and pragmatism that provide reductive rather than critical uses of concepts like matter and materialism.[230]

As cultural theory after the 'linguistic turn' relies heavily on the methods of comparative literature, theories that are mostly 'textual' and that do not require disciplinary knowledge in any specific field make claims that, for instance, race matters and bodies matter, just as surely as atmospheric carbon or television cartoons matter. How it is that they matter, to whom and why is less important than the assertion itself, which gives priority to the researcher's subject and claims. The notion that race matters, for instance, is hardly incidental to the hashtag Black Lives Matter. With the reinforcement of postmodern anti-humanism and anti-foundationalism, the mere existence of a phenomenon is enough to make arbitrary claims concerning its social significance.[231] Aesthetic, political or scientific discoveries and inventions are less significant to postmodernists than the idea that they are discursively produced. Contrary to the ravings of conservatives, discourse theory has made its inroads in academia to a large extent due to claims that Marxism can no longer account for contemporary problems. Post-structuralism replaces Marxism as an expedient means to subject the disciplines to political critique. For example, for a so-called cultural Marxist, Cornel West's lectures would be less important for what he has to say than for the way that, as a black intellectual, he combines philosophy with the oratorial style of a religious preacher. It is his black masculinity or his Christian patriarchy that are relevant, interesting or problematic. This is in marked contrast to a historical materialist like Reed, who criticizes his comrade as a race relations spokesman with no concrete political practice other than his leadership role in the DSA.[232]

Within neoliberal hegemony, the increasing polarization between right-wing and left-wing populism has resulted in woke culture wars that are being engineered and managed as a feature of the class war against the radical left. This explains the popularity of academics like Peterson. The controversy generated around Peterson relates to the fact that he objected to the way that nonbinary, genderqueer, transgender and gender nonconforming people request that people use gender-neutral pronouns when addressing them, since these ostensibly defy cisgender presuppositions.[233] Not everyone is as pusillanimous as Peterson, however. Writing for *Forbes* magazine, CEO David Galowich states: "Modern society now requires that we update the previously taught and accepted grammatical framework to be considerate of the intersections between gender, race, class and other complex layers of identity."[234] The fact that class is not a category of identity is irrelevant to people who are concerned with diversity for the sake of good business practices. This kind of social sensitivity is not limited to CEOs that have a vested interest in diluting class consciousness but is endemic on the postmodern left, as noticed for example in an article by Peter Frase, a member of the *Jacobin* editorial board. Although Frase has good enough sense to mention that there are legitimate leftist arguments to be made in favour of universality and against identity politics, he reduces class to an identity, arguing that "class first" politics claim class as "an identity superior to all others," which Frase, making good use of his thesaurus, dismisses as snobbish, academic, abstract, essentialist, reductionist, populist, obstructionist, outmoded and dull. "Emancipation of the working class," he writes, "means abolishing the class as such, and thus giving up the comforts of working-class identity."[235]

One presumes that once class has been abolished, humanity will be able to enjoy itself without the surplus of Marxist ideology, which is simply the obverse to the idea that leftists are unconcerned with issues of race or gender. The image of a future communist society is in this case viewed from the perspective of the cosmopolitan creative class. This is where the diversity mindset and neoliberal post-Fordism work in tandem to transform all of society into an extortionist dungeon, with virtue signalling as well as trolling the order of the day. In these circumstances, a seemingly progressive culture is one that actively works against the stabilization of social norms. In the social confusion that ensues, signifiers that are coded straight, white or male are appropriated and then enforced, in their "corrected" form, as the new abnormal. As Žižek points out, the notion of toxic masculinity, which is a social-ideological category, is now approached by the psychiatric profession as though an actually existing medical problem.[236] Rather than social norms of good behaviour, the idea of toxic masculinity presupposes and promotes norms of female behaviour. Contrary to the popularity of this seemingly feminist concept, Badiou has argued that behaviours associated with paternal responsibility are today devalued as men are increasingly relegated to an a-symbolic realm of eternal adolescence.[237] While this goes on, unbridled capitalism has transformed women's feminist independence from men into premature womanhood and the cynicism of competitive individualism. Michael Warner's critique of homonormativity could in this regard be faulted for suggesting that there are better or worse ways that gay men are supposed to experience subjectivity and reality.[238] A 2019 article by Greta LaFleur, for instance, criticizes South Bend Indiana mayor and Democratic presidential hopeful Pete Buttigieg's gay relationship as epitomizing not only homonormativity, but a "heteronormativity without women" that "weaponizes the immaterial power of whiteness," both of these defined as pernicious forms of power.[239] Buttigieg's Wall Street and Silicon Valley campaign funding in 2020 are not at issue in this article, nor are his gentrification projects or his rejection of single-payer health care. The fact that Buttigieg has a background as a Naval Reserve intelligence officer assigned to identify targets for death squads in Afghanistan is chalked up by this social justice advocate to his white heteronormativity without women.

Psychoanalysis disputes the notion of subjectivity as anything less than heterogenous and self-conflicted. Touré's notion of authenticity violations are therefore not matters of race, gender, sexuality or class, but of the degradation of social solidarity into the pseudo-ethics of masochistic self-culpabilization, as advocated for example by Simon Critchley.[240] Those who do not take politics seriously can thus refer to material reality as an excuse rather than an issue. As Reed reminds us, the scholarship on race science and eugenics demonstrates that when researchers look for evidence of racial difference, they always find something.[241] The kind of racist pseudo-science that once discovered as many as 18 basic racial groups is similar to today's administration of the proliferation of sexual identities. The paradox of such political correctness, as Žižek argues, is that the more marginal you are and the further away you are from the category of white heterosexual European male, defined as "the model of oppression of others," the more you are allowed to openly celebrate your way of life. Paradoxically, it is the prohibition of this social group that secures its status as the universal-neutral medium.[242]

Moralistic demands to abolish whiteness and white privilege treat racism as a form of injustice *sui generis* rather than an unaccountable trauma that is embedded in histories, social structures and the political economy. Such demands are consistent with the neoliberal philosophies that define democracy as a matter of economic incentivization.[243] This leads not only to the notion of ideology as an always provisional solution to social antagonisms but explains why it is that capitalism functions as the genus of the plurality of identity politics. In the book *Racecraft*, Karen and Barbara Fields describe how Obama's post-race agenda functioned in relation to the subterranean racism that remains a reality in American life.[244] For historical reasons, the facts of social and economic inequality associate African Americans with the category of race. The association of race with poverty, and the stereotypes of lazy blacks and illegal immigrants, make it more difficult to elucidate and eliminate inequality. Although perceived as a victory for black people, the Obama presidency did nothing to mitigate socio-economic inequality. Through the construct of post-race, Obama could both embody and avoid being thought of as a stand-in for all persons of African descent. Paraphrasing Stokely Carmichael, the Fields argue that Afro-Americans could not for all that have Barack Obama for lunch. It was a progressive agenda and not his black ancestry that was needed of him. In this sense, the slightest redistribution of wealth could have been criticized from the right as racially motivated. Obama did not brave the criticism of those who might think this way. Obama avoided being thought of as a *black* president so as to avoid welfare policies. His blackness was instrumentalized as a matter of convenience, to be claimed or discarded according to the needs of the occasion. This adversely affected both white and black working Americans. What the Fields describe as racecraft was used as a ready-made propaganda weapon against equality.[245]

The term that the Fields invented to understand the ideology of race and racism in American society does not only incidentally sound like the word witchcraft. Just as Martin Luther believed in witches and superstitions, race, they argue, is an imaginary construct that has material effects. Racecraft identifies the non-scientific notions of race that are presupposed by scientific and sociological discourses. Although the concept of race has no scientific basis, the statistical tabulation of social phenomena and disparities according to 'race' is a common instance of the everyday use of racist concepts. One example is the use of Personal Genetic Histories to determine one's African tribal ancestry. One thinks in this regard of Adrian Piper's self-portrait in *Thwarted Projects, Dashed Hope, A Moment of Embarrassment, 2012*, which announces that the artist has determined that her identity is neither black nor white, but 6.25 percent grey, due to her 1/16th African ancestry, a discovery that Piper says will lead to exciting new adventures in pointless administrative precision and futile institutional control. For the Fields sisters, the implication is that such racecraft involves both race concepts and racism. Racecraft is based on the belief that humans can be classified into biologically distinct groups of unequal social status. Racecraft therefore legitimizes social and legal double standards. As is the case in a witch trial, evidence for racecraft is never in short supply insofar as racism takes for granted the objective reality of race.[246] What then is the alternative to racecraft? If post-blackness operates as a kind of postmodern opportunism, the practice of racecraft could be charged with sociological relativism. After Louis Althusser's notion that ideology can be explained via reference to the totality of material structures and Raymond Williams' notion of culture as a "whole way of life," the structures and institutions that rely on racecraft could be said to perniciously transform black culture into a 'whole way of death,' to reference the work of Orlando Patterson.[247] All the more reason to not believe in racecraft.

One conundrum that the Fields identify is the fact that the topography of racecraft is effective even if you do not believe in it. If blindness to race is not the solution, deconstruction might seem to be the next best thing. A comparison with sexual difference may be of some help in this instance. Based on the Lacanian theory of sexuality as a fundamental antagonism that cannot be inscribed in the positive features of biological sex, Žižek argues that transgender people do not resolve the question of sexual difference but bring out into the open the anxiety and tension that characterizes every sexual identification and gender identity.[248] Gender norms contain and obfuscate this antagonism. Psychoanalysis considers that prior to all social identification, subjectivity coincides with an indeterminate guilt. Social symbolization seeks to conflate these primordial guilt feelings with specific narratives and social processes. A subject passively assumes a symbolic mandate through the interpassivity of belief in structures that free the subject from the constant pressure of having to decide what to believe. One identifies as male or female, white or black, straight or gay, in relation to the ways that such social categories are historically, materially and socially defined. This means that race matters *cannot* account for psychic processes that are associated with the unconscious, even if the psyche has a biological foundation.

The black freedom tradition calls on subjects to either embrace racial norms and identities, or to overcome race altogether through the rejection of race essentialism. Insofar as these choices are overdetermined by capitalism, only socialism offers a solution to the demands of abstract universality. Why is it then that socialist universality appears to so many as the worldview of people who are straight, white, male, heterosexual, European, able-bodied, and so on? This is the same as asking why it is that the cause of reparations is a capitalist politics. From the perspective of Cultural Studies, reality, knowledge and politics are contingent, contextual, provisional, relational, differential, multiple, etc.[249]

Such academic studies call on us to abandon notions like universality and emancipation as the refuse of European Enlightenment. Contrary to this view, class struggle, Žižek argues, traverses all social groups in such a way that it is impossible to distinguish between universal and particular demands: "The communist struggle for universal emancipation means a struggle which cuts into each particular identity, dividing it from within."[250] Insofar as someone else's struggle becomes my struggle as well, anti-capitalism and anti-racism are two moments of the same struggle. This universality is only operative, however, insofar as it is anti-capitalist. The discriminatory practices of one culture deserve to be denounced, but do not justify Napoleonic conquest. On this issue, Žižek cites Lenin's declaration of "war to the death" against "dominant-nation chauvinism."[251]

Cultural Marxists, if the term can be allowed as anything other than an alt-right slur, sometimes replace Marxist political economy with nebulous alternatives, like Georges Bataille's theory of expenditure or Jean-François Lyotard's concept of libidinal economy, both of which obscure production relations. More typically, cultural Marxists reject economic overdetermination and emphasize instead the relative autonomy of ideological superstructures, separating questions of agency and subjectivity, defined as cultural issues, from questions that are specific to economic analysis. For example, in her well-known essay titled "Merely Cultural," Judith Butler rejected the Marxist objection to the reduction of Marxist scholarship to the study of culture as well as Marxism's relegation of new social movements to the sphere of the cultural.[252] She not surprisingly but very unsatisfyingly attempted to solve this dilemma with a theory of criticism-as-performance. As a counterpoint, Nancy Fraser proffered a conciliatory politics of redistribution and recognition.[253] What Fraser could not anticipate at that time was the extent to which the politics of recognition would become neoliberalized and the injustice of misrecognition would become a strategy of both social justice warriors and the alt-right. In any event, Žižek thereafter solved the problem of exclusion and recognition, that is, of cultural norms, by rejecting the possibility of fixed positions. He also insisted on capitalism as the concrete universal that subtends micro-political identity struggles. For Žižek, post-politics describes the displacement of class antagonisms onto markers of social difference.[254] Even if activist academics are in denial about this, Žižek, and later the Anglo-American reception of Badiou, led the radical left project beyond the valley of postmodernism.

Contrary to the concept of *Kulturbolschewismus*, it is less the case that the Frankfurt School ignored matters of political economy than they avoided class politics.[255] Žižek has also avoided political identification with any class formation that is older than Lacan. By some cunning of reason, both the economistic Frankfurt School and culturalist postmodernists ended up in the politically woke quagmire. The alt-right has understood at least this much, even if it tends to systematically distort the insights of critical theory.[256] In this respect, the alt-right is more a byproduct of postmodern nihilism than its alternative. As a byproduct of critical theory, Cultural Studies made its peace with Marxism as a mostly post-Althusserian undertaking, setting out with its postmodern toolbox to advocate *n'importe quoi*. So-called French theory and Cultural Studies always had its challengers but by 2000 its political deficit as a perhaps unintentional or at least unforeseeable adjunct to the neoliberalization of culture and knowledge was challenged only by the Young Turks of the anti-globalization left. After the post-9/11 War on Terror was launched, the anarchist multitude and the usual leftist groups – trade unionists, NGOs, church groups, identity groups, affinity groups, collectives, socialist parties, progressives, ecologists – began to be acknowledged by academia, with some professors of critical theory pitching in.

The aughts were short-lived and educated activists quickly grew tired of leaderless assemblies and mic check hand signals. With the new social movements defeated for the most part by austerity and securitization, the academic left returned with a bid for social democracy rather than communism as the possible-impossible, with new materialisms subtending a New Age anthropo-scene. This 'global turn' was accompanied by the aforementioned decolonial critique of everything Eurocentric. Intellectuals who should know better smeared Badiou as anti-Semitic, Žižek as a Stalinist and Hardt and Negri as manarchists.[257] The debates around communism quickly lost their appeal after academics were given Trump and the alt-right to become obsessed with. For these people, it seems, Trump was better than sex. As the editors of the journal *Commune* stated in the editorial for their first issue:

> Everywhere morbid symptoms bloom. In the place of conservatism, we witness the rise of a white revanchism bent on rolling back the reforms of eras past until Jim Crow walks a landscape devoid of labor unions, until women are driven back to the kitchen, queer people back to the closet, trans people out of restrooms. On the left, we must admit, congruent nostalgias dominate.[258]

Whereas many in decolonial studies now go so far as to reject class analysis as well as French theory due to its white, Eurocentric and hetero-patriarchal masculinism – that is, at the same time that the CIA markets its diversity assets – *Commune* at least maintained the revolutionary charge against the liberal centre.[259]

The hobgoblin of cultural Marxism is made more complex by theories that directly link subjectivity to the mode of post-Fordist production.[260] For many in the anarchist camp, the 'vanguard' are billionaires like Elon Musk and Jeff Bezos, if not more intractable agents like global capital flows and network effects. Against this kind of reductionism, Žižek has mounted a spirited if somewhat solitary defence of dialectical materialism.[261] Working with his unique blend of philosophical confabulations, Badiou hailed the rebirth of History with a capital H, but just as soon, Joshua Clover argued that the decline of labour power leaves us with no other option but disorganized mass riots against the now militarized police.[262] The Invisible Committee, for their part, argued that the notion of networked resistance to the greater power of biocapitalist regimes is wrongminded and defeatist.[263] Since the decline of the alter-global multitude, the leftist initiative has gone over to populisms of various sorts, which, along with an increase in trade union resistance, environmentalist protest and electioneering, are beginning to consolidate a power bloc. The wave of mass protests in 2019 in Hong Kong, Czech Republic, France, Spain, Puerto Rico, Mexico, Haiti, Chile, Bolivia, Ecuador, Pakistan, Iran, Iraq, Algeria, Sudan, Lebanon, India and Sri Lanka indicate that radical demands continue to shape political resistance. The failures of Syriza, Podemos, Corbyn and Sanders, the COVID-19 pandemic, right-wing insanity and threats of World War Three make coordinated strike activity the only leftism that makes sense anymore.

CH.5: BLACK CAPITALISM AND EMBEDDED HISTORY

The totalitarian idea that there is no such thing as law, that there is only power, has never taken root. In England, such concepts as justice, liberty and objective truth are still believed in. They may be illusions, but they are very powerful illusions.

– George Orwell

If you don't stand for something, you'll fall for anything.

– Malcolm X cited on *The X-Files*

The politics of race and class in the United States are conditioned by what, from a Marxist point of view, is the more intractable question of the relation between class and politics. Race issues shape and delimit class politics. In her description of Barack Obama as a "race whisperer," Melanye T. Price argues that the former president used race to solidify black loyalty to the Democratic Party.[1] Obama's use of racial tropes as well as his cross-racial appeal allowed him to combine race specificity with the ideals of American liberalism. This then allowed him to avoid radical policy initiatives. But what about people who are not so quiet about race and class issues, who speak out against all forms of injustice? In the summer of 2016, the rapper M.I.A. criticized Black Lives Matter for its focus on American politics, stating:

> Is Beyoncé or Kendrick Lamar going to say Muslim Lives Matter? Or Syrian Lives Matter? Or this kid in Pakistan matters? That's a more interesting question. You can't ask it on a song that's on Apple, you cannot ask it on an American TV programme, you cannot create that tag on Twitter, Michelle Obama is not going to bump you back.[2]

Beyoncé and Jay-Z are billionaire friends of the Obamas. Beyoncé performed at Obama's inaugural ball and at Michelle Obama's 50th birthday party. Kendrick Lamar was hired by Obama for his My Brother's Keeper affirmative action programme. In contrast to such well-heeled talent, M.I.A. told reporters: "Sorry I'm not doin' Afropunk. I've been told to stay in my lane. Ha, there is no lane for 65 million refugees whose lanes are blown up! #nolanes."[3] Under threat of a boycott, M.I.A. was summarily dropped from the British strand of the Afropunk festival, an event that advertises itself as being opposed to sexism, racism, ageism, homophobia, fatphobia, transphobia and hatefulness. The question is: Why should M.I.A.'s criticism be thought to contradict these aims? The answer is: The embeddedness of progressivism in neoliberalism. The weakening of symbolic efficiency among contemporary audiences, such that millions of *Game of Thrones* fans demanded that the producers rewrite the final season, corresponds to the inability to sustain belief in anything that cannot be readily absorbed into mainstream networks.

In a similar case, the former San Francisco 49ers quarterback Colin Kaepernick was unofficially blacklisted from the National Football League for sitting down and 'taking a knee' during the playing of the National Anthem at the start of football matches. Kaepernick began doing this in August 2016 as a statement against police violence, sparked in particular by the murders of Alton Sterling and Philando Castile. His protests, which echoed the raised Black Power fists of Tommie Smith and John Carlos at the 1968 Olympics, earned him the support of teammates as he came under fire from the league and later from Donald Trump, who spewed invective at Kaepernick and demanded that he be fired.[4] As a star athlete in his prime, Kaepernick should not be prevented from playing sport. However, as a celebrity athlete, and now a *cause célèbre* for his stand on political issues, Kaepernick was drawn into the realm of advertising legend after he was sponsored by the sports company Nike, which created an ad campaign with the copy "believe in something, even it if means sacrificing everything," followed by the swoosh symbol and the Just Do It slogan. The black and white image emphasizes Kaepernick's voluminous afro, a Panther-like black turtleneck and the discrete edges of a gold chain emerging from underneath a black sports jacket. With Nike looking to increase its sales by making its brand appear more socially conscious, the ad soon became Internet meme fodder, with random celebrities and politicians believing in just about anything, and with perhaps the most sobering of these an image of young women working on a Nike assembly line with the tag: "Just do it, for $0.23 per hour."[5] Such materialist unveiling, however, does not fully capture the unreality that makes the ad ripe for satire.

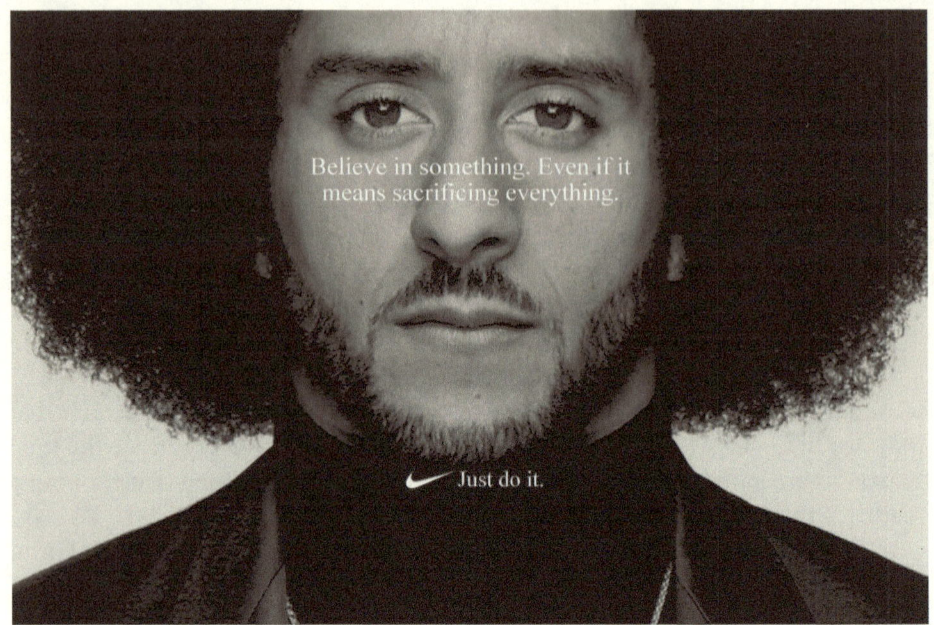

Nike advertisement featuring Colin Kaepernick, 2017. Despite a boycott by patriotic Trump supporters, Nike sales surged by 30 percent in the few days after a two-minute television version of the ad was broadcast.

Shortly after the "believe in something" ad campaign, Kaepernick advised Nike against their 2019 Fourth of July-themed sneakers, which shows the Betsy Ross 13 stars-in-a-circle flag on the heel of the shoe. After Kaepernick informed the company that the flag was commonly used by white nationalists and extremist right-wing movements as a substitute for the Confederate flag, and therefore serviceable as a pro-slavery symbol, the company decided to remove the shoe from circulation. *Rolling Stone* reporter E.J. Dickson argued that Nike acted less out of zeal for political correctness than with concern for their $134 billion market share.[6] As with the assembly line meme, demystification of 'the Big One' circumvents some of the issues that are in play. In contrast, the conservative website *National Review* accused Nike of being more successful than neo-Nazis in making the Betsy Ross flag into a symbol of racism.[7] Nike's removal of the product, according to Jonah Goldberg, seemed to concede to the alt-right a monopoly on semiotics. The writer has a point since Nike, like most Americans, did not know that the flag was used by white supremacists and so had no need to get into a panic. Nike could have reclaimed the symbol and used it to expand its considerable share of the African American market. Nike instead capitulated to what the author describes as the grievance politics of the "perpetually offended" who like to stir controversy, such that the culture war has yet another "idiotic fight on its hands."[8]

Despite the wishful thinking of conservatives, and according to the neoliberal version of the culture war, it is Nike and Kaepernick who made a woke touchdown. Having been awarded a W.E.B. Du Bois Medal from Harvard University in 2018, presented to him by Cornel West, the multi-millionaire athlete was hardly out in the cold, enjoying a career in philanthropy and countless other activities, even if for the time being shut out of the NFL.[9] A left perspective on this issue was written by Joseph Grosso for the website *CounterPunch* in a piece called "To Be or Not To Be Woke: The Follies of Political Correctness."[10] The "brutal tediousness" of American politics, he argues, is that much political correctness and identity politics is meaninglessly abstract. Nike's labour practices have in no way been improved by the media-manufactured controversy, but its market value jumped by $3 billion when it removed the Betsy Ross shoe from circulation. Liberals have to ask themselves how their virtue signalling about white privilege does anything to improve the lot of poor black and white people. Grosso mentions how it is that all-gender washrooms in North Carolina, a seeming success story due in part to the NBA pulling its 2017 All-Star game in protest against the state's Public Facilities Privacy & Security Act, does little to alter the fact that transgender people are twice as likely to live in poverty. He concludes: "Such is the luxury and price of becoming woke: the luxury of having a radical attitude without actually taking a radical position."[11]

Worthy Causes

The M.I.A. and Kaepernick episodes are not only part of the mainstreaming of protest politics, but also raise issues concerning art and identity, as well as art and class politics. As the Trump phenomenon suppurated, with Congress and the right wing of the Democratic Party conceding on most of his major policy offensives, the racialist camp intensified its rhetoric. Whereas one used to accuse someone of discrimination, with the belief that people could nevertheless change their racist attitudes, the charge now is white supremacy, which encodes absolute racial incommensurability within institutional structures. The extreme centre is now so politically bewitched, bothered and bewildered that leftist universalism is proscribed as inherently racist. Postmodern identitarians now have more in common with the Anti-Defamation League than the National Association for the Advancement of Colored People, protecting ethnic groups from criticism rather than discrimination. The racialist woke war has some typical features that are nevertheless instructive to anyone who is not satisfied to remain idle as authoritarian capitalism seeks to outlaw the last remaining vestiges of socialism.

These include: the reduction of culture to questions of identity; the denial of a common humanity and intercultural intelligibility; the reduction of distinctions between formal and popular culture for the sake of moral extortion rather than cultural and political expression; the reduction of distinctions between art and life to the business of opportunism rather than cultural and political emancipation.

If the rigid division of society along racial lines was once the purview of racists, today's identitarian intimidation, as Hiram Lee argues, uses the methods of the far right to advance the social, political and economic interests of whichever identity group.[12] For instance, complaints by mainstream newspapers that the Peter Farrelly film *Green Book* (2018) should not have been awarded Best Picture at the 2018 Oscars are decidedly off-kilter. One reviewer suggested that *Green Book* is "woefully retrograde and borderline bigoted" because it makes use of stereotypes in a *true story* about the overcoming of racial prejudice.[13] The message of the film is that culturally encoded class distinctions, which were structurally dominant in the early 1960s, are less about class conflict than they are occasions for racial and cross-class alliance. This message is difficult to perceive, however, insofar as the effects of contemporary class polarization confuse the issue as to whether today's middle strata of creative class workers and identitarians serve democracy or the skyrocketing salaries of millionaires. A neoliberal like Obama can thus appear democratic by simply proclaiming his appreciation of *Good Kid, M.A.A.D City*.

The conditions created by the woke culture and politics that sustain the military-industrial-entertainment-identity complex alter the sense of what it means to make history. Whereas war artists like Otto Dix depicted the horrors of war, embedded war artists and embedded journalists are today instructed by the military on what they can and cannot report. Artists and journalists are thus expected, like Facebook and Google 'cleaners,' to shield the public from reality rather than exposing lies and atrocities. One would not want to live in a society where there is no censorship at all, as Julian Assange argues.[14] Radicalism does not imply the elimination of societal norms in favour of nihilistic abandon. However, today's revisionism is not simply a matter of interpreting history, but rather, interpreting the present before it happens, such that cybernetic prediction, political predation and capitalist calculation shape what was, is and can be. If Marx's famous thesis eleven calls on people to not only interpret but change the world, neoliberal capitalism both interprets and changes the world according to the commercial needs of a social order whose new normal is the state of emergency. The difference between Walter Benjamin's notion of "homogenous empty time" and today's cynical realism is the fact that neoliberal capitalism makes claims to both making and witnessing history at the same time that it makes these activities subservient to social, economic, ecological, intellectual, cultural and moral decline.[15]

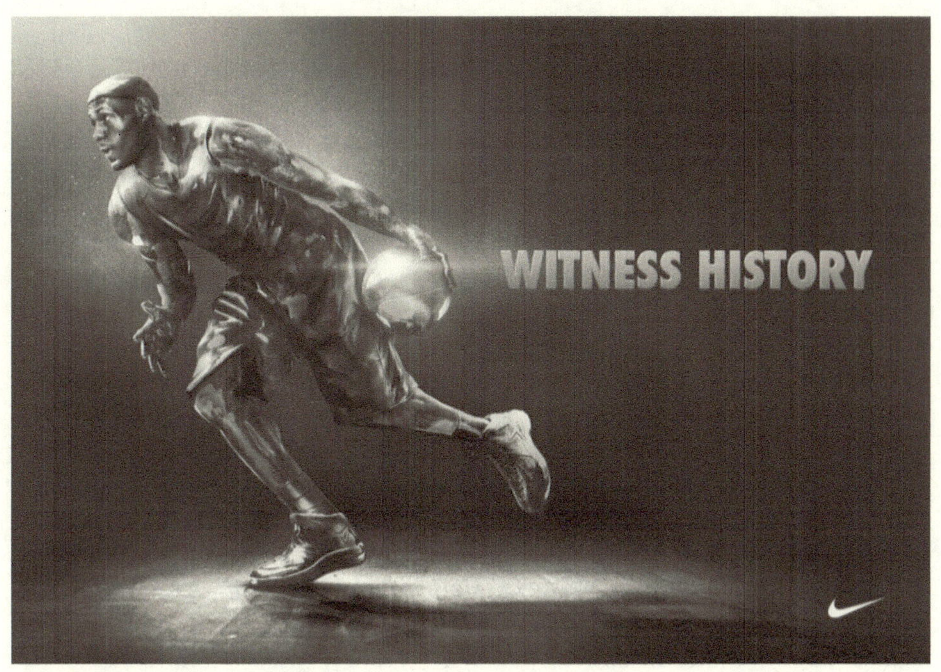

Nike "Witness" ad campaign featuring LeBron James. The 2013 ad celebrates James's entry into the NBA Finals with print, digital, television and grassroots marketing.

Beyond postmodernism's historicist pastiche, the simultaneous interpretation and changing of the world in the interest of capital accumulation and circulation advances a form of *embedded history* that instrumentalizes the notion of progress. In this context, black capitalism and celebrity culture draw on vernacular forms to heighten the profiles and enrich the portfolios of high-net-worth politicians, athletes and artists. An emblem of this contemporary condition of embedded history is Nike's The Witness (We Are All Witnesses) integrated marketing campaign, which features the Cleveland Cavaliers National Basketball Association player LeBron James. The campaign was started in 2005 with a billboard showing James in a Christ-like pose, with his arms outstretched and his face looking to the sky above. This initial advertisement did not feature any specific sports product but directly associated James himself with the Nike brand. As he skipped college basketball and went directly from high school to the NBA, James was crowned with a $90 million endorsement. Nike's June 2007 integrated marketing campaign celebrated his first NBA Finals appearance with digital, print, television and grassroots marketing. A black and white "We Are All Witnesses" television commercial was set to Bob Dylan's 'I Shall Be Released' and was sung by Marion Williams, an African-American gospel singer. James eventually went on a Witness History World Tour to China and the Philippines.

Such campaigns market sporting excellence and prowess in the interest of commodification. The extent to which they also reinscribe notions of ethno-national unity is incidental to the corporatization of culture. Across all of these campaigns, the implicit message is that capitalism is the only game in town, which in the U.S. makes the basketball court a fitting emblem of the two-party system. As if to seem like he is always on the winning side, Obama delivered a commencement speech in May 2020 in the company of LeBron James, now head of the philanthrocapitalist LeBron James Family Foundation. After having sabotaged the Sanders campaign, Obama gave a speech to high school students about systemic racism, economic disparity and lack of basic health care. In August, after players from all teams shut down the National Basketball Association playoffs to protest the police shooting of Jacob Blake, Obama advised James and the president of the Players' Association to end the strike and finish the playoffs. The collective protest, which had spread from the NBA to Major League Baseball, the National Hockey League, the National Football League, Major League Soccer and professional tennis, threatened to politicize a realm of fully corporatized spectacle that is partially funded by the Pentagon. Like Obama, Trump argued that the increasing politicization of professional sports is not a good thing. Choosing team Obama over team Trump, with a few symbolic concessions that owe more to virtue signalling than police reform, the athletes did little more than preserve the veneer of woke capitalism. The protests in the streets were prevented from interfering with sports business or the neoliberal agenda.

Nike's 2017 Kaepernick ad campaign was not only the highlight of the 30-year anniversary of its Just Do It slogan, but a blatant exercise in the corporate use of social justice issues. Popular with the global millennial market, wokewashing promotes compassionate capitalism. In 2018, for instance, the sports betting company Paddy Power sent a sponsored bus to the Brighton Gay Pride parade, calling it the official bus of gay professional footballers and making known the fact that none of the 500 professional league soccer players are openly gay. Like the 2017 Kendall Jenner Pepsi commercial that trivialized BLM activism, the stunt was condemned by gay rights groups. There might be more to complain about perhaps with the fact that Northrup Grumman, a maker of Intercontinental Ballistic Missiles and drone parts, is one of many companies celebrating Pride and Heritage months, along with the support of gender and racial diversity. Not to be left behind, the beer company Heineken marketed "unity, peace and understanding" in an ad showing a member of the alt-right debating politics with a black feminist.[16] The follies of woke, as Grosso has it, might not be so absurd if one accepts without question that making money is making history. The problems of embedded history and woke capitalism have deeper historical sources and more complex political and economic meanings than are typically allowed by the social and mass media. Knowledge of these problems is obstructed by a networked consciousness industry that is simultaneously conservative and destructive. As Benjamin said of the conspicuous consumption of the *fin de siècle*, "the pure consumer is the pure exploiter."[17] Having a 'national conversation' means setting the stage for a shouting match that makes little room for anything that comes close to education.

Because it dates from a critical moment in the shift away from socialist and labour politics towards neoliberalism, Ellen Meiksins Wood's *The Retreat from Class* is more relevant to contemporary radical politics than contemporary race brokers allow. Wood warned readers about the pitfalls of post-Marxism and anti-universalism.[18] The problem with post-Marxism, which could also be substituted for a term like new social movements, is that its connections to Marxism are so tenuous as to be effectively non-existent. Its premise is the abandonment of class struggle as the basis for understanding history and its replacement with an abstract notion of humanity. Instead of a theory that defines social relations on the basis of capitalist relations of production and exploitation, politics are concerned instead with electoral victories.[19] This explains why revolutionary enthusiasm has been replaced with victim politics and woke sentimentality. And that is the reason why Kaepernick's Nike ad was ripe for appropriation. As Wood puts it:

> The point is simply that none of these alternatives has been supported by a systemic reassessment of the social forces that constitute capitalism and its critical strategic targets. The typical mode of these alternative visions is voluntaristic utopia or counsel of despair – or, as is often the case, both at once: a vision of a transformed society without real hope for a process of transformation.[20]

On International Women's Day in 2018, McDonald's advertised the golden arches upside down on its packaging and uniforms. One could celebrate this latest version of the medieval world turned upside down, or Queen for a Day, with a gay milkshake and black Freedom fry. One would be surprised, nevertheless, to discover that such symbolism and democratic raw material is derived to a great extent from the influence of Maoism on European intellectuals as they adapted theorists like Antonio Gramsci, Louis Althusser and Nicos Poulantzas into "non-class" and lumpen countercultural theories of strategic social power that did little more to change the world, as Marx had proposed, than "bearing witness against the system."[21]

The characteristic of post-Marxism is its rejection of class essentialism and economic reductionism as well as its autonomization of politics and ideology. On this view, since there is no necessary and determinate connection between politics and economics, the working class is said to have no privileged position in the struggle for social progress. Radical social agents can therefore be found among people who are either relatively or absolutely autonomous from class issues. Such has been the premise of Eurocommunist intellectuals, the British Labour Party, Syriza, Podemos, the DSA and other "newer" lefts that may as well, according to Wood, be referred to as the "never" left. Having rejected, or "disarticulated" the primacy of class, and therefore the link between the working class and socialism, the progressive movement could be "rearticulated" as the popular alliance of social groups with different political objectives into a "democratic" struggle that does not oppose labour to capital, but rather distinguishes the public interest from the demands of the corporate state. Intellectual trends like discourse theory and radical democracy authorize a multitude of social agents who are perceived to be more likely to bring about change because they are less economically dependent and therefore less politically conservative than the working class. Post-Marxism not only abandons the class struggle but actively dismisses the working class on a cultural, social and political basis as anti-revolutionary, reformist and economistic.[22]

As post-Marxism concedes to social democracy and the view that capitalism is best able to meet social needs while at the same time promoting new subjectivities and lifestyles, anti-communism becomes acceptable to erstwhile militants. One historical paradox is the fact that post-Marxist Eurocommunism emerged at the same time that the New Right perceived and understood its struggle as a class conflict against the remaining vestiges of socialism. The upshot is that the neoliberalism of the Democratic Party and the Labour Party is part of the same assault on the working class as the neoconservatism of the Republican and Tory parties. The difference is that the New Right sought to win over the working class through chauvinism and anti-elitism while the New Left materially destroyed the working class by playing the game of de-unionization, government cutbacks, tax breaks and debt financing, capping this off with petty-bourgeois resistance, lifestyle and diversity. To add insult to self-injury, the dispossessed now considers itself the "new dangerous class."[23] Declassed intellectuals take to Twitter… In August 2019, Twitter cancelled some 200,000 accounts that discussed the mass protests in Hong Kong, an action similar to Facebook's censorship of Venezuelan news pages and Google's anti-left algorithms. Such artificial intelligence is shaped by the class struggle as we know it, which reduces the politics of the left to a non-class or class-neutral politics. Google algorithms also promote woke content and steer 'normative' search queries towards diversity content. This non-class character of post-politics becomes the bedrock of capitalist universality. While one could go on with Wood's assessment of the prospects of a socialist universality, a consideration of contemporary economic conditions better explains what it is that makes today's capitalism so different, so woke.

In a 2016 lecture-discussion between Robert Brenner and David Harvey, Brenner begins with an assessment of the falling rates of capitalist profit, which, without insisting on homology, one could relate to the autonomization of the cultural symbols of identity in their embedded, state-corporate modality.[24] Brenner correlates the upward distribution of income with the economic decline, low productivity, low wages and low consumption that have plagued low-growth capitalism since the late 1970s. The decline in advanced countries after the postwar boom is due to the entry of new economies on the world market and the dramatic reduction of production costs, forcing down prices and leading to a 40 percent drop in rates of profitability, especially in manufacturing. With lower demand for investment and for capital goods, the neoliberal solution to declining dynamism worldwide has been a hardline attack on wages and state spending. Lower demand is offset by government subsidy, reduced interest rates, tax breaks to corporations and wealthy individuals, government theft, bailouts, deficit spending, debt financing, financialization, as well as the liberalization of credit and the growth of consumer and household debt.[25] Where both Keynesian and free market solutions fail, asset bubbles are manipulated to drive up prices and satisfy shareholders. Government policy has protected the top earners while at the same time attacking workers through various means, including de-unionization, offshoring and policing. As a complement to this, social services are increasingly subject to privatization and consumer goods are subject to hyper-marketization. Marketing, one could say, is as illusory or as real as the strength of the deregulated economy. Just as conservative pundits can wax glib about these houses of cards, the political right can step into the political vacuum. Such "neoliberal excrescence," as Brenner calls it, was made possible by the mantra of TINA: there is no alternative. Now *they* are in office, he argues, and like all neoliberal administrations, from Carter to Obama, they will also fail to invest profitably. The one thing that governments have not tried, because they refuse to, is bringing the world economy under social and state regulation.

For his part, Harvey looks at the other side of falling rates of profit and addresses the ways in which global capital avoids disasters. As American labour is hollowed out by the reconfiguration of the global workforce, new skill sets are invented through technological changes, design innovation and the kind of regional and identity marketing that offsets low productivity and stimulates demand. Workers who took issue with Hillary Clinton's lectures to Goldman Sachs believed that they had little to benefit from the growth of the global labour force. Regardless, the value-added profitability of sales in the stronger economies of developed nations transfers the potential for struggles at the point of realization. Precarious employees at McDonald's, Amazon and Walmart are less worried about mortgage debt than they are about illness and homelessness. The elements of the picture we are seeing today were created by Bill Clinton's NAFTA economics, welfare reform and bank deregulation. Debt-accelerated Ponzi schemes, like university tuition, create growth at other sites of the circulation and distribution process, even if most of it is designed for investment rather than students. Little wonder that Trump is a property developer. There is therefore not much to gain, Harvey argues, from presuming that workers voted for Trump on the basis of either class or race.

The lack of a class perspective on the left greases the gears of the Identity Industry. Hardly a panacea, woke wars line the pockets of the one and ten percent who have no incentive to change life in any systematic or progressive way. The result is universal alienation in pseudo-conflicts of mutual shaming as well as alienation from oneself in rituals of humility or hostility. The hysteria of political correctness complements the excessively regulatory conditions of work. What is on offer as an alternative to this is the braggadocio of demagogues, who, as Harvey mentions, boast about how much money they make at the same time that they give voice to popular discontent. Brenner comments that verbiage about white privilege could be put to better use by describing the degradation that people have experienced as wages have stagnated for more than four decades. Refusing to vote for another candidate like Obama, who did not support a single social struggle for the simple fact that he supported economic inequality and the neoliberal status quo, people are desperately opting for rightist alternatives to neoliberalism, preferring the devils they know to wolves in sheep's clothing. For those who retain a sense of idealism, inept slogans like the DSA's 'Decarbonize, Democratize, Decommodify & Decolonize & Demand a Green New Deal' are unable to condense politics as effectively as a name you can trust and someone who will listen to your concerns. A decolonial activist is likely to cancel you if you're not ready to check your privilege. A neoliberal politician adjusts the problems created by the shift from industrial policy to financialization and trade wars with military Keynesianism.

My President

The marketing of Barack Obama as a cool president has alerted us to the way that woke candidates will be manufactured in such a way that the colour and gender lines in American society are used to deter the possibility of class politics. The black capitalism that Obama supports has developed over the last several decades alongside the marketing and celebritization of black success. After Obama's first term, his administration's shift away from economic stabilization through taxpayer bailouts and economic stimulus was marked by the hyping of black cultural signifiers, as with his rendition of Young Jeezy at the 2012 White House Correspondents' Association Dinner. As Michael Eric Dyson argues, the Prez wished to indicate that he had not forgotten his hip hop constituency: "The first thing Obama suggested about his administration's second term, joking or not, was an explicit embrace of hip hop by the commander in chief."[26] Turning to austerity and relinquishing his campaign of hope and change, Obama sought mass appeal through attitude. At the 2015 White House Correspondents' Dinner, he alluded to himself as a basketball player, saying that he was feeling "more loose and relaxed than ever before."[27] The cut 'n' mix president who likes Jay-Z especially could not only reach out to the hood for identification, but could make history even if he believed that history had officially ended. History is now made by commercial artists, basketball stars, film celebrities and corporate capitalists. And it goes down easy if you do it with style. Writing for the *New Yorker*, Vinson Cunningham noted Obama's code-switching ability: "As President, Obama was exceptional and relatable; aloof and an empath; a Bob Gates-style realist when it came to Syria and a Power-Rice interventionist in Libya; a global celebrity and a ponderous professor; a radical presence but somehow, simultaneously, a company man."[28] None of this conservative appropriation of countercultural cool was news after the preppy and yuppie eighties but all of that obnoxious display of upward mobility could now be enhanced through the unique signature of a black president.

Advertising Age named the Obama campaign Marketer of the Year in 2008. Some have suggested that brand Obama was a feel-good brand, but the view from the black ghetto is somewhat more nuanced. According to Michael P. Jeffries, hip hop changed dramatically from its origins in deindustrialized cities, where homegrown breakdancing, graffiti, DJing, rapping and MCing was eventually transformed into celebrity big business. By the 1980s and 90s, hip hop was glorifying wealth and conspicuous consumption at the same time as selling the notion of oppositional blackness and its occasionally gendered counterpoints.[29] As corporate music giants bought out independent labels, marketing black music to not only black middle-class households, but to a mass audience with a taste for what Jennifer Lena refers to as "puerile rap," investment increased alongside the homogenization of regional styles, overseen by a "white supremacist capitalist patriarchy."[30] Now a field of academic debate as well, accusations that hip hop sells alienated hedonism and avoids serious political engagement contrasts with the view that hip hop represents the epistemological and artistic challenges of a black vernacular that resists, critiques and challenges social domination. As Imani Perry puts it, the "open discourse" of hip hop allows it to express the complexity of black experience: "In the midst of a consumer culture that glorifies violence and eschews intellectualism, hip hop has both spewed American vices on the airwaves and aggressively introduced progressive politics, compelling artistic expression, emotion, and beauty into popular culture."[31]

While the figure of Obama can hardly determine whether the contradictory politics of hip hop are revolutionary or conformist, Jeffries thinks that hip hop is one way to assess the Obama phenomenon. Young Jeezy's 'My President' of 2008 brags that "my president is black" at the same time that the song boasts about the fact that the singer's Lamborghini is blue. A cameo by the rapper Nas on this song advises Obama to not lose his connection to the black popular agenda as he rises to power. Hip hop's moral injunction to not forget where you came from, according to Todd Boyd, has less to do with the politics of the Civil Rights generation and more to do with a notion of fidelity to the "post-soul" generation that came of age in the era of Reaganomics. Asserting their "playa hatin" independence and self-determination, the hip hop generation has either ignored the Civil Rights and Black Power paradigms or allowed them to be commercialized in exchange for global success and authority.[32] Although artists like Nas and Young Jeezy have no distinct politics and mark their distance from the Civil Rights movement through a boisterous oppositionality and black pride, Jeffries believes that Obama was able to bridge the black generation gap, especially as he cautioned the American public to not allow moral panics over hip hop to detract from the work required to improve social conditions. Obama's stylized luminosity was, according to Jeffries, a "complex cool" that eventually won the approval of artists like 50 Cent, Common, Ludacris and Talib Kweli. "We about to make history," rapped Ludacris in 'Politics (Obama Is Here),' presenting Obama's election victory as unavoidable. Obama's popularity with the hip hop generation, Jeffries concludes, had little to do with his politics and was rather due to his cool youthful affect. This complex cool, he says, invalidates the view of hip hop unflappability as shallowly self-defeating and rather affirms the courage to make public business out of the struggles of private life.[33] Obama, however, is both more than a symbol of integration into the American mainstream and less than black hip hop royalty. Obama is a by-product of the commodification of black culture and politics.

If Jeffries no doubt understands the capitalist morality of a nation weaned on *The Oprah Show* and *Cops*, his hip hop metaphysics are suitably matched to the ethnographic deference of Cultural Studies. In his introductory text to the first issue of the journal *Celebrity Studies*, Graeme Turner suggests that the exponential growth of entertainment and exploitation in a world of rapid news cycles has led to a "celebrity worship syndrome" that calls on academics to do more than relay the "celebrity-commodity" that is manufactured by media visibility and dispensed by journalists.[34] As Krista Thompson argues about the language of hip hop performance, the limelight of celebrity visibility, or 'bling,' coincides with the glorification of consumer values, sex, power, wealth and self-aggrandisement.[35] A slave sublime locates black subjectivity at the interstices of hypervisibility and disappearance in a propaganda of power – a hyper-masculinization and hyper-sexualization that she says is at play in the work of Kehinde Wiley. What is certain is that if Wiley plays with these codes, he did not invent them, nor has he done much to question them.

Celebrity branding is easily reversible. Blurring the lines between celebrity and politics, the branding of George W. Bush as 'W' and 'Dubya' in the 2004 election played on the notion that the Southern American accent is a sign of ignorance. His campaign "reclaimed" this prejudice to valorize a candidate and a politics that was perceived to be sub-standard. According to Jeremy Heckett, the reversal of this stereotype, as is the case with the reclamation of terms like the N-word and 'queer,' not only challenged prejudices but retained and redeployed them.[36] Dubya could therefore function as a symbolic condensation of various meanings: conservatism, religious values, white cultural heritage and 'love it or leave it' patriotism.[37] To the extent that it is successful, brand consciousness usurps the complexity of issues and politics into a personified symbol that is easy to market. The "disproportionate influence of symbolism," Heckett says, "threatens the democratic process."[38] American and global politics are reduced to culture wars and brand wars, a message discipline that altogether eclipses the fact that the terms of the struggle are entirely on the side of late capitalism.

Young Jeezy's song title 'My President' is fittingly similar to other iProducts and the kinds of 'emotional branding' and 'relationship marketing' that are designed to make rational people respond viscerally and emotionally to personalized products. After Run-DMC's 'My Adidas' practically saved the German company from market extinction due to competition from Nike and Reebok, the song also made the hip hop trio the first non-athletes to break into the million-dollar endorsement phenomenon. What impressed executives the most was the 1986 Madison Square Garden concert in which thousands of fans held their Adidas shoes aloft, much as concert fans do today with their mobile phones.[39] Celebrity as we know it today is part of the legacy of nineteenth-century Romanticism and bourgeois individualism. Celebrity also gestures towards the people who congregate around those who are deemed famous. If an athlete and a musician have fans, the celebrity politician is defined by the number of voters they can mobilize and their approval ratings. The celebritization of politics, however, leads to worries about manipulation. In a world of simulation and pseudo-events, the "complex cool" of a politician like Obama, according to Richard Dyer's notion of "constructed celebrity," combines ordinariness with extraordinariness. Fame therefore has as much to do with luck as it does with hard work.[40] The real person is not as important as the persona. As Daniel Boorstin long ago said of celebrities, the secret of the great man is God's secret.[41] The consequent God's eye view is a free trade agreement between celebrities and the media, mass-manufacturing voyeuristic access to the private life of popular individuals.

Olivier Driessens emphasizes the distinction between celebrification and celebritization. Whereas celebrification describes the process by which a person becomes notable if not famous, usually because they have excelled in their field of endeavour, celebritization addresses the other side of this process, where for example celebrity status can be thrust upon ordinary people. In electoral politics, celebritization is necessary if the process of political representation is to be considered legitimate, as is the case with slogans on both the right and left, with Trump's 'Make America Great Again' as well as Sanders' 'Not me, Us.'[42] Although celebritization is sometimes thought of as an effect of democratization, the shift from the kind of celebrity that derives from achievement towards media-driven entertainment has many downsides. Unless people take politics seriously, a celebrified activist politician like Sanders is disadvantaged by a celebritized clown politician like Trump, who openly promotes the inflation of self-importance through various means: de-professionalization and diversification into various fields like business, entertainment and politics; doing anything for attention; using emotionalism and personalization to create brand identification; avoiding the question of meritocratic achievement; using social media as platforms for self-branding; capitalizing self-display and celebrity hierarchy in consonance with the profit dynamics of consumer and corporate logics, as in Reality TV shows. According to Driessens, "[t]he self becomes a monetized commodity that is gradually unpacked and reduced to mere exchange value."[43] Joe Biden's 2020 No Malarkey campaign tour, for instance, replaced the missing crowds of supporters with the media sensationalism of a cranky old man attacking his constituents, all the while raising $1.183 billion in campaign donations.

If one wished to avoid hero worship and celebrate the ordinary greatness of everyday people, Amy Sherald's modest portraits are more successful than Wiley's "just-add-water," or rather, just-add-semen celebrity.[44] Both of them, nevertheless, have one foot in the shopping mall and the other in the bank. As art criticism and art institutions become more complacently racialist, the intellectual rigor, artistic daring and political challenge of work by artists like Romare Bearden, David Hammons, Charles Burnett, Adrian Piper, Renée Green and Fred Wilson takes a back seat to commercial work that is made almost exclusively for monetary reasons. These artists may very well enjoy the status of consecrated museum artists, but they achieved this incrementally by earning what Bourdieu referred to as "titles of nobility" and not merely by accumulating "marks of infamy." While it is undoubtedly true that even critical work reproduces the class function of the field of cultural production, their work does not simply flatter audiences with stimulants that are based on little more than good looks. They rather acknowledge social contradictions while at the same time radicalizing the forms of art.

One consequence of celebritization is that instead of politics being about the creation of the kind of world we want, the field is transformed into a space of consumerism, which gives more power to campaign consultants, advertisers, pollsters and pundits than it does to the citizens whose choices are made for them. These problems are compounded in the U.S. where citizens receive more reliable information about candidates from campaign advertisements than they do from the news media. With even a star candidate like Sanders, whose credibility as a progressive politician was head and shoulders above all of the other 2020 Democratic Party nominees combined, the Dems nevertheless produced in 2019 no fewer than 20 competitors for the leadership, as if to give the impression that Sanders was not a strong enough candidate to take on Trump. The establishment's strategy panned out as early as August 2019, when Michael Moore, the maker of such films as *Capitalism: A Love Story* (2009) and *Farenheit 11/9* (2018), stated that only Michelle Obama could beat Trump, thereby betraying his own politics, undermining the most socialist of nominees and propping up the neoliberal consensus.[45] Moore's defeatism did not invalidate the Sanders nomination, but rather suggested that Trump's celebrity can only be matched by someone who has a similarly nominal symbolic value, which would allow for identification across popular and elite sectors. Moore defined Michelle Obama as "somebody who is not a politician" but is a beloved American, as proven by the fact that her book tour was filling 15,000-seat arenas. Obama's strength, according to Moore, is that she would beat Trump in debates and would not allow him to bully her and call her names. While a Sanders leadership would be a one-round knockout, a Michelle-Donald event could last forever since these two contestants would turn politics not only into celebrity surplus for the networks but into a diversitarian's wet dream. Moore eventually endorsed Sanders at a Queens rally alongside Alexandria Ocasio-Cortez. Regardless, the logic of consumer spectacle that Moore knows all too well is the transgression of political conventions in the interest of those same conventions. Understanding how spectacle functions is not the same thing as fighting it. In this regard Michelle Obama is hardly the "street fighter" that Moore may have thought she was. If one was nevertheless to adopt a marketing perspective, it would have been foolhardy to choose Michelle Obama as the leader of the Democratic Party. Insofar as market communication functions according to conditioned stimulus through repeated exposure, and sociologists long ago proved that advertising does not modify behaviour, marketers argue that the potential advantage of a celebrity endorsement has to be evaluated against the potential hazards.[46] The question, in this case, is whether the brand 'match-up' is with the Democratic Party, the office of the President of the United States, or the American public.

If Obama maintained his market appeal over his two terms, he lost trustworthiness to the extent that support for the Democratic Party fell to the same low level as that of the Republicans, with Americans buying into the neo-fascist ravings of a self-styled demagogue. If marketers are correct that consumers prefer a low-involving and reasonable match-up between a celebrity they can trust and the endorsed product, then the match-up that is significant is not with the presidency or the party, but with the people. If Sanders proved to not be a low-involving and positive brand repositioning for the Democrats, it is because Americans were either not able to admit to themselves the hardships they are living through and causing worldwide, or they were unable to consider that a democratic socialist is a plausible match-up with what they think the U.S., and by extension themselves, can become. From Edward Bernays to Noam Chomsky, the marketing of politics has been shown to be as effective as it is nefarious.

Heavenly Compulsions

For many Americans, Obama's blackness meant that he could hardly fail as 'My President.' For all of his acquiescence to power and money, Obama was perceived to have run a good government, avoiding any cause for impeachment and over eight years gaining access to establishment circles worldwide. Like the kind of 'soft news' journalism that emerged in the 1970s, and that limited critical reporting, Obama's brand image combined the solemnity of news with entertainment and lifestyle. As Ellis Cashmore argues in *Celebrity/Culture*, consumer media have dissipated credibility at the same time that ideologically indistinguishable politicians are presented as entertainers as much as leaders.[47] Candidates must not only be ideologically but aesthetically acceptable and recognizable, a phenomenon exemplified by Ronald Reagan. Prior to his election in 2004, Arnold Schwarzenegger had no experience in politics. Celebrities who endorse the cause of a political candidate extend the culture of entertainment and philanthropy to the realm of government, serving the interests of the wealthy rather than criticizing them. In exchange, politicians surrender their independence to the system, with elections becoming yet another arena of hyperreality.

Before Barack Obama came along, the American public had already been conditioned by the logic of black blandness in the figure of golfer Tiger Woods. Whereas celebrity athletes like Muhammad Ali were known to challenge the political mainstream, athletes like Woods are comparatively tame but nevertheless retain the ability to captivate millions of followers. Woods became the highest paid sports endorser, earning more than $50 million annually in the early 2000s, up to over $80 million by the mid-aughts. Hardworking, honest and benign, Woods also promoted a "post-historical" view of the U.S. as a nation of immigrants and post-racial colourblindness.[48] An 'alpha male' with few vices, Woods combined celebrity with the quality of pliable manageability. As with politicians, celebrity athletes like Woods surrender their autonomy in exchange for multi-million-dollar endorsements.

Corporate interests have not completely subdued the 'authenticity' of character. Vices, prurience and wrongdoings are par for the course in the publicity machine, where convenience and profitability are shaped by the need to placate the fanaticism of audiences. This is certainly true in hip hop, where 'fresh' performers like Break Machine, Run-DMC and Salt-N-Pepa were marketed out of the field by bad boy acts like Grandmaster Flash and Beastie Boys. Aside from the political militancy of someone like Chuck D of Public Enemy, who learned to rap by imitating Grandmaster Flash and sports announcer Marv Albert, much rap art was influenced by Reagan Noir, as exemplified by the Wesley Snipes character in Leon Ichaso's 1984 film *Sugar Hill*, a story about two drug dealer brothers from Harlem who come up against the more established Italian crime gangs. Grandmaster Flash not only pioneered DJing, scratching and mixing in the mid-1970s, but his 1982 electro rap hit 'The Message,' produced by Sugar Hill producer Clifton Chase, provided a sensational music video exposé of inner-city violence, drugs and poverty, closing with a scene of the artist being arrested by the police. As if to underscore the white American view of black culture, 'The Message' was the first hip hop recording to be added to the Library of Congress National Recording Registry. The Sugar Hill record label, known in 1979 for the Sugarhill Gang's 'Rapper's Delight,' also produced music videos directed by Spike Lee, including 'White Lines' by Grandmaster Flash and the Furious Five, which mixes sex, money and drugs in a bipolar cautionary tale that is fitting of the exploitation genre developed by Lee since the 1980s.

By the late 1990s, ghetto pride was readily associated with big money. Grandmaster Flash appeared in a 1996 endorsement for Louis Vuitton by Helmut Lang, wearing Timberland boots, a Kangol hat and perched on a LV monogram DJ record case. The Vuitton campaign was designed to create a middle-class and youth market for its high-end luxury goods that had now gone street. The ad appeared in American *Vogue* to celebrate the company's centenary, endorsed for promotional purposes by Chrissie Hynde, Courtney Love, Johnny Depp and John Travolta. Bernard Arnault, the CEO and leading shareholder of Louis Vuitton, is the third wealthiest individual in the world, with a personal fortune worth over US $167 billion. Not only did Grandmaster Flash never receive his record case, as promised, but the company also exploits textile sweatshop workers worldwide. An owner of several newspapers, Arnault is friends with politicians across the spectrum, from Jacques Chirac and François Mitterrand to Nicolas Sarkozy and Emmanuel Macron. His earnings in one year would be enough to prevent starvation worldwide.

In the 1980s, the concept of 'crossover potential' was borrowed from the music industry, where Motown artists had been valued by business interests for their cross-racial appeal. Crossover potential was then transferred to the business of sports. This happened when Bo Jackson became the first athlete to be named an All-Star in both baseball and football. Considered one of the greatest athletes in history, 'Bo' also became known though Nike advertisements that promoted a cross-training athletic shoe, the Nike Air Trainer I. In 1987 Nike promoted its Air Max shoe in a television commercial that featured the Beatles recording of 'Revolution.' One year later it introduced the slogan 'Just Do It.' Nike's "Bo Knows" ad campaign was launched during the 1989 Major League Baseball All-Star Game, when Jackson was playing with the Kansas City Royals. Ronald Reagan pitched from the broadcaster's booth during the first inning. The ad is among the first to combine product innovation, a sports personality and the timing of a sporting event. Other Nike ads featured Wayne Gretzky and John McEnroe. Created by Jim Riswold of Wieden + Kennedy, the "Bo Knows" campaign is credited to have won Nike 80 percent of the cross-trainer shoe market, much of it later won over by Reebok. Nike ads went on to depict Jackson taking up other sports, including tennis, golf, luge, auto racing and even blues music, where Bo was staged alongside Bo Diddley. He was featured as an unstoppable Nintendo video game character and was also a Saturday morning cartoon character along with Wayne Gretzky and Michael Jordan.

By 1991, Bo Jackson and Michael Jordan were the most famous athletes in the world and Nike was the leading shoe manufacturer. Jackson, who few people today are familiar with, went on to earn a B.A. in science. For its part, Nike went on to become a brand that is as familiar as McDonald's, coca-colonizing the sports market through the celebrity endorsement of star athletes. Whereas in the 1960s a sponsored athlete used to receive free company footwear and gear, Nike pioneered the practice of paying athletes more for endorsements than their professional earnings. With most endorsements guaranteeing a four percent increase in sales, which for Nike resulted in profits of $3 billion annually for its Jordan brand products alone, consumer identification allows multinationals to avoid having to be concerned with higher wages and benefits for factory workers. Instead, just as Willie Nelson and Snoop Dog helped to change popular attitudes towards marijuana, endorsements have helped Nike avoid criticism of its use of sweatshop labour.[49] Nike also marketed its products to African-American youths by incorporating the worlds of street culture and rap music into its advertising, with additional promotion through the philanthropic construction of inner-city playgrounds and arenas.

By the 2000s, crossover potential had more to do with celebritization than with any recognized skill or merit in associated fields of endeavour. Sean Combs, also known as Puff Daddy, is both a rapper and TV producer, estimated in 2019 to be worth $740 million, making him the second wealthiest hip hop artist. His clothing line, produced by Sean John factories in Honduras, was revealed to have been violating labour laws. Combs's perfume, I Am King, is dedicated to Barack Obama, Muhammad Ali and Martin Luther King. He also sells GIRLS women's clothing, owns two restaurants, is involved in the Ciroc vodka brand and owns stock in a television network as well as an athletic beverage company.

The rapper known as 50 Cent, Curtis James Jackson III, is also an actor, TV producer, businessman and investor. 50 Cent's first major album, *Get Rich or Die Tryin*, made with Eminem and Dr Dre, has sold more than 30 million albums, winning him several awards. He has diversified business interests, including talent management, record-television-film production, footwear, apparel, fragrances, video games, mobile apps, book publishing, headphones, dietary supplements, real estate, financial markets, mining and metals industries in South Africa, boxing promotion, consumer electronics and fashion. He owns G-Unit Records, G-Unit Books and Reebok G-Unit sneakers, all of which, he says, revolve around his alter ego. Formula 50 water, a variant of VitaminWater, makes "water taste good" and earned him $100 million when sold to Coca-Cola. He also sells Pure 50 RGX body spray with Right Guard (with proceeds to HIV awareness), as well as a dietary supplement company created in conjunction with a 2007 film. He founded G-Unit Films and Cheetah Vision, which has over $200 million in funding and makes low budget action thrillers for the foreign film market. In 2011, with the proceeds from Street King purchases, a flavoured energy drink, 50 Cent launched a charity initiative to provide food for one billion starving people in Africa. His consumer electronics company, SMS Audio, has co-branding deals with Reebok, Marvel, Disney, Lucasfilms and Intel. He owns shares in Effen Vodka and has his own signature liquor brand. He has investments in FRIGO Revolution Wear, a luxury underwear brand. In 2007, 50 Cent was the second-wealthiest rapper after Jay-Z. In 2015 he had an estimated net worth of $155 million – though that same year he bankrupted on $32 million, which revealed that his true net worth was closer to $4 million.

Raymond IV, better known as Usher, is a singer and dancer. One of the best-selling pop musicians of the 2000s, selling more than 75 million records worldwide, Usher was considered by *Billboard* magazine to be the second most successful artist of the 2000s. A blockbuster phenomenon in pop music, he started his own record label, restaurants, fragrances, music streaming service and a school supply company called Yoobi, which mixes "street smarts with school smarts." Yoobi made $20 million in its first few years. Usher also owns shares in the Cleveland Cavaliers NBA basketball team as well as *Mass Appeal Magazine*. He has endorsed MasterCard, Belvedere Vodka, a Microsoft dance game, Samsung smart TV, Pepsi and Armani. He has combined with corporate philanthropy through the New Look Foundation and has supported Barack Obama as well as Hillary Clinton.

One can find similar cases of crossover marketing among athletes. Albert Pujols, a baseball player with the L.A. Angels and St. Louis Cardinals is a three-times National League MVP and nine-time All-Star. One of the top ten players in major league history, his Pujols Family Foundation NGO provides support for families who live with Down syndrome and aids the poor in the Dominican Republic. Such athletes compete not only on the court and on the field but also through their products and endorsements. The LeBron James basketball sneaker yielded $340 million in sales between January and December 2014. Comparatively, Kobe Bryant's Kobe 9 sold up to $100 million and the L.A. Clippers' Chris Paul raised $32 million. The process comes full circle when athletes engage in virtue signalling through shoe competition. In August 2019, L.A. Lakers player Kyle Kuzma brought attention to Amazon rainforest fires with a message written on his shoes.

According to Cashmore, sport is like culture in the sense that it has no obvious purpose.[50] Sociologically speaking, however, there is no reason to think that sport has less of a class function than aesthetics, least of all due to its corporatization, which channels the aleatory qualities of play into highly bureaucratized and mediated spectator events. The game that is played by managers is the capitalization of uncertainty and indeterminacy – precisely the quality of sport that is its most prized commodity.[51] The capitalization of sport both sustains and destroys it, transforming sport into a metaphor for capitalist social competition more generally, where risk is remade into an organizational principle. In the nineteenth century, sport in public schools emphasized the importance of physical training as a skilled art form. As a gentlemanly activity, sport differed from the routines of industrial work. Even for the working class, sport developed as a leisure activity that contrasted with the working day. Sport was subjected to regulation so that matches did not erupt into riots. It channelled hooliganism into ritualized outlets for aggressive behaviour and social tensions. Since a gentleman was not to profit from a free activity, the professionalization of sport emerged through industrial leagues, where notions like punctuality and precision were transferred from the realm of labour to athletics, socializing as well as capitalizing the process through which violence and rebellion are enacted and witnessed. By the twentieth century, the payment of wages to athletes radically transformed the world of sport, making the activity more professional and more oriented towards the spectacle of competition, with prizes for winners and record breakers. In the spirit of Olympian fame, elite athletes became part of the celebrity star system. In this way, sport came to reflect and reproduce the capitalist system.[52]

With regard to black athletes in particular, Cashmore cites Jack Olsen's 1968 book, *The Black Athlete*, which argues that professional athletes are symbols of failure insofar as the millions of aspiring wannabes will never make a living from a career in sport.[53] Athletes like Michael Jordan, Mike Tyson, Kobe Bryant, Tiger Woods and Serena Williams are perceived by the black masses as having escaped lives of poverty much in the same way that eighteenth-century prizefighting slaves could win their freedom. Sport is one of the ways in which blacks have crossed the colour line, especially in boxing, the NBA, the NBL and the NFL, competing with whites at the same time as challenging and reinforcing social Darwinist myths that displace material realities with pseudo-scientific notions of biological difference and natural ability. In a context where certain fields of endeavour have been inaccessible, sport and entertainment have allowed opportunities for a small elite of blacks to not only excel, but to be managed by corporations as icons of aspiration, ambition and economic success. In exchange, the marketability of a product endorsed by Michael Jordan, for example, allows a company to raise their stocks by billions of dollars annually. However, as a ticket out of poverty, a career in sport or entertainment curtails more realistic and likely alternatives for the majority, leading to despair while at the same time reinforcing Horatio Alger narratives of a well-earned good life at the expense of social and political solidarity. High-priced players and privately-owned teams are linked by media empires like Time Warner, Comcast and Disney to corporate sponsors and advertising agencies, connecting the business of sport with the interests of the billionaire class. Professional sport is thereby influenced by the corrupting influence and culture of big money. Nor are local and amateur sports leagues encouraged by the professionalization of sport.

As celebrities become obscenely wealthy, audiences and the mass media do as much to idolize them as to expose and embarrass them by exploiting their weaknesses and private lives. Desultoriness has long been part of tabloid sensationalism and celebrity blather, where serious social and political subjects mix with crassness and glitz. The former stripper, rapper and television personality Cardi B, who starred on the VH1 television series *Love & Hip Hop: New York*, released two successful mixtapes in 2016-17: *Gangsta Bitch Music, Vol.1 and 2.* With more than 123 million Instagram followers, Cardi B makes, as she puts it, "money moves." Included in *Time* magazine's 2018 top 100 list of most influential people in the world, Cardi B considers herself a feminist. Although she supported Clinton in 2016, in 2020 she supported Sanders, who applauded her for drawing attention to Social Security issues. As a field that is inherently controversial, artists and athletes who become involved in politics not only lend their celebrity to causes, but also reinforce the cause of celebrity as socially meaningful rather than simply the product of class inequality.

The queen of black music is Beyoncé. In 2009 Beyoncé serenaded Barack and Michelle Obama with the song 'At Last' from the 1942 film *Orchestra Wives*, later made famous by Etta James in the Civil Rights era when MLK gave his "Free at Last!" speech. Her partner, Jay-Z, is the most successful rap musician and the two epitomize the ascension of blacks to the class of super-rich. Beyoncé's first solo album after performing in Destiny's Child was *Dangerously in Love*, which sold more than 120 million copies. This ongoing $8 million annual music success has led her to diversify her album, CD, download and ringtone revenue into $80 million in annual returns from investments in film, commercials, fashion lines, lingerie, handbags, footwear, eyewear, soft drinks, cosmetics, jewellery, perfume and the endorsement of more products, in Cashmore's words, "than any other living person."[54] One might think that only an undead zombie would willingly become "the most valuable commodity" in the U.S. "Beyoncé is less a human being," Cashmore writes, and "more an ambulant brand, an advertisement for a new gilded age when commodities overpower everything – including race."[55] The highest paid black musician in history, she has been described by *Forbes* as the most powerful woman in entertainment in 2015 and 2017.

Black celebrities like Beyoncé join the ranks of celebrities like Oprah, Michael Jackson, Bill Cosby, Denzel Washington, Halle Berry, Mariah Carey and Kanye West who have rejected 'victim' status in favour of glamour, luxury, affluence, ostentatiousness and the validation of the American Dream as the product of individual and entrepreneurial zeal. As Cashmore argues, becoming a prodigious pitch(wo)man for commodities requires that one remain silent on political issues, especially the critique of capitalism. Like Jay-Z, who domesticated rap for family consumption, Beyoncé markets products to schoolchildren and cross-promotes her products for pre-college teens through her music. Whatever remains of racism is transferred in this celebrity remix of American politics to the market, where Beyoncé's biggest fans are American Express, General Mills, L'Oréal, Pepsi and Trident. Beyoncé's best product is less her music than it is the ideology of black capitalism and the myth of success that combine cupidity with power.

Although Cashmore's 2010 article criticizes Beyoncé's music for its neglect of black history, the artist thrilled fans in 2016 with the recording and Super Bowl performance of 'Formation,' a reference to the 50th anniversary of the formation of the Black Panther Party, whose symbolism is forbidden by the NFL. This was followed by the release of the film and album *Lemonade*, which relates her biography to the history of black struggles. An article on the website *Madame Noire* describes it as a combination of the kind of conspicuous consumption that celebrates the conservatism of Obama with the class consciousness of Cornel West and Adolph Reed. Within the terms of Super Bowl sponsorship, it participates in the kind of black 'firsts' that aspire, the article says, to the white supremacist power structure.[56] Selling more than 2.5 million copies in its first year alone, *Lemonade* combines contemporary art with activist protest and African goddess symbolism, not to mention its blending of musical genres and references, from classical music to gospel, R&B, blues, country, rock, soul, funk, reggae, hip hop, electronic and trap.

Dreams From Beyoncé

Cultural Studies scholars like Cashmore approach black celebrity in ways that are similar to racialists. In *Beyond Black: Celebrity and Race in Obama's America*, Cashmore argues that black celebrities, like Will Smith, Tyra Banks and Jamie Foxx, have successfully sold the post-racial notion that America is no longer tied to the history of slavery. According to Cashmore: "The election of Barack Obama in 2008 indicated that, even if the post-racial society had not materialized, there was at least evidence that it may do so over the next several years."[57] As an exercise in brand building, the Obama presidency made neoliberal bipartisanship into the stuff of consumer behaviour. Like most social constructionists, Cashmore argues that the crux of racial inequality is the reduction of racism to aberrant behaviour rather than social, historical and institutional processes. Insofar as the conservative values once propounded by Bill Cosby legitimize the politics of people like Colin Powell, the notion of racial equality is meaningless. If the fact of black success disproves the notion that white supremacy is a significant social force, the fact of racial hierarchy proves that it is, as argued for instance by the reactionary, anti-immigrant and pro-reparations hashtag movement #ADOS (African Descendants of Slavery), according to whom Obama is not black but rather "black," since he is not a descendent of West African slaves.[58] Whereas black freedom fighters once took racism for granted, the attitudes of black celebrities are more negotiated and situational. In the process, the goal of social equality has been traded for access to wealth and media attention. Little wonder that the birther movement that questioned Obama's citizenship was led by the host of *Celebrity Apprentice*. Trump's target was not so much Obama but the guilt feelings of white liberals towards blacks as a broad-based collectivity and Democratic Party demographic, against which he could make use of racism to reinforce the Republican ideology of self-interest.[59] This explanation, however accurate, tends to leave aside the question of black capitalism. As support for Obama assuaged white guilt, and as he could play to both sides of the colour line, he could all the more easily govern in the interest of corporate hegemony.

Cashmore notes that 75 percent of African Americans supported the War on Terror, which implies that Obama's imperialist targeting of Muslim nations, among other contemptible policy orientations, was not necessarily interpreted along racial lines. The path to a "more perfect union" therefore meant marketing brand Obama as an adequate match-up to brand USA as the leading corporate-state superpower – itself a celebrity nation on a planet of sycophantic fans and competitors. As Trump's trade wars against China, Iran and Venezuela make clear, the U.S. expects nothing less from other countries than the kind of 'parasocial interaction' according to which deluded fans like Australia and Israel pathologically fixate on Number One for the sake of empowerment and protection from the risks of isolation.[60] Just as criticism of Israel leads to accusations of anti-Semitism, criticism of the U.S. can be denounced as racist – a somewhat ridiculous accusation given that the U.S. is a multicultural society. The issue is rather one of politics. The contemporary, everyday version of parasocial interaction is depicted in Matt Spicer's 2017 film *Ingrid Goes West*, wherein a mentally unstable woman attempts to befriend her Instagram idol, a social media influencer whose seemingly perfect life seduces Ingrid into desperate acts of ingratiation and risk-taking imitation.

If branding has become a way to match politicians with consumers, today's media can also be said to be engineering fascism. For Cashmore, the success of brand Obama is the confluence of history and personality. Obama combined post-racialism with neoliberalism. After Trump, it became a mystery to many how it is that blackness could have been matched with an ostensibly white supremacist society. This was an after-effect of Trump. In political terms, all of the talk of having a leader that 'looks like me' reinscribed the classic formula of fascism in which the masses expect their leader to have the same traits and attitudes as them. One of the many Obama memes that emerged after the popular Shepard Fairey *Obama Hope* stencil design became well-known was a Fairey-like depiction of Obama as an alien from the 1988 John Carpenter film *They Live*, in which advertising subliminally commands people to obey, conform, consume, stay asleep, buy, watch TV and submit. Like the film, workers will need to convince their comrades to put on the shades that decode the messages of celebrities and the mass media. The drawn-out fight scene between Nada, the white protagonist, and Frank, his black blue-collar comrade, could feasibly be rewritten for the new Hollywood quota system in such a way that Frank, now

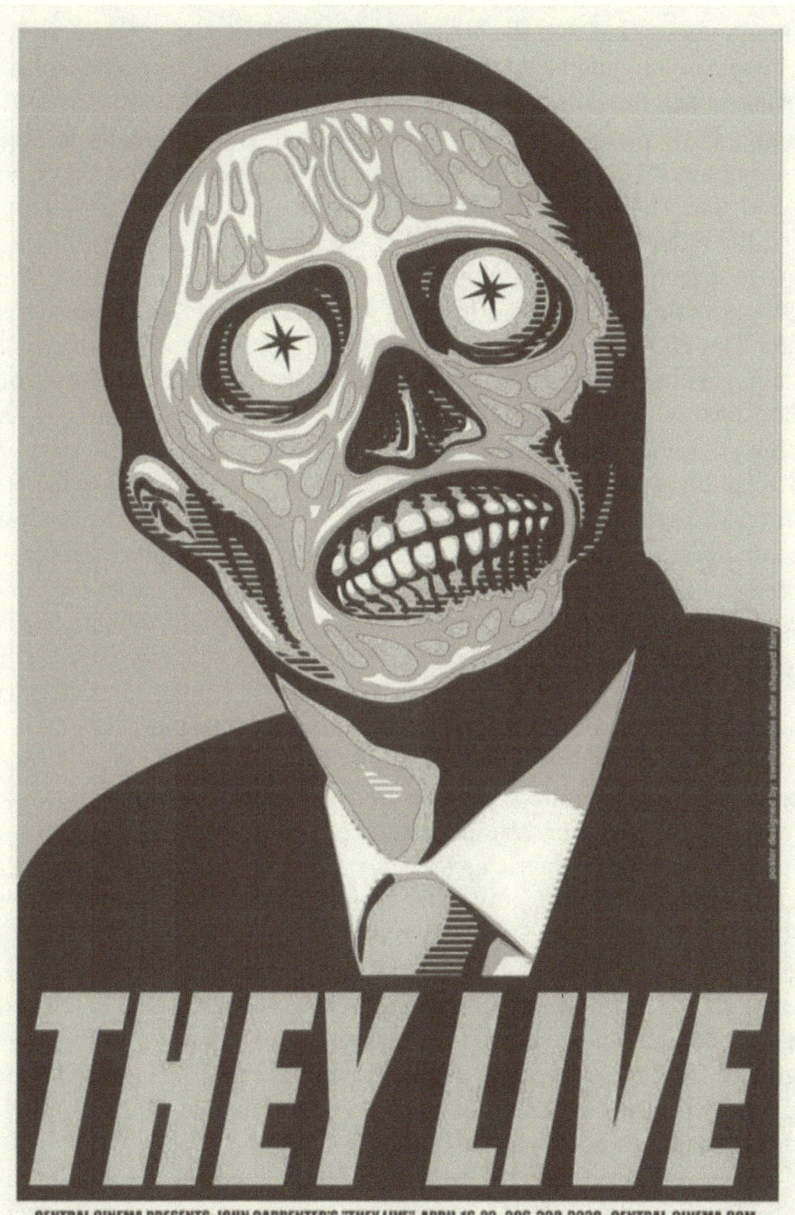

Marc J. Palm (swellzombie) parody of Shepard Fairey's Obama poster made on the occasion of a screening of John Carpenter's *They Live* at Central Cinema, 2010. The Seattle cinema avoided using the image in the context of its concurrent Black History film series. Courtesy of the artist.

wearing the glasses, points out how this black and white messaging does not say enough about race. Are the aliens colourblind?

People might think that Obama's branding problem has been resolved now that he has joined the presidents' club and receives $400,000 fees for delivering democracy boilerplate in as many as 50 speeches given annually to oligarchs and billionaires worldwide.[61] In a speech in South Africa, Obama cheerfully confessed that his bipartisan neoliberal policies exacerbated inequality and fostered the rise of the far right. In 2019, he received close to $600,000 for a conference speech in Bogotá, Columbia, in which he lectured on growth strategies through marketing. Regardless, his fans worship the least of his gestures, like drinking Tim Hortons coffee at a Toronto Raptors NBA game, where he was seen having a chat with the Canadian rapper Drake. Avoiding the thesis of false consciousness, we can safely say that within the two-party system, it is identity and lifestyle rather than socialist politics that have become the best way to mobilize an electoral majority against the Republican right.[62] To what ends?

Political satire about the 'banality of evil' acknowledges the ordinariness that characterizes fame and billion-dollar portfolios. Obama was a relief to everyone as his family's middle-class ordinariness minimized the spectacle of social climbing or the demand to jump and dance for your dinner. The consequence, however, was a 'complex' technocratic 'cool' that Cornel West defines as an attitude that is "well-adjusted to injustice."[63] A longstanding purveyor of everything black and American, and counterpoint to the whiteness of *Life* and *People*, the magazine *Ebony* featured Obama on its August 2008 cover, emerging from a government car like an action-ready G-Man. The crossover copy announces "swagger, confidence and effortless style." This "black cool," which is attributed to "America's hottest singles," who "date without drama," provides tips from "the 25 coolest brothers of all time" on how to "survive foreclosure" and navigate the "two Americas" that remain "separate and unequal" by listening to "the women of gospel." Similarly, an August 2016 cover of *Variety* magazine shows Michelle Obama in front of a photographer's screen with an antique, medallion-shaped portrait painting of an unidentified white lady in the background. The crossover copy reads: "Leading Lady" Michelle Obama uses "her passion, smarts, and entertainment savvy to transition from White House supporting player to beloved media star."

Obama marketed his cool status to "minority" voters like youth, students, women, single mothers, Hispanics, African Americans, Asian Americans and LGBTQ constituencies who feel oppressed by Republican values. In 2008 the John McCain campaign created an anti-Obama attack ad called "Celebrity," which showcased Obama alongside Britney Spears and Paris Hilton. Critics argue that McCain failed to understand that celebrity, rather than warnings of tax increases, was winning Obama votes as a civil rights crusader. During his second term, Obama's hobnobbing with the likes of Beyoncé and Ellen DeGeneres was not only, as Joanna Love argues, a smart combination of celebrity spectacle and hip consumerism, but also an aspect of his advancement by any means necessary.[64] Having won 80 percent of the non-white vote in 2008, and with most white men and half of white women favouring Mitt Romney, Obama targeted those demographics that were demanding government intervention. However, as Diana E. Sheets argues, Obama campaigned in 2012 on demographics rather than economic policy, which would have exposed the failings of his administration. Instead, he won by demonizing Romney and appealing to diversity.[65] Here then is the prejudice of liberal pragmatism against anything that could appear to be too radical and too demanding of citizens than America's next top role model. One would think that by 2018 the mainstream would have had some reason to question the hype. However, marketing often has little or nothing to do with the product. A vote for Obama is akin to an act of 'compensatory consumption' that has symbolic importance in proportion to its significance for social progress.[66] Obama's 2008 campaign strategists ran more negative attack ads than any previous candidate in American politics.[67] If the fallibility of a candidate is definitional of their acceptability, then white and black Americans are in collusion, accepting capitalism as the basis and the standard of everything and anything. Civil rights are reinterpreted in terms of market choice. It is therefore less the case that racism is attenuated through the accession of a black upper class into the ruling plutocracy, than that capitalism has remade race, gender and sexuality into a set of flexible terms whose significance is proportionate to their ability to serve the dominant social and political order. Short of a radical departure from capitalism, the meliorism according to which blacks are succeeding is a matter of *reductio ad absurdum*. The political task is not to become queer, post-racial or post-feminist but anti- and post-capitalist.

For commentators who are impervious to the problems of economic crisis and exploitation, the promise of black capitalism since the creation of Nixon's Office of Minority Business Enterprise and Carter's Minority Business Development Agency has been disappointing only inasmuch as it has failed to deliver.[68] The same system that created white wealth, it seems, should be able to do the same for the blacks who were previously excluded from equality of opportunity. Such ideologues hardly concern themselves with the fact that a black man presided over the destruction of wealth by a yearly average of $4,500 for those in the bottom 99 percent and an increase to the annual earnings of the top one percent by $4.9 million. As some nine million Americans lost their homes, many of them black families who were steered towards subprime loans and who are known by predatory lenders as "mud people," the wealthiest ten percent of black families saw their annual wealth increase by eight percent, or $78,000, 13 percent short of the wealthiest white families. One might think that Obama had to do what was needed to save the economy from meltdown but by 2016 the rate of foreclosures was higher than before he took office.[69] Obama's black capitalism meant the championing of conservative self-help philosophy, leaving most people with little more than S.O.S.[70]

The fact that Obama's record does not make good copy for the gospel of black capitalism has not prevented him from acceding to celebrity status, with more than half of Americans approving of his work in 2018. Post-presidency, the Obamas yacht with billionaires and are developing the same kind of crossover portfolio as Rihanna, earning multi-million dollar deals with corporations like Netflix and Pepsi. Obama now lectures on the democratic benefits of a free market that is loosened from control by government autocrats.[71] Pulitzer-prize winning historian David Garrow concludes his 2017 book *Rising Star: The Making of Barack Obama*, with the view that well before he became President, Obama was a hollow vessel, an assessment that confirms Reed's description of Obama as a vacuous-to-repressive neoliberal.[72] Obama's elevation of process over programme, according to Reed, gave identity politics a role to play in the same middle-class "reformism" that was advocated by Bill Clinton and Tony Blair.[73] His realist anti-ideology has been one of success and pragmatic accommodation to corporate power, leaving leftist goals of social justice to "cranks" and "zealots."[74] Anticipating a possible Trump comeback in 2024, even Sanders conceded to centrists by rebranding his political advocacy group, Our Revolution, with the conciliatory moniker, Pragmatic Progressives.

With the population having gained a sense that political rights in a system founded on economic inequality can hardly bring about radical change, Trump is the politician who seemed to have changed the name of the game – or rather, made sure that it does not change – by feeding the media with celebrity scandal and sending the politics of identity into a tailspin through overt chauvinism. Fighting fire with fire would do little to abate the pauperization of the American working class. According to N.D.B. Connolly, the "third worldization" of the U.S. cannot be resisted through black nationalism or consumer power, as was presumed for example by the Don't Buy Where You Can't Work campaigns.[75] Although black freedom fighters have viewed the public sector as an instrument of state power, the neoliberal privatization of black life demands solidarity rather complicity between blacks and whites. Celebrities of all sorts now have more money than they know how to handle and must hire money managers to diversify their assets and business accounts.[76] The less scrupulous you are with venture capital, the more your celebrity can lead to investments in any random company and business sector. Artists like Jay-Z have even started their own venture capital firms that give advice to other celebrity athletes and artists. People like Chris Bosh, Shaquille O'Neal, Carmelo Anthony, David Beckham, Bono and Elton John are as relevant today to the business page as they are to the sports and entertainment column.[77] When celebrities are not selling products, they champion diversity, fighting for gender equity and crusading for gay rights in an effort to connect with "politicized" millennials.[78] As brands increasingly appropriate political activism and as venture capitalists adorn their profiles with charitable philanthrocapitalism, wokewashing markets a cheap version of social movement justice. Krome brand jeans that are labelled 'Anarchy' allow companies to sell products to young people who want to look good fighting Trump. The clothes, which are made in Shanghai, are referred to by the parent company, Mischief International, as the kind of "fast fashion wokeness" that profits from politics and protest iconography in what is also known as "activism jacking."[79] As progressive messaging is increasingly used to sanitize neoliberal capitalism, politicians like Beto O'Rourke and Amy Klobuchar become barely distinguishable from bland celebrities like Justin Timberlake and Lena Dunham. After a few years in office, the activist candidate AOC began to be as interesting a politician as Selena Gomez is an actress. Her Trumpian nemesis was someone who became known as MTG, an alt-right troglodyte whose gaffes and improprieties made her a better candidate for reform school than Congress.

Various sectors of capitalist and racialist activism came together in a September 2020 issue of *Time* magazine, titled "The New American Revolution." The presentation of some twenty successful black Americans, from Congressman Jamaal Bowman to rising basketball star Mikey Williams, is themed by the Pharrell Williams and Jay-Z song 'Entrepreneur,' a celebration of black entrepreneurial loftiness that shows, in the mix, Obama endorsing his favourite soul food restaurant. That racialist black capitalism should be considered revolutionary is adumbrated by the statement made by Angela Davis to the effect that voting for an "imperfect candidate" like Biden would allow "our movements to flourish." What movement is this? At the same time that the issue was released, Biden had visited the city of Kenosha, where not only was Jacob Blake shot by police but so were two white protesters killed by the 17-year-old vigilante terrorist Kyle Rittenhouse, an ardent fan of Trump. Equally supportive of fascistic policing, Biden said nothing about the matter. Nor did his election platform promise anything to the more than 30 million Americans who were unemployed and the 40 million without health care. In a universe of post-representation, believing in something becomes the equivalent of sacrificing everything.

Not My President

Over the past several years the decolonial movement has demanded and worked with public authorities to remove symbols of America's colonial past that are considered racist or offensive to contemporary viewers. Despite the fact that the trend for such removals has intensified in the age of BLM, not all historical namesakes, monuments and artworks deserve the same sort of antipathy. With mounting enthusiasm for the toppling of symbols of the Confederacy, there has also been some undesirable spillover, such that protest fever leads to instances of copycat indignation. In 2018, the Frank Happersberger sculpture *Early Days*, which depicts a befallen Native American being taught salvation by a Catholic missionary, was removed from the San Francisco Civic Center Plaza. In this instance, the Counter-Reformation logic that conflates the Christian struggle of good over evil with the Jesuit mission of warrior priests, the Inquisition and the Index, merits correction. The question in such cases is what to do with the artwork – destroy it, relocate it to a less prominent site, or re-contextualize it with new signage or new artworks.

The revived passion for bronze statuary in the 1980s and 90s, which emerged after abstract sculpture had lost its radical edge and after postmodern art had restituted figuration and traditional materials, came about in part as a reaction to Maya Lin's 1982 *Vietnam Veterans Memorial*, which by all accounts is one of the most affecting war memorials. Like the conservative administrators who had Richard Serra's *Tilted Arc* removed from Federal Plaza, Reagan-era conservatives who could not tolerate the existence of a powerful anti-war monument in D.C. had to ruin the experience of the VVM by adding the nearby bronzes *The Three Soldiers* and the *Vietnam Women's Memorial*. These monuments were created around the same time that Sylvester Stallone was petitioning the Philadelphia Museum of Art to keep his Rocky Balboa likeness on the museum's monumental stairway, just a few hundred yards from the Rodin Museum. The desire of reactionaries to have the last word on even the war dead has led to at least two monumental abominations around the Washington Mall, the *Korean War Veterans Memorial* and the *Franklin Delano Roosevelt Memorial*. The abstraction versus realism issue in public art also informed 1980s debates about public sites of Holocaust commemoration, some of this devolving into disaster tourism. If imagined communities, as Benedict Anderson called them, are held together by institutions like the museum, the archive and the census, the universality that once allowed people to be considered the same in both their essence and in their inalienable rights gave way to variations on some rather dismal theme parks, from Auschwitz and Chernobyl to animal safaris and sex tourism.[80] For the conscientious, today's political correctness offers lessons in the kind of "mindful travel" that Dean MacCannell once referred to as the postmodern fantasy of consumption without exploitation.[81] After 9/11 and the War on Terror, and as labour precarity was taking its toll, the culture at large swung from its creative class museum and university expansion phase to its activist phase of the 2000s. Deconstructing museums gave way to protesting them. As hashtag activism became increasingly mainstream, protest art all but abandoned radical political aims, promoting issues in ways that are more snobbish than subversive.

While the American Museum of Natural History debated what to do with James Earle Fraser's 1940 Theodore Roosevelt Equestrian Memorial, the 2019 Fourth of July holiday was celebrated in Washington with General Trump's 'Salute to America' parade of warplanes, tanks and armoured cars.[82] Trump's donning of military regalia made it all the more inconceivable why the University of Indiana decided it was time to remove a 1933 Thomas Hart Benton mural titled *A Social History of Indiana*, which shows the Klu Klux Klan burning crosses in the midst of Depression era labour struggles, industry, racial poverty and mass entertainment. The murals also depict a lynching and a slave auction. The KKK, which remains active in Indiana, had been shown in the late 1920s to have ties to the government, not unlike the right-wing militias that stormed the Capitol building on January 6, 2021, and the far-right military agents who escorted the Canadian Freedom Convoy in February 2022. All the more reason to preserve the work. The massive murals have been defamed on the grounds that the school's diversity policy states that students have the right to freedom from discrimination.[83] One would think that the students are rather being protected from education and valuable artwork. The University of Notre Dame decided to cover up murals of the life of Christopher Columbus because they glorify European settlers at the expense of Native Americans. Despite the quality and interest of the work, the stand-alone figure of Columbus is low-hanging fruit by today's standards, when black mayors consider removing statues of even Abraham Lincoln.[84] A statue of Columbus in New York City's central park has so far been kept in situ, but one can anticipate that monuments to explorers and colonialist slavers may soon find themselves in something similar to Budapest's Memento Park, where Stalinist statues were rounded up for tourists to gawk at before their eventual destruction or auction.

With all of this getting our house in order, one might think that we are experiencing a new phase of iconoclasm, seemingly revolutionary, except for the fact that there is no Thermidorean Cult of the Supreme Being nor any newly formed International. Perhaps we have arrived at Aldous Huxley's brave new world, where in the Cathedral of Ford people are taught that history is bunk. In the age of biocapitalist activism, when musicians, novelists, playwrights, painters, filmmakers and museum personnel are being subject to cancelation and various other forms of reprisal, the perfect Twitter storm of progressive neoliberalism has less the whiff of Puritan bleach and more the odour of teen spirit: here we are now. Whereas the context for avant-garde experimentation more or less disappeared by the end of the recessionary 70s, with the 80s appetite for Victorian holidays and corporate hedonism filling the void, the universalist premises of progressive art and politics suffered a setback that is a society-wide problem now that the politics of difference is also wielded by the management.

Since academic postmodernists have assailed Enlightenment humanism for the sake of institutionalized capitalism rather than class struggle, politics is now conditioned by macro- and micro-fascist reinscription. One incident stands out as particularly revealing of today's woke wars. In June of 2019, the San Francisco Unified School District (SFUSD) Board of Education voted unanimously to destroy 13 Works Progress Administration murals made by Victor Arnautoff in 1936 for the George Washington High School. The *Life of George Washington Murals* depict episodes from the life of the revolutionary leader and first President of the United States. In addition to Robert Boardman Howard's exterior entrance low-reliefs of Thomas Edison, William Shakespeare and George Washington, the murals are integrated into the streamlined architecture of the building. There are also two 1936 murals in the school library, one by Lucien Labaudt and one by Ralph Stackpole, and another mural just outside the library painted by Gordon Langdon. There are in addition three monumental low-relief friezes that surround the school yard that depict athleticism. These were sculpted in 1941 by Sargent Johnson, one of the few African-American artists working in the WPA. The building was designed by Timothy Pflueger and J.R. Miller. Pflueger, who was one of the most acclaimed architects in San Francisco at that time, planned all of the murals and low-relief sculptures as part of an integrated whole. The main entrance lobby, where the Arnautoff murals are located, has not undergone any considerable changes since the building of the school eight decades ago. Although Arnautoff's other San Francisco mural projects from this period are protected as registered heritage sites, the effort to include the Washington murals as an integral part of the school building's landmark status had not materialized by the time the School Board decided to get rid of them.

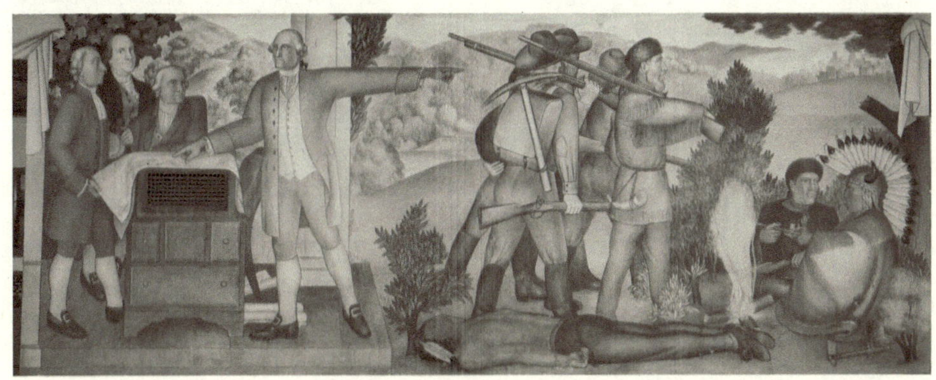

Victor Arnautoff, "Westward Vision," fresco mural, George Washington High School, San Francisco, 1936. Image courtesy of Dick Evans.

In the late 1960s, one of two murals was the cause of student complaints and these two murals are the reason why the Board decided in 2019 to destroy all 13 murals. One of these, titled "Westward Vision," shows Washington with members of his cabinet – Thomas Jefferson, Alexander Hamilton and Benjamin Franklin – overlooking the new constitution as though a map of the future of the country. A trained surveyor, Washington was also a skilled mapmaker. He points westward with his arm stretched out, almost like a statue of Lenin. In the centre-right of the mural, in this critique of Manifest Destiny, four pioneer explorers in *grisaille* walk over and to the side of a dead and prostrate Native American. The dead figure is larger than any of the other figures. His size alone underscores the anti-illusionistic and allegorical devices that Arnautoff used to encourage viewers to reflect on the meaning of the mural. On the far right of the panel, a frontiersman and a Native American chief sit at a campfire smoking a peace pipe. A tomahawk is laid at the feet of the chief and a white fabric is wrapped around a tree with a broken branch, which symbolizes the breaking of peace treaties. Insofar as the artist wished to emphasize colonial misadventures, as white settlers attempted but failed to enslave Native Americans, Arnautoff knowingly built into the work representations of the troubling realities of American history. The panel leaves no doubt that the artist was aware of the tragic aspects of westward expansion and so he planned the experience of this mural to have both a graphic and a reflexive character.

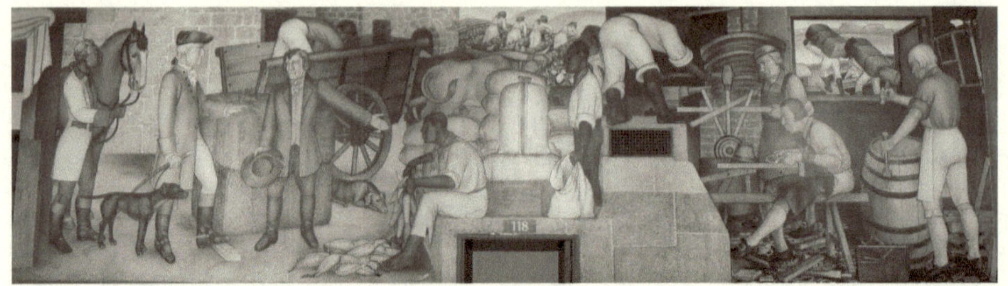

Victor Arnautoff, "Mount Vernon," fresco mural, George Washington High School, San Francisco, 1936. Image courtesy of Dick Evans.

The other controversial mural, titled "Mount Vernon," is a depiction of black slaves on Washington's plantation estate in Virginia. When Washington inherited Ferry Farm from his father, he also inherited ten slaves. After his half-brother's widow died, he became the owner of Mount Vernon, which he had been managing for a decade already, experimenting with as many as 60 different crops and exporting fish as well as flour and cornmeal. He hired indentured servants from Europe to train slaves in trade skills. By 1770, with some 300 slaves on his Virginia plantation, Washington was one of the wealthiest men in the state. On the right side of the panel, a black slave assists three white carpenters who are making barrels. At the far right, a window opens onto an outdoor vista where two other black slaves haul bundles on their backs. These are most likely cotton bales. Bales are repeated on the left side of the panel, where, in the foreground, Washington is leaning on two huge bundles and talking with his white straw boss as a black valet waits with his horse. This house slave looks up at another black man stooped over in a hay cart. The manager gestures towards a black slave worker who is seated and shucking corn. His co-worker is looking on, as though waiting for Washington to leave before resuming his chores. The size of the bales beside Washington gives an indication of their weight, which makes the strength of the workers one of the themes of the painting. The seated slave is pictured sitting on the 'natural' stone of the school building, which is unpainted in parts and integrates the reality of the school building, and those who built it, with the work of labourers in the past.

In addition to this already complex programme, Arnautoff included at the top and centre of the panel four black female slaves working in a cotton field in biomechanical formation. This vignette appears like an image within an image and functions as the 'boss' or keystone of the work. Its message is the dictatorship of the proletariat. One thinks of similar works like Dmitrii Moor's *Gather the Harvest* of 1931. As this frame looks like a picture on a wall, it alludes to the mural itself as an image about work. The most widely reproduced image in the nineteenth century, Jean-François Millet's 1857 painting *The Gleaners*, was a sentimental image of three peasant women gleaning the wheat left over from a harvest. Associated with socialism, and as such with revolutionary impulses, Millet's image was popular with the public but not with the ruling class. One thinks also of Kazimir Malevich's *Black Square*, which was hung like an icon in the corner of his *0.10* exhibition of Suprematist works in 1915. This picture within a picture is significant also in relation to the mural Arnautoff would make in 1939 for the Linden, Texas, post office, titled *Cotton Pickers*, which he is known to have made into lithographic reproductions at the same time that he lectured on the art made in the Russian village of Palekh, a miniature painting technique used for icons and boxes. Arnautoff's Mount Vernon cotton pickers thus allude to the political art and propaganda posters of the European and Soviet avant garde. As such, they could be said to serve various political interests: the Roosevelt administration; the social function of a typical vocational school; the cross-race solidarity of the labour and communist movement at that time; the prospects of international socialism. Fascism was on the rise throughout Europe when Arnautoff made these murals. The Popular Front against fascism and war had been proclaimed official policy by the Soviet Union, the U.S. and allied European nations. The Popular Front distinguished its use of symbols of patriotism and the defence of national independence from fascist chauvinism. This led the Communist Party (CPUSA), under the leadership of Earl Russell Browder, to supported FDR's New Deal at the same time that it encouraged American patriotism.

In terms of the race politics of these two panels, we are shown how white settlers, from the eighteenth through to the nineteenth century, justified African slavery and the dispossession of Native lands on the basis that Europeans were more hardworking than "savages." The virtues of labour exploitation and land use provided ideological justification for what was considered the dreadful but necessary violence of conquest and colonial expansion. The murals themselves, however, were produced in the midst of the Great Depression and at the height of the labour movement in the U.S., when white and black workers pitched their struggle together against capitalist interests in the North and South. The murals are therefore not only a monument to Washington, but to the class consciousness that was spearheaded by the socialist movement during the Red Decade and which, after the government crackdown on communism, correlated with the Civil Rights movement of the 1960s. The attention to the humanity of the Natives and blacks that are depicted in the murals is demonstrated through their manliness and physical strength, a common feature of both Socialist Realist art and Art Deco modernism, which idealize humanity's self-production and the possibility this creates for emancipation from the conditions of scarcity.

The objections to the Arnautoff murals are not merely due to their depiction of the most troubling aspects of American history, but the ways in which the works compel viewers to think critically about art and politics. The murals are a Federal Arts Project commission produced by a Russian emigre artist who moved to the U.S. in 1925, studied at the California School of Fine Art and later learned fresco painting with the famed Mexican muralist Diego Rivera. By the mid-1930s, Arnautoff was one the most recognized artists in San Francisco. The murals in the GWHS were made in the summer of 1936 and commissioned by the Works Progress Administration, a New Deal arts programme for unemployed artists. Using the wet plaster technique, or *buon fresco*, Arnautoff and his assistants George Harris and Gorden Landen produced nine feet of work every day, often working ten and twelve-hour days so that the plaster did not dry before the paint pigment could be applied. Made over the course of ten months, the murals cover more than 1,600 square feet and are in their very method of production a monument to labour. As with most social realist work from the 1930s, the murals situate its protagonist in the midst of a history from below and seen through the everyday lives of ordinary people. Arnautoff's realistic representation of slavery and allegorical representation of genocide is consistent with the radical sensibilities of leftists and progressives in that era. Like many artists who worked on WPA projects, Arnautoff was a member of several radical organizations, including the San Francisco Artists and Writers Union, the American Artists Congress and the Communist Party, which he joined in 1937. In 1956 he was investigated and interrogated by the House Un-American Activities Committee due to a "communist conspiracy" caricature he made of Vice-President Richard Nixon, who had at that time been involved in the McCarthyite persecution of communists. Arnautoff moved to the Soviet Union in 1963, where he died in 1979. Robert W. Cherny, a San Francisco State University professor who wrote a monograph about the artist, argued at a 2018 Board of Education meeting that with these murals Arnautoff was very consciously representing slavery and genocide in an effort to challenge the storybook representations of Washington that students were taught in the 1930s.[85]

Arnautoff's 1934 works for the Coit Tower in San Francisco was the first major New Deal art project and served as a model in the way that it combined the diversity of the American scene with the influence of the Mexican mural movement. According to Cherny, this included a preoccupation with the lives of working people and the advancement of social change through left-wing political causes.[86] As Arnautoff became more deeply involved in socialist struggles, his work was more readily understood as sympathetic to communism. Although he had been a cavalry officer in the White Army, he was partial to Lenin's New Economic Policy. Like Rivera, he was decidedly anti-Stalinist. His sympathy for communism was based on a feeling of solidarity with ordinary people but not on a picturesque and sentimental perception of them as victims. Unlike most of his contemporaries, he included in his works imagery of non-white workers. This, if nothing else, explains the presence of Native American workers in the corner of the triangular "American Revolution" panel in the stairwell of the school, and the black workers in the corner of the facing "Life of Washington" mural. In the latter, Native Americans occupy a central role alongside George Washington, who served as an officer for the Virginia Regiment. Hardly given to the grotesque, the mural introduces the *dramatis personae* of this phase of Washington's life, with care given to the accurate depiction of soldiers' uniforms and Native dress.

As not only a businessman but a socialite, Washington's political career began with his role in protests against the British taxation of the colonies. The Royal Proclamation that controlled the territories west of the Alleghenies and the Stamp Act that taxed printed matter so as to fund the British occupation of the colonies led to the Declaration of Independence and the American Revolution of 1776. In the centre of the "American Revolution" panel is a small depiction of the Boston Massacre of 1770, an incident in which British soldiers fired on a mob, killing five people. The bottom of the mural shows protests against the Townshend Acts of 1767-68, a series of taxation measures that led to the Boston Tea Party of 1773, which is alluded to in the upper left section of the mural. The two Indians who carry bundles onto a ship represent the Sons of Liberty who disguised themselves as Mohawk warriors to avoid detection. The image also demonstrates identification with the cause of independence. One of the beneficiaries of the Tea Act of 1773 was the British East India Company, a joint-stock company with holdings in the East Indies, Southeast Asia and China, which makes the connection between different versions of "Indian" labour throughout the British empire, East and West – a vast system of colonial rule that required the presence of colonial armies and administrations. Famine in Bengal India caused the East India Company to impose the Tea Act on the American colonies to avoid bankruptcy. Opposed to the East India Company's monopoly on tea, some 30 to 130 protesters dressed as Mohawk warriors, boarded three British ships and dumped some 300 bundles of tea into the Boston harbour. The British Parliament's punitive reaction then set off the American revolutionary war.

Having been nominated by John and Samuel Adams as commander in chief of the Continental Army, Washington is shown at the right of the "American Revolution" mural, where the assembled cheer the hoisting of the new American flag. The choice of Washington was due to the belief that he was best able to unite the colonies. The remaining episodes from during and after the Revolution are dispersed throughout the other smaller murals, with depictions of the arrival of Lafayette, von Steuben and Pulaski (in an homage to David's *Oath of the Horatii*), the winter at Valley Forge, the victory over the Hessians at Trenton, Washington's mediation as President of the views of Andrew Hamilton and Thomas Jefferson, Washington's effort to create a national university and Washington greeting Martha Washington. Washington eventually gave her his will, a document through which he awarded freedom to his slaves. Of the 317 slaves at Mount Vernon, Washington set free 123 individuals. Those slaves who could not be freed by law, because they had been part of Martha Washington's dower property, were provided with sick and elder care. Slave orphans were taught to read and trained in trade skills until the age of 25, when they could be freed. This was not an act of generosity on Washington's part, but an acknowledgement, against the perceptions of many educated men at that time, and against purely material interests, of the humanity of the black slaves who were bonded into forced labour on account of their second-class status. In addition to celestial phenomena, a ceiling mural shows Liberty placing thirteen new stars in the firmament. All of this imagery is presented in charmingly colourful drawings with simple outlines, modest naturalism and a modicum of modernist abstraction. A high school should be so lucky to be designed with art of this degree of interest and quality.

Like Arnautoff's 1934-35 murals in the Protestant chapel at the Presidio, the GWHS murals went against the stereotypical portrayal of Indians at that time. Like most of his social realist contemporaries, Arnautoff rejected art for art's sake and made art that he defined as "the materialization of human thought and emotion."[87] The murals are not incitements to racism, they are indictments of brutality and homages to the dignity of all humans. The GWHS murals represented the largest mural project in the Bay Area at the time and were funded through the Federal Arts Project component of the WPA, which created jobs for unemployed artists and commissioned works for public buildings. Arnautoff is not known to have said anything about his critical take on the schoolbook narrative about the founding fathers and westward expansion. Regardless, according to Cherny,

> Arnautoff's mural makes clear that slave labor provided the plantation's economic basis. On the facing wall Arnautoff was even more direct: the procession of spectral future pioneers move west over the body of a dead Indian, challenging the prevailing narrative that westward expansion had been into largely vacant territory waiting for white pioneers to develop its full potential. For Arnautoff, "the spirit of Washington's time" included not only the struggle for liberty and the founding of a new nation but also chattel slavery and the slaughter of Native Americans.[88]

Immediately after finishing the Washington murals, Arnautoff went to work as an instructor of fresco painting at the California School of Fine Arts where less than ten years previously he had been thought to be a "good student."[89] By this time, FDR's New Deal had begun to worry conservatives that the country was on a slippery slope towards socialism. Undeterred, Arnautoff joined the Communist Party (CPUSA) and shortly afterwards raised funds for the Republican campaign against Franco's fascists in the Spanish Civil War. In 1949 he taught courses at the California Labor School and Graphic Arts Workshop to working-class students who were interested in Marxism-Leninism and the latest theories of art, economics, management and psychology. Seminars focused on the relationship between culture, labour and social struggles, as well as the debasement of culture by monopoly capitalism. Lectures were given there by people like W.E.B. Du Bois, Paul Robeson, Pete Seeger, Edward Weston and Imogen Cunningham.

The more one learns about Arnautoff's work, the more one understands his humanistic feeling and his anti-fascist, socialist sensibilities, the less there is cause for wanting the murals removed. It is an irony of history that Arnautoff's defence of Anton Refregier's murals for a San Francisco post office, which depicted labour struggles as well as anti-Chinese violence, could be used in defence of his own murals today. Arnautoff wrote: "In our days of artificially created hysteria, it becomes somewhat of a distinction to be a target of political bigotry. If reactionary elements begin to attack someone or something – the target of the attack must be something worthwhile, something progressive."[90] Arnautoff was eventually placed under surveillance by the FBI and blacklisted by HUAC. The George Washington High School murals are an artistic testament to a radical leftist vision that today remains controversial and for that reason is all the more vital.

When the murals became the object of renewed controversy, the conservative members of the School Board established a review process that was biased in several ways: they ignored public opinion, the professional advice of the cultural sector and the majority of students, approximately 85-95 percent of whom were in favour of preserving the murals; they accepted and inflated the rhetoric of protesters that the murals cause trauma to students and promote racism; they manipulated mass media reporting to make the issue seem like more of a controversy than it is; they threatened the destruction of important and valued artworks as a means to raise their personal profiles as neoliberal technocrats. From a professional point of view, the so-called controversy is an open and shut case. However, and because the Arnautoff murals are not owned by the General Services Administration fine arts collection, they are subject to the decisions of School Board members, who have proven themselves better at public mismanagement and community consultation manipulation than they are in Art, History or Civics.

The consultation process was slanted from the start. The former School Board vice-president, now commissioner, Mark Sanchez, insisted that the Board is listening and learning from those people who claim that the murals are harmful.[91] Unfortunately, Sanchez and former Board president Stevon Cook did not learn from professional advice or from the community at large.[92] While the GWHS was under review by San Francisco Heritage as a historical landmark, these Board members worried that heritage status would prevent them from destroying the murals. They solved their problem by appointing a Reflection and Action Working Group community advisory committee to consider whether or not the allegorical depiction of genocide and realist depiction of slavery are offensive to Native Americans and African Americans. After several public meetings between December 2018 and February 2019, the Working Group, which consisted of school district representatives, school representatives, students, local Native American community representatives, local artists and historians, decided ten to one, with two abstaining, in favour of removing the murals on the hearsay that they contribute to the trauma of these two minority groups. The conclusive report that was issued by the Working Group states:

> We come to these recommendations due to the continued historical and current trauma of Native Americans and African Americans with these depictions in the mural that glorifies slavery, genocide, colonization, manifest destiny, white supremacy, oppression, etc. This mural doesn't represent SFUSD values of social justice, diversity, united, student-centered. It's not student-centered. It's not student-centered if it's focused on the legacy of artists, rather than the experience of the students. If we consider the SFUSD equity definition, the "low" mural glorifies oppression instead of eliminating it. It also perpetuates bias through stereotypes rather than ending bias. It has nothing to do with equity or inclusion at all. The impact of this mural is greater than its intent ever was. It's not a counter-narrative if [the mural] traumatizes students and community members.[93]

By July 2019, all 13 murals were to be destroyed. Their destruction was estimated to cost between $645,000 and $825,000, a significant amount for an insolvent school district. Some less destructive spirits suggested that appropriate signage or an off-campus interpretation centre could satisfy the concerns of Native American people in the Bay Area. However, the demolition that is at issue has less to do with the Arnautoff murals than with some Board members' perception of the suitability of George Washington as the namesake of the school, a race-first mentality that is supposedly concerned with combatting white supremacy, but that is better understood as part of a reactionary neoliberal agenda. The key indicator of this is the anti-Enlightenment and anti-revolutionary tenets of Board members who champion race fundamentalism for the sake of ruling-class power. Failing to appreciate the mural movement of the 1930s as a democratic offensive that worked to take art beyond the privileged realms of wealthy homes and museums, and into everyday realms, a clique of self-appointed representatives of minority constituencies was enabled by Board members to plan the destruction of valuable art and deny students a unique window on more than one era of American history.

As mentioned, controversy surrounding the murals is not new. In the late 1960s the school's Black Student Union, headed by Roosevelt Thomas, a member of the Black Panther Party, demanded that the SFUSD correct these depictions. Some 250 students protested in the fall of 1968, demanding that the murals be removed.[94] After students voted to save the murals, a decision to alleviate the situation was reached by commissioning the African-American muralist Dewey Crumpler to make new murals that celebrate Asian-American, Hispanic, Native-American and African-American culture. Titled *Multi-Ethnic Heritage: Black, Asian, Native/Latin American*, Crumpler's three-mural cycle was completed in 1974. Now a teacher at the San Francisco Art Institute, he says that in 1966-68 many African-American students who had been mobilized by race riots demanded that the Mount Vernon mural be destroyed and that Crumpler, who was a member of a Bay Area black arts organization, be commissioned to make a replacement work. Crumpler argues that black students at that time did not understand the work and were simply shocked to see a depiction of African-American slaves. He later studied mural painting in Mexico, where he met David Alfaro Siqueiros and Pablo O'Higgins. When he returned, he explained the Arnautoff works to his peers and refused to be involved in their destruction. At the dedication to his murals, one of the black student leaders stated to the assembled: "I want you to know, and I want this audience to know, that if I understood what Arnautoff was doing, I would never have reacted the way I did."[95] Other African-American students also issued an apology for having failed at the time of the protests to fully appreciate the value of the works. In response to the 2019 decision to destroy the murals, Crumpler argued that to destroy the Arnautoff murals is to destroy his as well.

Crumpler is not alone in defending the murals. Among the groups and institutions who defended these artworks was the California College of the Arts, the San Francisco Art Institute, the San Francisco Museum of Modern Art, the Fine Arts Museum of San Francisco, the United Public Workers for Action, the National New Deal Preservation Association, the *Los Angeles Times* Editorial Board, the San Francisco chapter of the NAACP, the College Art Association and the National Coalition Against Censorship.[96] An open letter and petition started by *Nonsite* was signed by as many as 400 scholars and artists.[97] Many of the GWHS teachers and students defended the murals as one of the best things about the school and a campaign to save them was launched by the George Washington High School Alumni Association.[98] A petition on Change.org was also started by the Russian Community Council of the USA. Defenders of the work argue that the murals were designed to make visible the injustices of colonial America and should not be confused with symbols of the Confederacy whose intent is to legitimize racism. The San Francisco Arts Commission has not advised on the conservation of the murals and defers to the SFUSD School Board since the latter has legal jurisdiction over them. Contrary to much news reporting, many Native Americans, chiefs, elders, one member of the American Indian Movement, African-American artists and concerned San Francisco professionals of various sorts supported the preservation of the murals.

School officials, a small number of students and parents, and some local Native Americans, were divided about the murals. Some insisted on their importance and the realities of history. Others argued that whitewashing the walls would provide reparation to descendants of slaves and Native Americans. Overall, those who argued against the murals, and who acted as representatives of community groups, had a decidedly much weaker case. Professional and public opinion was not on their side. The tenor of their confused complaints speaks volumes about the ways in which culture and politics are today conditioned by the logic of victimhood and not by solidarity across struggles. Although there had not been any further controversy since the heady days of 1968, the issue was revived in 2016 when Amy Anderson decided to enrol her son at the school. Noticing the murals, she unilaterally decided that they should be erased, enlisting in the process Mariposa Villaluna, an activist who helped to have the Happersberger statue removed. The two drafted a resolution that they sent to Sanchez, which resulted in the creation of the Reflection and Action Working Group Committee, which by many accounts was eager to do the bidding of the Board and the murals' critics. At a June 25 meeting, Anderson called on people to be racially and socially woke and to end white supremacy by taking down "a racist mural."[99] The sad reality is that the people at the meeting who were on the opposite side of the so-called debate with people like Anderson were either Indigenous themselves or educators who have likely taught students about nineteenth-century stereotypes of the vanishing Indian. Anderson's associate, Villaluna, who was a member of the advisory committee, has stated: "We all decided those are ideas we do not want to follow through with because we didn't want anybody to see or re-traumatize or get PTSD again. ... We don't want kids to go through the trauma anymore."[100] Although no research confirms that teenage students have suffered from PTSD or trauma on account of the murals, this storyline has been promoted by the School Board and the media. In addition, neither the Board nor the critics of the murals have made the slightest effort to distinguish between the alleged effects of the work and its meaning. The total absence of art theory and art history from the discussion was abetted by efforts to ontologize the reception of the murals along racial lines. Moreover, where history is in fact invoked by the murals' critics, the public sense of history is replaced by the uses of history to confer identity.

Among the many arguments and statements that have been made to the media by both school officials and community members, one finds the following claims: the murals are racist, stereotypical and defend white supremacist values; the imagery is harmful and miseducates students; there are better ways to teach history; there are other depictions of history available; destroying the murals will right the wrongs of the past; white artists do not have the right to depict the history of Indigenous and black people or tell them how they feel about the murals; Arnautoff's intentions cannot be known and are irrelevant. Those who argued that the murals portray Indians as defeated ignore the prominence of Indian warriors in the two entrance murals, which depict their participation in the Revolutionary wars. Those who focused only on black slaves ignored the co-presence of indentured white servants. In contrast, many pointed to the fact that the murals show very clearly that Washington was a slaver and was partly responsible for the genocide of First Nations.

Given the contrasting viewpoints, and beyond the question of whether or not any community group should have more say on the matter than the public at large, the reduction of history, art and politics to questions of identity and suffering leads to reductionist forms of race metaphysics. Identity, in this instance, serves two purposes: it covers over the shortcomings of the murals' critics and it gives cover to the regressive, neoliberal politics of the School Board. With all of the fraudulent concern shown for students, it is encouraging that most of them disagreed with the show trial atmosphere that was created. Among the 49 student freshmen who were asked by schoolteacher Barbara A. Brewer to write about the murals, only four thought they should be destroyed.[101]

The same sort of punditry that one finds in politics developed around the GWHS murals debate as tight-format news media presented both sides of the issue as though they have equal validity. If Obama was too black to fail, Arnautoff, in this latter-day HUAC show trial, would seem to be too much of a brocialist advocate of New Deal democratic socialism to succeed. Decisions about the murals should have been distributed across fields of competence and communities of interest rather than reduced to narrow uses of media visibility and manipulation. Mark Seltzer once suggested that trauma in the pathological public sphere is a normalized aspect of today's news and entertainment industry, interpreted by Arthur Kroker and Michael Weinstein in quasi-Marxist verbiage as the media's intoxication with "abuse value."[102] When people are treated and treat themselves as incompetent victims, the next step is the securitization of the classroom and the reduction of education to the capitalization of bland educational products and services. Regarding the San Francisco controversy, art critic Charles Desmarais says that he fears the day when the public sphere will be nothing more than an innocuous and commercial environment.[103] As Mark Lewis once wrote concerning public controversies, people in positions of authority often defer to an indefinite notion of 'the public' and 'public opinion' that can be colonized at the same time that the public's custodial role is both differentiated by democratic pluralism and objectified by capitalist interests.[104] In the era of global capitalism, the shock doctrine, as Naomi Klein calls it, construes controversies in such a way as to never let a good disaster go to waste.[105] Amidst the chaos that disaster capitalism creates, conservatives seek to finesse further concessions against democracy.

In 2016, Matt Haney, the former President of the San Francisco Board of Education had considered changing the names of those schools in the district that were named after slave owners.[106] Maya Angelou was considered as an alternative for the GWHS since she had studied there for a short while. This strategy was revived by the Board in July 2020 in the midst of the coronavirus pandemic and as governments were enforcing back-to-work and back-to-school policies. Meena Harris, the niece of Kamala Harris and Director of the Phenomenal Women Action Campaign, a woke branding company, started a Change.org petition to have the name of the GWHS changed to honour Angelou, who is memorialized elsewhere. This ridiculous suggestion was rejected by even Elliott Jones, Angelou's grandson.[107] A court order issued through the GWHS Alumni Association managed to suspend 44 possible name changes throughout the district.[108] There is clearly more to this case than the murals themselves. Some sense of what is happening can be related to the decision by Democratic Party operatives to remove the names of Thomas Jefferson and Andrew Jackson from their annual Jefferson-Jackson dinners.[109] In the spirit of diversity and inclusiveness, and as the DP abandons labour politics, replacing economic justice with identitarian liberalism, the names of the slaveholder Jefferson and the Jackson who authorized Indian removal policies stand in the way of progressive neoliberalism. The Jefferson who drafted the Declaration of Independence and supported the abolition of despotism, and whose social reformism has been associated with the New Deal, is now an embarrassment to a party that is dedicated to the interests of war hawks and the billionaire class.

Mojo Morality

The notion that the Arnautoff murals are racist is a dead letter that says more about the people who have been stirring controversy than the work itself. If there is an impact or effect attributed to the work, it is mostly because critics are simply on the wrong side of the issue. In addition to the facts about the murals themselves, the controversy was manipulated in various ways to further competing partisan agendas. The "centrist" journalist Bari Weiss cited Robby Soave, the author of a book on "panic attacks" in the age of Trump, who suggests that the demand for safe spaces, trigger warnings and top-down protection against microaggression cannot be extended from K-12 to all of society. Weiss argues: "By now stories of progressive Puritanism (or perhaps the better word is Philistinism) are so commonplace – snowflakes seek safe space! – that it can feel tedious to track the details of the latest outrage."[110] Similarly, conservative legal analyst and pundit Lionel (Michael William Lebron) conferred to the news network Russia Today that social justice warriors are turning history into hysteria, a moral panics that is no longer about delinquent teens, but that is being orchestrated in the name of teens who are not happy with the curriculum and anything that may trigger unhappiness, including the Egyptian pyramids, geometry and Shakespeare.[111]

The complaint that GWHS students have been known to say things like "let's meet under the dead Indian" second guesses their ability to distinguish between fact and fancy, leading to the kind of education where students are treated as passive clients rather than imaginative young adults. Various other conservatives fanned the flames of the culture war, defending American symbols from the sort of anti-discrimination policies that seek to guarantee protection from even the most innocuous of harms.[112] Much of this type of commentary reiterates Greg Lukianoff and Jonathan Haidt's rejection of "offendedness sweepstakes," where the taking of offence becomes the basis for an ever-diminishing level of acceptable speech.[113] Somewhat more constructively, Brian T. Allen focuses on the Board instead of the students, suggesting that better-informed trustees should self-correct so as to maintain standards and avoid stupid mistakes.[114] Despite some red-baiting, Allen is able to state the obvious: Arnautoff was a reputed artist who was commissioned by the WPA for important projects; his depictions of Washington are multi-layered and courageously include the realities of slavery and genocide; the murals remain relevant in new ways over time and people learn from them; the murals are integrated into important civic architecture; most students and most sensible people do not want the murals destroyed; the School Board is going against its mission of public service; the cost of destroying the murals is a ridiculous sum that would be better used for their conservation.

It is a sad state of affairs when the conservative right has a better sense of the value of radical artworks than "progressive" neoliberals who are in actuality doing the work of the fascist right. This situation led to the intervention of a few Democratic Party politicians who were worried that the School Board's decision was making Democrats seem out of touch, thereby giving ammunition to the Trump campaign during an election cycle. Former San Francisco mayor Willie Brown compared the protesters' bullying tactics to the behaviour of Trump supporters. A statement by Brown to the effect that shouting people down is no way to debate public issues was followed up with a CNN report on a shouting match in front of the murals.[115] Former mayor Dianne Feinstein also rejected the Board's decision. Democratic Party strategist Bob Shrum tweeted: "Just because others are nuts, doesn't mean we have to be."[116] Strategist Mike Semler proposed a ballot measure to save the murals and created an advocacy group to save New Deal art called the Coalition to Protect Public Art. Around this time, the international press compared the School Board to the Taliban.[117]

Despite their reasonableness, these Democratic Party defenders of the murals tend to ignore the problems of neoliberalism. Writing for the Internationalist Group and the League for the Fourth International, Jack Heyman reported that among the officials who have orchestrated this sham, the superintendent of the School District, Vincent Matthews, was once the principal of a for-profit charter school that was eventually closed in 2001 because it was purging the school of its minority poor and special-needs children. As a state administrator of the Oakland Unified School District, Matthews was known to be a union buster, denying pay raises for the lowest paid teachers and demanding increases to class sizes, causing problems for teachers' unions and students. Matthews is also connected to the charterization of schools through the Bill and Melinda Gates Foundation, the Eli and Edythe Broad Foundation and the Walton Family Foundation, organizations whose market-based goals for public education include standardized testing for students, merit pay for teachers and school closures for underperforming schools. These policies have been proven to disadvantage poor students.[118] Stevon Cook is also known to be anti-union and to promote privatization. Mark Sanchez used peer-assisted review programmes to target black, Latino and dissident teachers. Board commissioner Alison Collins, who argued that the murals are white supremacist and that its defenders are allies of the far right, is a promoter of charter schools in low-income communities and is married to the co-founder of a multi-billion-dollar development corporation with ties to Goldman Sachs.

The neoliberal policies of Board and School District members coincide with the racialist agenda of groups like Showing Up for Racial Justice (SURJ) who defended Board members on the basis of their minority identity and compared defenders of the murals to defenders of symbols of the Confederacy.[119] Along these lines, a short article titled "Dear San Francisco: Stop Honoring George Washington And His Bigotry" was written by members of the W.O.K.E. collective Sean Joseph Watson and Harry P. Chavez.[120] The article commends San Francisco for being a left-leaning city, lumping Harvey Milk and Nancy Pelosi in the same local heroes category. Arnautoff, they say, perpetuated the narrative that black people and Native people can only be victims and never heroes. More to the point, art, they say, has been white for too long. The implication here is that there is such a thing as white art and black art. What the Arnautoff case reveals very clearly is the way that neoliberal professionals cater to this racialist mentality.

In contrast to SURJ and the W.O.K.E. collective, the International Longshore and Warehouse Union held a panel discussion on the issue of the murals at a July 9, 2019, Labor Fest event. This same union, among the first to integrate, had a working relationship with the WPA in the 1930s and more recently shut down ports during protests against the Afghanistan and Iraq War. On May 1, 2015, the Union undertook a work stoppage in solidarity with Black Lives Matter. It also sent workers to the Standing Rock Indian Reservation to protest the Dakota Access Pipeline.[121] The goal of ending white supremacy is a class demand that Arnautoff, much to his credit, understood perfectly well, as did most unionists in the 1930s. This perspective has since then been abandoned for the rhetoric of diversity. The San Francisco Socialist Workers Party mayoral candidate, Joel Britton, had a better sense of the big picture when he argued that unbridled censorship tends to work against the working class and minorities.[122] While no one can argue that slavery exists today, at least officially, one can argue nonetheless that wage slavery has not been abolished. If slaves were punished for not meeting their work quotas, and their work quotas could be increased as soon as they were met, how different is this from Amazon warehouse workers who are monitored in their every activity and pressured to outperform one another? When the workers of this now largest employer in the U.S. meet faster fulfilment rates, these rates are increased to the point that employees fear taking the slightest rest break. Most eventually quit from injuries, overwork or are fired. Likewise, truckers working as independent contractors for companies like XPO Logistics and who are told they will eventually own their rig work full-time and end up indebted to what is in actuality an employer. The majority of the students at the GWHS come from working-class families. For reasons that are not difficult to understand, these students appreciate learning about the art of a muralist associated with the workers' movement.

The manipulation of sensitivity in the interest of corporations is now a mainstay of woke capitalism. The wokewashing of labour exploitation has now extended to public services like education. Among the complaints raised during the mural debates was the fact that teachers at the school are underpaid. Teachers across California were on strike in 2018 and 2019 as school budgets and teaching staff were slashed, largely in the interest of regressive tax cuts, leading to a period of school-based activism. There was more strike activity in the U.S. in 2018 than any previous year since 1986. About three quarters of this activity was by teachers in Michigan, Arizona, Colorado, Kentucky, North Carolina and Oklahoma. As with auto workers, there are teachers on strike worldwide. The strikes in California failed in part because teachers, who must sometimes work more than one job, are broke and are pressured by reprisals to not be on strike for very long. Overworked teachers are demanding better pay and smaller class sizes, as well as funding for support staff like librarians, nurses and counsellors. They also want to stop the privatization and charterization of schools. Although teacher salaries in California are relatively high by national standards, the overall cost of housing, cost of living and health care is exorbitant. The 'education wars' threaten charterization by corporate chains that siphon funds from public schools and downsize staff. Too many overpaid administrators and expensive consultants take priority away from the classroom and shift education towards a business model. Keith Brown, the president of the Oakland Education Association, says that school boards are now desperate to build ties with local communities in a struggle for the soul of public education.[123]

After an open house on August 1, 2019, when members of the public were allowed to visit the GWHS to view the Arnautoff murals first-hand, most people expressed their interest in saving them. After a deluge of emails and public pressure, including student opinion, the School Board made a decision that is the bureaucratic version of fetishistic disavowal. The Board made the wise choice to not destroy the murals. However, it followed this with a supplementary decision to cover the murals with boards and obscure them from view, which would allow for the possibility of adding images of "the heroism of people of colour in America" on top of them. This revised decision amounts to a denial of the fact that the school was named after George Washington, that the Crumpler murals already honour people of colour, and the fact that people want the Arnautoff murals saved so that they can be shown and taught as exemplary works of art.[124] Repeating on August 13 the same consultation scenario as the June 27 meeting, Cook manipulated the process a second time, iterated the same clichés about student trauma, SFUSD values and the false notion that the murals are racist and dehumanizing. Board member Collins insisted at the meeting that leftist defenders of the murals are of the same mind as alt-right supporters of the murals who argue that "marginalized kids should toughen up."[125] Collins ignores the fact that rightist views about student "snowflakes" were the product of corporate media sensationalism, which the Board encouraged when it decided to attack the murals on the say-so that they promote racism and cause trauma.

The hype that results from the conflation of leftist views with alt-right white supremacy changes nothing of the fact that it was right-wing capitalists who were sitting on this board, many of them members of minority groups proposing the destruction of important public art in the name of a privatization agenda that burdens the public with social inequality. What the San Francisco case amounted to was an assault by the managerial class to defund the public in the interest of the corporate plutocracy. The artworks, the students and the public were held hostage in a situation in which the corporatization of the curriculum is replacing social solidarity with woke fanaticism. More sensible people spoke out against the plan to cover over the murals. GWHS alumnus Danny Glover denounced the proposal as akin to book burning.[126] Noted author Alice Walker, whose daughter attended the school, and whose words had been used by Cook as justification for the Board's decision, told reporters that the murals should be used to teach history and that the destruction of art is ignorant and backwards.[127]

In a state where many people learn about history from a military-entertainment complex that glorifies superhero righteousness, the debates around the murals have been instructive if not also dispiriting. In July, after scholars had voiced their opposition to the destruction of the murals, the magazine *The Nation* published an article by Jennifer Wilson that reduced the issues and politics to questions of victimhood.[128] For Wilson, the only imaginable reason why someone would come to the defence of such work is because they are complicit with the right wing of the liberal establishment. Efforts to illustrate racism are said to instrumentalize the bodies of black people and represent a "tired understanding of allyship," she argues, "that prioritizes intent over effect."[129] If it were not for the ethnicity of the artist, her argument could be used against Steve McQueen's *12 Years a Slave* (2013), Ava DeVernay's *Selma* (2014), or any other work that depicts historical conflicts. The past here is not simply a foreign country, it is being subject to social, cultural, economic and political extortion.

A few weeks after the School Board decided to not destroy the Arnautoff murals, but to permanently cover them up instead, *The Nation* published an essay by the cultural theorist and prominent black scholar Robin D.G. Kelley. Despite countless articles that were published in time to save the murals from destruction, Kelley belatedly claimed that he had something to say about the issue that had not already been addressed by the mainstream press. Kelley defended Arnautoff's work and added a few new details on the context surrounding the commissioning of the Crumpler murals. However, he also came to the defence of the Board by suggesting that the decision to preserve *and* cover over the murals is an "eminently reasonable solution."[130] He also repeated the notion that left-wing and right-wing critics are "strange bedfellows," an obfuscation that was put across to the media on several occasions, and for all the wrong reasons, by board members Cook, Sanchez and Collins. Kelley could have followed up his own assertion with the suggestion that by attacking murals that are dedicated to the hero of the War of Independence, the SFUSD School Board are placing themselves in the tradition of Joseph Goebbels, the Nazi minister of propaganda, who said in 1933 that the goal of fascism was to erase 1789 from history. Kelley shows sympathy for the beleaguered Cook, who had suggested that the black men who served in Washington's army could be depicted in a new set of images, an idea that was put forward by the Black Student Union in 1968. Yet the matter was settled long ago with the Crumpler murals. It rather seems that Cook and his ilk were eager to leave their mark by destroying something that is beyond them. Luckily, the efforts of the GWHS Alumni Association and all those who defended the murals led to a ruling issued on September 24, 2021, by San Francisco County Superior Court Judge Anne-Christine Massullo, who determined that the School Board had violated California environmental laws. The ruling voided all unlawful actions taken by the Board to destroy or cover the murals. The judge reprimanded commissioner Alison Collins as well as Board members Gabriela López and Faauuga Moliga for bias in the kangaroo court they had established. The judge's decision was based on the fact that every School Board member had clearly announced their desire to destroy or cover the murals before initiating public proceedings. Further evidence of Board corruption is the fact that within two weeks of this CEQA ruling, it decided 6 to 1 to appeal the case, a decision that would further involve wasting public funds on legal counsel while SFUSD overspending was already at $116 million for the 2021-22 school year. In February 2022, a recall election allowed San Francisco voters to remove Collins, López and Moliga from the Board of Education. Citizens had had enough of conservative uses of woke anti-racism and fiscal incompetence in the context of a pandemic.[131] As for the Arnautoff murals, the California Art Preservation Act may yet prove to be effective in further consolidating their protected status.

You Ain't Got No Alibi

The mixing of woke celebritization and neoliberal racialism was on full display in the controversy surrounding the '1619 Project' that was launched as a 100-page issue of the *New York Times Magazine* on August 18, 2019. Initiated by staff writer Nikole Hannah-Jones, the project includes essays and literary texts by 17 African-American writers on the commemoration of the arrival of the first African slaves in the U.S. at Point Comfort, Virginia, in August 1619. The cover page, which shows the Atlantic Ocean seen from the shores of New England, states that because slavery was the most formative aspect of the U.S., its history begins in 1619. A short note by the editor of the magazine, Jake Silverstein, makes explicit the thesis of the Project that 1619 and not 1776 is the date of birth of the nation. The original wording in the August 2019 introduction states that the 1619 Project "aims to reframe the country's history, understanding 1619 as our true founding, and placing the consequences of slavery and the contributions of black Americans at the very center of the story we tell ourselves about who we are." A revised version from December 2019, which was not announced by the *Times*, despite criticisms, changed this to state: "It aims to reframe the country's history by placing the consequences of slavery and the contributions of black Americans at the very center of our national narrative."[132] Defined as the "original sin" of the country, slavery is said to have been based in anti-black racism and so racism is responsible for "nearly everything that has truly made America exceptional," including its economic power, political system and culture.[133] The founding fathers are referred to as "the men known as our founding fathers," a wording that raises suspicion about the Enlightenment in an effort to "reframe American history by considering what it would mean to regard 1619 as our nation's birth year."[134] The editor warns readers that the material in the issue is gruesome but that by confronting its reality, Americans can prepare for a more just future.

Making slavery rather than democracy the focus of American politics and culture leads one to think that a state of exception is being used to justify identitarian authenticity.[135] Recall that the notion of sin was mobilized by the *anti-philosophes* of the counter-Enlightenment, who affirmed the power of absolute authority by casting aspersion on those who made use of public reason in the name of humanity rather than particular interests. When the Enlightenment legacy came under renewed attack by the postmodern left, the kind of anti-racism that relies on cultural relativism ceded to the political status quo, inspiring hatred of Western culture and promoting a politics of Otherness – the cultural belonging of ethnicity (ethnos) over considerations of rights and democracy (demos).[136] Recall also that in anti-Enlightenment philosophy, from Cornelius de Pauw to Joseph de Maistre, Oswald Spengler, Martin Heidegger and Jean Baudrillard, America has long figured as a "degenerate image of Europe's own future."[137] The difference is that warnings against American democracy are now coming from the American neoliberal intelligentsia.

The leading text of the 1619 Project, "The Idea of America," is written by Hannah-Jones. This text in particular gives a sense of the confusion that the Project has propagated. The premise of her argument is that the founding ideals of the United States – liberty and equality – were false at the outset and that they are only true to the extent that black Americans have made them so. Black American patriotism is premised on the eventuality that America will one day live up to its ideals, even if to date that has not been the case. The African slaves who were brought to Virginia in 1619 were the first of 400,000 Africans who were sold to North Americans. The author makes no mention of the Native Americans who populated the Americas before the arrival of the first Europeans. There is nothing in the text to suggest that liberal definitions of freedom and equality have been subject to left criticism or that primitive accumulation should be subject to critique. Instead, the text celebrates the hard work that created the most successful colonies of the British Empire. Unlike the Arnautoff murals, the 1619 Project is framed from the perspective of Adam Smith's *The Wealth of Nations* rather than Karl Marx's *Das Kapital*. The article states that the writers of the Declaration of Independence did not believe that blacks were among those who are "created equal" and endowed with "inalienable rights."[138] It suggests that even if the founding fathers did not extend constitutional rights to all American citizens, black Americans nevertheless believed in the American Creed and its principles of freedom, equality and justice.

Hannah-Jones's argument is not entirely compatible with one of the tenets of radical democracy: the notion of the 'democratic idea,' which proposes that although the age of Enlightenment did not imagine that the same rights attributed to propertied white males could be extended to women, children, slaves and working men, it did establish the principles through which those rights would eventually be extended. The problem today is less whether people believe in these principles than the fact that in the absence of a socialist politics, liberal political freedoms are inoperative for the majority of people worldwide, even if they believe in them and even if these should be defended against conservative attack and postmodern relativism. In comparison with the 'idea of communism' interventions that were advanced by Alain Badiou, Tariq Ali, Boris Groys, Jodi Dean, Bruno Bosteels, Slavoj Žižek and others in the 2000s, Hannah-Jones's "The Idea of America" promotes a rearguard approach to *American* (read: capitalist) universality, subtending everything that is wrong with progressive neoliberalism and making this a cornerstone of school curriculum through the auspices of the Pulitzer Center. The author does not hesitate to turn the tables of history, suggesting that it is black Americans who are the true founding fathers of the nation.[139] Along these same lines, Obama at one time eulogized John Lewis, the Civil Rights activist turned Democratic Party hack, as a "founding father of a fuller, fairer, better America."[140]

"The Idea of America" makes two regressive moves. First, it denies the notion of revolutionary progress that leads from feudalism and capitalism to international socialism. Second, and on the basis of this arrested notion of historical transformation, it privileges black Americans among all of the other groups who were initially excluded from the democratic idea. Hannah-Jones argues that without the idealism of black Americans in particular, the U.S. might not be the democracy that it is today. Examples are provided with Crispus Attucks, the first person to die in the American Revolution, and the fact that black soldiers fought in every American war since then. One is led to think that the Vietnam War, the wars in the Middle East and the more than 150 foreign interventions perpetrated by the U.S. since 1850 have contributed to what constitutes American democracy. Vaunting racialist hutzpah, Hannah-Jones denies the fact that the U.S. does not have a global reputation as the 'land of liberty,' as she suggests. More prosaically, according to Wharton Best Countries, the U.S. ranks number one in global competitiveness and 121 out of 162 on the Global Peace Index. As a leading global power, the U.S. does not do especially well when it comes to trade, literacy, press freedom, health, economic equality, political equality, democracy and government transparency. These problems do not inform the kind of writing that mobilizes a racialist version of history instead of the history of radicalism.

The racial contradictions of the Revolutionary era are addressed by the 1619 Project, as is the development of racist science in the mid-nineteenth century, which protected the economic benefits of the slave economy. Hannah-Jones acknowledges that people like Thomas Jefferson blamed Great Britain for forcing slavery on the colonies but suggests that they were hypocritical when they argued that Americans were the slaves of Great Britain. The Declaration of Independence paved the way for the Constitution, which protected slavery in the name of property rights. At that moment, the "sin" of slavery could no longer be blamed on history or on England, but became the nation's own, she argues, making the racial caste system into an ideology that lasts to this day.[141] Nor does Abraham Lincoln figure well in this narrative as someone who suggested that freed blacks could be sent to Africa since black equality was unimaginable to him in America at that time. Preventing the secession of the South, the Civil War led to a short period of black involvement in American politics, a period of civil rights legislation that would be reversed by the advent of Jim Crow laws. The reason for this is explained through the *deus ex machina* of biological materialism: "Anti-black racism runs in the very DNA of this country, as does the belief ... that black people are the obstacle to national unity."[142] One is thankful that Hannah-Jones means this metaphorically and that she does not engage in the kinds of arguments that account for ethnic conflict as the result of genetics.[143] The "second slavery" of the period 1880s to 1930s was due to the racial apartheid that was defended by whites of all economic classes, she argues. Since racist ideology had been inscribed in the nation's founding, whites needed to discriminate against blacks to prevent them from thriving economically and excelling in education. New forms of inhumanity therefore justified the injustices of the past.

The exceptional nature of the U.S. that is proposed by Hannah-Jones's narrative lends credence to the notion of the exceptional nature of the black challenge to oppression. By struggling for civil rights, blacks laid the foundations for other modern rights struggles. This suggestion loses sight of the secular notion of universal human rights, which was unheard of in 1619 and which was essential to abolitionism and anti-racism through to the 1960s. Her argument does not address the limits of civil society and civil rights discourse as features of bourgeois ideology. It merely reframes them retroactively. Black capitalism thus claims exclusive rights of exception. It does not share emancipatory idealism and radicalism with whites but preserves it for those who were historically the most marginalized. "Our founding fathers," she argues, "may not have actually believed in the ideals they espoused, but black people did."[144] This logic takes vengeance on propertied white European males by making struggle and resistance a matter of biological determinism. It presumes that blacks resist inequality and never contribute to it. Whites, for the most part, are believed to do the opposite. And why is this? Because, as Hannah-Jones claims, only those who have not benefited from freedom can cherish it.[145] Vanished from this line of thought is the concept of inalienable rights. From there, she makes the specious argument that black Americans embrace democracy more than any other group, as evidenced by black support for progressive government programmes like universal health care and opposition to the death penalty. She does not address the fact that Africans and freed blacks can be and have been as ruthless in their treatment of other blacks as any black capitalist has been towards black workers or black slave owners towards black slaves. Blacks are surreptitiously made the secret custodians of post-Enlightenment ideals. And how do we know this? How is it that black Americans are not part of the problem, but are always part of, if not *the* solution? The proof, as her argument dwindles, is the "avant-garde" nature of black hairstyles and fashion.[146]

From September 2019 to January 2020, the *World Socialist Web Site* was the first and for the most part the only online newspaper to offer in-depth criticism of the 1619 Project, publishing several articles and conducting interviews with prominent American historians, including Gordon Wood, James McPherson, James Oakes, Victoria Bynum, Richard Carwardine and Clayborne Carson. This organ of the Trotskyist Socialist Equality Party was only reluctantly credited by those who followed their example. There are too many inaccuracies, omissions and falsifications in the 1619 Project to list all of them here. However, the main objections to the Project relate to five interrelated and false claims:

1) the American Revolution was fought to save the institution of slavery, 2) Lincoln was a racist and the Civil War was not fought to end slavery, 3) African Americans have single-handedly fought against racism, 4) racism is a timeless and necessary feature of the U.S., and 5) American history is defined by the struggle between blacks and whites.[147] In terms of contemporary research, the Project ignores the close connection between the Civil Right movement, the labour movement and socialist politics. Nor are the historical overlaps between the Black Power movement of the 1960s and the development of black capitalism acknowledged. This is to be expected since the Project, as a product of the establishment, ignores the shift within the Democratic Party towards neoliberal policy and identity politics.

For a lecture presentation delivered by Hannah-Jones at New York University, the school President, Andrew Hamilton, praised the 1619 Project for excellence in journalism. Hannah-Jones reiterated her theory about the "undemocratic" character of the American Revolution and the Constitution, adding to this her view that white working-class voters oppose social programmes because they wish to "punish black people." "We cannot get rid of that [racism]," she argued, later comparing the American South to Nazi Germany and suggesting that whereas the Germans have reckoned with what they did, Americans have not.[148] In response to detailed criticism of these claims, she smeared the *World Socialist Web Site*, tweeting: "You did what y'all keep doing – making things up to make a nonexistent argument." She also tweeted that Trump supporters have not harassed her and insulted her intelligence as much as "white men claiming to be socialists" who have revealed themselves as "anti-black folks."[149] She has also tweeted statements that balk at the notion that "white historians have produced truly objective history," adding to this the relativistic notion that "there is no such thing as objective history so complaints that the 1619 is an illegitimate reframing of history deny that all history is framed."

The least that one can say about Hannah-Jones is that she believes in the racialist agenda, not only dismissing all criticism, but especially criticism that issues from whites, from men or from socialists. On May 4, 2020, the liberal establishment awarded her a Pulitzer Prize. The prize was in the category of Commentary rather than History, which indicates that the committee discounted the Project as history writing, defining her contribution to it as a "personal essay." Further, the awarding of the History prize to Caleb McDaniel for his book, *Sweet Taste of Liberty: A True Story of Slavery and Restitution in America*, was a rebuke of Hannah-Jones's claims that "white historians" are unable to understand racism and African American history. When interviewed by Henry Louis Gates at the Hutchins Center on December 4, 2019, she jokingly asked the scholar-turned-television personality to not fact-check her.[150] So much for the MacArthur Genius fellowship that she received, unless the prize is meant to reward reverse discrimination and red-baiting. In the summer of 2021, the establishment rewarded Hannah-Jones with a professorship at Howard University and a chair in Race and Reporting that comes with $20 million in financing from several foundations. Like Robin DiAngelo, she is now offered c.$25,000 lecture fees from universities and her talent agency arranges for lavish speaking engagements, personal appearances and consulting work.

That the *New York Times* could publish such substandard journalism and meet with mostly conservative criticism in the mainstream press says less about the arguments put forward than the fact that the liberal class is satisfied to deregulate and privatize school curriculum along with everything else. When five historians, including Wood, Oakes, Bynum, McPherson and Sean Wilentz sent them a letter recommending that they make corrections to certain aspects of their narrative, especially the thesis that the U.S. sought independence from Britain in order to ensure slavery, Silverstein cited consultation with African-American historians and positive feedback from readers as reason enough to double down on the Project's false premises.[151] Silverstein said to the media that from the start the *Times* was prepared for a public reaction. This is no doubt true since the provocation of a historians' debate was sure to sell newspapers and generate academic buzz. It was revealed in March 2020 that the *Times* ignored the advice of a fact-checker, Leslie M. Harris of Northwestern University, which would have prevented the scandal. This proves that the newspaper intentionally manufactured the controversy. Although a minor update was made after this revelation, the change maintained the misguided effort to deny the emancipatory aspects of the American Revolution.[152]

Hannah-Jones was not the only person to hedge on facts and attack the identity of historians. Writing for *Rolling Stone*, Jamil Smith reduced criticism of the 1619 Project to the conservative backlash of "white men" who believe in the "inviolate greatness of other white men of the past," against which he argues for narratives by "people who look like me."[153] Similarly, Michael Harriot, writing for *The Root*, dismissed historians' criticisms, arguing that there is no such thing as American history and that these historians make whiteness the standard measure.[154] He caricatures these scholars as the League of Concerned Caucasians, the Legion of Extraordinary Revisionists and the White Power Rangers, reducing their claims to soundbites and to the query "but-what-about-wypipo?" Woke reactions are hardly a litmus test of radicalism. As Jodi Dean says about the idea of the comrade, anyone but not everyone can be a comrade, the measure of which is not whether someone looks like me or is like me, or even that they like me, but the fact that comrades are in a relation of political solidarity.[155] The proof is in the pudding. As the conservative journal *The New*

Criterion moved in on the *World Socialist Web Site*'s groundwork to claim the prize for itself, it denounced the 1619 Project as a "stupefying race-based fantasy about the origins of the United States."[156] The editors of *The New Criterion* cite historian Allen C. Guelzo, who argues that the 1619 Project seeks to tarnish capitalism by associating it with slavery. A more likely conspiracy is that the *New York Times* went all in on race to take the focus off of the failed Mueller investigation.

In response to criticism of the 1619 Project, the liberal press avoided recommending rectification, responding to the issue with careerist equanimity.[157] To underscore its racialist agenda, the *Times* ran an advertisement for the Project during the 2020 Academy Awards, a ceremony that was criticized by the press for the lack of non-white and gender representation. The ad shows actress Janelle Monáe in a designer dress at the edge of the Atlantic Ocean, explaining that America began in 1619 with the sale of African slaves to colonists. The ad closes with the copy: "The truth can change how we see the world. The truth is worth it." Monáe performed the opening musical number at the awards ceremony, interjecting: "I'm so proud to stand here as a black, queer artist telling stories. Happy Black History Month." Hollywood's support for this endeavour was concretized when Oprah Winfrey and Lionsgate announced that they would partner with Hannah-Jones to adapt the 1619 Project for film, television and a book series.

The 1619 Project fully entered the realm of the bipartisan culture wars when Trump announced that his department of education would cut funds to public schools using the 1619 Project in their classes.[158] With Oprah's endorsement and Trump's attacks, the Project was further politicized. A conservative columnist at the *Times* wrote in October that the Project's ambition to reframe American history exceeded the bounds of unbiased journalism and foolishly made itself the news.[159] His review of the case was disavowed by the newspaper's staff, editor and publisher. In January 2021, the Trump administration released its '1776 Report' on Martin Luther King Jr. day, a piece of propaganda that celebrates the American Revolution and the Civil War as events that ostensibly ensure the values of law and order, family and religion. Its insistence on cultural homogeneity does not refute the 1619 Project so much as provide a white Christian alternative.[160] That both of these documents speak to the deeply anti-left character of American democracy is evidenced by government attacks on voting rights, the right to protest, labour rights and the right to advocate for socialist ideas. Despite itself, the 1619 Project imagines how the exception to universal freedom tells us something about this same universality. However, by fixing the problem in racialist terms, it abandons nearly everything that makes the investigation relevant to emancipatory universality. What this kind of black capitalist populism leads to are acts of shaming for "sinful" behaviour and a race metaphysics, where, for example, whites are not allowed to wear dreadlocks and blacks are not supposed to like prog music.

Pride and competitiveness prevent blacks and whites from finding solutions to systemic injustices. Particularist theorizing, by itself, cannot adequately define justice. Instead, such notions as original sin produce an atmosphere of sorcery where safety can only be secured for the preachers and the exorcists. One gets a sense of who the thaumaturges are by examining the advertisements that accompany the introduction to the 1619 Project and the first essay by Hannah-Jones: a Broadway advertisement for the Aaaron Sorkin rewrite of Harper Lee's *To Kill a Mockingbird*, which prosecutes the lawyer Atticus Finch rather than Southern racism; an ad for the Fund II Foundation, a charitable foundation that is directed by Robert F. Smith, a former Goldman Sachs executive and the wealthiest black American; an ad for the NYU Winthrop Hospital that features Supreme Court Justice John Roberts, the man whose Citizens United decision engineered the deregulation revolution in campaign financing.[161] There is also an ad for Possible Plan, a philanthropic initiative that is owned by a company that wants to become the "Nike of cannabis." One of the directors of Possible Plan is Carry Twigg, a former Special Assistant to President Barack Obama and former Director of Public Engagement for Vice President Joe Biden. The name of this Curaleaf Holdings initiative is derived from the slogan of the cannabis company Select: "everything is possible." The history of Curaleaf involves a real estate scam that defrauded hundreds of thousands of dollars from investors. Its former CEO allegedly raped his wife's hairdresser on their wedding day.[162] Its current CEO is known to have intimidated women in the cannabis industry for sharing information about the incident through social media. Undeterred by bad press, the ad uses a line by the thirteenth-century poet Rumi, which entreats readers to "Come, even if you have broken your vows a thousand times." Needless to say, none of this is particularly instructive. It is not difficult to imagine that the *New York Times* would like to get cash-strapped schools hooked on its free product as the public education system is fighting tooth and nail against privatization. On the other side of content, Internet-threatened newspapers are leveraging their brand identity to diversify their product lines beyond journalism.[163] As it happens, the New York Times Company is highly invested in database consumer research that operates within the ideological spectrum that is suited to the Democratic Party. It is not concerned with journalism so much as framing the news. And now it wants to reframe American history by both displacing and confirming the nation's ideological foundations.

When one looks at the complete package of the 1619 Project one gains a better sense of "the idea of America" that motivates a newspaper known as much for its foreign policy bluster as for its crossword puzzles. Norman Mailer was close to the mark when he described America as vulgar and brutal. Its culture is like its cars, he once said – they wear out quickly because they are made to keep the economy running. As Sheldon Wolin argued, the politics of state-corporate power – which he referred to as inverted totalitarianism – is directly connected to the political demobilization of a citizenry that seems unaware of the consequences of its own ideology of exploitation.[164] The reasons for this obliviousness are thoroughly material. As U.S. capitalism became the model for unregulated Walmart labour and Wall Street speculation, supply-side economics leveraged global capital flows against consumer debt. According to Yanis Varoufakis, the more financialized the economy becomes and the more it is prone to crisis, the more that consent regarding the upward redistribution of wealth is produced through labour discipline.[165] Human labour resists being made into a commodity. Why is it then that the 1619 Project is not part of a history of labour exploitation? The simple answer is that the Project is not about history. It is rather part of a strategy to use identity politics as a ruling-class tactic to divide working people along racial lines. Insofar as it is about history, its purpose is to alienate working people from their own past.

The Umpteenth Brumaire of Louis Bonaparte

In "What Is National Socialism?" Leon Trotsky described Adolph Hitler as a self-assured mediocrity who was more adept at inflaming the petty bourgeoisie's desire for vengeance and arousing their anti-intellectualism than he was at defining a programme that could solve inflation and the high cost of living.[166] Nazi hostility to socialist politics raised the nation and the "zoological materialism" of race above history, replacing historical materialism with Aryan myths. What Hitlerism also provided was a means to return to economic liberalism. The 1619 Project and the fake controversies surrounding the Arnautoff murals similarly devolve collective social struggles into micro-political versions of the "sentimental formlessness" that reinforces the status quo.[167] Equality is not a fact that can be measured. It is an ideal that one strives for. By the same token, what makes something radical is not the depiction of social misery, but the depiction of what it is that causes and could change that reality. Those who decry the fact that the murals include the representation of slavery ignore the fact that the anti-racist works in question are dedicated to revolutionary themes. In contrast, the 1619 Project, which is also concerned with slavery and racial supremacy, dispenses with revolutionary themes. Sensibilities that have been trained to think of life as a sandbox of idiomorphic hokum prefer to approach culture and history in terms of free choice – a morality of the shopping mall.

It is less the case then that postmodernism represents an incredulity towards meta-narratives than it is the case that the meta-narrative of postmodernism is incredulity. History and reality are experienced as Oedipal trauma.[168] The Manifest Destiny of global capitalism can dispense with racial superiority only to the extent that it also replaces solidarity with race-first initiatives. The tech futurism of the social media environment in which these processes now occur does not indicate that we have progressed beyond the problems of modernity. Rather, the identitarian retrofit of the postmodern crisis of historicity, as MacCannell argues, is less forward-looking and innovative than it is a "violent trivialization" of culture, politics and history.[169]

The uses and misuses of art and history that are the stock in trade of postmodern artists plummeted to new depths in the 2019 poster campaign of the far-right Alternative for Germany (Alternative fur Deutschland), some of whose candidates were elected to the Bundestag in September 2017. As with the rise of right-wing parties across Europe, Eurasia, Latin America and North America, the AfD has created a base for itself in regions where previous Social Democratic Party and Left Party officials, now perceived to be anti-working class, have been implementing cutbacks to labour and welfare. To win back voters, the Christian Democrats and Social Democrats are now implementing AfD policies, including mass deportations. For those who voted for the AfD out of concern about the integration of refugees, it must come as a pleasant surprise to see posters that show Jean-Léon Gérome's 1866 painting *The Slave Market* with the tag line "So that Europe does not become 'Eurabia'." Devised to stoke anti-immigrant chauvinism, the term Eurabia was used by far-right terrorist Anders Breivik in his Islamophobic rhetoric. The poster is part of a series titled "Learn from Europe's History," which combines famous works of art with right-wing slogans. The combination of canonical artworks with xenophobic agitation produces a rightist version of the woke racialization of politics.

In terms of both art and politics, flirting with fascism is now part of a postmodern attitude that views everything as constructed. After the academic reception of both the avant garde and modernist reaction, the two can be approached by sophisticates as reversible tropes. However, the reflexivization of all 'social texts' is perhaps not as free-floating as one might think. Žižek argues that there are three aspects to today's normalization of fascism: 1) the relativization of the crimes of capitalism, communism and fascism; 2) the notion that fascism borrowed its worst aspects from communism; and 3) the notion that those who became fascist chose it in preference to communism.[170] The re-normalization of fascism in post-representational culture and politics can thus be defined in these terms: 1) there is no essential difference between avant-garde, modernist and totalitarian art; 2) fascist art was already inspired by the avant-garde; and 3) fascist art allowed for a more democratic, ethno-nationalist alternative to communism's idealization of proletarian internationalism. The fantasy of liberal capitalism is that economic growth does not produce a corresponding impoverishment and destruction – a reality that disputes the simplistic emphasis on economic dynamism. Such dynamism is pure ideology insofar as one perceives wealth creation from the perspective of those who profit, those who destroy nature, increase the rate of exploitation, intensify labour productivity, concentrate capital in the hands of fewer individuals and extend global markets in such a way that imperialism becomes inevitable.[171] Regardless, it is at the level of the critique of political economy that one finds the significant difference between communism and fascism, and also between radical art and woke aesthetics. Seemingly opposed to conservative values, woke culture wars spearhead the entrepreneurial offensive against class struggle. Woke culture is not tragic, Žižek would argue, because it does not betray the revolution. It simply has nothing to do with it.

Just as the neoliberal class is happy to do away with the welfare state, woke aesthetics is happy to do away with radical aesthetics and art theory in favour of institutional arrangements that are oriented towards profit-seeking. Since identity capitalism has already been ratified by neoliberalized museums and university departments, the last form of "regulation" that its advocates worry about now is the criticism of radical historians and theorists. One instance of this is an article published in the *New York Times* titled "The Dominance of the White Male Critic."[172] The authors, Elizabeth Méndez Berry and Chi-hui Yang, criticize the fact that many art critics who wrote unfavourable reviews of the 2019 Whitney Biennial, which featured many young women artists of colour, were unfamiliar with the "intellectual, conceptual and artistic ideas that underlie the work."[173] The attitude of white critics, they argue, is that the work of people of colour is not universal enough. As inequality and white supremacy increase, they say, the judgements of art critics determine whether or not people are locked in cages. White male critics who impose national myths reinforce segregation and fail to notice that the best art being made today is by BIPOC artists – black, Indigenous and people of colour. One indication of what these authors understand by aesthetics is noticed in their association of criticism with career advancement. "Reviews create momentum that shape economic and intellectual marketplaces," they argue, a statement that is no doubt true but which also recommends that critics give 'likes' to everything they see so as to not be preferential. They also recommend writing criticism in the interest of affirmative action.[174] They dismiss the work of professional critics in favour of social media conversation, where there are fewer barriers, they claim, for people who acknowledge issues of class, gender, sexual orientation and ability.

The de-professionalization of criticism assumes that only those who are not motivated by monetary considerations can be the true public servants and civic infrastructure. This idea contradicts the previous one which recommends that critics should pay more attention to the economic interests of marginal artists. Championing the "rollicking culture coverage" of marginalized "critics of colour," they argue that "old-school white critics" should step aside and let "diverse writers" hold court in mainstream outlets.[175]

One could question the progressivism of such racialist propaganda by recalling two versions of the right-wing reaction to the socialist and anarchist avant garde. One is the Futurist Manifesto issued by Marinetti in 1909. While borrowing most of their creative insights from French Cubism, the Futurists published their celebration of macho violence behind "enemy lines" in *Le Figaro*. Less a slap in the face of the international bourgeoisie than a chauvinist declaration of war, Marinetti's degrading attack has been the model for reactionary artists ever since, from *Entartete Kunst* to the SCUM Manifesto. Berry and Yang also conjure up the ghost of Stalin. The Lyssenko debates in the Soviet Union opposed 'bourgeois science' to 'proletarian science,' which sometimes resulted in the degradation of scientific knowledge in the name of anti-imperialist competition. In the realm of Socialist Realism, the use of outmoded forms of art, especially folk art, was permitted and even encouraged by the state in order to replace the idea of permanent revolution with nationalism. The claim by the Endnotes collective that class struggle is inoperative today and that the diversity agenda of groups like BLM is the only path through which to pursue radicalism is little more than a recalibration of Stalinism for post-Fordist times.[176] One could further suggest that today's political correctness substitutes woke wars for Cold War liberalism if it were not for the fact that in many cases it is no longer a matter of conformism versus rebellion, but of blacks and against whites, women against men and gays against straights, each of whom, on the basis of intersectionality, can be presumed to be anti-capitalist without having to be universalist.

Insofar as some artists respond to negative reviews with the argument that white critics do not understand the work of black artists, a radical materialism would find that at a fundamental level, no critic ever understands an artist's work fully, least of all because the aesthetic is indeterminate at the same time that it is thoroughly historical and social. One must add that no artist fully understands their own work and individuals do not fully understand themselves. This makes rather than dismisses the case for the social value of art theory, history and criticism. Whereas the leveraging of identity politics is now an embedded feature of neoliberalism, organs like the *New York Times* propagate the racialist agenda by making it appear to be the "left" wing in the struggle between progressive Democrats and conservative Republicans. When the critics who are being attacked are actual leftists, the issue devolves to a condemnation of their identity rather than their credibility. While the history of race and gender discrimination in cultural institutions is undisputable, and inclusivity remains a progressive goal, the problem today, according to David Walsh and Fred Mazelis, is that most mainstream critics are not critical enough and have over the years accommodated identity politics at the expense of radicalism.[177] The demand for quotas rests in part on the argument that black artists and critics have special access to a particularist aesthetic or to certain issues. This separatist strategy was pursued by women artists in the 1970s, only to unravel under the pressure of the critique of its exclusivity, later broadening to include women of colour and then male feminists. Feminism then acquiesced to commercialism as part of the postmodern critique of the left. Berry, as it happens, is the director of a Foundation that is funded by a $200 million estate donation. Yang works for the Ford Foundation. Walsh and Mazelis further note Berry's defence of black nationalism and her appeal to mainstream news outlets as well as capitalist philanthropy.[178] Such petty-bourgeois racialism, now advanced by the middle and upper class, reveals the contradictions of multiculturalism as a feature of capitalist ideology.[179] The cynical core of this belated postmodern ideology is to purge representation of a critical understanding of history, and with it, anything that might encourage a radical understanding of contemporary social relations. Ethnic identifications, understood as lifestyle communities if not as race nationalism and race fundamentalism, are not exceptions to Enlightenment reason, however, but its most advanced expression in terms of the economic form of the attachment to the concept of race.

With a political left comprised of racialists and other neoliberal identitarians, who needs right-wing pundits? Walsh has been far more accurate in his analysis of made-for-Twitter controversies than the prattle that is routinely served up by the neoliberal press. For instance, the denunciation in the *New York Times* of Gary Ross's *Free State of Jones* (2016) as a "white saviour" film, or the critique of Scott Frank's television series *The Queen's Gambit* (2020) because it does not include enough sexism, is considered by Walsh an indication of the political alliance between advocates of identity politics and upper-middle-class establishment constituencies.[180] The focus on issues of cultural appropriation and privilege, he argues, are designed to exacerbate ethnic tensions, prevent working-class alliances and give a progressive gloss to neoliberal politics. Middle and upper-class artists and scholars today seek to leverage historical and contemporary injustices to advance their careers. This trend develops alongside rather than in opposition to the imperialist culture of such films as Kathryn

Bigelow's *Zero Dark Thirty* (2012), Clint Eastwood's *American Sniper* (2014) or Seth Rogen and Evan Goldberg's *The Interview* (2014).

Today's anti-universalist reasonings provide an ideological defence for ethnicity-based irrationalism and anti-democratic prejudices that in the 1920s and 30s were part of the fascist ideology that celebrated patriotism, tradition, conformity and contempt for humanity. An anti-Enlightenment monarchist like Joseph de Maistre was a multiculturalist in the sense that he despised the abstract notion of 'man' and did not believe that there was anything that human beings had in common. One of the early ideologues of racism, Arthur de Gobineau, was disgusted by notions like equality and democracy, arguing that interracial mixing causes civilizational decline. The anti-communist national socialist Oswald Spengler anticipated postmodern relativism with his focus on difference and the incommensurability of perspectives on reality. Walsh associates the poor state of contemporary culture with these atavistic tendencies, which have re-emerged through the clichés of postmodernism: the obsession with otherness and identity; the rejection of objectivity, truth and universality; hostility to reasoned argumentation and generalization; the focus on technological invention and promotional bombast.

Walsh argues that the prevalence of pessimism, self-pity, pettiness and selfishness among artists and intellectuals is a symptom of declining social and historical knowledge. Why be accountable to others when you can simply serve your Nietzschean self? An instance of this postmodern fascism is the criticism of Dana Schutz's *Open Casket*, an abstract painting of Emmett Till, the 14-year-old black youth who was killed in Mississippi in 1955 for allegedly flirting with a white woman. Shown at the 2017 Whitney Biennale, Schutz's work came under fire by racialist critics. An open letter written by Hannah Black and signed by two dozen young black artists demanded that the work be destroyed so that Schutz cannot benefit from black suffering. Walsh compares the protests to the discriminatory communalism of Zionists. Such activism is fraudulently leftist, he argues, because it presumes that art and cognition cannot transcend cultural differences.[181] Why would Harriet Beecher Stowe's *Uncle Tom's Cabin* have been translated into 60 languages, he asks, if art could not convey universal truths. Similarly, Arthur Miller argued against cultural relativism on the grounds that his 1953 allegorical play about McCarthyite witch trials, *The Crucible*, was universally appreciated in the more than 70 countries in which it was shown. Walsh compares the thinking of Black and her co-signatories to the chauvinist rhetoric of Hans Severus Ziegler, a Nazi cultural official whose concern for "the soul of the people" and its "creative powers" could only be secured by protecting German music from the influence of non-Aryan artists like Bach, Beethoven and Mozart. Walsh applauds the decision by the Boston ICA and 80 prominent artists to defend Schutz's solo exhibition from protesters who demanded that her exhibition be cancelled.[182]

An artist who could be considered postmodernist, Coco Fusco, criticizes the puritanical, anti-intellectual tendency that places moral judgement before aesthetic understanding and that calls for the censorship and destruction of artworks.[183] Fusco faults the press for shirking the responsibility to analyse the arguments of protesters and smugly recirculating them. She also faults Black for presuming to speak for all black people and for the kind of black nationalism that in the past was rarely beneficial to the most disadvantaged African Americans. Mamie Till, the boy's mother, in contrast, stated that she wanted an open casket so that everyone could see what had been done to her son. Photographs of Till's funeral were circulated by the Civil Rights movement to encourage cross-race collaboration and to shame politicians into action. One could say the same about images of war, as revealed by Chelsea Manning's leak of the Collateral Murder videos, which are now censored from public view. The government of Emmanuel Macron has taken similar steps to make it illegal for citizens to record police misconduct. These cases make Fusco's fast and ready distinction between moral judgement and aesthetic understanding problematic. For Fusco, the policing of art and the intimidation of artists leads to narrow-minded populism by foreclosing "the effort to achieve interracial cooperation, mutual understanding, or universal anti-racist consciousness."[184] While this is true enough, one would not want to stretch the point to make excuses for artists who only purpose is the encryption of reactionary values. As we have seen, one person's anti-racism is another's anti-communism.

Aesthetic understanding can be manipulated as a pretext for apolitical moralism. Does Fusco's stance against censorship, which she also wields against the government of Cuba, have anything to do with the left, that is, beyond the familiar bourgeois freedoms? It is important to ask this question if advocacy is not to reproduce what Reed refers to as the James Brown Theory of Black Liberation.[185] What many embedded artists and critics have in common is the reduction of history to questions of subjective agency, a strategy that makes for dubious history and regressive politics. As Brown aligned himself with Nixon's policies, he advocated black self-help, making black progress a matter of will and hard work. Known as Soul Brother No.1 and later as the King of Soul, Brown advocated for dropout prevention in schools, eventually gaining the support of Nixon and later founding a trust for disadvantaged school children. Through James Brown Enterprises he helped to provide job opportunities for blacks in the business sector. He also advocated patriotism in the context of the Vietnam War. On the question of civil rights, and despite writing songs dedicated to black pride, Brown did not believe in defining people by their race and did not advocate race separatism. His 1969 song 'I Don't Want Nobody to Give Me Nothing' defended equal opportunity in terms of self-reliance. After Brown endorsed Nixon in the 1972 elections, black organizations began to protest his concerts.

Today's racialist criticism and politics is consistent with neoliberal attacks on social policy and promotion of individual entrepreneurialism and volunteerism, emphasizing agency over public issues. Reed notices this trend in films like Quentin Tarantino's *Django Unchained* (2012), which represents a rebellious figure liberating himself from slavery, and in Steven Spielberg's *Lincoln* (2012), which Reed argues is not a film about how slavery was ended but about how audiences would like to imagine slavery to have ended. Ava DuVernay's *Selma* (2015), he says, falsifies King's relation to the Johnson administration and the relation of the SNCC and the SCLC to King at that time. He contrasts these with Edward Zwick's film *Glory* (1989), which shows black slaves and freedmen combining their energies in a broad-based military campaign to destroy the institution of slavery. Today's films about race issues often have less to do with history and are rather informed by the kind of subaltern studies that deny the possibility of the oppressed to advance their own interests.[186] From out of this problematic assumption, political economy and class domination are replaced with multiculturalism and respect for differences, a phenomenon that Reed argues is rooted in the neoconservative project of Thatcher and Reagan.

The emphasis on social structures, political economy and historical materialism has never existed independently of problems of ideology, alienation, abstraction and subjectivity. Postmodern takes on history and materialism, however, tend to overestimate the realm of culture. In addition to the problems of the corporate state, those Nietzscheans of the right who emphasize ambition, willpower and vitality reject reason in favour of adventure and conflict. They devalorize history, society and politics by making identity into an absolute that is legitimized through violence. If rightists eventually earn the enmity and derision of society, it is largely because they destroy knowledge through their indeterminate transgressions.[187] The ideology of embedded history that is endemic to today's black capitalism constitutes a racialist version of the cultural nationalisms of the twentieth century. To defuse its logic, it is necessary to recognize that its sources are not contained in a mythic past, encoded in DNA or in ethnic rituals and paraphernalia, but rather in ideology.

The Israeli scholar and critic of Israeli policy, Zeev Sternhell, developed in the 1980s a theory of the ideological origins of fascism. Sternhell argues that fascism is a form of revolutionary conservatism that is not simply irrational but offers a fairly coherent and recognizable system of thought.[188] Fascism is typically opposed to Enlightenment, universality, liberalism, materialism and intellectualism. Although fascism is also against Marxism, it nevertheless borrows from the left aspects of its revolutionary ideology and theory of praxis. Contemporary debates around so-called social constructionism that appeal to leftist understandings of historical materialism as a critique of the ideological naturalization of social processes tend to abandon, along with this, notions of rights, autonomy, culture and history in favour of a determinism of the particular that separates cultures from one another in the interest of parochial specificity. These practices also separate culture and politics from the totality of social relations. Unwittingly or not, postmodern pessimism and identity politics have incubated the renewal of fascist tendencies, destroying both liberal and socialist universality, thereby justifying the political right and disarming the left. One notices this in media outlets like *Vice* magazine, for instance, where rightist values and capitalist excess are mixed with critiques of xenophobia and homophobia. One could even find fault with antifa notions of counter-violence, where punch-ups and the promotion of hatred against white supremacists leave most sensible people nonplussed. The issue does not come around to the wish for a perpetual peace, as identitarians argue, who instead want their perpetual pound of flesh, but to an organized resistance to capitalism that does not compromise on principles.

According to Sternhell, fascist ideology developed in France at the end of the nineteenth century but also has its sources in the German tradition of *volkisch* nationalism. During the *fin-de-siècle*, the anti-materialist reaction attacked the institutions of liberal democracy as well as its philosophical foundations in such Enlightenment principles as individualism, equal rights, utilitarianism, the state, democracy and majority rule. Rather than Jacobin values of excellence, the decadence movement privileged slumming and Rousseauian notions of the popular will. The exploited masses became a political force through which to enliven a sickly national spirit, which had been destroyed by economic calculation, industrialism and imperialism. Fascism is not simply an alternative to bourgeois ideology, however, but is also one of its contradictory tendencies, its illiberal obscene underside.

Fascism is complicated by the fact that it makes use of revolutionary ideology. Although turn of the century fascism attacked Marxism, many of its early proponents came from and were associated with leftist organizations, where they had absorbed leftist ideas and the materialist conception of history. Just as socialists criticized parliamentary deliberation, fascists considered elections and party politics to be agencies of corruption that weaken executive authority. Fascists attacked the established "disorder" and sought to impose a higher authority and organization of social life that emphasizes interdependence and that restricts individualist notions of liberty. Unlike bourgeois radicals, who had already achieved their goals and now lacked a revolutionary path forward, cultural nationalists could draw on the social Darwinist ideas of writers like Nietzsche, Renan, Taine, Le Bon, Boulanger, Michels, Bergson and others to justify a new morality. Theories of race were used to justify exploitation as well as historical, social and political concepts. Moreover, in the context of Freudian psychoanalysis, it was accepted that humans were irrational, in part, because they were confined by historical limitations and controlled from without by images and ideas.[189] In order to give some shape to human emotions, enthusiasm and unruly passions, a cult of the leader and an ideology of populism were to replace liberal institutions and laws. A mob, rather than liberal reforms or communist parties, could better regulate financiers. The mobilization of the masses through the nationalist conquest of scapegoats could be devised to overcome internal divisions and contradictions. A fascist leader is invariably a man of the people – less an exemplary representative and spokesperson than the embodiment of the will of the masses. Unlike the communist worker, who is a part of the whole, the fascist leader is a metonymic part that stands in for the whole. The totality in this case does not represent the possibility of a transition away from capitalism but is rather a nationally defined popular movement. Workers are enjoined to support their capitalist employers in a collaborative spirit that is typical of a wartime state of emergency. Fascist violence thus takes on the trappings of class warfare in its organizational effort to destroy the liberal order. Workers are mobilized as shock troops and soldiers. Heroism is glorified as an aspect of the dynamism and activism of the revolutionary will to power.

Among political ideologues, revisionism takes many forms, from liberals, who accept the unevenness of power between the establishment and the working masses, to syndicalists, who revise Marx on the basis of an anti-materialist moralism. The spiritualist activism of Georges Sorel, for instance, stressed vitalism against moral degeneration and Marxist rationality. Georges Valois added Christian values to his quest for a 'third way' beyond capitalism and socialism, calling for fraternity in the heroic construction of the national economy. In his political style, Valois adopted Mussolini's orchestration of grandiose settings and luxurious décors in his propaganda on the overcoming of communist symbols and programmes. The intellectual counterpart to this was historical revisionism.

Fascists accepted Marxism as an incomparable tool for the analysis of history. The Belgian politician Henri de Man argued in his book *The Remaking of a Mind: A Soldier's Thoughts on War and Reconstruction* (1919) that the experience of the First World War led to the realization that communism was not able to organize the working class as effectively as nationalism. He concluded that nationalism is a more revolutionary ideology than international socialism. Economic class struggle, on this view, does not adequately explain the movement of history and socialism can only come about through nationalism. Economic competition is better suited to the development of a synthetic national socialism than communist revolution. The bourgeois state must be modernized through authoritarian government and retention of the profit motive. Marx's theory of the economic laws of history were thus revised and redefined by fascist ideologues as a "neo-socialist" defence of private property. In *Beyond Marxism* (1927) and *The Idea of Socialism* (1929) de Man called for the liquidation of Marxist political economy in favour of the relativization of ideologies through institutions that emphasize moral decisions rather than scientific laws of historical becoming. Whereas for Marx the contradictions of capitalism have nothing to do with questions of morality, de Man advocated a non-Marxist socialism that reverses the Hegelian cunning of history through which capitalism produces a proletarian counter-force and instead expounded a spirit of sacrifice that is embodied in material means with the goal of destroying socialism through the conquest of bourgeois institutions and the *embourgeoisement* of the proletariat.[190] One finds here a displaced description of the shift from the formal to the real subsumption of labour. De Man's worker is not selling his labour in uneven exchange relations but is rather motivated by the instinct of self-esteem and a religion of work that offers a vision of the future presented to the masses as a matter of destiny. As industrial psychology replaces Marxism and as advertising replaces public culture, the instinctive feeling of self-respect generated by the culture industry provides the doctrine of will with a cultish pragmatism, a sense of movement and an ethics of personal satisfaction.

Another revisionist, Marcel Déat, advocated a form of neo-socialism with the designation "anti-capitalism," a theory for which Marxism is a flexible method. Since the middle class also suffers from the problems of capitalism, alliances should be made with the national bourgeoisie in a refashioning of the state. Because the middle class has a better sense of individuality and freedom, it remains for him the natural leader of the proletariat. Further, the state mode of production, or planned economy, implies that the dictatorship of the proletariat has evolved along nationalist lines, with intellectual cadres leading technological changes like automation and the managed productivity of large firms. Communities can thus be restored as a "harmonious aggregate" through social solidarity, from the family unit and local community to the region, the firm and the nation.[191]

Neo-socialist ideas are only a hop, skip and jump away from the anti-Marxist revisionism of Michel Foucault and his *à la carte* materialism, an interpretive method that has some affinities with Gilles Deleuze's 'transcendental empiricism.' Foucault's critical theory has contributed to the demobilization of the left by diversifying the notion of agency and by criticizing liberal political philosophy in favour of liberal economics. Opposed to the old left and perceiving the welfare state to be outdated, Foucault believed that economic liberalism would lead to a less disciplinary society, a view that has proven more useful to Wall Street and the Pentagon than to "the subject."[192] As Heiko Feldner and Fabio Vighi argue, the ubiquity of discourse theory in today's university-driven culture is due to the belief that it provides a more compelling alternative to the discredited paradigms of Marxist political economy and ideology critique.[193]

Foucault's neo-positivist and anti-dialectical theory of the subject of discourse abandons the notion of class antagonism in favour of difference and aesthetic self-fashioning. Power relations are not restricted to the level of the state and the economy but are rather defined as simultaneously diffuse and local. Symbolic regimes therefore have a materiality that is independent of social norms of meaning. They are part of a micro-physics of power that is specific to different orders of power/knowledge. On this basis, it is possible to develop 'technologies' of gender, race, sexuality and diversity that are defined without recourse to such Marxist notions as totality. With the collapse of the Soviet Union in 1989, Feldner and Vighi argue, the mass exodus from Marxism into various spin-offs of Gramscian hegemony, like post-colonial and queer theory, transformed Marxist history into relativistic and crypto-normative forms of historicism in which history writing could be associated with the formation of new identities.[194] With regard to Foucault's method, Žižek emphasizes the difference between historicism and historicity. Historicity has a dialectical relation with the Real, defined as the unhistorical traumatic kernel that interferes with every attempt to integrate society into a coherent symbolic order.[195] One finds examples of the Foucauldian approach to materiality in new social movement rhetoric against reason, laws, borders or limits and in favour of competing notions like affect, flows, spheres and assemblages. Foucault sought to avoid the contradictions of dialectical negation and the psychoanalytic notion of the unconscious. He emphasized instead the affirmation of problems of cause and effect, a principle of absolute immanence which has translated in postmodern quarters to the assertion of TINO: there is no outside. In practical terms, this takes the form of grudge matches and radical democratic agonism rather than solidarity across struggles.[196] It leads to efforts to master lack rather than working out a modus vivendi on what is reasonable and visionary.

After Napoleon's peace with the Catholic Church and the establishment of the new civil code, the Bourbon Restoration led to a mass revolt against the constitutional monarchy and the reign of the Citizen-King, Louis Philippe, which led to another mass revolt, suppressed by Louis-Napoleon Bonaparte, the president of the Second Republic, nephew of the former Emperor of France and forerunner of fascism. In his 1851 text, *The Eighteenth Brumaire of Louis Bonaparte*, Marx derided Louis-Napoléon as a "grotesque mediocrity" dressed in the costume of a hero. Men make history, Marx argued, but in circumstances not of their making. Paraphrasing Engels, Marx made the now famous assertion that history repeats itself, "first as tragedy, then as farce." In a book dedicated to this notion, Žižek comments on today's so-called materialists and argues that among the ways in which capitalist ideology is naturalized is the separation of the included and excluded through apartheid walls.[197] With the extension of systems of surveillance, these walls have become increasingly virtual. While it is possible that humanity will solve the problems of ecology, biogenetics and intellectual property, the notion of universal economic justice on a planet of slums defies any teleological notion of the overcoming of the contradictions of proletarianization. What difference does it make if one is penetrated by discourse if one is proletarianized as part of redundant surplus populations, no longer valuable as labour power and now without any meaningful rights of citizenship.

The global 'part of no part' that the capitalist rhetoric of diversity cannot incorporate into the social space except for a handful of politicians, academics, athletes, artists, Hollywood celebrities and CEOs, finds its expression in the appearance in 2018 of the Gilets Noirs, the immigrant counterpart to the Gilets Jaunes movement against precarity and the neoliberal regime in France. Although it eventually became a global movement, with similar protests worldwide, the Gilets Jaunes encountered its refracted self-image in the demands of *sans papiers* against the "Asylum and Immigration Law" and against a system that includes detention centres, forced labour, the black market, prisons for foreigners, deportation, and the deaths of migrants crossing the Mediterranean Sea.[198] In July of 2019, the Gilets Noirs occupied the Panthéon, a national monument and memorial site for French political figures like Rousseau, Voltaire, Émile Zola, Jean Jaurès and Simone Veil. They demanded recognition from Prime Minister Édouard Philippe to obtain their immigration papers. Marine Le Pen tweeted her indignation: "It is INADMISSIBLE to see militant undocumented workers occupying, with impunity, the great place of the Republic that is the Panthéon." Why it is that in this situation the Gilets Noirs did not seek to become active within the Gilets Jaunes is as important a question as why BLM has developed separately from OWS. The global division of labour that makes it such that embedded history can represent black capitalism but not socialism defines the politics of post-representation under capitalist globalization.

Today's racialism increasingly accepts the definition of equality in terms of access to middle-class and billionaire status rather than in terms of social equality. Production relations are then transposed to neoliberal notions of the free market. Social groups and individuals compete with one another in this world of markets. Because they do so their interests are more easily represented in the realm of culture, where history, agency, experience and attitudes are separated from the confrontation with capitalism. Tellingly, the Gilets Noirs do not wear vests and have no unifying symbol other than their black skin. Nor are there many women among them. One reason why the Gilets Noirs and BLM matter have no need for the Gilets Jaunes and OWS is because the latter, like them, possess little more than the shirts on their backs. As minor detachments of the demobilized proletariat, they cannot offer much more than their solidarity, or so it seems. Outside the hallowed halls of the Panthéon, the *tabula rasa* of decolonization is mediated by the digital realm. The healthy immune response of social movements to traditional organizational methods that Hardt and Negri say is a vestige of the centralism of the International are today an autoimmune disorder, organizing petty-bourgeois activism as a diversified constituent power.[199] No one speaks for these movements in what they tell everyone is a rejection of hierarchy. The immense majority of the colonized are oblivious because that which is most concrete is not race but the moral universe that is defined by the idealism that accepts capitalism as the immanent state of things and that transmutes class struggle into cultural fantasy.

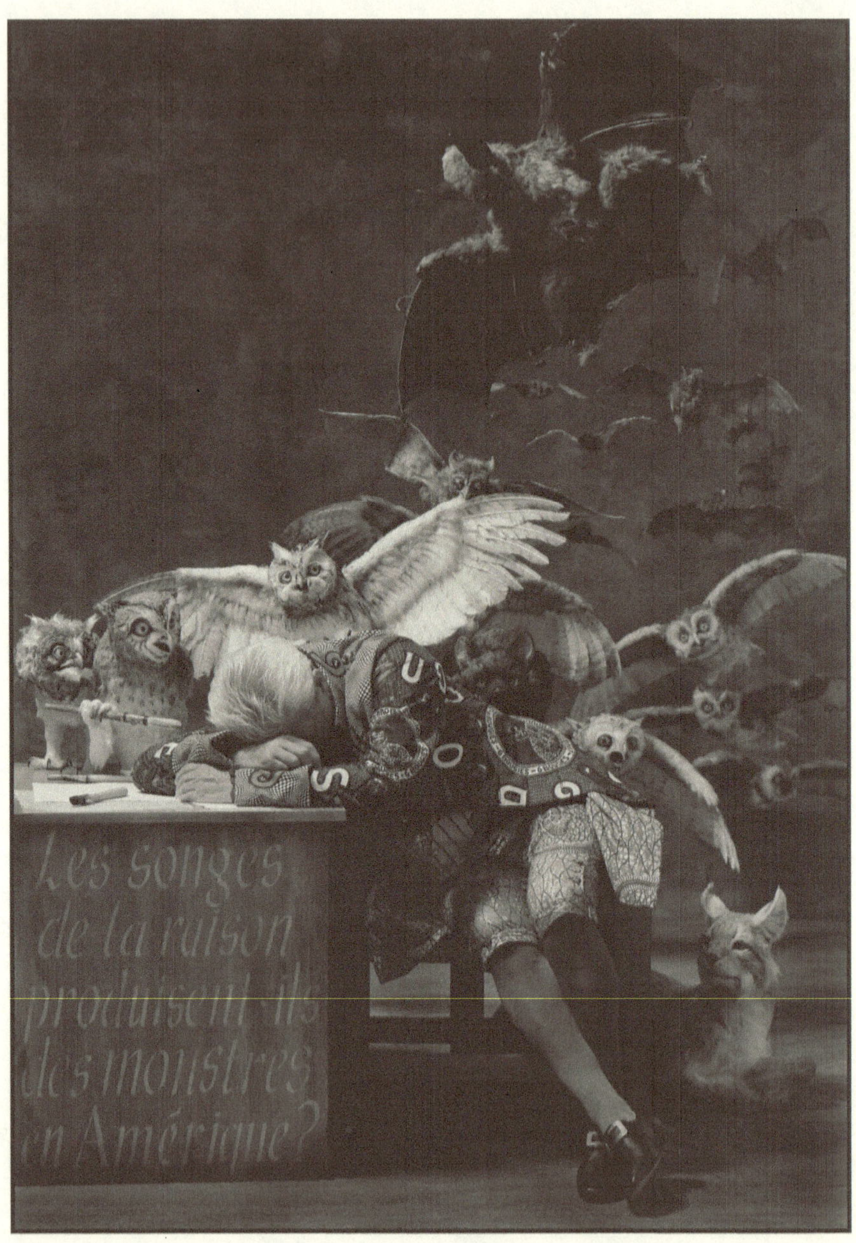

Yinka Shonibare, ***The Sleep of Reason Produces Monsters (America)***, 2008. 1 of 5. Based on Goya's *Los Caprichos*, 1797-98. Victorian tailoring in batik patterned cloth produced by Dutch and British factories with designs from Indonesia and sold in West Africa. © Yinka Shonibare CBE. Courtesy of the artist and James Cohan, New York.

CONCLUSION

From north and south / We come from east and west / Breathing as one / Living in fame or dying in flame / We laugh / Our mission is blessed / We fight for you / For freedom unforeseen / Thinking as one / Rolling along / To the beat of the drum

– Laibach, 'The Whistleblowers'

The Nigeria-born British artist Yinka Shonibare produced in 2008 a series of large-scale photographic prints that are based on Francisco Goya's 1799 etching *The Sleep of Reason Produces Monsters*, a work that depicts the artist asleep while behind him owls, bats and other nocturnal creatures allude to the nightmarish corruption of Spanish society. Shonibare quotes the image in five tableaux in which sleeping allegorical figures, dressed in colourful batik fabrics, represent Africa, America, Asia, Australia and Europe. The skin colour of each sleeper is not necessarily congruent with what is expected for the geographic region. By making the work global in scope rather than simply European, Shonibare relates the issues of Enlightenment reason and Romantic caprice to the history of colonization. These beautifully crafted images are simple and evocative enough to lead to multiple interpretations. At the same time, they make it impossible to ignore questions of race and culture in the history of colonial conquest. Whereas Goya's work was concerned with the traumas of the transition from Royalism to Parliamentarism, with the history of the Counter-Reformation a not-so-distant memory, Shonibare has as his subject the misadventures of global capitalism. One implication of such work is that by delving into the prestige with which Western culture has endowed its canonical artworks, contemporary art is recovering some of what has been pillaged from formerly colonized peoples. Progressive collectors, gallerists, curators and critics play their part by facilitating this global, cross-cultural redistribution of symbolic capital.

Like Shonibare's works, the Obama portraits are about the politics of global capitalism. When between 2021 and 2022 the Smithsonian NPG toured the Obama portraits across the country, this quote by Kehinde Wiley was prominently displayed as wall text: "What I'm doing here in this particular commission is dealing not only with the *idea* of power in a portrait but literal power in a portrait." If one was not to be asleep about the implications of Wiley's painting, one could suggest revising the label that accompanies his NPG portrait of Obama to read:

> Barack Obama, born 1961. Forty-fourth president, 2009-2017. Barack Obama made history by becoming the first African-American president. However, according to his post-race neoliberal ideology, History had already ended before he was elected. Clever marketing gave people the impression that there was some hope that Obama would alter the situation that led to the 2008 financial crisis. Instead, the former Illinois state senator catered to the donor class by failing to prosecute Wall Street corruption and overseeing a $20 trillion handout to renegade banksters. His cronyism was reflected in the increase in economic inequality over his two terms, adversely affecting poor black and minority communities in particular. Rather than institute universal health care, his Affordable Care Act handed millions of uninsured Americans over to the predatory health insurance companies and left millions more underinsured. The 2003 invasion of Iraq was perpetrated under false premises by the Republican administration of George Bush, implicating the United States in a war of aggression that violated Iraqi sovereignty – a war crime under the international laws that were established after the Nuremberg Trials. U.S. officials, including Obama, who continued the intervention by expanding the war into Syria and Libya, should have faced prosecution as war criminals. Obama ignored his legal obligation to investigate, prosecute and punish every act of torture committed by American soldiers and intelligence officers during these wars, in which millions of people died and which cost American taxpayers $8 trillion. In addition to controversial drone strikes and kill lists, the constitutional lawyer authorized the illegal assassination of American citizens. His failure to close the Guantánamo Bay prison and his assassination of al-Qaeda founder Osama bin Laden said more about the decline of U.S. democracy than about political leadership. This "woke" portrait by the businessman artist Kehinde Wiley alludes to the possibility that Obama is being sexually abducted by background foliage. The spermatozon on Obama's temple indicates that he has been "branded" by the artist. The cultural contradictions of racialist neoliberalism and the logic of embedded history that this work champions contributed to the weakening of the American left and the strengthening of the far right.

One of the problems with the reduction of politics to the quest for empowerment rather than the advancement of principles and programme is that power is an arbitrary measure. After the hoopla about the NPG paintings had died down, Obama attempted to distance himself from the kind of woke culture that defines his official portrait. On the occasion of a discussion with young adults at the Obama Foundation Summit in October 2019, Obama argued that someone who is politically woke and never compromises on their principles is simply judgemental and does not appreciate the messiness of the world. Reiterating his conservative ideology of meritocracy, he castigated call-out culture as lazy and ineffective, especially if someone wants to contribute to social change.[1]

Obama's statement on woke culture is similar to the remark he made in 2009 in response to the G20 protests in Pittsburgh: "focusing on concrete, local, immediate issues that have an impact on people's lives is what really makes a difference and … having protests about abstractions [like] global capitalism … is not really going to make a difference."[2] Whereas he was previously criticizing anti-globalization protesters, he is now scolding people who use social media to engage in Twitter spats. Obama is correct to satirize political wokeness. Contrary to what was suggested by Malaika Jabali in *The Guardian*, Obama's caricature of cancel culture is not mere conjecture.[3] As Michael Arceneaux mentioned in *The Independent*, many young people become aware of social issues and become involved in activism through social media.[4] What neither mention is the extent to which Obama enabled woke culture as the limit of progressivism within the Democratic Party, rejecting at every turn the grassroots movements that helped bring him to power and supporting instead the kinds of establishment politics that are not simply messy but unambiguously corrupt. The mainstream media, who are equally responsible for creating the culture of wokeness, praised Obama for "ripping" and "lashing out" at woke culture (*The New York Post*), "blasting" the idea of purity (*Fox News*), gaining bipartisan support by "bashing" and "shaming" cancel culture (*The Washington Post*), "laying" into people who are too judgemental (*Business Insider*), warning that becoming woke could be "dangerous" if you wish to make it as a professional politician (*Oprah Magazine*), telling young people not to be ideologically rigid but to "get over it" (*USA Today*) and making a rare foray into the cultural conversation by condemning cancel culture (*The New York Times*). Casting stones is "easy to do," Obama said, as he pretended to be sitting on a couch and pressing a television remote control. One might think that sending out remote-piloted drones to drop explosives on Afghani citizens is also easy to do.

The notion of political purity and perfection that Obama denounced is a strawman in an argument that avoids the agenda that his administration pursued and the problems that it exacerbated. As if Americans had not had enough of this agent of Wall Street and the Pentagon, Obama sought to interfere in the progressive debate created by the Sanders campaign by denouncing socialism. In November 2019, he told an audience of financial donors at the Democracy Alliance in Washington D.C.:

> This is still a country that is less revolutionary than it is interested in improvement. They like seeing things improved. But the average American doesn't think we have to completely tear down the system and remake it. […] There are a lot of persuadable voters and there are a lot of Democrats out there who just want to see things make sense. They just don't want to see crazy stuff. […] Even as we push the envelope and we are bold in our vision, we also have to be rooted in reality and the fact that voters, including the Democratic voters and certainly persuadable independents or even moderate Republicans are not driven by the same views that are reflected on certain, you know, left-leaning Twitter feeds. Or the activist wing of our party.[5]

Obama knows that his version of moderate is the reactionary radicalism of the extreme centre and its willingness to carry forward a programme of social inequality, austerity, war and ecological destruction. Politicians are political leaders. They are not, or rather, they should not be technocrats who manipulate voters to do the bidding of wealthy campaign donors. That is what lobbyists and public relations firms do. As for left-leaning Twitter feeds, one tweet issued in this context was Kyle Kulinsky's reminder that 90 percent of the people killed by Obama's drone strikes were civilians, a fact that was confirmed by drone pilot-turned-whistleblower Daniel Hale.[6] Although the media reported that Obama's November comments referred to the left-leaning candidates Sanders and Warren, it is more accurate to say that they directly targeted the Sanders 2020 campaign, which called for a "political revolution" in American politics. Sanders replied that his policy objectives are not equivalent to tearing down the system. They are essential reforms that could and should have been implemented decades ago.[7] Now that Obama no longer has to contend with the demands of the presidency, he more clearly demonstrates what his politics have been all along. Since 2017, he voiced his opposition to Elizabeth Warren's criticism of Wall Street and stated his intention to intervene in the 2020 primaries if Sanders got anywhere near the Democratic nomination. Alas, he came through on these promises.[8] Centrists like Obama are more concerned with fighting the activist wing of the Democratic Party than the Republican right, as evidenced by two failed attempts at impeachment and calls for bipartisan unity with Republican lawmakers who peddle Trump's fascistic 'big lie' that the 2020 election was stolen.[9] Like his billionaire friends and celebrity allies, Obama benefited from Trump's tax cuts for the wealthy. Yet it is his administration that oversaw the largest transfer of wealth in American history.

Can Americans be judged for the kind of government they choose for themselves? Yes, they can. If they could not, there would be no democracy and there would be no politics. Can politicians adequately represent people's needs and interests? Yes, they can. If they could not, there would be no democracy and no politics. Can politicians fully represent people's needs and interests? No, they cannot. If they could, there would be no democracy and no politics. This problem of representation distinguishes democracy from the ideology of fascism. It also distinguishes the neoliberal logic of post-representation from communism.

Romanticism reflects on the question of Enlightenment universality from the perspective of the particular. This counterpoint to universality does not represent its failure but its condition. Particularists who embrace capitalism tend to ignore how it is that universality conditions its exceptions. The only way to avoid such disavowal is for particularism to engage in self-criticism. Walter Benn Michaels argues that what anti-racists want is for Americans to be perceived as conservative and for conservatives to be racist. The racialist "left" is more concerned with apportioning blame, he contends, than eliminating inequality. In this process, one escapes rather than understands the condition of particularism. Such particularism tends to judge or acknowledge other particulars at the expense of common determinations. Having accepted that there are no alternatives to global capitalism, the problems of the totality are projected, like so many bats and owls, onto specific social groups. This phenomenon is especially acute in the U.S. insofar as people accept the myths of American exceptionalism. From this ideology is derived the phenomenon of black exceptionalism.

We live today at a moment when the possibility of universal social policies around labour rights, wages, a guaranteed basic income, pensions, health care, education, housing and ecology have the potential to revolutionize and overthrow the capitalist system. While the populist left considers that corporate elites are the main obstacle to this possibility, rather than the challenge of building the class organizations that could overthrow the existing world order, the need to build international class power is undermined by the post-politics of the professional-managerial class, which advances the interests of identity groups at the expense of the "essentialist" left. Conservatives have caught on to this fact and have fanned the flames of animosity against 'social justice warriors' of various stripes. Postmodern academics, activists and the liberal class have responded in kind, capitalizing on identity as a stake in social, cultural, political and economic competition. As the postmodern left continues to make culture and identity struggles into privileged sites of political conflict, it ignores the consequences of its own post-representational and post-ideological agenda. Seeking the socio-economic advantages of progressivism, but not its responsibilities, the petty-bourgeois activist sector ignores how it is that identity politics has become a ruling-class politics. As Reed puts it,

> I think it's imperative as well that we accept and not waver from an understanding that there's no splitting the difference between a) what's called anti-racism, the fundamentally brokerage, petition politics of racial representation, which assumes as it has ever since Booker Washington, that the pertinent locus of political agency for advancing "black interests" is the ruling class, which is therefore antiracism's natural ally, and which guarantees that antiracist politics is thus by definition a politics fully incorporated within neoliberalism, and b) an anti-capitalist politics centered on the broad working class.[10]

Advocating flexibilization in all facets of life, from education, job training and legal rights to social identity and human values, the postmodernized politics of pseudo-solidarity make diversity into a bludgeon against the international working class. The latter is limited to the status of the abstract labour that corresponds to the abstract universality of identities in the global marketplace. It is this abstract universality, or abstract particularism, that is valorized by capitalism. One cannot make identity struggles more 'concrete' without changing the system of capitalism. From out of this situation, populism emerges as an attempt to redress the elitism that is created by both the managerial class and the petty-bourgeois left.

Populism is inadequate to international class solidarity. What makes a political movement populist is its mobilization of 'the people' against an external enemy.[11] Elitist forms of progressive neoliberalism can thereby be expressed in populist terms. 'Black populism' emerges in the American context as one among other strategies that make use of bipartisan politics in a way that is seemingly class neutral, but that insists on the inherent antagonism between whites and blacks, or between the white power structure and black resistance. Since capitalist exploitation exists alongside civil rights and liberal democracy, the strategy of black populism is inadequate at the outset. Regardless, insofar as it accepts wealth inequality, it also accepts political inequality. Democracy is rejected in favour of the sovereignty of a particular social group whose goal has become the pursuit of political power and economic advantage. The activist pseudo-left tends to ignore this problem when it rejects democratic struggle as a politics of the state.

In the wake of OWS and the Arab Spring, the black left in the U.S., and now also the 'intersectional' and 'decolonial' left more generally, has been troubled by political disorientation. On the subject of the 1619 Project, the *Black Agenda Report* interviewed professor of African American Studies Josh Myers, who argued against the American exceptionalism that is implicit in the 1619 Project by making reference to the writings of Cedric Robinson.[12] In contrast to Nikole Hannah-Jones, Myers contends that blacks were never interested in becoming true patriots. They simply sought freedom from slavery, as evidenced by the fact that more blacks fought with the British, who promised them freedom, than with the American revolutionaries. Robinson's 1983 book, *Black Marxism: The Making of the Black Radical Tradition*, is one of the texts that one might look to for an alternative to the kind of revisionism that is served up by the *Times*.[13] The black radical tradition that Robinson champions, however, is presented as a critique of the historical limitations of the Marxist tradition. Robinson's combination of historicism with black separatism interprets Marxism as a form of Euro-Enlightenment domination. His concept of black Marxism maintains a focus on macro-political issues but, like the 1619 Project, is unfortunately committed to the notion that European culture is inherently racist. Robinson's return to a pre-Hegelian notion of dialectics and metaphysics is anathema to the intellectual foundations of Marxism and is as such compatible with bourgeois and postmodern notions of materialism. What Robinson posits as Marxism's failure to acknowledge the radical agency of peasants is, historically speaking, not the view of Lenin and Trotsky, but of the Mensheviks, who advocated a bourgeois-democratic revolution. One should rather think of Robinson's notion of black Marxism as a form of black populism that targets Europeans as the established elite group.

It is not for no reason that Robinson's scholarship has been put to dubious uses, as for example by the editors of the book *Futures of Black Marxism*, who associate the rise of neo-fascism with the white supremacy of the security state rather than with upper-class uses of authoritarianism to protect vested interests.[14] Twisting the slogan that the rise of every fascism is due to a failed revolution, the editors attribute neo-fascism to a failed anti-racism. Not surprisingly, they associate Robinson's concept of 'racial capitalism' with Trump but not with Obama. Although detrimental to Marxist praxis, the concept of racial capitalism serves to clarify how it is that emancipatory universalism is undermined by not only black capitalism but also by pseudo-Marxist and anti-Western theories that substitute solidarity for intersectionality, which Michaels refers to as the "opiate of the professional-managerial class."[15]

According to Robinson, Marx's method of historical materialism ignores the question of race, slave labour and the peasantry.[16] Robinson accuses Marxism of European exceptionalism and challenges its ability to explain history. One might have made this claim in 1860 but it hardly stands one century later when every formerly peasant nation has been incorporated into global capitalism. Robinson's work is premised on two notions: first, that Europeans are inherently "racialist," by which he means racist; and second, that Africans have never been integrated into the world system of slavery and capitalism but have retained through cultural means a particularism that defies the universalizing claims of Hegelian and Marxist totality. Regardless, Robinson claims, black radicals have been attracted to Marxism due to its "apparent universalism."[17] If Marxism was at one time an antidote to European racism and imperialism, he argues, its internationalism is an insufficient explanation of social and cultural forces. Robinson denounces the explanation of racism through historical and economic processes as Eurocentric. For him, slave revolts throughout history indicate that race is an organizing principle and an epistemology that better explains notions of authority, commerce and power.[18] The epistemology of race recovers dignity as it negates the world system and provides alternative forms of agency to that of a global proletariat.[19] Robinson disputes the Marxist critique of nationalism and falsely conflates the Soviet programme of 'socialism in one country' with this phenomenon.[20] One might not associate this revisionism with a regressive populism if it was not for Robinson's rejection of rationalism and Marxist science. Black radicalism, as a negation of Western civilization, has its roots in African life, he contends, which is expressed in forms of rebellion like marronage, in religious rituals like Obeah and in the ontology of black metaphysics more generally. This "demon" that Africans injected into the "normative" processes of primitive accumulation, he argues, "infected" the system of slave labour with its contradictions and syncretic revolts.[21]

Robinson's development of the notion of a revolutionary black intelligentsia, with his focus on the work of W.E.B. Du Bois, C.L.R. James and Richard Wright, is his least objectionable contribution in *Black Marxism*. Yet here too he transforms social struggle into "historical antilogic."[22] For instance, the notion that for James the radical black tradition is contained in the phatic traditions of African culture converts his anti-Stalinist humanism into a nascent postmodernism.[23] As James wrote in the introduction to his study of the Third International: "The ideas on which this book are based are the fundamental ideas of Marxism."[24] The essence of this was the solidarity of the international working class against national tradition and against the capitalist class of each respective country. One could not say the same thing for Richard Wright, who in his later years became an existentialist. What is surprising to today's reader, however, is how similar Robinson's 1983 text is to today's post-structuralist racialism. Myers is correct in this regard that Robinson's *Black Marxism* is an alternative to the 1619 Project, since, despite their common racialist perspective, Robinson is concerned with historical accuracy and relies on Marxist concepts.

The 1619 Project has less to do with American historiography than with postmodern art and simulation films – cultural forms that accept uneven power relations at the same time that they subvert conventions.[25] By attacking the political universalism that subtends claims to difference, postmodernism supports cultural and political relativism. As the micro-waving of the normalizing power of anything and everything failed to disrupt the power of the corporate state, the 2000s witnessed the rise of a macro-political rethinking of the end of History. Those artists and intellectuals who in the interim have taken no notice of the corporatization of diversity carry on with the fantasy that they are game-changing the spectacle one woke project at a time. Making a micro-narrative into a macro-narrative involves a political choice: you either repeat the ideology of bourgeois nationalism, or, if you reject Enlightenment, you repeat the ideology of fascism. Fascism, however, is not simply unrelated to Enlightenment. Writing in the 1930s, Marcuse argued that fascism replaces the notion of inalienable human rights with the naturalism of the volk. This worldview, according to Marcuse, maintains the capitalist economic system to save society from Marxian socialism and class struggle. Its "political existentialism" results in a "dehistoricization of the historical" and a "cynical realism" that extols the "metaphysical certainties" of race and a classless society.[26] Less overtly volkish, Robinson's theory of black Marxism would seem to allow adherents to have their Marxism and eat it too. His notion of black radicalism has no need for the Enlightenment or the notion of a common humanity. It rather resembles afro-pessimism in its extreme phenomenological reduction, even if Robinson argues that slaves never became slaves because their nature could not be reduced to their historical condition.[27]

Gregory Meyerson's critique of Robinson's *Black Marxism* is a welcome rejoinder.[28] Robinson's work, Meyerson argues, is typical of contemporary theories of race, gender and culture that eschew Marxist dialectics and misconstrue the theory of base and superstructure. The Marxist focus on class does not exclude women and people of colour or reduce them to secondary contradictions. What the centrality of class implies is the necessity of building multiracial, multi-gendered and international organizations that can fight all forms of oppression at the same time as capitalist exploitation. Race, class and gender do intersect and interact. However, in contrast to postmodern theories, Marxist class analysis explains how it is that different forms of oppression are structural but not determinant. Moreover, class analysis should not be conflated with economic reductionism. Meyerson contends that a dialectically non-deterministic Marxism offers a better explanation of both pre-capitalist forms of racism and those forms of racism that are caught up with contemporary capitalism. The worlds of 1619 and 2019 are not so easily conflated. However valid, psycho-cultural concepts fail to explain class domination and potentially conflate the interests of the working class and the ruling class. What is overlooked is the need of the dominant classes to sew discord among the dominated classes so as to secure their hegemony.

The potential for the political radicalization of social relations of production is not determined at the outset but can only come about through struggle.

Nationalism is not an effective a path towards the democratization of productive forces. Nor is the revolutionization of productive forces emancipatory if it leaves relations of exploitation intact. By politicizing only gender or race relations and leaving economic relations unchanged, Meyerson argues, difference politics provide a culturalist alternative to radicalism, which is denounced as something that is specific to white, European males. The political relevance of sexuality is even more difficult to make. Since sexuality has no determinate objectivity and is inherently aporetic, it easily serves the ideology of corporate capitalism.[29] Identitarians accuse Marxism of dissolving difference into the interpretive framework of Marxist theory and universalism. Contemporary culture and politics are therefore caught in a Chinese finger trap. The greater the need for a radicalization of the political economy, the more that various forms of identity are proffered as the most persistent problems and pressing issues of the day. This trap manifests the politics of post-representation.

The result of today's diversity populism reinforces the worst tendencies of neoliberal capitalism. As capitalism replaces internationalism with de-unionization and the rule of global markets, the professional-managerial class uproots the politics of culture and substitutes racialized and sexualized attacks on the 'old' left. Race and gender initiatives today bamboozle publics to accept a more perfect capitalism, embedding geographical and cultural differences, including radical challenges, into the machinations of technocratic domination. In contemporary educational and cultural institutions, a sorting process is underway in which people who are too woke to fail are populating the ranks of the managerial elite. The now fashionable notion of racial capitalism, Reed suggests, is less an oxymoron than one might presume.[30]

Today's postmodern racialism calls on us to accept the view that socialist radicals who struggle for a progressive agenda in the areas of labour, health care, housing, education, peace and ecology are relics of a politics that collapsed in 1989. The extreme centre that dispensed with postwar Keynesianism wields the kind of political power that has no tangible connection to the interests of the majority and that is unmoored from any ideological challenge to the belief that History has come to an end. In its wake, the notion of emancipatory universality has become suspect and recast as 'class reductionism,' a Marxist concept that is wielded by anti-Marxists who use Marxist theory against Marxists.[31] This ploy works with people who do not understand Marxism or who no longer accept its basic tenets. The charge of 'economism' is in part a communist critique of the social democratic limitation of revolutionary politics to the realm of trade unionism. Workers who act particularistically are concerned with only that which is in their narrow economic interest. Workers become a class-conscious proletariat when they act in the universal interest, that is, when they seek to transform all of humanity and abolish class society. The belief that neoliberal governance can contribute to racial and gender equity is a capitalist class politics. Unless neoliberal progressives are prepared to accept that they defend the same class interests as neo-fascists, they should recognize that the far right has understood the contradictions of identity better than they have. To those who ask us to ignore the politics of neoliberal artists and politicians, whether they come from minority constituencies or not, our answer is simple: no, we cannot.

NOTES

Introduction

1. Ta-Nehisi Coates, *We Were Eight Years in Power: An American Tragedy* (New York: One World, 2017) 11-18.
2. Martin Pengelly, "Barack Obama: 'Americans spooked by black man in White House' led to Trump presidency," *The Guardian* (November 12, 2020), https://www.theguardian.com/us-news/2020/nov/12/barack-obama-memoir-donald-trump.
3. The birther debate was incubated in the Hillary Clinton camp by the same people who invented the Bernie Bro stereotype. See Glenn Greenwald, "Democrats and Their Media Allies Impugned Biden's Cognitive Fitness. Now They Feign Outrage," *The Intercept* (March 9, 2020), https://theintercept.com/2020/03/09/it-was-democrats-and-their-media-allies-who-impugned-bidens-cognitive-fitness-yet-now-feign-outrage/.
4. The Zero Hour with RJ Eskow, "Adolph Reed Jr: The Left, Biden, and the Totalitarian Threat," *YouTube* (October 2, 2021), https://www.youtube.com/watch?v=1jncq76OivI.
5. Hillary Rodham Clinton, *What Happened* (New York: Simon & Schuster, 2017) eBook, 653.
6. Editors, "Who Will Fill Biden's Cabinet?" *The New York Times* (November 24, 2020), https://www.nytimes.com/2020/11/11/us/politics/biden-cabinet.html?auth=login-email&login=email.
7. These are the claims of Briahna Joy Gray, the former press secretary of the Bernie Sanders campaign, on Katie Halper, "Woke Imperialism With Rania Khalek & Briahna Joy Gray," *YouTube* (November 22, 2020), https://www.youtube.com/watch?v=IiI4xnRCOT8.
8. Pluckrose and Lindsay have offered a compelling critique of "applied postmodernism," albeit in defence of liberal and conservative ideology. Despite the moral panic that these authors elicit, they nevertheless make some valid criticisms of what they define as the "third stage" of postmodern thought, where concepts drawn from critical theory and postmodern anti-foundationalism are taken to be objective facts and "socially applied" through reified themes and practices. The result, they argue, is an authoritarian Social Justice Movement that perceives injustice in everything and transforms social existence into a zero-sum struggle around identity markers. See Helen Pluckrose and James Lindsay, *Cynical Theories: How Activist Scholarship Made Everything about Race, Gender, and Identity – and Why This Harms Everybody* (Durham: Pitchstone Publishing, 2020).
9. John Roberts, *The Reasoning of Unreason: Universalism, Capitalism and Disenlightenment* (London: Bloomsbury, 2018).
10. Roberts, *The Reasoning of Unreason*, 20.
11. Mikkel Bolt Rasmussen, *Trump's Counter-Revolution* (Winchester: Zero Books, 2019) 1.
12. Rasmussen, *Trump's Counter-Revolution*, 3.
13. Cited by Slavoj Žižek in *First as Tragedy, Then as Farce* (London: Verso, 2009) 73.

14. Jeffrey St. Clair and Joshua Frank, "Prelude: Barack Obama, Changeling," in St. Clair and Frank, eds. *Hopeless: Barack Obama and the Politics of Illusion* (Oakland: AK Press, 2012) 4.
15. St. Clair and Frank, "Prelude," 7.
16. Rasmussen, *Trump's Counter-Revolution*, 95.
17. Rasmussen, *Trump's Counter-Revolution*, 21.
18. Rasmussen, *Trump's Counter-Revolution*, 25.
19. Rasmussen, *Trump's Counter-Revolution*, 25.
20. Paul Frymer, "Race, Labour, and the Twentieth-Century American State," *Politics & Society* 32:4 (December 2004) 475-509.
21. Touré F. Reed, *Toward Freedom: The Case Against Race Reductionism* (London: Verso, 2020) eBook, 33.
22. See Max Horkheimer, "The Jews and Europe" (December 1939) in Stephen Eric Bronner and Douglas MacKay Kellner, eds. *Critical Theory and Society: A Reader* (New York: Routledge, 1989) 77-94.
23. Cited in Robert Kuttner, "Steve Bannon, Unrepentant," *The American Prospect* (August 16, 2017), http://prospect.org/article/steve-bannon-unrepentant.
24. Kim Sajet, "The Obama Portraits Have Had a Pilgrimage Effect," *The Atlantic* (February 12, 2019), https://www.theatlantic.com/entertainment/archive/2019/02/obama-effect-national-portrait-gallery/582457/.
25. Keeanga-Yamahtta Taylor, "Joe Biden's Success Shows We Gave Obama a Free Pass," *The New York Times* (March 4, 2020), https://www.nytimes.com/2020/02/05/opinion/Biden-Obama-2020.html?auth=login-email&login=email. See also Branko Marcetic, "Joe Biden Has Built a Career on Betraying Black Voters," *Jacobin* (March 5, 2020), https://www.jacobinmag.com/2020/03/joe-biden-black-voters-african-americans-betrayal.
26. For a discussion of the African American vote on Super Tuesday as an anti-Trump vote based on the perception of Biden's greater electability, and despite blacks' support for socialist policies, see Glen Ford, "The Corporations and Their Media Strangled Bernie, and Older Black Voters Tied the Knot," *Black Agenda Report* (March 12, 2020), https://www.blackagendareport.com/corporations-and-their-media-strangled-bernie-and-older-black-voters-tied-knot. Against the black "misleadership class" that promotes the Democratic Party as a ruling-class party, the Black Agenda Report advocated radical movement building and mass protests. See in contrast Kshama Sawant's call for forming a socialist third party in Sawant, "#DemExit: Time to Launch a New Party Of, By, and For Working People," *Socialist Alternative* (March 11, 2020), https://www.socialistalternative.org/2020/03/11/demexit-time-to-launch-a-new-party-of-by-and-for-working-people/. See also Jacobin Magazine, "Adolph Reed, Cedric Johnson, Willie Legette & Michael Brooks 'Bernie, South Carolina & Black Voters'," *YouTube* (April 10, 2020), https://www.youtube.com/watch?v=qwnb0xParBM&list=PLxlNhP2f0kUKLSP2cQ38b9xymXZInHzRn&index=3&t=0s.
27. Dan Kovalik, *Cancel This Book: The Progressive Case Against Cancel Culture* (New York: Hot Books, 2021) eBook, 288.
28. Alana Wise, "Biden Pulls Back On 'Cavalier' Remarks About Black Voters," *NPR* (May 22, 2020), https://www.npr.org/2020/05/22/861007175/biden-pulls-back-on-cavalier-remarks-about-black-voters.
29. Eric Levitz, "The GOP Coalition Is Getting More Working-Class. Its Agenda Isn't," *New York Magazine* (July 18, 2020), https://nymag.com/intelligencer/2020/07/rightwing-populism-post-trump-gop.html.

30. This relative autonomy of ideology from material concerns allows people to both intervene in economic relations as well as endure them. While class analysis is concerned with the study of class interests and struggle, culture and ideology are causally independent from economic structures and so both politics and culture must be oriented by those who struggle for progressive social change towards radical ends. See Vivek Chibber, "Rescuing Class from the Cultural Turn," *Catalyst* 1:1 (Spring 2017), https://catalyst-journal.com/2017/11/cultural-turn-vivek-chibber.
31. Jeffrey Goldberg, "Why Obama Fears for Our Democracy," *The Atlantic* (November 16, 2020), https://www.theatlantic.com/ideas/archive/2020/11/why-obama-fears-for-our-democracy/617087/.
32. The Hill, "Krystal Ball: The woke left tried to cancel me, that's why they keep losing," *YouTube* (April 24, 2020), https://www.youtube.com/watch?v=GxgUQ4ZVlUA.

1: A Trap for the Gaze

1. Although the reporting on the paintings emphasized the ethnicity of the artists, very few articles mentioned Wiley's gay sexual identity or, for that matter, Sherald's sexuality. A request for information I made to the NPG to know if the Wiley portrait is the first in the collection to be painted by a gay artist went unanswered. My inquiry was to know whether the museum collects data on the subject. Failure to respond likely indicates that the question seems unreasonable. I am not, with this, suggesting that such information should be collected. Beyond the comment by George M. Johnson that the mass media ignored the question of Wiley's sexuality in its reporting – a valid point since much of Wiley's work is expressly gay-themed and homoerotic – there are equally valid reasons why sexuality is not reducible to identity and why art need not be classified or interpreted according to the sexuality of the artist. See George M. Johnson, "Why Obama presidential portrait artist Kehinde Wiley's sexuality can't be ignored," *The Grio* (February 12, 2018), https://thegrio.com/2018/02/12/kehinde-wiley-obama-painting-gay/.
2. See the NPG web page for this painting at https://npg.si.edu/exhibition/former-president-barack-obama-artist-kehinde-wiley.
3. "Artist Kehinde Wiley Explains President Obama Portrait," *C-Span* (February 12, 2018), https://www.c-span.org/video/?c4714123/artist-kehinde-wiley-explains-president-obama-portrait; Lewis Corner, "Kehinde Wiley becomes the first black, gay artist to paint a US president's official portrait," *Gay Times* (February 13, 2018), https://www.gaytimes.co.uk/culture/99241/kehinde-wiley-becomes-first-black-gay-artist-paint-us-presidents-official-portrait/.
4. Taína Caragol et al., *The Obama Portraits* (Washington/Princeton: National Portrait Gallery/Princeton University Press, 2020).
5. Wiley cited in Corner, "Kehinde Wiley becomes the first black, gay artist to paint a US president's official portrait."
6. Wiley cited in Heidi Glenn, "Behind The Obama Portraits: Artists Put Their Own Spin On A Presidential Tradition," *NPR* (February 13, 2018), https://www.npr.org/2018/02/13/585299081/obama-portraits-unveiled-at-national-portrait-gallery. The reference to "young" people in this statement can also be thought of as a now common metaphor for LGBTQ constituencies.
7. Wiley cited in Maya Rhodan, "'A Game Changer': How a Painting of President Obama Broke the Rules," *Time* (February 14, 2018), https://news.yahoo.com/apos-game-changer-apos-painting-215612577.html.

8. Obama cited in Zameena Mejia, "5 things you may know about Kehinde Wiley, the artist behind Barack Obama's presidential portrait," *CNBC* (February 13, 2018), https://www.cnbc.com/2018/02/13/meet-kehinde-wiley-artist-behind-barack-obamas-presidential-portrait.html.
9. Obama cited in Roger Catlin, "Artists Kehinde Wiley and Amy Sherald Capture the Unflinching Gaze of the President and First Lady," *Smithsonian* (February 12, 2018), https://www.smithsonianmag.com/smithsonian-institution/artists-kehinde-wiley-amy-sherald-capture-unflinching-gaze-president-first-lady-180968142/.
10. Wiley cited in Sarah Lewis, "Celebration and Critique," in Thelma Golden et al., *Kehinde Wiley* (New York: Rizzoli, 2011) 88.
11. See Michel Foucault, *The History of Sexuality, Volume 1: An Introduction*, trans. Robert Hurley (New York: Pantheon Books, [1976] 1978).
12. See the NPG web page for this painting at https://npg.si.edu/exhibition/former-first-lady-michelle-obama-artist-amy-sherald.
13. Doreen St. Felix, "The Mystery of Amy Sherald's Portrait of Michelle Obama," *The New Yorker* (February 13, 2018), https://www.newyorker.com/culture/annals-of-appearances/the-mystery-of-amy-sheralds-portrait-of-michelle-obama.
14. Avery Matera, "Michelle Obama's Portrait Milly Dress Sends a Powerful Political Message," *Teen Vogue* (February 13, 2018), https://www.teenvogue.com/story/michelle-obama-portrait-milly-dress-political-message.
15. Kate Betts, *Everyday Icon: Michelle Obama and the Power of Style* (New York: Clarkson Potter, 2011).
16. Sherald cited in Sarah Moroz, "Painting the Obamas," *Modern Painters* (December 2017) 84.
17. Sherald cited in Marissa G. Muller, "Michelle Obama Dances With Parker Curry, Who Went Viral After Looking at Her Portrait," *W Magazine* (March 6, 2018), https://www.wmagazine.com/story/michelle-obama-dances-with-parker-curry.
18. See Blair Murphy, "Obamas Open Up About Their Newly Unveiled Official Portraits," *Hyperallergic* (February 12, 2018), https://hyperallergic.com/426582/obamas-official-portrait-unveiling-kehinde-wiley-amy-sherald/.
19. Michelle Obama cited in Catlin, "Artists Kehinde Wiley and Amy Sherald Capture the Unflinching Gaze of the President and First Lady." See also R. Eric Thomas, "The Obamas' Official Portraits Have Been Unveiled," *Elle* (February 12, 2018), https://www.elle.com/culture/art-design/a17045197/obama-michelle-national-portrait-gallery-wiley-sherald/.
20. Deana Haggag, "Why the Obamas' newly unveiled official portraits matter," *CNN* (February 12, 2018), https://www.cnn.com/style/article/barack-michelle-obama-official-portraits-unveiled/index.html.
21. See Betty Boyd Caroli, *First Ladies: From Martha Washington to Michelle Obama* (Oxford: Oxford University Press, 2010).
22. Christopher Knight, "How the Obama portraits cheerfully buck the trend of instantly forgettable presidential paintings," *The Los Angeles Times* (February 13, 2018), https://www.latimes.com/entertainment/arts/la-et-cm-obama-wiley-sherald-20180213-story.html.
23. Thomas Frank, *Listen, Liberal, or, What Ever Happened to the Party of the People?* (New York: Metropolitan Books, 2016).
24. Cited in Catherine Bigelow, "Kehinde Wiley, SF Art Institute alum, points its 2018 graduates to the future," *San Francisco Chronicle* (May 21, 2018), https://www.sfchronicle.com/style/article/Kehinde-Wiley-SF-Art-Institute-alum-points-its-12932287.php.

25. Patricia Nicol, "How Kehinde Wiley's paintings of the world's most famous African-Americans have made him a star in his own right," *Evening Standard* (July 25, 2018), https://www.standard.co.uk/lifestyle/esmagazine/kehinde-wiley-s-paintings-interview-a3894116.html.
26. Vinson Cunningham, "The Shifting Perspective in Kehinde Wiley's Portrait of Barack Obama," *The New Yorker* (February 13, 2018), https://www.newyorker.com/culture/annals-of-appearances/the-shifting-perspective-in-kehinde-wileys-portrait-of-barack-obama.
27. Peter Schjeldahl, "The Amy Sherald Effect," *The New Yorker* (September 16, 2019), https://www.newyorker.com/magazine/2019/09/23/the-amy-sherald-effect.
28. Steven Nelson, "The Obama Portraits and the History of African American Portraiture," *Hyperallergic* (March 14, 2018), https://hyperallergic.com/432420/obama-portraits-history-african-american-portraiture/.
29. Chiquita Paschal, "It's OK to Feel Ambivalent About Michelle Obama's Official Portrait," *Hyperallergic* (February 15, 2018), https://hyperallergic.com/427123/ambivalence-amy-sherald-michelle-obama-portrait/.
30. Ben Davis, "Here's the Bad News About Kehinde Wiley's Presidential Portrait of Barack Obama," *Artnet News* (February 13, 2018), https://news.artnet.com/art-world/barack-obama-portrait-kehinde-wiley-1222910.
31. Davis, "Here's the Bad News About Kehinde Wiley's Presidential Portrait of Barack Obama."
32. Davis, "Here's the Bad News About Kehinde Wiley's Presidential Portrait of Barack Obama."
33. Roland Barthes, *Mythologies*, trans. Annette Lavers (New York: The Noonday Press, [1957] 1972) 91.
34. Barthes, *Mythologies*, 92.
35. Pierre Bourdieu, *Photography: A Middle-Brow Art*, trans. Shaun Whiteside (Stanford: Stanford University Press, [1965] 1993).
36. Barthes, *Mythologies*, 93.
37. Avi Selk, "All we know about the White House portrait of Trump drinking Diet Coke with Abraham Lincoln," *The Washington Post* (October 16, 2018), https://www.washingtonpost.com/arts-entertainment/2018/10/15/all-we-know-about-white-house-portrait-trump-drinking-diet-coke-with-abraham-lincoln/?utm_term=.8becbcf997f2. Whereas the painter Andy Thomas owns the original painting, the print belongs to Darrell Issa, the Director of the United States Trade and Development Agency under Trump, and formerly the wealthiest serving member of Congress. Issa rejects the scientific consensus on climate change, favours repealing the Affordable Care Act and opposes same-sex marriage as well as abortion. Thanks to Caitlin Sanders, Digital Asset Librarian at The White House Historical Association, for her help with an information request on this issue.
38. Clement Greenberg, "Avant-Garde and Kitsch," in *Art and Culture: Critical Essays* (Boston: Beacon Press, [1961] 1989) 19.
39. J. Hoberman, "The Entertainer: Trump l'oeil," *j-hoberman* (November 29, 2016), http://j-hoberman.com/2016/11/the-entertainer-trump-loeil/.
40. Alex Melamid, "Blame Donald Trump's Rise on the Avant-Garde Movement," *Time* (May 12, 2017), available at http://time.com/4777118/avant-garde-koons-trump/.
41. Angela Nagle, *Kill All Normies: The Online Culture Wars from Tumblr and 4chan to the Alt-Right and Trump* (Winchester: Zero Books, 2017).
42. Joshua David Stein, "George W. Bush's talent as a painter finds an ironic muse: the combat veteran," *The Guardian* (March 6, 2017), https://www.theguardian.com/artanddesign/2017/mar/06/george-w-bush-art-painting-portraits-in-courage.

43. Eliza Relman, "'I love him to death': Michelle Obama says George W. Bush is her 'partner in crime' at official functions," *Business Insider* (October 11, 2018), https://www.businessinsider.com/michelle-obama-says-george-w-bush-is-her-partner-in-crime-2018-10.

44. See Boris Groys, *The Total Art of Stalinism: Avant-Garde, Aesthetic Dictatorship, and Beyond*, trans. Charles Rougle (Princeton: Princeton University Press, 1992).

45. Pierre Bourdieu, *The Rules of Art: Genesis and Structure of the Literary Field*, trans. Susan Emanuel (Stanford: Stanford University Press, [1992] 1996).

46. Pierre Bourdieu, *On the State: Lectures at the Collège de France, 1989-1992*, ed. Patrick Campaign et al., trans. David Fernbach (Cambridge: Polity Press, 2014).

47. See Bill Readings, *The University in Ruins* (Cambridge: Harvard University Press, 1996); Gerald Raunig, Gene Ray and Ulf Wuggenig, eds. *Critique of Creativity: Precarity, Subjectivity and Resistance in the 'Creative Industries'* (London: MayFlyBooks, 2011); Lane Relyea, *Your Everyday Art World* (Cambridge: The MIT Press, 2013).

48. Adolph Reed, Jr., "Race and Class in the Age of Obama," lecture delivered at Villanova University, November 6, 2015, *YouTube* (November 24, 2015), https://www.youtube.com/watch?v=iF6ruCDHxuU.

49. See Sylvère Lotringer and Christian Marazzi, eds. *Autonomia: Post-Political Politics* (Los Angeles: Semiotext(e), 2007).

50. Michael Hardt and Antonio Negri, *Multitude: War and Democracy in the Age of Empire* (New York: The Penguin Press, 2004).

51. Simon Tormey, "Occupy Wall Street: From Representation to Post-Representation," *Journal of Critical Globalisation Studies* #5 (2012) 135.

52. Tormey, "Occupy Wall Street," 133.

53. See for instance, Maude Barlow and Tony Clarke, *Global Showdown: How the Global Activists Are Fighting Global Corporate Rule* (Toronto: Stoddart, 2001).

54. David Harvey, *A Brief History of Neoliberalism* (Oxford: Oxford University Press, 2005) 13.

55. For a critique of some the themes addressed in *Multitude*, see Michael Hardt and Antonio Negri, *Assembly* (New York: Oxford University Press, 2017).

56. See Michael Hardt and Antonio Negri, *Empire* (Cambridge: Harvard University Press, 2000).

57. Hardt and Negri, *Multitude*, 101. Since the advent of Black Lives Matter, Hardt and Negri have taken a more radical democratic stance towards identity politics. See for example Michael Hardt and Antonio Negri, "Empire, Twenty Years On," *New Left Review* #120 (November-December 2019) 67-92. Note also that some have sought to further deconstruct the category of constituent power with the idea of a "destituent" power, which altogether refuses politics along with the constituted forms of power of the established political system. The purpose of revolt, in this case, is to suspend the exercise of political power and the circulation of money rather than replace it with something better. See Marcello Tari, *There Is No Unhappy Revolution: The Communism of Destitution*, trans. Richard Braude (Brooklyn: Common Notions, [2017] 2021).

58. See Giorgio Agamben, *The Coming Community*, trans. Michael Hardt (Minneapolis: University of Minnesota Press, 1993).

59. Hardt and Negri, *Multitude*, 237.

60. David Harvey, *The New Imperialism* (Oxford: Oxford University Press, 2003).

61. Slavoj Žižek, *Like a Thief in Broad Daylight: Power in the Era of Post-Humanity* (London: Allen Lane, 2018) 22, 42.

62. Laura Bazzicalupo, "Political Representation after its Deconstruction," *Instituto de Estudios Críticos* volume 3 (2012), available at https://quod.lib.umich.edu/p/pc/12322227.0003.003?view=text;rgn=main.
63. Bazzicalupo refers indirectly to the work of both Claude Lefort and Jacques Rancière. See Claude Lefort, *Essais sur le politique: XIXe–XXe siècles* (Paris: Seuil, 1986); Jacques Rancière, *Disagreement: Politics and Philosophy*, trans. Julie Rose (Minneapolis: University of Minnesota Press, [1995] 1998).
64. Slavoj Žižek, *The Indivisible Remainder: An Essay on Schelling and Related Matters* (London: Verso, 1996) 3.
65. Bazzicalupo, "Political Representation after its Deconstruction."
66. See Luc Boltanski & Eve Chiapello, *The New Spirit of Capitalism* (London: Verso, [1999] 2005).
67. Bazzicalupo, "Political Representation after its Deconstruction."
68. Bazzicalupo, "Political Representation after its Deconstruction."
69. Žižek makes the same observation, but about capitalism rather than the state. Slavoj Žižek, *In Defense of Lost Causes* (London: Verso, 2008) 337-8.
70. Alain Badiou, *The Communist Hypothesis*, trans. David Macey and Steve Corcoran (London: Verso, [2008] 2010). Despite his premature obituary, McAdams offers a useful analysis of the idea of the party and the history of its organizational problems. See A. James McAdams, *Vanguards of the Revolution: The Global Idea of the Communist Party* (Princeton: Princeton University Press, 2017).
71. Slavoj Žižek, *The Courage of Hopelessness: Chronicles of a Year of Acting Dangerously* (London: Allen Lane, 2017).
72. Slavoj Žižek, ed. *Lenin 2017: Remembering, Repeating, and Working Through* (London: Verso, 2017) xiv.
73. Slavoj Žižek, *Disparities* (London: Bloomsbury, 2017). See Henri Lefebvre's critique of Foucault's *The Order of Things* in Lefebvre, *Position: contre les technocrates* (Paris: Éditions Gonthier, 1967).
74. Hito Steyerl, "Politics of Art: Contemporary Art and the Transition to Post-Democracy," in *Wretched of the Screen* (Berlin: Sternberg Press, 2012) 93.
75. Hito Steyerl cited in Marvin Jordan, "Hito Steyerl | Politics of Post-Representation," *dismagazine* (June 2014), http://dismagazine.com/disillusioned-2/62143/hito-steyerl-politics-of-post-representation/.
76. Barthes, *Mythologies*, 143, 146.
77. Barthes, *Mythologies*, 148.
78. Alan Kirby, "The Death of Postmodernism and Beyond," *Philosophy Now* #58 (2006), https://philosophynow.org/issues/58/The_Death_of_Postmodernism_And_Beyond.
79. Steyerl cited in Marvin Jordan, "Hito Steyerl | Politics of Post-Representation."
80. Thibaud Izard, "[Pierre] Bourdieu – Entretien avec Günter Grass (1990)," *YouTube* (August 26, 2013), https://www.youtube.com/watch?v=aOTu98tW9Hk.

2: From Obamarama to the Drone Presidency

1. Paul Street, "How 'Black' Is Obama? Color, Class, Generation, and the Perverse Racial Politics of the Post-Civil Rights Era," in *Barack Obama and the Future of American Politics* (London: Routledge, 2009) 81. See also Paul Street, *Barack Obama and the Future of American Politics* (New York: Routledge, 2009).

2. Justice Center of The Council of State Governments, "Researchers Examine Effects of a Criminal Record on Prospects for Employment" (August 20, 2014), available at https://csgjusticecenter.org/reentry/posts/researchers-examine-effects-of-a-criminal-record-on-prospects-for-employment/.
3. Facundo Alvaredo et al., eds. *World Inequality Report* (Cambridge: Harvard University Press, 2018).
4. Nielsen (global measurements and data analytics), "Increasingly Affluent, Educated and Diverse: African-American Consumers" (September 17, 2015), available at https://www.nielsen.com/us/en/insights/news/2015/african-americans-are-increasingly-affluent-educated-and-diverse.html.
5. Nancy Fraser, "From Progressive Neoliberalism to Trump – and Beyond," *American Affairs* 1:4 (Winter 2017) 49.
6. Slavoj Žižek, "A Great Awakening and Its Dangers," *The Philosophical Salon* (November 20, 2017), https://thephilosophicalsalon.com/a-great-awakening-and-its-dangers/.
7. Adolph Reed, Jr. and Merlin Chowkwanyun, "Race, Class, Crisis: The Discourse of Racial Disparity and Its Analytical Discontents," *Socialist Register* #48 (2012) 169.
8. Matt Taibbi, "Obama Is the Best BS Artist Since Bill Clinton," *Rolling Stone* (February 16, 2007), available at http://www.smirkingchimp.com/thread/5533.
9. Hortense J. Spillers, "'All the Things You Could Be by Now, If Sigmund Freud's Wife Was Your Mother': Psychoanalysis and Race," in Elizabeth Abel, Barbara Christian and Helene Moglen, eds. *Female Subjects in Black and White* (Berkeley: University of California Press, 1997) 137.
10. Michael Eric Dyson, *The Black Presidency: Barack Obama and the Politics of Race in America* (Boston: Houghton Mifflin, 2016) 98.
11. Barack Obama, *The Audacity of Hope: Thoughts on Reclaiming the American Dream* (New York: Crown Publishers, 2006) 247.
12. Richard Hofstadter, "Reflections on Violence in the United States" (1970), *The Baffler* #28 (July 2015), http://thebaffler.com/ancestors/reflections-violence-united-states.
13. Adolph Reed, Jr., *Class Notes: Posing as Politics and Other Thoughts on the American Scene* (New York: The New Press, 2000) 13.
14. Ken Silverstein, "Barack Obama Inc.," *Harper's* (November 2006) 40. For a detailed study of Obama's progress from the state senate to the presidency, see David Remnick, *The Bridge: The Life and Rise of Barack Obama* (New York: Alfred A. Knopf, 2010).
15. Sharon Smith, "Obama and Abortion Rights," in Jeffrey St. Clair and Joshua Frank, eds. *Hopeless: Barack Obama and the Politics of Illusion* (Oakland: AK Press, 2012) 42-4.
16. Glen Ford, "Obama Subverts Social Security," *Black Agenda Report* (September 15, 2011), https://www.blackagendareport.com/content/obama-subverts-social-security.
17. Dave Lindorff, "Obama's Attack on Social Security and Medicare," in St. Clair and Frank, eds. *Hopeless*, 237-42.
18. Chris Hedges, "The Obama Deception: Why Cornel West Went Ballistic," *Truthdig* (May 16, 2011), https://www.truthdig.com/articles/the-obama-deception-why-cornel-west-went-ballistic/.
19. Thomas Frank, "Presidents Clinton and Obama Helped Make the Democrats a Wall Street Party," *The Real News* (December 28, 2017) and Frank, "Obama Chose Wall St Over Main St," *The Real News* (December 29, 2017), https://therealnews.com/stories/obama-chose-wall-st-over-main-st-thomas-frank-on-rai-8-9.

20. Matt Taibbi, "How Wall Street Killed Financial Reform," *Rolling Stone* (May 10, 2012), https://www.rollingstone.com/politics/politics-news/how-wall-street-killed-financial-reform-190802/. See also Matt Taibbi, "Secrets and Lies of the Bailout," *Rolling Stone* (January 4, 2013), https://www.rollingstone.com/politics/politics-news/secrets-and-lies-of-the-bailout-113270/.
21. John Cassidy, "An Inconvenient Truth: It Was George W. Bush Who Bailed Out the Automakers," *The New Yorker* (March 16, 2012), https://www.newyorker.com/news/john-cassidy/an-inconvenient-truth-it-was-george-w-bush-who-bailed-out-the-automakers.
22. Anna Clark, "'Nothing to worry about. The water is fine': how Flint poisoned its people," *The Guardian* (July 3, 2018), https://www.theguardian.com/news/2018/jul/03/nothing-to-worry-about-the-water-is-fine-how-flint-michigan-poisoned-its-people; usefulidiots, "Did Obama Know?" *YouTube* (January 28, 2022), https://www.youtube.com/watch?v=Mi9hHvRRz6Q.
23. Victoria Stanhope, "The Affordable Care Act: The Good, the Bad and the Ugly," *Affilia: Journal of Women and Social Work* 30:4 (2015) 423-6.
24. Howard Waitzkin and Ida Hellander, "Obamacare: The Neoliberal Model Comes Home to Roost in the United States – If We Let It," *Monthly Review* (May 1, 2016), https://monthlyreview.org/2016/05/01/obamacare/.
25. Dave Lindorff, "Obama's Attack on Social Security and Medicare," in St. Clair and Frank, eds. *Hopeless*, 237-9.
26. Vicente Navarro, "Obama's Mistakes in Health Care Reform," in St. Clair and Frank, eds. *Hopeless*, 72-81.
27. Henri Giroux, "Obama's Dilemma: Postpartisan Politics and the Crisis of American Education," *Harvard Educational Review* 79:2 (July 2009) 250-66.
28. Tavis Smiley and Cornel West, *The Rich and the Rest of Us* (New York: Hay House, 2012) eBook, 188.
29. Richard Mora, "Charter Schools, Market Capitalism, and Obama's Neo-Liberal Agenda," *Journal of Inquiry & Action in Education* 4:1 (2011) 93-111.
30. Kevin Alexander Gray, "The Novocaine President," in St. Clair and Frank, eds. *Hopeless*, 91-100.
31. David Macaray, "Friends Without Benefits," in St. Clair and Frank, eds. *Hopeless*, 217-21.
32. Gillian Russom, "Obama's neoliberal agenda for education," *International Socialist Review* #71 (July 2010), https://isreview.org/issue/71/obamas-neoliberal-agenda-education.
33. Ellen David Friedman, "What's Behind the Teacher Strikes?" *Jacobin* (May 27, 2018), https://jacobinmag.com/2018/05/teacher-strikes-labor-movement-education.
34. Jeffrey St. Clair, "Obama and the Man in the Hat," in St. Clair and Frank, eds. *Hopeless*, 53-9.
35. Ronnie Cummins, "Monsanto's Minions: The White House, Congress, and the Mass Media," in St. Clair and Frank, eds. *Hopeless*, 169-72.
36. Brian Tokar, "Politics as the Earth Burns: Obama and the Climate Crisis," in St. Clair and Frank, eds. *Hopeless*, 231-5.
37. Albert C. Lin, "A Sustainability Critique of the Obama 'All-of-the-Above,'" *Journal of Energy & Environmental Law* (Winter 2014) 17-25.
38. Bill McKibben, "Obama and Climate Change: The Real Story," *Rolling Stone* (December 17, 2013), https://www.rollingstone.com/politics/politics-news/obama-and-climate-change-the-real-story-104491/#ixzz2nt4eXg9c.
39. Alejandra Marchevsky and Beth Baker, "Why Has President Obama Deported More Immigrants Than Any President in US History?" *The Nation* (March 31, 2014), https://www.thenation.com/article/why-has-president-obama-deported-more-immigrants-any-president-us-history/.

40. Glen Ford, "Obama Prepares to Reinforce the Militarized Police Occupation of Black America," *Black Agenda Report* (July 28, 2016), https://www.blackagendareport.com/obama_reinforces_militarized_police. See also Radley Balko, *Rise of the Warrior Cop: The Militarization of America's Police Forces* (New York: Public Affairs, 2013).
41. Sam Morris, "Mass shootings in the US: there have been 1,624 in 1,870 days," *The Guardian* (February 15, 2018), https://www.theguardian.com/us-news/ng-interactive/2017/oct/02/america-mass-shootings-gun-violence.
42. Sibel Edmonds, "From State Secrets to War to Wiretaps," in St. Clair and Frank, eds. *Hopeless*, 45-50.
43. Bill Quigley, "Obama's Assault on Civil Liberties: Twenty Examples," in St. Clair and Frank, eds. *Hopeless*, 243-47.
44. Smiley and West, *The Rich and the Rest of Us*, 75.
45. Andrea Ó Súilleabháin, "Interview With Mary Ellen O'Connell, International Law Expert, on US Drone Policy," *The Global Observatory* (February 8, 2013), https://theglobalobservatory.org/2013/02/interview-with-mary-ellen-oconnell-military-expert-on-us-drone-policy/.
46. Henry Giroux, "War Colleges," in St. Clair and Frank, eds. *Hopeless*, 223-9.
47. Matt Taibbi on the Chris Hedges programme On Contact, "Deep rot in American journalism," *RT America* (May 5 and 12, 2019), https://www.rt.com/shows/on-contact/458410-matt-taibbi-american-journalism/.
48. Kathleen Christison, "The US as Israel's Enabler in the Middle East," in St. Clair and Frank, eds. *Hopeless*, 157-61.
49. William Pfaff, "Armed and Dangerous: The inexorable rise of American militarism," *Harper's* (August 2014), https://harpers.org/archive/2014/08/armed-and-dangerous/.
50. Jessica Saifee, "The War on Opium in Afghanistan," *The Huffington Post* (May 5, 2017), https://www.huffpost.com/entry/the-war-on-opium-in-afgha_b_9828506.
51. Franklin Spinney, "The Afghan War Question," in St. Clair and Frank, eds. *Hopeless*, 83-5.
52. Susan Fayazmanesh, "The Obama Administration and Iran," in St. Clair and Frank, eds. *Hopeless*, 201-6.
53. Intercepted, "American Dissident: Noam Chomsky on the State of the Empire," *The Intercept* (September 26, 2018), https://theintercept.com/2018/09/26/trump-united-nations-noam-chomsky/.
54. Ben Norton, "Media Erase NATO Role in Bringing Slave Markets to Libya," *FAIR* (November 28, 2017), https://fair.org/home/media-nato-regime-change-war-libya-slave-markets/.
55. Horace Campbell, "Imperialism and Anti-Imperialism in Africa," *Monthly Review* (July 1, 2015), https://monthlyreview.org/2015/07/01/imperialism-and-anti-imperialism-in-africa/.
56. Maximilian Forte, "The Top Ten Myths of the War in Libya," in St. Clair and Frank, eds. *Hopeless*, 249-64.
57. See Medea Benjamin, *Kingdom of the Unjust: Behind the U.S.-Saudi Connection* (New York: O/R Books, 2016) and Chris Gelardi, "Amnesiac Warmongers: Obama Staffers Launder their Culpability in Yemen," *The Baffler* (March 27, 2020), https://thebaffler.com/latest/amnesiac-warmongers-gelardi.
58. David Gordon, "The Failures of Obama's Foreign Policy," *Mises Wire* (January 19, 2017), https://mises.org/wire/failures-obamas-foreign-policy.
59. Jon Schwarz, "GOP Senator Says Trump Is Ready to Start War with North Korea, Which Would Be 'One of the Worst Catastrophic Events in History'," *The Intercept* (February 21, 2018), https://theintercept.com/2018/02/21/gop-senator-says-trump-is-ready-to-start-war-with-north-korea-that-would-be-one-of-the-worst-catastrophic-events-in-history/.

60. Conn Hallinan, "The Honduran Coup: A US Connection," in St. Clair and Frank, eds. *Hopeless*, 63-6.
61. Daniel Kovalik, "Obama's War for Oil in Columbia," in St. Clair and Frank, eds. *Hopeless*, 101.
62. Alex Emmons and Margot Williams, "After 15 Years, Prisoners at Guantánamo Face More Uncertainty than Ever," *The Intercept* (January 11, 2017), https://theintercept.com/2017/01/11/after-15-years-prisoners-at-guantanamo-face-more-uncertainty-than-ever/.
63. Chase Madar, "Torturing the Rule of Law at Obama's Gitmo," in St. Clair and Frank, eds. *Hopeless*, 119-25; Andy Worthington, "Guantánamo, Torture and Obama's Surrender," in St. Clair and Frank, eds. *Hopeless*, 273-8.
64. Sibel Edmonds, "From State Secrets to War to Wiretaps," in St. Clair and Frank, eds. *Hopeless*, 45-50.
65. Matthew Rosenberg, "Gina Haspel, C.I.A. Deputy Director, Had Role in Torture," *The New York Times* (February 2, 2017), https://www.nytimes.com/2017/02/02/us/politics/cia-deputy-director-gina-haspel-torture-thailand.html.
66. Steve Hendricks, "Obama and Rendition: Exporting Torture," in St. Clair and Frank, eds. *Hopeless*, 145-6.
67. Andy Worthington, "Guantánamo, Torture and Obama's Surrender," in St. Clair and Frank, eds. *Hopeless*, 273-8.
68. Glenn Greenwald, "Obama Killed a 16-Year-Old American in Yemen. Trump Just Killed His 8-Year-Old Sister," *The Intercept* (January 30, 2017), https://theintercept.com/2017/01/30/obama-killed-a-16-year-old-american-in-yemen-trump-just-killed-his-8-year-old-sister/.
69. Mollie Reilly, Ryan J. Reilly and Shadee Ashtari, "This Is What Eric Holder's Legacy Will Be," *The Huffington Post* (October 02, 2014), https://www.huffingtonpost.ca/2014/09/27/eric-holder-legacy_n_5889730.html.
70. Democracy Now, "Eric Holder's Complex Legacy: Voting Rights Advocate, Enemy of Press Freedom, Friend of Wall Street," *Democracy Now* (September 26, 2014), https://www.democracynow.org/2014/9/26/eric_holders_complex_legacy_voting_rights.
71. See David Adler, "Centrists Are the Most Hostile to Democracy, Not Extremists," *The New York Times* (May 23, 2018), https://www.nytimes.com/interactive/2018/05/23/opinion/international-world/centrists-democracy.html.
72. Pod Save America, "Barack Obama on 2020," *Crooked* (October 14, 2020), https://crooked.com/podcast/barack-obama-on-2020/. See also Secular Talk, "Obama Blames Democratic Voters For His Failures," *YouTube* (October 19, 2020), https://www.youtube.com/watch?v=2CxeXMYkWD4.
73. Chris Hedges, *Death of the Liberal Class* (New York: Nation Books, 2010) eBook, 22-5, 492.
74. See Tariq Ali, *The Extreme Centre: A Warning* (London: Verso, 2015).
75. Tariq Ali, *The Obama Syndrome: Surrender at Home, War Abroad* (London: Verso, 2010) 38.
76. See Mike Davis on Obama nostalgia in "The Great God Trump and the White Working Class," *Catalyst* 1:1 (Spring 2017), https://catalyst-journal.com/vol1/no1/great-god-trump-davis.
77. See Cornel West, *Black Prophetic Fire*, ed. Christa Buschendorf (Boston: Beacon Press, 2014).
78. See Luke Savage, "Barack Obama, The Hollow Icon: An Interview with Blair McClendon," *Jacobin* (September 13, 2021), https://www.jacobinmag.com/2021/09/barack-obama-photography-race-representation-mcclendon.
79. Carol E. Lee, "White House portrait ceremony may be the latest casualty of the political divide," *NBC News* (May 19, 2020), https://www.nbcnews.com/politics/politics-news/white-house-portrait-ceremony-may-be-latest-casualty-political-divide-n1209676?cid=sm_npd_nn_tw_ma.

80. Jodi Dean, "Donald Trump Is the Most Honest Candidate in American Politics Today," *In These Times* (August 12, 2015), http://inthesetimes.com/article/18309/donald-trump-republican-president. See also Joshua Gunn, "On Political Perversion," *Rhetoric Society Quarterly* 48:2 (2018) 1-26.
81. Trip Gabriel, Zolan Kanno-Youngs and Katie Benner, "As Trump's Language Grows More Heated, Fears Rise of Political Violence," *The New York Times* (October 15, 2020), https://www.nytimes.com/2020/10/15/us/politics/trump-election-violence.html.
82. Evan Hill, Mike Baker, Derek Knowles and Stella Cooper, "'Straight to Gunshot': How a U.S. Task Force Killed an Antifa Activist," *The New York Times* (October 13, 2020), https://www.nytimes.com/2020/10/13/us/michael-reinoehl-antifa-portland-shooting.html?auth=login-email&login=email; Ken Coleman, "Eric Trump won't campaign at gun shop where man accused in Whitmer murder plot worked," *Michigan Advance* (October 13, 2020), https://www.michiganadvance.com/blog/eric-trump-wont-campaign-at-gun-shop-where-man-accused-in-whitmer-murder-plot-worked/.
83. Éric Aeschimann, "Getting Beyond Hatred: An Interview with Jacques Rancière," *Verso Blog* (February 17, 2016), https://www.versobooks.com/blogs/2505-getting-beyond-hatred-an-interview-with-jacques-ranciere.

3: Woke Aesthetics

1. Michel Foucault, *The Order of Things: An Archaeology of the Human Sciences*, trans. Alan Sheridan-Smith (London: Routledge, [1966] 1970/2002) 3-18.
2. Foucault, *The Order of Things*, 3-4.
3. Benjamin H.D. Buchloh, "Farewell to an Identity," *Artforum* (December 2012) 253-61.
4. Jean-François Lyotard, "Presenting the Unpresentable: The Sublime," *Artforum* (April 1982) 64.
5. Jean Baudrillard, "The Order of Simulacra," in *Symbolic Exchange and Death*, trans. Iain Hamilton Grant (London: Sage, 1993) 50-86.
6. Paul Virilio, "From Superman to Superexcited Man," *Domus* #754 (November 1993) 22-5.
7. Dick Hebdige, "A Report on the Western Front: Postmodernism and the 'Politics of Style'," *Block* #12 (Winter 1986/87) 7.
8. Kobena Mercer, "Black Hair/Style Politics," *Welcome to the Jungle: New Positions in Black Cultural Studies* (Minneapolis: University of Minnesota Press, 1994) 97-128.
9. Meaghan Morris, "Banality in Cultural Studies," *Discourse* 10:2 (1988) 3-29.
10. Hal Foster, "Postmodernism: A Preface," in Foster, ed. *The Anti-Aesthetic: Essays on Postmodern Culture* (Seattle: Bay Press, 1983) xii.
11. Ernesto Laclau and Chantal Mouffe, *Hegemony and Socialist Strategy: Towards a Radical Democratic Politics* (London: Verso, 1985).
12. Gregory Sholette, "Delirium and Resistance after the Social Turn," *Field* #1 (Spring 2015), http://field-journal.com/issue-1/sholette.
13. Yates McKee, *Strike Art: Contemporary Art and the Post-Occupy Condition* (London: Verso, 2016) 9.
14. See Žižek's speech at OWS at http://muse.jhu.edu/journals/theory_and_event/v014/14.4Szizek.html.
15. Gina Dent, "Black Pleasure, Black Joy: An Introduction," in Dent, ed. *Black Popular Culture / A Project by Michelle Wallace* (New York: The New Press, 1983) 11, 18.
16. Dent, "Black Pleasure, Black Joy: An Introduction," 5.

17. See Michael Gardiner, *The Dialogics of Critique: M.M. Bakhtin and the Theory of Ideology* (London: Routledge, 1992).
18. Jasmine Weber, "In Times Square, Kehinde Wiley Unveils a Massive Monument to Black Identity," *Hyperallergic* (September 27, 2019) https://hyperallergic.com/519886/in-times-square-kehinde-wiley-unveils-a-massive-monument-to-black-identity/; Whitney Evans and David Streever, "Virginia's Massive Robert E. Lee Statue Has Been Removed," *NPR* (September 8, 2021), https://www.npr.org/2021/09/08/1035004639/virginia-ready-to-remove-massive-robert-e-lee-statue-following-a-year-of-lawsuit.
19. See Suzanne Lacy, ed. *Mapping the Terrain: New Genre Public Art* (Seattle: Bay Press, 1995).
20. See the classic essay by Howardena Pindell, "Art (World) & Racism: Testimony, Documentation and Statistics," *Third Text* #3/4 (Spring/Summer 1988) 157-90.
21. Cedric Johnson, "What Black Life Actually Looks Like," *Jacobin* (April 29, 2019), https://jacobinmag.com/2019/04/racism-black-lives-matter-inequality/.
22. Examples of the progressive populist critique of class reductionism can be found in Chantal Mouffe, *For a Left Populism* (London: Verso, 2018) and David I. Backer, "Uses and Abuses of Class Separatism," *Verso Blog* (January 1, 2019), https://www.versobooks.com/blogs/4201-uses-and-abuses-of-class-separatism.
23. See Micaela Giovannotti and Joyce B. Korotkin, *Neo-Baroque!* (Milano: Edizioni Charta, 2005).
24. Artsy Editors, "The Artsy Vanguard: Newly Established," *Artsy* (April 30, 2018), https://www.artsy.net/series/artsy-vanguard/artsy-editors-newly-established.
25. Anna Louie Sussman, "Demand Soars for Amy Sherald's Work Following Obama Portrait Reveal," *Artsy* (February 16, 2018), https://www.artsy.net/article/artsy-editorial-demand-soars-amy-sheralds-work-obama-portrait-reveal.
26. Jeremy Goodwin, "After Obama portrait, Amy Sherald seeks to 'reclaim time' for African-Americans," *St Louis Public Radio* (May 17, 2018), https://news.stlpublicradio.org/post/after-obama-portrait-amy-sherald-seeks-reclaim-time-african-americans#stream/0.
27. It might be a stretch to associate this work with a historical record about an emancipated slave who allowed herself to buy a blue dress with polka dots as a luxury item, previously denied to her, along with countless other freedoms. See Thavolia Glymph, *Out of the House of Bondage: The Transformation of the Plantation Household* (Cambridge: Cambridge University Press, 2008) 204.
28. Samra Khawaja, "Art Talk with Painter Amy Sherald," *Art Works Blog* (July 26, 2016), https://www.arts.gov/art-works/2016/art-talk-painter-amy-sherald.
29. Gina Sweeney, "What's Behind the Gray Skin Tones and Arresting Eyes in Amy Sherald's Portraits?" *Medium* (April 11, 2018), https://medium.com/high-museum-of-art/whats-behind-the-gray-skin-tones-and-arresting-eyes-in-amy-sherald-s-portraits-8d21477d6b40.
30. Dawoud Bey, "Being Themselves: The Portrait Paintings of Amy Sherald," in *Amy Sherald: A Wonderful Dream* (Chicago: Monique Meloche Gallery, 2016) 18.
31. Khawaja, "Art Talk with Painter Amy Sherald."
32. Rikki Byrd, "Amy Sherald on Her 'Gentle Presentation of Black Identity' and More," *Hyperallergic* (May 24, 2018), https://hyperallergic.com/443819/amy-sherald-contemporary-art-museum-st-louis/.
33. Goodwin, "After Obama portrait, Amy Sherald seeks to 'reclaim time' for African-Americans."
34. Victoria L. Valentine, "Portrait Artist Amy Sherald Discussed Her Practice at the National Gallery of Art: 'I Paint American People. Black People Doing Stuff'," *Culture Type* (November 7, 2017), https://www.culturetype.com/2017/11/07/portrait-artist-amy-sherald-discussed-her-practice-at-the-national-gallery-of-art-i-paint-american-people-black-people-doing-stuff/.

35. David Menconi, "Georgia-born artist is now a star," *AJC* (June 7, 2018), https://www.ajc.com/lifestyles/the-same-person-was-before-amy-sherald-michelle-obama-portrait-artist-star/T3IEFFM743vyE9uJrR9QdK/; Valentine, "Portrait Artist Amy Sherald Discussed Her Practice at the National Gallery of Art."
36. Sarah Cascone, "'There Is So Much You Go Through Just Trying to Make It': Amy Sherald on How She Went From Obscurity to a Museum Survey (and the White House)," *Artnet News* (June 20, 2018), https://news.artnet.com/art-world/amy-sherald-interview-1281740.
37. Ella Ceron, "Kentucky's Attorney General Slams Celeb Reactions to Breonna Taylor News," *Teen Vogue* (September 24, 2020), https://www.teenvogue.com/story/daniel-cameron-breonna-taylor-celebrities.
38. Jewél Jackson, "Why Black Women Like Breonna Taylor Still Need 'Say Her Name' Movement," *WFPL* (July 6, 2020) https://wfpl.org/why-black-women-like-breonna-taylor-still-need-say-her-name-movement/.
39. Kevin Cunningham, "Steph Curry dons custom Black Lives Matter golf shoes to honor Breonna Taylor at celebrity event," *Golf* (July 11, 2020), https://golf.com/news/steph-curry-golf-shoes-breonna-taylor-black-lives-matter/.
40 Mark Lilla, *The Once and Future Liberal* (New York: HarperCollins, 2017) eBook, 15.
41. Sherald cited in Miles Pope, "Amy Sherald on Making Breonna Taylor's Portrait – The artist, who painted Michelle Obama, took care to draw on details from Taylor's life," *Vanity Fair* (August 24, 2020), https://www.vanityfair.com/culture/2020/08/amy-sherald-on-making-breonna-taylors-cover-portrait.
42. Taylor Dafoe, "Amy Sherald Painted Breonna Taylor for the Cover of Vanity Fair's September Issue, Guest Edited by Ta-Nehisi Coates," *Artnet News* (August 24, 2020), https://news.artnet.com/art-world/new-amy-sherald-painting-breonna-taylor-featured-cover-vanity-fairs-september-issue-1903740.
43. Sherald cited in Pope, "Amy Sherald on Making Breonna Taylor's Portrait."
44. Terry Eagleton, *Culture* (New Haven: Yale University Press, 2016) 43.
45. Adolph Reed, Jr. and Merlin Chowkwanyun, "Race, Class, Crisis: The Discourse of Racial Disparity and Its Analytical Discontents," *Socialist Register* #48 (2012) 167.
46. Walter Benn Michaels and Adolph Reed, Jr., "The Trouble with Disparity," *Nonsite* (September 10, 2020), https://nonsite.org/the-trouble-with-disparity/.
47. Griselda Pollock, *Differencing the Canon: Feminist Desire and the Writing of Art's Histories* (London: Routledge, 1999) 13.
48. Pollock, *Differencing the Canon*, 26.
49. Bob Duggan, "Why All Kehinde Wiley Wants Is the World," *Big Think* (May 9, 2012), https://bigthink.com/Picture-This/why-all-kehinde-wiley-wants-is-the-world.
50. Touré Show, "Kehinde Wiley: How To Make It In Art Careers, Society & Culture," *DCP Entertainment* (January 3, 2018), https://podtail.com/en/podcast/toure-show/kehinde-wiley-how-to-make-it-in-art/.
51. Rachel Spence, "Kehinde Wiley's contemporary call to arms," *The Financial Times* (December 1, 2017), https://www.ft.com/content/2295b686-d10f-11e7-947e-f1ea5435bcc7.
52. Wyatt Mason, "How Kehinde Wiley Makes a Masterpiece," *GQ* (April 10, 2013), https://www.gq.com/story/kehinde-wiley.
53. Brandy McDonnell, "Tulsa's Philbrook Museum acquires a Kehinde Wiley painting," *Newsok* (December 13, 2017), https://newsok.com/article/5575755/tulsas-philbrook-museum-acquires-a-kehinde-wiley-painting.
54. Spence, "Kehinde Wiley's contemporary call to arms."

55. Wiley cited in Robert Hobbs, "Kehinde Wiley's Conceptual Realism," in Thelma Golden et al., *Kehinde Wiley* (New York: Rizzoli, 2011) 32.
56. Hobbs, "Kehinde Wiley's Conceptual Realism," 31.
57. "A Conversation with Kehinde Wiley and Peter Halley," in Thelma Golden et al., *Kehinde Wiley*, 162.
58. Christine Y. Kim, "Kehinde Wiley: Faux Real," *Issue Magazine* (December 2003), https://issuemagazine.com/kehinde-wiley-faux-real/#/.
59. Victoria Emily Jones, "Christian-themed portraits by Kehinde Wiley," *Art & Theology* (August 31, 2016), https://artandtheology.org/2016/08/31/christian-themed-portraits-by-kehinde-wiley/.
60. Wiley cited in David Emery, "Did Obama's Portraitist Paint an Image of a Black Woman Holding the Severed Head of a White Person?" *Snopes* (February 13, 2018), https://www.snopes.com/fact-check/kehinde-wiley-painted-black-woman-severed-head/.
61. Wiley cited in Christopher Beam, "How to Make It in the Art World," *New York Magazine* (April 22, 2012), http://nymag.com/arts/art/rules/kehinde-wiley-2012-4/.
62. Wiley cited in Morgan Brinlee, "The Artist Behind Obama's Official Portrait Makes Some Seriously Powerful Work," *Bustle* (February 12, 2018), https://www.bustle.com/p/who-is-kehinde-wiley-the-painters-work-challenges-perceptions-of-african-americans-8193251.
63. See John Tagg, *The Burden of Representation: Essays on Photographies and Histories* (Minneapolis: University of Minnesota Press, [1988] 1993) and Gen Doy, *Seeing and Consciousness: Women, Class and Representation* (Oxford: Berg, 1995).
64. Wiley cited in NPR interview with Roy Hurst, June 1, 2005, in Hobbs, "Kehinde Wiley's Conceptual Realism," 18-19.
65. Eugenie Tsai, "Introduction," in Tsai, ed. *Kehinde Wiley: A New Republic* (Brooklyn/Munich: Brooklyn Museum/Prestel, 2015) 13.
66. Touré, "Mugshot Study (2006)," in Tsai, ed. *Kehinde Wiley*, 52.
67. Walter Benjamin, *Charles Baudelaire: A Lyric Poet in the Era of High Capitalism*, trans. Harry Zohn (London: Verso, 1983) 36.
68. Brian Keith Jackson, "Quiet as It's Kept," in Golden et al, *Kehinde Wiley*, 116.
69. Wiley cited in Helen Stoilas, "Toppling the Ivory Tower," *The Art Newspaper* 17:8 (February 2008) 27.
70. Michael Upchurch, "Street Casting: Some Curious Parallels Between Diane Arbus and Kehinde Wiley," *Virginia Quarterly Review* 92:4 (Fall 2016) 202.
71. Sarah Lewis, "Celebration and Critique," in Golden et al, *Kehinde Wiley*, 87.
72. Wiley cited in Helen Stoilas, "Toppling the Ivory Tower," *The Art Newspaper* 17:8 (February 7, 2008) 28.
73. Micah Malone, "Kehinde Wiley," *Art Papers* 31:5 (September-October 2007) 70.
74. Wiley cited in Emery, "Did Obama's Portraitist Paint an Image of a Black Woman Holding the Severed Head of a White Person?"
75. Wiley cited in Christine Kim, "Faux Real: Interview with Kehinde Wiley," in Thelma Golden et al., eds. *The Figurative Impulse in Contemporary African American Art* (New York: The Studio Museum in Harlem, 2002) 53.

76. Wiley cited in Hobbs, "Kehinde Wiley's Conceptual Realism," 48. A contemporary interpretation of Adolph Loos's 1908 modernist tract, *Ornament and Crime*, was developed by the artist Yinka Shonibare in his 2019 curated exhibition, *Criminal Ornamentation*, which included a toile wallpaper by Timorous Beasties that depicts London crime scenes. In 1992 Renée Green collaborated with the Fabric Workshop and Museum in Philadelphia to produce *Mise-en-Scène: Commemorative Toile*, a fabric design with scenes from antebellum America and colonial Europe. The counterpart to Loos in the contemporary context is less anti-modernism than it is, as Hal Foster argues, the possibility that a historical dialectic would provide critical culture some chance to contest the disciplinarity of consumerism's "tweaked commodities and niched markets." See Hal Foster, *Design and Crime (and Other Diatribes)* (London: Verso, 2002) xiv.
77. Wiley cited in Lewis, "Celebration and Critique," 124.
78. Wiley cited in Touré Show, "Kehinde Wiley: How To Make It In Art Careers, Society & Culture."
79. Wiley cited in Touré Show, "Kehinde Wiley: How To Make It In Art Careers, Society & Culture."
80. Murray cited in Hobbs, "Kehinde Wiley's Conceptual Realism," 52-3.
81. Rebecca Walker, "Passing/Posing (Female Prophet Anne)," in Tsai, ed. *Kehinde Wiley*, 46.
82. Wiley cited in Lewis, "Celebration and Critique," 88.
83. Wiley cited in Brian Keith Jackson, "Quiet as It's Kept," 113.
84. Sarah Lewis, "De(i)fying the Masters," *Art in America* 93:4 (April 2005) 123.
85. Lewis, "De(i)fying the Masters," 124. Wiley's project could be thought of as a form of neoliberal reverse colonization. According to Frantz Fanon, "Colonialism is not satisfied merely with holding a people in its grip and emptying the native's brain of all form and content. By a kind of perverted logic, it turns to the past of the oppressed people, and distorts, disfigures and destroys it." Frantz Fanon, *The Wretched of the Earth*, trans. Constance Farrington (New York: Grove Press, [1961] 1963) 210.
86. David Greenberg, "Kehinde Wiley," *Art in America* 97:3 (March 2009) 134; Holland Cotter, "Art in Review: Kehinde Wiley," *The New York Times* (December 9, 2005) https://www.nytimes.com/2005/12/09/arts/art-in-review-kehinde-wiley.html.
87. Connie H. Choi, "Kehinde Wiley: The Artist and Interpretation," in Tsai, ed. *Kehinde Wiley*, 24. On this subject, see Henry Giroux, *Channel Surfing: Racism, the Media, and the Destruction of Today's Youth* (New York: St. Martin's Press, 1998).
88. Walter Benjamin, "Paris, Capital of the Nineteenth Century," in *Reflections: Essays, Aphorisms, Autobiographical Writings*, trans. Edmund Jephcott, ed. Peter Demetz (New York: Schocken Books, 1978) 157.
89. Killian Fox, "Kehinde Wiley: 'Creating the portrait of Obama is a huge responsibility'," *The Guardian* (November 26, 2017), https://www.theguardian.com/artanddesign/2017/nov/26/kehinde-wiley-creating-portrait-barack-obama-huge-responsibility.
90. Skye Sherwin, "Kehinde Wiley's Equestrian Portrait of King Philip II (Michael Jackson): classical kitsch," *The Guardian* (July 6, 2018), https://www.theguardian.com/artanddesign/2018/jul/06/kehinde-wiley-equestrian-portrait-of-michael-jackson. Grace Jones eventually opted out of becoming one of Wiley's models.
91. Wiley cited in Stoilas, "Toppling the Ivory Tower," 28.
92. Christopher Beam, "How to Make It in the Art World."
93. Wiley cited in Stoilas, "Toppling the Ivory Tower," 28.
94. Wiley cited in "A Conversation with Kehinde Wiley and Peter Halley," 162.

95. See the video PUMA, "PUMA presents: OF THE SAME EARTH," *YouTube* (January 26, 2010), https://www.youtube.com/watch?v=1dECwcdJMXg.
96. Matthew B. DiCenso, "A Long-Awaited Reboot: The FIFA Scandal and its Repercussions for Football's Governing Body," *Boston College International and Comparative Law Review* 40:1 (2017) 115-39.
97. "A Conversation with Kehinde Wiley and Peter Halley," 166.
98. Wiley cited in Arianna Rosica, "When Art Meets Sport and Design: Interview with Kehinde Wiley," *Flash Art International* 43:273 (July-September 2010) 50.
99. Wiley cited in Audie Cornish, "The Exquisite Dissonance of Kehinde Wiley," *NPR* (May 22, 2015), https://www.npr.org/2015/05/22/408558234/the-exquisite-dissonance-of-kehinde-wiley.
100. Wiley cited in "A Conversation with Kehinde Wiley and Peter Halley," 166-7.
101. Wiley cited in "A Conversation with Kehinde Wiley and Peter Halley," 165-6.
102. Wiley cited in Mark Mardell, "Kehinde Wiley: Paintings of a moment that never occurred," *BBC News* (September 2, 2012), https://www.bbc.com/news/world-us-canada-19454025.
103. Eugenie Tsai, "Introduction," in Tsai, ed. *Kehinde Wiley*, 19.
104. "A Conversation with Kehinde Wiley and Peter Halley," 165.
105. Davis cited in Wyatt Mason, "How Kehinde Wiley Makes a Masterpiece," *GQ* (April 10, 2013), https://www.gq.com/story/kehinde-wiley.
106. See Andrea Fraser, *2016 in Museums, Money, and Politics* (New York/San Francisco/Cambridge, MA: Westreich Wagner/CCA Wattis Institute/The MIT Press, 2018).
107. LL Cool J, "Kehinde Wiley," *Time* (2018), http://time.com/collection/most-influential-people-2018/5217612/kehinde-wiley/.
108. Wiley cited in Mardell, "Kehinde Wiley."
109. Chloe Wyma, "Kehinde Wiley," *Modern Painters* 27:2 (February 2015) 93.
110. Spence, "Kehinde Wiley's contemporary call to arms."
111. Jenni Sorkin, "Kehinde Wiley: Portraits, patterns and fashion; post-colonialism and mortality," *Frieze* (October 1, 2008), https://frieze.com/article/kehinde-wiley.
112. Molly McArdle, "'I Arrived at the Revolution Via Poetry': An Interview with the Mongrel Coalition Against Gringpo," *Brooklyn Magazine* (July 22, 2015), http://www.bkmag.com/2015/07/22/i-arrived-at-the-revolution-via-poetry-an-interview-with-the-mongrel-coalition-against-gringpo/.
113. Eileen G'Sell, "Kehinde Wiley's Painted Elegies for Ferguson," *Hyperallergic* (February 2, 2019), https://hyperallergic.com/481788/kehinde-wiley-saint-louis-saint-louis-art-museum/.
114. Wiley cited in Andrew Lasane, "Detailed Portraits of Tahiti's Third Gender by Kehinde Wiley Challenge Gauguin's Problematic Depictions," *Colossal* (May 25, 2019), https://www.thisiscolossal.com/2019/05/portraits-of-tahiti-third-gender-by-kehinde-wiley/.
115. Wiley cited in Kim, "Kehinde Wiley: Faux Real."
116. Klaus Ottmann interview with Jeff Koons published in *Journal of Contemporary Art* (October 1986), available at *Culture Night Los Angeles* (June 21, 2014), https://culturenightlosangeles.wordpress.com/2014/06/21/on-americas-wunderkind-artist-jeff-koons-articles-interviews-and-texts/; the full quote was formerly available at https://acourtfolio.wordpress.com/2014/04/24/jeff-koons-equilibrium-posters/.
117. Chris Wiley, "The Toxic Legacy of Zombie Formalism, Part 1: How an Unhinged Economy Spawned a New World of 'Debt Aesthetics'," *Artnet News* (July 26, 2018), https://news.artnet.com/opinion/history-zombie-formalism-1318352.
118. Hobbs, "Kehinde Wiley's Conceptual Realism," 52.

119. Slavoj Žižek, "What Is a Brand?: Marketing Redefines Our Lives in Strategic New Ways," *Playboy* (December 30, 2013) 256.
120. Victor Burgin, *The End of Art Theory: Criticism and Post-Modernity* (Atlantic Island, NJ: Humanities Press International, 1986).
121. Against those who would prematurely write off modernism entirely, see Raymond Williams, *The Politics of Modernism: Against the New Conformists* (London: Verso, 1989). See also Walter Benn Michaels' critique of the aesthetic and theoretical reduction of politics to identity in Michaels, *The Shape of the Signifier: 1967 to the End of History* (Princeton: Princeton University Press, 2004).
122. Jackson, "Quiet as It's Kept," 118.
123. See Ishmael Reed, "Post-Race Scholar Yells Racism," *CounterPunch* (July 27, 2009), https://www.counterpunch.org/2009/07/27/post-race-scholar-yells-racism/.
124. Robin Cembalest, "The Obscenity Trial," *Art News* (December 1990) 136-41.
125. Carole S. Vance, "The War on Culture," *Art in America* 77:9 (September 1989) 43.
126. Douglas Crimp, "The Boys in My Bedroom," *Art in America* 78:2 (February 1990) 47-8.
127. Douglas Crimp, "He's Dead Now, But…," in Gilles Godmer and Réal Lussier, eds. *Pour la suite du monde* (Montreal: Musée d'art contemporain de Montréal, 1992) 263.
128. Essex Hemphill, "The Imperfect Moment," *High Performance* 13:50 (Summer 1990) 18.
129. Kobena Mercer, "Skin Head Sex Thing: Racial Difference and the Homoerotic Imaginary," *New Formations* #16 (Spring 1992) 1, 15, 19.
130. Jane M. Gaines, "Competing Glances: Who Is Reading Robert Mapplethorpe's *Black Book*," *New Formations* #16 (Spring 1992) 20.
131. Mark Fisher, *Capitalist Realism: Is There No Alternative?* (Winchester: O Books, 2009).
132. "A Conversation with Kehinde Wiley and Peter Halley," 158.
133. Wiley cited in Elahe Izadi, "Who is Kehinde Wiley, the artist behind President Obama's official portrait?" *The Washington Post* (February 13, 2018), https://www.washingtonpost.com/news/arts-and-entertainment/wp/2018/02/12/who-is-kehinde-wiley-the-artist-behind-president-obamas-official-portrait/?utm_term=.45cc447eba3b.
134. Lewis Corner, "Kehinde Wiley becomes the first black, gay artist to paint a US president's official portrait," *Gay Times* (February 13, 2018), https://www.gaytimes.co.uk/culture/99241/kehinde-wiley-becomes-first-black-gay-artist-paint-us-presidents-official-portrait/.
135. Choi, "Kehinde Wiley," 30.
136. "A Conversation with Kehinde Wiley and Peter Halley," 165-6.
137. Hobbs, "Kehinde Wiley's Conceptual Realism," 18.
138. Hobbs, "Kehinde Wiley's Conceptual Realism," 46.
139. Hobbs, "Kehinde Wiley's Conceptual Realism," 43. See Michel Foucault, *Discipline and Punish: The Birth of the Prison*, trans. Alan Sheridan (New York: Vintage Books, [1975] 1995).
140. Wiley cited in Upchurch, "Street Casting," 202.
141. See Judith Butler, *Gender Trouble: Feminism and the Subversion of Identity* (New York: Routledge, 1990); *Bodies That Matter: On the Discursive Limits of "Sex"* (New York: Routledge, 1993).
142. Hobbs, "Kehinde Wiley's Conceptual Realism," 56.
143. Mercer, "The Dead Christ in the Tomb," in Tsai, ed. *Kehinde Wiley*, 81.
144. Spence, "Kehinde Wiley's contemporary call to arms."
145. Hobbs, "Kehinde Wiley's Conceptual Realism," 19.
146. Hobbs, "Kehinde Wiley's Conceptual Realism," 20.

147. See Daniel Zamora and Michael C. Behrent. eds. *Foucault and Neoliberalism* (Cambridge: Polity Press, [2014] 2016).
148. Wiley cited in Beam, "How to Make It in the Art World."
149. Wiley cited in Cornish, "The Exquisite Dissonance of Kehinde Wiley."
150. W.E.B. Du Bois, *The Souls of Black Folk*, ed. Brent Hayes Edwards (Oxford: Oxford University Press [1903] 2007) 8.
151. Frantz Fanon, *Black Skin, White Masks*, trans. Charles Lam Markmann (New York: Grove Press, 1967) 197.
152. Brian Holmes, "Unleashing the Collective Phantoms: Flexible Personality, Networked Resistance," *Unleashing the Collective Phantoms: Essays in Reverse Imagineering* (Brooklyn: Autonomedia, 2008) 16-21.
153. Paul Gilroy, *Against Race: Imagining Political Culture Beyond the Color Line* (Cambridge: The Belknap Press, [2000] 2001) 8, 21.
154. Du Bois, *The Souls of Black Folk*, 43.
155. Du Bois, *The Souls of Black Folk*, 188.
156. Du Bois, *The Souls of Black Folk*, 189.
157. Du Bois, *The Souls of Black Folk*, 193. Du Bois only began to take Marxism seriously in the mid-to-late 1920s. His 1931 book *Black Reconstruction* is nevertheless considered eclectic in its use of Marxist concepts. Du Bois was radicalized in the 1930s as a consequence of the rejection by the black masses of elitist black leadership.
158. Du Bois, *The Souls of Black Folk*, 76.
159. Du Bois, *The Souls of Black Folk*, 93.
160. Nina Power, *One-Dimensional Woman* (Winchester: Zero Books, 2009).
161. Power, *One-Dimensional Woman*, 6.
162. Sigmund Freud, *Totemism and Taboo*, trans. A.A. Brill (London: W.W. Norton, [1913] 1989).
163. Siegfried Kracauer, *The Salaried Masses: Duty and Distraction in Weimar Germany*, trans. Quintin Hoare (London: Verso, [1930] 1998) 12. See also Stuart Ewen's analysis of how prewar captains of industry marketed youthful promiscuity as a way to undermine working-class traditions of thrift along with the socialist movement as a whole in *Captains of Consciousness: Advertising and the Social Roots of the Consumer Culture* (New York: Basic Books, [1976] 2001).
164. Herbert Marcuse, *One-Dimensional Man: Studies in the Ideology of Advanced Industrial Society* (Boston: Beacon Press [1964] 1991) 52.
165. Marcuse, *One-Dimensional Man*, 5.
166. See Thomas Frank, *The Conquest of Cool: Business Culture, Counterculture, and the Rise of Hip Consumerism* (Chicago: University of Chicago Press, 1997).
167. Marcuse, *One-Dimensional Man*, 65, 70-1.
168. Marcuse, *One-Dimensional Man*, 74-5. See also Theodor Adorno et al., *The Authoritarian Personality* (London: Verso, [1950] 2019).
169. Marcuse, *One-Dimensional Man*, 75.
170. Hobbs, "Kehinde Wiley's Conceptual Realism," 48. Guy Debord and Gil Wolman, "Methods of Détournement," in Ken Knabb, ed. *The Situationist International Anthology* (Berkeley: Bureau of Public Secrets, 1981) 10.
171. Debord and Wolman, "Methods of Détournement," 9.
172. Debord and Wolman, "Methods of Détournement," 10.
173. Debord and Wolman, "Methods of Détournement," 8.
174. Debord and Wolman, "Methods of Détournement," 11.

175. Situationist International, "Détournement as Negation and Prelude," in Knabb, ed. *Situationist International Anthology*, 55. See also Oscar Negt and Alexander Kluge, *Public Sphere and Experience: Toward an Analysis of the Bourgeois and Proletarian Public Sphere*, trans. Peter Labanyi et al. (Minneapolis: University of Minnesota Press, [1972] 1993).

176. Mieke Bal and Norman Bryson, "Semiotics and Art History," *Art Bulletin* 73:2 (June 1991) 174-208; Michael Warner, *Publics and Counterpublics* (New York: Zone Books, 2002).

177. McKenzie Wark, *The Spectacle of Disintegration: Situationist Passages Out of the 20th Century* (London: Verso, 2013) 147.

178. Hobbs, "Kehinde Wiley's Conceptual Realism," 65.

179. On this issue, see Tiqqun, *Preliminary Materials for a Theory of the Young-Girl* (Los Angeles: Semiotext(e), 2012). See also the 2009 film by Alex Cox, *Repo Chick*, the story of a celebutante who finds a job as a repossessor in the midst of widespread credit collapse.

180. Maurizio Lazzarato, *The Making of Indebted Man*, trans. Joshua David Jordan (Amsterdam: Semiotext(e), 2012).

181. Artnet News, "Julie Mehretu and Kehinde Wiley Collaborated With American Express to Design the Company's New Platinum Card," *Artnet News* (January 21, 2022), https://news.artnet.com/art-world/american-expresss-kehinde-wiley-julie-mehretu-2062759.

182. See the *City of Ladies* project page on Zanny Begg's website, https://zannybegg.com/the-book-of-the-city-of-ladies/.

183. See Silvia Federici, *Caliban and the Witch: Women, the Body and Primitive Accumulation* (Brooklyn: Autonomedia, 1998) and *Revolution at Point Zero: Housework, Reproduction, and Feminist Struggle* (Oakland: PM Press, 2012).

4: Racialism and Its Discontents

1. Interview with Adolph Reed in Lynn Parramore, "Cheap Talk on Race and Xenophobia Keeps Americans from Confronting Economic and Political Problems," *Institute for New Economic Thinking* (November 2, 2018), https://www.ineteconomics.org/perspectives/blog/cheap-talk-on-race-and-xenophobia-keeps-americans-from-confronting-economic-and-political-peril.

2. See for example this article by a BLM activist who wilfully ignores the fact that there are legitimate leftist critiques of racialism: Mame-Fatou Niang, "France's racial spring," *Rosa Luxemburg Siftung* (August 26, 2020), https://www.rosalux.eu/en/article/1761.france-s-racial-spring.html.

3. See Fredric Jameson, *An American Utopia: Dual Power and the Universal Army*, ed. Slavoj Žižek (London: Verso, 2016).

4. Georg Lukács, *The Theory of the Novel: A Historico-Philosophical Essay on the Forms of Great Epic Literature*, trans. Anna Bostock (London: The Merlin Press, [1916] 1971), https://www.marxists.org/archive/lukacs/works/theory-novel/.

5. Trévon Austin, "US police have killed more than 30,000 people since 1980," *World Socialist Web Site* (October 2, 2021), https://www.wsws.org/en/articles/2021/10/02/upkm-o02.html.

6. Aaron Morrison, "Exclusive: Black Lives Matter issues a statement on Trump's election," *Mic* (November 15, 2016), https://www.mic.com/articles/159496/exclusive-black-lives-matter-issues-a-statement-on-trump-s-election.

7. Ibram X. Kendi, *How to Be an Antiracist* (New York: One World, 2019) eBook, 302-3.

8. On why black voters did not support Sanders in the South Carolina primaries, a conservative anti-union state, see Cedric Johnson, "Fear and Pandering in the Palmetto State," *Jacobin* (February 29, 2016), https://www.jacobinmag.com/2016/02/sanders-clinton-south-carolina-primary-black-voters-firewall/.
9. Adolph Reed, Jr., "Splendors and Miseries of the Antiracist 'Left'," *Nonsite* (November 6, 2016), https://nonsite.org/editorial/splendors-and-miseries-of-the-antiracist-left-2.
10. Reed, "Splendors and Miseries of the Antiracist 'Left'."
11. Paul Street, "What Would the Black Panthers Think of Black Lives Matter?" *Truthdig* (October 29, 2017), https://www.truthdig.com/articles/black-panthers-think-black-lives-matter/.
12. See Keeanga-Yamahtta Taylor, *From #BlackLivesMatter to Black Liberation* (Chicago: Haymarket Books, 2016).
13. Cedric Johnson, "The Triumph of Black Lives Matter and Neoliberal Redemption," *Nonsite* (June 9, 2020), https://nonsite.org/editorial/the-triumph-of-black-lives-matter-and-neoliberal-redemption. See also Cedric Johnson, "Don't Let Blackwashing Save the Investor Class," *Jacobin* (June 24, 2020), https://jacobinmag.com/2020/06/blackwashing-corporations-woke-capitalism-protests.
14. Kimberlé Crenshaw cited in Sydney Ember, "Bernie Sanders Predicted Revolution, Just Not This One," *The New York Times* (June 19, 2020), https://www.nytimes.com/2020/06/19/us/politics/bernie-sanders-protests.html; see also Jacobin Magazine, "Walter Benn Michaels & Jennifer Pan on the Trouble with Diversity," *YouTube* (July 3, 2020), https://www.youtube.com/watch?v=HT41gzsN7Ik;
15. Ralph Nader Radio Hour, "How To Fix Our Broken Democracy," *YouTube* (July 4, 2020), https://www.youtube.com/watch?v=NWBnarQkA6s.
16. Tracy Jan, Jena McGregor and Meghan Hoyer, "Corporate America's $50 billion promise," *The Washington Post* (August 23, 2021), https://www.washingtonpost.com/business/interactive/2021/george-floyd-corporate-america-racial-justice/.
17. Jan, McGregor and Hoyer, "Corporate America's $50 billion promise."
18. Tatiana Cozzarelli, "Class Reductionism Is Real, and It's Coming from the Jacobin Wing of the DSA," *Left Voice* (June 16, 2020), https://www.leftvoice.org/class-reductionism-is-real-and-its-coming-from-the-jacobin-wing-of-the-dsa.
19. Tom Carter, "The ideological foundations of Critical Race Theory," *World Socialist Web Site* (August 29, 2021), https://www.wsws.org/en/articles/2021/08/30/crit-a30.html.
20. Don McIntosh, "Talking Socialism | Catching Up with AOC," *Democratic Left* (March 19, 2021), https://www.dsausa.org/democratic-left/aoc/.
21. Cited in Carter, "The ideological foundations of Critical Race Theory."
22. See Félix Guattari, *Chaosophy*, ed. Sylvère Lotringer (Los Angeles: Semiotext(e), 1995).
23. See Pascal Robert, "The Great 'Awokening' and Ruling Class Uses for Racial Grievance Discourse," *Black Agenda Report* (June 9, 2021), https://www.blackagendareport.com/great-awokening-and-ruling-class-uses-racial-grievance-discourse.
24. Carter, "The ideological foundations of Critical Race Theory." See also Christian Parenti's somewhat flawed characterization of Marcuse but valuable critique of the 'Power Shuffle' in Parenti, "The First Privilege Walk," *Nonsite* (November 18, 2021), https://nonsite.org/the-first-privilege-walk/.
25. Carter, "The ideological foundations of Critical Race Theory."
26. Carter, "The ideological foundations of Critical Race Theory."
27. Marx cited in V.I. Lenin, *State and Revolution* (Chicago: Haymarket Books, [1918] 2014) 70.
28. Engels cited in Lenin, *State and Revolution*, 52.

29. Jo Freeman, "The Tyranny of Structurelessness" (1970), available at https://www.jofreeman.com/joreen/tyranny.htm.
30. Keeanga-Yamahtta Taylor, "Five Years Later, Do Black Lives Matter?" *Jacobin* (September 30, 2019), https://www.jacobinmag.com/2019/09/black-lives-matter-laquan-mcdonald-mike-brown-eric-garner.
31. David Roediger, "'Who's Afraid of the White Working Class? On Joan C. Williams's 'White Working Class: Overcoming Class Cluelessness in America'," *Los Angeles Review of Books* (May 17, 2017), https://lareviewofbooks.org/article/whos-afraid-of-the-white-working-class-on-joan-c-williamss-white-working-class-overcoming-class-cluelessness-in-america/#.
32. Gurminder K. Bhambra, "Brexit, Trump, and 'methodological whiteness': on the misrecognition of race and class," *The British Journal of Sociology* 68:1 (2017) 219, 225.
33. Daniel Denvir, "Beyond 'Race Relations': An Interview with Barbara J. Fields / Karen E. Fields," *Jacobin* (January 17, 2018), https://www.jacobinmag.com/2018/01/racecraft-racism-barbara-karen-fields.
34. Richard Seymour, "What's the Matter with the 'White Working Class'?" *Salvage* (February 2, 2017), https://salvage.zone/online-exclusive/whats-the-matter-with-the-white-working-class/.
35. Kwame Anthony Appiah, "The Politics of Identity," *Daedalus* 135:4 (Fall 2006) 21.
36. Barbara Ehrenreich, "Dead, White and Blue: The Great Die-Off of America's Blue Collar Whites," *Tom Dispatch* (December 1, 2015), http://www.tomdispatch.com/blog/176075/.
37. Eric London, "The myth of the reactionary white working class," *World Socialist Web Site* (November 12, 2016), https://www.wsws.org/en/articles/2016/11/12/pers-n12.html.
38. Mike Davis, "The Great God Trump and the White Working Class," *Catalyst* 1:1 (Spring 2017), https://catalyst-journal.com/vol1/no1/great-god-trump-davis.
39. Michael Bray, "The 'White Working Class' Does Not Exist: Thinking Through Liberal Postracialism," *Historical Materialism* (September 20, 2017), http://www.historicalmaterialism.org/blog/white-working-class-does-not-exist-thinking-through-liberal-postracialism.
40. See Amber A'Lee Frost, "The Poisoned Chalice of Hashtag Activism," *Catalyst* 4:2 (Summer 2020), https://catalyst-journal.com/vol4/no2/the-poisoned-chalice-of-hashtag-activism.
41. Michael Bray, "The Sanders Antinomies: Strategic Questions for Uncertain Times," *Historical Materialism* (April 17, 2019), http://www.historicalmaterialism.org/blog/sanders-antinomies-strategic-questions-for-uncertain-times.
42. See Ian F. Haney-López, "Is the 'Post' in Post-Racial the 'Blind' in Colorblind?" *Berkeley Law Scholarship Repository* #32 (2010) 807-31.
43. Haney-López, "Is the 'Post' in Post-Racial the 'Blind' in Colorblind?" 828.
44. Haney-López, "Is the 'Post' in Post-Racial the 'Blind' in Colorblind?" 829.
45. Touré, *Who's Afraid of Post-Blackness?: What It Means to Be Black Now* (New York: Free Press, 2011).
46. Touré, *Who's Afraid of Post-Blackness?*, 53.
47. Wiley cited in Touré, *Who's Afraid of Post-Blackness?*, 61.
48. See for example Michel Foucault's wrongminded defence of sadism, and of Nazism, as "not sadistic enough" in "Sade, Sergeant of Sex," in *Aesthetics, Method, and Epistemology, Volume Two*, ed. James D. Faubion, trans. Robert Hurley et al. (New York: The New Press, [1994] 1998) 223-7. See, comparatively, Slavoj Žižek's rejection of Sadean perversion as a supposed "ethics" of self-humiliation in Žižek, "Kant and Sade: The Ideal Couple," *Lacanian Ink* #13 (1998), https://www.lacan.com/zizlacan4.htm.
49. Touré, *Who's Afraid of Post-Blackness?*, 60.
50. Touré, *Who's Afraid of Post-Blackness?*, 70.

51. Touré, *Who's Afraid of Post-Blackness?*, 234.
52. Touré, *Who's Afraid of Post-Blackness?*, 109.
53. Touré, *Who's Afraid of Post-Blackness?*, 438.
54. The classic essay that became of the basis of privilege theory is Peggy McIntosh, "White Privilege: Unpacking the Invisible Backpack." The article, which has many iterations, was first published in 1989.
55. On this subject, see Holly Lewis, *The Politics of Everybody: Feminism, Queer Theory, and Marxism at the Intersection* (London: Zed Books, 2016).
56. See the keynote lecture by Immanuel Wallerstein at the American Sociological Association conference on the Political Economy of the World-System, April 10, 2014, available at PittGlobalStudies, "Immanuel Wallerstein - Dilemmas of the Global Left," *YouTube* (September 5, 2014), https://www.youtube.com/watch?v=rTG5TQSZ1FY.
57. John McWhorter, *Woke Racism: How a New Religion Has Betrayed Black America* (New York: Portfolio/Penguin, 2021) eBook.
58. McWhorter, *Woke Racism*, 204.
59. Scott cited in McWhorter, *Woke Racism*, 205.
60. McWhorter, *Woke Racism*, 252.
61. McWhorter, *Woke Racism*, 255.
62. McWhorter, *Woke Racism*, 240.
63. McWhorter cited in Neal Conan, "Linguist John McWhorter Makes the Case for Obama," *NPR* (October 28, 2008), https://www.npr.org/transcripts/96215276.
64. McWhorter cited in Lydia Lum, "The Obama Era: A Post-racial Society?" *Diverse* (February 4, 2009), https://www.diverseeducation.com/home/article/15088210/the-obama-era-a-post-racial-society.
65. John McWhorter, "Despite Mixed Heritage, President Obama Is Hardly Post-Racial," *New York Magazine / Intelligencer* (August 2, 2012), https://nymag.com/intelligencer/2012/08/obama-hardly-post-racial.html.
66. John McWhorter, "It's about time Obama stuck up for his 'respectability politics'," *The Washington Post* (May 14, 2015), https://www.washingtonpost.com/posteverything/wp/2015/05/14/its-about-time-obama-stuck-up-for-his-respectability-politics/.
67. John McWhorter, "The Upside of Obama," *The Manhattan Institute* (October 26, 2006), https://www.manhattan-institute.org/html/upside-obama-0125.html; John McWhorter, "What Are President Obama's Black Critics Talking About?" *The New Republic* (October 29, 2012), https://newrepublic.com/article/109357/what-are-president-obamas-black-critics-talking-about.
68. John McWhorter, "The real cause of Trump isn't Obama," *CNN* (March 16, 2016), https://www.cnn.com/2016/03/16/opinions/obama-isnt-the-cause-of-trump-opinion-mcwhorter/index.html.
69. John McWhorter, "Trump is a disaster, but talk of a 'whitelash' is misguided – and counterproductive," *Vox* (November 15, 2016), https://www.vox.com/the-big-idea/2016/11/15/13631980/trump-racism-demographics-whitelash.
70. For a discussion of these four forms of politics – meta, para, archi and ultra – see Slavoj Žižek, "The Lesson of Rancière," in Jacques Rancière, *The Politics of Aesthetic*, trans. Gabriel Rockhill (London: Continuum, [2000] 2004) 69-79.
71. Adolph Reed, *Class Notes: Posing as Politics and Other Thoughts on the American Scene* (New York: The New Press, 2000) xxvii.
72. Reed, *Class Notes*, xxi.

73. Johnny Bernard Hill, *The First Black President: Barack Obama, Race, Politics, and the American Dream* (New York: Palgrave Macmillan, 2009) 1.
74. Hill, *The First Black President*, 8.
75. Du Bois, *The Souls of Black Folk*, 67.
76. Hill, *The First Black President*, 138-9.
77. Ta-Nehisi Coates, *We Were Eight Years in Power: An American Tragedy* (New York: One World Press, 2017).
78. Coates, *We Were Eight Years in Power*, 207.
79. Coates, *We Were Eight Years in Power*, 15.
80. Coates, *We Were Eight Years in Power*, 525.
81. Coates, *We Were Eight Years in Power*, 166.
82. See Étienne Balibar's discussion of "neo-racism" in Étienne Balibar and Immanuel Wallerstein, *Race, Nation, Class: Ambiguous Identities*, trans. Chris Turner (London: Verso, [1988] 1991). See also Jacques Rancière's analogous theory of neoliberal "cold racism" in Rancière "Politics, Identification, and Subjectivization," *October* #61 (Summer 1992) 58-64.
83. Coates, *We Were Eight Years in Power*, 272.
84. Coates, *We Were Eight Years in Power*, 114, 540.
85. Coates, *We Were Eight Years in Power*, 546.
86. Ta-Nehisi Coates, "Obama's Robot Army," *The Atlantic* (December 28, 2011), https://www.theatlantic.com/politics/archive/2011/12/obamas-robot-army/250584/.
87. See Touré F. Reed, "Between Obama and Coates," *Catalyst* 1:4 (Winter 2018), https://catalyst-journal.com/vol1/no4/between-obama-and-coates.
88. Coates, *We Were Eight Years in Power*, 661.
89. Coates, *We Were Eight Years in Power*, 668.
90. West cited in Hope Reese, "Cornel West: Neoliberalism Has Failed Us," *JSTOR Daily* (December 25, 2017), https://daily.jstor.org/cornel-west-interview/.
91. Cornel West, "Ta-Nehisi Coates is the neoliberal face of the black freedom struggle," *The Guardian* (December 17, 2017), https://www.theguardian.com/commentisfree/2017/dec/17/ta-nehisi-coates-neoliberal-black-struggle-cornel-west.
92. Coates, *We Were Eight Years in Power*, 358.
93. Daniel Zamora, "Bernie Sanders and the New Class Politics: An Interview with Adolph Reed," *Jacobin* (August 8, 2016), https://www.jacobinmag.com/2016/08/bernie-sanders-black-voters-adolph-reed-trump-hillary.
94. Cedric Johnson, "An Open Letter to Ta-Nehisi Coates and the Liberals Who Love Him," *Jacobin* (February 03, 2016), https://www.jacobinmag.com/2016/02/ta-nehisi-coates-case-for-reparations-bernie-sanders-racism/. See Ta-Nehisi Coates, "Why Precisely Is Bernie Sanders Against Reparations?" *The Atlantic* (January 19, 2016), https://www.theatlantic.com/politics/archive/2016/01/bernie-sanders-reparations/424602/, and Coates, "Bernie Sanders and the Liberal Imagination," *The Atlantic* (Jan 24, 2016), https://www.theatlantic.com/politics/archive/2016/01/bernie-sanders-liberal-imagination/425022/.
95. Johnson, "An Open Letter to Ta-Nehisi Coates and the Liberals Who Love Him."
96. Michael Eric Dyson, *The Black Presidency: Barack Obama and the Politics of Race in America* (Boston: Houghton Mifflin Harcourt, 2016) ix.
97. Dyson, *The Black Presidency*, 117.
98. Dyson, *The Black Presidency*, 55.

99. Democracy Now, "Eric Holder's Complex Legacy: Voting Rights Advocate, Enemy of Press Freedom, Friend of Wall Street," *Democracy Now* (September 26, 2014), https://www.democracynow.org/2014/9/26/eric_holders_complex_legacy_voting_rights.
100. Dyson, *The Black Presidency*, 65.
101. Dyson, *The Black Presidency*, 68.
102. Glen Ford, "Why They Hate Cornel West: Michael Eric Dyson's attack on Cornel West signals the bankruptcy of the black political class," *Jacobin* (April 24, 2015), https://www.jacobinmag.com/2015/04/cornel-west-dyson-obama-glen-ford. See also Dyson's attack piece against Cornel West, "The Ghost of Cornel West," *The New Republic* (April 19, 2015), https://newrepublic.com/article/121550/cornel-wests-rise-fall-our-most-exciting-black-scholar-ghost.
103. Michael Eric Dyson, "What Donald Trump Doesn't Know About Black People," *The New York Times* (December 17, 2016), https://www.nytimes.com/2016/12/17/opinion/sunday/what-donald-trump-doesnt-know-about-black-people.html.
104. Michael Eric Dyson, "Barack Obama, the President of Black America?" *The New York Times* (June 25, 2016), https://www.nytimes.com/2016/06/26/opinion/sunday/barack-obama-the-president-of-black-america.html.
105. Michelle Alexander, *The New Jim Crow: Mass Incarceration in the Age of Colorblindness* (New York: The New Press, 2010).
106. Adolph Reed, Jr., "How Racial Disparity Does Not Help Make Sense of Patterns of Police Violence," *Nonsite* (September 16, 2016), https://nonsite.org/editorial/how-racial-disparity-does-not-help-make-sense-of-patterns-of-police-violence.
107. Reed, "How Racial Disparity Does Not Help Make Sense of Patterns of Police Violence."
108. West cited in Thomas Frank, "Cornel West: 'He posed as a progressive and turned out to be counterfeit. We ended up with a Wall Street presidency, a drone presidency,'" *Salon* (August 24, 2014), https://www.salon.com/2014/08/24/cornel_west_he_posed_as_a_progressive_and_turned_out_to_be_counterfeit_we_ended_up_with_a_wall_street_presidency_a_drone_presidency/.
109. West cited in Frank, "Cornel West: 'He posed as a progressive and turned out to be counterfeit. We ended up with a Wall Street presidency, a drone presidency."
110. Cornel West, "Black Prophetic Fire: Cornel West on the Revolutionary Legacy of Leading African-American Voices," *Democracy Now* (October 6, 2014), https://www.democracynow.org/2014/10/6/black_prophetic_fire_cornel_west_on.
111. The Real News, "The Betrayal of the Black Elite with Chris Hedges and Cornel West," *The Real News* (August 11, 2015), https://therealnews.com/stories/daysofrevolt0811cwest2.
112. West cited in Reese, "Cornel West: Neoliberalism Has Failed Us."
113. Walter Benn Michaels, "The Trouble with Diversity," *The American Prospect* (August 13, 2006), https://prospect.org/article/trouble-diversity. See also Michaels, *The Trouble with Diversity: How We Learned to Love Identity and Ignore Inequality* (New York: Metropolitan Books, 2006).

114. When Bernie Sanders kicked off his 2016 nomination campaign, one of the arguments that circulated in the mainstream media was that at age 78 Sanders is too old to be President. Although Donald Trump was close behind and only five years younger, Trump's age was never an issue in the criticisms emerging from the same mainstream. Instead of directly attacking Sanders' socialist policies, the neoliberal press first attacked his identity and only criticized his socialist values around the time that Biden became the sure bet. See Mehdi Hassan, "Critics Say Bernie Sanders Is Too Old, Too White, and Too Socialist to Run for President in 2020. They're Wrong," *The Intercept* (December 19, 2018), https://theintercept.com/2018/12/19/bernie-sanders-2020-election/.
115. Pamela Newkirk, "Diversity Has Become a Booming Business. So Where Are the Results?" *Time* (October 10, 2019), https://time.com/5696943/diversity-business/.
116. Frank Dobbin and Alexandra Kalev, "Why Diversity Programs Fail," *Harvard Business Review* (July-August 2016), https://hbr.org/2016/07/why-diversity-programs-fail; Matt Martin, "5 reasons diversity training usually fails," *Fast Company* (August 3, 2020), https://www.fastcompany.com/90535289/5-reasons-diversity-training-are-not-successful-as-anticipated.
117. See Matt Taibi, *Hate Inc.: Why Today's Media Makes Us Despise One Another* (New York: O/R Books, 2019).
118. Film at Lincoln Center, "Joel Coen, Denzel Washington, Frances McDormand & More on The Tragedy of Macbeth," *YouTube* (September 27, 2021), https://www.youtube.com/watch?v=gNcGggqJhCY.
119. Michaels, "The Trouble with Diversity."
120. Walter Benn Michaels, "On the Trouble with Diversity," *n+1* (December 13, 2006), https://nplusonemag.com/online-only/online-only/magical-capitalism/.
121. See Park Center for Independent Media, "Recognize Race Reductionism with Scholars of Sociology, History," *YouTube* (May 26, 2021), https://www.youtube.com/watch?v=n-wCSs0T5Tbk.
122. Bhaskar Sunkara, "Let Them Eat Diversity: An Interview with Walter Benn Michaels," *Jacobin* (January 1, 2011), https://jacobinmag.com/2011/01/let-them-eat-diversity/.
123. Walter Benn Michaels, "The Political Economy of Anti-Racism," *Nonsite* (February 11, 2018), https://nonsite.org/article/the-political-economy-of-anti-racism.
124. Michaels, "The Political Economy of Anti-Racism."
125. Michaels, "The Political Economy of Anti-Racism."
126. Adolph Reed, Jr., "The limits of anti-racism," *Left Business Observer* #121 (September 2009), http://www.leftbusinessobserver.com/Antiracism.html.
127. Adolph Reed, Jr., "Black Politics After 2016," *Nonsite* (February 11, 2018), https://nonsite.org/article/black-politics-after-2016.
128. Reed cited in Zamora, "Bernie Sanders and the New Class Politics."
129. Adolph Reed, Jr., "Unravelling the Relation of Race and Class in American Politics," in Diane E. Davis, ed. *Political Power and Social Theory* (Bingley: Emerald Publishing Limited, 2006) 270.
130. Adolph Reed, Jr., "Rejoinder," in Davis, ed. *Political Power and Social Theory*, 310.
131. Adolph Reed, Jr., "Adolph Reed on Sanders, Coates, and Reparations," *New Politics* (February 5, 2016), https://newpol.org/adolph-reed-sanders-coates-and-reparations/.
132. Reed, "The limits of anti-racism."
133. Adolph Reed, Jr., "What Materialist Black Political History Actually Looks Like," *Nonsite* (January 8, 2019), https://nonsite.org/editorial/what-materialist-black-political-history-actually-looks-like.

134. Adolph Reed, Jr., "Nothing Left: The long, slow surrender of American liberals," *Harper's* (March 2014), https://harpers.org/archive/2014/03/nothing-left-2/. Note that Reed's criticism of the false representativity of race leaders works more readily as a critique of politics than of aesthetics and activism, where the question of political representation is in some ways dissimulated, depending also on the art and activism in question. This observation, however, only raises the stakes of the problem of political representation and strategy.
135. Adolph Reed, Jr., "The James Brown Theory of Black Liberation," *Jacobin* (October 6, 2015), https://jacobinmag.com/2015/10/adolph-reed-black-liberation-django-lincoln-selma-glory.
136. Adolph Reed, Jr., "The Real Problem with *Selma*: It doesn't help to understand the civil rights movement, the regime it challenged, or even the significance of the voting rights act," *Nonsite* (January 26, 2015), https://nonsite.org/editorial/the-real-problem-with-selma.
137. Reed, "Adolph Reed on Sanders, Coates, and Reparations."
138. Reed, "Adolph Reed on Sanders, Coates, and Reparations."
139. Reed, "Nothing Left."
140. Reed, "Black Politics After 2016."
141. Reed, "What Materialist Black Political History Actually Looks Like." On the cancelation of a talk that Reed was supposed to give to the NYC DSA by the chapter's steering committee and the DSA Socialists of Color Caucus, see Class Unity, "Spiraling anti-Marxism in the DSA," *Class Unity* (June 4, 2020), https://classunity.org/2020/06/04/spiraling-anti-marxism-in-the-dsa/; Michael Powell, "A Black Marxist Scholar Wanted to Talk About Race. It Ignited a Fury," *The New York Times* (August 14, 2020), https://www.nytimes.com/2020/08/14/us/adolph-reed-controversy.html.
142. See in particular, Ellen Meiksins Wood, *Democracy Against Capitalism: Renewing Historical Materialism* (Cambridge: Cambridge University Press, 1995).
143. Ellen Meiksins Wood, "The Imperial Paradox: Ideologies of Empire," lecture delivered at SOAS, University of London, October 29, 2008, *YouTube* (April 11, 2013), https://www.youtube.com/watch?v=mzaAoRx6uH4.
144. Ellen Meiksins Wood, "Class, Race, and Capitalism," in Davis, ed. *Political Power and Social Theory*, 276.
145. Wood, "Class, Race, and Capitalism," 281.
146. Ellen Meiksins Wood, "Capitalism and Human Emancipation: Race, Gender, and Democracy," in Nancy Holstrom, ed. *The Socialist Feminist Project: A Contemporary Reader in Theory and Politics* (New York: Monthly Review Press, 2002) 277.
147. Wood, "Capitalism and Human Emancipation," 291. Reed's critique of Wood in *Political Power and Social Theory* argues that her conclusions are premised on idealist, or structuralist, formulations and are not historical enough – a charge that she disputes convincingly. Reed's critique is repurposed for feminist uses in Cinzia Arruzza, "Logic or History? The Political Stakes of Marxist-Feminist Theory," *Viewpoint Magazine* (June 23, 2015), https://www.viewpointmag.com/2015/06/23/logic-or-history-the-political-stakes-of-marxist-feminist-theory/ and Arruzza, "From Women's Strikes to a New Class Movement: The Third Feminist Wave," *Viewpoint Magazine* (December 3, 2019), https://www.viewpointmag.com/2018/12/03/from-womens-strikes-to-a-new-class-movement-the-third-feminist-wave/. See also Cinzia Arruzza, Tithi Bhattacharya and Nancy Fraser, *Feminism for the 99%: A Manifesto* (London: Verso, 2019).
148. Wood, "The Imperial Paradox."

149. Chris Chen, "The Limit Point of Capitalist Equality: Notes Towards an Abolitionist Antiracism," *Endnotes* #3 (September 2013), https://endnotes.org.uk/issues/3/en/chris-chen-the-limit-point-of-capitalist-equality.
150. Chen, "The Limit Point of Capitalist Equality."
151. See for instance in David I. Backer's unhelpful contrast between "class unity," which for him includes identity politics, and "class separatism," which he says excludes identity issues from left politics. David I. Backer, "Uses and Abuses of Class Separatism," *Verso Blog* (January 1, 2019), https://www.versobooks.com/blogs/4201-uses-and-abuses-of-class-separatism.
152. Monthly Review, "An Interview with Ellen Meiksins Wood," *Monthly Review* (May 1999) 82. See also Ellen Meiksins Wood, "Why Class Struggle Is Central," *Against the Current* (September/October 1987) 7.
153. For one of the most advanced discussions of this issue, see especially Slavoj Žižek, "Postmodernism or Class Struggle? Yes Please!" in Judith Butler, Ernesto Laclau and Slavoj Žižek, *Contingency, Hegemony and Universality: Contemporary Dialogues on the Left* (London: Verso, 2000) 90-135.
154. Asad Haider, *Mistaken Identity: Race and Class in the Age of Trump* (London: Verso, 2018) eBook.
155. Haider, *Mistaken Identity*, 24.
156. Haider, *Mistaken Identity*, 101.
157. Haider, *Mistaken Identity*, 190.
158. Haider, *Mistaken Identity*, 189.
159. Melissa Naschek, "The Identity Mistake," *Jacobin* (August 28, 2018), https://www.jacobinmag.com/2018/08/mistaken-identity-asaid-haider-review-identity-politics.
160. The CRC cited in Naschek, "The Identity Mistake."
161. Naschek, "The Identity Mistake."
162. Nikhil Pal Singh and Joshua Clover, "The Blindspot Revisited," *Verso Blog* (October 12, 2018), https://www.versobooks.com/blogs/4079-the-blindspot-revisited.
163. Adolph Reed, Jr., "Response to Backer and Singh," *Verso Blog* (October 10, 2018), https://www.versobooks.com/blogs/4073-response-to-backer-and-singh.
164. Adolph Reed, Jr., "Which Side Are You On?" *Common Dreams* (December 23, 2018), https://www.commondreams.org/views/2018/12/23/which-side-are-you. After the routing of the Sanders campaign in 2020, the DSA-affiliated *Jacobin* magazine created the Center for Working-Class Politics (CWCP) and issued a research report titled *Commonsense Solidarity: How a working-class coalition can be built, and maintained.* The report was based on surveys which concluded that working-class voters prefer messaging that presents policy ideals in universal rather than woke terms. However, the report's research agenda also made room for the prospect that woke messaging is a more effective electoral strategy in urban and middle-class districts. See Center for Working-Class Politics, *Commonsense Solidarity: How a working-class coalition can be built, and maintained* (2021), https://images.jacobinmag.com/wp-content/uploads/2021/11/08095656/CWCPReport_CommonsenseSolidarity.pdf. See also my critique of the study in Léger, "Working-Class Politics at the Margins," *Blog of Public Secrets* (November 17, 2021), https://legermj.typepad.com/blog/2021/11/working-class-politics-at-the-margins.html.
165. Haider, *Mistaken Identity*, 20, 200.
166. Red May TV, "Asad Haider - Mistaken Identity: Race and Class in the Age of Trump," *YouTube* (May 27, 2018), https://www.youtube.com/watch?v=6vaZGh5CIPY. See Leo Bersani, "Is the Rectum a Grave?" *October* #43 (Winter 1987) 197-222.

167. See Judith Butler, *The Psychic Life of Power: Theories in Subjection* (Stanford: Stanford University Press, 1997); Wendy Brown, *States of Injury: Power and Freedom in Late Modernity* (Princeton: Princeton University Press, 1995). See also Wendy Brown, "Resisting Left Melancholy," *Boundary* 2:26 (Autumn 1999) 19-27.
168. Henri Lefebvre, *Vers un romantisme révolutionnaire* (Paris: Éditions Lignes, [1957] 2011).
169. Haider, *Mistaken Identity*, 50.
170. Henri Lefebvre, *Le Marxisme* (Paris: Presses Universitaires de France, [1948] 1997) 58.
171. Adolph Reed, Jr., "From Jenner to Dolezal: One Trans Good, the Other Not So Much," *Common Dreams* (June 15, 2015), https://www.commondreams.org/views/2015/06/15/jenner-dolezal-one-trans-good-other-not-so-much.
172. David Roediger, *Class, Race, and Marxism* (London: Verso, 2017) eBook.
173. Roediger, *Class, Race, and Marxism*, 44.
174. See David Harvey, *Seventeen Contradictions and the End of Capitalism* (London: Profile Books, 2014).
175. Roediger, *Class, Race, and Marxism*,15.
176. See my discussion of Harvey's views on identity politics in Marc James Léger, *Vanguardia: Socially Engaged Art and Theory* (Manchester: Manchester University Press, 2019).
177. Roediger, *Class, Race, and Marxism*, 49, 60.
178. Roediger, *Class, Race, and Marxism*, 60.
179. Ellen Meiksins Wood, *The Retreat from Class: A New 'True' Socialism* (London: Verso, [1986] 1998).
180. Roediger, *Class, Race, and Marxism*, 70.
181. Roediger, *Class, Race, and Marxism*, 91. Roediger also takes issue with the writings of more moderate critics of anti-racism such as Paul Gilroy, Orlando Patterson, Antonia Darder, Rudy Torres, Loïc Wacquant and Pierre Bourdieu.
182. F.T.C. Manning, "Same Path, Different Weather?" *Syndicate Network* (April 11, 2015) https://syndicate.network/symposia/theology/seventeen-contradictions-and-the-end-of-capitalism/.
183. See Erik Olin Wright, *Understanding Class* (London: Verso, 2015) 122-4.
184. Roediger, *Class, Race, and Marxism*, 57. My emphasis.
185. Roediger, *Class, Race, and Marxism*, 49.
186. Mark Fisher, "Exiting the Vampire Castle," *The North Star* (November 22, 2013), available at https://www.opendemocracy.net/en/opendemocracyuk/exiting-vampire-castle/.
187. Fisher, "Exiting the Vampire Castle."
188. David E. Roediger, *The Wages of Whiteness: Race and the Making of the American Working Class* (London: Verso, [1991] 2007).
189. See Esme Choonara and Yuri Prasad, "What's wrong with privilege theory," *International Socialism* #142 (April 2, 2014) 22, http://isj.org.uk/whats-wrong-with-privilege-theory/#esmeyuri142.
190. Reed, *Class Notes*, 191.
191. Roediger, *Class, Race, and Marxism*, 119.
192. Roediger, *The Wages of Whiteness*, 95.
193. Roediger, *The Wages of Whiteness*, 151.
194. Roediger, *The Wages of Whiteness*, 180.
195. Roediger, *Class, Race, and Marxism*, 153.
196. Vivek Chibber, "Rescuing Class from the Cultural Turn," *Catalyst* 1:1 (Spring 2017), https://catalyst-journal.com/vol1/no1/cultural-turn-vivek-chibber.
197. Roediger, *The Wages of Whiteness*, 126.

198. The sixth chapter of *Class, Race, and Marxism* opens with an epigraph by Chandra Talpade Mohanty: "Solidarity is … the result of an active struggle to construct the universal on the basis of particulars." In Roediger, *Class, Race, and Marxism*, 276.
199. Brown University, "Whiteness in the Time of Trump," *YouTube* (April 20, 2018), https://www.youtube.com/watch?v=96m8FzPkUIc.
200. As if the minimum wages of whiteness were not enough, Jonathan M. Metzl has written a book on how it is that middle and lower-income white Americans are also killing themselves by attacking health services. See Jonathan M. Metzl, *Dying of Whiteness: How the Politics of Racial Resentment Is Killing America's Heartland* (New York: Basic Books, 2019).
201. Cedric Johnson, "The Wages of Roediger: Why Three Decades of Whiteness Studies Has Not Produced the Left We Need," *Nonsite* #29 (September 9, 2019), https://nonsite.org/article/the-wages-of-roediger-why-three-decades-of-whiteness-studies-has-not-produced-the-left-we-need.
202. Slavoj Žižek, "The Need to Traverse the Fantasy," *In These Times* (December 28, 2015), http://inthesetimes.com/article/18722/Slavoj-Zizek-on-Syria-refugees-Eurocentrism-Western-Values-Lacan-Islam.
203. See Pierre Bourdieu, *Distinction: A Social Critique of the Judgement of Taste*, trans. Richard Nice (Cambridge: Harvard University Press, [1979] 1984).
204. Wood, *The Retreat from Class*, xii-xiii, 5.
205. Žižek, "The Need to Traverse the Fantasy."
206. Žižek, "The Need to Traverse the Fantasy."
207. Roediger, *Class, Race, and Marxism*, 281.
208. Roger Lancaster, "Identity Politics Can Only Get Us So Far," *Jacobin* (August 3, 2017), https://jacobinmag.com/2017/08/identity-politics-gay-rights-neoliberalism-stonewall-feminism-race.
209. See for example, Strike MoMA Working Group of International Imagination of Anti-national, Anti-imperialist Feelings (IIAAF), *Strike MoMA Reader* (2022), available at https://static1.squarespace.com/static/605790cc083be87e4278c493/t/61ecb49314a9390a4ef503b4/1642902692411/StrikeMoMAReader_Final..pdf.
210. Dan Kovalik, *Cancel This Book: The Progressive Case Against Cancel Culture* (New York: Hot Books, 2021) eBook, 78-148.
211. See Marc James Léger, *Bernie Bros Gone Woke: Class, Identity, Neoliberalism* (Leiden: Brill, 2022).
212. Bhaskar Sunkara, "When American democracy crumbles, it won't be televised," *The Guardian* (January 6, 2022), https://www.theguardian.com/commentisfree/2022/jan/06/us-democracy-capitol-attack-january-6.
213. Jan Sowa, "Forget Postcolonialism, There's a Class War Ahead," *Nonsite* (August 12, 2014), https://nonsite.org/article/forget-postcolonialism-theres-a-class-war-ahead.
214. Jean-Luc Nancy, *The Inoperative Community*, ed. Peter Connor, trans. Peter Connor et al. (Minneapolis: University of Minnesota Press, 1991). See also Achille Mbembe, *Necropolitics* (Durham: Duke University Press, 2019).
215. David Walsh, "The socioeconomic basis of identity politics: Inequality and the rise of an African-American elite," *World Socialist Web Site* (August 30, 2016), https://www.wsws.org/en/articles/2016/08/30/pers-a30.html. One such genealogy can be found in Sylvia Wynter, "Unsettling the Coloniality of Being/Power/Truth/Freedom: Towards the Human, After Man, Its Overrepresentation – An Argument," *The New Centennial Review* 3:3 (Fall 2003) 257-337.

216. See for example Richard Florida's infamous "tech-innovation-gay-bohemian-talent-melting-pot-diversity-creativity index" in his calculations of the value of human and creative capital in regional economic growth, in Florida, *The Rise of the Creative Class, And How It's Transforming Work, Leisure, Community and Everyday Life* (New York: Basic Books, 2004).
217. Sven Lütticken, "Cultural Marxists Like Us," *Afterall* #46 (Autumn/Winter 2018) 72.
218. Empire Files, "Debunking Jordan Peterson's 'Cultural Marxism' with Richard Wolff," *YouTube* (May 27, 2019), https://www.youtube.com/watch?v=liT7e5M6XfY; Democracy at Work, "Understanding Marxism: Q&A with Richard D. Wolff," *YouTube* (June 13, 2019), https://www.youtube.com/watch?v=eU-AkeOyiOQ.
219. Žižek-Peterson debate at the Sony Centre, April 19, 2019, available at Ippolit Belinski, "Slavoj Žižek vs Jordan Peterson Debate – Happiness: Capitalism vs. Marxism (Apr 2019)," *YouTube* (April 20, 2019), https://www.youtube.com/watch?v=gYGnd99McHM.
220. Slavoj Žižek, "Why Secondary Contradictions Matter: A Maoist View," *The Philosophical Salon* (January 7, 2019), https://thephilosophicalsalon.com/why-secondary-contradictions-matter-a-maoist-view/.
221. Slavoj Žižek, "Class Struggle Against Classism," in *Heaven in Disorder* (London: O/R Books, 2021) 164.
222. See for instance: Angela Davis, *Women, Race, and Class* (New York: Random House, 1981) and Lise Vogel, *Marxism and the Oppression of Women: Toward a Unitary Theory* (New Brunswick, NJ: Rutgers University Press, 1983).
223. Simone de Beauvoir, *The Second Sex*, trans. H.M. Parshley (London: Jonathan Cape, [1949] 1956) 273.
224. Monique Wittig, "One Is Not Born a Woman," in *The Straight Mind and Other Essays* (Boston: Beacon Press, 1992) 9-20.
225. See for example Elizabeth Grosz, *Space, Time, and Perversion: Essays on the Politics of Bodies* (New York: Routledge, 1995). See also Samantha Bankston, *Deleuze and Becoming* (London: Bloomsbury Academic, 2017).
226. Deb Kelsh, "Desire and Class: The Knowledge Industry in the Wake of Poststructuralism (Part 1 and Part 2)," *Cultural Logic* Volume 2 (1998), https://ojs.library.ubc.ca/index.php/clogic/article/view/192713.
227. See David Tomas' comparison of global academic theory to the ivory harvested by Joseph Conrad's Kurtz in Tomas, *Live rightly, die, die...* (Montreal: Dazibao, 2012).
228. See David Graeber, *The Utopia of Rules: On Technology, Stupidity, and the Secret Joys of Bureaucracy* (Brooklyn: Melville House, 2015).
229. Henri Lefebvre, *Dialectical Materialism*, trans. John Sturrock (Minneapolis: University of Minnesota Press, [1940] 2009) 117.
230. Lewis, *The Politics of Everybody*, 214.
231. See for example Sara Ahmed's advocacy of "diversity work" in Ahmed, *On Being Included: Racism and Diversity in Institutional Life* (Durham: Duke University Press, 2012).
232. Reed, *Class Notes*, 86.
233. Robin Dembroff and Daniel Wodak, "If someone wants to be called 'they' and not 'he' or 'she,' why say no?" *The Guardian* (June 4, 2018), https://www.theguardian.com/commentisfree/2018/jun/04/gender-neutral-pronouns-they-he-she-why-deny.
234. David Galowich, "How To Respectfully Use Gender Pronouns In The Workplace," *Forbes* (August 2, 2018), https://www.forbes.com/sites/forbescoachescouncil/2018/08/02/how-to-respectfully-use-gender-pronouns-in-the-workplace/#23d750e06c40.

235. Pete Frase, "Stay Classy," *Jacobin* (June 26, 2014), https://jacobinmag.com/2014/06/stay-classy.
236. See JOE, "Slavoj Žižek interview: Boris Johnson, Jo Cox, Greta Thunberg," *YouTube* (September 26, 2019), https://www.youtube.com/watch?v=IaF2_rDOLw8.
237. See Alain Badiou, *The True Life*, trans. Susan Spitzer (Cambridge: Polity Press, [2016] 2017).
238. See Michael Warner, *The Trouble with Normal: Sex, Politics, and the Ethics of Queer Life* (London: The Free Press, 1999).
239. Greta LaFleur, "Heterosexuality Without Women," *Los Angeles Review of Books Blog* (May 20, 2019), https://blog.lareviewofbooks.org/essays/heterosexuality-without-women/.
240. Simon Critchley, *Infinitely Demanding: Ethics of Commitment, Politics and Resistance* (London: Verso, 2007).
241. Adolph Reed, Jr., "Marx, Race, and Neoliberalism," *New Labor Forum* 22:1 (2013) 51.
242. Slavoj Žižek, "The Sexual Is Political," *The Philosophical Salon* (August 1, 2016), http://thephilosophicalsalon.com/the-sexual-is-political/.
243. Reed, "Marx, Race, and Neoliberalism," 53-5.
244. Karen E. Fields and Barbara F. Fields, *Racecraft: The Soul of Inequality in American Life* (London: Verso, 2012).
245. Fields, *Racecraft*, 283-6.
246. Fields, *Racecraft*, 17. Lewis has modelled a concept of sexcraft that draws on the theory of racecraft. See Lewis, *The Politics of Everybody*, 198-201. See also Elena Louisa Lange, "Gendercraft: Marxism-Feminism, Reproduction, and the Blind Spot of Money," *Science & Society* 85:1 (January 2021) 38-65.
247. Orlando Patterson, *Slavery and Social Death: A Comparative Study* (Cambridge: Harvard University Press, 1982).
248. Slavoj Žižek, "Reply to My Critics," *The Philosophical Salon* (August 5, 2016), https://thephilosophicalsalon.com/a-reply-to-my-critics/.
249. Lawrence Grossberg, *We All Want to Change the World: The Paradox of the U.S. Left, a Polemic* (London: Lawrence & Wishart, 2015) 217-18.
250. Žižek, "Reply to My Critics."
251. See Vladimir Lenin, "Memo Combating Dominant-Nation Chauvinism" (1922) in Slavoj Žižek, *Lenin 2017: Remembering, Repeating, and Working Through* (London: Verso, 2017) 111.
252. Judith Butler, "Merely Cultural," *Social Text* 15:3-4 (Fall/Winter 1997) 265.
253. Nancy Fraser, "Heterosexism, Misrecognition, and Capitalism," *Social Text* 15:3-4 (Fall/Winter 1997) 280.
254. This concern is found throughout Žižek's work. See for example Žižek, "Too Radical for Democracy?" in *Iraq: The Borrowed Kettle* (London: Verso, 2004) 88-102.
255. Although it is not often acknowledged, Žižek's work has a great deal in common with Western Marxism and the Frankfurt School. See Perry Anderson's classic study, *Considerations on Western Marxism* (London: New Left Books, 1976).
256. See Andreas Huyssen, "Breitbart, Bannon, Trump and the Frankfurt School: A Strange Meeting of Minds," *Public Seminar* (September 28, 2017), http://publicseminar.org/2017/09/breitbart-bannon-trump-and-the-frankfurt-school/. See also James Lindsay's disingenuous effort to discredit Hegel as the linchpin of Marxism, the Frankfurt School, postmodernism and woke culture warriors, in New Discourses, "Hegel, Wokeness, and the Dialectical Faith of Leftism," *YouTube* (May 28, 2021), https://www.youtube.com/watch?v=uf4R0gX7g3w.

257. See for instance the rather jaunty treatments of Badiou and Žižek in Bruce Robbins, "Balibarism," *n+1* #16 (Spring 2013), https://nplusonemag.com/issue-16/reviews/balibarism/ and Martin Jay, "Fidelity to the Event? Lukács' History and Class Consciousness and the Russian Revolution," *Studies in East European Thought* (July 2018) 195-213.
258. Commune, "Introducing Commune," *Commune* #1 (Fall 2018), https://communemag.com/introducing-commune/.
259. See for example Ramón Grosfoguel, "The Epistemic Decolonial Turn: Beyond political-economy paradigms," *Cultural Studies* 21:2-3 (March/May 2007) 211-223. See also Julian Borger, "CIA forges unity in diversity: everybody hates their 'woke' recruitment ad," *The Guardian* (May 4, 2021), https://www.theguardian.com/us-news/2021/may/04/cia-woke-recruitment-ad.
260. See for instance Franco 'Bifo' Berardi, *Precarious Rhapsody: Semiocapitalism and the Pathologies of the Post-Alpha Generation* (Williamsburg: Minor Compositions, 2009). On this subject, see David Harvey's critique of the notion of a neoliberal habitus in Democracy at Work, "Anti-Capitalist Chronicles: How Do We Break from Neo-Liberalism?" *YouTube* (December 16, 2021), https://www.youtube.com/watch?v=_-CRMfZ3Y50. See also Marc James Léger, *Don't Network: The Avant Garde after Networks* (Wivenhoe: Minor Compositions, 2018).
261. Slavoj Žižek, *Less Than Nothing: Hegel and the Shadow of Dialectical Materialism* (London: Verso, 2012); Žižek, *Absolute Recoil: Towards a New Foundation of Dialectical Materialism* (London: Verso, 2014); Žižek, *Disparities* (London: Bloomsbury, 2016).
262. Alain Badiou, *The Rebirth of History: Times of Riot and Uprising*, trans. Gregory Elliott (London: Verso, [2011] 2012); Joshua Clover, *Riot. Strike. Riot: The New Era of Uprisings* (London: Verso, 2019).
263. The Invisible Committee, *To Our Friends*, trans. Robert Hurley (Los Angeles: Semiotext(e), [2014] 2015).

5: Black Capitalism and Embedded History

1. Melanye T. Price, *The Race Whisperer: Barack Obama and the Political Uses of Race* (New York: New York University Press, 2016).
2. Jazz Monroe, "M.I.A.: 'Is Beyoncé or Kendrick Lamar Going to Say Muslim Lives Matter?'," *Pitchfork* (April 21, 2016), https://pitchfork.com/news/64968-mia-is-beyonce-or-kendrick-lamar-going-to-say-muslim-lives-matter/.
3. Guardian music, "MIA says she won't play Afropunk festival after Black Lives Matter," *The Guardian* (June 21, 2016), https://www.theguardian.com/music/2016/jun/21/mia-says-she-wont-play-afropunk-festival-black-lives-matter-comments. On the subject of identitarian reductionism in the music industry, as noticed for example in the work of Taylor Swift, Janelle Monáe, Frank Ocean, Beyoncé, Jay-Z, Kendrick Lamar, Dixie Chicks, Solange, Justin Bieber, Eminem and Kanye West, see Jason King, "Activism, Identity Politics, and Pop's Great Awokening," *Pitchfork* (October 11, 2019), https://pitchfork.com/features/article/2010s-pops-great-awokening-black-lives-matter-beyonce-kendrick-lamar-solange/.
4. Dave Zirin, "Taking a Knee Is Not About Abstract Unity but Racial Justice," *The Nation* (September 26, 2017), https://www.thenation.com/article/taking-a-knee-is-not-about-abstract-unity-but-racial-justice/.

5. Cas Carter, "Nike working hard to look 'woke'," *Stuff* (September 11, 2018), https://www.stuff.co.nz/business/106953301/nike-working-hard-to-look-woke. For a critique of the uses of black liberation imagery in contemporary media, see Adolph Reed Jr., "The Retrograde Quest for Symbolic Prophets of Black Liberation," *The New Republic* (February 17, 2021), https://newrepublic.com/article/161124/retrograde-quest-symbolic-prophets-black-liberation.
6. E.J. Dickson, "Why Is Everyone So Upset About the Betsy Ross Flag?" *Rolling Stone* (July 2, 2019), https://www.rollingstone.com/culture/culture-features/betsy-ross-flag-nike-colin-kaepernick-patriot-movement-ku-klux-klan-854612/.
7. Jonah Goldberg, "Nike Fans the Flames of the Culture War," *National Review* (July 5, 2019), https://www.nationalreview.com/2019/07/nike-betsy-ross-sneakers-colin-kaepernick-culture-war/.
8. Goldberg, "Nike Fans the Flames of the Culture War."
9. Kehinde Wiley also received the W.E.B. Du Bois Medal on this occasion, October 11, 2018.
10. Joseph Grosso, "To Be or Not To Be Woke: The Follies of Political Correctness," *CounterPunch* (August 2, 2019), https://www.counterpunch.org/2019/08/02/to-be-or-not-to-be-woke-the-follies-of-political-correctness/.
11. Grosso, "To Be or Not To Be Woke: The Follies of Political Correctness."
12. Hiram Lee, "The New York Times on race and art," *World Socialist Web Site* (April 4, 2016), https://www.wsws.org/en/articles/2016/04/04/race-a04.html.
13. Brooks Barnes, "In 'Green Book' Victory, Oscar Critics See an Old Hollywood Tale," *The New York Times* (February 25, 2019), https://www.nytimes.com/2019/02/25/business/media/green-book-spike-lee-reaction.html.
14. See the discussion between Julian Assange and Slavoj Žižek from July 2, 2011, available at Frontline Club, "Julian Assange in conversation with Slavoj Žižek moderated by Democracy Now's Amy Goodman," *YouTube* (August 1, 2012), https://www.youtube.com/watch?v=j1Xm08uTSDQ.
15. Walter Benjamin, "Theses on the Philosophy of History," in *Illuminations: Essays and Reflections*, ed. Hannah Arendt, trans. Harry Zohn (New York: Schocken, 1968) 261. See also Alain Deneault, *Mediocracy: The Politics of the Extreme Centre*, trans. Catherine Browne (Toronto: Between the Lines, [2016] 2018).
16. Brian Boyd, "Nike's Kaepernick ad is corporate 'woke washing'," *The Irish Times* (September 5, 2018), https://www.irishtimes.com/opinion/nike-s-kaepernick-ad-is-corporate-woke-washing-1.3619149.
17. Benjamin, "The Image of Proust," in *Illuminations*, 210.
18. See the 1998 introduction to the revised edition of Ellen Meiksins Wood, *The Retreat from Class: A New 'True' Socialism* (London: Verso, [1986] 1998) xii.
19. On this subject, see Sarah Mason and Robert Cavooris, "Search for a Mass Politics: The DSA Beyond Bernie," *The Bullet* (August 6, 2019), https://socialistproject.ca/2019/08/search-for-mass-politics-dsa-beyond-bernie/.
20. Wood, *The Retreat from Class*, 15.
21. Wood, *The Retreat from Class*, 17.
22. Wood, *The Retreat from Class*, 7.
23. Guy Standing, *The Precariat: The New Dangerous Class* (London: Bloomsbury, 2011).
24. Lecture at The Graduate Center, CUNY, New York City, December 1, 2016, available at Reading Marx's Capital with David Harvey, "David Harvey and Robert Brenner: What now? The roots of the economic crisis and the way forward," *YouTube* (December 3, 2016), https://www.youtube.com/watch?v=8fhTGm4Dbpw.

25. See David Graeber, *Debt: The First 5000 Years* (Brooklyn: Melville House, 2011).
26. Michael Eric Dyson, *The Black Presidency: Barack Obama and the Politics of Race in America* (Boston: Houghton Mifflin Harcourt, 2016) 53.
27. Kia Makarechi, "Obama's Best White House Correspondents' Dinner Jokes," *Vanity Fair Hive* (April 26, 2015), https://www.vanityfair.com/news/2015/04/obama-whcd-jokes-2015.
28. Vinson Cunningham, "The Shifting Perspective in Kehinde Wiley's Portrait of Barack Obama," *The New Yorker* (February 13, 2019), https://www.newyorker.com/culture/annals-of-appearances/the-shifting-perspective-in-kehinde-wileys-portrait-of-barack-obama.
29. Michael P. Jeffries, *Thug Life: Race, Gender, and the Meaning of Hip Hop* (Chicago: University of Chicago Press, 2011) 2.
30. Jeffries, *Thug Life*, 12.
31. Imani Perry, *Prophets of the Hood: Politics and Poetics in Hip Hop* (Durham: Duke University Press, 2004) 1-2.
32. Todd Boyd, *The New H.N.I.C. (Head Niggas in Charge): The Death of Civil Rights and the Reign of Hip Hop* (New York: New York University Press, 2002) 5, 11-13.
33. Jeffries, *Thug Life*, 203.
34. Graeme Turner, "Approaching Celebrity Studies," *Celebrity Studies* 1:1 (March 2010) 12.
35. Krista Thompson, "The Sound of Light: Reflections on Art History in the Visual Culture of Hip-Hop," *Art Bulletin* 91:4 (December 2009) 501.
36. Jeremy Heckett, "Brand 'W' and the Marketing of an American President: Or, Logos as Logos," *Westminster Papers in Communication and Culture* 2:2 (2005), 79. Heckett cites Judith Butler, *Excitable Speech: A Politics of the Performative* (New York: Routledge, 1997).
37. Heckett, "Brand 'W' and the Marketing of an American President," 80-1.
38. Heckett, "Brand 'W' and the Marketing of an American President," 90.
39. Steve Stoute, *The Tanning of America: How Hip-Hop Created a Culture That Rewrote the Rules of the New Economy* (New York: Gotham Books, 2011) 14-23.
40. See Jo Little, "Celebrity," in Toby Miller, ed. *The Routledge Companion to Global Popular Culture* (Abingdon: Routledge, [2014] 2015) 119-27.
41. Daniel J. Boorstin, *The Image: A Guide to Pseudo-Events in America* (New York: Atheneum, [1961] 1975) 45.
42. Olivier Driessens, "The Celebritization of Society and Culture: Understanding the Structural Dynamics of Celebrity Culture," *International Journal of Cultural Studies* 16:6 (2013) 641-59, http://eprints.lse.ac.uk/55742/1/__lse.ac.uk_storage_LIBRARY_Secondary_libfile_shared_repository_Content_Driessens%2C%20O_Celebritization%20of%20society%20culture_Driessens_Celebritization%20society%20culture_2014.pdf.
43. Driessens, "The Celebritization of Society and Culture."
44. Maxwell Williams, "Kehinde Wiley: The Transcontinental Breadth of a Contemporary Master," *Flaunt* #114 (2011) 137.
45. MSNBC, "Michael Moore: To crush Trump, Michelle Obama needs to run," *MSNBC* (August 1, 2019), https://www.msnbc.com/msnbc/watch/michael-moore-to-crush-trump-michelle-obama-needs-to-run-65031749700.
46. Abdullah Malik and Bushan D. Sudhakar, "Brand Positioning Through Celebrity Endorsement – A Review Contribution to Brand Literature," *International Review of Management and Marketing* 4:4 (2014) 259-75. See also Michael Schudson, *Advertising, The Uneasy Persuasion: Its Dubious Impact on American Society* (New York: Basic Books, [1984] 1986).
47. Ellis Cashmore, *Celebrity/Culture* (New York: Routledge, 2006) 211.
48. Cashmore, *Celebrity/Culture*, 232.

49. Daniel Morgan, "The Rise of Celebrity Branding," *Cannabiz Journal* (June 7, 2017), formerly available at https://www.cannabizjournal.com/volume-2-issue-2-june-2017/2017/6/7/the-rise-of-celebrity-branding; Peter Isackson, "Reading the News: Branding and Celebrity as the Anchor of Late Capitalism," *Fair Observer* (June 27, 2017), https://www.fairobserver.com/region/north_america/celebrity-advertising-branding-marketing-culture-economics-news-10001/.
50. Ellis Cashmore, *Making Sense of Sports* (London: Routledge, [1990] 2005) 1.
51. Cashmore, *Making Sense of Sports*, 4.
52. Cashmore, *Making Sense of Sports*, 98.
53. Cashmore, *Making Sense of Sports*, 205.
54. Ellis Cashmore, "Buying Beyoncé," *Celebrity Studies* 1:2 (July 2010) 136.
55. Cashmore, "Buying Beyoncé," 138.
56. Charing Ball, "Beyoncé's Formation And The Failed Strategy Of Black Capitalism," *Madame Noire* (February 8, 2016), https://madamenoire.com/613117/beyonces-formation-and-the-failed-strategy-of-black-capitalism/.
57. Ellis Cashmore, *Beyond Black: Celebrity and Race in Obama's America* (London: Bloomsbury, 2012) 10.
58. Debra J. Dickerson, "Colorblind: Barack Obama would be the great black hope in the next presidential race – if he were actually black," *Salon* (September 24, 2010), https://web.archive.org/web/20100924194645/https://www.salon.com/news/opinion/feature/2007/01/22/obama/; Talib Kweli Greene, "Why #ADOS Is Trash. Receipts Attached," *Medium* (April 10, 2019), https://medium.com/@TalibKweli/why-ados-is-trash-receipts-attached-5a337f46f10.
59. Cashmore, *Beyond Black*, 26.
60. The concept of parasocial interaction is derived from a 1956 article by Donald Horton and Richard Wohl in the journal *Psychiatry*. See Cashmore, *Making Sense of Sports*, 413.
61. Leo Panitch and Paul Jay, "Obama Joins the Club of the Super-Rich – Defends Global Capitalism in Lecture," *The Real News* (July 30, 2018), https://therealnews.com/stories/obama-joins-club-of-the-super-rich-defends-global-capitalism-in-lecture.
62. Perry Anderson, "Homeland," *New Left Review* #81 (May-June 2013), https://newleftreview.org/issues/II81/articles/perry-anderson-homeland.
63. Audie Cornish, "Cornel West Doesn't Want to Be a Neoliberal Darling," *The New York Times Magazine* (November 29, 2017), https://www.nytimes.com/2017/11/29/magazine/cornel-west-doesnt-want-to-be-a-neoliberal-darling.html.
64. Joanna Love, "Branding a Cool Celebrity President: Popular Music, Political Advertising, and the 2012 Election," *Music & Politics* IX:2 (Summer 2015), https://quod.lib.umich.edu/m/mp/9460447.0009.203/--branding-a-cool-celebrity-president-popular-music-political?rgn=main;view=fulltext. See also Nicholas A. Yanes and Derrais Carter, eds. *The Iconic Obama 2007-2009: Essays on Media Representations of the Candidate and New President* (Jefferson: McFarland & Company, 2012).
65. Diana E. Sheets, "Obama's 2012 Victory: The Demographic Becomes the Narrative," *HuffPost* (February 20, 2013), https://www.huffpost.com/entry/obamas-2012-victory-the-demographic-becomes-the-narrative_b_2341438.
66. The concept of compensatory consumption is attributed to David Caplovitz. See Cashmore, *Beyond Black*, 93.
67. Jeremy W. Peters, "Aggressive Ads for Obama, at the Ready," *The New York Times* (May 8, 2012), https://www.nytimes.com/2012/05/09/us/politics/obamas-media-team-has-aggressive-ads-at-the-ready.html.

68. Gillian B. White, "The Unfulfilled Promise of Black Capitalism," *The Atlantic* (September 21, 2017), https://www.theatlantic.com/business/archive/2017/09/black-capitalism-baradaran/540522/.
69. Matt Bruenig and Ryan Cooper, "How Obama Destroyed Black Wealth," *Jacobin* (December 7, 2017), https://jacobinmag.com/2017/12/obama-foreclosure-crisis-wealth-inequality.
70. Lance Selfa, "Booker T. Washington and Black Capitalism," *Socialist Worker* (May 11, 2012), https://socialistworker.org/2012/05/11/booker-washington-and-black-capitalism.
71. Matt Taylor, "Dear Obama, Spare Us the Lectures," *Vice* (July 18, 2018), https://www.vice.com/en_us/article/ywkvqv/dear-obama-spare-us-the-lectures.
72. Paul Street, "Obama: a Hollow Man Filled With Ruling Class Ideas," *CounterPunch* (June 2, 2017), https://www.counterpunch.org/2017/06/02/obama-a-hollow-man-filled-with-ruling-class-ideas/. See also Paul Street, *The Empire's New Clothes: Barack Obama in the Real World of Power* (Boulder: Paradigm Publishers, 2010) and *Hollow Resistance: Obama, Trump and the Politics of Appeasement* (Petrolia: CounterPunch, 2020).
73. See Megan Garber, "Kapitalism, With Kim Kardashian," *The Atlantic* (July 29, 2014), https://www.theatlantic.com/entertainment/archive/2014/07/lessons-in-capitalism-from-kim-kardashian/375252/.
74. Paul Street, "Obama's Audacious Deference to Power," *Black Agenda Report* (January 31, 2007), https://www.blackagendareport.com/content/obamas-audacious-deference-power.
75. N.D.B. Connolly, "Black and Woke in Capitalist America: Revisiting Robert Allen's *Black Awakening* … for New Times' Sake," *Items* (March 7, 2017), https://items.ssrc.org/reading-racial-conflict/black-and-woke-in-capitalist-america-revisiting-robert-allens-black-awakening-for-new-times-sake/.
76. Paul Schrodt, "Inside the Strange and Fascinating World of Celebrity Money Handlers," *Time* (November 29, 2017), http://money.com/money/5039650/inside-celebrity-money-handlers/.
77. Dana Sanchez, "10 Hip Hop Artists And Black Athletes Investing In Startups," *Moguldom* (May 26, 2017), https://moguldom.com/7141/10-hip-hop-artists-and-black-athletes-investing-in-startups/; Dan Smith, "10 of the UK's most notable celebrity investors," *Growth Funders Blog* (August 10, 2017), https://blog.growthfunders.com/celebrity-investors-in-the-uk-whos-invested-their-money.
78. Arwa Mahdawi, "Woke-washing brands cash in on social justice. It's lazy and hypocritical," *The Guardian* (August 10, 2018), https://www.theguardian.com/commentisfree/2018/aug/10/fellow-kids-woke-washing-cynical-alignment-worthy-causes.
79. Kyle Chayka, "The Resistance Will Be Merchandised," *GQ* (June 13, 2017), https://www.gq.com/story/the-resistance-will-be-merchandised.
80. See Benedict Anderson, *Imagined Communities: Reflections on the Origin and Spread of Nationalism* (London: Verso, [1983] 1991); Michael Sorkin, ed. *Variations on a Theme Park: The New American City and the End of Public Space* (New York: Hill and Wang, 1992); Kyo Maclear, *Beclouded Visions: Hiroshima-Nagasaki and the Art of Witness* (New York: State University of New York Press, 1999).
81. Anu Taranath, *Beyond Guilt Trips: Mindful Travel in an Unequal World* (Toronto: Between the Lines, 2019); Dean MacCannell, *Empty Meeting Grounds: The Tourist Papers* (London: Routledge, 1992).

82. Nick Mirzoeff, "How Do We Address a Statue of President Roosevelt That Affirms Racist Hierarchies?" *Hyperallergic* (September 24, 2019), https://hyperallergic.com/517774/how-do-we-address-a-statue-of-president-roosevelt-that-affirms-racist-hierarchies/; David Smith, "'Great country!' Trump flaunts US military might at jingoistic jamboree," *The Guardian* (July 5, 2019), https://www.theguardian.com/us-news/2019/jul/05/donald-trumps-july-4th-jamboree-symbolic-jingoistic-and-untraditional.
83. Sarah Cascone, "Students Rally to Remove a Thomas Hart Benton Mural Depicting the KKK at Indiana University," *Artnet News* (October 31, 2017), https://news.artnet.com/art-world/thomas-hart-benton-mural-indiana-1133765.
84. The Associated Press, "Fate of Honest Abe statues under review in Chicago, honestly," *ABC News* (February 18, 2021), https://abcnews.go.com/Entertainment/wireStory/fate-honest-abe-statues-review-chicago-honestly-75973288.
85. Sarah B., "Historic WPA murals at George Washington High School are facing destruction due to controversial depictions of Native Americans and African-Americans," *Richmond District Blog* (April 9, 2019), https://richmondsfblog.com/2019/04/09/historic-wpa-murals-at-george-washington-high-school-are-facing-destruction-due-to-controversial-depictions-of-native-americans-and-african-americans/.
86. Robert W. Cherny, *Victor Arnautoff and the Politics of Art* (Urbana: University of Illinois Press, 2017) 96.
87. Cherny, *Victor Arnautoff and the Politics of Art*, 105.
88. Cherny, *Victor Arnautoff and the Politics of Art*, 109-10.
89. Cherny, *Victor Arnautoff and the Politics of Art*, 49.
90. Cherny, *Victor Arnautoff and the Politics of Art*, 158-9.
91. Samantha Maldonado, "San Francisco School Board Votes to Paint Over Controversial George Washington Mural," *Time* (July 4, 2019), https://news.yahoo.com/san-francisco-school-board-votes-213451527.html.
92. An online posting by the former President of the Board, Stevon Cook, shows letters of support that were sent to him along with his statement: "I support the decision to remove the mural, but I am listening to everyone's point of view." Stevon Cook, "Letters to Commission Cook #002," *Medium* (April 6, 2019), https://medium.com/@stevon.cook/letters-to-commission-cook-002-b1a8e4e37043. For evidence that Cook ignored the meaning of the murals in favour of racialist interpretation, see Stevon Cook, "Keep Those Slaves on that Wall!" *Medium* (July 11, 2019), https://medium.com/@stevon.cook/keep-those-slaves-on-that-wall-5369a63a2a7. For further evidence of the ways in which Cook's thinking combines black nationalism with American imperialism and technocratic capitalism, see Stevon Cook, "Series B," *Medium* (June 3, 2019), https://medium.com/@stevon.cook/series-b-33cb39970b85.
93. Cited in Sarah B., "Historic WPA murals at George Washington High School are facing destruction due to controversial depictions of Native Americans and African-Americans."
94. tpoletti, "Defending Victor Arnautoff's WPA-era murals at George Washington High School," *Timothy Pflueger Blog* (April 23, 2019), https://blog.timothypflueger.com/2019/04/23/defending-victor-arnautoffs-wpa-era-murals-at-george-washington-high-school/.
95. Cited in Ben Davis, "This Artist Painted the Black Radical Response to the George Washington Slaveholder Murals. Here's Why He Stands Against Destroying Them," *Artnet News* (July 10, 2019), https://news.artnet.com/art-world/san-francisco-mural-victor-arnautoff-dewey-crumpler-1596409.

96. See National Coalition Against Censorship, letter to Superintendent Matthews, May 6, 2019, https://ncac.org/wp-content/uploads/2019/06/NCAC-Letter-to-G-Washington-High-School-5.6.2019.pdf

97. "An Open Letter on the Proposed Destruction of a Mural Cycle," *Nonsite* (July 2, 2019), https://nonsite.org/editorial/open-letter-on-the-proposed-destruction-of-a-mural-cycle.

98. Online activity by the GWHS Alumni Association to save the murals was formerly available at http://www.sfgwhsalumni.org; #SaveTheMurals, #SaveOurMurals.

99. See laborvideo, "Arnautoff Mural Debate At SFUSD Board Meeting Over Proposed Destruction of Murals," *YouTube* (June 20, 2019), https://www.youtube.com/watch?v=rG6x4JS76j0.

100. Cited in Thomas K. Pendergast, "Mural Opponents Meet Defenders at Tour of George Washington H.S. Artwork," *Richmond Review/Sunset Beacon* (May 4, 2019), https://sfrichmondreview.com/2019/05/04/mural-opponents-meet-defenders-at-tour-of-george-washington-h-s-artwork/.

101. Carol Pogash, "These High School Murals Depict an Ugly History. Should They Go?" *The New York Times* (April 11, 2019), https://www.nytimes.com/2019/04/11/arts/design/george-washington-murals-ugly-history-debated.html.

102. Mark Seltzer, "Wound Culture: Trauma in the Pathological Public Sphere," *October* #80 (Spring 1997) 3-26; Arthur Kroker and Michael A. Weinstein, *Data Trash: The Theory of the Virtual Class* (Montreal: New World Perspectives, 1994). From a liberal perspective, see also Neil Postman, *Amusing Ourselves to Death: Public Discourse in the Age of Show Business* (New York: Viking, 1985).

103. Charles Desmarais, "High school mural debate a reminder that destroying art destroys our culture," *Datebook* (June 20, 2019), https://datebook.sfchronicle.com/art-exhibits/high-school-mural-debate-a-reminder-that-destroying-art-destroys-our-culture.

104. Mark Lewis, "The Technologies of Public Art," *Vanguard* 16:5 (November 1987) 14.

105. Naomi Klein, *The Shock Doctrine: The Rise of Disaster Capitalism* (Toronto: Knopf, 2007).

106. KPIX 5, "SF Official Calls for Renaming Of Schools Named After Slaveholders," *CBS SF BayArea* (September 7, 2016), https://sanfrancisco.cbslocal.com/2016/09/07/sf-official-calls-for-renaming-of-schools-named-after-slaveholders/.

107. Meena Harris, "Over 20,000 People Want to Rename the High School Maya Angelou Attended After Her," *Glamour* (July 7, 2020), https://www.glamour.com/story/rename-george-washington-high-school-maya-angelou; Phil Matier, "SF may erase presidents' names from schools: Washington, Jefferson, Lincoln and FDR could all go," *San Francisco Chronicle* (July 26, 2020), https://www.sfchronicle.com/bayarea/philmatier/article/SF-may-erase-presidents-names-from-schools-15433452.php; Elliott Jones, "Which Monuments Should Come Down And What Should Replace Them?" *SFist* (July 27, 2020), https://sfist.com/2020/07/27/op-ed-taxpayers-continue-to-fund-racist-symbols-and-messaging/.

108. Vanessa Romo, "San Francisco School Board Rescinds Controversial School Renaming Plan," *NPR* (April 7, 2020), https://www.npr.org/2021/04/07/984919925/san-francisco-school-board-rescinds-controversial-school-renaming-plan.

109. Jonathan Martin, "State by State, Democratic Party Is Erasing Ties to Jefferson and Jackson," *The New York Times* (August 11, 2015), https://www.nytimes.com/2015/08/12/us/politics/state-by-state-democratic-party-is-erasing-ties-to-jefferson-and-jackson.html.

110. Bari Weiss, "San Francisco Will Spend $600,000 to Erase History," *The New York Times* (June 28, 2019), https://www.nytimes.com/2019/06/28/opinion/sunday/san-francisco-life-of-washington-murals.html.

111. "'Snowflakes' or empowered youth? RT debates student uproar over George Washington mural," *Russia Today* (May 5, 2019), https://www.rt.com/usa/458364-washington-mural-school-debate/.
112. Selwyn Duke, "School May Remove George Washington Mural that 'Traumatizes' Students," *The New American* (May 7, 2019), https://www.thenewamerican.com/culture/item/32217-school-may-remove-george-washington-mural-that-traumatizes-students.
113. Greg Lukianoff and Jonathan Haidt, "The Coddling of the American Mind," *The Atlantic* (September 2015), https://www.theatlantic.com/magazine/archive/2015/09/the-coddling-of-the-american-mind/399356/.
114. Brian T. Allen, "San Francisco's Board of Education: Anti-Art Fools," *National Review* (July 6, 2019), https://www.nationalreview.com/2019/07/san-francisco-board-of-education-george-washington-murals/.
115. Willie Brown, "The new America: Those who yell loudest win," *The San Francisco Chronicle* (July 13, 2019), https://www.sfchronicle.com/bayarea/williesworld/article/The-new-America-Those-who-yell-loudest-win-14092264.php?psid=d5ouo; CNN, "Screaming match erupts over vote to remove mural," *CNN* (July 27, 2019), https://www.cnn.com/videos/media/2019/07/27/school-board-votes-to-remove-historic-mural-san-francisco-smerconish-vpx.cnn.
116. Cited in Carla Marinucci, "Move to erase George Washington mural sparks firestorm among Dems," *Politico* (July 22, 2019), https://www.politico.com/story/2019/07/22/george-washington-mural-san-francisco-1424425.
117. Serge Halimi, "The Taliban of San Francisco," *Le Monde diplomatique* (August 2019), https://mondediplo.com/2019/08/01edito.
118. Labor Video Project, "SFUSD Board & Superintendent Matthews Cutting $300,000 From MLK Middle School," *Indybay* (September 12, 2019), https://www.indybay.org/newsitems/2019/09/12/18826177.php.
119. Julie Roberts-Phung, Brandee Marckmann and Scott Bravmann, "Open Letter on the Life of George Washington" *SURJSF* (June 2019), available at https://www.surjsf.org/open-letter-on-the-life-of-washington-murals. See also the statement by Teachers 4 Social Justice, "Teachers 4 Social Justice Statement on Washington Murals," *Medium* (July 30, 2019), https://medium.com/@t4sjsf/teachers-4-social-justices-statement-supporting-the-painting-down-of-the-life-of-washington-c508113b5acb.
120. Sean Joseph Watson and Harry P. Chavez, "Dear San Francisco: Stop Honoring George Washington And His Bigotry," *Medium* (May 9, 2019), https://medium.com/@thewokerise/dear-san-francisco-stop-honoring-george-washington-and-his-bigotry-eb37fd69a2a6.
121. Jack Heyman, "Whitewashing American History: The WPA Mural Controversy in San Francisco," *The Internationalist* (July 20, 2019), http://www.internationalist.org/whitewashing-american-history-arnautoff-murals-1907.html.
122. Holly Matkin, "School Board To Spend Over $375k To Remove 'Racist' George Washington Mural," *The Police Tribune* (June 23, 2019), https://policetribune.com/school-board-to-spend-over-375k-to-remove-racist-george-washington-mural/.
123. Bryce Covert, "The Oakland Teachers' Strike Revealed California's Education Crisis," *The Nation* (March 18, 2019), https://www.thenation.com/article/the-oakland-teachers-strike-revealed-californias-education-crisis/.

124. Associated Press, "San Francisco will keep but cover up George Washington mural," *The Morning Call* (August 13, 2019), https://www.mcall.com/what-now-for-george-washington-mural-in-san-francisco-story.html. An equally egregious case developed at the Vermont Law School in 2020 when a few students caught up in BLM iconoclasm compelled their classmates and the administration to destroy the Sam Kerson murals titled *The Underground Railroad, Vermont and the Fugitive Slave*. See Marc James Léger, "Artist Sam Kerson will continue to fight Vermont Law School effort to cover up murals commemorating abolition of slavery," *World Socialist Web Site* (October 27, 2021), https://www.wsws.org/en/articles/2021/10/28/mura-o28.html. On the artist's efforts to save the murals, see his reportage series of artworks at "The Muralist Imagines the Destruction of His Work" (2020-ongoing) at https://dragondancetheatre.wixsite.com/underground-railroad/imagined.

125. Toby Reese, "San Francisco school board proposes 'compromise' in move to suppress historic Depression-era murals," *World Socialist Web Site* (August 15, 2019), https://www.wsws.org/en/articles/2019/08/15/mura-a15.html.

126. Drew Costley, "San Francisco native and actor Danny Glover against removal of mural at Washington High School," *SFGATE* (August 13, 2019), https://www.sfgate.com/bayarea/article/danny-glover-life-washington-mural-removal-sfusd-14302359.php.

127. Caroline Goldstein, "Author Alice Walker Decries the Efforts to Censor San Francisco's George Washington Murals as 'Ignorant and Backwards'," *Artnet News* (August 20, 2019), https://news.artnet.com/art-world/alice-walker-mural-interview-san-francisco-1630942.

128. Jennifer Wilson, "Black People Don't Need Murals To Remember Injustice," *The Nation* (July 9, 2019), https://www.thenation.com/article/san-francisco-school-mural/. For an article that similarly argues for the universality of the condition of victimhood, see Kevin Baker, "Whiteout," *Harper's* (November 2019), https://harpers.org/archive/2019/11/whiteout/.

129. Wilson, "Black People Don't Need Murals To Remember Injustice."

130. Robin D.G. Kelley, "We're Getting These Murals All Wrong," *The Nation* (September 10, 2019), https://www.thenation.com/article/arnautoff-mural-life-washington/.

131. Jill Tucker, "S.F. school board faces more legal costs with appeal of lawsuit over controversial mural decision," *San Francisco Chronicle* (October 7, 2021), https://www.sfchronicle.com/sf/article/S-F-school-board-faces-more-legal-costs-with-16517552.php; Thomas Fuller, "In Landslide, San Francisco Forces Out 3 Board of Education Members," *The New York Times* (February 16, 2022), https://www.nytimes.com/2022/02/16/us/san-francisco-school-board-recall.html.

132. Jake Silverstein, "The 1619 Project/Introduction," *The New York Times Magazine* (August 18, 2019) 4. For an account of Nikole Hannah-Jones' denial of her lead essay's original claims, see Tom Mackaman and David North, "The New York Times and Nikole Hannah-Jones abandon key claims of the 1619 Project," *World Socialist Web Site* (September 22, 2020), https://www.wsws.org/en/articles/2020/09/22/1619-s22.html.

133. Silverstein, "The 1619 Project/Introduction," 4.

134. Silverstein, "The 1619 Project/Introduction," 4-5.

135. See Richard Wolin, "Carl Schmitt: The Conservative Revolutionary Habitus and the Aesthetics of Horror," *Political Theory* 20:3 (August 1992) 432.

136. Richard Wolin, *The Seduction of Unreason: The Intellectual Romance with Fascism from Nietzsche to Postmodernism* (Princeton: Princeton University Press, 2004) 1-2, 6-8, 22.

137. Wolin, *The Seduction of Unreason*, 278. Wolin's inclusion of Žižek in this discussion of anti-Americanism, on the basis of his post-9/11 book, *Welcome to the Desert of the Real*, fails to make the argument that Žižek's work has anything in common with postmodern relativism.

138. Nikole Hannah-Jones, "The Idea of America," *The New York Times Magazine* (August 18, 2019) 16. For a discussion of how the three-fifths clause was devised to weaken the power of slave states, see Tom Mackaman, "Historian Jack Rackove on American history writing and the falsifications of the 1619 Project and its defenders," *World Socialist Web Site* (January 19, 2022), https://www.wsws.org/en/articles/2022/01/20/rako-j20.html.
139. Hannah-Jones, "The Idea of America," 17.
140. Aris Folley, "Obama lauds Lewis' civil right legacy: A 'founding father of that of a fuller, fairer, better America," *The Hill* (July 30, 2020), https://thehill.com/homenews/house/509834-obama-lauds-john-lewis-civil-rights-legacy-in-eulogy-he-will-be-a-founding.
141. Hannah-Jones, "The Idea of America," 19.
142. Hannah-Jones, "The Idea of America," 21.
143. See W. Carson Byrd and Matthew W. Hughey, "Born that way? 'Scientific' racism is creeping back into our thinking. Here's what to watch out for," *The Washington Post* (September 28, 2015), https://www.washingtonpost.com/news/monkey-cage/wp/2015/09/28/born-that-way-scientific-racism-is-creeping-back-into-our-thinking-heres-what-to-watch-out-for/.
144. Hannah-Jones, "The Idea of America," 21.
145. Hannah-Jones, "The Idea of America," 21.
146. Hannah-Jones, "The Idea of America," 26. These contradictions concerning the exceptional role of blacks in relation to the American Creed is supported by the influence of *Ebony* magazine editor Lerone Bennett, Jr. and by Gerald Horne's racialist rejection of the American Revolution in *The Counter-Revolution of 1776* (2014). See Fred Schleger "Gerald Horne's counter-revolution against 1776," *World Socialist Web Site* (March 17, 2021), https://www.wsws.org/en/articles/2021/03/18/horn-m18.html. For a critique of the book version of the 1619 Project, see Tom Mackaman, "*The New York Times 1619 Project: A New Origin Story*: History as the emanation of race," *World Socialist Web Site* (February 21, 2022), https://www.wsws.org/en/articles/2022/02/21/proj-f21.html.
147. Tom Mackaman and David North, "American Historical Review publishes letter on 1619 Project," *World Socialist Web Site* (April 20, 2020), https://www.wsws.org/en/articles/2020/04/20/ahrr-a20.html. Articles published by the *World Socialist Web Site* that critique the 1619 Project are available at https://www.wsws.org/en/topics/event/1619/. Most have been anthologized in David North and Thomas Mackaman, eds. *The New York Times' 1619 Project and the Racialist Falsification of History: Essays and Interviews* (Oak Park: Mehring Books, 2021). See also Michael Guasco, "The Fallacy of 1619: Rethinking the History of Africans in Early America," *Black Perspectives* (September 4, 2019), https://www.aaihs.org/the-fallacy-of-1619-rethinking-the-history-of-africans-in-early-america/. For a rebuttal to the assertions made in Matthew Desmond's contribution to the 1619 Project, see John Clegg, "How Slavery Shaped American Capitalism," *Jacobin* (August 28, 2019), https://jacobinmag.com/2019/08/how-slavery-shaped-american-capitalism. See also James Oakes, "What the 1619 Project Got Wrong," *Jacobin* 2:3 (December 17, 2021), https://catalyst-journal.com/2021/12/what-the-1619-project-got-wrong?fbclid=I-wAR2Hl3V6l_Ha3W3V1td7X9jZlcmhHCjLFM11cK6zgGRmGjIw0v3aBrPMLyA#po-fn.
148. Eric London and David North, "Nikole Hannah-Jones, race theory and the Holocaust," *World Socialist Web Site* (November 26, 2019), https://www.wsws.org/en/articles/2019/11/26/1619-n26.html.

149. Eric London, "Audio recording refutes Hannah-Jones' claim that she was falsely quoted by the World Socialist Web Site," *World Socialist Web Site* (November 27, 2019), https://www.wsws.org/en/articles/2019/11/27/hann-n27.html; Tom Mackaman, "An Interview with historian Gordon Wood on the New York Times' 1619 Project," *World Socialist Web Site* (November 28, 2019), https://www.wsws.org/en/articles/2019/11/28/wood-n28.html; Tom Peters and John Braddock, "An interview with historian Dolores Janiewski on the New York Times' 1619 Project," *World Socialist Web Site* (December 23, 2019), https://www.wsws.org/en/articles/2019/12/23/inte-d23.html.
150. In February 2020, Gates told the *New York Times* that Michael Bloomberg, a billionaire that he associates with, could beat Trump in the general election. As mayor of New York City, Bloomberg championed "stop and frisk" policies that targeted millions of black and Latino youth and had a 0.1 percent conviction rate. Gates defended Bloomberg, stating: "I think black people want him." See David Marchese, "Henry Louis Gates Jr. on what really happened at Obama's 'beer summit'," *The New York Times* (February 3, 2020), https://www.nytimes.com/interactive/2020/02/03/magazine/henry-louis-gates-jr-interview.html?auth=login-email&login=email.
151. See Adam Serwer, "The Fight Over the 1619 Project Is Not About the Facts," *The Atlantic* (December 23, 2019), https://www.theatlantic.com/ideas/archive/2019/12/historians-clash-1619-project/604093/.
152. See Eric London, "New York Times ignored objections raised by 1619 Project fact-checker," *World Socialist Web Site* (March 9, 2020), https://www.wsws.org/en/articles/2020/03/09/nyti-m09.html; Tom Mackaman, "New York Times Magazine editor Jake Silverstein attempts to slither away from central 1619 Project fabrication," *World Socialist Web Site* (March 16, 2020), https://www.wsws.org/en/articles/2020/03/16/nyti-m16.html.
153. Jamil Smith, "The 1619 Project's Patriotic Work," *Rolling Stone* (August 21, 2019), https://www.rollingstone.com/politics/political-commentary/1619-project-critics-874781/.
154. Michael Harriot, "#NotAllHistorians: Some White People Are Upset That the New York Times' 1619 Project Isn't Centered in Whiteness," *The Root* (December 23, 2019), https://www.theroot.com/notallhistorians-some-white-people-are-upset-that-the-1840616511. See also Eric Levitz, "The '1619 Project' Isn't Anti-American – It's Anti-White Identity Politics," *New York Magazine* (August 23, 2019), http://nymag.com/intelligencer/2019/08/the-1619-project-isnt-unpatriotic-its-just-anti-whiteness.html.
155. Jodi Dean, *Comrade: An Essay on Political Belonging* (London: Verso, 2019) eBook, 145.
156. Editors, "1619 & all that," *The New Criterion* 38:5 (January 2020) 1, https://newcriterion.com/issues/2020/1/1619-all-that.
157. See for instance Alex Lichtenstein, "From the Editor's Desk: 1619 and All That," *The American Historical Review* (January 23, 2020), https://academic.oup.com/ahr/advance-article/doi/10.1093/ahr/rhaa041/5714757.
158. Oliver O'Connell, "Trump says he opposes using the 1619 Project to teach about slavery because 'we grew up with a certain history'," *The Independent* (September 8, 2020), https://www.independent.co.uk/news/world/americas/us-politics/1619-project-slavery-america-revisionist-history-cancel-culture-b405094.html.
159. Brett Stephens, "The 1619 Chronicles," *The New York Times* (October 9, 2020), https://www.nytimes.com/2020/10/09/opinion/nyt-1619-project-criticisms.html.
160. Tom Carter, "The Trump Administration's 1776 Report. The far right attempts to seize opening from the 1619 Project," *World Socialist Web Site* (January 30, 2021), https://www.wsws.org/en/articles/2021/01/30/1776-j30.html.

161. See Casey Cep, "The Contested Legacy of Atticus Finch," *The New Yorker* (December 10, 2018), https://www.newyorker.com/magazine/2018/12/17/the-contested-legacy-of-atticus-finch; Jeffrey Toobin, "Money Unlimited: How Chief Justice John Roberts orchestrated the Citizens United decision," *The New Yorker* (May 14, 2012), https://www.newyorker.com/magazine/2012/05/21/money-unlimited.
162. Mike Rogoway "Cura Cannabis, Portland's billion-dollar marijuana company, has a tortured past," *The Oregonian/Oregon Live* (May 1, 2019), https://www.oregonlive.com/business/2019/05/cura-cannabis-portlands-billion-dollar-marijuana-company-has-a-tortured-past.html.
163. See Paul Starr, "Goodbye to the Age of Newspapers (Hello to a New Era of Corruption)," *The New Republic* (March 4, 2009) 28-35.
164. Sheldon S. Wolin, *Democracy Incorporated: Managed Democracy and the Specter of Inverted Totalitarianism* (Princeton: Princeton University Press, 2008) x.
165. Yanis Varoufakis, *The Global Minotaur: America, the True Origin of the Financial Crisis and the Future of the World Economy* (London: Zed Books, 2011) 30.
166. Leon Trotsky, "What Is National Socialism?" (1933) available at https://www.marxists.org/archive/trotsky/germany/1933/330610.htm.
167. Trotsky, "What Is National Socialism?"
168. See Alexander Kluge and Oskar Negt, *History and Obstinacy*, trans. Richard Langston et al. (Brooklyn: Zone Books, [1981] 2014) 354.
169. Dean MacCannell, *The Tourist: A New Theory of the Leisure Class* (New York: Schocken, [1976] 1989) xiii.
170. See the May 5, 2015, lecture by Slavoj Žižek at the Institute for Human Sciences, Vienna, available at IWMVienna, "Slavoj Zizek: What does it mean to be a great thinker today?" *YouTube* (May 6, 2015), https://www.youtube.com/watch?v=-MoLdQA7aSg.
171. See Chris Harman, *Zombie Capitalism: Global Resistance and the Relevance of Marx* (London: Bookmarks Publications, 2009).
172. Elizabeth Méndez Berry and Chi-hui Yang, "The Dominance of the White Male Critic," *The New York Times* (July 5, 2019), https://www.nytimes.com/2019/07/05/opinion/we-need-more-critics-of-color.html.
173. Berry and Yang, "The Dominance of the White Male Critic."
174. Berry and Yang, "The Dominance of the White Male Critic."
175. Berry and Yang, "The Dominance of the White Male Critic."
176. Endnotes, "Onward Barbarians," *Endnotes* (December 2020), https://endnotes.org.uk/other_texts/en/endnotes-onward-barbarians. See also Jan Calloway, "Where Do Identity Politics Come From?" *Damage* (July 7, 2021), https://damagemag.com/2021/07/07/where-do-identity-politics-come-from/.
177. David Walsh and Fred Mazelis, "Racialism and money-grubbing: The New York Times explains why 'more critics of color' are needed," *World Socialist Web Site* (July 9, 2019), https://www.wsws.org/en/articles/2019/07/09/mend-j09.html.
178. Walsh and Mazelis, "Racialism and money-grubbing."
179. Slavoj Žižek, "Multiculturalism, or, the Cultural Logic of Late Capitalism," in *The Universal Exception: Selected Writings, Volume Two*, eds. Rex Butler and Scott Stephens (London: Continuum, 2006) 151-82.

180. David Walsh, "Should art by judged on the basis of race and gender?" *World Socialist Web Site* (April 27, 2017), https://www.wsws.org/en/articles/2017/04/27/sdsu-a27.html; Fred Mazelis, "New York Times, Washington Post feminist critics disparage The Queen's Gambit," *World Socialist Web Site* (December 10, 2020), https://www.wsws.org/en/articles/2020/12/11/com2-d11.html.
181. David Walsh, "The foul attempt to censor and suppress Dana Schutz's painting of Emmett Till," *World Socialist Web Site* (March 24, 2017), https://www.wsws.org/en/articles/2017/03/24/till-m24.html.
182. David Walsh, "Another reactionary attack on artist Dana Schutz, this time in Boston – and a healthy response," *World Socialist Web Site* (August 10, 2017), https://www.wsws.org/en/articles/2017/08/10/schu-a10.html.
183. Coco Fusco, "Censorship, Not the Painting, Must Go: On Dana Schutz's Image of Emmett Till," *Hyperallergic* (March 27, 2017), https://hyperallergic.com/368290/censorship-not-the-painting-must-go-on-dana-schutzs-image-of-emmett-till/.
184. Fusco, "Censorship, Not the Painting, Must Go."
185. Adolph Reed, Jr., "The James Brown Theory of Black Liberation," *Jacobin* (October 6, 2015), https://jacobinmag.com/2015/10/adolph-reed-black-liberation-django-lincoln-selma-glory.
186. On this subject, see Vivek Chibber, *Postcolonial Theory and the Specter of Capital* (London: Verso, 2013).
187. Henri Lefebvre, *Hegel-Marx-Nietzsche, ou le royaume des ombres* (Tournai: Casterman, 1975) 48-54.
188. Zeev Sternhell, *Neither Right Nor Left: Fascist Ideology in France*, trans. David Maisel (Princeton: Princeton University Press, [1983] 1986).
189. Sternhell, *Neither Right Nor Left*, 36.
190. Sternhell, *Neither Right Nor Left*, 129.
191. Sternhell, *Neither Right Nor Left*, 129.
192. See Mitchell Dean and Daniel Zamora, *The Last Man Takes LSD: Foucault and the End of Revolution* (London: Verso, 2021).
193. Heiko Feldner and Fabio Vighi, *Žižek Beyond Foucault* (New York: Palgrave Macmillan, 2007).
194. In terms of aesthetic theory, see for example Janet Wolff, *The Aesthetics of Uncertainty* (New York: Columbia University Press, 2008).
195. Feldner and Vighi, *Žižek Beyond Foucault*, 18.
196. See for instance Chantal Mouffe, "Deliberative Democracy or Agonistic Pluralism," *Social Research* 66:3 (Fall 1999) 745-58.
197. Slavoj Žižek, *First as Tragedy, Then as Farce* (London: Verso, 2009) 91.
198. Gilets Noirs, "The Gilets Noirs are coming for the Prime Minister," *Verso Blog* (July 1, 2019), https://www.versobooks.com/blogs/4367-the-gilets-noirs-are-coming-for-the-prime-minister. By 2020, there were more than 20,000 reported migrant deaths due to overseas travel, which is now a part of the informal economy.
199. Michael Hardt and Antonio Negri, *Assembly* (New York: Oxford University Press, 2017) 6. See also: Hardt and Negri, "The Multiplicities within Capitalist Rule and the Articulation of Struggles," *tripleC* 16:2 (2018) 440-8; Stefano Harney and Fred Moten, *The Undercommons: Fugitive Planning & Black Study* (Wivenhoe: Minor Compositions, 2013).

Conclusion

1. Emily S. Rueb and Derrick Bryson Taylor, "Obama on Call-Out Culture: 'That's Not Activism'," *The New York Times* (October 31, 2019), https://www.nytimes.com/2019/10/31/us/politics/obama-woke-cancel-culture.html.
2. HuffPost, "Obama: G-20 Protests Too Abstract To Make A Difference," *The Huffington Post* (November 21, 2009), https://www.huffingtonpost.com/2009/09/21/obama-calls-g-20-protests_n_293620.html.
3. Malaika Jabali, "Barack Obama thinks 'woke' kids want purity. They don't: they want progress," *The Guardian* (November 1, 2019), https://www.theguardian.com/commentisfree/2019/nov/01/does-obamas-critique-of-radical-politics-help-bring-about-the-change-he-wanted.
4. Michael Arceneaux, "I respect you immensely, Barack Obama, but I don't need lessons about 'being woke' and 'cancel' culture," *The Independent* (October 30, 2019), https://www.independent.co.uk/voices/obama-woke-meaning-michelle-cancel-culture-foundation-chicago-a9178436.html.
5. Grace Segers, "Obama says average American doesn't think we have to 'tear down the system and remake it," *CBS News* (November 16, 2019), https://www.cbsnews.com/news/obama-says-average-american-doesnt-think-we-have-to-tear-down-the-system-and-remake-it/; Guardian staff and agencies, "Democratic candidates reject Obama's warning of going too far," *The Guardian* (November 17, 2019), https://www.theguardian.com/us-news/2019/nov/17/democratic-candidates-obama-warns-going-too-far-left; Eliza Relman, "Obama indirectly rebukes Bernie Sanders and Elizabeth Warren by warning donors not to be 'deluded' into thinking voters want radical change," *Business Insider* (November 18, 2019), https://www.businessinsider.sg/obama-warns-donors-not-be-deluded-pushing-radical-change-2019-11/.
6. Secular Talk, "Obama Goes After 'Left Leaning Twitter Feeds'," *YouTube* (November 18, 2019), https://www.youtube.com/watch?v=a-emrsUkcvA; Jeremy Scahill, "Drone Whistleblower Daniel Hale Is a Truth-Teller in a Time of Systemic Deceit and Lethal Secrecy," *The Intercept* (July 30, 2021), https://theintercept.com/2021/07/30/daniel-hale-drone-whistleblower/.
7. Guardian staff and agencies, "Democratic candidates reject Obama's warning of going too far."
8. See Jonathan Allen and Amie Parnes, *Lucky: How Joe Biden Barely Won the Presidency* (New York: Crown, 2021).
9. Ryan Lizza, "Waiting for Obama: The Democratic establishment is counting on him to stop Trump and, perhaps, stave off Bernie as well. But can his cerebral politics still galvanize voters in an age of extremes?" *Politico* (November 26, 2019), https://www.politico.com/news/magazine/2019/11/26/barack-obama-2020-democrats-candidates-biden-073025; Luke Savage, "The Real Barack Obama Has Finally Revealed Himself," *Jacobin* (November 27, 2019), https://www.jacobinmag.com/2019/11/obama-socialism.
10. Adolph Reed, Jr., "Why Black Lives Matter Can't Be Co-opted," *Nonsite* (July 23, 2021), https://nonsite.org/why-black-lives-matter-cant-be-co-opted/.
11. Slavoj Žižek, "Against the Populist Temptation," *Critical Inquiry* #32 (Spring 2006) 553.
12. Black Agenda Radio with Nellie Bailey and Glen Ford, "NYT '1619 Project' More Pro-American Exceptionalism than Anti-Slavery," *Black Agenda Report* (October 14, 2019), https://www.blackagendareport.com/nyt-1619-project-more-pro-american-exceptionalism-anti-slavery.
13. See Cedric J. Robinson, *Black Marxism: The Making of the Black Radical Tradition* (Chapel Hill: The University of North Carolina Press, [1983] 2000).

14. See Gaye Theresa Johnson and Alex Lubin, "Introduction," in Johnson and Lubin, eds. *Futures of Black Marxism* (London: Verso, 2017) eBook, 46. For a class perspective on the rise of neo-fascism and far-right movements in countries like Italy, the Philippines, Indonesia, Malaysia, Singapore, Chile, India and Thailand, see Ben Wray, "'We Have to Move to a Post-Capitalist System': An Interview with Walden Bello," *Jacobin* (October 28, 2019), https://jacobinmag.com/2019/10/walden-bello-interview-capitalism-china.
15. Walter Benn Michaels, "It's Not Racism vs. Anti-Racism; It's Capitalism vs. Socialism," *Common Dreams* (December 18, 2016), https://www.commondreams.org/views/2016/12/18/its-not-racism-vs-anti-racism-its-capitalism-vs-socialism.
16. Robinson, *Black Marxism*, xxvix.
17. Robinson, *Black Marxism*, xxx.
18. Robinson, *Black Marxism*, xxxi.
19. Robinson, *Black Marxism*, 43. The question of dignity is the focus of Francis Fukuyama's neoliberal theory of identity conflicts in Fukuyama, *Identity: The Demand for Dignity and the Politics of Resentment* (New York: Farrar, Straus and Giroux, 2018).
20. Robinson, *Black Marxism*, 63-4.
21. Robinson, *Black Marxism*, 122. Along these lines, see also the specious thinking of Robin D.G. Kelley in *Yo' Mama's Dysfunktional! Fighting the Culture Wars in Urban America* (Boston: Beacon Press, 1997).
22. Robinson, *Black Marxism*, 240.
23. Robinson, *Black Marxism*, 145.
24. C.L.R. James, *World Revolution 1917-1936: The Rise and Fall of the Communist International*, ed. Christian Høgsbjerg (Durham: Duke University Press, [1937] 2017) 63.
25. See Jean Baudrillard, *America*, trans. Chris Turner (London: Verso, [1986] 1989).
26. Herbert Marcuse, "The Struggle Against Liberalism in the Totalitarian View of the State" (1934) in *Negations: Essays in Critical Theory*, trans. Jeremy J. Shapiro (London: MayFlyBooks, 2009) 16, 19, 21.
27. Robinson, *Black Marxism*, 124, 168. For a critique of similar postulates in afro-pessimism, see Bruce A. Dixon, "Intersectionality is a Hole, Afro-Pessimism is a Shovel. We Need to Stop Digging, Part 1," *Black Agenda Report* (January 25, 2018), https://www.blackagendareport.com/intersectionality-hole-afro-pessimism-shovel-we-need-stop-digging-part-1-3; "Looking Down That Deep Hole: Parasitic Intersectionality and Toxic Afro-Pessimism, Part 2 of 3," *Black Agenda Report* (February 1, 2018), https://www.blackagendareport.com/looking-down-deep-hole-parasitic-intersectionality-and-toxic-afro-pessimism-part-2; "Are Intersectionality Or Afro-Pessimism Paths to Power? Probably Not. Part 3 of 3," *Black Agenda Report* (February 16, 2018), https://www.blackagendareport.com/are-intersectionalism-or-afro-pessimism-paths-power-probably-not-part-3-3.
28. Gregory Meyerson, "Rethinking Black Marxism: Reflections on Cedric Robinson and Others," *Cultural Logic* 3:2 (Spring 2000), https://www.academia.edu/8104602/Rethinking_Black_Marxism_Reflections_on_Cedric_Robinson_and_others.
29. Slavoj Žižek, "For-show female empowerment & gender fluidity are simply the latest instruments of corporate capitalism," *Russia Today* (November 5, 2019), https://www.rt.com/op-ed/472680-women-empowerment-gender-mustaches/.
30. See the contribution of AR in Nonsite, "N+1 and the PMC: A Debate about Moving On," *Nonsite* (October 21, 2019), https://nonsite.org/feature/n1-and-the-pmc-a-debate-about-moving-on.
31. See Adolph Reed, Jr., "The Myth of Class Reductionism," *The New Republic* (September 25, 2019), https://newrepublic.com/article/154996/myth-class-reductionism.

INDEX

www.ingramcontent.com/pod-product-compliance
Lightning Source LLC
LaVergne TN
LVHW050921080826
845145LV00001B/159

* 9 7 8 1 9 2 6 9 5 8 3 6 1 *